Hollywood Heroines

Hollywood Heroines

The Most Influential Women in Film History

Laura L. S. Bauer, Editor

An Imprint of ABC-CLIO, LLC
Santa Barbara, California • Denver, Colorado

Library of Congress Cataloging-in-Publication Data

Names: Bauer, Laura L. S., editor.
Title: Hollywood heroines : the most influential women in film history / Laura L. S. Bauer, editor.
Description: Santa Barbara, California : Greenwood, an Imprint of ABC-CLIO, LLC, [2019] | Includes bibliographical references and index.
Identifiers: LCCN 2018029246 (print) | LCCN 2018036595 (ebook) | ISBN 9781440836497 (ebook) | ISBN 9781440836480 (hard copy : alk. paper)
Subjects: LCSH: Women in the motion picture industry—California—Los Angeles—Biography. | LCGFT: Biographies.
Classification: LCC PN1995.9.W6 (ebook) | LCC PN1995.9.W6 H68 2019 (print) | DDC 791.43/6522—dc23
LC record available at https://lccn.loc.gov/2018029246

ISBN: 978-1-4408-3648-0 (print)
978-1-4408-3649-7 (ebook)

23 22 21 20 19 1 2 3 4 5

This book is also available as an eBook.

Greenwood
An Imprint of ABC-CLIO, LLC

ABC-CLIO, LLC
130 Cremona Drive, P.O. Box 1911
Santa Barbara, California 93116-1911
www.abc-clio.com

This book is printed on acid-free paper ∞

Manufactured in the United States of America

For my mother, Inja Lee, who demonstrated what feminism was before I knew what it was called.

For my mother-in-law, Aleta Bauer, who showed me that love and kindness were the toughest forms of power and strength.

For my lifelong friend, Hana Ingle, whose shared love of stories got me into this entire mess in the first place.

Contents

Preface

Hollywood Heroines: The Most Influential Women in Film History is an ambitious project that aims to highlight the contributions exceptional women have made throughout the history of Hollywood cinema in every major occupation of filmmaking. Together, these trailblazers represent a uniquely broad range of categories, that consist of the following: actresses, casting directors, cinematographers, costume designers, directors, editors, feature animators, makeup and hairstyling artists, music (including composers, a songwriter, and a music supervisor), producers, production designers, screenwriters, sound designers, studio heads and executives, stuntwomen, and visual and special effects supervisors and producers. Every woman written about in this volume is an award winner in her respective craft—and in some cases, across multiple professions. Not only does this book incorporate an academic perspective on each of these women, but in many of these categories the reader can hear directly from the women themselves through interviews in which they share their experiences, advice, and wisdom.

Many of the categories and women in this collection have been underappreciated or unrecognized in previous works on the subject of women in Hollywood. Enhancing the visibility and representation of women whose contributions have helped shape the course of Hollywood film history is the motivating force behind the creation of *Hollywood Heroines*. This book is also particularly distinctive in that it provides comprehensive and wide-ranging categories not often found together in a single volume on film, thus helping to bring the study of film closer to the realities of the Hollywood film industry.

The main introduction eases readers into the broad yet complex subject of women in Hollywood cinema. It outlines the rationale and criteria used for the women selected and provides readers with a general context for understanding some of the central issues that permeate the subject of women in film.

The table of contents contains categories of women based on their primary profession, listing each filmmaker alphabetically by last name. These female filmmakers have been classified based on the trade in which they are most professionally recognized. It is important to note that some of the women belong to multiple categories and are not necessarily limited to the one profession they are listed under.

A short introduction to each profession will precede the individual essays for the section. These short introductions will provide a brief history as well as the recent developments for each profession and touch on the location of women across the different periods of Hollywood film history. The section introductions will also provide a description of the occupation itself and the role it plays in filmmaking.

The individual essays that follow the section introductions have been written by industry professionals, scholars, and students doing advanced graduate work and explain the role, significance, and contributions of each woman who has been selected for this volume. Each entry concludes with recommended print and online resources, as well as cross-references to related entries. These "See also" lists will direct readers to other women with whom the entry's subject worked directly, other women who worked during the same chronological period as the entry subject, and other women who are mentioned within the entry at hand. When provided, interviews will appear at the end of each section that feature a filmmaker who has been selected for the book and discussed in the section. They will provide, in their words, invaluable knowledge about their experience and vocation.

The content of this book should appeal to a vast array of users. Readers will find value in the volume's thorough coverage of the subject whether they are a member of the general reading public broaching the wide-ranging subject of film for the first time, are a seasoned film student performing research, or an individual considering a future career in the entertainment industry. Students beginning film studies will find this work particularly useful, not only for specific information on the subject of women in film but for the broader applications it holds as well. The unique scope of this work provides a comprehensive introduction to all of the major filmmaking positions, including descriptions about what they are, discussions on their role within filmmaking and the industry, and each position's historical context. Film students specializing in the emerging field of industry studies may also discover useful information within these pages.

Those with an interest in women and gender studies will find this book informative, as the majority of these women successfully navigated male-dominated occupations without a road map or female mentors and proved resilient against rampant and blatant sexism. It will also be interesting to note how specific occupations have been gender-coded differently throughout Hollywood film history. Jobs traditionally more inviting to female talent include editing, screenwriting, costume design, and casting, whereas jobs in executive positions at the studio, sound design, cinematography, and directing continue to be disproportionately male occupied.

Finally, it is incumbent upon the reader to be aware of the forces shaping Hollywood that are inextricably linked to the subject of this book. The major studios, which retain a dominant presence in media production and distribution, are today owned by major conglomerates whose purpose is profit. Cultivating an awareness of Hollywood as a business and familiarizing oneself with the tools utilized to promote passive consumption and viewership can be considered a way to inoculate oneself against forces that threaten consumer/audience agency and autonomy. The connection between women in Hollywood, the stories that make it to the silver screen, the market forces of supply and demand, and capitalism in general is a large and complex one that isn't visibly obvious or easily understood, nor is it inherently bad or good. It can, however, be easily obscured, and therein lies a serious danger for all involved. As our world economy, technology, and visual complexity increase at a rapid rate, so, too, will our passive consumption if we don't remain mindful of the forces that seek to control our attention and influence our desires and decisions.

Acknowledgments

I am indebted to the generous participation of many scholars and industry professionals whose time and talents made this project possible.

I would like to thank each of my consulting editors. Dr. Scott Strovas provided substantial assistance with the music section by writing the introduction, assembling contributors, and editing the entries for each composer listed. Dr. Brian McCabe contributed significantly by providing feedback, editing many entries (including my own writing), and furnished an entry on director Jane Campion. Lauren Hartle Morrison edited and consulted on many entries as well as wrote an entry on screenwriter Lillian Hellman. Finally, Dr. Jonathan Dickstein edited and consulted on numerous entries throughout the project as well.

My heartfelt appreciation to Carrie Tupper, whose enthusiasm and knowledge of the largely unexplored history of women in animation was so compelling that I had to add a section on feature animation. In addition to writing the introduction, Mrs. Tupper wrote every entry in the animation section as well as conducted the interview with Vicky Jenson. Professor Deborah Nadoolman Landis, the founding director and chair for the David C. Copley Center for Costume Design at the University of California, Los Angeles, consulted on the name selection for the costume designers, wrote the introduction to the costume design section, and edited several entries in the section. Susan Cabral-Ebert, the president of the Make-up Artists and Hair Stylists Guild, IATSE Local 706, supplied information on the history of makeup and hairstyling artists and provided the introduction to the Makeup and Hairstyling Artists section.

On a personal note, my deepest appreciation and gratitude go to my life partner and husband, Aaron Bauer, for his endless support throughout this journey. This book would not exist without our many long discussions on the subject, and I was grateful for his patience as I undertook such an ambitious project. Not a day passes that I do not feel incredibly fortunate to have him in my life.

I also owe an enormous thanks to Dr. Cari Beauchamp, the Pickford Foundation's Resident Scholar at the Mary Pickford Foundation, for her invaluable feedback regarding the table of contents and for sharing her research to the benefit of several entries, especially the ones on Marion Frances and Anita Loos. Professor Jane M. Gaines, at Columbia University's School of the Arts and founder of the Women Film Pioneers Project, helped solicit several contributors and provided helpful feedback. My advisor, Dr. Wendy Martin, has been my mentor and gave me the opportunity to co-edit *All Things Dickinson: An Encyclopedia of Emily Dickinson's*

World (2014) with Dr. Karen Strovas. Without that experience, conceiving this project would not have been feasible. Also, thank you to my editor, Catherine Lafuente, at Greenwood whose patience and guidance throughout the process was incredibly helpful, and to my former editor, Rebecca Matheson, who got me started on this project. My assistant editor, Sara Flores, helped on a number of entries, and I greatly appreciated her work. Additionally, my thanks to the librarians and staff at the Honnold-Mudd Library of the Claremont University Consortium in Claremont, California, for assisting with accessing materials for research.

My endless gratitude goes to all the writers whose scholarship contributed to creating this book and to all the amazing award-winning women who provided interviews in order to give this book an industry perspective. I am so grateful to have their voices included in this project.

Introduction

Hollywood Heroines: The Most Influential Women in Film History is being published at a time when sexual harassment and gender inequality seem to be the predominant topic of public discussion in the entertainment industry. It is a sobering reminder that the progress of gender equality throughout history has been complicated and rarely, if ever, follows a linear path. By representing female filmmakers who have contributed to their craft and Hollywood film history in significant and meaningful ways, *Hollywood Heroines* aims to celebrate the women who carved out their own routes to power. They succeeded on their terms, not through manipulation or force, but with a tremendous amount of resilience, courage, persistence, skill, hard work, talent, and in many cases, some luck and kindness. Herein lie examples of talented women whose gender and ethnicity are important to represent. It is also crucial, however, to recognize these individuals not as *women* filmmakers but as great filmmakers, period.

Many, many women deserving of recognition were not included simply due to the physical limitations of this project or extenuating circumstances. In some instances, important entries on women such as Brianne Murphy, who was the first woman to join the American Society of Cinematographers; Ida Koverman, who was Louis B. Mayer's instrumental executive secretary at Metro-Goldwyn-Mayer (MGM); and Harriet Parsons, one of the first women producers in Hollywood, as well as many more, could not be included. An entire section on agents, managers, and publicists that would have featured women such as legendary super-agent Sue Mengers had to be cut due to volume constraints. The word "influential" was carefully selected for the title of the book, as there is no pre-existing consensus on who the most prominent women in each field are and also because the definition of success isn't straightforward. Scholars and industry professionals may provide slightly different answers depending on who is asked to share an opinion. Each woman's degree of influence is based on the historical context and period in which they existed, the impact they may have had setting a precedent for future generations, and the combined significance of the movies in their filmography—which was sometimes based on the level of artistry, other times on box office revenue, and was often a combination of the two.

The notion of success can be a tricky issue to navigate. After all, not everyone aspires to the same measures of success. This book focuses on the professional lives of these women—whether they succeeded or valued fulfillment in their personal lives is a matter that can be more difficult to address. Some women's paths to professional success arrived through powerful men they knew or pre-existing connections they had to Hollywood royalty, while others started out with absolutely no connections in the industry. However, this is true of life in general, and many influential women (and men) can trace their path back to an initial fortunate opportunity, connection they had, or any number of advantages they had starting out. So, the criteria for selecting these women did not take those considerations into account. The focus was primarily on the quality and impact of the work these women performed and the historical contexts in which they existed.

The need to represent these female filmmakers and their contributions to film history can't be stressed enough. As Stacy Smith's study of "Inequality in 900 Popular Films" points out, there is an "epidemic of invisibility" when it comes to women in front of and behind the camera. Of the 900 top-grossing films from 2007 to 2016, the overall ratio of male to female filmmakers was 2.3 to 1, only 34 women total worked as directors, and only 30 percent of the speaking characters were female. Of the 30 percent of speaking roles for women who do appear onscreen, most only exist to serve a conventional heterosexual male-driven storyline. Noticing this, American cartoonist Alison Bechdel created the rules now recognized as "the Bechdel test" in 1985, designed as a quick way to gauge the level of gender inequality in any given work of fiction (Bechdel 2013). The Bechdel test can be easily applied to movies and names three criteria the film must pass in order to be considered feminist or simply gender neutral: (1) there must be at least two women present (2) who speak to each other (3) discussing something other than a man. This may sound simplistic, but the disconcerting truth is that the failure rate of this test is absolutely staggering. Not only are women's real experiences being unfairly represented onscreen, women's presence behind the scenes in film is sorely lacking as well. Dr. Martha Lauzen's 2014 study "The Celluloid Ceiling" discovered that women only made up 17 percent of all key creative content-producing jobs such as directors, writers, producers, executive producers, editors, and cinematographers who worked on the top 250 domestic-grossing films. These statistics illustrate that traditional male-driven storylines continue to be the norm, and the two most common roles for women in the heteronormative white male experience involve a woman who is in need of male protection or a woman who is the object of desire as the romantic interest. Both roles are typically passive and vulnerable, positioned as secondary to the man in the narrative, whose autonomy and agency drive the plot forward.

Women's stories and female leads, especially women of color, are routinely devalued in Hollywood due to a pervasive myth that teenage boys drive box office revenue. It is a belief that has long existed in the Hollywood film industry when it comes to greenlighting films with the largest budgets. The outcome is that films with a high production value follow a predictable cycle that consistently features male leads and in which stories are created by men, for men. Of course, that is not to say that men are not capable of authentically expressing the female experience, and this is where the topic becomes more complex. There are plenty of examples of female leads in big-budgeted Hollywood films that have been directed by men, and some of them feature a female protagonist with an authentic motivation that makes her character, and the story, ring true. The setting or genre of the film is immaterial to this discussion—what matters is the female protagonist herself and her motivation. Does her character, fictional or not, express something true about the female experience? A fantastic example of this is James Cameron's character Ellen Ripley in *Aliens* (1986). Ripley is a female action heroine whose motivation to face down the horrifying alien queen in the movie's infamous climax is driven by a maternal instinct to save a young girl nicknamed Newt. Ripley's large and lasting fan base is a testament to the resonance of this character. Conversely, women have also been able to effectively tell stories about the male experience. The first woman to win an Academy Award for Best Directing was Kathryn Bigelow for her film *The Hurt Locker* (2008), in which she explores the varying psychological reactions of seven male soldiers to the extreme stresses of combat during the Iraq War (2003–2011).

A growing number of lucrative films have been challenging the "teenage boy box office" myth in recent years, proving that women and diversity can translate into box office success. The emergence of female-led blockbuster films such as *The Hunger Games* film series (2012–2015), *Star Wars: The Last Jedi* (2017), and especially *Wonder Woman* (2017), directed by Patty Jenkins, which was the highest-grossing live-action film of all time upon its release, show that traditional male-driven narratives in the action genre are not the only stories that sell. These box office numbers have sparked a conversation about the underrepresentation of women in major Hollywood films. Likewise, the enormous success of *Black Panther* (2018) has raised similar protests toward Hollywood's prevailing attitudes about presenting more diversity in film, as it features a predominantly black cast and crew, including African American director, Ryan Coogler. UCLA's publication "Hollywood Diversity" (2018), a report that examines the relationship between diversity and Hollywood profits, suggests that American audiences increasingly prefer films with more diversity as audiences themselves become more diverse.

These films demonstrate that the broader inclusion of different voices in cinema produces content that is new and exciting as well as commercially viable. Significantly, *Black Panther* has a number of women in key filmmaking positions, many of whom are included in *Hollywood Heroines* and whose work was so skilled that audiences and critics admired the look of the film not knowing it was mostly created by the women behind the scenes. Victoria Alonso, producer for the Marvel Cinematic Universe (listed in the producer section of this book), was one of the executive producers of *Black Panther* and has publicly stated she makes a point of hiring the best people for the job, so it is meaningful that the majority of key filmmaking positions on this movie went to women (Cipriani 2018). Ruth E. Carter, whose entry and interview for this book can be found in the costume design section, based her designs on indigenous African clothing and expertly integrated her inspiration with the modernized science and technology look and theme of the film. Rachel Morrison, the first woman ever to be nominated in the history of the Academy Awards for Best Cinematography in 2017 for *Mudbound* (whose entry is in the cinematography section), was the director of photography on *Black Panther*. Hannah Beachler who, as the production designer for the film, was hired by Coogler to bring the world of the movie to life, and Camille Friend, the hair department head, created memorable hairstyles for the film. Not only was there an ideal number of female content creators represented behind the camera on *Black Panther*, but the film also happens to pass the Bechdel test with flying colors.

It is important to note that the classification of women as a group can itself be problematic. First, not all women have the same life experiences; they have faced different triumphs and challenges based on their identity and position in the world. The challenges facing women of color are different from those of white women; the experience of the poor does not encompass the experiences of the rich; and the experiences of heterosexuals are different from the lesbian, gay, bisexual, transgender, and queer (LGBTQ) experience.

Second, the dialogue about "women" in this book immediately sets up a binary categorization, meaning the use of the category itself presupposes the existence of two possibilities (women and men) when, in reality, gender and identity exist on a broad continuum. At the same time, the use of "women" as a category is imperative to advancing the discussion on the subject of women in film. So, the two must co-exist in a constant negotiation with one another for the sake of conversation and the purposes of this book. A similar tension can be present when it comes to representing identity. In the description of the women involved with making *Black Panther*, for example, it's important to note that Victoria Alonso is Latina; Ruth E. Carter, Hannah Beachler, and Camille Friend are all African American; and Rachel Morrison's sexuality also means she is the first lesbian to be nominated for Best Cinematography (Zonkel 2018). These identities should be represented, and their inclusion ought to enrich the conversation about these talented filmmakers and not limit discussion by focusing solely on the fact that they are women of color or that one belongs to the LGBTQ community.

Third, the perils of essentialism are also present when we discuss women's stories as a general category. The concept of essentialism, for our purposes, refers to the belief that certain characteristics are part of the foundational identity or essence of a person. A common mistake is to attribute qualities to a group of people that are either socially constructed or vary significantly among the individuals within the category. That is not to say biological differences do not exist, but biology does not inevitably lead to a predictable set of gendered characteristics and behaviors. For example, the Victorian belief that the "delicate nature" of women made them unsuitable for public life was used as a rationalization against them to prevent women from exercising their right to vote up until 1920, which, shockingly, was still less than 100 years ago at the time of this writing. Essentialization is dangerous, and even today women still battle the stereotypes that surround them and encourage them to believe they are incapable, passive, emotional—which is often weaponized code for being unreasonable and unintellectual—and weak.

The best way to challenge the harmful cycles of gender inequality is to increase the visibility of women as well as the quality of their representation, and that is exactly what *Hollywood Heroines* aims to do. This project has been a joy to create, and it is exciting to share the scholarship of each of the writers who contributed to making this book possible. *Hollywood Heroines* is also extremely fortunate to present interviews with 16 of the women featured in this book, including actress and director Jodie Foster, casting director Avy Kaufman, cinematographer Nancy Schreiber, costume designer Ruth E. Carter, editor Lynzee Klingman, feature animation directors Brenda Chapman and Vicky Jenson, makeup artist Ve Neill, producer Donna Gigliotti, sound mixer Deb Adair, sound editors Karen Baker Landers and Gwendolyn Yates Whittle, former studio head and executive Sherry Lansing, stuntwoman Zoë Bell, and visual and special effects supervisors Lindy De Quattro and Karen Goulekas. The reader will get to hear directly from these award-winning filmmakers as they speak about the industry, their craft, and the challenges they have overcome and continue to face in their own words. It is a privilege to hear them discuss these issues and an inspiration to see how far film has come and where it is going due to their pioneering efforts. Again, this book is not meant to provide an exhaustive list of women in Hollywood film history, it is just a part of an ongoing conversation that will hopefully continue to flourish as time goes on.

FURTHER READING

Bechdel, Alison. 2013. "Testy." Dykes to Watch Out For, November 8. http://dykestowatchoutfor.com/testy

Bordwell, David, and Kristin Thompson. 2010. *Film Art: An Introduction*. New York: McGraw-Hill.

Cipriani, Casey. 2018. "How 'Black Panther' Producer Victoria Alonso Is Making Sure Marvel Hires More Women to Make Its Movies." Bustle, February. https://www.bustle.com/p/how-black-panther-producer-victoria-alonso-is-making-sure-marvel-hires-more-women-to-make-its-movies-8407723

Hunt, Darnell, and Ana-Christina Ramón. 2018. "Hollywood Diversity Report 2018: Five Years of Progress and Missed Opportunities." UCLA College of Social Sciences, February. https://socialsciences.ucla.edu/wp-content/uploads/2018/02/UCLA-Hollywood-Diversity-Report-2018-2-27-18.pdf

Lauzen, Martha M. 2015. "The Celluloid Ceiling: Behind-the-Scenes Employment of Women on the Top 250 Films of 2014." Center for the Study of Women in Television & Film Accessed May 2, 2018. https://womenintvfilm.sdsu.edu/research

Smith, Stacy L., Marc Choueiti, and Katherine Pieper. 2017. "Inequality in 900 Popular Films: Examining Portrayals of Gender, Race/Ethnicity, LGBT, and Disability from 2007–2016." USC Annenberg School for Communication and Journalism, July. Accessed May 2, 2018. https://annenberg.usc.edu/research/aii

Zonkel, Phillip. 2018. "'Black Panther' Cinematographer Rachel Morrison Makes Oscar History with 'Mudbound.'" Q Voice News, February 17. https://qvoicenews.com/2018/02/17/black-panther-cinematographer-rachel-morrison-makes-oscar-history-with-mudbound

Actresses

Introduction

The craft of acting can be traced back to ancient Greek theater. Although the words "actress" and "actor" are binary terms used to distinguish a female performer from a male performer today, this has not always been the case, as a fair number of actresses and actors have portrayed the opposite sex in cross-gender acting across history, from the theater stage to the cinema screen. Of all the professions detailed here, "actress" is the only job description that remains gendered.

The difference between good and bad acting is highly subjective and easily debatable, but it is largely understood that the goal of good acting is to make the audience believe that the actress is the character she portrays. It may sound simple, but acting at its highest level is actually quite difficult. The greatest actresses seem to successfully balance preparation and improvisation, as well as the art of make-believe and truth. They do not imitate emotion; they engage empathy in order to better portray the emotion of their characters in authentic performances.

To claim that the women documented here are the most influential actresses in cinema history would be categorically false. And yet, no book on the most influential women in Hollywood would be complete without a discussion of at least a few of the most iconic actresses and their role in the history of cinema. It is imperative that one considers the list that follows as a sample of great actresses who are indicative of the time period in which they existed. Hollywood film history is generally organized into four categories in film criticism. As is the case with trying to define movements, there is some overlap of years and the timelines are not exact but are instead meant as approximations.

THE SILENT ERA (1890s–EARLY 1930s)

Theda Bara (1885–1955) and Norma Talmadge (1894–1957) were two major film stars of the silent era, when there was no synchronized recorded sound to accompany the film. It is hard to communicate with audiences without sound, and because relying solely on visual storytelling is harder, silent film actresses had to overemphasize their body language and facial expressions. This exaggerated acting technique may strike modern audiences as melodramatic. A shift in acting technique occurred with the development of the close-up in cinema. Framing an actress from the shoulders to the head enabled them to transition from vaudevillian, stagelike performances to a more naturalistic style. Lillian Gish pioneered many new film performance techniques and has been credited with being the "First Lady of the American Cinema" for this reason.

CLASSICAL HOLLYWOOD (1920s–LATE 1960s)

Classical Hollywood cinema, also known as the golden age of Hollywood, encompasses the transition of the silent era to the sound era. Many actresses' careers did not survive the transition from silent cinema to the "talkies," but two notable actresses who did make the transition successfully were Greta Garbo and Marlene Dietrich. The major studios created the studio system, giving them unrivaled control over the vast majority of film production and distribution, which afforded them enormous power. Actresses (and other studio employees) would generally sign long-term contracts, and once a contract was signed, the studios took control of the actresses' public persona by shaping, promoting, and exploiting their image to maximize profit—known as the "star system." Morality clauses were commonly included in these contracts, which held actresses to a behavioral standard in public. There is also the emergence of a preparatory approach to acting, a technique called "method acting," which endeavors to help the actress emotionally identify with the character she portrays (Marlon Brando's performance in *A Streetcar Named Desire* in 1951 is a famous example of this). Bette Davis, Katharine Hepburn, Ingrid Bergman, and Hattie McDaniel all participated in films indicative of this era.

NEW HOLLYWOOD (1960s–EARLY 1980s)

New Hollywood Cinema, also known as the American New Wave, was characterized as breaking with conventions of narrative filmmaking due to the decline of the studio system. The studios began to hire young, nontraditional filmmakers who became "auteurs" (the idea that the director was the "author" of a film). Innovative storylines and characters emerged, and political activism and artistry got entangled in Hollywood cinema in an unprecedented way due to the countercultural revolution of the 1960s and 1970s. As second-wave feminism gained momentum and society's attitude toward women began to change, so, too, did the stories and characters of women on screen. Many of the characters actresses portrayed in the 1960s and 1970s were revolutionary. Faye Dunaway (1941–) starred in films such as *Chinatown* (1974) and *Bonnie and Clyde* (1967) that are definitive of the era. Likewise, Jane Fonda starred in films such as *Klute* (1971) and *Tout Va Bien* (1972) that helped define the period with morally ambiguous characters and unresolved endings. Actress Pam Grier, who starred in the Blaxploitation film *Foxy Brown* (1974), would be an important precursor for the iconic female action heroines that were to come.

BLOCKBUSTER ERA (1980s–PRESENT)

As the name would imply, the Blockbuster Era has been known for films that were extremely financially lucrative at the box office. However, most of these popular action-packed blockbusters such as *Jaws* (1975), *Back to the Future* (1985), and *The Empire Strikes Back* (1980) were largely dominated by male leads. However, a very popular new archetype for women would emerge during this time as well: the female action heroine. The sequel to two franchises in particular ushered in lead roles for two of the most iconic female action heroines to date: Ellen Ripley in *Aliens* (1986) starring Sigourney Weaver and Sarah Connor of *Terminator 2: Judgment Day* (1991) played by Linda Hamilton. This tradition continues today with Charlize Theron's portrayal of Furiosa in *Mad Max: Fury Road* (2015) and films such as *Wonder Woman* (2017) starring Gal Gadot. Paradoxically, the Blockbuster Era also encompasses the rise of independent American cinema. As recent technologies democratized filmmaking in an unprecedented way, films with a lower budget have begun to proliferate. Meryl Streep and Jodie Foster are commonly considered two of the greatest actresses of our time, and their performances have contributed to some of the most iconic films in the last few decades. Both are transitional figures who began to act in the 1970s and have successfully evolved and stayed relevant in an industry occupation that is notorious for devaluing women as they age.

Laura L. S. Bauer

Bara, Theda (1885–1955)

One of the most popular American film stars prior to the First World War, Theda Bara is also one of the very few of that era to retain any presence in cultural memory. Born Theodosia Goodman in Cincinnati, Ohio, Bara is frequently given the highly contestable designation in popular literature of cinema's first sex symbol. With her waist-length black hair, pale skin, and copiously kohl-lined eyes, Bara was typecast as the vamp: a predatory seductress of uncertain ethnicity who uses her sexual allure to entrap and bring ruin or death to male victims.

Between 1915 and 1919, Bara starred in 39 feature films for the emerging Fox Film Corporation. Of those, two are known to survive, along with a feature and a short from her unsuccessful comeback attempt in the mid-1920s. Among those lost films, most destroyed in a 1937 storage vault fire, are Bara's major star vehicles, in which she played Carmen, Madame Du Barry, Camille, Salome, and the role with which she is still most identified: Cleopatra. Hundreds of surviving still images convey something of Bara's allure. Photos from *Cleopatra* (1917) in particular, in which she wears sometimes startlingly fetishistic and body-revealing costumes, have sparked interest among subsequent generations of audiences unable to see her films.

More plausible than the claim that Bara was cinema's first sex symbol is the assertion by film historians that Bara was the first film star constructed from publicity rather than onscreen appearances. Bara contracted with Fox in 1914 to play "the Vampire" in the studio's adaptation of the hit play *A Fool There Was*, in which her home-wrecking femme fatale gleefully destroys a wealthy diplomat who falls under her spell. Even in this founding period of the Hollywood studio system, publicity departments were integral to the business, and Fox's publicists built a campaign to generate interest in the unknown actress that was unprecedented in its convoluted extravagance.

Central to this publicity was the promotion of Bara as an exotic mystery woman, born in Egypt "in the shadow of the Sphinx" to French and Italian parents (contrary to later, more exaggerated accounts that claim she was touted as the daughter of an Egyptian dancing girl or Arabian sheikh). She was said to practice the occult arts, and men were reportedly driven to suicide out of unrequited love for Bara, who the press suggested was the reincarnation of notorious historical figures such as Lucrezia Borgia and Elizabeth Báthory. Photos of her crouching over skeletons, stroking ravens, or gazing into crystal balls amplified this colorful hype.

At the same time she was being promoted as "the wickedest woman in the world," however, press reports were also assuring audiences that Bara was in truth a bookish, reserved "misunderstood good woman" who lived with her parents (Courtlandt 1917, 59). Supposedly the only actor in early cinema to have a college education, Bara did in fact lead a private life remarkable solely for its complete lack of scandal. The frequency with which she is referred to in print and online as "just a nice Jewish girl from Cincinnati" suggests that the ironic duality of her persona has amused audiences for decades.

In a 1917 interview, Bara declared herself a "feministe," stating, "Women are my greatest fans because they see in my vampire the impersonal vengeance of all their unavenged wrongs" (May 1980, 106). The implications of Bara's star image for feminist politics have been a matter of contention for a century, and the passage of time and distancing of that image from its original context have inspired reevaluations of what her film roles and publicity gimmickry signify for female audiences, then and now. What to make of a whore with a heart of coagulated cobra venom who lounges wantonly on leopard skins, smokes cigarettes in long holders, and commands besotted men to "kiss me, my fool," her famed line from *A Fool There Was* (1915)? Opinions tend toward the extreme. Feminist film critic Molly Haskell dismisses Bara as a "comical carnivore" (Haskell 1974, 103), and cultural critic Bram Dijkstra regards her as a dangerously misogynistic embodiment of male fears of sexually active women. Problematic, yet intriguing enough for feminist interrogation, Bara also has been "reclaimed" as a symbol of female unruliness, and many contemporary fans find the independence, subversion, unwillingness to submit to male authority, and unapologetic sexuality they see in her image empowering.

Bara's phenomenal box office success was short-lived. With postwar jadedness, audiences lost interest in the vamp, now regarded as a ludicrously naïve embodiment of Victorian prudery, but were unable to accept Bara in other types of roles. Unlike many other stars with a rapid rise and fall, however, Bara had an apparently comfortable postfame life married to director Charles Brabin—who, in another disconcerting contrast between Bara and her manufactured star image, did not countenance a wife working outside the home. Aside from her commercial, if decidedly not critical, success appearing in the notoriously awful Broadway play *The Blue Flame* in 1920, a couple of performances on California stages in the 1930s, and some radio cameos into the 1940s, Bara's postfilm life was contentedly private until her death from stomach cancer in 1955.

Considering the almost total inability to reassess her cinematic oeuvre, Bara's continuing circulation in popular and online cultures is all the more remarkable. For a century her name has been synonymous with histrionic silent film acting, heavy-handed seductiveness, and Orientalist outrageousness. She has been the object of countless parodies and the butt of jokes, but she has also been iconic to the countercultural movements of the 1960s, the goth subculture, and some third-wave feminists as a sexual subversive in a period of extreme repression. Certainly Bara's star image, with its brazen eroticism and ambiguous ethnicity, has better corresponded with changing attitudes and resonates with many present-day audiences more than the virginal, lily-white star images of contemporaneous actresses such as Mary Pickford and Lillian Gish, and for many the fascination with Bara has much to do with the perception of her as the foremother of the cinematic bad girl.

Mark Andrew Hain

See also: Dietrich, Marlene; Garbo, Greta; Pickford, Mary; Talmadge, Norma

Further Reading

Courtlandt, Roberta. 1917. "The Divine Theda." *Motion Picture Magazine*, April.

Craig, Joan, with Beverly F. Stout. 2016. *Theda Bara, My Mentor*. Jefferson, NC: McFarland, 59.

Dijkstra, Bram. 1996. *Evil Sisters: The Threat of Female Sexuality and the Cult of Manhood*. New York: Alfred A. Knopf.

Genini, Ronald. 1996. *Theda Bara: A Biography of the Silent Screen Vamp, with a Filmography*. Jefferson, NC: McFarland.

Golden, Eve. 1996. *Vamp: The Rise and Fall of Theda Bara*. Vestal, NY: Emprise Publishing.

Haskell, Molly. 1974. *From Reverence to Rape: The Treatment of Women in the Movies*. New York: Holt, Rinehart and Winston, 103.

May, Lary. 1980. *Screening Out the Past: The Birth of Mass Culture in the Motion Picture Industry*. New York and Oxford, UK: Oxford University Press, 106.

Bergman, Ingrid (1915–1982)

In 1939, Ingrid Bergman arrived in America with 11 Swedish films to her name. By the late 1940s, the Swedish-born actress had become one of the most popular movie stars in America and a household name across the globe. Her onscreen persona embodied a universally refreshing combination of sophisticated modesty and captivating beauty. Critics and audiences alike agreed that "when Ingrid played women of questionable virtue . . . her innate goddess seemed to show through . . . and when she played women of high virtue . . . she appeared to be displaying aspects of herself" (Leamer 1986, 1). Bergman actively worked against this correlation and Hollywood's tendency to typecast actresses. Nevertheless, this conception of wholesomeness further permeated through her private life and would later cost her the support of the American public following personal scandal; her abandonment of both family and Hollywood marked the beginning of a seven-year absence from the United States. Despite such hindrances, Bergman would continue to artistically persevere internationally, and this recognition led to her eventual return to Hollywood. She procured three Academy Awards, four Golden Globes, two Emmys, and one Tony Award over a 48-year career.

Bergman's 1936 performance in *Intermezzo* caught the attention of David O. Selznick (1902–1965), the Hollywood producer who advanced the careers of various actors and produced the epic *Gone with the Wind* (1939). Under his wing, her Hollywood image became that of the "first natural actress": minimal, wholesome, and pure (Smit 2012, 42). The two signed a seven-year contract, but Bergman would only star in two Selznick productions: the American remake of *Intermezzo*: *A Love Story* (1939) and Alfred Hitchcock's *Spellbound* (1945). The other nine pictures made during this time were done so on loan-out to other studios, three of which earned her the Academy Award nomination for Best Actress in their respective years: *For Whom the Bell Tolls* (1943), *Gaslight* (1944), and *The Bells of St. Mary's* (1945). She would receive her first of three Oscars for *Gaslight.*

During this time, Bergman became the quintessential female romantic lead, the most memorable of her characters being Ilsa Lund in Warner Bros.' *Casablanca* (1942). Typecasting actors and actresses alike—that is, assigning them the same type of role in various films—was the common practice of the Hollywood studio system. However, Bergman actively worked to maintain some personal control over her own career. Alongside conventional melodramatic roles, Bergman would opt for parts more "divergent" from her "Swedish milkmaid image" as an attempt to avoid Hollywood's all too habitual path of typecasting economically viable stars. She believed that acting "meant the certainty of change" and was constantly looking to "get inside somebody else's skin" (Bergman and Burgess 1980, 109). Thus, she was often attracted to showcased deviance or rebellion, and she notably exhibited both in films such as *Dr. Jekyll and Mr. Hyde* (1941), *Saratoga Trunk* (1945), and Alfred Hitchcock's *Notorious* (1946). Nevertheless, because the public seemingly saw some form of inherent goodness within her cinematic persona, no matter the character, this artistic straying from the conventional path was publically accepted and critically praised.

As the Selznick-Bergman era ended toward the end of the 1940s, so, too, did Bergman's beloved relationship with her American public, though this occurred much more instantaneously. Hers immediately became an image attached to scandal as she traveled to Rome and became professionally and romantically involved with Italian Neorealist director Roberto Rossellini. Such was the price of America's conflation of her onscreen image with her personal life that the public could see her as "pure" no longer.

Bergman and Rossellini collaborated on six films together. *Stromboli* (1950), *Europa '51* (1951), and *Viaggio in Italia* (1954) have since been taken up by critics and scholarship alike and are considered some of the final films of the Italian Neorealist movement. This continued success away from Hollywood speaks to the greater international appeal of Bergman and her versatile career. Her desire for and willingness to take on diverse roles transcended limitations of cultural difference. Possessing some mastery of four different languages, Bergman worked with acclaimed French director Jean Renoir (1894–1979), and she later starred in Ingmar Bergman's (1918–2007) *Autumn Sonata* (1978), a role that earned Ingrid Bergman her last Academy Award nomination.

In 1956, 20th Century Fox offered Bergman the lead in the production of *Anastasia*. Producers and critics believed that enough time had passed and that the scandal with Rossellini could be forgotten—a decision that worked in their favor. Not only did this role reunite Bergman with Hollywood, but it also secured another Academy Award for Best Actress. She would later receive her third and final Academy Award for her supporting role in *Murder on the Orient Express* (1974).

Despite this rejuvenation of American success, Bergman retained this international mode of work, performing in film, television, and theater throughout Hollywood, Sweden, Italy, and the United Kingdom. Almost half of the 46 film roles throughout her career are international productions, many of which are performed in their respective language. Ingrid Bergman was able to successfully navigate both the dominant and international film market. Thus, she is ultimately a figure of geographical duality. Though seemingly forced to leave the United States because of personal failure, she did so with the intention of expanding her own artistry and agency as an actress at odds with studio typecasting. Her international appeal is a product of her search for professional individuality. Bergman is contemporarily remembered as both Hollywood actress and international sensation. Ironically, her search for artistic change and willingness to work outside of Hollywood subsequently produced even further enamored success within Hollywood itself. Bergman battled cancer for several years before passing away on her 67th birthday in her London home on August 29, 1982.

Kelsey E. Moore

See also: Davis, Bette; Garbo, Greta; Hepburn, Katharine; McDaniel, Hattie

Further Reading

Bergman, Ingrid, and Alan Burgess. 1980. *Ingrid Bergman: My Story.* New York: Delacorte Press.

Leamer, Laurence. 1986. *As Time Goes By.* New York: Harper and Row.

Lindström, Pia, and Isabella Rossellini. 1996. *Ingrid Bergman Remembered,* DVD. Directed by Gene Feldman. Tappan, NY: Janson Media.

Quirk, Lawrence J. 1970. *The Films of Ingrid Bergman.* New York: Citadel Press.

Smit, David. 2012. *Ingrid Bergman: The Life, Career, and Public Image.* Jefferson, NC: McFarland.

Davis, Bette (1908–1989)

Born Ruth Elizabeth Davis in Lowell, Massachusetts, Bette Davis played an impressive array of film and television roles in a career spanning 58 years. Beginning in theater, Davis made her Hollywood debut with *The Bad Sister* (1931) and appeared onscreen for the last time in *Wicked Stepmother* (1989). In between, she became famous for playing characters that Molly Haskell describes as "superfemales":

women too astute and ambitious to be limited by the roles of wife and mother that society allots them (Haskell 1987, 214). Davis strained against constrictions both in front of and behind the camera, fighting Warner Bros. for better parts and even filing a lawsuit in 1937 to free herself from her contract—she lost the suit, but made future legal action easier for talent subject to the draconian rules of the classical Hollywood studio system. The epitaph on her tombstone, suggested by Joseph L. Mankiewicz (1909–1993) after he directed her in *All about Eve* (1950), reads "She did it the hard way" (Davis and Stine 1974, 3). The way may have been hard, but Davis did something right along it: she received a grand total of 10 Academy Award nominations, winning 2 awards for Best Actress for *Dangerous* (1935) and *Jezebel* (1938). She won a Best Actress award at the Cannes Film Festival for *All about Eve* and an Emmy for *Strangers: The Story of a Mother and Daughter* (1979). In 1999, the American Film Institute (AFI) voted her the second-greatest Hollywood actress of all time, superseded only by Katharine Hepburn.

Arriving at Warner Bros. in 1932 following a brief, unpromising stint at Universal, Davis was largely wasted in her early years at the studio. It was not until the late 1930s and 1940s (ironically, after her failed lawsuit) that the roles she craved, and are now best known for, began coming in: the brittle Southern belle in *Jezebel*, the socialite grappling with an inoperable brain tumor in *Dark Victory* (1939), the dowdy spinster turned glamour girl in *Now, Voyager* (1942). Her breakout role was as the shrewish Mildred in *Of Human Bondage* (1934). It was a part that other actresses had avoided for fear of alienating audience sympathy, but Davis leapt at the opportunity to play a villainess and show off her range. She persuaded director John Cromwell to let her apply her makeup herself. In her words, "I intended to be convincing-looking. We pulled no punches and Mildred emerged as a reality—as immediate as a newsreel and as starkly real as a pestilence" (Spada 1993, 102–107). Reviews of her performance were rapturous. Officially, Davis was overlooked for an Oscar nomination, but that year Academy of Motion Picture Arts and Sciences (AMPAS) voters took it upon themselves to add her name to the ballot as their personal choice for Best Actress. The award ultimately went to Claudette Colbert (1903–1996) for *It Happened One Night* (1934), but Davis's write-in nomination led to changes in Academy voting procedures that continue to this day (Bona and Wiley 1986, 55–58).

From *Of Human Bondage* on, Davis often gleefully resisted likable roles. She clashed with William Wyler on the set of *The Little Foxes* (1941), as he wanted to soften her aristocratic matron Regina. Davis, on the other hand, preferred portraying a character who kills her sick husband by forcing him to crawl upstairs to fetch his medicine as evil incarnate. Richard Dyer argues that Davis is the most mannered of independent woman–type stars like Hepburn, Joan Crawford, Rosalind Russell, and Barbara Stanwyck. As he says, "With most stars, their particular manner is seen as a spontaneous emanation of the personality; but Davis is hard to treat in the same way since her manner is so obviously 'put on.' In certain films—*Jezebel*, *The Little Foxes*, *Dark Victory*, *Now, Voyager*, *All about Eve*—this sense of the artifice of social performance meshes with notions of social expectations and requirements, of women and/or of class" (Dyer 2007, 59). Davis, like her great rival Crawford, dominated mannered melodramas aimed primarily at female viewers.

Despite her indelible association with the "woman's film" genre, Davis could also be effortlessly funny, as in the glorious wartime screwball comedy *The Bride Came C.O.D.* (1941).

During the Second World War (1939–1945), Davis cofounded and served as the hard-driving president of the Hollywood Canteen, which provided free refreshments, entertainment, and the company of stars to almost 3 million U.S. servicemen on their way overseas. It proved so popular that it spawned a film, *Hollywood Canteen* (1944), in which Davis and scores of other stars appeared as themselves, and garnered her a Distinguished Civilian Service Medal from the Department of Defense. After the war, Davis's long career cycled through a series of peaks and troughs. Finally released from her Warner Bros. contract when *Beyond the Forest* (1949) bombed at the box office, Davis came roaring back with *All about Eve*. In 1962, she took out a *Variety* advertisement under the heading "Situations wanted—women artists" in which the actress half-jokingly requested "steady employment in Hollywood." Employment came calling that same year with *What Ever Happened to Baby Jane?* (1962), the searing, wildly successful story of two sisters, played by Davis and Crawford, going to seed in their decaying Los Angeles mansion. In 1977, Davis became the first woman to receive the AFI's Lifetime Achievement Award. In 1941, she had been the first female AMPAS president as well. A trailblazer for her sex, Davis undermined industrial and social structures designed to keep women in their place throughout her work and her life. Her toughness, her style, and her tremendous intelligence created a powerful model for legions of fans to follow.

Ila Tyagi

See also: Bergman, Ingrid; Dunaway, Faye; Garbo, Greta; Head, Edith; Hellman, Lillian; Hepburn, Katharine; McDaniel, Hattie; Streep, Meryl

Further Reading

Bona, Damien, and Mason Wiley. 1986. *Inside Oscar: The Unofficial History of the Academy Awards.* New York: Ballantine Books.

Davis, Bette, and Whitney Stine. 1974. *Mother Goddam: The Story of the Career of Bette Davis.* New York: Hawthorn Books.

Dyer, Richard. 2007 (1979). *Stars.* London: BFI Publishing.

Haskell, Molly. 1987 (1974). *From Reverence to Rape: The Treatment of Women in the Movies.* Chicago: University of Chicago Press.

Spada, James. 1993. *More Than a Woman: An Intimate Biography of Bette Davis.* New York: Little, Brown.

Dietrich, Marlene (1901–1992)

Marlene Dietrich was not the first European star to become a Hollywood icon, but her position in Hollywood is legendary. Dietrich created a unique and daring screen persona that she managed to uphold for decades. Her eroticized but not objectified image, which encouraged queer or gender-bending interpretations, was connected to her unique features as a European actress, as well as her lifestyle of constant travel and a symbolic identification with exile and displacement.

In 1931, *Motion Picture Magazine* described "newcomer" Marlene Dietrich as the "answer to any producer's prayer," one who possessed "the glamour of Garbo, the appeal of a Bow, the mind of a Chatterton" (Reid 1931, 43). This was high praise for a German actress, who added to this already attractive package a dash of the maternal *hausfrau* and a staunch "Prussian" work ethic. Already a relatively successful actress of the Berlin stage and German silent cinema, Dietrich became a candidate for international stardom after appearing in Austrian director Josef Von Sternberg's bilingual production of *Der Blaue Engel* in 1930. There, she played Lola, a fabulous but fatal cabaret temptress, whose rise was "paralleled in real life by the rise of Marlene Dietrich and the fall of Emil Jannings," the film's German top-billed star (Sarris 1966, 25). Her first American sound release was the oriental yarn, *Morocco* (1931), where she again played a cabaret entertainer/prostitute. Her cross-dressed performance and a kiss on the mouth with another female character made the film's *and* Dietrich's reputation.

Dietrich's role and agency in the creation of her now-legendary star image have been the subject of much debate. She has been understood as "a pure vehicle for [Director Von Sternberg's] fantasies and formalist concerns" but also as an example of (feminist) resistance to male sexual objectification (Dyer 1980, 179–180). However, even though the synergy was quite real, Dietrich should not be reduced to the flesh puppet of a director's fantasies. In her studied and deliberate bid for stardom prior to working with Von Sternberg, Dietrich's agency can clearly be established. Moreover, as various biographies have convincingly illustrated, she was in control of her star persona throughout her long career. Her image deliberately combined masculine and feminine traits, which was pleasing to audiences and suggested a playful and flexible sense of gender and sexual identities. This has encouraged queer readings, as indeed "role after role Dietrich acts as if heterosexuality were a huge bore or charade" (Kuzniar 2007, 248), and the actress publicly had various affairs with both men and women. Again, despite her erotic image, she did not cast herself "[as] a sex object but [as] a sexual and sexualized *subject*" (Garber 1993, 16, emphasis added). Of course, Dietrich's penchant for playing promiscuous or morally corrupt characters had the Production Code Administration, the office founded to make sure studios handled sex, violence, and religion according to industry rules, working overtime.

However, an often-underappreciated aspect of her persona was her sense of humor. The sophisticated comedy *Desire* (1936) played up Dietrich's funny side and worked at humanizing the untouchable, Euro-glamorous creature she had become in the Von Sternberg films. The films she made for Universal (with producer Joe Pasternak) in the late 1930s and early 1940s continued the by then well-established Dietrich character (the cabaret singer/entertainer with either a heart [of gold], a maternal instinct, or a sense of honor) but played up Dietrich's self-awareness and comic instincts.

Dietrich had worked and lived outside her native country from the early 1930s onwards, thus symbolically embodying displacement and international mobility. For U.S. audiences, Dietrich was always explicitly known as a non-American actress (and she usually played international characters), and she always claimed that her Prussian origins were to thank for her virtues and discipline. Nevertheless, when Dietrich visited Germany after the war, she was met with hostility and contempt and was even "hounded to the grave" when she was buried in Berlin in 1993 (Koch 1993, 11). Dietrich had always been critical of Nazism and in the late 1930s refused several offers to come back to Germany to become queen of its domestic film industry. Instead, Dietrich applied for American citizenship in 1937 (which was granted in 1939) and later helped other fellow compatriots flee Germany when war was impending. During the war she sold United States war bonds and entertained American troops, and she arrived in a defeated Germany in an American uniform. (She would receive the Medal of Freedom in 1947 and the French Legion d'Honneur in 1950 for her war efforts.) Public statements made by Dietrich that "Germany deserved everything" that was coming to it and was in fact "guilty" (Bach 2000, 299), coupled with her appearances in patriotic films such as *Pittsburgh* (1942) or in critical pictures such as *A Foreign Affair* (1948) and *Judgment at Nuremberg* (1961), did not improve relations with her native country. Most tellingly, what made Germany's position vis-à-vis Dietrich so troublesome was the fact that she made void the apologetic "explanation" that the German people had been helplessly seduced by their political leader and had naively and unwittingly supported an inhumane regime. She was living proof of an alternative path, the embodiment of the "Good German" (Koch 1993, 12).

Throughout her career Dietrich was a most flexible actress and entertainer who moved across nations, genres, gender and identities, media and venues (cinema, television, and theater). She made bold (political) choices, and her long-lasting career was made possible through tireless determination, self-knowledge, and both an affective and rational intelligence, still discernible in her pictures today.

Anke Brouwers

See also: Bara, Theda; Dunaway, Faye; Garbo, Greta; Talmadge, Norma

Further Reading

Bach, Stephen. 2000. *Marlene Dietrich. Life and Legend.* New York: Da Capo Press.

Basinger, Jeanine. 1993. *A Woman's View. How Hollywood Spoke to Women, 1930–1960.* Hanover and London: Wesleyan Press.

Dietrich, Marlene. 1966. *Marlene Dietrich's ABC.* New York: Ungar Publishing.

Dyer, Richard. 1980. *Stars.* London: British Film Institute, 179–180.

Garber, Marjorie. 1993. "From Dietrich to Madonna: Cross-Gender Icons." In *Women in Film: A Sight and Sound Reader.* Edited by Pam Cook and Philip Dodd. Philadelphia: Temple University Press, 16–20.

Garncarnz, Joseph. 2007. "Playing Garbo: How Marlene Dietrich Conquered Hollywood." In *Dietrich Icon.* Edited by Gerd Gemünden and Mary Desjardins. Durham and London: Duke University Press, 103–118.

Gemünden, Gerd. 2008. *A Foreign Affair. Billy Wilder's American Films.* Oxford: Berghahn Books.

Gemünden, Gerd, and Mary Desjardins. 2007. *Dietrich Icon.* Durham and London: Duke University Press.

Hastie, Amelie. 2007. *Cupboards of Curiosity. Women, Recollection and Film History.* Durham and London: Duke University Press.

Koch, Gertrud. 1993. "Exorcised: Marlene Dietrich and German Nationalism." In *Women in Film: A Sight and Sound Reader.* Edited by Pam Cook and Philip Dodd. Philadelphia: Temple University Press, 10–15.

Kuhn, Annette. 1994. *Woman's Pictures: Feminism and Cinema*. London: Verso.

Kuzniar, Alice A. 2007. "'It's Not Often That I Want a Man': Reading for a Queer Marlene." In *Dietrich Icon.* Edited by Gerd Gemünden and Mary R. Desjardins. Durham and London: Duke University Press, 239–258.

Loewenstein, Joseph, and Lynne Tatlock. 1992. "The Marshall Plan at the Movies. Marlene Dietrich and Her Incarnations." *The German Quarterly.* 65(3/4): 1492–1992: Five Centuries of German-American Interrelations (Summer–Autumn): 429–344.

Reid, Laurence. 1931. Editor. *Twentieth Year*, Vol. XLI, No. 3: 43.

Riva, Maria. 1992. *Marlene Dietrich.* New York: Alfred A Knopf.

Sarris, Andrew. 1966. *The Films of Josef Von Sternberg.* New York: Museum of Modern Art.

Spoto, Donald. 1992. *Blue Angel. The Life of Marlene Dietrich.* New York: Doubleday.

Studlar, Gaylyn. 1988. *In the Realm of Pleasure. Von Sternberg, Dietrich and the Masochistic Aesthetic.* New York: Columbia University Press.

Studlar, Gaylyn. 2007. "Marlene Dietrich and the Erotics of Code-Bound Hollywood." In *Dietrich Icon.* Edited by Gerd Gemünden and Mary R. Desjardins. Durham and London: Duke University Press, 211–238.

Dunaway, Faye (1941–)

Faye Dunaway is an American actress. Active since the 1960s on stage and in film, her breakout role was in *Bonnie and Clyde* (1967), where she starred alongside Warren Beatty and earned her first Academy Award nomination, as well as a British Academy of Film and Television Arts (BAFTA) Award and a David di Donatello Award. She was nominated again for her work in Roman Polanski's *Chinatown* (1974) and finally won the Academy Award for Best Actress (as well as a Golden Globe Award, Kansas City Film Circle Critics Award, and David di Donatello Award) for her role as television executive Diana Christensen in *Network* (1976). Dunaway has worked with many European directors, including Barbet Schroder, Roman Polanski, Richard Lester, and Franco Zeffirelli. The recipient of many other television and film awards, Dunaway stands out for her acting range across multiple film genres, studios, and televisual mediums.

More reminiscent of the major stars of the 1920s and 1930s than of her own contemporaries (such as Barbra Streisand or Meryl Streep), who have been stronger box office draws, Faye Dunaway has famously acted with brilliant energy, often portraying women who were more than a match for their male counterparts. These men included the biggest stars of the mid-1960s and 1970s, including Jack Nicholson, Robert Redford, and Warren Beatty. Dunaway's strength recalls earlier stars such as Marlene Dietrich and Greta Garbo, though her toughness might have worked to the detriment of her career (Schur, 2010, 138).

For example, playing against Jack Nicholson in the neo-noir *Chinatown*, Dunaway brings to mind earlier femme fatales, such as Lauren Bacall in *The Big Sleep* (1946) and Jane Greer in *Out of the Past* (1947). However, Dunaway's character Evelyn Mulwray is the opposite of cool. Apprehensive and psychologically camouflaged, Dunaway's performance is frightening but also extremely vulnerable, and this admixture attested to the cultural anxieties of men in the film and in the audience (Maxfield 1996, 126). Similar to Joan Crawford's formidable presence in such noir films as *Mildred Pierce* (1945) and *Possessed* (1947) but adding her own fine emotional detail in films such as *Three Days of the Condor* (1975) and *Barfly* (1987), Dunaway's complexity as a film artist is difficult to define but always powerful.

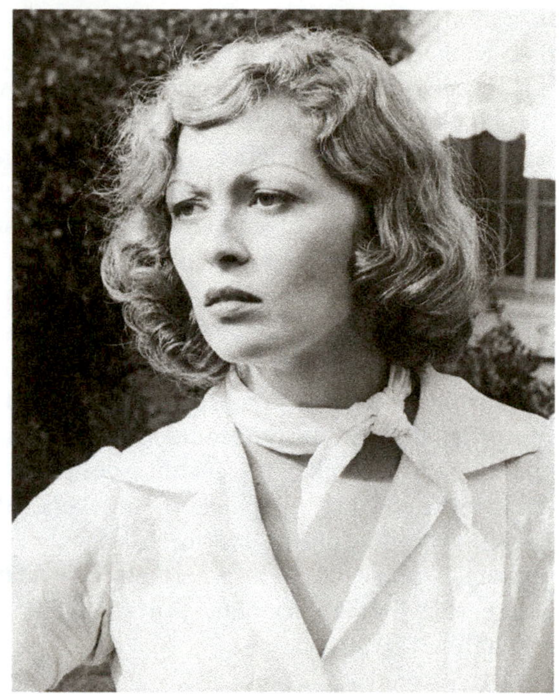

Academy Award-winning actress Faye Dunaway as femme fatale Evelyn Mulwray in Roman Polanski's neo-noir *Chinatown* (1974). Dunaway is noted not only for her elegance and sensuality, but for her ability to portray complex characters onscreen. She starred in several films considered emblematic of the New Hollywood era of the American film history. (Silver Screen Collection/Getty Images)

Dunaway even played Joan Crawford in *Mommie Dearest* (1981). Reception to the film and often to Dunaway's performance was generally poor, though some critics did praise her acting. The outlandish role of an aging, abusive, and psychotic-seeming Crawford has come to be seen as a cliché in film. The elements of camp and melodrama are extremely strong in *Mommie Dearest*, and whether the film has added or detracted from Dunaway's overall reputation remains to be seen. Crawford herself had written a decade before, in her autobiography *My Way of Life* (1971), that "of all the actresses, to me, only Faye Dunaway has the talent and the class and the courage it takes to make a real star" (quoted in Dunaway and Sharkey 1995, 335).

Dunaway has also worked on stage and on television. She won the Golden Globe for her work on the television miniseries *Ellis Island* (1984) and an Emmy Award for the episode of *Columbo* entitled, "It's All in the Game" (1993). She won another Golden Globe for the HBO movie *Gia* (1998). On stage, Dunaway played the opera singer Maria Callas in Terrence McNally's play *Master Class*. In 1994, she was ready to take over for Glenn Close in the musical *Sunset Boulevard*, but the show abruptly shut down before Dunaway was to join the cast. The producers and Dunaway went to court with each other over the premature ending of the production. She has also appeared in less successful films, such as *Supergirl* (1984) and *Don Juan DeMarco* (1995), and smaller roles in other television series, including *Grey's Anatomy*, *The Starlet*, and others.

Though her prolific film career has had its share of missteps, Dunaway's achievements are rare. In an era when independent filmmakers as well as major studios were creating a new vision for American film, Dunaway's acting style was unique. She is not often described as an intense Method actor, like Shelley Winters or Ellen

Burstyn. Yet neither is her acting entirely redolent of classical Hollywood actresses like Katharine Hepburn or Bette Davis. Her acting impulses are always surprising, even when she is cast as a stereotypical love interest, and during the period of the 1960s and 1970s, when feminine and masculine gender roles in film were being exploded, Dunaway's deft combinations of intimate emotional vulnerability and concealed anger helped to complicate her roles in very important ways.

It is unsurprising, given the range of her characters, that Dunaway is given relatively scant critical attention in books on film. Her work has not been of a single kind or note, and she has tended to work with very different directors on various projects. But perhaps the connection between old and new Hollywood that Dunaway represents in film is an important legacy in its own right. Her idiosyncratic performances provide a bridge between the different eras of Hollywood glamor, European cinema, and the renaissance of American independent films in the 1960s. Theadora Van Runkle, the costume designer for *Bonnie and Clyde* (she would go on to make costumes for Dunaway in several other films), recalled seeing the young Dunaway's photo during casting sessions for the film. Her opinion of Dunaway was extremely prescient. In an interview with Mark Harris, Van Runkle said, "[S]he was perfect for the spirit of the thirties and perfect for the spirit of the sixties" (Harris 2008, 213).

Nicholas Tamarkin

See also: Allen, Dede; Bergman, Marilyn (Songwriter); Davis, Bette; Dietrich, Marlene; Fonda, Jane; Garbo, Greta; Hepburn, Katharine; Sharaff, Irene; Streep, Meryl; Sylbert, Anthea; Van Runkle, Theadora

Further Reading

Dunaway, Faye, and Betsy Sharkey. 1995. *Looking for Gatsby: My Life*. New York: Simon and Schuster.

Harris, Mark. 2008. *Pictures at a Revolution.* New York: Penguin.

Maxfield, James F. 1996. *The Fatal Woman.* Madison, NJ: Fairleigh Dickinson University Press.

Schur, Thomas. 2010. "Faye Dunaway: Stardom and Ambivalence." In *Hollywood Reborn.* Edited by James Morrison. Piscataway, NJ: Rutgers University Press, 138–157.

Smith-Rowsey, Daniel. 2013. *Star Actors in the Hollywood Renaissance.* New York: Palgrave Macmillan.

Fonda, Jane (1937–)

Jane Seymour Fonda was born on December 21, 1937, in New York City at Doctors Hospital. Jane Fonda began her acting career in the theater and made her stage debut alongside her father, Henry Fonda, himself a Hollywood star, in *The Country Girl* in Omaha in 1955. She made her first Hollywood film debut with *Tall Story* in 1960. Fonda has had a wide-ranging career, including Oscar-winning performances in film, leading roles on the stage, creating and starring in her own home workout videos, and most recently starring in an original Netflix television series *Grace and Frankie* (2015–2018) and a feature-length Netflix film *Our Souls at Night* (2017). Her film career spans classical Hollywood cinema through New Hollywood, which includes films such as *Klute* (1971), as well as starring in European films for directors like Roger Vadim and Jean-Luc Godard. Besides starring in films as an actor, Fonda has produced and executive-produced some of her own productions and set up her production company, IPC Films, to make some of her projects starting in the 1970s (Bosworth 2011, 477). In her career she has been nominated for an Oscar for Best Actress five times, and she has won two Academy Awards for Best Actress for *Klute* (1971) and *Coming Home* (1978), and received an Emmy award for her role in *The Dollmaker* (1984). In addition to being known worldwide as a movie star, Fonda is known as a controversial political activist who championed a number of causes in the 1970s, including Native American rights, supporting the Black Panthers, and, most famously, as an activist who used her celebrity to publicly oppose U.S. involvement in the Vietnam War.

Despite being the daughter of Hollywood star Henry Fonda, acting was not something that Jane initially pursued. After her stage debut with her father in *The Country Girl* (1955), she showed enough promise for her father to take note of her talent. Once she decided that she wanted to be an actor like her father, she began studying at the Actors Studio with Lee Strasberg. Fonda began studying with Strasberg in his private classes in New York City. Strasberg had become famous for his "Method" technique, and he had an impressive list of students, among them Marlon Brando and Marilyn Monroe. During the time she was studying with Strasberg, she had begun modeling for high-fashion magazines as a way to make a living and became well known as a fashion model in New York City. Fonda's break into Hollywood came in the form of her screen test with Josh Logan, who put her under contract for $10,000 a year. Her first film was *Tall Story* (1960), a college comedy made for Warner Bros., where she played opposite Anthony Perkins. Fonda made a conscious decision to break away from the good-girl image that she had at the time in her next role as Kitty Twist, a high-class prostitute in *Walk on the Wild Side* (1962). She also bought her contract back from Josh Logan for $250,000 to ensure her artistic freedom (Fonda 2005, 135).

After buying back her contract, Fonda said that she never wanted to make another Hollywood picture again. She got her chance to make films outside the Hollywood system when she agreed to star in a film in France, *Joy House* (1964), opposite Alain Delon for director Rene Clement. Fonda moved to France and said one of the reasons she took the part was that France was then at the height of the French New Wave and she could distance herself from her father's image. The French *Nouvelle Vague,* or New Wave, featured films by young directors with unique stylistic breakthroughs, like the jump cut in *Breathless* (1960) by Godard. Other representative directors like Truffaut and Vadim were making films with their own authorial stamps. Fonda would go on to make films with Roger Vadim and eventually marry him. The first film they made together, *Circle of Love* (1964), established Fonda as a sex symbol in Europe and America. Fonda was not exclusively making films in France during this period and flew back to Hollywood to make films like *Barefoot in the Park* (1967) starring opposite Robert Redford. The most famous collaboration between Fonda and Vadim was the sex science fiction-comedy *Barbarella* (1968). This film, based on a French soft-core comic, would cement Fonda's sex symbol image around the world. It was after the shooting of *Barbarella*, while pregnant with her and Vadim's daughter, Vanessa, that Fonda would see television coverage of the Vietnam War in France, which would lead to the beginnings of her political activism against the war.

Fonda went back to Hollywood to shoot *They Shoot Horses, Don't They?* (1969). The film was based on a novel of the same name written by Horace McCoy in 1935 and told the story of Depression-era marathon dances. Fonda threw herself into the character of Gloria, working out intensely and living at the studio in order to better inhabit her character. The hard work paid off with great critical reviews and Fonda's first Academy Award nomination for Best Actress. It was during this time that Fonda began to take a serious in interest in political activism and embarked on a cross-country road trip with her friend from France, Elisabeth Vailland. They visited Native American reservations and G.I. coffeehouses, where she would speak out against the Vietnam War. Because of these activities, the FBI opened a file on her, and this led to her deliberately being harassed and arrested numerous times. Fonda had accepted a part in the film *Klute* (1971), which began filming in New York City after the road trip. This film would be part of a style of Hollywood film that would become known as the "New Hollywood." New Hollywood films would become known for on-location shooting, smaller budgets, and techniques influenced by other forms of cinema, like the French New Wave. Her brother, Peter Fonda, who had also become an actor, made one of the first New Hollywood films, *Easy Rider* (1969), which he wrote and starred in. In *Klute* Fonda portrayed a call girl named Bree Daniel opposite Donald Sutherland, a private investigator who tries to figure out who is stalking Bree. Fonda spent time with working prostitutes in preparation for the role and had her hair cut by Vadim's stylist in New York in a trademark shag cut that shed much of her previous blond sex symbol image. Fonda's performance in *Klute* was a mixture of the research she had done and elements of her own self. Her performance again won her favorable critical reviews, and for *Klute* she won her first Academy Award for Best Actress in 1972. In keeping with her new, radical outlook, she agreed to make a film for Godard about a factory strike in France opposite Yves Montand, *Tout Va Bien* (1972). She later admitted that she was not thrilled at making the Maoist polemic film for Godard.

Fonda found a way to integrate her political beliefs with her own films in the latter part of the 1970s into the 1980s with her own productions with films like *The China Syndrome* (1979), about the danger of nuclear power, and *9 to 5* (1980) about women's rights in the workplace. These films were top performers at the box office, and around this time she became a highly successful businesswoman when she virtually created the home video market with her home workout videos. The success of the first video, which sold 17 million copies, led to mass purchasing of VCRs in the United States (Fonda 2005, 394). ,In addition, she was instrumental in making *On Golden Pond* (1981), the only picture she starred in with her father, and the only film for which Henry Fonda won an Oscar, for Best Actor, in 1982. Fonda took a 15-year hiatus from acting starting in 1990; during this time she married media mogul Ted Turner. She resumed making films with the comedy *Monster-in-Law* (2005), and her most recent film, *Our Souls at Night* (2017), paired her onscreen with Robert Redford once again.

Eric Pellerin

See also: Dunaway, Faye; Sylbert, Anthea

Further Reading

Bosworth, Patricia. 2011. *Jane Fonda*. New York: Houghton Mifflin Harcourt.

Fonda, Jane. 2005. *My Life So Far*. New York: Random House.

Kiernan, Thomas. 1973. *Jane: An Intimate Biography of Jane Fonda*. New York: G. P. Putnam Sons.

Pramaggiore, Maria. 2010. "Jane Fonda: From Graylist to A-List." In *Hollywood Reborn: Movie Stars of the 1970s*. Edited by James Morrison. New Brunswick, NJ: Rutgers University Press, 16–38.

Ross, Steve J. 2011. *Hollywood Left and Right: How Movie Stars Shaped American Politics*. New York: Oxford University Press.

Foster, Jodie (1962–)

At 12 years of age, Jodie Foster took on the contentious role of a child prostitute in *Taxi Driver* (1976), and her performance garnered her the first of many Academy Award nominations to come. Acting since age three, Foster was featured in many commercials, television shows, and Disney productions prior to *Taxi Driver,* including her first feature-length film, *Napoleon and Samantha* (1972), in which she played the title character Samantha. Foster's departure from an innocent child star to the sexualized role she embodied in *Taxi Driver* challenged the cultural norms and public perception of what type of content films were permitted to engage in. For much of her career, the characters Foster chose to play and the woman she would become continued to challenge people on issues of gender, sexuality, and power. Regardless of how audiences past or present may be divided, Foster's daring to take on potentially controversial and complex characters that push conventional boundaries are what sets Foster apart from other actresses and cements her as an important cultural icon and tour de force.

Prior to her ground-breaking role in *Taxi Driver,* Foster broke with the mold—especially in how unfeminine she appeared as a child star. While many other female child actresses were pegged into typical gender-conforming roles, playing up girlish charms, Foster's roles between 1972 and 1977 were typified by tomboy characters. It became a poignant characteristic that defined much of Foster's career, also fueling the debate surrounding her sexuality in later years (Hollinger 2006). Her most noted role during this time was the tomboyish Aubrey who gets high on "Ripple" in *Alice Doesn't Live Here Anymore* (1974). The strong and complicated female characters she became known for as an adult were clearly rooted in her child-star years.

Foster has been just as cautious selecting roles in her adult career as she was as a child star, opting for character portrayals that set her apart. She carefully selects roles that fit the purview of her career goals, but not without consequences. The growing sexualized persona of Foster's teen years got the attention of John Hinckley, Jr., who became obsessed with Foster after he watched *Taxi Driver*; in 1981, Hinckley attempted to assassinate then-president Ronald Reagan hoping to gain Foster's affection. At the time, Foster had traded in the film industry for the college experience, graduating cum laude from Yale University in 1985 with a BA in literature. The assassination attempt not only sparked national outcry but also represented a moment of change for Foster's image. Foster took the opportunity to write an essay entitled "Why Me?" presenting the image of a woman who was made the victim of a man's obsession. A few years after her graduation from Yale, she took the role of rape victim Sarah Tobias using the legal system against her rapists in *The Accused* (1988). Her portrayal won her a Golden Globe and her first Academy Award for Best Actress and established her official transition from child star to serious Hollywood star and actress.

Her portrayal of victim/survivor characters took a turn when she played FBI agent Clarice Starling in the titular film *The Silence of the Lambs* (1991). Foster won her second Golden Globe and Academy Award for this role. However, with the awards also came controversy. A figurehead for the feminist movement for her nonconformist gender roles and challenges to notions of beauty and glamour in Hollywood, and a de facto member of the gay community with widespread rumors about her sexuality since she was a teen, Foster split the community with this film. Feminist scholars and activists praised Foster for Clarice, who was not sexualized against her male counterparts as the romantic female lead and who was presented as a strong-willed woman who did not adhere to the typical Hollywood film narrative of female characters in need of saving. However, the gay community, upset by the representation of the killer James "Buffalo Bill" Gumb as an LGBTQ man murdering women for their skin to create a new "body suit," called on Foster, stating that even if she wanted to remain in the closet, it didn't mean she had to support a homophobic film. The controversy was exacerbated since Foster always remained quiet about her sexuality. It wasn't until December 2007 that Foster acknowledged Cydney Bernard as her partner, whom she had been in a relationship with for a significant amount of time. In April 2014, Foster married photographer Alexandra Hedison.

Following *The Silence of the Lambs*' critically acclaimed character portrayal of Clarice, Foster's roles into the 1990s saw more gender-conforming roles such as the female romantic lead alongside Mel Gibson in *Maverick* (1994). In *Nell* (1994) she co-starred with Liam Neeson as the title character, playing an isolated woman who speaks her own made-up language. While those character representations were received with mixed reviews, Foster's representation of Nell earned her a fourth Academy Award nomination for Best Actress as well as her fourth Golden Globe nomination. Additional notable roles played by Foster include Eleanor Arroway in *Contact* (1997), Anna in *Anna and the King* (1999), Meg Altman in *Panic Room* (2002), Elodie Gordes in *A Very Long Engagement* (2004), Kyle Pratt in *Flightplan* (2005), Madeline White in *Inside Man* (2006), Erica Bain in *The Brave One* (2007), Meredith Black in *The Beaver* (2011), and Delacourt in *Elysium* (2013). Even with the differing opinions about the broader sociocultural value of the numerous female roles and characters portrayed by Foster, there isn't doubt that her characters hold a strength and tenacity that she has carried throughout all her roles, which sets her apart from traditional representations in Hollywood.

While Foster's acting career has been marked by controversy, her path as a producer and director has been more straightforward, albeit not any less important than her acting career. In 1991 she directed (and starred in) her first feature film, *Little Man Tate*, before starting her production company, Egg Pictures (which produced *Nell*), in 1992. While the film was received well, Foster did not meet the expectations of feminists who were hoping Foster's foray into producing and directing would lead to more radical and feminist representations of women. In *Little Man Tate*, Foster also starred as Dede, mother of a genius boy who tried to give him a "normal" childhood. Even as Foster played a single, working-class mother, her character seemed more like a gender-conforming role and was not considered a "radical refashioning of the representation of women onscreen" (Hollinger 2012, 51). Foster followed up her directorial debut with *Home for the Holidays* (1995), which was not as critically acclaimed as her first film. Foster didn't return to directing until *The Beaver* (2011) in which she co-starred alongside Mel Gibson again. While her directorial projects in film have not come off as radical representations overall, Foster did direct two episodes of *Orange Is the New Black* (2013–), a show first released on Netflix that has gained wide popularity in the LGBTQ community for its representations of women in prison. She also directed an episode of the popular and original Netflix series *House of Cards* (2014–), a political drama noted for its unconventional sexual representation of a heterosexual power couple. Foster has continued to flourish in her new role, directing the feature *Money Monster* in 2016 and an episode in 2017 for yet another popular series released on Netflix, *Black Mirror* (2011–). Foster has stated that she finds being able to present a picture from her own perspective as a director a rewarding passion that she will continue to craft (Bio 2015; Hollinger 2006).

Foster has continued to successfully claim her identity throughout the many challenges and controversies surrounding her impressive career as an actress, producer, and director. Judging her work by its quality and groundbreaking contribution to the industry, it should come as no surprise that in 2013 she was awarded the honorary Golden Globe Cecil B. DeMille Award for "outstanding contributions to the world of entertainment" (Bio 2015). Her unapologetic ownership of both typical and radical female roles, as well as the films she helms from behind the camera, makes her a Hollywood heroine.

Elaine Venter

See also: Arrighi, Luciana (Production Designer); Atwood, Colleen; Briesewitz, Uta; Kaufman, Avy; Streep, Meryl; Vincent, Amy

Further Reading

Bio. 2015. "Jodie Foster." Accessed March 14, 2015. http://www.biography.com/people/jodie-foster-9299556

Crimp, Douglas. 1992. "Right On, Girlfriend!" *Social Text* 33: 2–18. http://www.jstor.org/stable/466431

Erb, Cynthia. 2010. "Jodie Foster and Brooke Shields 'New Ways to Look at the Young.'" In *Hollywood Reborn Movie Stars of the 1970s*. Edited by James Morrison. New Brunswick, NJ: Rutgers University Press, 82–100.

Hollinger, Karen. 2006. "'A Perfect Acting Machine': Jodie Foster." In *The Actress: Hollywood Acting and the Female Star*. New York: Routledge, 141–164.

Hollinger, Karen. 2012. "Jodie Foster Feminist Hero?" In *Pretty People: Movie Stars of the 1990s*. Edited by Anna Everett. New Brunswick, NJ: Rutgers University Press, 43–64.

Wettach, Gabriel. 2011. "For the Love of Jodie Foster: Star Demystification and National Configuration." In *The Star and Celebrity Confessional*. Edited by Sean Redmond. London: Routledge, 96–112.

Garbo, Greta (1905–1990)

In Billy Wilder's 1951 *Sunset Blvd.*, fictional former silent film star Norma Desmond derides current Hollywood royalty, sneering, "We didn't need dialogue. We had *faces!*" And during the peak of Hollywood's silent era, no face shone more luminously or expressed so evocatively as Greta Garbo's. The eyes had it: heavy-lidded, large, bright, the key to her thoughts. Those eyes have held audiences captive for generations, pulling them in even as she grew to isolate herself from the business that had made her famous. She did not wind up an icon for having died young and pretty, but in the eyes of Hollywood, she may as well have: she abruptly retired from the screen in 1941 at the age of 36. In 1955 she became the youngest person to receive an honorary Oscar, given for her "luminous and unforgettable screen performances." She did not attend the ceremony and continued to stay out of the spotlight until her death in 1990.

Born in Stockholm, Sweden, in 1905, Garbo first came to prominence acting under noted Swedish director Mauritz Stiller. Hollywood was out scoping for international talent, and Metro-Goldwyn-Mayer (MGM) studio head Louis B. Mayer was encouraged to attend a screening of Stiller's 1924 film *The Saga of Gösta Berling.* Accounts differ as to whether Mayer was entranced by Garbo's performance in the film and wanted to sign only her but had to agree to bring her mentor Stiller along as well, or whether Mayer begrudgingly signed Garbo because Stiller would not leave Sweden without her. Either way, Garbo's stardom quickly rose and Stiller's diminished after they arrived in Hollywood in 1925. Once Garbo became an established star—thanks mostly to an explosive turn opposite John Gilbert in 1926's *The Flesh and the Devil*—she would use her homeland as leverage: when offered parts she found unsuitable, she would intimate that perhaps she ought to return to Sweden. Desperate not to lose such a huge star—one who was appealingly exotic to American audiences while also immensely popular abroad—MGM acquiesced to her requests as best they could. Wielding the sort of control that few actors working within the studio system could claim, Garbo was often able to choose her cameramen, set photographers, directors, and even leading men.

As a teenager she had adored the films of Mary Pickford, and working in Hollywood, she frequented Lillian Gish's sets to watch the great actress perform. Though no doubt inspired by the tremendous skills of these women, during the silent period Garbo was able to cultivate a screen image more daring than Pickford's moppets and Gish's suffering saints: a woman who was both womanly and assertive. She could command contempt and sympathy, exuding a delicate vulnerability in one scene and steely self-reliance in the next.

In the United States, it was the mystery of Garbo that was just as (if not more) alluring to filmgoers as her acting. The classical Hollywood era was home to myriad fan magazines, bursting with stories and interviews about the biggest screen personalities. Every performer was expected to do their part for publicity, but Garbo was at odds with this particular period dictate and refused to grant interviews. She valued her privacy and though she belonged to the most esteemed stable of stars of the era—MGM boasted they had "more stars than there are in heaven"—she did not care to identify as part of the MGM family. Keeping her distance only stewed the public fervor more, and MGM's publicity department wisely built up this enigma as part of her appeal.

When sound came to Hollywood in the late 1920s, one of the major problems it presented was the question of what to do with foreign movie stars. The transition was difficult enough for many native English-speaking actors, several of whom saw their careers ruined, but was all the more challenging for actors who could not speak English very well or whose voices were deemed too heavily accented. Garbo ran the risk of being such an actress, and was thus MGM's only major star not to be included in their *Hollywood Revue of 1929*, essentially a series of sketches meant to show off their actors' voices to the viewing public.

Garbo would not make her sound debut until *Anna Christie* in 1930, three years after *The Jazz Singer*, the first "talkie," had been released. Her relevance had not waned during that time; if anything, the wait to hear her voice only ratcheted up further audience attentiveness. When Garbo's first spoken line of dialogue was heard—"Gimme a whiskey. Ginger ale on the side. And don't be stingy, baby"—rough, raspy, and sensual, viewers were not disappointed (*Anna Christie* 1930).

The issue arose after the initial excitement of "Garbo Talks!" wore off and it turned out that, largely, talkies didn't give Garbo much worth saying. Her greatest gift and contribution to screen acting were her unmatched ability to infuse the most melodramatic parts, poses, and affects with sincere intellect and emotion. The thoughtfulness put into expressing her characters' innermost feelings was sometimes hindered by dialogue in a language whose intricacies Garbo was still learning. All the same, she received Academy Award nominations for Best Actress four times during this period: for tragic roles in *Romance* (1930), *Anna Christie* (1930), *Camille* (1936), and a deadpan comedic turn in *Ninotchka* (1939).

Billed as "Garbo laughs!," *Ninotchka* proved such a success that MGM quickly put Garbo into another comedy. Unfortunately, *Two-Faced Woman* (1941) lacked *Ninotchka*'s witty script and was the first categorical letdown of Garbo's career. This first failure coupled with the closing of key war-torn European markets led to Garbo's premature retirement from the screen. Her ethereal image didn't mesh with the American sensibilities of the time, which desired relatable screen characters. By removing herself so consciously and early from film, Garbo cemented her legacy and has left generations of film aficionados yearning for the collaborations that might have been.

Chelsea Gibbs

See also: Bara, Theda; Bergman, Ingrid; ;Davis, Bette; Dietrich, Marlene; Dunaway, Faye; Hepburn, Katharine; Marion, Frances; McDaniel, Hattie; Talmadge, Norma

Further Reading

Anna Christie, DVD. 1930. Directed by Clarence Brown. Metro-Goldwyn-Mayer.

Conway, Michael, Dion McGregor, and Mark Ricci 1964. *The Films of Greta Garbo*. New York: Cadillac Publishing Company.

Garbo, DVD. 2005. Directed by Christopher Bird and Kevin Brownlow. Turner Classic Movies.

Vieira, Mark A. 2005. *Greta Garbo: A Cinematic Legacy*. New York: Harry N. Abrams.

Hepburn, Katharine (1907–2003)

Following her 1932 Broadway premiere in *The Warrior's Husband,* Katharine Hepburn caught the eye of some of Hollywood's most prominent directors. Both John Ford and George Cukor ordered respective screen tests, and Hepburn was eventually cast in George Cukor's *A Bill of Divorcement* (1932) later that year. This film established the varying reception that she would face by both audience and industry: although most found her strong-willed personality and mannerisms refreshing, others found her "modern" attitude difficult and tenacious. Hepburn's wardrobe, which generally consisted of "tomboyish" trousers, defied standard Hollywood glamor. She was a unique star of the day in that she was a figure who "[wasn't] what a star should be, and yet she [was] a star" (Britton 1984, 22). After a series of commercial failures, she was labeled "box office poison" by 1938. Nevertheless, Hepburn continuously defied societal expectations and facilitated her own Hollywood comeback vis-à-vis MGM's *The Philadelphia Story* (1940). From thereon out, she would continue to bring to the screen a strong female presence that "is always more radical than her films" (Britton 1984). This presence enabled her to stand her ground opposite talented male forces such as Humphrey Bogart, Henry Fonda, and, perhaps most unforgettably, Spencer Tracy. Throughout her 66-year career, she received four Academy Awards (the record number of any performer), one Emmy, a Lifetime Achievement Award from the Screen Actors Guild, and the Kennedy Center Honors.

Hepburn won public praise and her first Academy Award for her third RKO film, *Morning Glory* (1933). However, though later RKO films such as *Little Women* (1933), *Stage Door* (1937), and *Bringing Up Baby* (1938) were critically acclaimed, they were unsuccessful at the box office. Arguably, her professional decline during the late 1930s may be due to RKO's misplacement of her "modern" personality in various costume dramas. Her popularity with the public had also dwindled due to her difficult relationship with the press. Hepburn, now labeled "box office poison," bought herself out of her RKO contract and returned to Broadway to star in Philip Barry's *The Philadelphia Story.* Barry had written the part of Tracy Lord specifically with Hepburn in mind; the role therefore highlighted Hepburn's vivacious, modern attitude that previous scripts had disregarded. She would later purchase its film rights following the story's success on the stage, thereby initiating her own Hollywood comeback.

To bring *The Philadelphia Story* to the screen, Hepburn partnered with George Cukor and MGM. The film was one of most successful films of 1940, and its Academy nominations and record-breaking numbers instantly appealed to Louis B. Mayer and company. Hepburn was later placed on contract at MGM and was largely responsible for the development of her subsequent project, *Woman of the Year* (1942) opposite Spencer Tracy. This film, directed by George Stevens, established the Hepburn-Tracy onscreen team, as well as a private offscreen romance that endured 26 years. During their relationship, Hepburn's professional career slowed as she cared for Tracy and his declining health. However, choice projects ensured the public that Hepburn's determination would not slow with age. In 1951, Hepburn starred in *The African Queen* alongside Humphrey Bogart, and she starred in *Long Day's Journey into Night* (1962) the following year. Both performances received

Academy Award nominations. Nevertheless, audiences were predominantly attracted to the Hepburn-Tracy duo. The two would star in nine films together, including *Adam's Rib* (1949), *Pat and Mike* (1952), and, in later years, *Guess Who's Coming to Dinner* (1967). Tracy died shortly after filming, and Hepburn received her second Academy Award for their last performance together.

Following Tracy's death, Hepburn continued to sustain success in film, Broadway, and, for the first time, television. She received her third Academy Award for *The Lion in Winter* (1968) in which she played opposite Peter O'Toole. In 1969, Hepburn returned to Broadway to star in the musical *Coco*, which is based upon the life of Coco Chanel. Though her first and only musical, she received a Tony Award nomination for Best Actress. Four years later, she made her first television appearance in Tennessee Williams's *The Glass Menagerie* (1973). Hepburn would continue to star in various successful television movies, yet her screen appearances throughout the 1970s were reviewed as mediocre at best. However, similar to her career's beginnings, a comeback was imminent. In 1981, Hepburn starred opposite Henry Fonda in *On Golden Pond,* a film that was met with tremendous acclaim. At 74 years old, Hepburn was awarded her fourth and final Academy Award.

Katharine Hepburn's career is in every aspect a challenge to Hollywood convention. From her filmic beginnings, Hepburn brought forth a new type of female to the American screen, both in fashion and mannerisms. She is a "key presence within classical Hollywood, a consistent, potentially radical disturbance" to the conventional studio system (Britton 1984, 6). Offscreen, she pioneered various artistic projects and directed her own personal image, an attitude that enabled a career that successfully spanned 66 years. Her enduring onscreen appeal is evident: she received a total of 12 Academy Award nominations (a record that has since been surpassed only by Meryl Streep), and 3 of her Academy Awards were received for performances throughout her later years. Furthermore, Hepburn continuously challenged herself through the exploration of other media outlets and found a place in both Broadway and television. Thus, her career is one of unconventional sustainability. Despite various setbacks, including early box office condemnation and various reprieves from the screen, Hepburn has since become one of the female trailblazers of American classical cinema.

Kelsey E. Moore

See also: Bergman, Ingrid; Davis, Bette; Dunaway, Faye; Garbo, Greta; Marin, Mindy; McDaniel, Hattie; Streep, Meryl

Further Reading

Britton, Andrew. 1984. *Katharine Hepburn: Star as Feminist.* New York: Columbia University Press.

Dickens, Homer. 1971. *The Films of Katharine Hepburn.* Secaucus, NJ: Citadel Press.

Edwards, Anne. 1985. *Katharine Hepburn: A Remarkable Woman.* New York: St. Martin's Press.

Hepburn, Katharine. 1992. *Me: Stories of My Life.* New York: The Random House Publishing Group.

Samelson, Judy. 2010. "Katharine Hepburn on Stage." In *Playbills to Photoplays: Stage Performers Who Pioneered the Talkies.* Edited by Brenda Loew. Bloomington: New England Vintage Film Society.

McDaniel, Hattie (1895–1952)

Hattie McDaniel was an African American singer, dancer, and actor of quality. Born in 1895 into an artistic family from Kansas, she inherited her talents from her parents. In her early teens, Hattie was already an established entertainer writing lyrics, singing, and dancing/acting with touring troupes. Her exceptional knack for spectacle earned her unparalleled repute and catapulted her name to national headlines.

Hattie moved to Los Angeles in 1931. All in all, she played in over 100 pictures with many unbilled appearances. After a 1939 apogee, McDaniel's silver-screen stint ground to a halt in the 1940s. All her artistic activities were tragically cut short after being diagnosed with breast cancer in 1951, to which she finally succumbed in October 1952. McDaniel reaped many awards and honors in recognition of her contributions to the big screen and the airwaves.

Yet McDaniel's ascension to nationwide fame was an arduous journey. Her artistic talents did not guarantee her an auspicious beginning. The pre-war, racially stratified movie industry hampered her progress. Nevertheless, Hattie's inventive renditions of the help stereotype engendered far-reaching changes in Hollywood, allowing her to become a trailblazer who lit the path for generations of gifted black artists to come.

Actress Hattie McDaniel, holding the plaque-style Oscar she received for winning Best Supporting Actress in *Gone With The Wind* (1939). McDaniel was the first African American to ever win an Academy Award. The ceremony was held at the Ambassador Hotel in Los Angeles on February 29, 1940, and after her memorable acceptance speech, McDaniel was escorted back to a segregated table due to the hotel's "no-blacks" policy at the time. (John D. Kisch/Separate Cinema Archive/Getty Images)

By and large, Hattie's film career in Hollywood can be divided into three phases. The first phase stretched from 1932 to 1934 when she was still unknown to filmmakers. Unable to land many roles during the Great Depression, McDaniel toiled as a real-life maid for $7 a week washing 3 million dishes in the process. She made only 15 uncredited appearances as a "loyal, unobtrusive" (Bogle 2001, 83) reel maid, including Mammy Lou in *The Golden West* (1932), Edna in *Goodbye Love* (1933), and Aunt Dilsey in *Judge Priest* (1934).

McDaniel witnessed the height of her success between 1935 and 1939. During this most productive phase of her career, she played in

51 features. Far from the earlier innocuous and repetitive stereotype, the maid image of this phase is serious and pregnant with protest. The Mammy stereotype had clearly undergone a radical transmutation in the second half of the 1930s when McDaniel embarked on a journey of calculated breaking of her casting type.

The Mammy figure, as refashioned by McDaniel, is resilient and uplifted. Her persona exhibits differences that are worthy of remark. Together, her interpretations of the stereotype amount to an iconoclastic "anti-Mammy" figure (Wallace-Sanders 2008, 48–49). As the hired maid Malena in *Alice Adams* (1935), she pokes fun at her white employers, mocking their pretentious manners and laying bare their false claims to social status and wealth. In *The Mad Miss Manton* (1938), her character Hilda is further emancipated to the point of throwing a water pitcher in Henry Fonda's face.

The epitome of a transformed Mammy, however, is portrayed in the Civil War epic *Gone with the Wind* (*GWTW*) (1939). McDaniel managed to decisively convert her slave persona into a well-rounded character. Unlike the nostalgic figure of antebellum slavery, Mammy here is an updated character who resists the relegation to the screen recesses and shows little fealty in having drinks with her white master. She unflinchingly shoulders the heavy burden of running the white man's world with matchless dignity, taking charge of the plantation and becoming the pivot of the O'Haras' Southern universe. All this has enhanced the air of equality the McDaniel's celluloid persona evinces, which unsettled the deep-rooted (mis) conceptions of the white supremacy/black inferiority binary. In brief, Hattie successfully midwifed a counter-stereotype that cannot be relegated to the bottom of Hollywood's totem pole anymore.

How McDaniel infused her onscreen character with an air of defiance and pride equally affected the movie industry behind the camera. Her commitment struck a chord with both black and white performers and white studio executives. In relation to *GWTW*, McDaniel and other black actors pressured studio executives into making important alterations to the movie script. In response, David Selznick agreed to omit the racial epithets from the dialog. He further erased all references to the Ku Klux Klan found in the original text and made changes to accommodate Hattie's metamorphosing brand of the enslaved maid.

The most eloquent testimony to McDaniel's success in modifying the movie industry is unquestionably her Oscar triumph. She won the 1940 Academy Award for Best Supporting Actress for her outstanding rendering of Mammy in *GWTW*, garnering national acclaim as the first black performer to receive such a coveted trophy. This storied career capstone was a watershed in (black) film history. Despite her exclusion from the segregated *GWTW* premiere in Atlanta and her sitting in the rear of the Coconut Grove ballroom in the Ambassador Hotel at the 12th Academy Awards held in Los Angeles in 1940, Hattie proved she could make a difference. In her acceptance speech, she hoped to always be a credit to her "race." This momentous achievement set the seal on a remarkable Hollywood career and elevated Hattie to such an exalted position that no black entertainer had ever attained before.

After this pinnacle, McDaniel's career waned. She obviously failed to ride the crest of her success due to a chain of unfavorable circumstances. Most harmful of all was her bitter feud with the National Association for the Advancement of Colored People's (NAACP) executive secretary Walter White. This vendetta caused her to become reclusive after her name figured on the blacklist of the House Un-American Activities Committee, which reduced the roles offered to her to only 21 films in the 1940s.

Hattie's third-phase appearances were not particularly singular, except for two roles. Her Minerva Clay in *In This Our Life* (1942) is a socially advanced family maid with a house of her own and a son attending a law school. In *Since You Went Away* (1944), Fidelia is a reminiscence of the revamped caretaker character. Endowed with a defiant gaze, she enjoys eating a takeout cake with her white employers. Nonetheless, the two characters did not fare well with wartime America. McDaniel eventually left Hollywood to play Beulah, a wild maid with unaccented English, over the airwaves for approximately five years. The ether gave Hattie more leeway to enact her favorite part without impositions.

In sum, there is no denying that what McDaniel achieved set the wheels of change in motion. She succeeded in demonstrating that there was a place for black performers in Hollywood. Her curtain-raising struggle helped open doors for more black actors. She believed it her duty to help newcomers into the movies. McDaniel certainly deserves her place in the pantheon of divas who have shaped the history of Hollywood. Her Academy Award shook the walls of the cinematic apartheid and set her down in the cinema annals as the heroine who portrayed only minor characters. She was posthumously inducted into the Black Filmmakers Hall of Fame in 1975 and given two stars on the Hollywood Walk of Fame for cinema and radio works. In 2006, a commemorative U.S. postage stamp was issued bearing a still of McDaniel from the Academy Awards night. Though the plaque-style Oscar statuette she received was lost, her lasting legacy is constantly found to be illustrious of unprecedented success against overwhelming odds.

Yet a final question remains: Have all the Oscars won ever since changed the situation for black actors? It seems little has improved, as they are still remarkably underrepresented as nominees and very few of them actually win. Black women in particular still win Oscars for playing degrading stereotypes. It is such a bizarre coincidence that Hattie's last part as Minnie in *The Big Wheel* (1949) is almost duplicated by Octavia Spencer in her Oscar-winning role of the maid Minny in *The Help* (2011). Does the survival of the anachronistic Mammy stereotype into the 21st century not perpetuate a negative conception of black women at large?

Ali M. Amri

See also: Bergman, Ingrid; Davis, Bette; Garbo, Greta; Hepburn, Katharine

Further Reading

Bogle, Donald. 2001. *Toms, Coons, Mulattoes, Mammies, and Bucks: An Interpretive History of Blacks in American Films.* London: Continuum.

Bogle, Donald. 2006. *Bright Boulevards, Bold Dreams: The Story of Black Hollywood.* New York: One World Ballantine Books.

Brideson, Cynthia, and Sara Brideson. 2015. *Also Starring . . . : Forty Biographical Essays on the Greatest Character Actors of Hollywood's Golden Era, 1930–1965.* Albany, GA: BearManor Media.

Dreher, Kwakiutl L. 2008. *Dancing on the White Page: Black Women Entertainers Writing Autobiography.* Albany: State University of New York.

Hobson, Janell. 2014. "The Fantasy of Mammy, the Truth of Patsey." *Ms. Magazine*, March 5. http://msmagazine.com/blog/2014/03/05/the-fantasy-of-mammy-the-truth-of-patsey

Jackson, Carlton. 1990. *Hattie: The Life of Hattie McDaniel.* Lanham, MD: Madison Books.

Leff, Leonard J. 1999. "'Gone with the Wind' and Hollywood's Racial Politics." *The Atlantic*, December 9. https://www.theatlantic.com/magazine/archive/1999/12/gone-with-the-wind-and-hollywoods-racial-politics/377919

Otfinoski, Steven. 2010. *African Americans in the Performing Arts.* New York: Facts on File.

Wallace-Sanders, Kimberly. 2008. *Mammy: A Century of Race, Gender, and Southern Memory.* Ann Arbor: University of Michigan Press.

Streep, Meryl (1949–)

In a 1998 interview with CBS News, Meryl Streep said, "[I]t's difficult to find that niche which tells a true story about a fully dimensional woman and at the same time is screen worthy and going to bring people into the theater" (Streep 1998). Meryl Streep has devoted her talent to making the stories of complex women, both real and fictional, vibrant and visible within the Hollywood machine of moviemaking. Universally acknowledged as one of, if not the greatest actress of this generation, she is certainly considered Hollywood royalty and destined to be remembered as a silver-screen legend among the likes of Bette Davis and Katharine Hepburn. Streep's stunning acting has garnered 19 Academy Award nominations, the most of any performer in the history of the Academy; she has won three times.

Meryl Streep's talent was crafted and cultivated from a young age. Once her parents realized she had a naturally gifted voice, she began taking opera singing lessons from Estelle Liebling. She starred in high school plays and eventually enrolled at Vassar College for her undergraduate education. She would go on to earn an MFA from Yale School of Drama, where she stood out as a star of the stage. Streep never intended to get into films; she preferred the raw energy that came from live acting in plays. However, meeting and falling in love with actor John Cazale changed the course of her life forever.

In an effort to be as close as possible with her boyfriend, ,who was dying of cancer, Meryl Streep agreed to play Linda in Michael Cimino's Oscar-winning picture *The Deer Hunter* (1978). While the character of Linda was initially written to be very demure, Cimino's loose script gave Meryl the freedom to cultivate more nuances to her character. This practice of adding dimensions to her characters through costume design input, rewriting lines of dialogue, and even improvisation became a staple of her acting method and an integral aspect of her development as an actress. Streep received her first Academy Award nomination for her role as Linda; this would be the start of a now four-decade-long career as one of Hollywood's most distinguished talents.

Meryl Streep's relationship with John Cazale ended with his death in 1978 of cancer. Streep's grief was overwhelming. She would later go on to marry sculptor Don Gummer, whom she is still married to; they have four children together.

Streep's role as a mother and wife has had a profound impact on her career as an actress. She's been dubbed a "reluctant superstar" because she's managed to keep her personal life very private and because she is extremely humble about her talent and success. In the early 1990s it seemed as though her career took a turn from Oscar-worthy, serious dramas to trashy comedies with the likes of *She-Devil* (1989) and *Death Becomes Her* (1992). However, having a stable location to raise her children and have a family life was a major component to the roles she took on during this time. What is important to note is that despite the surfaced camp of some of these less prestigious roles, Streep always focused on bringing depth to every female character she played. Her role as Madeline Ashton in *Death Becomes Her* transcends the comedy and computer-wizardry of the film as it offers an allegorical tale about how women in Hollywood and in general are often turned into disposable objects once they reach a certain age and are no longer youthful. Streep's natural comedic timing coupled with her own experience as an actress in Hollywood entering her forties informed her performance of Madeline and the film's commentary on a culture obsessed with youth and beauty.

While Streep insists that she has no particular method of acting, she does make a habit of doing significant research into what she interprets as the background to the lives of her characters. It's critical to Streep to understand her characters as real in order to breathe into them a certain authenticity of aliveness. She once said, "[A]cting is total immersion into possibility; a life I could imagine I've lived, and that's infinitely interesting to me" (Streep 1998). Her passion to bring complexity to the women she plays is key to her successful transformations and immersions into the spectrum of female characters she performs. An aptitude for memorizing scripts quickly and a gift for mastering a multitude of accents have been fundamental to the range of characters she has been able to play and are skills that speak to the longevity of her career as well as her continued success.

Meryl Streep continues to make cinematic history as she holds the record for the most Academy Award nominations for any performer in the Academy's history. She has beaten her own record six times to date with a total of 19 nominations and 3 wins. She has earned 29 Golden Globe nominations with 8 total wins. She boasts three primetime Emmy Award nominations with two wins. She's also been a one-time Tony Award nominee and a four-time Grammy Award nominee. Meryl Streep has the rare capacity to glide through genres from drama to comedy to musicals and levels of productions from independent projects to huge blockbusters. Her unique style, chameleon nature, and immense talent have allowed her to give defining performances throughout different stages of Hollywood's film movements. She understands that real women exist in all ages, and she is unafraid to embrace and explore the intricacies of female characters, regardless of age.

Erendira Espinoza-Taboada

See also: Chenoweth, Ellen; Davis, Bette; Dunaway, Faye; Foster, Jodie; Hepburn, Katharine

Further Reading

Longworth, Karina. 1980. *Meryl Streep: Anatomy of an Actor* New York: Phaidon Press.

Maychick, Diana. 1984. *Meryl Streep: The Reluctant Superstar.* New York: St. Martin's Press.

Pfaff, Eugene E., and Mark Emerson. 1987. *Meryl Streep: A Critical Biography*. Jefferson, NC: McFarland & Co.

Streep, Meryl. 1998. "Rare Meryl Streep Interview (1998)." YouTube video, 9:29. Posted by "The Meryl Streep Forum," December 2, 2011. https://www.youtube.com/watch?v=bdY3tgPBLgg

Talmadge, Norma (1894–1957)

Norma Talmadge was an actress-producer of the silent era whose professional accomplishments were the result of a staunch work ethic and solid career management. Her films, which from 1916 onwards would be produced by her self-named production company, boasted excellent production values and surrounded the star with talented creative professionals. Her (deliberately) underdetermined screen persona allowed Talmadge to cover a wide array of ethnic, racial, and social identities in her roles. This adaptability was considered proof of her greatness as an actress despite the fact that she made only two talking pictures before retiring in 1930.

Norma Talmadge was among the first silent film stars—along with Mary Pickford and Douglas Fairbanks Sr.—to leave handprints and footprints in front of Grauman's Chinese Theatre in 1927. This alone should alert us to Talmadge's monumental popularity and commercial importance during the silent era, even if she is one of those great silent film stars who are largely forgotten today.

Urged by paternal absence and financial necessity, it was Talmadge's enterprising mother Margaret, or "Peg," Talmadge who realized the potential of her attractive daughter and who nudged Norma toward a career in film. Norma had two younger siblings, Constance and Nathalie, the former of whom would become a successful movie star in her own right. Norma's film career took off in 1910 when, at the age of 14, she started to work for the New York–based Vitagraph Company, a studio dubbed the "university of the screen" (*Motion Picture Classic* 1919, 12). Here she nurtured her as-yet undeveloped acting skills in small parts, usually of the ingénue kind. In 1916 she married Joseph M. Schenck, an exhibitor turned producer 15 years her senior. Schenck was a smart businessman, and in 1917 the Talmadge-Schenck tandem founded the Norma Talmadge Film Corporation, which released its pictures via Lewis J. Selznick's Select Pictures. This self-producing venture makes Talmadge a good example of a very successful second group of screen actors who understood the creative and commercial benefits—story influence and profits percentage—of owning their own company. Mostly female stars dominated this trend. In 1918, the Norma Talmadge Film Co. moved to First National, which had many other actress-producer initiatives (as well as Charlie Chaplin) under its wings. Always aided by her ambitious and watchful manager-mother, her devoted manager-husband, and her own work ethic, Talmadge saw her popularity and bankability grow steadily during these years.

Talmadge was not the most remarkable beauty, nor did she possess a unique screen persona like several other great stars of the silent era. In fact, Talmadge rather lacked a stable, familiar, and easily classifiable type or trait such as those which defined the diminutive and doll-like Mary Pickford ("little Mary"); the fragile, perpetual ingénue Lillian Gish; or the fashionably glamorous and feisty Gloria

Swanson. Her success thus relied on her intelligence and professionalism as well as on her naturalness and sincerity in acting, a fact frequently noted by critics and fan magazines at the time. When watching Talmadge's films today one is struck by her skill at portraying subtle emotions through the slightest of facial expressions. If *Photoplay* labeled her an "emotional actress" (1922, 16), there was certainly no implication of Talmadge overacting or being overly mannered. The "emotional" quality of her work lay principally in the story material or in the genres she appeared in, now broadly classifiable as "woman's films," or films applying a melodramatic mode of address (Basinger 1999, 140; Smith 1996, 5).

The early-to-mid-1920s mark Talmadge's most successful years: her popularity was at its peak (she was voted the most popular box office attraction in 1924 in *Photoplay*), and she made a string of commercially and artistically successful pictures. In several of these, Talmadge managed to display her dramatic range in playing either double roles, playing younger and older versions of one and the same character or via transformation narratives (stories in which a character undergoes radical physical or psychological changes). Talmadge collaborated with reliable directors such as Sydney Franklin for *Smilin' Through* (1923) and Frank Borzage for *Secrets* (1923) and *The Lady* (1926), and always selected attractive but never scene-stealing leading men. She engaged excellent screenwriters who understood her range and abilities, and she looked for variety and prestige in her story material (literary or Broadway adaptations) and found it easy as well as commercially prudent to move between social, ethnic, and racial identities. Additionally, Talmadge possessed a keen understanding of her public and the market: she indulged in audience expectations, which liked her dressing in expensive frocks or wearing stunning jewelry. She advanced the idea of the availability and respectability of modern fashion, selling the notion that her style (and by extension her success) was democratic and could be attained by all "new women" and/or all of her fans.

After the conversion to sound, her career came to an end, despite the fact that she had taken one year off for voice lessons and had made two sound films: *New York Nights*, directed by Lewis Milestone in 1929 and *Dubarry: Woman of Passion*, directed by Sam Taylor in 1930. After these, Talmadge officially retired and walked away with her memories and her money, and as legend would have it, never looked back. It was a gracious exit and a perfect coda to a career marked by professionalism, versatility, and prestige.

Anke Brouwers

See also: Bara, Theda; Dietrich, Marlene; Garbo, Greta; Mathis, June

Further Reading

Basinger, Jeanine. 1999. *Silent Stars*. Hanover and London: Wesleyan University Press.

De Groat, Greta. 2001. "Rediscovering Norma Talmadge" *Griffithiana* 71: 82–109.

Hall, Gladys. 1931. "Going. . . . Going. . . . Near the End of the Road. Norma Talmadge Looks Back." *Motion Picture Classic* (February): 38–39, 92.

Hallet, Hilary. 2013. *Go West, Young Women! The Rise of Early Hollywood.* Berkeley: University of California Press.

Loos, Anita. 1978. *The Talmadge Girls: A Memoir.* New York: The Viking Press.

Mahar, Karen Ward. 2008. *Women Filmmakers in Early Hollywood.* Baltimore: Johns Hopkins University Press.

Motion Picture Classic. 1919. Vol VII, No. 1. (March): 12.

Photoplay. 1922. Vol XXI, No. 5. (August): 16.

Smith, Greg M. 1996. "Silencing the New Woman: Ethnic and Social Mobility in the Melodramas of Norma Talmadge." *Journal of Film and Video* 48(3): 3–16.

Spears, Jack. 1971. *Hollywood: The Golden Era.* New York: A. S. Barnes.

Interview with Jodie Foster

At its highest level, what does great acting accomplish? Does your answer shift depending on whether you're answering this as an actress or as a director?

As an artist (both as an actor and as a director) I always ask myself one fundamental question before anything else: "Is this choice true?" Through the exploration of that question we all hope to connect the dots between the personal and the collective. A performance, a scene, an idea, a character that is "true" has the ability to move people, to create a communication with the audience that sparks discovery. I ask the "truth" question of every detail in an effort to know myself. Hopefully, through this act I can get better as a human instead of worse. By reaching out to others through performance, you hope that others are with your journey and they get better instead of worse too.

Since you began acting at such a young age, did you have a mentor or someone key in your life who offered guidance?

My mother Evelyn was my everything. Being raised by a single mom makes for a complicated and singular relationship with a parent. She was also my manager until my late twenties who read every script, who chose every role, who crafted every career strategy, especially in my younger years. She talked me through every decision every step of the way. These career lessons were about wanting me to be respected, to be ethical, to be strong, to be independent. I can see now that there was a vicarious element to her goals for me. As a woman born before the feminist movement, she came to her sense of self through tough circumstances. She wanted more for me than what she had lived. She believed that my creative gifts could be redemptive. For me that was a profound blessing in my life and also an odd point of view for a small child, a big responsibility I felt I had to live up to. Still, her belief in me gave me the confidence to chart a meaningful path as an artist.

How would you describe your relationship to acting or your experience as an actress in general?

I have a strange relationship with acting because I was born into it; I didn't choose it. I'm not sure I have the personality that would have chosen acting as my path. I was always more of an intellectual, a ruminator, a practical dissector, an introvert. I was not and am not naturally outwardly emotional. Although I have been acting since I was a toddler, which has given me the advantage of Gladwell's "10,000 hours," I see now that my innate personality can be a blessing and a curse. My work as an actor has a singular quality because of my "un-actor-like" makeup. But I will always struggle with a job not entirely geared for my personality.

How would you locate yourself in the landscape of Hollywood filmmaking today?

I have run the gamut as an actor in Hollywood for the last 50 some odd years. I've participated in the highest levels of that profession and now feel like my goals as an actor have mellowed. I just want to act in things that move me personally. Where that takes me, who knows. My priority has shifted to directing now. My career goals as a director are different than the ones I had as an actor in the past. I've only made four features as a director and a handful of television shows. I am excited about learning, about telling my stories in the way that I find personally provocative. I have no desire for abstract career goals as a director. I just feel blessed to explore the stories that touch me. So, as a director, I'm not sure I'm interested in paying attention to the Hollywood landscape. I just want to explore what's meaningful to me and hope that that connects to others somehow.

How would you explain your job in your capacity as a director?

Directing is about a full vision, the big picture. Every single choice on screen is a reflection of your point of view. The music you hear, the colors you see, the tone, the characters, the details big and small. They are all parts of you. Organizing your thoughts and feelings through the course of directing is actually about communicating who you are. You do this by inspiring technicians and artists to contribute with their own crafts. This, too, is an act of understanding on their parts. They interpret what you are trying to say, they try to "know" you. A director uses every tool, every detail, every decision, every thought to say, "This is what I believe to be true." But you are never entirely in control of what goes onscreen. You are a guide. You have to notice, to be flexible enough to recognize truth as it emerges, to let the movie assume the shape it is meant to assume. Kind of like being a good parent. You make the rules, the structure, but you have to embrace that your child is independent of you and has to be free enough to tread his or her own course.

Do you feel you have had any specific insights or advantages making the transition to directing due to your background in acting?

Oh yes. I am so lucky to have come up being an actor. Best film school in the world. No one on a movie set understands a scene the way an actor does. It is an exquisite place to learn what makes a scene or a moment work. But actor/directors sometimes struggle with mastering the big picture. I still think actors make the best transition to directing.

What major differences are there between directing for film versus directing for television?

I feel very lucky to have had some experience in both mediums. For features, the director is the first and last word on the vision of the film. It is an awesome responsibility that falls entirely on the director and no one else. At least that is how it should be. Directing television is really about serving the creator's vision, contributing your voice to articulate the writer/producer's idea. But that doesn't diminish the contribution. I love serving smart people. My experience as an actor comes in handy there. When directing television, it's interesting to explore a genre and tone that might not be entirely your own. You get to stretch into something outside your chosen path as an artist. But you definitely need to strengthen your collaboration muscles.

Do you believe women tell stories differently? If yes, then how so?

Yes and no. Jonathan Demme was an excellent feminist director who was always drawn to mining the complexity of the underdog. Kathryn Bigelow has been exploring the masculine psyche through the connection of brotherhood for decades. Both of these filmmakers subvert the artistic ideas we have for their genders. But yes, in many cases, the female experience does color an understanding of psychological complexity, of the subtleties of human interaction. Psychology is traditionally women's territory because we've had to hone those skills to survive the culture intact. I think very often women are interested in different parts of narrative than men simply because we have lived with a different pair of glasses. Female protagonists come with different history than male protagonists. It would be untruthful not to factor that in. But that doesn't mean that we want to reduce characters down to obvious gender stereotypes. On the contrary, considering the history of gender can help make the character richer with human idiosyncrasies.

Casting Directors

Introduction

It may seem obvious to state that the cast for any given film is essential to its outcome and yet, historically, casting directors seem to have been undervalued for their contribution to filmmaking. Casting directors are responsible for selecting the right actress or actor to fill a particular character role in a screenplay. While ostensibly straightforward, casting involves a great deal of work, and a great casting director can see potential in an unknown actress that others cannot see, which is an inexplicable talent in and of itself.

The profession of casting directors as we know it today is relatively new and did not emerge until the late 1950s. This was due in large part to the decline of the Classical Hollywood studio system, a time when actresses who had previously been under contract with the studios were becoming free agents. Two individuals during this transitional period in history are credited with developing the profession: Marion Dougherty and Lynn Stalmaster.

The Casting Society of America (then known as the American Society of Casting Directors) was not founded until 1982 and is a professional society rather than an industry union. Regardless of several attempts to get the Academy of Motion Picture Arts and Sciences to recognize casting for Oscar consideration, the academy has resisted. Stalmaster received an Academy Honorary Award in 2016 for his achievements in casting, but that is the extent to which the academy has formally recognized the contributions of the profession. Attempts to get them to recognize Dougherty's contributions to date have failed. Despite the lack of formal recognition, however, casting directors are clearly in demand for good reason, and many have created a name for themselves.

Laura L. S. Bauer

Chenoweth, Ellen (Unknown–)

Ellen Chenoweth was working as an office manager in the late 1970s at The Actors Studio, where she watched how directors such as Lee Strasberg, Elia Kazan, and

Arthur Penn talked, worked, and otherwise interacted with actors. At the time, she was in charge of putting together small plays at the Studio, and soon found that people would turn to her for casting suggestions. It was then that she decided to pursue the career of casting director full time. Chenoweth has since led the casting of Oscar contenders such as *Terms of Endearment* (1983), *Broadcast News* (1987), and *Bugsy* (1991) and developed consistent collaborations with contemporary directors like Barry Levinson, George Clooney, Clint Eastwood, Tony Gilroy, and the Coen brothers.

Based out of New York City, Chenoweth is known for giving stage actors their breakout onscreen roles. While assisting casting director Mike Fenton on the 1980 TV film *City in Fear*, she brought in Mickey Rourke, whom she knew from The Actors Studio, for his first screen performance. She gave Ellen Barkin and Kevin Bacon their breakout roles during her second job as casting director, for Barry Levinson's film *Diner* (1982). Likewise, Chenoweth has been responsible for Annette Benning's attention-grabbing turn in *Valmont* (1989) and Bill Pullman's debut in *Ruthless People* (1986), both of whom she discovered in the New York theater scene.

Chenoweth has been nominated for the Artois award from the Casting Society of America (CSA) 21 times over the last 20 years. In 2010, she was granted the Hoyt Bowers Award by the CSA, an annual award given for outstanding contribution to the casting profession. That year she also was nominated for an Emmy for casting the HBO film *You Don't Know Jack* (2010). Finally, along with film directors Joel and Ethan Coen and the main cast, Chenoweth won the Robert Altman Award for best ensemble cast at the 2010 Independent Spirit Awards for *A Serious Man* (2009).

Casting directors are the only above-the-line role that cannot be nominated for an Academy Award. Three times over the last two decades, casters have unsuccessfully proposed to the Academy Award rules committee that an award for their role be added. Former Academy executive director Bruce Davis claimed that the reason against this was that "there's no easy way to tell who did the casting in a movie" since producers and directors have considerable influence over casting and since big-studio projects sometimes come with a movie star attached long before a casting director is hired (Johnson 2011). Some find this distinction unsatisfying, however, because Oscars are awarded to roles that often receive substantial input from directors or producers, such as editing. Another argument against this category is that the job of a caster is essentially collaborative—but so are costume and set design. In 2008, two of the five nominees for Best Picture, including eventual winner *No Country for Old Men* (2007), were cast by Chenoweth. At the time, she spoke out on the lack of awards for casters, saying it was an important contribution to a film on par with those roles that are recognized. "When you see all the other categories," she noted, "it doesn't really make sense to me that we're not included" (Painter Young 2008).

Given its association with secretarial duties, historically casting has been considered women's work in Hollywood. Scholars estimate that female casters outnumber male casters by as much as three to one, a significant disparity in the otherwise male-dominated arena of film production (Mayer 2011, 132). Due to these traditionally feminine associations, casters are often required to perform various duties considered "emotional work." In addition to looking for the dramatic potential in each actor's skill set, they must nurture and mold this talent to best fit the requirements of producers. Casters thus act as both gatekeepers and mediators between talent and executive producers. Chenoweth describes her work as "a United Nations juggling act" in that she has to be very diplomatic and weigh in everyone's interests in making decisions (Wiseman 2011). Her repeated participations with directors such as Barry Levinson and Tony Gilroy evidence the long-lasting relationships casters maintain with those they work with.

Nowhere is her ability to manage both exorbitant demands and directors' personalities better exemplified than in Chenoweth's continued collaborations with the Coen brothers, with whom she has worked since *O Brother, Where Art Thou?* (2000). She was directly responsible for convincing the brothers to cast two of the leads for *No Country*, Josh Brolin and Kelly Macdonald (Painter Young 2008). For the Coens' Oscar-nominated films *A Serious Man* and *True Grit* (2010), Chenoweth and her associate Rachel Tenner were tasked with finding previously unknown actors for the leading roles, including considering more than 15,000 actresses before the Coens finally settled on Hailee Steinfeld as Mattie in *True Grit* (Chetwynd 2011). Furthermore, auditioning for the Coens is no easy feat. Chenoweth has to manage the directors' stoic managerial style with novice actors' expectations. "They don't very often have someone do a scene again," she explains, "I know that's hard for actors, and actors always want to talk to them and tell them how much they like their movies [but] it's just sort of not their thing. They're not chatty like that" (Painter Young 2008). Managing contrasting expectations and differing personalities is thus an integral part of Chenoweth's daily job and, ultimately, the key to success for actors, directors, and casters.

Juan Llamas-Rodriguez

See also: Streep, Meryl

Further Reading

Chetwynd, Josh. 2011. "Casting Directors Follow Instinct." *Variety*, January 10. http://variety.com/2011/film/awards/casting-directors-follow-instinct-1118029711

Dawes, Amy. 2013. "Casting Directors Often Play a Starring Role." *Los Angeles Times*, December 10. http://articles.latimes.com/2013/dec/10/entertainment/la-et-mn-casting-directors-20131210

Johnson, Reed. 2011. "No Oscar Love for Casting Directors." *Los Angeles Times*, February 21. http://articles.latimes.com/2011/feb/21/entertainment/la-et-casting-directors-20110221

Mayer, Vicki. 2011. *Below the Line: Producers and Production Studies in the New Television Economy*. Durham, NC: Duke University Press.

Painter Young, Jamie. 2008. "The Winners Should Be . . ." *Backstage*, February 26. http://www.backstage.com/news/the-winners-should-be

Simonson, Robert. 2009. "The Other Chenoweth: Casting Director Gives Stage Actors Their Film Careers." *Playbill*, September 21. http://www.playbill.com/features/article/the-other-chenoweth-casting-director-gives-stage-actors-their-film-careers-164225

Wiseman, Andreas. 2011. "Ellen Chenoweth." *Screen Daily*, June 2. http://www.screendaily.com/features/one-on-one/ellen-chenoweth/5028318.article

Dougherty, Marion (1923–2011)

Often referred to by a variety of monikers such as "the Mozart of casting" and "the grand matriarch of modern casting," Marion Dougherty was one of the first casting directors in American film history—male or female. In somewhat broad terms, the role of a casting director is "to collaborate with producers, directors, network and studios executives to cast the best talent for each role" (London 2018). In other words, like most other cast and crew members working on a film, casting directors aim to "fulfill the creative vision of a team of artists" and to "bring the vision of productions to life through their casting choices" (London 2018). Drawing on this understanding of what a casting director is and does, Dougherty can perhaps be best described as one of the many pioneers of modern casting, as she ultimately "brought the vision of films to life" for nearly four decades, and she remains one of the most well-known and influential individuals to ever work as a casting director in the history of the medium.

Marion Caroline Dougherty was born in Hollidaysburg, Pennsylvania. Dougherty later attended Penn State University, where she began her career in the performing arts as an actress at the Cleveland Playhouse. From there, Dougherty moved to New York in the hopes of becoming a set designer. In the late 1950s, while Dougherty was designing window displays at Bergdorf Goodman, a fellow Penn State alum, who had recently been hired in the casting department at *Kraft Television Theatre*, hired her as an assistant. Consequently, Dougherty's first casting credits were several television shows, including *Kraft Television Theatre* (1957), *Ellery Queen* (1958), *Naked City* (1961–1963), and *Route 66* (1963–1964)—where she gave many budding male actors of the late 1950s and early 1960s some of their first notable guest star roles, including Martin Sheen and Robert Duvall. After her work in television casting, in 1961 Dougherty moved to casting for films (she was the "casting executive" on two Herbert B. Leonard–produced dramas). In 1970, Dougherty's career in film casting became more noteworthy as she cast for two Best Picture Oscar nominees: *Midnight Cowboy* (1969) and *Butch Cassidy and the Sundance Kid* (1969).

In 1965, in the midst of her transition to casting for film, Dougherty also formed her own casting company, Marion Dougherty Associates, in a brownstone on 30th street in New York City (nicknamed "The Brothel" because all of her employees were women). In 1972, Dougherty became the first casting director to be given a single-card screen credit for *Slaughterhouse-Five*. In 1976, Dougherty moved to Hollywood at the request of former United Artists president David Picker, where she became the vice president of casting at Paramount. From 1979 to 1999, Dougherty worked at Warner Bros. as the vice president of casting (where she ended her career), and some of her last film casting credits include *Three to Tango* (1999) and *Venus and Mars* (2001). Dougherty also has earned a producing credit for her role as an executive producer for *Smile* (1975).

In terms of historical and industrial context, it is important to point out that casting in Hollywood continuously evolved throughout the 20th century and that the "casting director" did not always exist in Hollywood, which makes Dougherty's role in the pioneering of the profession that much more significant. During the silent era (circa 1908), producers started to sign actors to longer contracts and "the star system" was developed as a way to give audiences recognizable faces across films. This led to audiences forming attachments to certain stars/star personas from film to film, and stars themselves became a major draw for viewers to go to the movies, which then garnered certain stars favor in being casted and given contracts. In the 1930s and early 1940s, studios often signed stars to seven-year contracts, and the producers could put them into as many films at they wanted—whether the stars approved of the projects or not.

In the 1960s and early 1970s, with the repeal of the Motion Picture Production Code and the decline of the studio system (also known as the Classical Hollywood era—from the 1930s to the early 1960s), in a period that is often referred to as Post-Classical Hollywood or the New Hollywood era, Marion Dougherty (along with the acclaimed casting director Lynn Stalmaster—her male counterpart in L.A. at the time) brought about a more complex way of casting films that revolutionized what kinds of actors were cast, as well as how the casting processes was carried out. In the early days, actors were often cast based on their appearance (also known as typecasting). With rise of independents and free agents during this period, however, actors were being "discovered" at regional theaters, off-Broadway, and local playhouses—rather than being top-down decisions made by studio executives, producers, and contract agreements.

It was in these more independent and unconventional performance spaces that Dougherty first came into contact with countless acting talents looking to break into the film business (one of the first actors she cast is James Dean—who studied at The Actors Studio in New York). Dougherty's decision to make casting choices based on acting abilities, as opposed to casting based on appearance, or typecasting, is what revolutionized film casting during this period more specifically (in conjunction with the decline of the studio system and the rise of independents and actors as free agents). Interestingly, Dougherty also kept an extensive collection of index cards from her nearly 45-year career that contain some her first impressions/insightful notes on a multitude of famous actors who read/auditioned for her over the years. Dougherty's process of "cataloguing" actors on index cards is also a somewhat revolutionary approach to casting that she can be credited with bringing into mainstream filmmaking.

During her time in New York and later in L.A., along with James Dean, Dougherty went on to "discover" some of the most influential Hollywood actors of the next four decades. The list of Hollywood stars who got their first big breaks by Dougherty over the course of her career is seemingly endless, but some of her most well-known and commercially successful casting decisions include the casting of the following; Jon Voight and Dustin Hoffman in 1969's *Midnight Cowboy* (the Best Picture winner, and both actors received Oscar nominations for their performances), Al Pacino in *Me, Natalie* (1969) and *The Panic in Needle Park* (1971), Robert Redford in *Butch Cassidy and the Sundance Kid* (1969), Bette Midler in *Hawaii* (1966), Glenn Close in *The World According to Garp* (1982), Diane Lane in *A Little Romance* (1979), Tim Burton's *Batman* (1989), and four *Lethal Weapon* films throughout the late 1980s and 1990s (she catapulted Danny Glover to stardom and helped to diversify the Hollywood film landscape by casting him as the other half of the buddy cop duo in this film franchise alongside Mel Gibson).

In addition to paving the way for many of the New Hollywood era's A-list stars, Dougherty helped pave the way for future female casting directors such as Juliet Taylor, Amanda Mackey, Nessa Hyams, Phyllis Huffman, and Wally Nicita. As a way of recognizing and celebrating her work, a rather large cohort of A-list actors and directors (including Clint Eastwood, Woody Allen, and Al Pacino) famously campaigned for Dougherty to be given an Honorary Lifetime Achievement Oscar in 1991, but their efforts were ultimately unsuccessful. In fact, to this day, one of Dougherty's only casting awards was from the Casting Society of America, in 1987, when she received the Hoyt Boyd's Award. However, in 2012, HBO broadcasted the feature-length documentary entitled *Casting By*, which primarily centers on the life and career of Dougherty and can be considered a tribute to her (and the previously "untold story" of the important role that casting directors have played in film history in general). The documentary features a plethora of A-list star interviews, Jon Voight as one of the most notable examples, who single out Dougherty and express their appreciation for her consideration in casting them in their first big film roles.

Dougherty's legacy is that she quite literally "changed the faces of Hollywood" in her tenure as a casting director. It is also particularly important to recognize that Dougherty is the first in a long line of men and women who have come to shape the filmmaking industry with their casting choices. There is currently still no Oscar consideration given to casting directors, but with the continued recognition and discussion of the work of people like Dougherty in academia and popular culture, the future of casting directors may one day be acknowledged and respected on the same level as actors, directors, and writers. Perhaps one day Dougherty will also be given her long-overdue recognition at the Oscars, but only time will tell. Regardless of her lack of "tangible" accolades, Dougherty's influence in the world of film and casting will live on and continue to prosper for many years to come through the countless men and women who are working in the film industry today, thanks to her decision to take a chance on them.

Stephanie Oliver

See also: Taylor, Juliet

Further Reading

Georgakas, Dan, and Kevin Rabalais. 2000. "Fifty Years of Casting: An Interview with Marion Dougherty." *Cineaste* 25(1): 26.

London, Lisa. 2018. "What Does a Casting Director Do?" *Backstage*. January 16. https://www.backstage.com/advice-for-actors/backstage-experts/what-does-casting-director-do

Thompson, Kristin, and David Bordwell. 1994. *Film History: An Introduction*. 3rd ed. New York: McGraw-Hill.

Kaufman, Avy (Unknown–)

With over 250 credits to her name in both film and television, Casting Director Avy Kaufman has emerged as one of the best artists in her field. Through her work on such critically acclaimed films as *The Sixth Sense* (1999), *Brokeback Mountain*

(2003), and *Lincoln* (2012), Kaufman has cemented her place as one of the most prolific and talented casting directors working today.

As artists draw inspiration from their surroundings, Avy Kaufman proves no different. Based in New York City, Kaufman has a refined view of the people who inhabit the area. Her early work in such films as *The Super* (1991), *The Basketball Diaries* (1993), and *Searching for Bobby Fischer* (1995) showcase the diversity that New York offers. Films like Ridley Scott's *American Gangster* (2006) display the inner workings of Harlem's drug trade during the 1970s and the array of groups—African Americans, Italians, and police—struggling to control it. Recent work, such as the acclaimed HBO miniseries *The Night Of* (2016), exhibits a wide range of Manhattan denizens from all walks of life, including the protagonist, a Pakistani American college student living in Queens, New York.

The Artios Awards, given by the Casting Society of America, recognizes the best within the casting community. Fellow casting directors celebrate not only those in their business but also the art of casting in film, television, and theater. As of 2017, Kaufman has received an impressive 27 Artios Award nominations for her work in both film and television, winning four awards in the years 2001 for the film *State and Main* (2000), 2005 for the HBO miniseries *Empire Falls* (2005), 2006 for *Brokeback Mountain* (2005), and 2009 for *Sunshine Cleaning* released in 2008. As well, Kaufman has been lauded by the Academy of Television Arts and Science for her work within the television industry and has received nominations for her work with such miniseries as *Empire Falls* (2002) and *The Night Of* (2016). Kaufman won the Emmy for casting excellence in the FX network's pilot episode of *Damages* (2007).

Casting director Avy Kaufman has cast hundreds of film and television productions during her career, working with a number of critically acclaimed filmmakers such as Ang Lee and Steven Spielberg. Her many accolades include two Primetime Emmy Awards and four Artios Awards from the Casting Society of America. (Photo by Charles Nesbit)

Kaufman recognizes that collaboration is key in creating a cast for motion pictures and television shows, stating: "I think the writing has a lot to do with it. It's the writers and it's the director and everybody going, 'Well, what if we do *this*?' And then you hope they say yes." (Li 2016). This collaboration shines through in many areas, especially when bringing historical period dramas to life. Films such as *Lincoln* (2012) are a prime example of this. On the challenges of casting Spielberg's Lincoln, Kaufman notes that "[b]ecause it's a piece of history, I tried to get the honest living person in resemblance and personality" (Lehman 2012). This collaboration between artists ensures that the film has authenticity but gives respect to the historical figures portrayed. It is in the careful and thought-out casting that Avy Kaufman's art shines through.

Acclaimed actress and director Jodie Foster is no stranger to the artistry of Kaufman, having worked with her on all four of her directing efforts spanning over 25 years from 1991's *Little Man Tate* to 2016's *Money Monster*. Her continued collaboration with Kaufman speaks to the respect and trust that Foster has in her. On the importance of casting, Foster exclaimed, "The casting director is the director's first pair of eyes shaping the vision of the movie once the process of film making has started. Avy Kaufman has always been the first person I look to help bring the script from possibility to reality" (Teamsters Joint Council 2017). It's no wonder that Kaufman and her work is not only acclaimed, but her talent in casting is in repeat demand by Foster and other directors such as Ang Lee (*The Ice Storm*, *Ride with the Devil*, *Life of Pi*), Robert Redford (*Lions for Lambs*, *The Conspirator*), and Steven Spielberg (*AI: Artificial Intelligence*, *Lincoln*). Kaufman's work with Lee, in particular, has been fruitful. In casting Lee's 2016 film *Billy Flynn's Long Halftime Walk*, Actor Joe Alwyn was a last-minute read for the lead role. Kaufman's eye for talent and determination for Alwyn to read for the role won out in the end. Remarking on Kaufman's casting acumen and dogged insistence, even with last-minute reads, Lee notes that "she's done that to me quite a few times in the past and she's always right" (InqPOP 2016).

When she received her lifetime achievement award for casting at the Subtitle European Film Festival in 2013, Kaufman remarked, "It's the visionaries that take you through a different style of life" (SubtitleFest 2013). While she was humbly referring to the talent she has encountered in her career, this statement could describe the artistry and career of her as well. Avy Kaufman's 30+ years in the industry represent not only excellence in the field of casting but also speaks to continued success and an ever-growing reputation for excellence.

Shawn Driscoll

See also: Foster, Jodie

Further Reading

Artios Awards. n.d. Accessed January 20, 2018, from http://www.castingsociety.com/awards/artios

InqPOP. 2016. "Young British Actor Marks Film Debut with 'Billy Lynn's Long Halftime Walk?'" *InqPOP!*, November 7. http://pop.inquirer.net/2016/11/young-british-actor-marks-film-debut-with-billy-lynns-long-halftime-walk

Lehman, D. 2012. "Avy Kaufman, Casting in Gold." *TWC Guilds*, November 24. http://twcguilds.com/filmmaker/avy-kaufman-casting-in-gold

Li, S. 2016. "Hollywood Casting Directors Say Asian Movie Stars Are on Their Way." *Entertainment Weekly,* November 9. http://ew.com/article/2016/11/09/asian-representation-casting-directors-whitewashing

SubtitleFest. 2013. "Subtitle 2013—Jim & Avy." YouTube video, 2:18, December 11. https://www.youtube.com/watch?v=706uGJS-ndI

Teamsters Joint Council 16. 2017. "Hollywood Greats' Quotes on Casting." Teamsters Joint Council, July 19. http://teamsters.nyc/2017/07/19/hollywood-greats-quotes-casting

Lewis, Ellen (Unknown–)

Ellen Lewis is a casting director who is best known for creating some of Hollywood's most memorable films. She cites casting as the craft of working with human beings, putting together the faces and talents that create stories the audience has loved (Peikart 2015). For her work, she has earned two Primetime Emmys, first for Outstanding Casting of Miniseries, Movie or Special for *Wit* (2001) and for Outstanding Casting of a Drama Series for *Boardwalk Empire* (2010). These are two of many accolades that Lewis has won, primarily for her work with Steven Spielberg, Woody Allen, and Martin Scorsese. She has helped produce some of Hollywood's most vibrant casts; her work is defined by the care that she puts in each project, by the stories that she tells through the faces she puts forth.

Ellen Lewis was born near the north side of Chicago, Illinois, to parents Audrey and Norman Lewis. Together, her parents owned the William A. Lewis clothing store and gave her early exposure to arts—dance, theater, symphonies, and film. Lewis attended Francis Parker School in Chicago for 12 years and then briefly attended School of the Art Institute for painting and textile design and later Columbia College for filmmaking. Lewis made her first significant connection when she began working at St. Nicholas Theater with fellow Francis Parker alum David Mamet in 1984. Despite not knowing what the job of casting director entailed, she added it to her resume at the suggestion of her friends. When Mamet learned of this, he arranged for Lewis to meet with Juliet Taylor, who was seeking an assistant. This was the beginning of what is now being described as a "legendary career" (Peikart 2015).

Within a week of being hired by Taylor, Lewis was helping cast variety acts for Woody Allen's *Broadway Danny Rose* (1984). Lewis worked under Taylor for eight years, assisting with and casting more than 25 films. Notable works during these years included *Working Girl* (1988), *Goodfellas* (1990), and *A League of Their Own* (1992). During this time, Lewis was also nominated for the Casting Society of America's Artois Award for her work on *Barton Fink* (1992). Despite not working under Taylor after these eight years, the pair frequently collaborated with each other throughout the 1990s and early 2000s. Taylor was also essential in helping Lewis forge connections with Martin Scorsese and Woody Allen, whose films she still casts for today. Lewis claims that her biggest takeaway from working with Taylor was learning how to be kind to actors, but what Taylor really did for Lewis was inviting her to become part of a casting family (Buder 2016).

The casting family that Lewis joined is one that is primarily female run. Casting directors are rarely recognized or interviewed, but they serve as liaisons for actors and directors. They are the ones whose minds are an archive of faces, names, and talents. They scout for talent, create connections, and make sure that they are building a story with the people they cast. For Lewis, her favorite part of casting is working with people and helping the director fulfill their vision. She imagines casting as painting with faces and loves trying the right people to fill the screen (Buder 2016). For directors like Scorsese and Spielberg, who consider Lewis their go-to casting director, her long-time connections help her find the perfect talents. Lewis is traditional in her methods, as she finds roles based on the relationships she builds with people. She likes meeting people in person and talking on the phone;

even though casting is now frequently done over video, Lewis still casts primarily through in-person connection.

These methods have served Lewis well, as she has cast some of the most well-known films and shows in Hollywood. Currently, she holds casting credits for just under 90 productions. Films that she cast have frequently earned Oscar and Emmy nominations. She herself has been nominated for three Primetime Emmy Awards, winning for both *Angels in America* (2003) and *Boardwalk Empire* (2011). Twice these nominations were in Outstanding Casting of a Miniseries, Movie or a Special for *Wit* (2001) and *Angels in America* and once in Outstanding Casting of a Drama Series for *Boardwalk Empire*. Like many casting directors, Lewis believes that casting deserves an Oscar category. For Lewis, this is especially bothersome, as many of the films for which she has been in charge of casting, such as *Forrest Gump* (1994) or *Wolf of Wall Street* (2013), have been nominated for or won Academy Awards. Despite the lack of recognition in the Academy, Lewis's resume is not short on other awards. Lewis won the Online Film and Television Association Award for Best Casting both in 2005 and 2007, and was nominated in 1999 and 2014. She has been nominated for the Casting Society of America's Artois Award for Best Casting no fewer than 15 times, winning in 1993, 2011, and 2015. She has also won the Hoyt Bowers Award for Best Casting and the New York Television and Film Muse Award.

With a decorated career that spans nearly 40 years, Lewis is now known as one of casting's greats. She embodies the "unique spirit, ideals, and creativity" that drives casting directors. She is known for attention to relationships and loving actors, believing there is no small role and always making sure that actors or actresses are comfortable during castings. She says that "you have to love actors to do this work" because "we are all working toward the same ends" (Peikart 2015). World building is important to Lewis because casting is building a world where all the characters seem like they fit in. Casting is a tricky craft for Lewis because it is working with human beings who you hope can tell the story that directors, writers, and rest of the team imagine. However, after years of honing the craft, Lewis treats casting like a puzzle that she comes back to again and again.

Keshia L. McClantoc

See also: Marshall, Penny; Taylor, Juliet

Further Reading

Buder, Emily. 2016. "Painting with Faces: Trade Secrets from Legendary Casting Directors." *NoFilmSchool*, April 25. https://nofilmschool.com/2016/04/casting-masterclass-ellen-chenoweth-ellen-lewis

Casting By, DVD. 2013. Directed by Tom Donahue. New York: HBO Documentary Films.

Dinello, Dan. 1999. "Ellen Lewis Brings Stars into the Light for Director Scorsese." *Chicago Tribune*, October 26. http://articles.chicagotribune.com/1999-10-26/features/9910260354_1_ving-rhames-roles-actors

Ford, Rebecca. 2017. "Casting Pros Debate Harassment, Whitewashing and Why the Term 'Casting Couch' Is Offensive." *The Hollywood Reporter*, December 5. https://www.hollywoodreporter.com/features/casting-pros-debate-harassment-whitewashing-why-term-casting-couch-is-offensive-1063312

IMDb. 2017. "Ellen Lewis." Accessed January 12, 2017. http://www.imdb.com/name/nm0220984

Lee, Veronika. 2017. "10 Secrets of Casting Directors." *Mental Floss*, July 27. http://mentalfloss.com/article/502068/10-secrets-casting-directors

Peikart, Mike. 2015. "Artios Awards 2015: Ellen Lewis on Her Legendary Career." *Backstage*, January 20. https://www.backstage.com/interview/artios-awards-2015-ellen-lewis-her-legendary-career

Marin, Mindy (1960–)

For over three decades, Mindy Marin has consistently been a dominating female presence in the film and television industry as a casting director and producer. Marin's work often showcases her affinity for casting actors/actresses to play against type and her penchant for investing her time in projects that present challenging and original stories to mainstream audiences. In the words of Marin herself, a casting director's job is to "bring life to film scripts through actors" and to ultimately "paint with humanity" (Malone 2015). Every film has to have a casting director, but casting directors have gone largely unrecognized for their contribution to the filmmaking process. Marin's ability to identify individuals whose innate human qualities will translate on screen is a unique skill that is shaping the Hollywood filmmaking culture of the future.

Marin began her career in casting in the television division of Paramount Pictures in 1985. After two years with Paramount, Marin moved to Warner Brothers Television, where she was first given her own casting projects. In 1989, Marin formed her own casting company, Casting Artists, Inc. Since founding her own casting company, Marin has accumulated over 75 film credits that span a wide range of topics and film genres. Apart from her early work in television, Marin most commonly serves as a casting director for feature-length Hollywood narrative films. Unlike a film director or writer who has various common stylistic or thematic threads visible across their body of work, Marin's work is perhaps most notable for how her casting choices often showcase actors and actresses who push their abilities to fill roles that are in opposition to the kinds of roles they are known for up to that point (what is often referred to as "playing against type"). For example, the Oscar-winning film *Juno* (2007) stars Ellen Page as the titular character. As the character Juno, Page portrays a witty and cynical teenage girl who gets pregnant and decides to give the baby up for adoption. The film proved that Page could play a leading lady in a mainstream film and strengthened her abilities as a fast-talking, rebellious, and relatable actress who could balance comedic wit and dramatic gravitas all in one role.

Marin's ability to transform an actor's career is also evidenced by her choice to cast Aaron Eckhart as the male lead in the 2005 satirical comedy film *Thank You for Smoking*, which she also produced (Marin began producing films in 1996 and she has six producing credits as of 2006). Before this film, Eckhart had only appeared in supporting roles and independent films. But after Marin cast Eckhart in his first mainstream leading role as the smooth-talking tobacco spokesperson Nick Naylor, a man at odds with himself as he struggles to reconcile his job with his responsibilities as role model for his 12-year-old son, he proved to be an actor who could be considered for roles that required him to play more conflicted and complex characters. For example, in 2008 (three years after *Thank You for Smoking*), Eckhart was cast in the dual role of Harvey Dent/Two Face in Christopher Nolan's *The Dark Knight*. Marin's choice to cast Jake Gyllenhaal (who was known for somewhat more mild-mannered and demure character actor performances at the time) in the gritty neo-noir thriller *Nightcrawler* (2014) as Louis Bloom (a Los Angeles–based "crime journalist" who takes advantage of other people's misfortune to turn a profit) is also demonstrative of her ability to successfully cast actors against type and her ability to open up actors/actresses to a wider range of casting possibilities as they move forward in their careers.

Interestingly, Marin's films often have large casts and rely on her ability to choose an "ensemble" of actors that complement each other and work together to make the world of a film "come to life" for the audience. For example, the 2011 romantic comedy *Crazy, Stupid, Love* features a complex world of interconnected love stories that primarily focuses on the relationship between the recently separated and repressed family man Cal (Steve Carell), the womanizing and perpetually charismatic sex guru Jacob (Ryan Gosling), and the quirky and effervescent law student Hannah (Emma Stone). This film was the first film to feature Ryan Gosling and Emma Stone as an onscreen couple, whose chemistry was thought to be so strong and believable by other casting directors that they went on to star in/play love interests in two other films, *Gangster Squad* in 2013 and *La La Land* in 2016.

Considering the success of *Crazy, Stupid, Love* at the box office and in the reception of the film's casting of Gosling and Stone, this film is particularly important to discuss in relation to Marin's accomplishments as an innovative and influential casting director. While many fans of the film may not know who she is, Marin is directly responsible for originally pairing Gosling and Stone together. This ostensibly created an onscreen couple that has somewhat resurrected the trend of continuously casting the same actors as love interests in multiple films that audiences obsessively idolize and rush out to theaters to see. This was a commonplace strategy used by the studios in the Classical Hollywood era with well-known onscreen couples such as Spencer Tracy and Katharine Hepburn, Humphrey Bogart and Lauren Bacall, and Rock Hudson and Doris Day—who all became big box-office draws whenever they appeared in films together. While it can be surmised that Marin did not intentionally cast Gosling and Stone in the hopes of creating a cultural phenomenon, their success as an onscreen duo after working with her further demonstrates Marin's abilities to recognize chemistry and change the way casting directors and audiences have come to view certain stars and their acting prowess.

In addition to the films discussed in this entry, there are countless other credits in Marin's filmography that demonstrate both how and why she has gained a reputation as one of the most influential casting directors of her generation. Throughout her career, Marin has shown that she is dedicated to helping other people realize their potential by finding the right actor for the role with each project she has been responsible for casting and that she wanted to be involved in the casting process on her own terms when she founded her own company. In the words of one writer for *The Hollywood Reporter*, casting is sometimes referred to as "the invisible art" or "the art of distinguishing talent from a lack of talent" (Empty 2009). This is yet another way of describing Marin's unique artistic capabilities, as her films consistently show that she has an "eye for actors" and "the diplomacy to steer a filmmaker toward the right performer," which will be interesting to witness in the coming years as she continues to evolve her craft and cast films that test actors' abilities and audience's expectations (Empty 2009).

Stephanie Oliver

See also: Hepburn, Katharine

Further Reading

Empty. 2009. "Casting Director Profiles." *The Hollywood Reporter*, March 30. https://www.hollywoodreporter.com/news/casting-director-profiles-81588

Malone, Tyler. 2015. "Painting with Humanity: Casting a Light on the Role of the Casting Director with Mindy Marin." *PM Magazine*, Winter. http://pmc-mag.com/2015/02/mindy-marin/?full=content

Taylor, Juliet (1950–)

In 1979, an article in *New York* magazine called Juliet Taylor "the best and by far the most important of the casting directors" (Curtis Fox 1979, 44). After graduating in theater from Smith College, Taylor soon began working as a secretary for casting legend Marion Dougherty, whose company Taylor managed after Dougherty became a producer in 1973. Taylor left the company in 1977 to work for Paramount Pictures and casted independently from 1978 onwards both in California and in New York.

Taylor is particularly known for her collaboration with Woody Allen over the course of 45 films from 1975 until she retired in 2016. In an open letter to help establish an Oscar from the Academy of Motion Picture Arts and Sciences for casting directors in 2013, Allen explained: "In my case certainly, the casting director plays a vital part in the making of the movie. My history shows that my films are full of wonderful performances by actors and actresses I had never heard of and were not only introduced to me by my casting director, Juliet Taylor, but, in any number of cases, pushed on me against my own resistance" (Allen 2013). Allen continues to acknowledge his own clumsiness in the process of finding the perfect fit for a role: "If it were up to me we would use the same half dozen people in all my pictures, whether they fit or not" and contributes the success of his films partially to Taylor.

Casting remains a "classic behind the scenes profession" (Curtis Fox 1979, 46), although, as can be seen from Allen's enthusiasm, a crucial one. Perhaps due to its invisibility and the lesser degree of fame (and consequentially money) attached to it, it is largely a female profession. Casting directors make a selection of suitable actors and present them to the directors, but they also have to negotiate with screenwriters, producers, actors, and agents to manage a specific time frame and budget. Taylor herself recognizes that "[b]oth the actor and the director have to feel they are brought together under the right circumstances. Before I bring an actor to a reading, I'll go over what they've done, what I've seen, what I think they can do" (Curtis Fox 1979, 46). In this pre-production process, casting directors select a

Casting director Juliet Taylor attends the New York premiere of the HBO documentary *Casting By* at HBO Theater on July 29, 2013, in New York City. Taylor has been the recipient of many prestigious awards over the course of her long career, and is perhaps best known for her collaboration with Woody Allen. The two were introduced by casting legend Marion Dougherty. (Michael Loccisano/Getty Images for HBO)

number of different suitable actors. While also working with agencies that are presented with concise versions of the script and/or character descriptions and then are able to respond with suggestions on their part, casting professionals like Taylor frequent the theaters. In this way, Taylor was able to suggest Meryl Streep to Fred Zinnemann for his film *Julia* (1977), which became Streep's door to Hollywood. Streep had been a promising theater actress in New York City at the time but was unknown to the movie world. Paul Mazursky, whom Taylor had also been working with, particularly for his film *An Unmarried Woman* (1978), appreciated Taylor's honest and sincere ways. "She will not do things like, if the part's written for a big, beefy cop, say 'What about someone who's really *shy*?'" he told Terry Curtis Fox in an interview (Curtis Fox 1979, 46).

While Taylor is well known for casting most of Woody Allen's movies, she is also responsible for the cast in other well-known Hollywood movies from *Taxi Driver* (1976) to *Schindler's List* (1993). Her work for the HBO miniseries *Angels in America* (2003) won the Emmy Award for outstanding casting in 2004. The American Casting Society recognized Taylor's work for *Hannah and Her Sisters* (1987), *Mississippi Burning* (1988), *Sleepless in Seattle* (1993), and *Bullets over Broadway* (1995) with the prestigious Artios Award. Furthermore, Taylor won the Independent Film Tribute Award in 1995 (Gotham Independent Film), the Muse Award in 1996 (New York Women in Film), and the Crystal Award in 2001 (Women in Film Crystal Awards). However, the Academy Awards have not yet created a section for the Oscars for casting. Following Tom Donahue's documentary *Casting By* (2012) in which Taylor is also interviewed, the Academy announced a casting director branch, elevating casting directors to full membership with three seats on the board of governors.

Andrea Zittlau

See also: Dougherty, Marion; Lewis, Ellen; Streep, Meryl

Further Reading

Allen, Woody. 2013. "Woody Allen Pens Rare Open Letter to Hollywood." *Hollywood Reporter*, October 31. https://www.hollywoodreporter.com/news/woody-allen-pens-rare-open-651493

Casting By, DVD. 2012. Directed by Tom Donahue. New York: First Run Features.
Curtis Fox, Terry. 1979. "The Casting Director." *New York Magazine*, June 4: 44–47.

Interview with Avy Kaufman

How would you explain your profession and its contribution to a film? What does your work schedule look like from day to day or even over the course of a year?

As a casting director I am responsible for casting all speaking parts in projects I work on in film and television. There are exceptions where I am asked to cast non-speaking roles when a director or producer feel they need an actor in a part. My work schedule varies from project to project. My office usually puts in long days. I am proud of the projects that come my way and the directors I am asked to collaborate with.

How did you know you wanted to do this? Any failures or setbacks you're willing to share and, if so, how did you overcome or move past them? What advice would you give someone trying to break into your field?

I came to New York City to become a dancer, which did not turn out! I fell into casting, which feels very organic for me. When I began casting I was not aware of internships; I would suggest being an intern in a casting office to get a feel [for] what casting is about.

Yes, I have had setbacks in my time. I am still trying to figure out the best way to deal with setbacks! It feels like a lifelong journey figuring out how to deal with any situation that isn't easy to deal with!

How did you get your start?

I fell into casting by being offered a casting position in advertising. I was quite lucky in building a career quickly in advertising. I loved working with actors but missed storytelling and knocked on many doors to assist casting directors in film but did not land a job. I then started at the bottom, [working] with a casting office doing extras casting. This was quite different from advertising, including the hours. Hours in casting extras for film were being on set some mornings as early as 4 a.m. and staying in the office as late as 11 p.m. I then moved on to location casting. John Sayles asked me to work on *Matewan*. I worked with John and his team for a few years doing location casting, which I loved, as I would not only cast local actors wherever we were shooting but often find nonactors, which was interesting. I was offered a film called *Miss Firecracker*, which was the first feature film I cast, then I met with Jodie Foster for her directorial debut with *Little Man Tate*, which started my path.

Did you have a mentor?

I did not have a mentor, which I had wanted—it just did not happen for me the way I had wanted when starting my career.

If you have children or dependents, how do you manage career and family (does a partner help with domestic labor and childcare, any hired help, is there a support system at work, etc.)?

I have two incredible sons, so juggling my career when they were growing up was not easy, but when the day was done and I could go home and be with my family and I knew how lucky I was. My children have always been understanding and proud of my work.

I have been rewarded with those I have known to support me. Directors and producers who have asked me to work with them over and over, which is wonderfully fulfilling.

I am still on my path. I take nothing for granted. I love many directors and producers I have been lucky enough to work with.

Cinematographers

Introduction

A cinematographer is also known as the director of photography, or "DP," because they are responsible for crafting images with light that communicate the narrative. A great cinematographer understands that she is responsible for conveying story and emotion through visuals, not just to create a pretty picture. A cinematographer is essential to any film production and collaborates very closely with the director.

A high level of technical skill is involved in becoming a cinematographer. She must understand camera movement and placement, focus, composition, and lighting in order to support the narrative and convey emotion. Realism is not effortlessly captured when the camera records—it must be manufactured since places and people often appear differently on camera than they do in person.

The way we tell stories has evolved alongside advancements in cinematography. The precursors to cinematography stretch back to the 1800s with inventions such as the zoetrope and kinetoscope. Early filmmakers such as Georges Méliès did everything themselves from creating the sets, to directing, to camera work, to acting—this system of production was termed the "cameraman system." Cinematography has been a male-dominated field since the silent era. One significant exception during this time was Francelia Billington, a silent film actress who was also an accomplished camera operator.

As films began to be composed of more shots, a need for people to specialize as camera operators grew. The monochrome films of the late 1800s made a slow transition to color by 1950, and shooting on 35mm film at the beginning of the century evolved into digital cinematography by the 2010s. Despite the relatively long history of cinematographers, it was not until 1980 that Brianne Murphy became the first female cinematographer to be hired to work on a major studio film, as well as the first female member of the American Society of Cinematographers that same year. Thirty-seven years later, in 2017, Rachel Morrison would become the first woman ever nominated for an Oscar in cinematography (for reference, the first Academy

Awards ceremony was held in 1929). However, cinematography is an area of Hollywood filmmaking where women remain severely underrepresented.

Laura L. S. Bauer

Alberti, Maryse (1954–)

Maryse Alberti is a French cinematographer based in the United States. She moved to Hollywood in 1973 and started working as a cinematographer in the mid-1980s, a time when the field was almost exclusively dominated by men. As a self-taught independent and documentary cinematographer, Alberti has pivoted between documentary and fiction film throughout her career. Today, she has over 40 years of experience in the field and approximately 90 cinematography credits to her name. She is mostly known for her work in documentaries such as *H2-Worker* (1990), *Crumb* (1994), and *Taxi to the Dark Side* (2007) and in fiction films such as *Happiness* (1998), *Velvet Goldmine* (1998), and *The Wrestler* (2008).

At the age of 19, Alberti came to the United States to see her childhood hero Jimi Hendrix in concert, who unexpectedly died while Alberti was en route. She decided to stay, however, working as an au pair during the day and binge-watching movies at night. After a few months, she found a job as a photographer, taking pictures for the *New York Rocker*. Her first experience on a movie set was not much later, when she was introduced by a friend as a still photographer in the X-rated film industry. According to Alberti, "[T]hey were paying something like $75 a day, which was great money" (Mulcahey 2015). Later, Alberti worked as an assistant on several low-budget features. The first full-length documentary Alberti shot was *H-2 Worker* (1990) by filmmaker Stephanie Black, for which she won the Cinematography Award at the Sundance Film Festival. In 1995, Alberti won her second Sundance Award for her work in Terry Zwigoff's documentary *Crumb* (1994). In a conversation with the International Documentary Association in 1991, Alberti expressed her biggest frustration in the field of contemporary documentary-making at that time as a lack of spontaneity and realism. She said, "[W]hat you end up with is a kind of illustration for the essay. You don't find the film as you are filming it, you find it in your research. [. . .] I think we should emphasize the cinematic aspects of the medium more" (Alberti 1991).

During those first years of her career she was asked to work on the first English-language feature film by Chilean-born French-based filmmaker Raul Ruiz, *The Golden Boat* (1990). A year later, Alberti was able to work with the independent film director Todd Haynes on his science fiction horror film *Poison* (1991). In *Poison* she implemented radically new visual techniques and worked with different kinds of film stock for different scenes (Alberti 1991). Later on, Alberti collaborated two more times with Haynes, on his feature films *Dottie Gets Spanked* (1993) and *Velvet Goldmine* (1998), the latter of which she won an Independent Spirit Award for in 1999. Despite her successes with feature film, she identifies the documentary as her favorite form of filmmaking: "I always think of the feature process as a more intellectual process. There is a lot of reflection and thought put into the movie, whereas with a documentary you rely more on instinct" (Di Mattia 2015).

In 2005 Alberti began a long-time collaboration with the American documentary film director Alex Gibney on films including *Enron: The Smartest Guys in the Room* (2005), *Taxi to the Dark Side* (2007), and *We Steal Secrets: The Story of WikiLeaks* (2013).

Alberti is repeatedly linked to and appreciated for the degree of realism throughout her work. In 2008, because of her formal realist style, Darren Aronofsky wanted her to be the director of photography for *The Wrestler* (2008). This film, for which she won her second Independent Spirit Award (in 2008), fluently makes use of deep focus and long focal lenses and is praised for its long-take aesthetics. "I think you don't need to rely on movie editing to dictate emotion," Alberti expressed in an interview with *Variety* (Tapley 2015). The fighting scene in Ryan Coogler's *Creed* (2015), one of Alberti's more recent films, is famous because it consists mainly of one extended take, without any post-production stitching. According to Tapley (2015), the incredible immersive scene is the result of 12 takes—of which the 10th eventually ended up in the film. Apart from her realist working method, Alberti is well known for her eclectic style. For example, in Todd Solondz's *Happiness* (1998), a film that deals with the subject of pedophilia, the camera is reserved, whereas in another of her films of that exact same year, *Velvet Goldmine* (1998), the camera is abundant. "If *Velvet Goldmine* is an exercise in excess," Alberti herself argues in an interview with *The New York Times* (Lee 1998), "*Happiness* is an exercise in restraint."

Finally, Maryse Alberti was the first woman on the cover of the *American Cinematographer* in 1998. Alberti has succeeded in creating a space for herself within the male-dominated world of cinematography, making it possible for more women to enter the field today, even though there's clearly still a long way to go. In a 2015 interview, when Alberti was confronted with the fact that not one woman has ever been nominated for, let alone won an Academy Award for, Best Cinematography and that there still are not many women in the American Society of Cinematographers (ASC), she answered pragmatically: "Before the Oscars, before the ASC, before all that, let's get women to work. That's what we need" (Hannett 2015).

Camille Bourgeus

See also: Morrison, Rachel

Further Reading

Bernstein, Paula. 2015. "Groundbreaking DP Maryse Alberti on Shooting 'Freeheld,' 'Creed' and 'The Visit.'" *IndieWire*, September 15. http://www.indiewire.com/2015/09/groundbreaking-dp-maryse-alberti-on-shooting-freeheld-creed-and-the-visit-58141

Di Mattia, Joseph. 1991. "Shooting from the Hip: An Interview with Cinematographer Maryse Alberti." *IDA*, April 1. https://www.documentary.org/feature/shooting-hip-interview-cinematographer-maryse-alberti

Hannett, Michelle. 2015. "Cinematographer Maryse Alberti Talks Creed and Women in Film." *We Are Movie Geeks*, December 29. http://www.wearemoviegeeks.com/2015/12/cinematographer-maryse-alberti-talks-creed-and-women-in-film

Lee, Linda. 1998. "Framing a Vision, Invisibly Maryse Alberti, an Independent Force in Independent Films." *The New York Times*, December 10. http://www.nytimes.com

/1998/12/10/movies/framing-vision-invisibly-maryse-alberti-independent-force-independent-films.html

Mulcahey, Matt. 2015. "'Found Footage with Style': Cinematographer Maryse Alberti on M. Night Shyamalan's The Visit." *Filmmaker Magazine*, September 21. http://filmmakermagazine.com/95734-found-footage-with-style-cinematographer-maryse-alberti-on-m-night-shyamalans-the-visit/#.WiaDfLSdWfU

Tapley, Kristopher. 2015. "Yes, That Dazzling Boxing Sequence in 'Creed' Really Was One Shot." *Variety*, December 1. http://variety.com/2015/film/awards/yes-that-dazzling-boxing-sequence-in-creed-really-was-one-shot-1201650969

Briesewitz, Uta (1967–)

Uta Briesewitz is a German cinematographer and director currently working in Hollywood. Briesewitz, born in Leverkusen, Germany (Federal Republic of Germany, or "West Germany," at the time), in 1967, moved to the United States in the 1990s to study at the American Film Institute in Los Angeles. She is best known for her cinematographic work in Brad Anderson's *Vanishing on 7th Street* (2010), Jason Winer's *Arthur* (2011), and most notably for shooting the pilot and two and a half seasons of David Simon's *The Wire* (2002–2008). Since 2010 Briesewitz has also been active as a television director. She collaborated on Hollywood series including *Hung*, *Orange Is the New Black*, *Awkward*, *The 100*, *Jessica Jones*, and *The Deuce*. In 2007, Briesewitz was recognized by Women in Film Crystal + Lucy Awards for her achievements in cinematography. In 2010 she was nominated for a Primetime Emmy for the pilot episode of *Hung*, and in 2014 she was nominated for an Online Film & Television Award for Best Direction in a Comedy Series for her work on *Orange Is the New Black*. Since 2013 Briesewitz has been a member of the American Society of Cinematographers.

German American cinematographer Uta Briesewitz attends Women in Film's 2007 Crystal and Lucy Awards, held at the Beverly Hilton Hotel in Beverly Hills, California. Briesewitz won the 2007 Kodak Vision Award presented at the event for her outstanding achievements in cinematography. (Starstock/Dreamstime.com)

Uta Briesewitz has expressed that for her, film is all about the experience of working together intensively in a team: "Film is all about creating an illusion, and I have to admit, the bigger it gets the more fun it can be . . . I thoroughly enjoy the process and the privilege of being able to put everybody's hard work and vision up on the screen" (Briesewitz 2011). As a child, Briesewitz was oriented toward painting, but the experience of isolation and lack of collaboration would soon lead her to film, with a specific fascination for the Nouvelle Vague and Italian Neorealism (Briesewitz 2011). After finishing high school, Briesewitz started as an intern at a TV production company in Cologne, mostly shooting sporting events such as soccer, tennis, and ice hockey. "Once you have to follow a puck on the ice, you learn how to make quick decisions as an operator," she says, humorously referring to the skills she obtained during those years (Briesewitz 2011). She there learned to operate long lenses and specialized in super-slow-motion photography. Briesewitz left the company after three years to study at the German Film and Television Academy in Berlin while financing her education with regular assignments for television. She graduated in the summer of 1990 and decided to move to the United States to continue studying at the American Film Institute in Los Angeles under the supervision of Denise Brassard, Robert Primes, and Russell Carpenter.

In 1998, even before graduating from the American Film Institute, Briesewitz shot her first feature film, the romantic comedy *Next Stop Wonderland* by Brad Anderson, starring Hope Davis and Philip Seymour Hoffman. After graduating, she started working on low-budget, independent films such as Brad Anderson's *Session 9* (2001) and the indie film *XX/XY* (2002) shot on video and starring Mark Ruffalo. Around that time Briesewitz was asked to work on David Simon's television series *The Wire*, an American crime series focusing on the Baltimore drug scene through the eyes of both drug dealers and police officers. From 2002 to 2005 she was the main director of photography on the popular series, shooting the pilot and two and a half seasons, which totaled 29 episodes. Although definitely a career breakthrough and according to Briesewitz herself a series that changed her life (Anderson 2008), she testifies that "(w)hen I took *The Wire*, some of my indie friends said, 'Oh that's bad—don't do television or you'll never do another movie again' " (Briesewitz 2011). Briesewitz replied: "I see so many independent scripts, and just because they're independent doesn't mean they're great. If I see a good TV script, I prefer to do that. TV helped me make a living. TV helped me survive" (Briesewitz 2011). In an interview with *HD Pro Guide*, Briesewitz talks about style and expresses how series such as *The Wire* allowed her to experiment with natural light. She describes how she observed the city of Baltimore at night "bathed in an orange sodium vapor glow" and how she tried to depict those colors truthfully (Solis 2016). "As a DP [Director of Photography] I constantly observe light, how it moves, how it changes, how it differs from one city or country to the next" (Briesewitz 2016).

After *The Wire*, Briesewitz continued shooting television series, including *LAX* (2004–2005) and *Thief* (2006), as well as some feature films: *Walk Hard: The Dewey Cox Story* (2007), a comedy directed by Jake Kasdan; the post-apocalyptic thriller film *Vanishing on 7th Street* (2010); and the romantic comedy *Arthur* (2011), directed by Jason Winer and starring Helen Mirren, Jennifer Garner, and Russell Brand. Since 2010 Briesewitz started directing as her main activity. She now has 22 credits to her name as a director, having collaborated on several Hollywood series, including *Hung* (three episodes, 2010–2011), *Awkward* (four episodes, 2014–2015),

The 100 (two episodes, 2015–2016), *Orange Is the New Black* (four episodes, 2013–2017), *The Deuce* (one episode, 2017), and *Jessica Jones* (two episodes, 2015–2018). When asked what she thinks of the all-female director team of *Jessica Jones*' second season, she replies: "Listen, this is about a female superhero, maybe just a couple of women should tell the story?" (Weisbrod 2017). However, to *Vulture*'s next question, "Who can tell which story?" Briesewitz replied: "But there also are a credible amount of writers and authors who imagine worlds and lives that they have not lived, and that they either researched very well or completely imagine. I think at one point you also just have to look at the work itself" (Weisbrod 2017).

Camille Bourgeus

See also: Foster, Jodie

Further Reading

Anderson, John. 2008. "Uta Briesewitz. Communal Artist." *Variety*, October 29. http://variety.com/2008/scene/markets-festivals/uta-briesewitz-2-1117994911

Briesewitz, Uta. n.d. 2011. "Uta Briesewitz Shines Light on 'Arthur.'" *Panavision*, Accessed April 17, 2018. http://www.panavision.com/spotlight/uta-briesewitz-shines-light-arthur

Heuring, David. 2014. "Uta Briesewitz, ASC Eyes the Director's Chair." *ASC Magazine*, April 8. https://ascmag.com/blog/parallax-view/uta-briesewitz-asc-eyes-the-directors-chair

Solis, Michelle. 2016. "A Conversation with Uta Briesewitz." *HD Pro Guide*, July 22. http://www.hdproguide.com/a-conversation-with-uta-briesewitz-asc

Weisbrod, Lars. 2017. "The Deuce Director on How Men Often Direct Sex Scenes Differently than Women." *Vulture*, October 8. http://www.vulture.com/2017/10/the-deuce-director-uta-briesewitz-masturbation-scene.html

Kuras, Ellen (1959–)

Ellen Kuras is a director of photography and director whose body of work ranges from documentary to narrative film and from big-budgeted studio productions and commercials to independent and experimental films. As a director of photography, she has worked with visionary directors such as Martin Scorsese, Spike Lee, Michel Gondry, and Rebecca Miller, among other celebrated directors. For each film that she has collaborated with as a director of photography, she has been able to successfully adapt the visual language contained in the mind's eye of each director. She has shot in various formats, including film, HD video, and miniDV.

Kuras's career follows an unusual path to becoming one of the most esteemed cinematographers of both Hollywood and the independent film world. She studied anthropology and semiotics at Brown University and photography at Rhode Island School of Design. During her studies in anthropology, she was intrigued by documentary filmmaking because of its power to move audiences while portraying the lives of real people and its ability to speak to the human condition. Kuras's body of work is thus strongly rooted in documentary filmmaking techniques and illustrates her fascination with how meaning is constructed visually through image, color, light, perception, and movement.

In Rebecca Miller's directorial debut *Angela* (1995), Kuras portrays the world from a child's viewpoint, blending reality and fantasy through the use of a lyrical vintage aesthetic. The film revolves around 10-year-old Angela who invents imaginary narratives of sin and cleansing in order to cope with her increasingly dysfunctional family. The soft colors employed by Kuras create a dreamlike environment throughout the film, and the shallow depth of field aids the audience in viewing the film world environment from Angela's perspective. According to a review from *The New York Times*, the "early scenes [that] beautifully capture a childhood intuition of a world where bogeymen lurk and angels hover" are when the film is "at its best" (Holden 1996).

Kuras's next collaboration with Miller, *Personal Velocity: Three Portraits* (2002), was shot completely on video. The film is a triptych narrative; each frame reveals a woman striving toward self-realization. Three stories are visually distinct: Kuras brings a separate palette of colors into each story, in accord with the personal crisis that the main character is experiencing. The camerawork varies from a handheld cinéma verité style (a technique of documentary filmmaking invented by Jean Rouch) to static tripod shots. Kuras's mastery of lighting brings a poetic look to *Personal Velocity* even though the film was recorded on miniDV. The video medium allowed for long takes in which the actors could stay in character longer without disruption. For both collaborations with Miller, Kuras won the Cinematography Award at Sundance Film Festival. Having also won the Cinematography Award for *Swoon* (1992), Kuras is the first cinematographer to have received this Sundance award three times.

After winning the Sundance Film Festival's Cinematography Award for *Swoon*, Kuras caught the attention of several prominent Hollywood directors. In Spike Lee's *Summer of Sam* (1999), Kuras's evolution from a modest and lyrical independent cinematographer to a director of photography orchestrating a large Hollywood production is evident. The film's high-speed tempo incorporates dynamic dolly and crane shots, mirroring the urban energy of the disco era and punk music, as well as the anxiety caused by the serial killer known as the Son of Sam that pulsed throughout New York City in 1976. Kuras's use of lighting conveys the sensory experience of synesthesia as the audience can almost feel the intense heat and suffocating humidity of New York summer nights, while her use of saturated color scheme alludes to the 1970s and the dynamism of the story's young characters.

Perhaps one of the most interesting director-cinematographer collaborations in Kuras's career is *Eternal Sunshine of the Spotless Mind* (2004) directed by Michel Gondry. When Gondry and Kuras sat down to discuss how to translate the script into the visual realm, Gondry said he wanted to shoot the film with a handheld camera aesthetic and without any film lights. As a result, Kuras had to be innovative and resourceful with lighting and camerawork. For instance, she utilized lamps in the scenes as light sources by cutting holes in their shades on the side facing away from the camera toward the actors. When the protagonist's memories of his girlfriend are being erased, the camerawork speeds up to construct an energetic chasing scene. In order to achieve this, Kuras used two mobile handheld cameras as two master shots instead of a more conventional setup that would use one master and one for coverage. She choreographed the actors' movements so that each camera would capture the complete action. During the editing process, two takes could be intertwined together to produce a unique effect. Kuras's experience as a documentary cinematographer was a critical component of this ambitious scene, and she often had to make rapid decisions on the fly about camera positions and movement. To complement the documentary look of the film, visual illusions were also created as in-camera effects rather than in post-production, a technique reminiscent of the magic tricks created during the early cinema era. Kuras rose to the challenge of Gondry's artistic demands, and stunning cinematography was produced as a result.

Kuras's career as a director of photography has thrived over the years alongside her continued interest in exploring cultures and communities. She was both the director of photography and co-director (with Thavisouk Phrasavath) of the documentary *The Betrayal—Nerakhoon* (2008), a film about Laotian refugees in her neighborhood of Providence, New York. *The Betrayal* was nominated in 2009 for an Oscar as well as an Independent Spirit Award. Kuras continues to explore questions of representation, meaning, subtext, and symbolism in film language.

Beyza Boyacioglu

Further Reading

ASC. n.d. "Director of Photography Ellen Kuras, ASC Helps Spike Lee Explore a Serial Killer's Impact on New York in Summer of Sam." Accessed March 25, 2015. https://www.theasc.com/magazine/june99/psycho/pg1.htm

Guerrasio, Jason. 2009. "Director Ellen Kuras on *The Betrayal*." *Filmmaker Magazine*, January 19. http://filmmakermagazine.com/4761-ellen-kuras-the-betrayal-nerakhoon-by-nick-dawson-2

Hart, Hugh. 2009. "The Silent Witness." *Brown Alumni Magazine*, March/April. http://www.brownalumnimagazine.com/content/view/2216/40

Holden, Stephen. 1996. "Angela (1995) Film Review: Dark Fantasy as a Refuge from a Manic-Depressive Mother." *The New York Times*, April 17. http://www.nytimes.com/movie/review?res=9A02E5D81F39F935A15752C0A960958260

Internet Encyclopedia of Cinematographers. n.d. "Ellen Kuras." Accessed March 25, 2015. http://www.cinematographers.nl/PaginasDoPh/kuras.htm

Pavlus, John. 2004. "Forget Me Not." *American Cinematographer*, April. http://www.theasc.com/magazine/april04/cover

Torneo, Erin. 2002. "Cinematography as Poetry: Ellen Kuras Talks about the DV Challenges of 'Personal Velocity.'" *IndieWire*, November 25. http://www.indiewire.com/article/interview_cinematography_as_poetry_ellen_kuras_talks_about_the_dv_challenge

VanAirsdale, S. T. 2008. "Shooting at Will." *The Reeler*. January 9. http://www.thereeler.com/features/shooting_at_will.php

Walker Art Center. 2010. "Filmmakers in Conversation: Ellen Kuras." March 17. https://www.youtube.com/watch?v=bHnVrb4aPOI

Morano, Reed (1977–)

The youngest-ever inductee into the American Society of Cinematographers (ASC) and one of only 17 active female members as of 2018, Reed Morano is not only one of the most talented and prolific cinematographers today, she has also become an award-winning director and often functions as the producer on more recent projects. A master conductor of visual tone, Morano shoots on film "wherever possible" and firmly believes that a cinematographer relies on intuition and artistry, rather than any technological formula (Collins 2011).

Morano was born in Omaha, Nebraska, and attended New York University's Tisch School of the Arts, prompted by the recommendation of her father, and earned her degree in undergraduate film and television, followed by an MFA in cinematography and a few years of teaching cinematography there as well. Morano's breakout project as a cinematographer—after mainly working on short films—was the 2008 Oscar-nominated film *Frozen River*, directed and written by Courtney Hunt. By 2011, after only a few more feature films, including *Little Birds* (2011), which she shot during her third trimester of pregnancy; and *Yelling to the Sky* (2011), Morano won the Kodak Vision Award for Cinematography at the Women in Film Crystal + Lucy Awards. In the few years that followed, Morano has functioned as director of photography on a colorful array of films, including a documentary film about LCD Soundsystem called *Shut Up and Play the Hits* (2012), the Rob Reiner–directed *The Magic of Belle Isle* (2012), and the comedy-drama *The Skeleton Twins* (2014) starring *Saturday Night Live* alumni Bill Hader and Kristen Wiig.

Morano commits herself to visual storytelling in the vein of cinema vérite, which she studied to prepare for her career in cinematography. She gravitates toward the use of handheld, naturalistic lighting, extreme wide shots, and very tight close-ups; however, Morano does not want to be limited by these visual signatures, nor be limited to any one particular style. Instead, she pushes herself to adapt to every movie and "disappear into each story" (Robinson 2015).

By 2014, Morano emerged as a major force in television as well, acting as head of cinematography for numerous HBO original series, starting with the entire first season of *Looking* (2014), which explores the lives of three 30-something gay men in San Francisco. The following year, she did the series cinematography for five episodes of *Vinyl* (2015) that immediately followed the Martin Scorsese–directed pilot episode. Morano has spoken about how intimidating it was to try and mirror Scorsese's powerful filming style (O'Falt 2017). The tables turned on her next project, and in the reverse, Morano directed the pilot episode of the Sarah Jessica Parker–helmed series *Divorce* (2016), for which she earned an Emmy nomination for Outstanding Cinematography for a Single-Camera Series. During this golden age of television, Morano advocated for the provocative power of a single-director model that lent a singular vision to the program (O'Falt 2017).

In 2017, Morano became the first woman to win an Emmy for Outstanding Directing since 1995, for her work on an episode of Hulu's *The Handmaid's Tale* (2017). Adapted from Margaret Atwood's novel, the series presents an American dystopia that many find frighteningly relevant to current politics, one of many factors attributing to the show's success. Morano's stylistic choices set the tone for the overall series, marrying the audience's point of view with that of lead character Offred (Elisabeth Moss) through signature, extreme close-ups, and voice-over. The series pushes the boundaries of televisual narrative, emphasizing a higher-level symbolism in the image more often associated with film texts. Morano uses traditional Technicolor techniques, for instance, signaling rebellion through the blood red of the handmaidens' cloaks that boldly punctuate the bleak landscape of Gilead.

Morano debuted her directorial skills as a filmmaker with *Meadowland* (2015), which journals how one couple (Olivia Wilde, Luke Wilson) deals with the guilt and anguish following the abduction of their young son. Morano also did the cinematography on the film, for which she was nominated for an Independent Spirit Award. She operates as both director and DP for her current film as well, the dystopic *I Think We're Alone Now* (2018), for which she was awarded the Special Jury Award for Excellence in Filmmaking at the 2018 Sundance Film Festival, where it premiered.

Christina Parker-Flynn

Further Reading

Collins, Stacey. 2011. "Reed Morano Relies on Intuition." *Variety*, February 11. http://variety.com/2011/film/news/reed-morano-relies-on-intuition-1118031771

Desowitz, Bill. 2017. "'The Handmaid's Tale': How a Classic Technicolor Technique Made the Color Red a Political Act." *IndieWire*, May 25. http://www.indiewire.com/2017/05/the-handmaids-tale-technicolor-the-color-red-political-1201831792

O'Falt, Chris. 2017. "'Handmaid's Tale' Director Reed Morano Had to Mimic Martin Scorsese on 'Vinyl,' and Other TV Challenges." *IndieWire*, August 23. http://www.indiewire.com/2017/08/handmaids-tale-reed-morano-directing-1201868878

Robinson, Tasha. 2015. "*Frozen River* DP Reed Morano on Making Audiences 'Feel Everything' with Her Directorial Debut." *The Dissolve*, April 28. https://thedissolve.com/news/5536-frozen-river-dp-reed-morano-on-making-audiences-fe/

Morrison, Rachel (1978–)

Raw, fresh talent is the constant infusion that provides the lifeblood of filmmaking. If lucky, an artist can come along that has independent film credibility and talent and translate that into big-budget Hollywood films. In cinematographer Rachel Morrison, filmmaking has received an exciting new talent, but has also received notice that the status quo in the male-dominated field of cinematography has now been upended and brought to the forefront of discussion.

Morrison's education and background is found in the art of photography. Steeped in formal education, Morrison's journey took her from New York University, with a bachelor of arts in both film and photography, and a master's degree from the American Film Institute's cinematography program. Yet it is her love of photography that sustains her creativity. Morrison remarked, "I've always liked very photo-realistic photography, even in a very lit and collaborative film world. I try to see what is at the heart of the story and the character at a given moment, and let story and emotion be the factors that inform the technique" (Heuring 2018). Morrison further notes that "photography can distill the human spirit, capture human emotion in its raw, pure form, and freeze a moment in time that can then take on its own life" (Heuring 2018). Seeking new avenues of artistry, her transition from photography to cinematography seemed inevitable and was much needed in the field of cinematography.

While early in her career, Morrison has found a great collaboration with director Ryan Coogler. Having worked with Coogler on his debut film, 2013's *Fruitvale Station*, and his follow-up films *Creed* (2015) and the Marvel superhero film *Black Panther* (2018), Morrison has found a creative companion in the world of film. Noting their first film collaboration Morrison said that "*Fruitvale* set the bar for what I wanted to do with my career, which was to make films that had consciousness and messaging in an entertaining package" (Feeney 2018). Further commenting on her creative symmetry with Coogler, Morrison noted, "It should feel like [the filmmakers] are all speaking the same language" (Horton 2018).

Morrison's quick rise and accompanying talent amplified the long-standing argument of gender inequality in field of cinema, cinematography in particular. Not that there have not been female cinematographers before Morrison. However, Morrison's work and her much-deserved Academy Award nomination for Dee Rees's 2017 film *Mudbound* brought the discussion into the forefront of debate. Speaking to the history of the debate, writer Steve Zeitchik wrote that "Membership in the ASC (America Society of Cinematographers), which confers the cachet that attracts employers, has grown painfully slowly for women. The first woman joined in the 1980s—more than 60 years after the group was founded—and as of 2005, the group had only five women out of some 350 members. Today there are 18, still a fraction of the roughly 375 members" (Zeitchik 2018). Morrison's take on the subject is insightful and hopeful, noting that "[t]he job speaks to things women do inherently well: empathy, alertness to the emotions of others, multitasking. I'm surprised [the gender ratio of cinematographers] is not 60–40 in our favor" (Feeney 2018). With Morrison's star in ascension, and the discussion of inequality front and center, others in the film industry are beginning to take notice and weigh in. Of this debate, Netflix Chief Content Officer Ted Sarandos said, "There are a lot of barriers that should have fallen down a long time ago, and cinematography is a big one. I hope we'll soon see a lot more women getting behind the camera" (Zeitchik 2018).

Rachel Morrison has blazed a trail for women, yet even with the well-earned accolades, she represents a small minority in a field dominated by male cinematographers. Yet her presence and talent will serve as a clarion call for other females to enter into the art form. As Morrison succinctly pointed out in a 2018 interview, "I'm realizing that I've become a role model and then that visibility is giving a lot of women the courage to keep going, or the courage to get started, or it feels like a light at the end of the tunnel" (Zeitchik 2018).

Shawn Driscoll

See also: Alberti, Maryse; Carter, Ruth E.

Further Reading

Feeney, Mark. 2018. "Rachel Morrison, from 'Mudbound' to 'Black Panther' to the Oscars." *The Boston Globe*, February 27. https://www.bostonglobe.com/arts/movies/2018/02/27/rachel-morrison-from-mudbound-black-panther-oscars/a6OfjYGr9oQSwMnreCUmrN/story.html

Heuring, David. 2018. "Mudbound's Morrison Uses Still Photography Skills." *Variety*, February 22. http://variety.com/2018/film/awards/rachel-morrison-breaks-barriers-on-mudbound-1202707956

Horton, Robert. 2018. "Interview with Cinematographer Rachel Morrison." *Film Comment*, March 5. https://www.filmcomment.com/article/modern-painter-rachel-morrison-mudbound-fruitvale-station

Zeitchik, Steven. 2018. "Why Cinematography May Be the Most Gender-Biased Job in Hollywood." *Washington Post*, March 6. https://www.washingtonpost.com/news/business/wp/2018/03/06/why-cinematography-may-be-the-most-gender-biased-job-in-hollywood

Schreiber, Nancy (1949–)

Nancy Schreiber is an accomplished American cinematographer, a member of the American Society of Cinematographers (ASC), and the first and only woman to ever receive the prestigious President's Award from the ASC in 2017. Prolific in various audiovisual media (film, music video, television) and cinematic genres (period drama, documentary, crime), Schreiber has established her cinema veteran status with over 100 film credits during the 30 years of her career in the industry. Her mastery of both the equipment she uses and the cinematic style she employs

Award-winning cinematographer Nancy Schreiber. Her versatility has enabled her to shoot numerous features, music videos, documentaries, and television shows in different mediums throughout her illustrious career. Schreiber was the fourth woman in history to join the American Society of Cinematographers, in 1995. (Photo by Marie Chao)

earned her a place in various projects of both mainstream Hollywood and independent cinema. Schreiber's cinematography is versatile, yet in almost every case she manages to present stories through her own lens in subtle but recognizable ways.

Given her art history degree from the University of Michigan, Schreiber unsurprisingly cites Vermeer, Rembrandt, Van Gogh, and Matisse as influences. She also mentions Asian art and landscape architecture, Bauhaus, and music of almost any genre as inspiration. The epic *Lawrence of Arabia* (1962) was one of the films that affected her greatly when she was younger.

Schreiber is the recipient of two major awards: the ASC President's Award and the Susan B. Anthony Award ("Failure Is Impossible"), for which she was the first cinematographer to receive the prize, in 2017. She also won a Kodak Vision Award in 1997, which she shared with Judy Irola. She also received the Best Cinematography Award at Sundance for *November* (2004) and earned an Independent Spirit Award nomination for *Chain of Desire* (1992), followed by an Emmy nomination for *The Celluloid Closet* (1996), a documentary about gay people in the American film industry.

Schreiber was born on June 27, 1949, in Detroit, Michigan. Her mother was an academic and occasional art dealer, and her father died when she was young. The cinematographer mentions that she remembers her father's interest in photography and the fact that he used mainly 8mm and 16mm film. With little formal training in cinematography, she had the advantage of having an outsider look, which has given her the freshness in her cinematic approach and helped her through the ranks in film production. Schreiber began her career as a gaffer and advanced to a camera assistant and, eventually, director of photography. She got her first job as a production assistant in New York, responding to a *Village Voice* ad. Since the production was undercrewed, she found herself in the electric department. The fact that she knew very little about the power structure of male-dominated Hollywood helped her develop as a freelance cinematographer in New York and, later, in Los Angeles.

Her extensive film credits include *Your Friends and Neighbors* (1998), *Dead Beat* (1994), *The Nines* (2007), and *It's a Disaster* (2012). She also worked as director of photography in numerous shorts, including *Serena* (2012), *Rules of Love* (2002), and her debut *Am I Normal?: A Film about Male Puberty* (1979). Schreiber established her status in television movies such as *Filthy Gorgeous* (2006), *Thicker than Blood* (1998), and *Lessons Learned* (2000); documentaries (*Visions of Light, Through the Wire,* and *Eva Hesse*); and, more recently, in series such as ABC's *The Family* (2016), FX's *Better Things* (2016–), and HBO's *The Comeback* (2005).

In numerous interviews Schreiber admits to being a big music fan. She has served as director of photography of over 100 music videos for such stars as Aretha Franklin, Sting, Pink Floyd, and Billy Joel. According to the cinematographer, one of the most significant moments in her career was shooting behind-the-scenes footage during Amnesty International's human rights world tour starring Sting, Bruce Springsteen, Tracy Chapman, and Peter Gabriel.

Schreiber's experience in both Hollywood productions and New York independent films speaks volumes about her openness as a cinematographer. Her cinematic style can be described as eclectic and diversified. She employs a wide range of angles and types of lighting. Her close-ups in *Your Friends and Neighbors* and landscape shots in *Girl in the Cadillac* (1995) and *Nevada* (1997) have proven her skills as a director of photography. Schreiber is inventive and capable of bringing out the best of every camera she is given. In an interview, Schreiber said she is "equipment unbiased" (Kodakery 2017). As a cinematographer, Schreiber works almost like a chameleon with lighting that articulates textures in such films as *Lush Life* (1994) and *Every Day* (2010). Convincing in both cold (*American Gun*, *November*) and warm palettes (*Shadow Magic*, *The Nines*), Schreiber seems to prefer shooting in deeply textured and atmospheric low key (*Filthy Gorgeous*, *Chain of Desire*).

As one of the few women cinematographers in the industry, Schreiber unceasingly paves the way for other women like her. Throughout her career, Schreiber was a member of The National Association of Broadcast Employees and Technicians as the first female gaffer in history, and in 1995 she joined ASC as the fourth woman ever in the association's history. She has been a board member of the Women in Film Foundation and a member of the Academy of Motion Picture Arts and Sciences.

Lidia Kniaź

Further Reading

Caranicas, Peter. 2017. "Cinematographer Nancy Schreiber to Receive Susan B. Anthony Award at High Falls Film Festival." *Variety* (blog), October 31. http://variety.com/2017/artisans/markets-festivals/cinematographer-nancy-schreiber-better-things-courteney-cox-to-receive-susan-b-anthony-award-at-high-falls-film-festival-1202603055

The Kodakery. 2017. "Cinematographer Nancy Schreiber, ASC." The Kodakery (podcast)." Accessed February 9, 2018. https://player.fm/series/the-kodakery/cinematographer-nancy-schreiber-asc

Krasilovsky, Alexis, Harriet Margolis, and Julia Stein. 2015. *Shooting Women: Behind the Camera, Around the World.* Bristol, UK: Intellect.

Marko, Bobby. 2015. "Life as an Independent Cinematographer, an Interview with Nancy Schreiber." *ProVideo Coalition* (blog), September 9. https://www.provideocoalition.com/life-as-an-independent-cinematographer-an-interview-with-nancy-schreiber-asc

"Nancy Schreiber—Cinematographers." n.d. Accessed January 27, 2018. http://www.cinematographers.nl/PaginasDoPh/schreiber.htm

Schreiber, Nancy. 2017. "Things I've Learned as a Moviemaker: Cinematographer Nancy Schreiber." *MovieMaker Magazine* (blog), February 1. https://www.moviemaker.com/archives/series/things_learned/cinematographer-nancy-schreiber/

Stuart, Sophia. 2017. "Lighting Legacy." *HD Video Pro*, January 23. https://www.hdvideopro.com/film-and-tv/feature-films/lighting-legacy

Valentini, Valentina I. 2017. "First Woman to Receive ASC's Presidents Award Helps Pave Way to Equality for Cinematographers." *Variety* (blog), January 25. http://variety.com/2017/artisans/production/cinematographers-equality-asc-1201968908

Warren, Matt. 2017. "Cinematographer Nancy Schreiber on Awards, Changing Technology and Instagram." *Film Independent* (blog), February 17. https://www.filmindependent.org/blog/cinematographer-nancy-schreiber-awards-changing-tech-take-perfect-instagram-pic

Vincent, Amy (1959–)

Amy Vincent is one of the few female directors of photography working on narrative feature films in Hollywood today. In an area of film production traditionally populated almost exclusively by men, Vincent has crafted a distinctive body of work and forged a number of successful artistic collaborations. Her lush, tactile photography in such films as *Eve's Bayou* (1997), *Hustle & Flow* (2005), and *Black Snake Moan* (2006) paints a portrait of the American South that is unique in Hollywood over the past two decades. Vincent is also notable for being a white woman best known for several films that chronicle the African American experience in the Deep South; she brings an uncommon eye for capturing the joy and pain of black life in the United States.

Amy Vincent (credited as "Amy Vincent" early in her career) was born in Boston in 1959. She attended the University of California, Santa Cruz, where she received her degree in theater arts and film. Vincent concentrated on lighting design in college, as she explains in the documentary *Cinematographer Style* (2006). Throughout the late 1980s and early 1990s she made her way up through the ranks as camera loader, camera operator, and second assistant cameraperson, working for notable cinematographers like Robert Richardson and Bill Pope on such films as *Natural Born Killers* (1994) and *Clueless* (1995).

Vincent's first major feature film as the director of photography came in 1997 with *Eve's Bayou.* The film is a melodramatic coming-of-age tale of a young African American girl Eve (Jurnee Smollett-Bell) navigating the contentious marriage of her parents (Samuel L. Jackson and Lynn Whitfield) against the backdrop of the Louisiana bayou in the 1960s with its attendant Creole influences, including voodoo. Vincent, in collaboration with Kasi Lemmons, created a muted color palette of greens and browns that captures the environment of southern Louisiana, thick with humidity and the specters of history. Vincent renders many of the memory sequences in a stark, high-contrast black-and-white that calls attention to them as constructed images.

Critic Roger Ebert, who named *Eve's Bayou* the best film of 1997 in his year-end list, took note of the cinematography in his glowing review: "The film has been photographed by Amy Vincent in shadows and rich textures, where even a sunny day contains dark undertones; surely she looked at the Bergman films photographed by Sven Nyvist in preparing her approach" (Ebert 1997). Nyvist's painterly style used to capture the lives of Swedish director Ingmar Bergman's deeply flawed and disturbed characters translates particularly well to the setting of the American bayou, permeating the film with a sense of the Southern Gothic—an aesthetic subgenre that can be traced through the writings of William Faulkner and Flannery O'Connor, films like *The Night of the Hunter* (1955) and *Hush . . . Hush, Sweet Charlotte* (1964), and on to such recent television shows as the first season of *True Detective* (2014). This work, in articulating a contemporary visual grammar of the Southern Gothic, contributed to Vincent receiving the Women in Film Kodak Vision Award in 2001.

Vincent began her creative partnership with director Craig Brewer in 2005 with her work on *Hustle & Flow.* Set amidst the poverty of Memphis, Tennessee,

Vincent again displays her knack for photographing the vibrancy of black life in the South. This story of a small-time pimp pursuing his dreams of becoming a rapper, played by Terrence Howard, called for a visual style that would be evocative of the specific socioeconomic conditions of the characters. Vincent described to Kodak's *In Camera* magazine the look that she and Brewer were trying to achieve in the film: "You could photograph Memphis in a much more somber way but we chose to go for a very contrasty look and saturated colors. . . . All the elements were unbelievably beautiful, including locations, set dressings, wardrobe, the various skin tones, and how beautifully the sweat glistened on the faces of the characters in close-ups" (*In Camera* 2005, 25). Vincent contributes a more contemporary sheen to this present-day tale of urban struggle, in contrast to the historical milieu of *Eve's Bayou*, but the film nonetheless contributes its own mythologization of the American South. For her work on *Hustle & Flow,* Vincent was presented with the Cinematography Award at the 2005 Sundance Film Festival following its enthusiastic critical reception.

Vincent collaborated with Brewer again the following year on *Black Snake Moan,* a controversial film that infamously includes an extended sequence of a promiscuous young white woman, played by Christian Ricci, chained to a radiator by a middle-aged black man (Samuel L. Jackson) in the name of Christian morality. The film sees Vincent once more engaging with the lurid sexuality of the Southern Gothic, a theme that connects it to antecedents in American film history such as Elia Kazan's *Baby Doll* (1956). For such provocative material, Brewer and Vincent decided to take a fairly classical approach: "We could have photographed it with random handheld swish pans and hard light," she told the *Los Angeles Times*, "But I think if there is a deliberate, careful, specific choice in each frame, it forces the audience to believe that the decisions the director is making are conscious and guiding the story in an intended direction" (Crabtree 2007). The restrained, methodical formal style works in dialectical contrast with the grotesque violence of the film's content.

Vincent has tried her hand at documentary feature cinematography with *This Film Is Not Yet Rated* (2006), an exploration of the hypocrisies in the Motion Picture Association of America's ratings system. She continued her fruitful partnership with director Craig Brewer on the 2011 remake of the 1980s hit *Footloose*, the classic tale of a small town that outlaws dancing.

Jason LaRivière

See also: Foster, Jodie

Further Reading

Crabtree, Sheigh. 2007. "The Sympathetic Eye." *Los Angeles Times*, January 22. http://articles.latimes.com/2007/jan/22/entertainment/et-snake22

Ebert, Roger. 1997. "Eve's Bayou." *Chicago Sun Times*, November 7. http://www.rogerebert.com/reviews/eves-bayou-1997

In Camera. 2005. "Making Hustle & Flow." *In Camera Magazine*, April 29. http://www.motion.kodak.com/motion/uploadedFiles/hustleFlow.pdf

Tindall, George B. 2006. "Mythic South." *The New Encyclopedia of Southern Culture, Vol 4: Myth, Manners, Memory.* Edited by Charles Reagan Wilson. Chapel Hill: University of North Carolina Press.

Walker, Mandy (1963–)

Few women in the world of cinematography have risen to the heights of Mandy Walker, ASC, ACS, the first female director of photography (DP) to shoot a film with a budget of over $100 million and the first woman elected to the board of governors of the Academy of Motion Picture Arts and Sciences to represent cinematographers. "Be brave" is the advice she gives to young people.

When the industry began its 2017 Oscar nomination speculation, *Hidden Figures* (2016) appeared on a number of lists. Would this be the year that a woman, Mandy Walker, would finally be recognized in the cinematography category? Unfortunately, the film's three nods did not include Walker, and to date, the Oscars have never nominated, let alone awarded, a woman in the role of DP. However, her skill is widely appreciated in an industry in which women accounted for only 5 percent of the cinematographers working on the top 250 domestic grossing films of 2016 (Lauzen 2017). That is only one point more than the number almost 20 years ago in 1998.

Despite the rarity of women in her field, Walker feels that attitudes have changed a good deal in the last few years. The "tradition" of male cinematographers only has become a more public issue in the press, the union, and in Academy and American Society of Cinematographers (ASC) diversity initiatives. She herself takes on many female mentees and interns, teaching and training the next generation to lead the lighting, grip, and camera departments as they deliver the visual realization of a director's vision. After a 2014–2015 academic stint as artist-in-residence at UCLA, she received the 2015 Kodak Cinematography Mentor of the Year Award.

Walker, selected for both the ASC and Australian Cinematographers Society), started out in Australia at age 18 as a runner, then a film loader, and moved up the ladder quickly, earning her first director of photography credit by age 25. She was noticed internationally when the independent feature *Australian Rules* (2002) made a splash at the Sundance Film Festival, also winning the Film Critics Circle of Australia Award for cinematography. After shooting primarily low-budget short dramas, documentaries, and music videos, this led to work on the Lionsgate release *Shattered Glass* (2003), starring Hayden Christensen, Chloë Sevigny, and Peter Sarsgaard, which garnered Walker a 2004 Independent Spirit Award nomination for cinematography.

By 2006, after working on high-end commercials for Chanel No. 5, Virgin Atlantic, and American Express, *Variety* named her one of "Ten Cinematographers to Watch," noting, "Australian Cinematographer Mandy Walker [. . .] has quietly made a name for herself as an avid collaborator with a patient eye for nuance and as much technical acumen as emotional verve" (Lyons 2006, A11). Those words capture her style as both artist and technician, the combined elements that make her a powerhouse example for other DPs to emulate. In the industry today, it is that balance between science and art that all top cinematographers must master.

When choosing a shooter for *Australia* (2008), the Twentieth Century Fox period romantic adventure starring Nicole Kidman and Hugh Jackman, director Baz Luhrmann went with Walker, further introducing her to the international stage. Luhrmann said of Walker, "Her work was so good I simply couldn't ignore it" (Gray

2008, 54). She went on to snag the Best Cinematography Award from the Film Critics Circle of Australia, Satellite Award from the International Press Academy, and Cinematographer of the Year at the Hollywood Film Festival. Women in Film honored Walker with their Kodak Vision Award for her achievements, and *Variety* predicted that she was poised for an elusive Oscar nomination. Then another Australian adventure/drama, *Tracks* (2013, starring Mia Wasikowska), earned her recognition by peers in the Australian Cinematography Society with a Gold prize at the Australian Cinematography Society Awards, along with a nomination from the Australian Academy of Cinema and Television Arts Awards.

Walker faced extreme Australian camera conditions at 122-degree temperatures and wild dust storms shooting *Tracks* and epic-scale horse action in *Australia*, both producing trademark gorgeous scenery. *Hidden Figures*, on the other hand, required re-creating the time period of the segregated American South in the late 1950s and early 1960s. In the film, she delivered beautiful color primarily in cramped indoor locations for the feature about three female African American mathematicians who were critical to the success of NASA, conveying a story about oppression and triumph. Like Walker, these women broke into a traditionally male field, with the added barriers of segregation, racism, and the much greater sexism of the time.

Although the *Hidden Figures* Oscar nomination did not come her way, the film afforded Walker status as the first female cinematographer to shoot a movie with a budget of over $100 million. In 2017, Walker won election to the board of governors of the Academy of Motion Picture Arts and Sciences, outpacing three male candidates to become the first woman to represent cinematographers, and joined the board of governors of the American Society of Cinematographers as an alternate. Although only in her fifties, she has already been inducted into the Australian Cinematographers Hall of Fame.

Walker next lensed Twentieth Century Fox's October 2017 release *The Mountain between Us*, the plane crash romance starring Idris Elba, Kate Winslet, and Beau Bridges. Although the film received mixed reviews, Walker's finesse is called out for praise with phrases like "stunning location cinematography," "spectacular cinematography," and "stunningly shot." These came despite the challenges of shooting in the snow on top of a mountain in extreme cold. We will next see Walker's work in the live-action *Mulan* film for Disney (2019).

Angela Beauchamp

Further Reading

Gray, Simon. 2008. "Thunder Down Under: Mandy Walker, ACS Lends Sweep and Scope to Baz Luhrmann's Period Drama *Australia*." *American Cinematographer* 89(11): 54–63.

Lauzen, Martha M. 2017. "The Celluloid Ceiling: Behind-the-Scenes Employment of Women on the Top 100, 250, and 500 Films of 2016." *Center for the Study of Women in Television and Film*, Accessed April 18, 2018. http://womenintvfilm.sdsu.edu/wp-content/uploads/2017/01/2016_Celluloid_Ceiling_Report.pdf

Lyons, Charles. 2006. "Mandy Walker: 10 Cinematographers to Watch." *Daily Variety* 293(24): A11.

Interview with Nancy Schreiber

What does your work schedule typically look like?

I am a freelancer. Pretty much everyone is. We go from job to job, and there can be a lot of uncertainty about what is next. When I'm doing a film or television show, I am totally committed to that, generally five day a week schedule. And I can go for months without work. One just never knows. I prefer either short cable television series or movies. I admire the cinematographers that can do network series that go on for nine months. But I just couldn't do it. It's so grueling. We generally have 12 and a half hour days, and usually they're longer. I like to get to work a good hour in advance, to meet with the director or just figure out if my camera and lighting plan will hold, as this is usually the first opportunity to see the set or location dressed.

Would you say that your path to cinematography was conventional?

I came up in New York, and at that time people out in Los Angeles generally came up through the camera department. You would work your way up from loader to second assistant to first assistant to operator to DP. But in New York, I came up through the electric department, from best boy to gaffer to director of photography, a path that is a bit more common today. Yes, the term was and still is "best boy."

When you were working as an electrician and gaffer, did you already have your eye set on cinematography, or was it something you became interested in?

I had absolutely no idea I would do something like this. I had moved to New York to follow a boyfriend one summer. I had just graduated with a psychology degree from the University of Michigan in Ann Arbor and was running an avant-garde movie theater called the Alley Cinema that only showed foreign films and some American classics.

The Alley Cinema was like my film school. It was also during the women's movement, and I'd been working with the Women's Film Collective, which first introduced me to filmmaking. When I moved to New York, I took a class with a fantastic teacher, Jim Pasternak, who I still know today and now teaches in Los Angeles. I then answered an ad in the *Village Voice* and got on a real feature film but they were very undercrewed. I was put in the electric department knowing nothing, but I was a good student and learned quickly. I also had an art background because my mother was an art dealer and I had been an exchange student in Holland during high school and would spend hours in the museums there. I already had an appreciation for art and had been shooting still photography. Somehow, my interests and background merged into finding this profession where lighting was the key element to making art.

Any thoughts on why cinematography remains so male-dominated?

The term "cameraman" has existed since the beginning of film history. The director of photography is running three departments: the camera crew, the grip, and the electric crew. We really have a lot of power, and power in Hollywood is a tricky area.

It's still shocking to me, Laura, when I go on the set of a movie or on a TV show and members of the crew say, "You're the first woman cinematographer I've ever worked with." I've been doing this for a gazillion years! It's complicated and it's not just our industry. This gender bias goes back to how we bring up our children, where those values are first instilled.

I know that there are these mandates now to hire with diversity in mind. Real change where women are seen as equal will take time; we have a long way to go. We just have to continue doing our best and be better. Often, we're very much under the microscope to see how we perform. We can't have those temper tantrums that you hear about certain male directors having; otherwise, we're called a "bitch." We have to be assertive, not aggressive. I think my personality has been suited for this career because I think I'm basically a kind person who is easy to work with and a team player.

I never take my work for granted and feel privileged to keep getting hired. Many women like me who have worked for years understand how to create an inclusive, harmonious set. It's important that we stay on time and on budget if we are to keep getting hired. We make our art with technology, although we're making a "product." There is always a magic to what we do.

What were the greatest obstacles you faced transitioning from film to digital?

The big difference is the monitor. The monitor is God, and so people can sit there at the monitors at Video Village and say, "Oh, that's too dark," or "Why are you doing that?" Whereas before, the video monitors at Video Village were standard def, and one knew that it didn't look like what the film was going to look like. There was a mystique, that cinematographers had this craft and this magical skill and nobody really could visualize what it was going to [look] like. And now there is a danger of having too many cooks in the kitchen, so to speak. I have seen and heard of a lot cinematographers getting their vision taken away, because people wanted the work to be safe. Not so much now, but during the transition to digital, this was more common.

Also, the actors are understandably concerned because who wants to be seen in 6K? It's too much reality. Cinematographers always try to put their stamp on the film by manipulating the negative or the digital medium in fun ways, so that has not changed. We're still trying to screw up the digital to make it less present, less like the news.

I was able to shoot film recently as a lab just opened in New York in the spring of 2017. The big difference I found with shooting *Mapplethorpe* was that the film stocks are much slower than digital, so we have been using fewer and much smaller lighting units in digital. But when digital came out everybody said, "Oh! You don't need any light!" That's ridiculous! There's still an art to the lighting, it's just that the units have changed and have become more "green," especially with improvement in LED technology.

Is there ageism in cinematography?

Yes, there is definite ageism. You would think that one would want someone with more experience. But Hollywood's always [looking] for what's new and what's hot. Not only when it comes to cinematographers but with directors too. I think maybe's there is this perception by some producers that more experienced people will want more lights, more crew, and will take more time or that somehow they won't be able to control us. And it's not just women [who] are experiencing ageism, it's definitely the men too. There is a lot of ageism, but it is not discussed openly.

When I was coming up as a young cinematographer, if I had paid attention to the fact that I was a woman, I wouldn't be here talking to you. I just had to say, "Okay. That's the way it is. I don't care, I'm going to do it!" It's the same thing for ageism: "I don't care! I will find my niche! Okay, I'm shooting small movies right now." That's the way it is. I'm happy that people hire me. I just worked with a 30-year-old director. I am the same age as his parents. But he hired me and we had a great rapport. He found me because I had worked with the producer 20 years ago, who recommended me. You just keep going and don't look back. For people wanting to be cinematographers, men and women, you have to have a thick skin. You can't take anything personally. You might think you are more well suited and experienced when you go out for a job than the person who actually gets it. And there's no rhyme or reason why. It may still hurt a bit when I don't get a job, especially if I thought I aced the meeting. But I always know there's another project coming, and I just let go and move on to the next opportunity and challenge.

Costume Designers

> "If the designer can make the audience feel the actress is the character, then it's a good job of costuming."
>
> —Edith Head

Introduction

The role of the costume designer is simple: costume designers design the people in the movie. Their contribution to the story is more profound than providing the clothes for a production. The word "costume" works against the field. "Costume" is invariably associated with Halloween, fancy dress, parades, theme parks, Mardi Gras, and carnivals. Adding to the confusion is an uncertainty about the fundamental purpose of costume design. Film costuming serves two equal purposes: the first is to support the narrative by creating authentic characters (people), and the second is to provide balance within the frame by using color, texture, and silhouette. In addition, costume designers help paint each "frame" of film. If the dialogue is the melody of a movie, the color provides the harmony, a satisfying visual cohesiveness and "style." And a costume must move; costume designers work in a kinetic art. A successful costume must be subsumed by the story and be woven seamlessly into the narrative and visual tapestry of the movie. Costumes, like the characters they embody, must evolve within the context of the story and the arc of the character within it. Every costume is created for a certain moment in the arc of a film, to be lit in a certain way, to be seen on one set, on one actor.

Costumes are also tools a filmmaker uses to tell a story. A designer's challenge is to realize the director's vision and bring that script to the screen. A designer's work is inextricable from the theatrical context and collaborative interrelationships in which they work—the dialogue, the actor, the cinematography, the set, the weather, the season, the time of day, the choreography of movement, and a dozen other dilemmas all present challenges. Costumes embody the psychological, social, and emotional condition of the character at a moment in the script. For any film to work, the audience must be able to say absolutely, "I recognize that person." Ironically, the career of almost every costume designer is dominated by the design of modern dress films. High or low budget, all motion pictures utilize a combination of bought, rented, and manufactured costumes. Optimally, a costume designer will alter, refit, dye, and age modern clothes to look well worn. The fact that films are released about one year after they have finished shooting makes it nearly impossible for costume designers to be deliberate about influencing fashion. A costume becomes iconic when the public falls madly in love with the movie. The pool of incredible talent in the field of costume design is expanding exponentially. Costume designers represent a legion of inspired international film artists who are enriching popular culture, igniting fashion trends, and making television and cinematic history.

Deborah Nadoolman Landis

Atwood, Colleen (1948–)

Costume designer Colleen Atwood has established herself as one of the most versatile and bold designers working in entertainment today. Few costume designers in Hollywood hold such an intimidating creative portfolio as Atwood. Her credits range from handsome period dramas, to provocative musical adaptations, to whimsical and gothic fantasies. She has costumed two Academy Award–winning films for Best Picture (*The Silence of the Lambs*, 1991, and *Chicago*, 2002) and has been awarded four Oscars and another eight Academy Award nominations for her designs. Speaking to her transferable professional experience, Atwood has said, "To me, when you do one thing, you learn something that you can bring to something else" (Calhoun 1994). In addition, Atwood has worked with some of the most colorful auteurs whose distinct styles have cemented their legacy and pervasiveness in popular culture.

Born in Yakima, Washington, in 1948, Colleen Atwood studied painting at Cornish College of the Arts in Seattle, Washington, and worked in retail in the early 1970s. She later worked as a fashion advisor before moving to New York City to continue her studies at New York University. Transitioning from fashion to film and theater, she obtained a position as a production assistant on Milos Forman's *Ragtime* (1981). She subsequently served as an assistant to costume designer Patrizia von Brandenstein for Bruce Paltrow's *A Little Sex* and worked as the costume designer on musician Sting's "Bring on the Night" world tour.

Atwood has contributed to the unique styles of several acclaimed filmmakers. Her first major hit came with director Jonathan Demme's sly crime comedy *Married to the Mob* in 1988. She continued to work with Demme on several projects in the 1990s, including *The Silence of the Lambs*, *Philadelphia* (1993), and *Beloved* (1998). During her work on *Joe versus the Volcano* in 1990, production designer Bo Welch introduced her to director Tim Burton. This meeting commenced her enduring and current collaboration with Burton. She served as costume designer on nine of his strikingly grotesque films starting with *Edward Scissorhands* (1990) and continuing with *Ed Wood* (1994), *Planet of the Apes* (2001), *Big Fish* (2003), and *Dark Shadows* (2012). She received Oscar nominations for her work on Burton's *Sleepy Hollow* (1999) and *Sweeney Todd: The Demon Barber of Fleet Street* (2007) and won the Academy Award for *Alice in Wonderland* (2010). Additionally, she has costumed all but one of Rob Marshall's theatrical films, winning Oscars for *Chicago* (2002) and *Memoirs of a Geisha* (2005) and nominations for the film adaptations for the Broadway musicals *Nine* (2009) and *Into the Woods* (2014). She has also costumed and received Oscar nominations for *Little Women* (1994), the children's fantasy *Lemony Snicket's The Series of Unfortunate Events* (2004), and the visually opulent retelling of the Grimm Brothers' fairy tale, *Snow White and the Huntsman* (2012). Her latest Oscar win was in 2017 for the feature film *Fantastic Beasts and Where to Find Them* (2016).

Atwood's research methods are as multifaceted as the films she costumes. She often finds inspiration from looking through various fabrics, but sometimes goes straight to the drawing board. For Burton's *Ed Wood*—a biopic of the 1950s low-budget camp filmmaker in the 1950s—she not only viewed Wood's films but also utilized *Life* magazines from the era and photographs of 1950s Hollywood for inspiration and accuracy. During production on the period drama *Memoirs of a Geisha*, she explained in an interview with *Entertainment Weekly* magazine that after consulting Japanese historians and artists, she used Japanese fabrics as base layers but took liberties to simplify patterns. For costuming the many ensemble members in the medieval fantasy epic *Snow White and the Huntsman*, she traveled to the armor exhibition at London's Wallace Collection Museum. Because many of her films rely heavily on computer-generated imagery, she must consider the need to costume the actors physically while working in concert with visual effects artists.

Atwood's work extends beyond the cinema into television, Broadway, and other ancillary entertainment markets. She received an Emmy for costuming Rob Marshall's TV special "Tony Bennett: An American Classic." She has also worked on the Royal and the San Francisco Ballets. More recently, she costumed the Broadway production of *Breakfast at Tiffany's* in 2013. Her designs for *Snow White and the Huntsmen* inspired a clothing and accessory collection presented on the Home Shopping Network. The project included several renowned international designers such as Rhanjana Khan and Deborah Lippmann. Working for nearly 30 years in various entertainment industries, Atwood has produced designs that have transcended a singular style, location, and era.

Robert Sevenich

See also: Foster, Jodie

Further Reading

Calhoun, John. 1994. "Colleen Atwood". *TCI*, November 1994. Academic OneFile. July 30, 2015. http://go.galegroup.com/ps/i.do?id=GALE%7CA15873718&v=2.1&u=social_main@it=r&p=AONE&sw=w&asid=16490b7af45eabb7983e4957650d

Galas, Marj. 2015. "Colleen Atwood on Designing 'Into the Woods.'" *Variety*, February 13. http://variety.com/2015/artisans/production/colleen-atwood-on-designing-into-the-woods-costumes-1201432677

Leung, Marianaa. 2012. "Exclusive Interview: Oscar-Winning Costume Designer Colleen Atwood." *Ms. Fabulous*, June 1. https://www.msfabulous.com/2012/06/exclusive-interview-oscar-winning.html

Miller, Julie. 2012. "From Sketch to Still: Colleen Atwood on Her Rooster-Feather, Chainmail, and Suede Designs for Snow White and the Huntsman." *Vanity Fair*, May 17. https://www.vanityfair.com/hollywood/2012/05/snow-white-and-the-huntsman-kristen-stewart-charlize-theron-chris-hemsworth-colleen-atwood-costume-gallery

Schwartz, Missy. 2005. "Behind the Seams of 'Memoirs of a Geisha." *Entertainment Weekly*, November 11. http://ew.com/article/2005/11/11/behind-seams-memoirs-geisha

Canonero, Milena (1946–)

A three-time Oscar winner, Milena Canonero is a celebrated Italian costume designer as well as the inspired hand behind the creation of some of the most enduring and iconic designs onscreen. Apart from the role that costumes play in cinema, such as denoting character or narrative progression, they can also indelibly mark a film and determine how it is evoked in public consciousness. Canonero's career is full of such designs, having made their respective films immediately recognizable, from the Droogs white frocks with black hats and codpieces in *A Clockwork Orange* (1971), to the pastel-colored exuberance of *Marie Antoinette* (2006), among many other examples.

The Italian designer applied her academic studies in the fields of art, design history, and costume design to her cinematic work, patent through her use of color, pattern, and texture, in order to imbue characters with implicit meaning. Born in Genoa, Italy, Canonero moved to England to complete her studies. After working in advertising, her film career started with Stanley Kubrick, for whom she designed costumes for three of his films: *A Clockwork Orange*, *Barry Lyndon* (1975), and *The Shining* (1980). Throughout her career Canonero worked with Alan Parker (*Midnight Express*, 1978), Hugh Hudson (*Chariots of Fire*, 1981), Francis Ford Coppola (*The Cotton Club*, 1984; *The Godfather III,* 1990), Sydney Pollack (*Out of Africa*, 1985), Warren Beatty (*Dick Tracy*, 1990; *Bulworth*, 1998), Roman Polanski (*Carnage*, 2011), and Manoel de Oliveira (*Belle toujours*, 2006). Recently, she has worked with auteurs such as Sofia Coppola (*Marie Antoinette*, 2006) and Wes Anderson (*The Life Aquatic with Steve Zissou*, 2004; *The Darjeeling Limited*, 2007; *The Grand Budapest Hotel*, 2014). Her working relationship with the Coppola family has continued, as Canonero designed the costumes for Eleanor Coppola's *Bonjour Anne* (2016).

Working frequently within the paradigm of a certain kind of prestige, independent American cinema, Milena Canonero's body of work has been consistently linked to directors with precise, and sometimes idiosyncratic, visions. Kubrick, for example, who appreciated controlling all aspects of his movies, placed his complete confidence upon Canonero, as her costuming is characterized by being precise and meticulous. Similarly, Canonero remarks, in Matt Zoller Seitz's book *The Wes Anderson Collection: The Grand Budapest Hotel*, "Wes is particular about details, and so am I" (Zoller Seitz 2015).

Her movies have also frequently been marked by situations, both historically and geographically speaking, that influenced the costuming work: "her professional forte has been period costumes, both of the past and the near future" (Gross 1986). Her pursuit of a "feeling of authenticity" propels her to be attentive to every detail, and as a stickler for historical accuracy, she often combines real pieces whenever possible. In the case of *Marie Antoinette*, the challenge was "to show the essence of the period without being too academic" (Avins 2006). As was the case with *The Grand Budapest Hotel*, where subjective aesthetics trumped historical accuracy, Canonero's inventiveness flourished by staying true to the epoch's cuts but experimenting with color combinations, accessories, and other accouterments.

Apart from the aesthetic beauty of her costumes, Canonero is a master of narration through clothes, interlacing character development into her costumes. As the Fandor film essay *Women in Film: Milena Canonero* points out, the work of the Italian costume designer utilizes inventive interplays of color and texture that cleverly and purposely express the internal, emotional journeys of a film's character in each given scene.

Beyond her cinematic endeavors, Milena Canonero has also designed costumes for theater and opera director Otto Schenk for *Il trittico* (Vienna State Opera, 1979), *As You Like It* (Salzburg Festival, 1980), *Die Fledermaus* and *Andrea Chénier* (Vienna State Opera, 1980 and 1981, respectively), and *Arabella* (Metropolitan Opera, 1983). For the late Swiss film and theater director Luc Bondy, Milena Canonero created costumes for innovative productions of Puccini's *Tosca* (Metropolitan Opera, 2009) and of Euripides's *Helena* (Burgtheater, Vienna, 2010).

Canonero's many accolades and awards include nine nominations and four wins at the Academy Awards, all in the category of Best Costume Design. She first won for Kubrick's *Barry Lyndon*, in 1976, an award shared with Ulla-Britt Söderlund. Later, in 1982, her work for Hugh Hudson's *Chariots of Fire* garnered her a second Oscar. In 2007, Sofia Coppola's *Marie Antoinette* and its pastel-infused costumes provided her third win. Her last Oscar came in 2015 for Wes Anderson's *The Grand Budapest Hotel* and its refined uniforms. Canonero was also nominated for her costume design work in *Out of Africa* (1985), *Tucker: The Man and His Dream* (1988), *Dick Tracy* (1990), *Titus* (1999), and *The Affair of the Necklace* (2001).

She has three British Academy of Film and Television Arts (BAFTA) Awards, having won for *Chariots of Fire* in 1976, *The Cotton Club* in 1986, and *The Grand Budapest Hotel* in 2015, all for Best Costume Design. Canonero also won three Costume Designer Guild awards: in 2001, for Career Achievement in Film; in 2005, for *The Life Aquatic with Steve Zissou* in the category of Excellence in Contemporary Film (she was also nominated in the same category for *Ocean's Twelve* [2004]); and in 2015 for *The Grand Budapest Hotel* in the category of Excellence in Period Film. In 2017, the Berlin Film Festival paid tribute to the Italian costume designer with its Golden Bear for Lifetime Achievement. Dieter Kosslick, the Berlinale festival director, praised Canonero for being "an extraordinary costume designer," stating that her designs had "contributed decisively to the style of many cinematic masterpieces" (Roxborough 2017).

Ana Cabral Martins

See also: Coppola, Sofia

Further Reading

Avins, Mimi. 2006. "The Style to Which She's Accustomed." *Los Angeles Times*, September 10. http://articles.latimes.com/2006/sep/10/entertainment/ca-marieclothes10

Fandor. 2017. "Women in Film: Milena Canonero." YouTube video, 4:09, April 17. https://www.youtube.com/watch?v=amhbbO_5nzg

Gross, Michael. 1986. "Milena Canonero: Fashion On and Off the Big Screen." *The New York Times*, February 11. https://www.nytimes.com/1986/02/11/style/milena-canonero-fashion-on-and-off-the-big-screen.html

Roxborough, Scott. 2017. "Berlin: Costume Designer Milena Canonero to Get Lifetime Achievement Honor." *The Hollywood Reporter*, January 31. https://www.hollywoodreporter.com/news/berlin-golden-bear-grand-budapest-hotel-shining-costume-designer-milena-canonero-970496

Zoller Seitz, Matt. 2015. *The Wes Anderson Collection: The Grand Budapest Hotel.* New York: Abrams.

Carter, Ruth E. (1960–)

Ruth E. Carter has had a remarkable career in costume design. Just a few years after finishing her Bachelor's in Fine Arts at Hampton University, Carter received nominations for the Academy Award for Best Costume Design for *Malcolm X* (1993) and *Amistad* (1998), making her the first African American to receive the honor. Accolades continued with the Career Achievement Award from the American Black Film Festival (2002), the Costume Design Guild Award for *Selma* (2014), and an Emmy Award for Outstanding Costume Design for *Roots* (2016). Carter served as the 2016–2017 Swarovsky Designer in Residence at the David C. Copley Center for Costume Design at the University of California Los Angeles. She is experiencing new popularity with her most ambitious costuming work on the record-breaking science fiction/comic book adaptation *Black Panther* (2018). Carter's accomplishments make her essential to any serious history of black filmmaking in the United States.

Carter began developing her costume design skills in Hampton's theater department, where she learned how costuming could shape theater performances. College theater quite often involves minimalist stages and resources, which puts greater pressure on costume designers to enrich the characters, scenes, and overall story. Carter translated this early stage work to moving film images and grew more sophisticated through her additional research into art history. Her commitment to her craft prepared her to design costumes for film, television, and video in the genres of comedy, action, melodrama, science fiction, biography, comic book adaptations, the Western, and others.

The diversity of Carter's work has not stopped her from consistently tackling specific themes. Carter distinguishes herself by consistently designing for stories that reimagine African American icons and historical events such as Tina Turner; Lysistrata; Malcolm X; Martin Luther King, Jr.; Thurgood Marshall; the 1923 community of Rosewood, Texas; and the kidnapped Africans who revolted on 1839 slave ship in the film *Amistad* (1997). A committed student of African diasporic history, Carter combines her costuming expertise with her general cultural knowledge and detailed research on her film projects in order to bring familiar or unknown figures back to life. Carter has consistently worked on films that are at once exhilarating and educational.

Costume designer Ruth E. Carter onstage during the 2018 Essence Festival at Ernest N. Morial Convention Center in New Orleans, Louisiana. Carter was the first African American costume designer to be nominated for an Academy Award for her work on *Malcolm X* (1992), and would receive another nomination for *Amistad* (1997). Her costumes for Marvel's blockbuster *Black Panther* (2018), in particular, attracted an extraordinary amount of media attention for their contribution to the film. (Paras Griffin/Getty Images for Essence)

For this reason, Carter makes costume design something more than selecting, sewing, aging, weathering, or dyeing fabrics. The designer makes costumes convey the motivations and moods of the characters. In an interview Carter says, "There is a certain psychology of costume design—you are helping the actor create the character and to enhance the story." (Landis Nadoolman 2003). In *Kidnap* (2017), Halle Berry's character, Karla Dyson, demonstrates how Carter puts this technique to work. The film begins with Dyson wearing a sleeveless, golden t-shirt that matches a cheerful day with her son at a fair. Dyson's shirt morphs into a mother's battle armor as she faces car chases, armed assailants, head-on collisions, and hand-to-hand combat. The shirt is so ordinary, so readily available, and so unremarkable that any working mother could imagine herself in Dyson's shoes as the hero who recovers her kidnapped child. On this film and others, Carter draws viewers into the film's core conflicts.

If this were not enough to secure her place in black film history, Carter has also collaborated with some of the most notable black American filmmakers. When Spike Lee recruited Carter for his first feature-length film *School Daze* (1988), they began a more than 20-year partnership that created over 13 films, including *Do the Right Thing* (1989), *Mo' Better Blues* (1990), *Summer of Sam* (1999), *Bamboozled* (2000), and *Chi-Raq* (2015). Another influential filmmaker, John Singleton, incorporated Carter into his film family. Their professional collaboration led to several successful film projects, including *Shaft* (2000), *Baby Boy* (2001), and *Four Brothers* (2005). In the decades between 1980 and the 2000s several other African American directors hired Carter for their classic films, such as Robert Townsend's *I'm*

Gonna Git You Sucka (1988), *B*A*P*S* (1997), and *The Meteor Man* (1993), as well as Reginald Hudlin's *House Party* (1991), *The Great White Hype* (1996), and *Marshall* (2017). Carter has contributed her talents to African American women directors such as Ava DuVernay's *Selma* (2014) and Gina Price-Bythewood's *Love & Basketball* (1999). Her costuming has draped some of the most awarded actors in modern American cinema, including Ruby Dee, Ossie Davis, Forest Whittaker, Lonette McKee, Jamie Foxx, Oprah Winfrey, and Lupita Nyong'o, just to name a few. Carter's costume design work is inseparable from a constellation of U.S.-based directors, screenwriters, actors, directors of photography, and production designers making the most influential films that focus on African diasporic life.

Kwanda M. M. Ford

See also: DuVernay, Ava; Morrison, Rachel

Further Reading

Landis Nadoolman, Deborah. 2003. *Screencraft: Costume Design.* Waltham, MA: Focal Press.

Miller, Monica L. 2009. *Slaves to Freedom: Black Dandyism and the Styling of Black Diasporic Identity.* Durham, NC: Duke University Press.

Scott, Ellen. 2013. "More than a 'Passing' Sophistication: Dress, Film Regulation, and the Color Line in 1930s American Films." *Women's Studies Quarterly* 41(1/2, Spring/Summer): 60–86.

Williams, Linda. 2000. "Film Bodies: Gender, Genre, and Excess." In *Film and Theory: An Anthology.* Edited by Robert Stam and Toby Miller. Malden, MA: Blackwell Publishing, 207–221.

Head, Edith (1897–1981)

Edith Head's 58-year career spanned from the silent era to talkies, through the golden age of Hollywood and into the early 1980s. During her career, this iconic costume designer was associated with over 1,100 films, received 35 Academy Award nominations, and was awarded 8 Academy Awards for costume design, a record that, at this writing, still remains unbroken. Beginning in 1948, the Academy of Motion Picture Arts and Sciences allowed two awards for Best Costume Design: one for black-and-white films, and one for color films. Head was awarded two Academy Awards simultaneously in 1950 for the black and white film *All about Eve* as well as *Samson and Delilah,* which appeared in Technicolor. She also received Oscars for *The Heiress* (1949), *A Place in the Sun* (1951), *Roman Holiday* (1953), *Sabrina* (1954), *The Facts of Life* (1960), and *The Sting* (1973).

Head understood that making films was a collaborative effort. Author David Chierichetti, who interviewed Head and became a close friend, explains, "Edith could work with anybody. She went beyond simply listening to everybody's point of view and somehow synthesizing it into a garment; like a psychologist, she was able to draw from her coworkers that which they often could not verbalize" (Chierichetti 2003, 57). Commenting about her attitude as a costume designer, she remarked, "I believe you should allow an actor or actress to discuss and criticize" (Jorgensen 2010, 72).

Head was born as Edith Claire Posener on October 28, 1897 in San Bernardino, California, to Max Posener and Anna E. Levy. In 1901, her mother married mining engineer Frank Spare, and her stepfather's job required the family to move from one remote mining location to another. With few playmates, Edith hosted tea parties, dressing up her animals: burros, cats, dogs, and even a horned toad. "All of my intensive imagination in child's play had to be connected into activities I could pursue alone. In later years, struggling as a dress designer, I used to tell myself, 'Anyone who can dress a horned toad, can dress anything!'" (Jorgensen 2010, 14). Head attended Los Angeles High School and was accepted to UC Berkeley. In 1919, she graduated with a BA, with honors in French, and in 1920, she graduated from Stanford University with an MA in Romance languages.

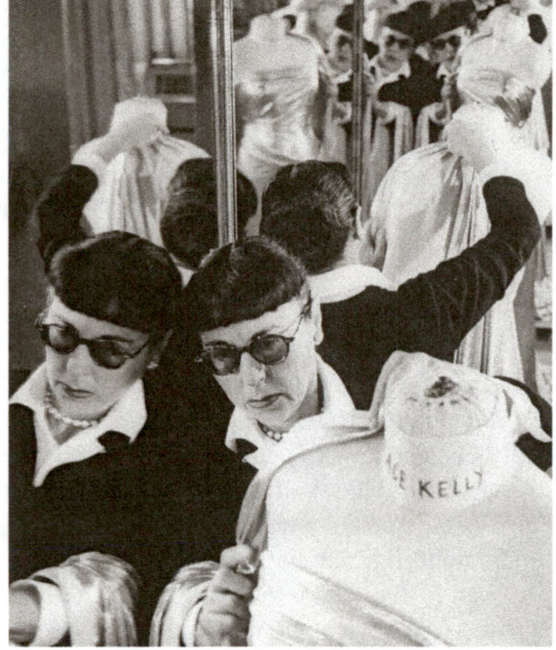

Edith Head drapes material over a mannequin to create a costume for actress Grace Kelly. Head won eight Academy Awards for Best Costume Design during her career and is regarded as one of the most significant designers in Hollywood film history. Head collaborated extensively with Alfred Hitchcock, creating iconic looks for many of his most popular and critically acclaimed films. (Allan Grant/The LIFE Picture Collection/Getty Images)

After graduating from Stanford, Head taught French and art at the Hollywood School for Girls. To improve her skills, she took night classes at Chouinard Art Institute. A classmate introduced Edith to her brother, Charles Head, and they were married in 1923. That summer, Head answered an advertisement for a sketch artist at the Famous Players-Lasky Studios (later Paramount Studios). She borrowed her classmates' drawings for an interview with head designer, Howard Greer.

Howard Greer taught Head how to sketch like him, and she worked in a pool with other sketch artists. When Greer would ask the artists for additional ideas for DeMille, Head recalled, "The others would make one and I'd make three or four" (Chierichetti 2003, 14–15). Her work ethic was noticed, and Greer and newly hired designer, Travis Banton, began to trust Head with her own assignments. Banton assigned Head to dress Clara Bow, Hollywood's "It" girl, for the film *Wings* (1927). Head also designed for Jean Harlow in *The Saturday Night Kid* (1929), where she created the white satin gown cut on the bias, an adaptation of Madeline Vionnet's design, that hugged Harlow's curves. Head's linguistic skills cemented her career at Paramount. "The only reason I survived to stay on his [Greer's] staff as a sketch girl was that fact that I had a background in speaking foreign languages. They were making foreign versions of films and I was the only one who could talk readily with foreign stars" (Jorgensen 2010, 24). Head spoke Spanish to Lupe Vélez and sketched her Spanish-style wardrobe for *The Wolf Song* (1929), eventually charming the star with her designs.

Head's first full screen credit came with designing gowns for the legendary Mae West in *She Done Him Wrong* (1933), who instructed, "Make the clothes loose enough to prove I'm a lady, but tight enough to show 'em I'm a woman (Jorgensen 2010, 41–42). In 1938, Head replaced Travis Banton as head of the costume design department at Paramount. That same year, she filed for divorce from her husband, who had a drinking problem. In 1940, she married art director, Wiard Boppo Ihnen. They shared a close relationship until his death in 1979.

Wearing her trademark dark glasses, a simple chignon with bangs, and classically elegant suits in neutral colors, Head dressed to fade into the background so the star would dominate the mirror at a costume fitting. Her design skills accentuated a star's positive traits, while disguising the negative ones. Head instinctively understood that the most important aspect of costume design was capturing the essence of the character, explaining that in costuming, "What we do is a cross between magic and camouflage" (Jorgensen 2010, 7). To ensure that her designs would not look dated once a film premiered, she shied away from using trendy details or popular prints in her wardrobes, and instead concentrated on the line and shape of the finished product. Head's most notable designs include Dorothy Lamour's sarong for *Jungle Princess* (1936), Ingrid Bergman's midriff-bearing top in *Notorious* (1946), Bette Davis's sable-trimmed cocktail dress in *All about Eve* (1950), Elizabeth Taylor's white gown in *A Place in the Sun* (1951), Grace Kelly's costume ball gown in *To Catch a Thief* (1955), and Kim Novak's white coat in *Vertigo* (1958). Although Head claimed to have designed the black cocktail dress that Audrey Hepburn wore in *Sabrina*, in 1983, Hubert de Givenchy confirmed that the black dress and the white ball gown that Hepburn wore in *Sabrina* were his designs.

Head realized that longevity in the film industry depended on publicity. In 1945, Art Linkletter asked her to appear regularly on his radio show *House Party.* The popular show moved to television in 1952 and ran until 1969. In 1959, Head published *The Dress Doctor*, which became a bestseller; her second book, *How to Dress for Success,* was published in 1967. In 1974, Head was honored with her own star on the Hollywood Walk of Fame.

Head joined Universal Studios in 1967. She was familiar with Universal because she had designed costumes for nine of Alfred Hitchcock's films, beginning with *Rear Window* in 1954. Her workload at Universal was not as demanding as it had been at Paramount, and Head had other business interests. Beginning in 1951, Head and her business partner, June Van Dyke, had been touring her costume collection across the United States for fashion shows, which she continued to do while at Universal. In 1974, Head signed a contract with *Vogue* patterns.

Head's final film was *Dead Men Don't Wear Plaid* (1982). In this film, she came full circle in her career because the project required designing 1940s fashions, including copying some of her original designs from the era. Head had never let anyone on the set know that she was seriously ill, and just two weeks after finishing the film, she died on October 24, 1981. She left her estate to the Motion Picture and Television Fund, to charities for animals, and to Native American children.

Edith Head's legacy is still a part of the public consciousness. Author Jay Jorgensen informs readers that "[b]oth Paramount and Universal studios named their wardrobe buildings after her" (2010, 391). An Edith Head commemorative postage stamp was issued by the U.S. Postal Service on February 25, 2003. In 2013, to honor her 116th birthday, a Google Doodle commemorative search bar logo featured Edith Head along with six sketches of her most famous costumes.

Edith Head's life story reads like a movie script. She evolved from a little girl who lived miles from playmates so she entertained herself by dressing animals in her clothing creations, to graduating from both UC Berkeley and Stanford, and became a celebrated, Academy Award–winning designer whose influence is still recognized in the film industry today.

Donna R. Phillips

See also: Davis, Bette

Further Reading

Alston, Isabella, and Kathryn Dixon. 2014. *Edith Head.* Charlotte, NC: TAJ Books International.

Claassen, Susan. 2015. "A Conversation with Edith Head." Accessed May 9, 2018. http://www.edithhead.biz

Chandler, Charlotte. 2006. *It's Only a Movie: Alfred Hitchcock: A Personal Biography.* Montclair, NJ: Applause Theatre & Cinema Books.

Chierichetti, David. 2003. *Edith Head: The Life and Times of Hollywood's Celebrated Costume Designer.* New York: HarperCollins.

Head, Edith, and Paddy Calistro. 2008. *Edith Head's Hollywood.* 25th Anniversary Edition. Santa Monica, CA: Angel City Press.

Jorgensen, Jay. 2010. *Edith Head: The Fifty-Year Career of Hollywood's Greatest Costume Designer.* Philadelphia: Running Press Book Publishers.

Rose, Helen (1904–1985)

Helen Rose was one of the most prolific costume designers who worked within the studio system during Hollywood's golden years. She designed costumes for over 200 films at MGM Studios between 1943 and 1966, a time period during which movie stars exemplified glamour and the studios ensured that the most talented designers were hired to cater to each individual star. Unlike in contemporary cinema where the stars often are dressed in clothes that are purchased from the racks of department stores, film professionals of the studio era felt that costume design needed to be original and often elaborate since it was an integral part of the creation of a character and even the film itself. Rose perfected her style of costume design during her lengthy career at MGM by developing an understanding of which materials and fabrics looked best on screen while simultaneously creating costumes that accentuated the attributes and camouflaged the flaws of the stars. In addition, she mastered the skill of using costume to bring out the traits of a particular character that an actor played. This ability was especially important for the form of narrative cinema in which she worked. Rose's talent gave her the opportunity to work with the most celebrated actresses of the period, including Elizabeth Taylor, Grace Kelly, Judy Garland, Lauren Bacall, and Lana Turner, to name just a few. Her talent earned her two Oscars and eight additional Academy Award nominations, as well as numerous other accolades. Equally important to her screen work, Rose was asked to design the wedding gowns for some of the most significant women in Hollywood, including Grace Kelly and Elizabeth Taylor. In this era, the studios worked diligently to construct a star's image not only on the screen but off as well. A wedding was an ideal publicity opportunity for a star to demonstrate her glamour to fans, and it is unsurprising that Rose dressed Kelly and Taylor on this occasion. The designer continued to make clothes that were worn outside of films with the establishment of Helen Rose Couture.

Helen Rose began her designing career in Chicago as a student at the Chicago Academy of Fine Arts and went on to design costumes for shows at the Chez Pierre night club. In 1929, she moved to California where she found work at the costume company of Walter and Ethel Israel, who produced costumes for films, and she became a designer for the movie theater stage shows of Fanchon and Marco, who gave her the opportunity to design a costume for child performer Frances Gumm, who would later be known as Judy Garland. Rose also designed costumes for the Ice Follies of Shipstad and Johnson before breaking into movies.

Before defining herself as one of the most important costume designers of the classical period of film history at MGM, Rose went to work at 20th Century Fox in 1942 designing costumes for Betty Grable in the film *Coney Island.* Even after her career at MGM began, the designer was loaned to 20th Century Fox in 1956 and 1966 after Lana Turner and Debbie Reynolds personally requested that she design their costumes for their respective films, *Rains of Ranchipur* and *Goodbye, Charlie* (Rose 1976, 44). After Louis B. Mayer discovered Rose's film work he quickly recruited her to MGM since he did not want such a talented designer working for a rival studio. She filled a significant void, as she was essentially replacing the enormously successful designer Adrian (Adrian Adolph Greenberg), who had recently left the studio.* Mayer's intuition proved correct since Rose went on to win Oscars for *The Bad and the Beautiful* (1952) and *I'll Cry Tomorrow* (1955) and was nominated for *The Great Caruso* (1951), *The Merry Widow* (1952), *Dream Wife* (1953), *Executive Suite* (1954), *Interrupted Melody* (1955), *The Power and the Prize* (1956), *The Gazebo* (1959), and *Mister Buddwing* (1966). In addition to previously mentioned stars, she designed for Ava Gardner, Esther Williams, Cyd Charisse, Barbara Stanwyck, Lucille Ball, Joan Crawford, and Lena Horne during her time at MGM. In addition to her role as a costume designer, Rose unofficially served in the capacity of saleswoman, advocate for the triumph of the artistic over the financial and the political, and confidant to many of the actresses with whom she worked.

Rose had a philosophy of costume design that served her well throughout her career. Like many successful designers, she avoided utilizing popular trends and fads in her films since it was very likely that they would already be out of style by

---

* The costume designer Irene replaced Adrian in 1941 before Helen Rose took over as costume director at MGM.

the time the film was released, which could sometimes be a year or two after films were made. The designer felt that timeless fashions that would always seem glamorous were the most logical and effective options for the cinema. Additionally, she believed it was men who dictated women's fashion, and therefore paid special attention to their opinions. In addition to these rules, Rose understood that a film costume did not always have to be glamorous, but it needed to fit the character at all times. When an actress plays a unfashionable character, it is the designer's task to create simple costumes that do not interfere with the film's narrative. However, when she designed for a stylish character, it was Rose's goal to create original, trendy clothes that female audiences would desire to include in their own wardrobes.

In 1958 Helen went on to open her own couture business, creating the Helen Rose label. This endeavor allowed her to extend her reach beyond film, creating gowns for women of high society. However, her film career contributed to the success of her company when she created "The Cat Dress," based on the white chiffon dress worn by Elizabeth Taylor in *Cat on a Hot Tin Roof* (1958). The dress was a part of her first couture collection. Rose's "Butterfield 8" dress, influenced by a dress worn by Elizabeth Taylor in a film of the same name (1960), was also popular with her clients.

Jennifer A. Zale

Further Reading

Rose, Helen. 1976. *Just Make Them Beautiful.* Santa Monica, CA: Dennis-Landman Publishers.

Rose, Helen. 1983. *The Glamorous World of Helen Rose.* Riverside, CA: Rubidoux Printing Company.

Vintage Fashion Guild. 2010. "Helen Rose." Accessed May 17, 2016. http://vintagefashionguild.org/fashion-history/helen-rose

Sharaff, Irene (1910–1993)

In a career spanning more than 50 years, Irene Sharaff was responsible for some of the most iconic designs and costumes of stage and screen. She earned 15 Oscar nominations for over 40 films and 7 nominations for 60 Broadway shows. Sharaff also designed for the American Ballet Theater, the Royal Ballet in London, and the New York City Ballet, as well as television. She earned Oscars for *The King and I* and *West Side Story.* Sharaff's influence was great and saw her clothing stars such as Marlene Dietrich, Elizabeth Taylor, Frank Sinatra, and Barbra Streisand. She was one of the most influential costume designers of her time and one of the highest-paid costume designers in Hollywood.

Irene Sharaff was born January 23, 1910, in Boston, Massachusetts. Her early interest in art led her to study at the New York School of Fine and Applied Arts, the Arts Students League, and the Grand Chaumiere in Paris. After her education, she became a fashion illustrator, and her work was featured in *Vogue* (U.S.) and *Harper's Bazaar.*

Sharaff also apprenticed for Aline Bernstein, the first female member of the designers union, at The Civic Repertory Theatre (CRT) in 1928 in New York City, where Bernstein was art director. The Civic Repertory Theatre, founded by actress-director-producer-writer Eva La Gallienne, was an all-women-run theater aimed at providing professional theater at low prices. Sharaff worked with Bernstein at CRT until the American stock market crash of 1929 left the theater without patrons. Sharaff then moved to Paris and learned to create haute couture. In 1933, the theater reopened and Sharaff returned as the designer of scenery and costumes for Gallienne's *Alice in Wonderland*. Using the original illustrations by John Tenniel as her guide, Sharaff mimicked the brushstrokes and pen lines of his drawings, infusing them with bright color and drama. The play was successful, and Sharaff became highly sought after on Broadway, despite the theater closing shortly thereafter.

After working on shows such as *Union Pacific* and *Peepshow*, Sharaff worked on the 1951 production of *The King and I*, an ambitious and elaborate show. Sourcing Thai silk as well as Chinese, Indian, and Japanese textiles, Sharaff's sumptuous designs began a trend on Broadway and off-stage as Thai silk became immensely popular. The show also earned Sharaff her first Tony Award nomination and only win. Five years later, Sharaff earned her second Oscar for Samuel Goldwyn's film adaptation of the play.

Sharaff was no stranger to creating international fashion trends. Earlier, in a production of *On Your Toes*, Sharaff created fishnet stockings, asking hosier Jessie Zimmer to create a tight that looked like coarse black mesh. This design, along with Zimmer's innovative elastic net fabric, was soon manufactured in Paris and other fashion epicenters.

Lyricist and MGM producer Arthur Freed helped find Sharaff a place in Hollywood, as the studio was developing its reputation as the musical powerhouse. Her first film was with Vincente Minnelli (also a transplant from the stage) called *I Dood It* (1943). Her second film with Minnelli, *Meet Me in St. Louis* (1944) utilized the new technology of Technicolor to its greatest advantage. The iconic scarlet velvet gown worn by Judy Garland not only established Sharaff as a formidable fashion designer, but it also changed Garland's star image from a perpetually young girl to that of a grown woman.

In 1951, Sharaff was hired by Freed, Minnelli, and Gene Kelly to create the costumes for the iconic ballet of *An American in Paris*. Sharaff designed the costumes and the set designs to match the vision of Impressionism. Kelly choreographed the ballet in order to serve the costumes and set to the fullest. This film earned Sharaff her first Oscar.

Sharaff also designed the costumes for the stage and screen productions of *West Side Story*. She won an Academy Award in 1962 for the film. Her Tony nominations include her work in *Shangri-La* (1957), *Candide* (1957), *Happy Hunting* (1957), *Small War on Murray Hill* (1957), *Flower Drum Song* (1959), *The Girl Who Came to Supper* (1964), and *Hallelujah, Baby!* (1968).

In 1963, Joseph L. Mankiewicz took over directing duty from Rouben Mamoulian for the epic, *Cleopatra*. Along with a budget increase of $3 million (for a total of $5 million), Mankiewicz hired Sharaff to contribute to the film's more opulent direction. The costume design team consisted of Renié Conley and Vittorio Nino Novarese who created 26,000 costumes for the film, while Sharaff worked exclusively on Elizabeth Taylor's wardrobe who had sixty-five costume changes alone. Sharaff did intensive research for the film, basing her designs on Egyptian sculpture, tomb paintings, and other ancient sources. The centerpiece of the film was a gown made out of gold lamé and lined with gold bullion, which allegedly cost $2,000. Sharaff won her fourth Oscar for *Cleopatra.* The costumes' plunging necklines created controversy, but Taylor was so pleased with the gowns that she commissioned Sharaff to design her wedding dress for her marriage to co-star Richard Burton.

Working once again with Taylor and Burton, Sharaff designed the costumes for *Who's Afraid of Virginia Woolf?* in 1966. Though Taylor was 15 years younger than the 50-year-old character she was playing, producer-screenwriter Ernest Lehman gave Taylor full control of casting co-stars, the director, hairdresser, and costume designer so that she would feel comfortable in the role. To help age herself, Taylor also gained weight, had a hairdresser make her a gray wig, and hired Sharaff to make her wardrobe, complete with added padding to transform her figure. The production became the most expensive black-and-white film at the time, and Sharaff won a fifth Oscar for her work.

After that film, Sharaff slowly made her way toward retirement with a few smaller films and television specials on her resume. The most notable film after *Who's Afraid of Virginia Woolf?* was *Hello, Dolly!* in 1969. *Mommie Dearest* (1981), starring Faye Dunaway as Joan Crawford, was Sharaff's last film as a costume designer. According to the memoir of Rutanya Alda, who played the housekeeper Carol Ann in *Mommie Dearest,* Sharaff walked off the set of the film, upset by Dunaway's costume wardrobe changes and erratic behavior on set (Longworth 2017).

Sharaff had a long-time relationship with Chinese American painter and writer Mai-Mai Sze (birth name: Yuen Tsung Sze). The women lived together in New York, and existing correspondence shows they often signed both their names in letters to friends. They traveled together and were seen in society circles together. Though neither of the women mention one another in their autobiographies, it is clear their partnership was an important aspect of their lives.

After Sze's and Sharaff's deaths in 1992 and 1993, respectively, their book collection was donated to the New York Society Library. The collection contains about 1,000 texts. They also established a trust to support research and education, including the Needham Research Institute and Lucy Cavendish College at Cambridge University.

The Theater Development Fund (TDF)/Irene Sharaff Lifetime Achievement Award was established in 1993, named for Sharaff, the inaugural recipient of the award. It is awarded annually to a costume designer with significant contributions and artistic vision in theater, film, opera, or dance.

Diana E. Martinez

See also: Dietrich, Marlene; Dunaway, Faye

Further Reading

Alford, Holly Price, and Anne Stegemeyer. 2014. *Who's Who in Fashion.* New York: Bloomsbury Publishing.

Jorgensen, Jay, and Donald L. Scroggins. 2015. *Creating the Illusion (Turner Classic Movies): A Fashionable History of Hollywood Costume Designers.* Philadelphia: Running Press.

Longworth, Karina. 2017. "The Illusion of Perfection." *Slate*, December 17. http://www.slate.com/articles/podcasts/you_must_remember_this/2016/09/faye_dunaway_in_mommie_dearest_the_real_story.html

Sharaff, Irene. 1976. *Broadway and Hollywood: Costumes Designed by Irene Sharaff.* New York: Van Nostrand Reinhold Company.

Sylbert, Anthea (1939–)

Anthea Sylbert is a two-time Academy Award–nominated costume designer for film, television, and theater. She began her career in film after the demise of Hollywood's studio system, working between 1967 and 1978, during a period now known as "New Hollywood." Throughout the decade, she designed 21 feature films, and her impressive credits include *Rosemary's Baby* (1968), *Chinatown* (1974), *Shampoo* (1975), and *Julia* (1977). Her design philosophy was to create costumes in the service of the story and characters, not to create flashy designs for their own sake. "A costume designer really is an extension of the writer, the director, and the actor," Sylbert once said, "If you do your job correctly and if you have done your thinking correctly, you have helped them; if not, you have sabotaged them" (Sylbert 1983, 155). Highly respected among her filmmaker colleagues, she later enjoyed a successful career as a studio executive, movie producer, and screenwriter.

Born Anthea Gianna Kouros in Brooklyn, New York, Anthea Sylbert grew up in a close-knit Greek family. She enjoyed drawing and painting, and her grandmother taught her how to sew; as a child, she would redesign her doll's clothes. Although her father expected her to be a lawyer or architect, she chose to study art history at Barnard College, where her interest in costumes helped advance her degree—she found that one of the best clues for periodizing a painting was through dating people's clothing. Sylbert went on to study fashion at Parsons School of Design but dropped out when she was offered a job as a research assistant on a Broadway theater production. This opportunity led to costume designing, although her productions were often small and offered scant wages. She found more financial success in the fashion world, designing ready-to-wear clothes for small boutiques and for the dancewear company, Capezio.

Anthea Sylbert's entrée into film, *The Tiger Makes Out* (1967), came through her first husband, fellow Brooklyn native Paul Sylbert, an established production designer and director. The Sylberts socialized with a group of intellectuals whose work would become synonymous with the post-studio system world. Their cohort included New York theater and film directors, as well as a number of Hollywood icons: film directors and writers Mike Nichols and Elaine May, actor and director Warren Beatty, actor Jack Nicholson, Polish director Roman Polanski, and others who described themselves as Hollywood "outsiders" even though they were working on what we now recognize as some of the most significant films of the decade.

Rosemary's Baby was Anthea's second film assignment, and it launched her career. Director Polanski wanted his lead actress (Mia Farrow) dressed in a cheerful and child-like style to contrast with the increasingly sinister storyline. Anthea designed a number of cotton baby doll dresses in florals and pastels. Echoing the rising hemlines of 1960s fashion, Sylbert subtlety shortened Rosemary's dresses throughout the script (starting below the knee up to mid-thigh), leaving the young pregnant heroine looking vulnerable by the end of the picture. The film was a big hit with critics and the box office, and Farrow's costumes received considerable attention from the fashion press.

Anthea worked constantly in the ensuing decade. For Mike Nichols, she designed the costumes for films such as *Carnal Knowledge* (1971) and Broadway productions including *The Real Thing* (1984) for which she received a Tony Award nomination. Throughout her career as a costume designer, Anthea's creative collaborators recognized her as a valuable member of the team and solicited her input on other aspects of the films they were making. When Nichols was at an impasse, she legendarily encouraged him to scrap a film—even though the studio had already invested a few million dollars into the production. Sylbert was unaware that costume designers were not supposed to offer their opinion on the script or other areas of the production, which was technically out of their jurisdiction. These rigid professional boundaries eluded her, since she thought it sensible to improve her productions in any way she could.

Sylbert's most challenging production, *Chinatown*, directed by Polanski, was a neo-noir story about private investigator Jake Gittes (Jack Nicholson) and his mysterious married client Evelyn Mulwray (Faye Dunaway). Instead of using fashion magazines from the time period, Anthea rooted her research in historical newspapers and photographs solicited from friends and family members. The film was a major success and received 11 Academy Award nominations, including 1 for Best Costume Design.

Chinatown was immediately followed by more strong films. *Shampoo,* the story of a Beverly Hills hairdresser (Warren Beatty) whose professional ambitions are thwarted by his womanizing lifestyle, was another big success. Although she made a point of avoiding attention-grabbing costumes, the fashion press went wild for the floor-length, high-collared black sequin gown Sylbert designed for Jackie (Julie Christie). The dress said volumes about the character when she turned onscreen to reveal it was backless. *Julia*, a drama depicting playwright Lillian Hellman (Jane Fonda) and a childhood friend, Julia (Vanessa Redgrave), was told in flashbacks from the 1930s to the present day. Anthea earned her second Academy Award nomination for the film by creating period clothes with a timeless feel, based on photographs of the real Lillian Hellman.

It was not a surprise to many in the industry when Anthea was offered and accepted a job as vice president of production at Warner Bros. A few years later, she moved into a similar executive position at United Artists. One of Anthea's strengths was her ability to resolve conflicts between filmmakers and the studio, whose adversarial relationship had developed in the New Hollywood era. As an executive, Anthea worked with Goldie Hawn on the highly successful film *Private Benjamin* (1980), and a few years later, they decided to create the Hawn/Sylbert Movie Company. Together they made many films, including *Protocol* (1984) and *Something to Talk About* (1995), before dissolving their partnership. Afterwards, Anthea won an Emmy award for producing the presidential bio-pic *Truman* (1995).

She eventually added screenwriter to her résumé, penning two scripts with her husband, actor Richard Romanus.

Natasha Rubin

See also: Dunaway, Faye; Fonda, Jane

Further Reading

Nadoolman Landis, Deborah. 2007. *Dressed: A Century of Hollywood Costume Design.* New York: HarperCollins.

Sylbert, Anthea. 1983. *Filmmakers on Filmmaking: The American Film Institute Seminars on Motion Pictures and Television, Volume 1.* Edited by Joseph McBride. Los Angeles: J. P. Tarcher.

Van Runkle, Theadora (1928–2011)

When Theadora Van Runkle began working on her first film, *Bonnie and Clyde* (1967), she had no prior experience as a costume designer. Unlike the costume designers of Hollywood's golden age she was not trained and brought up through the studio system. Van Runkle had no formal training as a designer, though she had briefly attended art school. Though Van Runkle was anxious, she felt she was prepared to take on this new role because, "I knew fashion. I knew style. I knew construction. I sewed by hand and by machine. I learned construction from *Vogue* patterns" (Jorgensen and Scoggins 2015, 303). That year, Van Runkle was nominated for the Academy Award for Best Costume Design, an auspicious start for a first attempt. Her costume designs for *Bonnie and Clyde* launched trends that would influence fashion throughout the late 1960s and early 1970s. The image of Faye Dunaway as Bonnie Parker in a midi skirt and beret has been embedded in the American collective imagination as an aesthetic symbol for 1930s rebellious chic and 1970s fashion. The seemingly effortlessly cool realism of Van Runkle's costumes that then influenced and entered the contemporary fashion market is a pattern that would continue and define most of her career as a costume designer.

Before she became Theadora Van Runkle, she was Dorothy Schweppe, born on March 27, 1928, in Pittsburgh, Pennsylvania. At the time of her birth, her mother, Eltsey Adiar, was not married to her father, Courtney Bradstreet Schweppe, an heir to the Schweppes carbonated drink family. Eltsey moved them both to Beverly Hills, California, when Dorothy was two. Dorothy spent her childhood in Beverly Hills, eventually dropping out of Beverly Hills High School and marrying Robert Van Runkle at 16. After the birth of her second child, she taught herself how to paint and draw and started to call herself Theadora. The marriage did not last, but she kept the name and worked as a department-store illustrator.

In 1964, Van Runkle was looking for a change, and after meeting Oscar-winning Hollywood costume designer Dorothy Jeakins at a party, Van Runkle was hired to be one of her sketch artists on the historical epic *Hawaii* (1966). The arrangement did not last. After a month, Van Runkle was let go. However, Jeakins did recommend her for a film at Warner Brothers that Van Runkle initially thought would be a flop. That film ended up being *Bonnie and Clyde*, a film that became a cultural phenomenon and has been heralded as starting the "New Hollywood" era.

The gritty and violent realism of *Bonnie and Clyde* ushered in a new wave of counter-culture films that redefined Hollywood. Van Runkle's costumes had an equally monumental impact, both on and off the screen. "I did not know how to do a movie or anything," she said, but after reading the script, "I knew exactly what I'd do after I read the first page (Finstad 2005, 366)." While shopping for the film, Van Runkle ran into Edith Head, the legendary costume designer. When asked what she was working on, Van Runkle explained that it was a film set in the 1930s and the characters were escaping from a bank robbery. Edith Head's advice was to "do everything in chiffon. You'll have no problems" (Fox 2011, B19). Instead, Van Runkle followed her own instincts and created costumes that perfectly captured the image of the romantic and tragic Depression-era gangsters presented in this revisionist version of the true-crime story. Dunaway was initially reluctant to trust Van Runkle's choice to put her in calf-length skirts. But soon after the film's release, maxiskirts replaced miniskirts, the production of traditional French berets increased, and women all around America began to search vintage stores and their grandmothers' closets for 1930s vintage pieces. The double-breasted suits worn by Warren Beatty as Clyde Barrow also brought a retro style back into 1970s menswear.

Van Runkle worked with Dunaway again when she created 29 costume changes for her in *The Thomas Crown Affair* (1968). Dunaway's co-star in *The Thomas Crown Affair* was Steve McQueen, whom Van Runkle had just worked with on *Bullitt* (1968). For *Bullitt*, Van Runkle collaborated with McQueen to create costumes that solidified his style status as the "king of cool." The costume design for both of these films had an immediate and lasting impact on fashion. For someone whose costumes influenced contemporary style to the extent that Van Runkle's did, she was not particularly interested in fashion. "I'm not interested in clothes off the screen. I'm interested in clothes only to the extent that they describe or express feelings" (Chase 1975, 195). What made Van Runkle so successful as a costume designer was that she always remained faithful to the script; her costumes became stylish off the screen because they were authentic, capturing a character that the public would want to imitate, whether that was an on-the-run 1930s outlaw or a present-day tough-guy detective.

The authenticity that defined Van Runkle's style was not always understated or serious. The costumes she designed for films like *Mame* (1974), *Myra Brekinridge* (1979), and *The Best Little Whorehouse in Texas* (1982) were dazzling, outrageous, and in many ways reminiscent of "Old Hollywood" glamour. One of Van Runkle's last films was *Troop Beverly Hills* (1989). The costumes designed for the film's heroine, Phyllis Nefler (Shelley Long), are the epitome of over-the-top quintessentially 1980s style. Long felt that, "When I put the dress on, I knew who Phyllis was, and that was perfect, and that had never happened to me before, where a costumer showed me who my character was (Long 1989)." When a judge asks troop leader Phyllis Nefler who designed her stunning outfit she declares, "It's a Van Runkle, isn't it fabulous?" (Long 1989).

Erin Fabian

See also: Dunaway, Faye

Further Reading

Chase, Donald. 1975. *Filmmaking: The Collaborative Art*. Boston: Little, Brown.

Finstad, Suzanne. 2005. *Warren Beatty: A Private Man*. New York: Harmony Books.

Fox, Margalit. 2011. "Theadora Van Runkle, Costume Designer, Dies at 83." *The New York Times*, November 7. https://www.nytimes.com/2011/11/08/arts/theadora-van-runkle-costume-designer-dies-at-83.html

Jorgensen, Jay, and Donald L. Scoggins. 2015. *Creating Illusion: A Fashionable History of Hollywood Costume Designers*. Philadelphia: Running Press.

Long, Shelley. 1989. "Shelley Long Remembers 'Troop Beverly Hills.'" *Troop Beverly Hills*, Blu-ray. Directed by Jeff Kanew. Culver City, CA: Sony Pictures Home Entertainment.

West, Clare (1879–1961)

Clare West is widely credited as one of the first costume designers to gain fame in Hollywood. Most prominently, she is noted for elevating the position of "head of wardrobe" to that of "head of studio," a far more involved job that included creating a unique creative vision for the films (Stamp 2015, 44). Since costume design was uncredited in silent films, many facts about West's early work are impossible to verify; however, it is largely accepted that she designed costumes for D.W. Griffith's *The Birth of a Nation* (1915), and it is known that she spent two years working on Griffith's *Intolerance* (1916) and was then in a successful collaboration with Cecil B. DeMille on at least 10 films. She was born Clara Belle Smith in Missouri in 1879 and married Otis Oscar Hunley in 1898. They divorced in 1902, and in 1903 she married Marshall Elmer Carriere. In 1912 West and Carriere relocated from the Midwest to Los Angeles and divorced soon after. Her first entrée into Hollywood was in 1914.

There has been some speculation that in the years that followed West's divorce she received formal training in costume design in New York and Paris, but there is no evidence to substantiate that. What is documented is that the studios heavily promoted West's work, in part selling the films based on West's outré designs. West quickly became known for her extravagant gowns that flattered the female figure, and the films' promotional materials liberally attributed West's talents to her Parisian training.

Whether West received training in France or while growing up in the Midwest, her original dress designs afforded her opportunities to collaborate with the most prominent filmmakers of the day, drawing attention from the top film stars and delighting audiences. What started with costume designs for the stars soon became the fashion of the time. In fact, West is often credited as the first costume designer to influence contemporary clothing style.

Initially, however, West gained respect from D. W. Griffith and Cecil B. DeMille for reasons that had nothing to do with contemporary fashion. West elevated the stature of the profession with her commitment to authenticity and historical accuracy. While designing for D. W. Griffith, it is suspected that much of the two years she spent working on his epic film *Intolerance* involved researching clothing across the centuries and creating costumes for every cast member. *Intolerance* was the first film in which every actor was costumed; in earlier films, the more minor characters wore clothing from their own wardrobes, hence the name "wardrobe department." West's work on *Intolerance* was rewarded with the unprecedented accomplishment of being included in the credits with the title of "studio designer" (Munich 2011).

West began her partnership with Cecil B. DeMille in 1918. At the time, he was working with high-profile stars like Gloria Swanson, and he knew that the three most important ingredients for a film's success were "sex, sets, and costumes." DeMille was quoted as saying that he hired West because of her "lavish hand," and over the course of their seven-year collaboration West's dresses became significantly more lavish. They were extravagant, formfitting, and daring to expose more skin than was customary at the time. DeMille instructed West to make costumes that would "make people gasp," reportedly telling her, "Don't design anything that anyone could buy in a store." The expectation was that West would costume the star of a film in a new gown in every scene, each more magnificent than the last. Her costumes were regularly reviewed in the most popular film fan magazines of the time, and the public was eager for her "dazzling" designs. She became known for her "sweeping drapery, tightly wrapped cloth, sumptuous headgear, and ornate beading" (Stutesman 2016).

This reputation West developed for creating high fashion for women is especially interesting when one considers how fashion has played into the representation of gender roles on screen throughout the years. Though West is not credited on the film *Why Change Your Wife* (1920), trade publications from the time suggest that she was the costume designer (Motion Picture News 1919). Gloria Swanson's character goes through a transformational makeover in that film, from the frumpy discarded wife to the reimagined stylish beauty. Though certainly West isn't credited with the story arc for the film, this general "pretty woman" concept with sultry off-the-shoulder gowns and manicured hair has been played out repeatedly in the past century. West's vision for what a "woman made over" might look like has long lasted on screen.

Unfortunately, West's career in the studios ended somewhat abruptly. In the years that followed her time with DeMille, she contracted as the dress designer for Norma and Constance Talmadge, and then for a brief period, she operated her own clothing store in Los Angeles. According to her grandchildren, West struggled with her mental health in her later years. She died at the age of 82 in a mobile home community in Ontario, California.

Anna Weinstein

Further Reading

Benstock, Shari, and Ferriss, Suzanne. 1994. *On Fashion.* New Brunswick, NJ: Rutgers University Press.

Butchart, Amber Jane. 2016. *The Fashion of Film: How Cinema Has Inspired Fashion.* New York: Hachette.

Jorgensen, Jay, and Scoggins, Donald L. 2015. *Creating the Illusion: A Fashionable History of Hollywood Fashion Designers.* Philadelphia: Running Press.

Landis, Deborah N. 2007. *Dressed: A Century of Hollywood Costume Design.* New York: HarperCollins.

Motion Picture News. November–December 1919.

Munich, Adrienne. 2011. *Fashion in Film.* Bloomington: Indiana University Press.

Stamp, Shelley. 2015. "Women and the Silent Screen." In *American Film History: Selected Readings, Origins to 1960.* Hoboken: Wiley-Blackwell. Edited by Cynthia Lucia, Roy Grundmann, and Art Simon.

Stutesman, Drake. 2016. "The Silent Screen." In *Costume, Makeup, and Hair.* Edited by Adrienne McLean. New Brunswick, NJ: Rutgers University Press.

Interview with Ruth E. Carter

How would you explain your profession and its contribution to a film?

On any film or television project, a costume is seen in every frame as long as there is an actor in it. Consequently, costumes play a big part and are an important contribution to the film medium. The costume adds color, style, texture, and the overall support of the story. As a costume designer, you are a part of the collaborative team. That team includes a key artist, like the director, who makes all the final decisions; the production designer, who designs all of the sets that become the backdrop; and finally the DP, or the director of photography, who adds color and depth through film lighting. The costume designer works with this team to create the overall composition on the film.

How did you know you wanted to do this? What advice would you give someone trying to break into your field?

I really figured out that costume design was a good fit for me in college. I went to Hampton University as a theater arts major. However, the department only focused on performance. There wasn't a costume course or curriculum. I decided that if I was going to learn this, I would have to go to the library and get information on the profession and do everything I could do to learn. So, I did. By the time I graduated from college I had designed plays on campus in a little theater, the dance troupe, and outfits for step shows for sororities and fraternities. So, that's my advice. Just do it! Commit to the idea, find out what it takes, and go for it. Don't worry about whether the project is high profile. Find something that you will enjoy creating. Then, it will never feel like work.

What kind of support did you have on your journey?

After I graduated, I had family support. I went home to Springfield, Massachusetts, and did an internship at a local theater. There, I thought I would be living at home while doing the internship. But they actually provided housing. So my first apartment was provided free of charge by the local theater (in exchange for long hours of work). Then, months later, I applied for a second internship at the Santa Fe Opera in New Mexico. I was granted the internship, and in the summer of 1986 I drove my VW Rabbit across the country to begin a fascinating summer at the opera. There I was given housing with other interns. From there, after the summer was over, I moved to Los Angeles where I stayed with family and pursued my professional career.

How have you had to adapt over the course of your career to stay relevant?

Because I started as an intern, I like to hire interns. They are usually college students or people new to the field. Working with pop culture keeps my ideas fresh and up to date. It also keeps me relevant. I like being in the mix of new, young talent. I like the independent spirit of it all. Maybe it's from my Spike Lee days. I also like to keep up with fashion trends, music, and the arts in general. I work on many projects that require a lot of research. That makes it easier to stay relevant because you are creating what "was" or what "could be," and you are in control of that.

Have you ever felt discriminated against in your field simply because of your gender or identity?

I know that prejudice in all forms exists everywhere in life. And as a black woman, you choose your mode of defense. Your profession is no exception. I tended to ignore stupid comments and keep forging ahead. The effect of how I am perceived, I cannot do anything about, for I know it has nothing to do with personal appearance. There were times when I was hired to pick out costumes, or clothing, for white people and an actor or producer would say to me, "Don't buy anything really bright." For a moment, I would think, "Maybe that was said because I am black?" It certainly burned like any racist statement does. But prejudice when presented within the face of an opportunity for me was far less important than proving that I will not only buy you that bright wardrobe, you will love it more than the dull one! I'm sure there are many, many people who would like to see half of the opportunities that I have been blessed with and just can't break through the barriers of racism, sexism, identity, ageism. And to them I say, show your greatness by any means necessary.

Is your field is male dominated?

Fortunately, my field is dominated by females. That is the up side only because I am a female and that means [there are] more opportunities for me. But the down side is that costume designing is like other female-dominated professions such as secretaries, nurses, or teachers where the pay, the human rights, and the job status are considered "lower tier" than the male-dominated professions like production design, directors, writers, and DPs. There are no residuals for costume designers, yet directors and DPs get them. The pay is much higher for production designers, and yet the amount of work and overall contribution to the project of a costume designer are as great or greater. Yet we have broken into many male-dominated roles in this field. Ava DuVernay is an example with *A Wrinkle in Time*; Rachael Morrison is another with *Black Panther*. We continue to make strides. And hopefully, for costume designers, we will see more breakthroughs.

Directors

Introduction

Films are considered by their nature to be a collaborative process, and a film director is typically credited as the individual with the most authorial influence in the entire filmmaking process. A director is responsible for the film's final appearance, sound, feel, and story quality, which is a measure of how successfully the director has translated the screenplay into the realm of visual storytelling. There are many pressures that frequently bear down on directors, and the endurance required to direct a feature film is staggering.

The director presides over a film's creative and logistical aspects by harnessing the technical skills of their crew and the theatrical talents of their actresses and actors in order to render her vision of the script onto the screen. In the pre-production stages, the director may be involved in script development, production planning, casting, and other aspects of production planning. When it comes to the actual day-to-day activities of the director while shooting during production, it is the director who makes the most important decisions about staging, lighting, sound, performance, and framing or shot composition (often heavily relying on and collaborating with the director of cinematography) and who watches dailies with the film's editor (with whom they will typically continue to collaborate closely in post-production). Although a director will have help, they are ultimately responsible for staying within the parameters of a shooting schedule and budget while simultaneously juggling whatever logistical challenges and creative differences may arise.

Greta Gerwig has been only the fifth woman in history to receive an Oscar nomination for Best Director, in 2018 for *Lady Bird* (2017). Lina Wertmüller was the first woman to be nominated in 1977 for her film *Seven Beauties* (1975), followed by Jane Campion's *The Piano* (1993) in 1994, and Sofia Coppola's *Lost in Translation* (2003) in 2004. The first Oscar win for a woman in Best Directing was Kathryn Bigelow for *The Hurt Locker* (2009) in 2010. And, despite Patty Jenkins's success directing *Wonder Woman* (2017), the highest-grossing live-action, female-directed film to date, women are still grossly underrepresented when it comes to directing opportunities from the major studios.

Laura L. S. Bauer

Arzner, Dorothy (1897–1979)

Dorothy Arzner's fame as the first "woman director" was obtained both in her lifetime and posthumously in contemporary film studies. The sound era in Hollywood began in 1919 with the installation of the first Paramount sound studio in New York. This period provided Arzner with new opportunities, as she quickly established herself as an influential director of "talkies" as early as 1926. Film scholars, especially Judith Mayne and Anthony Slide, note that the early 20th-century lore surrounding Arzner's pioneering of Hollywood was a bit misleading. In one respect, the documentation that could help verify a more complete history of women making movies—such as film credits and trade papers—did not exist in the silent film era. As a consequence, film historians have a limited understanding of how many women were active in early Hollywood. Arzner's claim to fame at Paramount may not be unique but rather an example of one career within a long unrecorded history of women filmmakers. In another respect, the *Los Angeles Daily Times* article in 1926 named two other noteworthy female directors, Lois Weber and Ida May Parks, who were important figures preceding Arzner. Her singular status as "the woman director" can be understood as the result of a late 20th-century "rediscovery" of Arzner's work, which occurred near her death in the 1970s and again in the 1990s. Arzner's directorial career was the most noteworthy and distinctive out of all the other women working in Hollywood because her large body of work endured throughout the 20th and 21st centuries.

Dorothy Arzner's success has inspired different interpretations. One of these accounts would cite her keen ability to network within the studio system, which allowed her to rise to the ranks of director. But Arzner did not gain her success immediately within Hollywood. Despite her later status as a "darling" of the film industry, Arzner humbly began her film career in 1919 with Famous Players-Lasky (later Paramount) as a typist of scripts. This job, which only lasted three months, was provided to Arzner because of her connection to William de Mille. From 1915 to 1917, Arzner left the University of Southern California to volunteer with the Los Angeles Emergency Ambulance Corps. It was through a chance encounter with de Mille, the head of this agency during World War I, that Arzner found a contact within the film industry. De Mille, an important filmmaker along with his younger brother Cecil B. DeMille, introduced Arzner to the ins and outs of filmmaking, an opportunity she readily grasped. Not only did Arzner decide to become a director during these three months, she also took this time to learn everything she could about the filmmaking process.

Another account of Arzner's success functions more as an industry myth. Her father, Louis Arzner, was the manager of the Los Angeles restaurant the Hoffman Café, an establishment much frequented by Hollywood elites such as actor Charles Chaplin and directors D. W. Griffith and James Cruze. A young Dorothy Arzner would visit her father at work and peer unseen at these influential film figures, until one day James Cruze invited her to sit at a table. It was here that Arzner absorbed the stories of these hallowed Hollywood movers and shakers, and soon became dedicated to the idea of directing. Judith Mayne offers a more realistic rendition of this story. She connects Arzner's interest in her father's illustrious clientele to a desire to become a financially independent woman. Historically speaking, a woman's motivation to gain independence was not uncommon in an era marked by the passage of the Nineteenth Amendment in 1920, the important legislation that gave women in the United States the right to vote. For Arzner, being a "modern woman" was closely aligned to her maverick attitude toward filmmaking; in other words, she could autonomously wield her creative energy and influence as a woman director. What followed after her directorial debut in *Fashions for Women* (1927) is an expansive oeuvre of films that for many contemporary film scholars became examples of a modern woman making movies for modern women.

Dorothy Arzner is undoubtedly most well known for the cinematic development of *the women's film*. This popular genre is characterized by narratives that foreground and privilege female experiences, relationships, and everyday hardships. Her contributions were the subject of a Directors Guild of America tribute in 1975. Arzner's women's films characteristically display the anxieties of modern women, who seek to balance career and the pursuit of marriage, as well as female-only companionship and male-centered romantic attachments. Three noteworthy films display these tensions: *Get Your Man* (1927), *The Wild Party* (1929), and *Dance, Girl, Dance* (1940).

Arzner herself remained ambivalent to the conventional love and marriage stories popularized by her women's films. The female characters within these films may quest to find the perfect mate, but the attainment of marriage is narratively replaced with the promise of matrimony—not the real thing. Film scholar Donna R. Casella notes that the lack of a marriage ceremony within Arzner's films—as well as no depiction of marital home life—underscores the social conventions surrounding love and marriage as somewhat illusionary or intangible.

The legacy of Dorothy Arzner resonates in her ability to break the accepted conventions of the Hollywood system and the meaning of the moniker "woman director." After her death in 1979, she was remembered as much more than an exceptional figure in film history but a pioneer in her own right. She established a powerful place for women in Hollywood and diversified the types of representations of women that could be viewed on screen. The bulk of her filmic legacy is currently housed in the Film and Television Archive at the University of California, Los Angeles.

Jessica Ziegenfuss

See also: Lupino, Ida

Further Reading

Berlant, Lauren. 2008. *The Female Complaint: The Unfinished Business of Sentimentality in American Culture*. Durham, NC: Duke University Press.

Casella, Donna R. 2009. "What Women Want: The Complex World of Dorothy Arzner and Her Cinematic Women." *Framework: The Journal of Cinema and Media* 50(1): 235–270.

Kenly, William S. 1987. "Paramount: The Early Sound Years." Museum of Modern Art. 44: 6–7.

Mayne, Judith. 1994. *Directed by Dorothy Arzner*. Bloomington: Indiana University Press.

Mercer, John, and Martin Shingler. 2004. *Melodrama: Genre, Style, Sensibility.* New York: Columbia University Press.

Slide, Anthony. 2012. "Early Women Filmmakers: The Real Numbers." *Film History* 24(1): 114–121.

Williams, Linda. 1991. "Film Bodies: Gender, Genre, and Excess." *Film Quarterly* 44(4): 2–13.

Bigelow, Kathryn (1951–)

Kathryn Ann Bigelow is a renowned American director, film producer, screenwriter, and television director. Bigelow has succeeded in establishing herself as an auteur working within the traditionally male-dominated action genres. Bigelow's films consistently question the constructs of masculinity, particularly the impact of violence, a convention in action films, while also serving as a source of entertainment. Through point of view, as well as through narrative strategies, Bigelow's films push spectators to focus on the crisis of masculinity. Bigelow's films employ, in the words of Anna Powell (1994), "stunning and expressionistic visuals, rapid narrative pacing, visceral scenes of eroticized violence and physical action," providing all the thrilling expectations of the action film genre.

Bigelow's oeuvre includes many works that span multiple genres, illuminating her range and abilities. Her first and most avant-garde film about a gang of 1950s

Kathryn Bigelow directing on the set of *Strange Days* (1995). With her film *The Hurt Locker* (2008), Bigelow became the first woman in Hollywood film history to win an Academy Award for Best Director. As a director, Bigelow is noted for her ability to create action films that both work with and transcend formulaic design. (20th Century Fox/Photofest)

bikers, *The Loveless* (1982), was followed by a Western horror film *Near Dark* (1987). She also directed the noted action film *Point Break* (1991), which has garnered a cult following. She followed this prominent film with *Strange Days* (1995), *The Weight of Water* (2000), and *K-19: The Widowmaker* (2002). Her breakout works, the war film *The Hurt Locker* (2008) and the action war film *Zero Dark Thirty* (2012) propelled her career to new heights.

The Hurt Locker became Bigelow's most awarded and lauded work, winning the 2009 Academy Award for Best Picture and the BAFTA Award for Best Film while also being nominated for the 2009 Golden Globe Award for Best Drama. With this film Bigelow became the first woman to win the Academy Award for Best Director, the Directors Guild of America Award for Outstanding Directing, the BAFTA Award for Best Direction, and the Critics' Choice Movie Award for Best Director. She was also the first woman to win the Saturn Award for Best Director in 1995 for the film *Strange Days*.

Set in the 1950s, Bigelow's first feature film, *The Loveless*, draws on the influence of mainstream biker movies of the period. Because of its stylized compositions and deliberately slow pace, it has been frequently described as an anti-action film. The film's slow pace is all the more striking given that it is film about men traveling on motorcycles. Drawing from Jean-Luc Godard's *Breathless* (1959), Bigelow's film uses a bold color palette, painstakingly choreographed tracking shots, and lush deployment of consumer images. In the film, the focus is often on the objects that belong to the biker gang members, such as their leather jackets and the comb in the opening scene. Bigelow's slow and deliberate focus on these masculine objects shows that masculinity is a continual performance and its "naturalness" is called into question.

The Hurt Locker continues to show Bigelow's critique of masculine ideology in action genres by working within them, in this case, the war film. The film gratifies the audience's desire for entertainment even as it subverts and questions that need. *The Hurt Locker* uses a quick editing style, utilizing mostly handheld shots from multiple perspectives with quick pans, zooms, and canted angles to mimic all the soldiers' understandable anxiety and fear of sudden, potential danger. This type of filmmaking also reflects the constant vigil soldiers must keep in the oppressive heat, but instead of explicitly addressing the politics of the Iraqi war, the film focuses on the experience of counterinsurgency warfare and the effects of what it does to those who wage it. Bigelow presents a film where there are no clear antagonists, limited acts of heroism in the traditional sense, and the narrative reaches no climax. There is gripping suspense without any catharsis, and the ever-looming threat of immediate death is always present. The heightened excess in Bigelow's films serve as commentary on the genre of the war film and the masculine culture it celebrates.

Regardless of gender, in order for a director to qualify as an auteur, they must be seen as able to successfully manipulate and work within the constraints of the film industry, while also putting across their personal agenda and style, which are often perceived as going against the expectations of the film industry itself. Bigelow herself asserts that what is needed is a radical change in conceptions of women working in the Hollywood industry and a breaking down of the generic categories to which they have traditionally been cosigned. Deliberately using graphic sexual and violent material allows Bigelow to confront issues of representation before much larger audiences, even if that use is controversial. Bigelow has stated, "Conventionally, hardware pictures, action oriented, have been male dominated, and more emotional material has been women's domain. That's breaking down. This notion that there's a women's aesthetic, a woman's eye, is really debilitating" (Hillier 1992).

Although Bigelow's films are not historical fictions, they use pastiche extensively. Pastiche is the imitation of the style, character, or other references to the work of another artist or collection of artists intended to praise their influence (Jameson 1991). By quoting from other movies and mixing genre and styles, often male-oriented action films, Bigelow appropriates the work of other filmmakers, past and present, in order to produce her own distinctive style. She has cultivated a reputation as a director unwilling to accept categorization of her work in traditional gender terms. She emulates the style of high-profile action directors such as (her former husband) James Cameron, Sam Peckinpah, and Oliver Stone, refusing to be restricted. However, the extent to which Bigelow's tactics of pastiche have either enabled Bigelow to retain a clear identity and voice in mainstream Hollywood or whether she has lost her own style as a result remains a point of debate. This sort of argument, however, is rarely a source of contention for male directors.

Bigelow's treatment of nostalgia differs from great iconic directors such as Martin Scorsese, in that there is a nostalgic homage in films like *The Loveless*, but instead of presenting a desire to retrieve a glorified past, the intention seems to use the images from the past in order to rewrite history from a distinct contemporary perspective. Bigelow uses those images to create new meanings. Her approach overturns the accepted account of the past and its values to create new, exciting possibilities in the arena of gender and representation. Bigelow's work raises fundamental questions of how we are to approach the past, deconstructing and reconstructing its presence in cinema.

Bigelow's feature films are all characterized by collaboration, particularly collaboration with influential men. *The Loveless* was directed and scripted with Monty Montgomery. She collaborated with Eric Red on the scripts of *Near Dark* and *Blue Steel*, and with James Cameron on *Point Break* and *Strange Days*, to whom she was married to from 1989 to 1991. She claims to have been influenced exclusively by male filmmakers, only citing Susan Sontag as a strong female influence, one of the professors she studied under at Columbia University. Bigelow's work suggests that how we conceive of feminism must be constructed by both filmmakers and audiences. Bigelow has asserted she sees no reason why female directors should be confined to women's pictures, or men to hard-core action movies.

Danielle Cofer

See also: Campion, Jane; Coolidge, Martha; Ellison, Megan; Jenkins, Patty; Meyers, Nancy; Pascal, Amy

Further Reading

Cook, Pam. 2005. *Screening the Past: Memory and Nostalgia in Cinema.* London: Routledge.

Grant, Barry Keith. 2010. *Shadows of Doubt: Negotiations of Masculinity in American Genre Films.* Detroit: Wayne State University Press.

Hillier, Jim. 1992. *The New Hollywood.* London: Studio Vista.

Jameson, Frederic. 1991. *Postmodernism, or, the Cultural Logic of Late Capitalism*. Durham, NC: Duke University Press.

Pomerance, Murray. 2010. "Review: *Auteurs and Authorship: A Film Reader*. Edited by Barry Keith Grant. Maldwell, MA: Blackwell Publishing, 2008." *Quarterly Review of Film and Video* 27: 3.

Powell, Anna. 1994. "Blood on the Borders—*Near Dark* and *Blue Steel*." *Screen* 35: 136.

Rascaroli, Laura. 1997. "Steel in the Gaze: On POV and the Discourse of Vision in Kathryn Bigelow's Cinema." *Screen* 38: 232.

Campion, Jane (1954–)

Director-writer Jane Campion was born in 1954 in Waikanae on the north coast of Wellington, New Zealand, to Richard and Edith Campion, who jointly established the touring theater company The New Zealand Players in 1952. Her father Richard was a well-established theater and opera director. According to her volume in *Contemporary Film Directors*, Campion grew up immersed in the world of New Zealand theater. Campion's interest in the creative arts blossomed throughout her childhood, and in 1976, Campion chose to attend art school at the Chelsea School of Arts in London. Subsequently, in 1981, she earned a

New Zealand film director Jane Campion on the set of her film *Bright Star* (2009). Campion was the second woman in the history of the Academy to be nominated for Best Director. As of 2018, she was the only female director ever to win the Cannes Film Festival's Palme d'Or, which is one of the most prestigious awards in the film industry. Both the Oscar nomination and Palme d'Or were in recognition of her film *The Piano* (1993). (Pathe/Photofest)

graduate diploma in Visual Arts—Painting from Sydney College of the Arts at the University of Sydney. Of her education in the two art schools, Campion cites painter Frida Kahlo and sculptor Joseph Beuys as significant influences on her work.

Dissatisfied with painting as a medium, she turned to film and, in 1980, created her first short work, *Tissues*. She described it as "this black comedy about a family whose father has been arrested for child molestation. I was absolutely thrilled by every inch of it, and would throw my projector in the back of my car and show it to anybody who would watch it" (Diekmann and Tabb 2012). She recalled, however, that when someone remarked that the film had no wide shots in it, "I said, 'Wide shots? What are they?' That comment kind of blew my whole world apart, and I realized that I did not have any idea of what I was up to" (Diekmann and Tabb 2012). Thus, in 1981, Campion made the move to formally study filmmaking at the Australian Film, Television and Radio School, where she made several more short films, graduating in 1984.

Campion's first professional short film, *Peel* (1982), also known by the title *An Exercise in Discipline—Peel,* won her the Short Film Palme d'Or award at the 1986 Cannes Film Festival, making her the first woman to win the prestigious prize. *Peel*'s initial reception helped shape Campion's vision as a filmmaker, she says: "The people at the [Australian Film and Television School] loathed *Peel* when they saw a first cut of it. They told me not to bother finishing it. I was quite vain so I found that really upsetting, but it was good for me. I cut out everything that was remotely extraneous and made the film a lot better" (Stiles 1984). *Passionless Moments* (1983), written and directed with Gerard Lee, was screened at Cannes that same year in the "Un Certain Regard" section. The year 1989 saw Campion's feature debut with *Sweetie*, also co-written with Lee; the film was considered so highly that it was one of 50 Australian films selected for preservation as part of the National Film and Sound Archive of Australia's Kodak/Atlab Cinema Collection Restoration Project. In 1990, Campion again proved her skill, this time in the form of *An Angel at My Table*, based on the three-part autobiography of author Janet Frame (aka Nene Janet Paterson Clutha), which garnered much praise and several awards including second prize at the Venice Film Festival, six New Zealand Film and Television awards, and the International Critics' Award from the Toronto International Film Festival.

In 1993, Campion received even more recognition, this time for *The Piano* (which she both wrote and directed), starring Holly Hunter and Anna Paquin (in her first acting role). The film is about a mute woman living in the 1850s, sent to New Zealand with her young daughter and her piano for an arranged marriage to a wealthy landowner. Among the accolades the movie received was critic Roger Ebert's high praise: "*The Piano* is as peculiar and haunting as any film I've seen" and "one of those rare movies that is not just about a story, or some characters, but about a whole universe of feeling" (Ebert 1993). Via the film, Campion became the first woman to receive the Cannes Film Festival overall Palme d'Or, and subsequently the film won Best Actress, Best Supporting Actress, and Best Screenplay at the 1994 Academy Awards. In total, the film won or was nominated for some 65 major international film awards.

Several powerful but polarizing films followed for Campion: *The Portrait of a Lady* (1996), *Holy Smoke!* (1999), *In the Cut* (2003), and *Bright Star* (2009), which was also shown at Cannes. As much as her filmmaking and its influence had grown, however, Campion began to think smaller, as it were, venturing into work for television. In a 2017 interview with *IndieWire*, Campion shared her discontent with the silver screen in Australia and New Zealand: "Cinema in Australia and New Zealand has become much more mainstream. It's broad entertainment, broad sympathy. It's just not my kind of thing . . . to make money out of entertaining doesn't inspire me. But in television, there is no concern about politeness or pleasing the audience. It feels like creative freedom" (Erbland 2017). In proof of fact, Campion's *Top of the Lake* (2013–) has been a smash hit, premiering at the 2013 Sundance Film Festival—the first miniseries to play at the festival—and eventually playing on the Sundance Channel in the United States and BBC Two in the UK a few months later. *Top of the Lake* has received several Emmy nominations, including for Best Mini-Series, Best Direction, and Best Writing, as well as nominations for Outstanding Lead Actress in a Miniseries or a Movie (Elisabeth Moss) and Outstanding Lead Actor in a Miniseries or a Movie (Peter Mullan).

Writing of Campion and her work in Routledge's Film Notebooks series, Deb Verhoeven says, "By any standards she is the most successful woman working in the contemporary film industry" (Verhoeven 2009). If output is any indicator, Verhoeven's assessment is not wrong; Campion holds credits as writer (12), director (18), producer (8), cinematographer (1), casting director (1), editor (1), and even as actress (2—one for 1995's *Operavox* and another for 1989's *The Audition*).

Brian F. McCabe

See also: Bigelow, Kathryn; Coolidge, Martha

Further Reading

Campion, Jane, and Virginia Wright Wexman. 1999. *Jane Campion: Interviews*. Conversations with Filmmakers Series. Jackson: University Press of Mississippi.

Cinema Axis. 2013. "The Auteurs: Jane Campion." *Cinema Axis*, September 30. http://cinemaaxis.com/2013/09/30/the-auteurs-jane-campion

Diekmann, Katherine, and Michael Tabb. 2012. "New Again: Jane Campion." *Interview*, May 30.

Dowd, A. A. 2014. "1993 Is the First and Last Time the Palme Went to a Woman." *The A.V. Club*, February 13. https://film.avclub.com/1993-is-the-first-and-last-time-the-palme-went-to-a-wom-1798266132

Ebert, Roger. 1993. "The Piano." Rogerebert, November 19. https://www.rogerebert.com/reviews/the-piano-1993

Erbland, Kate. 2017. "Jane Campion Isn't Excited about Film Anymore: 'Now, the Really Clever People Do Television.'" *IndieWire*, July 25. http://www.indiewire.com/2017/07/jane-campion-film-television-top-of-the-lake-1201859592

Freiberg, Freda. 1987. "The Bizarre in the Banal: Notes on the Films of Jane Campion." In *Don't Shoot Darling!: Women's Independent Filmmaking in Australia*. Edited by Annette Blonski, Barbara Creed, and Freda Freiberg. Richmond: Greenhouse Publications.

Hawker, Philippa. 1989. "Jane Campion—An Interview by Hawker, Philippa. Includes a Selected Filmography." *Cinema Papers* 73(73): 29–30.

McHugh, Kathleen Anne. 2007. *Jane Campion*. Contemporary Film Directors series. Urbana: University of Illinois Press.

Pulver, Andrew. 2014. "Jane Campion: 'Life Isn't a Career.'" *The Guardian*, May 12. http://www.theguardian.com/film/2014/may/12/jane-campion-interview-cannes-the-piano

Stiles, Mark. 1984. "Jane Campion." *Cinema Papers*, December: 434–435, 471.

Verhoeven, Deb. 2009. *Jane Campion*. Routledge Film Guidebooks. London: Routledge.

Coolidge, Martha (1946–)

Martha Coolidge is one of a group of female directors who gained prominence in the 1980s, and is perhaps best known for raising the bar for the "teen film" genre. Along with contemporaries Amy Heckerling and Penelope Spheeris, she brought a new perspective and her own brand of cool to Hollywood, creating cult classics that defined an era. From intensely personal documentaries, to indie films and major studio releases, the through line of Coolidge's career has been creating fully developed female characters with authentic voices and motivations. When she found these stories lacking in motion pictures, she went to television to tell a wider variety of stories, but her focus on presenting interesting women characters continued.

Raised in Connecticut by her architect mother, Martha's artistic leanings were encouraged and she pursued both singing and art, which led her to attend the Rhode Island School of Design and New York University's Tisch School of the Arts. In an interview with *The Hollywood Reporter*, she recalled that while applying to NYU, she was told it was pointless for her to study directing, because she was a woman and there were no women directors (Grove 1988). She ignored this "advice" and went on to direct several award-winning documentaries before making a move to Hollywood. In her later years as an established director, she came to believe that the best directors had traits that are generally attributed to both men and women (Silverstein 2011).

Throughout her most notable works, from the 1976 docudrama *Not a Pretty Picture*, to the films *Valley Girl* (1983), *Rambling Rose* (1991), *Angie* (1994), and later, *Introducing Dorothy Dandridge* (1999), women are the center of the story. *Not a Pretty Picture* details the director's own date rape experience, through re-enactments performed by an actress who herself had been a victim of rape. The film makes a powerful personal and political statement about violence against women, especially given how taboo the topic was at the time. Her first studio film, *Valley Girl,* was meant to be a low-budget throwaway film, a teen-sex comedy along the lines of the popular *Porkys* film series. With Coolidge at the helm, however, it became a punk rock romantic comedy about teenage love, peer pressure, and life in early 1980s Los Angeles that resonated with moviegoers and became a surprise hit upon its release. Now considered a cult classic, it gave Nicolas Cage his first leading role and shined a spotlight on the early 1980s punk and New Wave scene. At its core, though, the film is about the main character, Julie, and her struggle to stand up for what she wants. She does this at the beginning of the film, breaking up with her "boring" jock boyfriend, to the horror of her friends, and in the end when she chooses Randy (played by Cage), the punk boy she loves over the objections of the same friends.

Throughout Coolidge's films, a common thread of interesting and realistic female characters can be found. Her most critically acclaimed film, *Rambling Rose*, is the story of a damaged and misunderstood young woman who looks for love from men but finds kindness and support from the mother of the family who hires her. Both main actresses in the film were nominated for Academy Awards, and Coolidge was nominated for a Directors Guild of America (DGA) award for best director. *Angie* (1994), a film starring Geena Davis, follows a woman who shocks the neighborhood by refusing to marry the father of her baby and instead sets out to find a better life for herself. A later film, *The Prince & Me* (2004), is a lighthearted romantic comedy with a twist. The girl falls in love with a prince but chooses to pursue her professional dreams instead of conforming to the role of princess. In all of these films, we see women who struggle and ultimately succeed in standing up for themselves.

In 2002, Coolidge earned the distinction of becoming the first woman president of the DGA. She had been an active member of the organization for years, joining in 1983, serving as co-chair of the Guild's Creative Rights Committee since 1992, the first vice president since 1995, and was previously elected to their Western Directors Council in 1984. Notably, during this era three of the largest and most influential guilds in Hollywood, the DGA, the Screen Actors Guild (SAG), and the Writers Guild of America (WGA), were all headed by women. Coolidge has long been a vocal advocate of increasing diversity in Hollywood, especially behind the camera. In 2013, she wrote an opinion piece for *The New York Times* in which she frankly discussed the lack of realistic and relatable sex scenes in motion pictures. In her view, sex on films would continue to focus on the male perspective as long as men continued to dominate filmmaking. The solution, she argued, is to put more women in creative roles and have equitable hiring within the industry (Coolidge 2013).

Coolidge's work was recognized by the organization Women in Film, who awarded her with its Crystal Award for Excellence in Film in 1992. She received the DGA's Robert B. Aldrich Award in 1998 for "extraordinary service to the Directors Guild of America and to its membership" (Directors Guild of America 1998). She scored her first Emmy nomination for directing for the HBO original movie *Introducing Dorothy Dandridge*, as well as a DGA Award nomination for Best Director. She currently directs a variety of film and television projects while also teaching at Chapman University, where she is a professor of film and media arts.

Rachel Rohac Bernstein

See also: Bigelow, Kathryn; Campion, Jane; Coates, Anne V.

Further Reading

Coolidge, Martha. 2013. "Put Women behind the Camera to Make Sex Scenes More Realistic." *The New York Times*, June 16. https://www.nytimes.com/roomfordebate/2013/06/16/making-love-in-the-movies/put-women-behind-the-camera-to-make-sex-scenes-more-realistic

Directors Guild of America. 1998. "Martha Coolidge to Receive DGA's Robert B. Aldrich Award." Directors Guild of America, March 5. https://www.dga.org/News/PressReleases/1998/0305-Martha-Coolidge-to-Receive-DGAs-Robert-B-Aldrich-Award.aspx

Gregory, Mollie. 2002. *Women Who Run the Show*. New York: St. Martin's Press.

Grove, Martin A. 1988. "Hollywood Report." *The Hollywood Reporter*, June 16.

Hurd, Mary G. 2007. *Women Directors and Their Films*. Westport, CT: Praeger Publishers.

Kiefer, Peter. 2002. "Coolidge New DGA President." *Variety*, March 11.

Silverstein, Melissa. 2011. "Martha Coolidge Talks Valley Girl and Female Directors." *IndieWire*, June 9. http://www.indiewire.com/2011/06/martha-coolidge-talks-valley-girl-and-female-directors-212276

Vimeo. 2010. "Martha Coolidge—Director's Reel." Accessed November 19, 2007. https://vimeo.com/12063033

Deren, Maya (1917–1961)

Maya Deren, born Eleanora Derenkowskaia, was an experimental American filmmaker, choreographer, dancer, film theorist, poet, lecturer, writer, and photographer. Her most notable films include *Meshes of the Afternoon* (1943), *At Land* (1944), *A Study for Choreography for Camera* (1945), *Ritual in Transfigured Time* (1945–1946), *Meditation on Violence* (1947), and *The Very Eye of Night* (1959). She also wrote several books, *Divine Horsemen: The Living Gods of Haiti* (1953) and *An Anagram of Ideas on Art, Form and Film* (1946).

In 1946, Deren was awarded a Guggenheim Fellowship for "Creative Work in the Field of Motion Pictures" and won the Grand Prix Internationale for 16mm experimental film at the Cannes Film Festival for *Meshes of the Afternoon*. She created a scholarship for experimental filmmakers: the Creative Film Foundation. Through her use of camera techniques like jump cutting, superimposition, multiple exposure, and slow motion, Deren has become known for creating a sense of continued motion through discontinued space, while distorting the expectations of physical space and time, giving her work a stream-of-consciousness quality.

Deren, a legendary figure in the world of experimental film, is considered a founding force in the emergence of the avant-garde film movement in New York, beginning in the 1940s, and reaching her critically acclaimed peak throughout the 1960s. *Meshes of the Afternoon*, Deren's most notable 1943 film, is considered a seminal work in the avant-garde tradition and has been cited as an inspiration and model for subsequent generations of experimental filmmakers. Deren's initial cinematic interest was on the individual woman's psychological experience, with a focus on presenting a female subjective voice. Expanding her interest from the individual woman to what she saw as women's collective experience, Deren also explored myths and rituals, combining her interests in dance, Haitian vodun, and subjective psychology. Traveling to Haiti often, Deren's work in Haitian vodun, or voodoo, practices eventually led to her publication of an influential anthropological study of Haitian vodun culture. Throughout her career, Deren used the genre of cinema as a means for personal expression and successively stands as a representative figure of the woman filmmaker's evolving function in the American avant-garde.

Born in Russia in 1917, Deren's family fled the country in 1922 due to increasing anti-Semitism, finally settling in Syracuse, New York. Her father shortened the family name to "Deren" after they arrived. Deren immigrated to the United States; was educated in Geneva, Switzerland, and Syracuse University and New York University; and began her career in dance, writing, and filmmaking by accompanying a dancer-choreographer, Katherine Dunham, on a national tour in the early 1940s.

While studying journalism at Syracuse University, Deren also became active in the Trotskyist Young People's Socialist League (YPSL). Through the YPSL she met Gregory Bardacke, her first husband, whom she married at the age of 18. After relocating to New York City, they soon became active in various socialist causes, and Deren graduated from New York University with a bachelor's degree in literature and separated from Bardacke. She also attended the New School for Social Research and received a master's degree in English literature at Smith College.

Deren's short films adapted strategies from other art forms, as well as challenged the aesthetic expectations of Hollywood filmmaking. In 1943, Deren purchased a used 16mm Bolex camera with some of the inheritance money she received after her father's death. Filmed in Los Angeles, this camera captured her first and most critically acclaimed film, *Meshes of the Afternoon* (1943), shot in collaboration with Alexander Hammid. *Meshes of the Afternoon* is recognized as a pioneering American avant-garde film, with critics noting its autobiographical tone focusing on women and the individual. Shot originally as a silent film with no dialogue, music for the film was later composed by Deren's third husband, Teiji Itō, in 1952. The film is surrealistic, featuring dramatic camera angles and innovative editing, and investigates the ephemeral ways in which the protagonist's unconscious mind works and makes connections between objects and situations. Playing "The Woman," Maya Deren appears as the star. (Deren appeared in several of her films but never credited herself as an actress, choosing instead to downplay her roles.) Deren takes a stroll to her friend's home in Los Angeles, slips into a deep sleep, and has a dream. The sequence of approaching the gate on the partially enshrouded road restarts several times, resisting conventional narrative expectations. The film ends in various situations inside the house. Focusing on the movement from the wind, shadows, and the steady music sustain the rhythm of the dream. Recurring symbols appear on the screen, including a mirror-faced, cloaked figure and a key, which becomes conflated with a knife. Deren's symbolism "was very simple. Maya had the capacity to speak more directly about what everyone else was being very pompous about—that is, symbolism, particularly psychological symbolism" (Brakhage 1989).

Deren shatters any expectation of a conventional narrative, using repetition and rhythm to heighten the surreal experience. Initially the camera avoids capturing her face, preventing the viewer from identifying a particular woman. Playing with the expected subject position, Deren presents multiple selves, shifting between the first and third person. Deren's clear objective is to explore a woman's subjectivity and her relationship with elements present in the external world. With regard to space, the film depicts a woman whose subjectivity in domestic space is explored, foregrounding Deren's interests in feminism and politics via self-representation.

Deren further navigates conflicting identity politics as the self and the "other," developed through the splitting, doubling, multiplication, and synthesis of the woman in the film. Following a fantastical quest with allegorical complexity, *Meshes of the Afternoon* also draws on both the film noir and domestic melodrama genres.

At Land, filmed in Port Jefferson and Amagansett, New York, in the summer of 1944, focuses on an environmental psychologist's perspective. Starring in another one of her films, Deren washes ashore on the beach and climbs up a piece of driftwood that leads to a lit room filled with men and women smoking. Crawling across the featured table in the shot, Deren is invisible to the people seated. Her body then moves seamlessly onto a new frame as she crawls through foliage. She continues to crawl following the natural pattern of water on rocks, a man across a farm, a sick man in bed, through several doors, as she finally arrives on a cliff. Walking farther away from the camera, through the sand dunes, Deren collects rocks along the shore. Coming across two women playing chess in the sand, she appears perplexed, pushing her to return to her point of origin, running back through the entire sequence. The jump-cuts make it appear as though she runs into her doppelganger, heightening her sense of split identity as her earlier self sees the other self running through the scene. By focusing on the character's own inner subjectivity in her physical environment, as well as outside her subconscious, her interest in identity politics is stylistically consistent.

But Deren very much possessed an entrepreneurial spirit in addition to a creative calling, which became evident as she began to screen and distribute her films throughout the United States, Canada, and Cuba. Unable to secure continued financial backing for her films, Deren assumed the roles of lecturer, teacher, publicist, and organizational administrator in order to create a feasible environment for independent filmmaking. She also developed and organized economic bases for the production and reception of a radical film aesthetic. Deren consistently advocated for contemporary artists, also calling them to assume social and economic responsibility for artistic reception. Booking the Village's Provincetown Playhouse for a major public exhibition in February 1946, Deren's project, titled *Three Abandoned Films*, showed *Meshes of the Afternoon*, *At Land,* and *A Study in Choreography for the Camera.* The event was completely sold out and over maximum capacity, inspiring Amos Vogel's formation of Cinema 16, the most successful film society of the 1950s, which forced the public to take avant-garde seriously.

Deren also had several significant and formative friendships with other notable artists and performers. Back in New York City in 1944, her social circle included such notable names as Marcel Duchamp, André Breton, John Cage, and Anaïs Nin. Deren has been cited as a muse and inspiration to such up-and-coming avant-garde filmmakers as Curtis Harrington, Stan Brakhage, and Kenneth Anger, who channeled her fiercely creative, independent, and entrepreneurial spirit.

Danielle Cofer

Further Reading

Brakhage, Stan. 1989. *Film at Wit's End: Eight Avant-Garde Filmmakers*. New York: Documentext.

Petrolle, Jean, and Virginia Wright. 2005. *Women and Experimental Filmmaking*. Urbana: University of Illinois.

Rabinovitz, Lauren. 1991. *Points of Resistance: Women, Power & Politics in the New York Avant-Garde Cinema, 1943–71.* Urbana: University of Illinois.

Robinson, David. 1973. *The History of World Cinema.* New York: Stein and Day.

DuVernay, Ava (1972–)

Widely considered the forerunner of a new generation of African American filmmakers, Ava DuVernay was born on August 24, 1972, in Long Beach, California. She grew up in Compton and Alabama, where she was raised by her mother and stepfather. She graduated from UCLA with a double BA major in English literature and African American studies and worked as a journalist and a publicist. In 1999 she founded The DuVernay Agency, which marketed movies specifically for African American audiences, before taking up directing documentaries and movies.

Her first film was a short of 12 minutes in 2005 called *Saturday Night Life,* which depicted a trip to the local discount grocery store by a single mother and her three

Ava DuVernay (middle) directing David Oyelowo and Lorraine Toussaint on the set of *Selma* (2014). As a director, DuVernay has achieved a number of noteworthy industry firsts. She was the first African American woman to win Best Director at the Sundance Film Festival, for her work on *Middle of Nowhere* (2012). For *Selma*, she became the first African American female director nominated for a Golden Globe award. DuVernay was also the first African American female director to be given a budget of over $100 million to direct a studio film, for *A Wrinkle in Time* (2018). (Paramount Pictures/ Photofest)

children based on her mother's experiences. DuVernay's concerns with what she calls "her own house" could be seen in her subsequent efforts: in the short *Compton in C Minor* (2007) and the alternative hip hop documentary *This Is the Life* (2008), which showcased the history of L.A.'s Good Life Cafe's arts movement (Martin 2014).

To contextualize DuVernay, Michael T. Martin situates her in a history of black cinema that extends from the "race movies" screened in segregated theaters. These films can be traced to the new realism that marked the black independent cinema of the 1960s and the 1970s, especially in the documentary format as seen in William Greaves, Madeline Anderson, and St. Claire Bourne; or the L.A. school that included Charles Burnett, Julie Dash, Billy Woodberry, and Haile Gerima; or the Black Arts movement with Larry Neal and Amiri Baraka. DuVernay has also stated that her biggest frustration about Hollywood is the abysmally low number of female studio directors.

Her earliest films, such as *I Will Follow* (2010) and *Middle of Nowhere* (2012), feature strong women characters who not only have agency but also complex subjectivities which magnify a black identity that also carries the burden of cultural transmission and generational memories. *Middle of Nowhere* showed a young woman and her inner experiences as she cared for her husband who had been sentenced to eight years in prison. The tangled racial complexity and history of incarceration would be taken up by DuVernay in the *13th* (2013) as well, but for *Middle of Nowhere*, DuVernay won the 2012 Independent Spirit John Cassavetes Award. The film also premiered in the 2012 Sundance Festival, winning the U.S. Directing Award: Dramatic, making her the first African American woman to win the prize.

Her most famous film perhaps, *Selma* (2014), dramatized the 1965 protests for voting rights in Alabama led by Martin Luther King, Jr. It won DuVernay accolades and critical acclaim, making her the first African American to be nominated for a Golden Globe and a Best Picture Oscar. *Selma* faced criticism, as some felt the representation of Martin Luther King, Jr. and President Lyndon Johnson was not historically accurate. However, DuVernay specified that she is neither a historian nor a "custodian of anyone's legacy" but a storyteller. Indeed the representation of diversity in DuVernay's films is what is paramount, and as the lack of diversity became a heated point of discussion at the Academy Awards that year. Prominent African American actors and directors, including DuVernay, have pointed out that this problem is very systemic.

While the themes and subject matter of her films reflect her positions clearly, it is her unique handling of these themes that rearrange and rework the relation between history and narrative that has defined her position as a filmmaker who speaks politically about black empowerment. In 2016, she created *August 28: A Day in the Life of a People*, which was commissioned by the Smithsonian's National Museum of African American History and Culture. It portrayed six events in African American history that occurred on August 28, such as William IV's royal assent to the UK Slavery Abolition Act in 1833, the release of Motown's first number-one song, "Please Mr. Postman" by The Marvellettes, Martin Luther King, Jr.'s "I Have a Dream" speech, and the night then-Senator Barack Obama won the Democratic nomination for president at the 2008 Democratic National Convention. The film featured a variety of stars, including Don Cheadle, Angela Bassett, and Lupita Nyong'o, among others.

Her next endeavor was a documentary entitled the *13th* (2016). For that she received an Oscar nomination in the feature documentary category and won a Peabody Award in 2017. The title is a reference to the Thirteenth Amendment to the U.S. Constitution that abolished slavery. It dealt with the complex issue of criminalization and the disproportionate number of African Americans in the U.S. prison system. In charting out the different historical and legal injustices that exploited the black body, the documentary reflects on the present and the irony of history that repeats itself.

Her latest feature, *A Wrinkle in Time* (2018), is a science fiction/fantasy film based on the eponymous novel by Madeline L'Engle. With this project, she became the first woman of color to direct a live-action film with a budget of more than $100 million and only the second woman to do so after Patty Jenkins, who directed *Wonder Woman* (2017). The film was lauded for its message of female empowerment and diversity.

DuVernay has expressed a desire to cultivate a black cinematic image in "an organized and consistent" way, to have a niche market for such films which DuVernay defines as being "self-determining." This self-avowed activism can be seen in DuVernay's other enterprises, such as the AFFRM (African-American Film Festival Releasing Movement), which she started in 2010 to distribute films made by or on black people. DuVernay has referred to AFFRM as "a call to action" (Martin 2014). DuVernay's production company, called Forward Movement, also espouses a similar desire for a commercial space that allows her to tell stories from her "narrative point of view" (Martin 2014).

The DuVernay test, the race equivalent to the Bechdel test, was suggested by *The New York Times* film critic Manohla Dargis and asks whether "African-Americans and other minorities have fully realized lives rather than serve as scenery in white stories" (Dargis 2017).

Susan Haris

See also: Carter, Ruth E.; Gardner, Dede; Jenkins, Patty

Further Reading

Cieply, Michael. 2011 "Building an Alliance to Aid Films by Blacks." *The New York Times*, January 7. https://www.nytimes.com/2011/01/08/movies/08urban.html

Dargis, Manohla. 2017. "Sundance Fights Tide with Films Like 'The Birth of a Nation.'" *The New York Times*, December 21. www.nytimes.com/2016/01/30/movies/sundance-fights-tide-with-films-like-the-birth-of-a-nation.html

Harris, Mark. 2015. "How 'Selma' Got Smeared." Grantland, January 28. www.grantland.com/features/selma-oscars-academy-awards-historical-accuracy-controversy/

Martin, Michael T. 2014. "Conversations with Ava DuVernay—'A Call to Action': Organizing Principles of an Activist Cinematic Practice." *Black Camera* 6(1): 57–91.

Milliken, Mary. 2015. "'Selma' Director Makes History before Awards Are Bestowed." Reuters, January 6, www.reuters.com/article/us-film-selma-duvernay/selma-director-makes-history-before-awards-are-bestowed-idUSKBN0KF1W620150106

Siegel, Tatiana. 2015. "Ava DuVernay on Advocating for Female Directors, Her 'Low' 'Selma' Moment." *The Hollywood Reporter*, November 18, www.hollywoodreporter.com/news/ava-duvernay-advocating-female-directors-840942

Guy-Blaché, Alice (1873–1968)

Alice Guy-Blaché was one of the most prolific female filmmakers of the silent era and a key figure in the development of narrative film. She directed and produced hundreds of films in her lifetime, predominantly narrative shorts, many of which are lost. At least one critic has attributed Guy-Blaché's "disappearance" from film history to the scant availability of her films, a great number of which have been found worldwide since the 1980s, fueling renewed critical interest in this leading figure (Hastie 2002, 29–59). She is famously known as the first and only woman to build and own a production studio, the Solax Film Company in New Jersey, and maintains a dominant place in feminist film history and criticism.

In her native France, Guy-Blaché worked with a central figure of the early film movement, the inventor and motion picture pioneer Léon Gaumont, for whose studio she wrote, directed, and produced one of the earliest narrative films, *La Fée aux Choux* [*The Cabbage Fairy*] (1896). Her relationship to Gaumont and access to his recording studio subsequently paved the path to work on a great number of narrative films, which she wrote and directed, persistently refining her skill to render onscreen genres ranging from comedies, to dramas, to historical fiction. Guy-Blaché additionally oversaw the now-iconic hand tinting of color films like *Le depart d'Arlequin et de Pierrette* [*Pierrette's Escapades*] (1900) for Gaumont. One central theme that threads through her work during this period is that of the juxtaposition of folk wisdom with the demands of modern life, which especially shows in her famous satire about the cravings of pregnant women in *Madame a des envies* [*Madame Has Her Cravings*] (1900). Because of Gaumont's experiments with early sound motion picture technology, especially his invention of the synchronous sound recording technology with the Chronophone, Guy-Blaché additionally became exposed to and was one of the earliest directors to work with sound.

Guy-Blaché married another Gaumont employee, Herbert Blaché, in 1907. Although the couple would eventually divorce in 1920, Herbert Blaché's move to Cleveland in order to begin a Gaumont Chronophone franchise the same year of their marriage signaled Guy-Blaché's departure from Paris, France, as well. Shortly after her arrival in the United States in 1907, Guy-Blaché established what from 1912 onward became the Solax film studio, a state-of-the-art facility that channeled natural light through glass ceilings and enabled better filming conditions. Within the first years at Solax, Guy-Blaché produced hundreds of short films. She was a recognizable figure in the industry and among the movie audiences of the time. Guy-Blaché's productivity was recognized already during her lifetime when a 1912 *New York Clipper* article noted her to be the second most prolific film producer and director.

Despite her tireless dedication to filmmaking, Guy-Blaché and her studio chiefly produced short one-reelers and could not meet the demands of the rise in popularity of the longer, multireel narrative film in the mid-1910s. Her signature comedies produced and directed in this period—which recall the gentle and playful characterization of fairies, children, and gentle female figures from her time with Gaumont—include relationship comedies in which couples work out false infidelity claims such as seen in *A House Divided* (1913). Though popular in their own right, these comedies were not financially lucrative ventures in comparison to feature films.

Solax's financial struggles forced Guy-Blaché to direct films for other film studios such as Popular Plays and Players. She additionally became affiliated with what would within a decade become one of the largest distribution companies, Metro Pictures. Such ties to other industry giants, coupled with her brand-name recognition that she harnessed through her work with Solax, brought her in touch with the star actress Olga Petrova. In collaboration with Petrova, Guy-Blaché directed a number of films, including *The Tigress* (1914), *The Vampire* (1915), and *What Will People Say* (1916)—all of which featured strong female characters (Slide 1996, 26).

Although Guy-Blaché was not singularly interested in exploring and depicting the struggle of women in her films, a great number of the surviving features, especially the later narrative films such as those that included Petrova, do precisely that. Women comprised the majority of the film audience in the 1910s, and actresses enjoyed an equal (if not exceeding) popularity when compared to that of their male counterparts (Musser 2009, 81). Guy-Blaché herself famously remarked on the role of women in film and film production, referencing this strong influence of female audiences in a much-cited passage from a 1914 *Moving Picture World* essay: "There is nothing connected to the staging of a motion picture that a woman cannot do as easily as a man, and there is no reason why she cannot completely master every technicality of the art" (Guy-Blaché 2014, 329). For Guy-Blaché, the film industry formed an opportunity for women to explore the potential of this new medium, to make it their own. She, along with pioneering American female director Lois Weber, would lead by example. However, the film industry made it difficult for Guy-Blaché to maintain her reputation. Guy-Blaché's name frequently was left out from advertisements and other promotional materials for her films, which steadily marginalized her in the industry.

Unlike her ex-husband, Alice Guy-Blaché never remarried, choosing instead to return to France after the divorce, where she would lecture on film and write magazine fiction and novelizations of film scripts for the next 30 years. Guy-Blaché returned to the United States in 1964 to stay with one of her daughters and passed away on March 24, 1968, at the age of 94.

Ervin Malakaj

See also: Shipman, Nell; Weber, Lois

Further Reading

Guy-Blaché, Alice. 2014. "Woman's Place in Photoplay Production." In *Film Manifestos and Global Cinema Cultures: A Critical Anthology*. Edited by Scott MacKenzie. Berkeley: University of California Press, 328–330.

Hastie, Amelie. 2002. "Circuits of Memory and History: The Memoirs of Alice Guy-Blaché." In *A Feminist Reader in Early Cinema*. Edited by Jennifer M. Bean and Diane Negra. Durham, NC: Duke University Press, 29–60.

McMahan, Alison. 2002. *Alice Guy-Blaché: Lost Visionary of the Cinema.* New York: Continuum.

Musser, Charles. 2009. "The Wages of Feminism: Alice Guy-Blaché and Her Late Feature Films." In *Alice Guy-Blaché: Cinema Pioneer.* Edited by Joan Simon. New Haven, CT: Yale University Press, 81–101.

Simon, Joan. 2009. "The Great Adventure: Alice Guy-Blaché, Cinema Pioneer." In *Alice Guy-Blaché: Cinema Pioneer.* Edited by Joan Simon. New Haven, CT: Yale University Press, 1–33.

Slide, Anthony. 1996. *The Silent Feminists: America's First Women Directors.* London: Scarecrow Press.

Jenkins, Patty (1971–)

Patty Jenkins, who started as a screenwriter and director in the realm of independent American cinema, has worked steadily in television and reached a career pinnacle as she progressed to the upper echelons of blockbuster filmmaking. Hollywood in the new millennium is marked by the major studios' intensified blockbuster efforts. As the director of *Wonder Woman* (2017), Jenkins became the first female director of a studio superhero movie and now belongs to a group of contemporary Hollywood directors who can be trusted with valuable, and profitable, intellectual property.

After studying painting, Patty Jenkins, a self-described "army brat," quickly changed her goals after taking an experimental film class and changed her major. Between graduating from The Cooper Union for the Advancement of Science and Art in 1993 and receiving her master's in directing from the American Film Institute (AFI) in 2000, Jenkins worked as a camera operator, honing her filmmaking skills on countless commercials and music videos. After directing several short films at AFI, such as *Velocity Rules*—her AFI thesis film, which won in the Short Film category at the 2001 Telluride Indiefest—and *Just Drive* (also from 2001), Jenkins secured funding for her first feature film, the character study *Monster* (2003), an indie drama about a female serial killer that earned protagonist, Charlize Theron, an Oscar for her performance.

While *Monster* was a success that opened up opportunities for Jenkins, most of them either fell apart or were postponed. After becoming a mother, Jenkins began steadily working in television. She shot episodes of *Arrested Development* and *Entourage*, among other shows. Her Emmy-nominated pilot of *The Killing*, the American version of the Danish television show, regained her critical applause. Shortly after, at the behest of Natalie Portman, Patty Jenkins was hired by Marvel Studios to helm the maligned superhero blockbuster *Thor: The Dark World* (2013), but the collaboration quickly fell through. Although she argues that she "can't take on the history of 50 percent of the population because [she's] a woman," Patty Jenkins has been careful in selecting projects due to gender politics. Alluding to Marvel's tentpole movie from which she walked away, Jenkins considers that directing a project that she knew was troubled would have been a "big disservice to women" and would have sent "a very bad message" (Siegel 2017).

After Michelle MacLaren exited the production of *Wonder Woman* (2017) over creative differences, Warner Bros. hired Jenkins to direct the $150 million superhero movie. As it was widely reported at the time, Warner Bros. was under pressure to commit to hiring a woman to direct its upcoming female superhero movie. As part of a trend regarding the employment practices of contemporary major Hollywood studios, Jenkins follows in the footsteps of other directors who were plucked from independent cinema straight into blockbuster filmmaking with no previous experience directing big-screen action, such as Colin Trevorrow (*Jurassic World*, 2015) or Jon Watts (*Spider-Man: Homecoming*, 2017). Her gender being "important" but not "critical" to the project, Patty Jenkins brought her vision to the *Wonder Woman* film, shaped alongside screenwriter Allan Heinberg, one that has been described as "post-feminist," as Jenkins "strove to temper the character's traditional strength with vulnerability" (Siegel 2017). At the same time, the director had to work within Warner Bros.' already established extended universe of comic book movies, adhering to a certain code of tone, tempo, and style set by Zack Snyder in *Batman v. Superman: Dawn of Justice* (2016), wherein this iteration of Wonder Woman (Gal Gadot) made her debut.

A resounding success, Jenkins's *Wonder Woman*—the first female-led superhero film in more than a decade—became the highest-grossing superhero movie led by a female character, as well as the highest-grossing live-action film directed by a woman. Jenkins is only the second female director to make a movie with a budget of more than $100 million (the first was Kathryn Bigelow with 2002's *K-19: The Widowmaker*), and she now holds the record for the largest opening of all time for a female director, with *Wonder Woman* taking in an estimated $100.5 million at the box office.

Influenced by 1970s filmmaking, Jenkins considers herself an "emotional filmmaker" instead of a visual filmmaker such as David Fincher, so even though she's "very educated in visuals" she comes at her craft from a completely "emotional place" (Horowitz 2006, 118–119). Working within the constraints of the superhero origin story, *Wonder Woman* was heralded for its distinctive gaze as female bodies are celebrated yet not ogled or objectified. Fights were choreographed and shot in an unusual way, more akin to a dance, staged without disproportionate editing and with a focus on showcasing different styles according to the characters' particular abilities.

Some of Patty Jenkins's accolades include an Independent Spirit Award, in 2004, for Best First Feature, which she won for her work in *Monster*, having also been nominated for Best Screenplay. That same year, the director also received the Franklin J. Schaffner Alumni Medal from the American Film Institute. For her direction in the pilot episode of *The Killing*, Jenkins was nominated for an Emmy, in 2011, for Outstanding Directing for a Drama Series. In 2012, Patty Jenkins received two nominations from the Directors Guild Awards. For the pilot of *The Killing*, she was nominated, and won, in the category of Outstanding Directorial Achievement in Dramatic Series. She was also nominated for the segment "Pearl," for Outstanding Directorial Achievement in Movies for Television/ Mini-Series in *Five*, which explored the impact of breast cancer in different people's lives.

Ana Cabral Martins

See also: Bigelow, Kathryn; DuVernay, Ava

Further Reading

Bell-Metereau, Rebecca. 2015. *Star Bodies and the Erotics of Suffering.* Detroit: Wayne State University Press.

Horowitz, Joshua. 2006. *The Mind of the Modern Moviemaker: Twenty Conversations with the New Generation of Filmmakers.* London: Penguin.

Hurd, Mary G. 2007. *Women Directors and Their Films.* Westport, CT: Greenwood Publishing Group.

McCreadie, Marsha. 2006. *Women Screenwriters Today: Their Lives and Words.* Westport, CT: Greenwood Publishing Group.

Siegel, Tatiana. 2017. "The Complex Gender Politics of the 'Wonder Woman' Movie." *The Hollywood Reporter*, May 31. https://www.hollywoodreporter.com/features/complex-gender-politics-wonder-woman-movie-1008259

Lupino, Ida (1918–1995)

In the midst of a successful acting career, Ida Lupino co-founded a production company for which she wrote, produced, and/or directed eight films during the early to mid-1950s; she was the only female director of this period. By the end of the decade, Lupino had moved on to acting and directing for television, a medium in which she primarily remained for the rest of her career. It is, however, the five films she directed and wrote (or co-wrote) during the end of the Classic Hollywood period that make up Lupino's greatest contribution to the world of film.

Born on February 4, in London, England, to a family with a long history on the stage, Ida Lupino began her own acting career at the age of 13 while studying at the Royal Academy of Dramatic Arts. She appeared in a number of British films in the early 1930s before coming to Hollywood with a Paramount contract. Several years, and films, later, she switched over to Warner Bros.

It was while Lupino was under contract at Warner Brothers that she began to consider the creative process behind the camera. While Lupino insisted that she created her own style of filmmaking, she did admit to taking inspiration from directors Raoul Walsh, William Wellman, Stanley Kramer, Robert Rossen, Louis de Rochemont, Charles Vidor, Robert Aldrich, Fritz Lang, Michael Curtiz, and Roberto Rossellini, as well as cinematographer George Barnes.

Lupino ended her contract with Warner Brothers in 1948 and formed Emerald Productions, an independent film company, with her second husband, Collier Young, and John Anson Ford. Lupino's entrance into the world of film direction came as a matter of expediency. Early in the production of *Not Wanted* (1949), Emerald Productions' first film, director Elmer Clifton suffered a heart attack; Lupino took over and finished the film, on time and under budget. She did not take screen credit on the film and always insisted that she only stepped in to save money. Lupino adjusted the script written by Malvin Wald and turned it into a sympathetic portrayal of an unmarried mother. She used unknown talent for the lead roles, shot on location, and insisted on racial diversity in her casting—all elements that became part of Lupino's pattern.

Following the 1949 release of *Not Wanted*, Eleanor Roosevelt invited Lupino on to her radio show to discuss the film. Most of the mail Emerald Productions received after the interview was positive. The same year, Lupino became a member of the Screen Directors Guild of America, making her the second female member (and the only one working) of the organization after Dorothy Arzner, and immediately began work on her next film.

Never Fear, also released in 1949, uses the same lead actors as *Not Wanted* to portray the effects of polio on the life and relationship of a dancer, a topic close to Lupino's heart since she suffered a mild case of polio herself in the 1930s. Continuing the pattern set up in the previous film, Lupino used a documentary style, working-class characters, and scenes shot in a rehabilitation unit with actual polio patients and medical staff. As part of the promotion for *Never Fear*, Lupino and Young announced in *Variety* that they planned to "explore new themes, try new ideas, [and] discover new talents" (Silver and Ursini 2012, 225).

In early 1950, the company changed its name to The Filmmakers; Lupino served as vice president, producer, screenwriter, director, actor, and, occasionally, set and costume designer. This level of involvement in her company's films gave Lupino control to a degree that would have been impossible within a major studio, a fact she readily admitted. Working outside the studio system also gave her the ability to pick her own projects and themes. While it was not unusual for a movie star to start a production company during this time period, Lupino stands out because of both her gender and her success as a director. Lupino later remembered The Filmmakers period as "thrilling days" and the "happiest of her life" in which she co-wrote, co-produced, and directed films with "pretty daring" topics, each in less than two weeks and with a budget of less than $200,000 (Heck-Rabi 1984, 239; Koszarski 1977, 375). She also starred in four films for other companies during this time, primarily to help finance projects at The Filmmakers.

Lupino's third film, *Outrage*, built on her previous pattern of using unknown leads, shooting on location, and including racial diversity in the cast. This time, Lupino sympathetically addressed the issue of rape; the violence occurred offscreen. By the time *Outrage* was released in mid-1950, The Filmmakers had signed a deal with Howard Hughes and his studio, RKO. About this time, Ford left the company and Wald came on board.

Because of the edgy subject matter of her films: teenage pregnancy, rape, bigamy, etc., Lupino often found herself at odds with the Production Code Administration (PCA); however, Lupino maintained a civil relationship with the members of the PCA and even managed to keep some elements considered problematic by most Americans in her films. In fact, film historian Annette Kuhn argues that "the independently-minded and multi-talented Lupino evidently flourished in such challenging conditions" (Kuhn 1995, 6). Lupino and her team at The Filmmakers also appear not to have been cowed by the House Committee on Un-American Activities (HUAC) or other "patriotic pressure groups" (Stewart 1980, 76).

Lupino's first film with RKO is a bit of a departure from her earlier films. *Hard, Fast and Beautiful* (1951) is the first of her films with a lead, Claire Trevor, already well known to movie audiences. Additionally, Hughes's influence is apparent in the movie's title. In January 1951, during production of *Hard, Fast and Beautiful*,

Lupino received an award from *Holiday* magazine, recognizing her as "the woman in the motion-picture industry who has done the most to improve standards and to honestly present American life, ideals and people to the rest of the world" (Heck-Rabi 1984, 232).

It was nearly two years before another Lupino-directed film hit theaters, although Lupino was busy with other aspects of her production company in the interim. When she did return to her place behind the camera, the resulting film once again took Lupino into uncharted territory. *The Hitch-Hiker* (1953) was the first film noir picture directed by a woman and featured a nearly all-male cast of unknown actors. In this film, Lupino continued her dedication to racial diversity by depicting Mexican civilians and police in an authentic and positive light. Using her usual documentary style, Lupino wrote a screenplay based on the actual crimes of a serial killer, keeping so many of the details the same that she ran into trouble not only with the PCA but also with the Federal Bureau of Investigation (FBI). Lupino later rated *The Hitch-Hiker* one of her favorite films.

Lupino's last directed film with The Filmmakers also came out in 1953. *The Bigamist* is significant as the first film in which a woman directed herself. Lupino found this dual role difficult, but eventually considered this film to be one of her favorites. While *The Bigamist* differed from Lupino's other films in that it had well-known leads: Joan Fontaine, Edmund Gwenn, and Lupino herself, in many other aspects the film followed Lupino's pattern. She portrayed the title character sympathetically, used working-class settings, rejected glamorous and villainous female characters, and injected humor into the tense storyline.

At about this time, Lupino's partners, despite her objections, decided to attempt distribution of their own films, including *The Bigamist*. By the time the company folded in 1954, it had produced 12 movies; Lupino directed or co-directed 6, wrote or co-wrote 5, co-produced 1, and acted in 3. Following the dissolution of The Filmmakers, Lupino turned to television, where she enjoyed a successful career as a director, producer, and actor. She returned to film directing a final time in 1966 with Columbia's *The Trouble with Angels*. This film, staring Rosalind Russell and Hayley Mills, is a much different style of movie than Lupino made previously; however, it still addresses women's issues. Ida Lupino died of cancer on August 3, 1995.

When taken as a group, Lupino's films during this period reveal several similarities. She turned film noir on its head by portraying men in the irrational and dangerous roles usually reserved for women in this movie genre. Lupino's characters are unsure of how to act once they are outside the familiar, safe environment set up at the beginning of her films; they are passive and nearing breakdown in the face of these difficult situations. Always sympathetic, Lupino portrayed these characters with what film historian Ronnie Scheib calls an "almost maternal concern" (Kuhn 1995, 55). Lupino used the lives of individuals to comment on the social problems of her day. Lupino is often described as Neorealist, portraying female characters devoid of glamour, members of the working class, and inexperienced in the ways of the world. According to Kuhn, Ida Lupino is important because she "is the least invisible face in an entire hidden army of women working in various media production jobs in these years: scriptwriters, editors, continuity girls, and many more" (Kuhn 1995, 7).

Rebekah A. Crowe

See also: Arzner, Dorothy

Further Reading

Hannsberry, Karen Burroughs. 1998. *Femme Noir: Bad Girls of Film*. Jefferson, NC: McFarland.

Heck-Rabi, Louise. 1984. *Women Filmmakers: A Critical Reception.* Metuchen, NJ: Scarecrow Press.

Hurd, Mary G. 2007. *Women Directors and Their Films.* Westport, CT: Praeger.

Kay, Karyn, and Gerald Peary. 1977. *Women and the Cinema: A Critical Anthology.* New York: Dutton.

Koszarski, Richard. 1977. *Hollywood Directors: 1941–1976.* New York: Oxford University Press.

Kuhn, Annette, ed. 1995. *Queen of the 'B's: Ida Lupino Behind the Camera.* Westport, CT: Greenwood Press.

Silver, Alain, and James Ursini, eds. 2012. *Film Noir: The Directors.* Milwaukee: Limelight Editions.

Stewart, Lucy Ann Liggett. 1980. *Ida Lupino as Film Director, 1949–1953: An Auteur Approach.* New York: Arno.

Marshall, Penny (1943–)

Penny Marshall started her career in network television, where she starred in several popular series such as *The Odd Couple*, *Mary Tyler Moore*, *All in the Family*, *Happy Days*, and *Laverne & Shirley.* Marshall found success as Laverne DeFazio in *Laverne & Shirley*, earning three Golden Globe nominations. In the late 1970s, she directed four episodes of the show. In 1986, she made her first foray into film, directing her first feature film, *Jumpin' Jack Flash.* This was the start of a limited but illustrious career. Despite numerous production obstacles with her first two films and limited cinematic directorial credits in her career, Marshall is a trailblazer for women pursing directorial positions in a male-dominated film industry.

Due to problems early in production, Howard Zieff, director of *Jumpin' Jack Flash,* needed to be replaced. After attending a birthday dinner for the lead actor in the film, Marshall was offered the position. Unsure if she wanted to commit, she asked her brother, director Garry Marshall, for advice. He told her, "It's a strange business; they pay you to learn" (Marshall 2012, 204). Despite being unfamiliar with the process, she heeded her brother's advice and agreed to direct the film, which ended up being a life-changing decision.

Before Marshall found success, however, she struggled. *Jumpin' Jack Flash* was not well received, including criticisms regarding Marshall's ability to manage a feature film. Vincent Canby (1986) of *The New York Times* wrote, "Miss Marshall directs "Jumpin' Jack Flash" as if she were more worried about the decor than the effect of the performance." Echoing Canby, Roger Ebert (1986) argued that even "under the shaky hand of director Penny Marshall, the story doesn't even achieve coherence." Despite these negative reviews, *Jumpin' Jack Flash* served as Marshall's education. Taking what she learned, Marshall ensured that her next film was big, really *Big* (1988).

With *Big*, Marshall became the first woman to direct a film that grossed over $100 million (Silverstein 2013, ix). Like *Jumpin' Jack Flash,* however, Marshall had difficulties. Marshall struggled to find a lead, as many bankable stars turned down the role: Tom Hanks, Kevin Costner, and Dennis Quaid. Marshall was elated when she convinced Robert De Niro to consider the part, but she was soon disappointed that Fox would not pay him what she considered a fair wage. Frustrated, she turned to her Hollywood family and friends for advice, including Jim Brooks, who recommended she give De Niro her salary.

Eventually, Tom Hanks agreed to play the role, but production problems followed. Marshall admits that *Big* was a learning process, and there were numerous instances in which she had to reshoot scenes. In addition to problems during production, she suffered a miscarriage during this time. After medical treatment, she returned to set where she finished directing "while lying on the floor" (Marshall 2012, 224).

After her success with *Big*, Sony Pictures courted Marshall. She recalled them saying, "If you come with us we'll even let you do that girls movie" (Marshall 2012, 248). That "girls movie," *A League of Their Own* (1992), would be an impressive follow-up to *Big*, also grossing over $100 million. At the time, however, Marshall did not know that this "girls movie" would be her greatest achievement.

A League of Their Own was groundbreaking for a variety of reasons. It was a major film with a mostly female cast and a female director, and the plot focused on an all-women baseball team during World War II. Its popularity across demographics debunked the belief that men were uninterested in movies starring mostly women—a belief that plagued female storytellers for years. Not only did audiences like *A League of Their Own*, but they were also inspired by it, and its impact remains today. Geena Davis, who played Dottie Hinson, reflects on the movie, "I still have the same number of girls and women telling me they play sports because of that movie now as I did then. It's like a rite of passage to see this movie. It's got remarkable longevity" (Olsen 2017).

Sony, however, did not see the movie as a surefire hit, and Marshall had to fight for her creative choices. Reflecting proudly on the movie, she recounts Steven Spielberg asking her if he could use a similar ending for his upcoming picture, *Schindler's List* (1993). He was impressed that Marshall ended the movie not with actors Geena Davis or Tom Hanks, but with the women who had played in the All-American Girls Professional Baseball League. While her own studio president was unhappy with this decision, Marshall persisted and was rewarded in positive test screenings, box office success, and Spielberg's admiration. Marshall wanted the movie to be about the women who inspired the movie—to show how their story is important and inspiring.

Marshall would go on to direct 10 movies and is probably best remembered for *A League of Their Own*. Another celebrated movie, *Awakenings* (1990), received three Oscar nominations, although Marshall herself was not nominated. In her book, she notes being "left out of celebrations," hosting a non-nominee party (Marshall 2012, 246). Her lack of acclaim, however, did not matter, as she had already solidified herself as a pioneer and Hollywood heroine.

Melissa Vosen Callens

See also: Lewis, Ellen; Pascal, Amy

Further Reading

Canby, Vincent. 1986. "Screen: Whoopi Goldberg in 'Jumpin' Jack Flash.'" *The New York Times*, October 10. http://www.nytimes.com/movie/review?res=9A0DE2DD113FF933A25753C1A960948260?&mcubz=1

Ebert, Roger. 1986. "'Jumpin' Jack Flash.'" October 10. http://www.rogerebert.com/reviews/jumpin-jack-flash-1986

IMDb. 2017. "Penny Marshall." Accessed December 17, 2017. http://www.imdb.com/name/nm0001508

Marshall, Penny. 2012. *My Mother Was Nuts: A Memoir*. New York: Houghton Mifflin Harcourt.

Olsen, Mark. 2017. "On 'A League of Their Own's' 25th Anniversary, Geena Davis Still Isn't Afraid to Say 'Feminist.'" July 1. http://www.latimes.com/entertainment/movies/la-et-mn-geena-davis-a-league-of-their-own-25th-anniversary-interview-20170701-htmlstory.html

Silverstein, Melissa. 2013. *In Her Voice: Women Directors Talk Directing*. Women and Hollywood.

Riefenstahl, Leni (1902–2003)

Leni Riefenstahl was a German director, producer, screenwriter, and actress who remains most known for her propaganda film *Triumph des Willens* ("Triumph of the Will," 1935) and German documentary film *Olympia* (1938). This film, though noted for its framing, editing, and direction, is a subject of controversy, as it glorified Adolf Hitler during the 1934 Nazi Party Congress in Nuremberg. The film is still classified as among the most effective propaganda films of all times.

An active child, Riefenstahl participated in swimming and fine arts before becoming a celebrated dancer. She performed as a dancer throughout continental Europe before becoming an actress. After starring in five successful films between 1925 and 1929, she directed herself in the 1932 film *Das Blaue Licht* (*The Blue Light*). This narrative film, written in part by Hungarian Jewish academic Béla Balázs, featured Riefenstahl in the starring role of Junta, a young woman considered to be a witch by her fellow townspeople. After she misplaces her trust in an outsider who steals all of her crystals, she falls to her death. The film, which was heralded by European right-wing publications and denounced by left-wing writers, achieved moderate success as an example of Alpine cinema. The Venice Film Festival awarded the film its Silver Medal, and American publications such as *The New York Times* praised its pictorial beauty. The film's depiction of nature in the Alps is said to have contributed to Hitler's commissioning Riefenstahl to make propaganda films.

As an unofficial executive producer for *Triumph des Willens*, Adolf Hitler demonstrated his support for Riefenstahl's filmmaking career. In this film, Riefenstahl pioneered techniques such as moving cameras, aerial photography, and long-focus lenses. With his and Joseph Goebbels's (the Reich Minister of Propaganda) support, Riefenstahl was able to plan and diagram the Congress's actions and was able to rehearse movements and speeches endlessly. On a technical level, she was also deeply concerned with how the soundtrack paired up with and influenced the effects of the visual images. Film historians estimate that when editing for a two-hour propaganda film, Riefenstahl had over 61 hours' worth of material from which to work.

Triumph des Willens was an immediate success in Germany, becoming among the most profitable films of 1935. For her work, Riefenstahl received the German Film Prize, the Venice Biennale's gold medal, and the World Exhibition's Grand Prix. Though filmmakers and critics outside of Germany acknowledged the impressive technical aesthetic, most were wary of the overt propagandistic themes.

Following the Nazi Party's acceptance and celebration of *Triumph des Willens*, Riefenstahl was again called upon in service to the state, to record and document the 1936 Olympic Games in Berlin. The resultant film, *Olympia*, like its propagandistic predecessor, received widespread acclaim for its innovative shot composition and editing. The film used unusual camera angles, smash cuts, extreme close-ups, and tracking shot rails on bleachers. Released in 1938, two years after the Olympic Games, the film was the first documentary to be made of any Olympic Games. Additionally, the film influenced Olympic history by introducing the torch relay as a feature of the Olympic pageantry. The film also won several notable awards, including the National Film Prize, the Best Film of the Venice International Film Festival, and the Olympic Gold Medal awarded by the Comité International Olympique.

After World War II, the Allied Forces imprisoned Riefenstahl for four years for being a Nazi sympathizer. She was permanently blacklisted from the film industry for her role in making such an effective propaganda film and died more than 68 years after *Triumph des Willens* premiered. She unsuccessfully tried to make more films, most notably with French director Jean Cocteau and Scientology founder L. Ron Hubbard, but she was met with widespread resistance. Following her blacklist, she developed an interest in Africa and traveled repeatedly to Kenya and Sudan, living among and photographing the Nuba tribes. She published two bestselling photography books, *Die Nuba* (*The Last of the Nuba*) in 1973 and *Die Nuba von Kau* (*The Nuba People of Kau*) in 1976. She also served as a photographer at the 1972 Olympic Games in Munich and was invited as a guest of honor to the 1976 Olympic Games in Montreal.

As a director, Riefenstahl only made eight films, of which only two are commonly known outside of Germany. For a young female director during the time period, her work is impressive but cannot be divorced from its political context. Some are able to overlook the underlying thematic focus on the German state under Hitler, pointing especially to Riefenstahl's heroic framing of Jesse Owens in the film *Olympia*. Nevertheless, throughout her life Riefenstahl claimed to have no knowledge of the concentration camps. Throughout the remainder of her life she battled libel cases that claimed she was a Nazi, declaring that the biggest regret of her life was meeting Adolf Hitler.

Riefenstahl is a controversial figure because of her relationship to Adolf Hitler and the Nazi Party. While her propaganda films were very successful within Germany, film historians have found unclear evidence as to whether or not her films helped to convert any apathetic or anti-Nazi Germans into Nazi proponents or apologists. Her films, though aesthetically stunning, do, however, present Hitler and the Nazis as reified superhumans, able to bring Germany back to glory. The very fact that *Triumph des Willens* depicts no scenes with explicit anti-Semitism demonstrates the insidiousness of an immoral institutional system that blinded its citizens and the outside world to the horrors enacted by the Nazi Party.

When she died of cancer on September 8, 2003, Riefenstahl was 101 years old. Her obituary was carried by the world's most prominent news organizations, all of which commented both on the political nature of her propaganda and on the importance of her work as a technical innovator and as a young female director in a male-dominated industry and society.

Eleanor M. Huntington

Further Reading

Bach, Steven. 2007. *Leni: The Life and Work of Leni Riefenstahl.* New York: Knopf.

Gunston, David. 1960. "Leni Riefenstahl." *Film Quarterly* 14(1): 4–19.

Soussloff, Catherine M., and Bill Nichols. 1996. "The Power of the Image." *Discourse* 18(3): 20–44.

Shipman, Nell (1892–1970)

Nell Shipman, born Helen Foster Barnham, was a pioneer of the silent film era of early Hollywood as an actress, screenwriter, producer, and director. She owned her own production company and wrote, starred in, and produced the highest-grossing Canadian silent film of all time entitled *Back to God's Country* (1919), taking plenty of liberty with its source material to execute her own vision. Yet this woman's film career came almost to standstill in 1925, only six years after the immense success of *Back to God's Country* and four after the opening of her own company. The difficulties she experienced with her company were not those of a woman filmmaker so much as an independent one; however, both qualities were detrimental to Shipman's career and company when Hollywood became an industrialized business. Her legacy was largely forgotten, though recently she has been remembered for the wilderness themes and female heroines who featured in her films.

With the rise of cinema in the early 20th century had come an astonishing number of women working in the industry. For this, film historians credit its inheritance from vaudeville and the stage (areas in which women had been prominent), a more casual attitude toward division of production roles, the idea that women's perceived moral superiority would combat cultural worries about the moral value of films, and the power of the star actress. These factors meant women were able to work across most aspects of filmmaking, and even in independent production, as some established stars went out on their own.

Initially an actress, having joined a traveling show at the age of 13, Shipman's early career trajectory in the industry appears almost accidental. In 1912, pregnant and unable to act, she started writing scenarios (the outline of a film's story) on a suggestion from her first husband. Her first job directing in 1914 was reportedly the result of the director of the film running off with the lead actress. Shipman was then called to take up the megaphone, as she had written the scenario. Despite this rather reactive turn of events, Shipman did not lack ambition and soon was calling the shots on her career. Still mostly an actress, Shipman made her name starring in the high-grossing *God's Country and the Woman* (1916), based on the work by popular novelist James Curwood. A year later, she was offered a seven-year acting contract. Her rejection is emblematic of Shipman's resistance of Hollywood hegemony and her ambition to be more than an actress. She had made an exclusive contract with James Curwood to star in and produce films of his books. This partnership would make Shipman's most successful film, *Back to God's Country* (1919)—however, the film was to be more Shipman's vision than Curwood's.

As screenwriter, Shipman wrote an adaptation of Curwood's book with which he was reportedly unhappy, rewriting the story to feature a female character that she would play. Though reflective of Shipman's interest in empowered action heroines, this also shows her savvy understanding of her craft. She recognized that Curwood's novel, a character study of a dog, did not work as a film. It is evident that Shipman had clear ideas of what made a good film and was unwilling to conform to conventional storytelling; after the completion of the film, Shipman decided "the picture needed animal sequences to lift it from the humdrum human triangle" of "Bad Man wants Girl, Good Man loves Girl, Saves Her" and accordingly shot extra scenes (Shipman 1987, 80).

Her partnership with Curwood dissolved after *Back to God's Country*, and Shipman opened Nell Shipman Productions in 1921. Based in Canada, and far from the center stage of filmmaking in Hollywood, Shipman valued her independence and protected her vision fiercely. When *The Girl from God's Country* (1921) was cut down, she sent an advertisement out to every trade paper in the industry, begging them not to book the altered film. Her control over her films was increased by her tireless involvement in almost every aspect of filmmaking. In addition to writing and starring in her films (and taming the animals), she took on the role of co-director with partner Bert Van Tuyle for almost all the films her company produced. She would work closely with Joseph Walker, a cinematographer she had recruited for his first feature film in *Back to God's Country* (he would go on to be nominated for four Academy Awards). Shipman was interested in incorporating new and technically difficult shots, such as a psychedelic montage in *Back to God's Country*, and the double exposure used for the twin characters she played in *The Girl from God's Country*. After the shooting was complete, she would edit her films and attempt to distribute them.

From 1916, however, the film industry had begun focusing on business-minded systems, shutting independent companies out as the "majors" grew in power, holding monopoly over film production and distribution. Shipman struggled to continue producing films, as it became more difficult to distribute her films and so to finance new ones. Bankrupt, her company closed in 1925. This was the fate of many independent production companies, yet it was the female filmmakers who found themselves shut out of positions of power in the industry as the divisions of labor became rigid. Additionally, the silent films for which Shipman was known were now being driven out by the era of sound. Despite this discouragement, Shipman never stopped trying to return to the film industry. In 1935, she wrote the Paramount film *Wings in the Dark*, and in 1945 produced *The Clam Digger's Daughter*. However, she never again directed or had the control she had held as one of the earliest female filmmakers.

Jess Donohoe

See also: Guy-Blaché, Alice

Further Reading

Armatage, Kay. 2003. *The Girl from God's Country: Nell Shipman and the Silent Cinema*. Toronto: University of Toronto Press.

Mahar, Karen W. 2006. *Women Filmmakers in Early Hollywood*. Baltimore: Johns Hopkins Press.

Shipman, Nell. 1987. *The Silent Screen and My Talking Heart: An Autobiography*. Edited by Tom Trusky. Boise, ID: Boise State University.

Weber, Lois (1879–1939)

Lois Weber was arguably the most important female artist working during the early years of the America film industry. The multitalented Weber worked as a director, screenwriter, producer, and film actress throughout her lengthy career that spanned more than 25 years. During this time she directed and wrote over 40 feature-length films and over 100 short films. Although she is undoubtedly one of the most significant female directors within the history of American cinema, it would be incorrect to place all emphasis on the fact that she was a woman. During the silent era she was indeed one of the most gifted directors, regardless of gender, and many of her works rivaled those of the greatest directors, such as D. W. Griffith and Cecil B. DeMille. Due to the fact that Weber often occupied multiple roles in the making of her films, she exercised nearly complete control over her works, which made her a true auteur. It was not uncommon for her to have the lead role, direct, and write the screenplay for the same film. This type of authorship was unique during a time in which the American film industry was adopting vertical integration into its business practices. Weber's films were often dramas centered around Progressive politics and social issues, such as class, ethnicity, gender roles, immigration, alcoholism, and drug use. Another common theme in her films was family life, and she dealt with problems that sometimes developed due to marriage and raising children. Her films, which typically included morals and life lessons, did not match audience desires during the loose Jazz Age of the 1920s, and she found it increasingly difficult to make films around this time. Weber was largely written out of film history for many years; however, recent cinema scholars have rediscovered her work and its importance not only within the American cinema industry but also within cinema history at large.

Lois Weber got her creative start as a singer and stage actress after moving from her hometown in Allegheny City, Pennsylvania, to New York City in 1904. It was during her acting career that she met Phillips Smalley, who would become her husband as well as her collaborator in the cinema. Weber began her film career in New York with Gaumont Talking Pictures where she simultaneously wrote, directed, and played lead roles. Smalley eventually joined her, and they collaborated on a large group of films. In 1910, Weber and her husband left Gaumont and joined the Rex Motion Picture Company where they worked with the celebrated director Edwin S. Porter. By 1913 she moved to Los Angeles, the city that was quickly becoming the capital of the American film industry. Around this time she became a part of the Universal Film Manufacturing Company that had taken over Rex. In 1914, Weber moved on to Bosworth, Inc., where she wrote and directed feature films that helped to form her image as an auteur who was concerned with the craft of filmmaking. She was a proponent of cinematic techniques such as double exposure, and had a firm understanding of the need for detailed storytelling, the psychological development of characters, and the role that the art of proficient acting plays in a film. Weber was likewise recognized for the realism that she brought to her films as well as the feminine perspective that she brought to her subject matter. The director differed from her contemporaries, in that she often used the previously mentioned cinematic techniques and methods to critique rather than reinforce bourgeois viewpoints. She eventually returned to Universal before establishing Lois Weber Productions, her own independent company, in 1917. Up until this point she had been primarily associated with the social-problem films that made up the bulk of her repertoire; however, with the emergence of her independent company Weber's focus changed to sexuality and issues related to home life. As the 1920s progressed Weber's career waned as fewer opportunities were given to female writers, directors, and producers, and Weber's moralistic style of filmmaking became outmoded during the Roaring Twenties. In 1934, she wrote and directed her final film, *White Heat,* a vehicle about an interracial relationship that was shot on location in Hawaii. It was the only film that Weber directed in synch sound and, unfortunately, did not fare well with audiences.

The director has many notable films to her name, including *A Japanese Idyll* (1912) and *Suspense* (1913) in which she questions the status quo regarding the female image. Weber directed and starred in both of these films. In the latter vehicle she is famous for demonstrating the novel split-screen technique to convey different events to the audience simultaneously. Weber was the first American woman (in collaboration with Phillips Smalley) to direct a full-length feature film, an adaptation of William Shakespeare's *The Merchant of Venice* (1914). The director also wrote the screenplay and acted in the film. She was given this unprecedented opportunity to direct by producer Carl Laemmle who was impressed with Weber and Smalley's directorial work (she also acted and wrote the screenplay) on the three-reel film, *A Jew's Christmas* (1913), which dealt with overcoming religious prejudice. The director and screenwriter dealt with social issues such as religious hypocrisy, poverty and wage inequality for women, abortion, and birth control in *Hypocrites* (1915), *Shoes, Where Are My Children* (1916), and *The Hand that Rocks the Cradle* (1917). Weber and Smalley also acted in the final film. Another important film that deserves special mention is *The Dumb Girl of Portici* (1916), an adaptation of Esprit Auber's opera, *La Muette de Portici.* Finally, it is necessary to single out *The Blot* (1921), one of the most important films that Weber directed and wrote for Lois Weber Productions. This film centers on the issue of poverty that afflicts the family of a highly educated professor who is underpaid for his meaningful contributions to society. During the production Weber utilized location shooting, natural lighting, and several nonprofessional actors as she was inclined to do throughout her career.

Weber was one of the earliest examples of a celebrity filmmaker, and she was able to use her renown to advocate for improvements, such as the necessity of quality screenplays, in the creation of movies by taking on leadership positions throughout her career, including her tenure as the mayor of Universal City. She was also a founding member of the Photoplay Authors League that was established in 1914. As time went on her image as a star maker began to overshadow her most significant accomplishments as a director and screenwriter. As Weber's career continued into the late 1910s and 1920s Hollywood began to place a strong emphasis on the glamour of its female stars, and this reinforced the notion that women belonged in front of the camera rather than behind it as a directors, producers, or scriptwriters. During the earlier years of Weber's career this mentality was quite different and it was more acceptable for women to work behind the scenes. This ideological shift helps explain why the director's star maker status was increasingly emphasized during the second half of her career. This downplaying of her arguably most important talents, namely directing and screenwriting, helped to launch Weber into obscurity. Another factor that contributed to her unfortunate fate was that her name was sometimes conflated with or even obscured by that of her husband. While there is overwhelming evidence that Weber was the main force behind the vast majority of their collaborations, Smalley sometimes received an unfair amount of recognition since he was a man. Despite Weber's neglect within cinema history, scholars have come to acknowledge her important position as one of the few female directors from cinema's inception to the present day who can be considered an auteur of the highest caliber.

Jennifer A. Zale

See also: Guy-Blaché, Alice; Marion, Frances

Further Reading

National Women's History Museum. "Lois Weber." Accessed June 8, 2016. https://www.nwhm.org/education-resources/biography/biographies/lois-weber

Slide, Anthony. 1996. *Lois Weber: The Director Who Lost Her Way in History.* Westport, CT: Greenwood Press.

Stamp, Shelley. 2015. *Lois Weber in Early Hollywood.* Oakland: University of California Press.

Wertmüller, Lina (1928–)

Lina Wertmüller is an Italian filmmaker whose films are known for her deeply political subject matter and the humor with which she treats them. She is the first woman filmmaker nominated for an Academy Award for Directing for *Seven Beauties* (1975). Wertmüller openly expresses her politics and philosophy through her films, often with low-class anarchist or communist characters. The self-claimed socialist and feminist filmmaker credits her success to her commitment to making a "popular kind of cinema" (that is, not elitist or intellectual) (Bachmann 1977, 3): Wertmüller's films are stories of "a man in relation to his society or in conflict with it, a man who arrives unprepared, naïve, and is confronted with the machinery of a certain society which he is forced to make peace with" (7). There is a wide divergence in critical receptions of her work worldwide, ranging from high praise for her originality to harsh criticisms on her political inconsistency. Wertmüller remains one of the most significant and controversial filmmakers of the 20th century.

Lina Wertmüller trained and worked in theater before she started working in film and television. Wertmüller's big break came in 1962 when she joined Federico Fellini, one of the most significant filmmakers of Italian cinema and of the 20th century, as his assistant director for the production of the now-classic *8½* (1963). Wertmuller's apprenticeship with Fellini led to her impressive debut as a director one year later, in *The Lizards* (1963), "a satiric take on provincial life and its endemic apathy" (Bullaro 2006, xv), marking the beginning of themes of social consciousness and the setting of southern Italy that recur in her films.

Wertmüller's most representative works are the four films she wrote and directed in the 1970s: *The Seduction of Mimi* (1972), *Love and Anarchy* (1973), *Swept Away by an Unusual Destiny in the Blue Sea of August* (1974), and *Seven Beauties*. *The Seduction of Mimi* and *Love and Anarchy* were nominated for the Palme d'Or at the Cannes Film Festival in 1972 and 1973, respectively. *Seven Beauties* was nominated for four Academy Awards in 1977 for Best Director, Best Writing, Best Foreign Language Film, and Best Actor in a Leading Role (for the performance of Giancarlo Giannini, who starred in the other three films as well). It received a Golden Globe Award nomination for Best Foreign Film too. Wertmüller continued to have a prolific career: *A Night Full of Rain* (1978), Wertmüller's 10th film and her first work with original dialogue in English, was nominated for the Golden Bear at the 28th Berlin International Festival in 1978, and *Camorra (A Story of Streets, Women and Crime)* (1986) would be nominated for the same award eight years later.

At the time of their release, the Wertmüller films of the 1970s were met with praise akin to religious fervor in the United States. The Italian filmmaker was "enthroned as a cinematic goddess by many for her unique, radical and controversial treatment of serious subjects" (Michalczyk 1986, 263). Although critic Gina Blumenfeld concurs that such enthusiasm for Wertmüller's films existed in the United States, Wertmüller's American fame was a subject of ridicule in Italy, as she was dubbed "Santa Lina de New York" by the press in her mother country (Bachmann 1977, 6).

To determine why Wertmüller's cinema became so popular in the United States, one should consider the difference in the cultural contexts of Italy and the United States at the time. Wertmuller's films in the eyes of the American public were unprecedented in their radicalism. However, the issues her films deal with, such as unemployment, poverty, fascism, and government corruption, were commonly seen in Italian films, particularly in *commedia all'italiana*, the Italian-style comedy that is closely tied to the collective social awareness of Italians. Lucy Quacinella, a self-claimed Italian and a former assistant of Wertmüller, believed that the filmmaker "adds nothing new to the genre other than the pretense of a leftist political analysis" (Quacinella 1976, 16).

In Wertmüller's words, cinema is defined first and foremost as "a social service" despite being a product; filmmakers are artisans, and not necessarily artists (Bachmann 1977, 3). Her artisanal commitment is to making a popular cinema, in which the "works are not made by the people but they belong to them" (4). Her comic approach is representative of this philosophy: we should treat political matters with humor, not seriousness, for "power itself requires this seriousness to be terrifying. In order to retain our capacity for criticism, we need to see the familiar, ridiculous aspect of power as well" (Wertmüller, McIsaac, and Blumenfeld 1976, 7). Thus in her films, humor becomes a critical and subversive device, for "cheerful vulgarity is the wit of the poor, their last and extreme defense" (Biskind 1974, 3).

Despite criticisms, critics and scholars agree on her originality: "a Wertmüller film remains unmistakable" (Bullaro 2006, xix). Furthermore, the controversial filmmaker introduced strong female characters to the genre of Italian comedy that was previously occupied by men (xix). In 1985, she received the Crystal Award, presented by the Women in Film organization, for her help in expanding the role of women in the entertainment industry through her outstanding work.

Ennuri Jo

Further Reading

Bachmann, Gideon. 1977. "Look, Gideon . . ." *Film Quarterly* 30(3): 2–11.

Biskind, Peter. 1974. "The Politics of Private Life." *Film Quarterly* 28(2): 10–16.

Blumenfeld, Gina. 1976. "The (Next to) Last Word on Lina Wertmüller." *Cinéaste* 7(2): 2–5.

Bullaro, Grace Russo. 2006. *Man in Disorder—The Cinema of Lina Wertmüller in the 1970s.* Leicester, UK: Troubador Publishing.

Michalczyk, John. 1986. *The Italian Political Filmmakers.* Rutherford, NJ: Fairleigh Dickinson University Press.

Quacinella, Lucy. 1976. "How Left Is Lina?" *Cinéaste* 7(3): 15–17.

Wertmüller, Lina, Paul McIsaac, and Gina Blumenfeld. 1976. "You Cannot Make the Revolution on Film: An Interview with Lina Wertmüller." *Cinéaste* 7(2): 6–9.

Editors

Introduction

The early films of the 1890s were stills and continuous shots and did not contain any editing. The power of editing as a film language was refined early on by filmmakers such as D. W. Griffith in his film *The Birth of a Nation* (1915). While many of the formal techniques established in narrative cinema have been attributed to Griffith, history has ignored the contributions a female editor named Rose Smith may actually have made to the development of film language. Smith worked with her husband, James Smith, in the cutting room of many of Griffith's films, including *The Birth of a Nation.* Early filmmakers realized that a story could emerge by selecting and arranging individual shots and scenes. Many film editing techniques and rules have been developed to create actions that appear to flow continuously across shots and scenes to avoid jarring visual inconsistencies; the common technique in service of this purpose is known as continuity editing.

The history of women in editing is very interesting, in that, unlike many other key filmmaking positions, editing is a profession that was occupied primarily by women in the early years of Hollywood cinema. Before the use of editing systems, someone had to physically cut and paste the pieces of a film together from the positive copy of a film's original negative. During the silent era, it was women who performed the tiresome work of cutting negatives and assembling reels from thousands of feet of film and who were often referred to as "cutters." At the time, the meaning of "editor" varied and could also refer to women who adapted written stories (in the form of proposals or novels) into film scripts, which was considered more creative than technical. With very few exceptions, most of these working women were unacknowledged in the credits of the films on which they worked.

The technology of film editing has advanced substantially since its inception. Editors have gone from having to cut film footage and splice it together by hand to transferring footage to a computer's hard drive, liberating them to manipulate footage much faster using digital editing software (today's standard practice). The editing process is both collaborative and solitary and typically begins during production as editors work closely with the directors to review and discuss the raw footage being generated each day (called "dailies"). Once production wraps up, the film commonly undergoes three stages before it is considered complete: the first cut, or "rough cut," is known as the editor's cut; the second version is more refined and known as the director's cut; and the final cut is not ready until the director and producers are in agreement that the film is ready to be released to the public.

The first Academy Award for Best Film Editing was awarded in 1934 and Anne Bauchens, longtime editor for Cecil B. DeMille, was nominated for editing *Cleopatra.* Bauchens would later become the first female editor to win an Oscar for *North West Mounted Police* in 1940. The fact that, historically, the awards for Best Editing strongly correspond to the films that win for Best Picture speaks volumes about the powerful contribution editing makes to a film.

Laura L. S. Bauer

Allen, Dede (1922–2006)

One of the rare female screenwriters of the 1960s, Jay Presson Allen changed her birth name of Jacqueline to the simpler and more gender-ambivalent Jay. Writing came easy for Allen, a "chronic reader" and avid filmgoer from her early years who became a writer "by default" (McGilligan 1997, 15). Her first major authorial act was when she published her debut novel, *Spring Riot,* in 1948. But Allen eschewed the idea of having "literary aspirations" and often referred to the profound ignorance and naïveté she exhibited during her early writing career. Instead, Allen set out to write as a means to "make some money and have some fun" (McGilligan 20). Witty and scornful of intellectualism, her unvarnished attitudes seemingly aided her career endeavors and earned her a reputation for having a no-nonsense approach. Despite her unassuming remarks, Allen became an award-winning writer for television, film, and Broadway, whose career spanned more than 50 years.

After only a few years writing for television and the stage, Allen grew frustrated with writing. Part of that frustration may have been due to a reader who rejected one of Allen's plays while working for producer Bob Whitehead, who had optioned it. Soon after, that reader would become Allen's second husband, Broadway and film producer Lewis Allen. Family trumped writing for a while after she remarried and had her daughter, Brooke. Under constant demand from Whitehead to write something for him to produce, Allen discovered Muriel Spark's short novel *The Prime of Miss Jean Brodie* (1961) and strongly believed in her ability to make it into a play. Soon, Allen would be back to work writing at the encouragement of Lillian Hellman, adapting the novel into a film featuring Maggie Smith in the title role, which earned her the Best Actress Oscar in 1969. This adaptation became one of Allen's most widely acclaimed and operated as the springboard for her enduring future success in Hollywood and on Broadway.

Alfred Hitchcock helped jumpstart her career in Hollywood screenwriting; after reading an early pre-production draft of Allen's *Prime of Miss Jean Brodie* script, Hitchcock summoned her to Hollywood to write the screenplay for *Marnie* (1964). Allen admits to not even knowing what a screenwriter was previous to working with Hitchcock, who, she says, taught her more about screenwriting on the *Marnie* project than she learned throughout the rest of her career, especially in the realm of visual shorthand (Allen 2002, 210). She would become close friends with Hitchcock and his wife, Alma, and would write for him an unproduced adaptation of J. M. Barrie's *Mary Rose* (1920), a passion-project Hitchcock was never able to realize on film.

The expediency of her career was reflected in the equivalently automatic nature of her writing. Allen admitted that she liked to be "blinkered" when she wrote, "almost a trance, really. There's nothing else, nothing else, nothing else." Not one to be humble about facilities for writing, Allen, when asked if she ever had trouble writing offered the response, "I did. I couldn't type fast enough." Helen Dudar of *The Washington Post* claims that Allen's "speed writing record" is held by *The Prime of Miss Jean Brodie*, which, after her only experience of writer's block, only took three and a half days to write (Dudar 1981).

Through the 1970s, Allen was one of only two female screenwriters to have had more than two films produced. Her films of that decade include *Travels with My Aunt* (1972), directed by George Cukor, and *Funny Lady* (1975), a sequel to Barbra Streisand's Oscar-winning *Funny Girl* (1968). Yet her most famous script of the 1970s was the Bob Fosse–directed *Cabaret* (1972). To write it, Allen went back to Christopher Isherwood's novel *Goodbye to Berlin* (1939), the source text for *I Am a Camera* (1955), from which *Cabaret* was meant to be adapted. Allen followed her own staunch advice on the matter of adaptation, "not to throw out the baby with the bath water. You can change all kinds of things, but don't muck around with the essence" (Corry 1982). Often cited as one of the first Hollywood films to actually celebrate homosexuality, Allen considered it a matter of fact that the main character, Brian Roberts (Michael York), was a homosexual—"that's what the story was," she emphasized, staying true to the character's genesis (Epstein and Friedman 1996). Allen's screenplay for *Cabaret* was Oscar-nominated for Best Adapted Screenplay and won the Writers Guild of America (WGA) award for Best Adapted Comedy in 1973.

By the early 1980s, she was the highest-paid woman writer in Hollywood. Allen had occasion to turn her own novel, *Just Tell Me What You Want*, into a film. Directed by friend and frequent collaborator Sidney Lumet, it won the David di Donatello Award for Best Foreign Screenplay (1980). The following year, Allen and Lumet collaborated once more on the gritty police procedural *Prince of the City* (1981), about NYPD narcotics detective Robert Leuci and his work exposing corruption within the department, for which they earned an Oscar nomination for Best Adapted Screenplay. Leuci advised the writing directly; a testament to Allen's no-nonsense approach to life and writing, Leuci confirmed that she didn't pull any punches. She referenced this film, which she called a "very serious movie," in particular, to show that she had fortitude for writing male characters too.

Allen refuted the idea that she exhibited a propensity for writing tough, trademark women. Allen did, however, help create some memorable female characters, like the romantic yet intrepid Miss Jean Brodie, an award-winning role for many of the actresses who played it, and her updated version of Isherwood's Sally Bowles in *Cabaret*, played by Liza Minnelli. Yet ultimately, Allen claimed she could not care less whether a character was a man or a woman, as long as she found the character interesting (McGilligan 1997, 35).

Allen would become one of the first female screenwriters who also acted as producer—she considered it essential in the latter part of her career—on films like *Just Tell Me What You Want*, *Prince of the City*, and *Deathtrap* (1982). In 1982, Allen was awarded the Women in Film Crystal Award, which honors recipients for their endurance and excellence in the industry and for their help expanding the role of women in the entertainment industry. But she continued working through the 1980s and early 1990s on an eclectic mix of projects, many that included her family members. Allen wrote the script for *The Lord of the Flies* (1990), produced by her husband, Lewis (who also produced the 1963 British film version), and she co-wrote and directed *The Big Love*, a one-woman show for Tracey Ullman, with her daughter Brooke (1991).

At the same time, and after over 30 years in the business, Allen began to prefer acting as a consultant, or "script doctor," as her final act—a job that usually offered little to no public credit but lots of monetary reward. In 1997, she earned one of the top honors for a Hollywood writer, the Writers Guild's Ian McClellan Hunter Award for career achievement. Jay Presson Allen died on May 1, 2006, in New York City.

Christina Parker-Flynn

See also: Hellman, Lillian

Further Reading

Acker, Ally. 2009. *Screenwriters on Screenwriting.* New York: Reel Women Media. Kanopy Streaming.

Allen, Richard. 2002. "An Interview with Jay Presson Allen." *Framing Hitchcock: Selected Essays from the Hitchcock Annual.* Edited by Sidney Gottlieb and Christopher Brookhouse. Detroit: Wayne State University Press.

Corry, John. 1982. "Broadway; Angela Lansbury Returns in Comedy Next Season." *The New York Times,* April 23. http://www.nytimes.com/1982/04/23/theater/broadway-angela-lansbury-returns-in-comedy-next-season.html

Dudar, Helen. 1981. "The Prime of Jay Presson, the Serious Screenwriter." *The Washington Post*, October 18. https://www.washingtonpost.com/archive/lifestyle/style/1981/10/18/the-prime-of-jay-presson-the-serious-screenwriter/cf9530ce-4fe9-47ac-9b8c-839071b6cf7a

Epstein, Rob, and Jeffrey Friedman, dir. 1996. *The Celluloid Closet*, DVD. Tokyo: Sony Pictures Classics.

McGilligan, Patrick. 1997. *Backstory 3: Interviews with Screenwriters of the 1960s.* Berkeley: University of California Press.

Booth, Margaret (1898–2002)

Margaret Booth was one of the most influential people working in Hollywood, though few outside the film industry knew her name. Her career spanned a remarkable 71-year period, from 1915 when she began work as a film joiner, until her retirement in 1986. In her role as editor and, later, supervising editor, Booth helped to establish the techniques of continuity editing and the seamless style that are associated with Hollywood film.

Booth began her film career straight out of high school following the death of her brother, actor Elmer Booth. The director D. W. Griffith spoke at her brother's memorial and offered 17-year-old Booth a job at his studio. There she worked as a film joiner and negative cutter, preparing film negatives for Griffith's editors, James and Rose Smith, from 1915 until 1919, when Griffith shut down his Los Angeles studio and moved his production facilities to New York.

After a brief stint working at Paramount, Booth went to work for Louis B. Mayer at Mayer Pictures in 1921. There she worked closely with the director, John Stahl, who would screen the dailies with Booth and tell her what he wanted to use from which take. At the end of the day, after her work with Stahl was done, Booth would use the director's outtakes to practice editing. In later interviews, she would credit Stahl with teaching her the craft of editing, advising her to use long shots and cut to a close-up for emphasis. By 1922, her position in the field was well established enough that she was elected chair of the film cutters' convention in Chicago.

When Mayer's studio merged with Goldwyn Pictures and the Loews theater chain to become Metro-Goldwyn-Mayer (MGM) in 1924, Booth was among the two dozen editors—and one of only two women—working for the studio. There she worked under the studio's head of production, Irving Thalberg. Thalberg is credited with streamlining the production process at MGM, introducing efficiency through the division of labor and the specialization of roles. Under Thalberg's leadership, it became less common for directors to oversee the editing of the films they had directed, and Booth edited films for a variety of directors under the supervision of the studio's producers. At MGM, she made the transition from editing silent films, which permitted relative freedom in selecting takes, to sound film, for which she had to work with sound engineers who knew a great deal about the new technology and very little about filmmaking.

As an editor at MGM, Booth attended test screenings with Thalberg and other MGM producers, including Bernie Hyman and Harry Rapf. Together, they would gauge audience responses to the preview, identifying where a film lagged, where it was confusing to audiences, and whether it would be necessary to reshoot scenes. After discussing the test screening with the producers, Booth would return to the studio and re-edit the film in preparation for its release. The films she edited at MGM included *Bombshell* (1933), directed by Victor Fleming; *Mutiny on the Bounty* (1935), directed by Frank Lloyd, for which she was nominated for an Academy Award; and *Camille* (1936), directed by George Cukor. In 1937, when Britain's new film quotas necessitated overseas production, Booth sailed to England to work as supervising editor on *A Yank at Oxford* (1938), directed by Jack Conway.

Following her return to the United States, Booth became the supervising editor for MGM studios. From 1939 onward, she oversaw post-production on every film that MGM released until the studio's collapse in 1968. She assigned editors to films, and no film was released until she had approved the final editing of sound and image. Reporting directly to Louis B. Mayer, Booth screened the rushes for the studio's films and directed the editors to make any changes she saw necessary. During this period, she did not receive credit for the numerous films that she worked on, though in 1977 the Academy of Motion Picture Arts and Sciences awarded her an Honorary Oscar for her 62 years of service to the industry.

In 1968, shortly before Kirk Kerkorian purchased MGM and all but eliminated film production there, Booth left the studio where she had worked for over 40 years. At the age of 70, she was hired by Ray Stark to become the supervising film editor for Rastar Productions. Working with Stark, she oversaw the editing of a number of films starring Barbra Streisand, including *The Owl and the Pussycat* (1970), directed by Herbert Ross; *Funny Lady* (1975), directed by Herbert Ross; and *The Way We Were* (1973), directed by Sydney Pollack, as well as others written by Neil Simon, including *The Sunshine Boys* (1975), *The Goodbye Girl* (1977), and *California Suite* (1978), all directed by Herbert Ross. During the time that she was working for Stark, she was placed at number three in *Film Comment*'s list of top 10 editors.

In 1986, nearing the age of 90, Margaret Booth retired. Four years later, in 1990, the American Cinema Editors (ACE) awarded her a Career Achievement award, and the Editors Guild commemorated her work on the occasion of her 100th birthday in 1998. Hers was a remarkable career that spanned the transformation of Hollywood film from the silent era, before the studios were well established in Hollywood, through the post-studio era.

Kristen Hatch

See also: Smith, Rose

Further Reading

Booth, Margaret. 1938. "The Cutter." In *Behind the Screen: How Films Are Made.* Edited by Stephen Watts. London: A. Barker.

Hatch, Kristen. 2013. "Cutting Women: Margaret Booth and Hollywood's Pioneering Female Film Editors." In *Women Film Pioneers Project.* Edited by Jane Gaines, Radha Vatsal, and Monica Dall'Asta. Center for Digital Research and Scholarship. New York: Columbia University Libraries, September 27. https://wfpp.cdrs.columbia.edu/essay/cutting-women

Lewis, Kevin. 2012. "The Moviola Mavens and the Moguls: Three Pioneering Women Editors Who Had the Respect of Early Hollywood's Power-Broker's." *Archive Today,* September 5. http://archive.is/FAR8

Coates, Anne V. (1925–2018)

Anne V. Coates worked as an editor in the film industry for over 70 years, starting at Pinewood Studios in England after World War II, but with much of her career spent in Hollywood. During the course of her long career, she found critical and popular success in a profession largely dominated by men. She has worked with many directors and in many genres, ranging from action and adventure films that feature stars such as Arnold Schwarzenegger to David Lean's epic *Lawrence of Arabia,* generally conceded to be the pinnacle of her work. She continues to work as an editor at the present time (2018) well into her nineties.

Coates was born on December 12, 1925, in Reigate, England. After graduating college, she worked briefly as a nurse for the Red Cross before securing a job at Religious Films, a Christian production company that edited devotional films for churches across England. A short time later, Coates secured a job in the editorial

Oscar-winning veteran British editor Anne V. Coates, pictured at age 83 editing the film *Extraordinary Measures* (2010) at her editing station at CBS Radford Studios in Studio City, Los Angeles, on September 21, 2009. She rose to fame for editing David Lean's epic *Lawrence of Arabia* (1962), for which she won the Academy Award for Best Film Editing. Coates was regarded as a top film editor in Hollywood and enjoyed a distinguished career. (Ken Hively/Los Angeles Times via Getty Images)

department at Pinewood Studios. Her uncle, J. Arthur Rank, was one of the biggest figures in Britain's mid-20th-century film industry, as owner of Pinewood Studios and the Odeon theater chain. She had ambition to become a director but quickly made a name for herself in Pinewood's editing department.

Coates's first credit as editor came in 1952 for *The Pickwick Papers*. She edited about a film a year on average during the 1950s, a pace that would more or less be sustained throughout her long career. During this time, she married and started a family; her husband and three children all had careers in Hollywood. In 1957, Coates edited a film for a female director, Muriel Box, something she would do twice more in her career, with Martha Coolidge and Sam Taylor-Johnson. When asked why women, largely excluded from many aspects of Hollywood filmmaking, have a track record of opportunity and success in editing, Coates joked that, "We're mothers, and we're used to dealing with fractious kids," also adding, "I do think women are more painstakingly patient, generally speaking" (Verini 2016).

The early part of the next decade showcased her work in back-to-back critically reviewed films: *Lawrence of Arabia* (1962) and *Becket* (1964). Consistently, Coates cited the former as among the more difficult projects of her career: "[T]he most challenging film I cut was 'Lawrence,' because we had such a huge amount of film (I believe it was 31 miles!) which gave me an abundance of choices" (Stafford n.d.). This film is most often noted for its beautiful cinematography, although the editing is equally as spectacular, including one of the most famous cuts in cinematic history, the well-known head and shoulder shot of T. E. Lawrence blowing out a match to the sun rising over the Arabian peninsula. Coates and her editing team won an Academy Award for Film Editing for *Lawrence of Arabia* and were nominated for *Becket*, *The Elephant Man*, *In the Line of Fire*, and *Out of Sight*.

During the latter part of the 1960s and 1970s, Coates was active, although attached to a series of lesser-known films. Working with David Lynch on *The Elephant Man* in 1980 signaled a return to prominence, in regard to both critical and popular success. She worked with a great many notable directors over the course of her career, including David Lean, Carol Reed, Sidney Lumet, John Sturges, David Lynch, Frank Oz, Richard Attenborough, and Frank Marshall. Many of these directors had nice things to say about her. When it came to screening the test footage for *Lawrence of Arabia*, the director Sir David Lean gave her high praise indeed when he declared: "I don't think I've ever before seen anything cut exactly the way I would have cut it myself," making it clear that he wouldn't have cut it any differently had he edited the film himself (Verini 2016). And Sir Carol Reed told her that, "I've worked with many good editors, but you're the one with the most heart" (Verini 2016).

Starting in the 1990s, she gained the reputation of editing sexualized films, including *Striptease* (1996), *Unfaithful* (2002), and *Fifty Shades of Gray* (2015). According to Coates, the latter film was not sexual enough: "I tried to make 'Fifty Shades' a little more sexy, but they were worried they wouldn't get the R rating. I would have had her trussed up like a suitcase and hoisted to the ceiling. I tried and tried to get that in" (Keegan 2016). She also worked on films featuring strong women, several of which were directed by Steven Soderbergh: *Out of Sight* (1998) and *Erin Brockovich* (2000). The former was during a difficult time in Coates's career, as it marked her transition to digital editing. She used this opportunity, however, to try new approaches and evolve her work. *Out of Sight* contains many well-edited scenes, including one between the leads (Jennifer Lopez and George Clooney) in which they flirt in a bar, which is interspersed with a daydream about where they hope their forbidden relationship might take them.

In addition to winning the Academy Award for *Lawrence of Arabia*, Coates won a BAFTA Fellowship in 2007 and an Honorary Academy Award in 2016, only the second editor ever to receive this honor. She was also named an Officer of the British Empire in 2003. Coates had a long and successful career, working up until she passed away on May 8, 2018, at the age of 92 (she had been attached to a project set for release in 2018). In reflecting upon her career after being asked what made her a successful editor, she responded, "You have the courage of your convictions" (Verini 2016).

Andrew Howe

See also: Coolidge, Martha

Further Reading

Keegan, Rebecca. 2016. "From 'Lawrence of Arabia' to 'Fifty Shades of Grey,' Anne Coates Is Hollywood's Premiere Editor." *Los Angeles Times*, November 10. http://www.latimes.com/entertainment/movies/moviesnow/la-et-mn-anne-coates-governors-award-20161104-story.html

Murch, Walter. 2000. "Walter Murch Interviews Anne V. Coates." May. http://filmsound.org/murch/coates.htm

Stafford, Jeff. n.d. "Interview with Anne V. Coates, Oscar Winning Film Editor for 'Lawrence of Arabia.'" *Turner Classic Movies* http://www.tcm.com/this-month/article/67245%7C0/Interview-with-Anne-V-Coates-Oscar-winning-editor-.html

Verini, Bob. 2016. "Lawrence of Arabia Editor Anne Coates on Why So Many Great Editors Are Female." *Variety*, November 11. http://www.variety.com/2016/film/spotlight/anne-coates-lawrence-of-arabia-editor-honorary-oscar-1201915294

Fields, Verna (1918–1982)

Verna Fields was endearingly referred to as "Mother Cutter," which Steven Spielberg explains they called her because she was "very maternal" and because she cut her films in her own pool house, which he refers to as a very "heimishe" workplace, the Yiddish word for homey (Apple 2004). By all accounts a nice Jewish woman, Fields was also one of the most revered and successful film editors in the early 1970s New Hollywood era—her most famous work being her last, on Spielberg's *Jaws* (1975), which many refer to as a master class in editing. Though she began her career in film somewhat accidentally, Fields soon developed her skill in sound and image editing, established her belief in film as a political tool, and later became a tireless studio executive until the time of her passing.

Born in St. Louis, Missouri, Verna Fields (née Hellman) moved to Hollywood with her family at an early age so that her father, Samuel Hellman, could work as a screenwriter (credits include *Little Miss Marker* [1934] and *My Darling Clementine* [1946]). Educated at Le College Féminin de Bouffemont and later earning a BA in Journalism from the University of Southern California (USC), Fields began her film career when she was inadvertently "discovered" by Fritz Lang. On canteen duty with her friend, Margie Johnson, they would visit Johnson's boyfriend at the studio, where he worked as an assistant editor. Fields started "hanging out there to be with the cute guy" who would later become her husband, Sam Fields (Acker 1993, 223). Despite her lack of knowledge or experience, Lang hired Fields to be his sound apprentice. She worked as his assistant sound editor on *The Woman in the Window* (1944), and over a decade later would be the sound editor on Lang's noir film *While the City Sleeps* (1956).

Like many women in the industry during the mid-century, Fields stopped working after her 1946 marriage to Sam Fields, taking time to start a family and raise her two sons (Richard Fields would later become a film editor himself). However, after the sudden death of her husband in 1954, Fields went back to work as a sound editor in television from 1954 to 1960, working on series such as *Sky King* and *Fury*. She continued to sound edit in film as well, from 1959's *The Savage Eye* to *Pickup on 101* in 1972. In 1961, Fields was awarded the Motion Picture Sound Editing Golden Reel award for her work on Anthony Mann's epic film, *El Cid*.

Her illustrious career as a full-fledged film editor in Hollywood began largely after meeting director Irving Lerner, who asked Fields to edit his film adaptation of James T. Farrell's novel trilogy, *Studs Lonigan* (1960). Lerner mentored Fields, and his trust led to her developing greater confidence in her skills. Fields soon developed an interest in "using film as social reform," perhaps influenced by Lerner's leftist politics (Peary 1980). In 1965, Fields was drafted into Lyndon B. Johnson's Great Society, and in 1968 she made a United States Information Agency–sponsored documentary film called *Journey to the Pacific*. She hired two editors to help on the project: George Lucas and Marcia Griffin, his soon-to-be wife. Lucas had been a student of Fields during the year she taught at USC, and Fields would later edit, along with Marcia, one of Lucas's first feature films, *American Graffiti* (1973).

Fields did her most influential work in film editing during what she referred to as the Era of the Director, or what many would call the New Hollywood Era of the 1970s, and she was the editor of choice for many major directing figures of the period. Aside from George Lucas, Fields had a firmly established working relationship with Peter Bogdanovich; she worked on the sound for his first film, *Targets* (1968), and then went on to edit some of his most major works, including *What's Up, Doc?* (1972), *Paper Moon* (1973), and *Daisy Miller* (1974). Most notably, Fields formed a partnership with Steven Spielberg, editing his directorial debut, *The Sugarland Express* (1974). Her last and best-known film would be Spielberg's *Jaws* (1975), one of the first and most influential blockbusters ever made in Hollywood.

Some of Fields's editorial choices on *Jaws* proved instrumental in the film's overwhelming success. First, Fields suggested displaying the killer shark in quick, teasing cuts, a major textual element in terms of the film's building of suspense and anxiety. The choice was also based out of utility, since the quick editing distracted attention from the unrealistic aspects of the mechanical sharks (which were, it seems, constantly breaking down during filming). In addition, Fields made the pivotal decision to hold the shot longer before Ben Gardner's disembodied head pops up in the cloudy water, to increase the slow build and spectatorial shock response (the shot was filmed in Fields's own swimming pool). Her work on all aspects of *Jaws*—not only did she edit the film but she also acted tirelessly as the liaison between Spielberg and the studio—earned her the confidence of executives at Universal, where she then became a feature-production vice president.

Fields did not believe in having a recognizable "editing style" and preferred the more informal and direct occupational label "cutter" to "film editor." In a 1975 interview, Fields stated "that film creates its own style. . . . [W]hat I think that you develop is an approach to film that perhaps differs from one editor to another" (Macklin and Pici 2000, 239). She also admitted in an interview that she wished "the word 'editing' had never been invented . . . because the word 'editing' implies correcting, and it's not. [. . .] You're mounting the film" (Fields 1975). However, she made notable contributions to the artistry of film editing, specifically regarding her use of the "wipe-by" or the "wipe-by cut": "a long-lens shot picks out a figure, and then something closer to the camera . . . slides into view; cut as our view is completely masked; when the obtrusion leaves the frame, we have a closer framing of the figure" (Bordwell 2002, 18).

In 1981, Verna Fields was awarded the Women in Film Crystal Award honoring outstanding women who have helped to expand the influence of women in the entertainment industry. Sadly, Fields died the following year of cancer, in Encino, California. In her honor, Universal Studios named the building on their Universal City lot immediately across from the Alfred Hitchcock Building the Verna Fields

Building. In addition, the Women in Film Foundation established a Verna Fields Memorial Fellowship for female graduate students at UCLA, to assist with the editing and screenwriting of their thesis projects.

Christina Parker-Flynn

Further Reading

Acker, Ally. 1993. *Reel Women: Pioneers of the Cinema 1896 to the Present.* New York: Continuum.

Apple, Wendy, dir. 2004. *The Cutting Edge: The Magic of Movie Editing.* Meridian: Starz Encore Entertainment.

Bordwell, David. 2002. "Intensified Continuity: Visual Style in Contemporary American Film." *Film Quarterly* 55(3): 16–28.

Fields, Verna. 1975. "Cutting for Impact: A Conversation with Verna Fields." *American Film Institute*, December 3. https://web.archive.org/web/20120204052526/http://www.fathom.com/feature/122531

Keil, Charlie, and Kristen Whissel, eds. 2016. *Editing and Special/Visual Effects.* New Brunswick, NJ: Rutgers University Press.

Macklin, Tony, and Nick Pici, eds. 2000. *Voices from the Set: The Film Heritage Interviews.* Lanham, MD: Scarecrow Press.

Peary, Gerald. 1980. "Verna Fields." *The Real Paper*, October 23. http://www.geraldpeary.com/essays/def/fields-verna.html

Klingman, Lynzee (1943–)

Editor Lynzee Klingman is best known for her work on the film adaptation *One Flew over the Cuckoo's Nest* (1975) of the novel of the same name by Ken Kesey. The feature got her an Oscar nomination and an Eddie nomination from American Cinema Editors (an honorary society of film editors) and earned the award for best film editing from the British Academy of Film and Television Arts (BAFTA). Her prolific career spans from the mid-1970s to 2011, throughout which she mainly worked on big Hollywood productions following a debut in documentary film.

Now probably best known for New Hollywood (1960s–1980s) comedy dramas, biopics, and children's films, Klingman learned how to edit on the job in New York after graduating from Columbia University with a bachelor's degree in history and no formal film education. After struggling to get hired as one of the few women in the industry—she did not meet any other female editors the first three years on the job—she started a two-year apprenticeship at an editorial house that worked on a variety of films. She was hired to cut negatives and picked up some technical background, after which she visited a friend who studied film at UCLA, alongside of whom she further developed her editing skills. Around 1968, Klingman went back to New York and became assistant editor in a commercial house. She supported the women's rights and the anti-war movements and, through her political engagement, met Emile De Antonio, a documentary filmmaker who gave her the opportunity to work on his Vietnam documentary *In the Year of the Pig* (1968).

De Antonio's film was Klingman's first big project and received an Academy Award nomination for Best Documentary. After a few years of working on

Film editor Lynzee Klingman attends the 3rd Annual Diane Von Furstenberg Oscar Luncheon honoring the female nominees of the 88th Academy Awards on February 24, 2016, in Beverly Hills, California. Klingman edited *One Flew Over the Cuckoo's Nest* (1975), and received an Oscar nomination and the award for Best Film Editing from the British Academy of Film and Television Arts (BAFTA) for the film. (Donato Sardella/Getty Images for DVF)

commercials, Klingman worked on her second major project, *Hearts and Minds* (1974), an anti-war documentary directed by Peter Davis and produced by Bert Schneider. The film won an Academy Award and would be Klingman's last documentary, as she shifted her attention to fiction. The acclaimed *One Flew over the Cuckoo's Nest* was her first cooperation with Miloš Forman and a pivotal moment in her career. It was nominated for all the major Academy Awards, including her first nomination for editing. After this success she went on to work on other major narrative Hollywood productions, the most notable being the biopics *Man on the Moon* (1999), a film about performer Andrew Kaufman, for which she received another nomination by ACE, and the more recent *Ali* (2001), for which she was nominated for a Phoenix Film Critics Society award. She also worked on a large number of well-known comedy dramas like *The War of the Roses* (1989), family movies like *Matilda* (1996), and the rural drama *A River Runs Through It* (1992).

As she learned on the job and had no family in the industry, the most profound influences on her career were the directors and other colleagues she worked alongside. In an interview, Klingman says she had a positive experience working for Forman, who encouraged her to learn through trial and error. Today, Klingman influences a new generation of editors and filmmakers as an editing mentor at the University of Southern California (USC) and the American Film Institute (AFI) and is an esteemed member of American Cinema Editors. She has also been an invited lecturer in the course "The Film Industry: Career Challenges and Choices for Women" organized by USC colleague Bonnie Bruckheimer.

Research addressing the films to which Klingman has contributed rarely displays explicit attention for the editing as it relates to the rest of her oeuvre. The two anti-war documentaries are the most well-researched topics (notably, editing is often considered to be applied to its greatest advantage in documentary). *In the Year of the Pig* and *Hearts and Minds*, which was researched by Wilder, Grosser, and Blaylock, crosscut between shots of suffering Vietnamese and interviews with American veterans recalling the war, often resulting in dialectical irony.

Mainly adhering to an editing style common to the genres and time frame within which she worked, Klingman's fiction has some interesting attributes. The films Klingman worked on often exhibit the same dark humor through juxtaposition seen in her early documentary work, exemplified in *Man on the Moon* in a matchcut from Kaufman's little sister to a man in a dark bar for whom he is performing the same comedy routine over 10 years later. In *One Flew over the Cuckoo's Nest,* a rather upbeat scene predominated told through medium shots and close-ups is suddenly interrupted by an overhead view of the boat the patients stole aimlessly circling, as everyone has abandoned the helm. Klingman has a keen sense of rhythm, as exhibited in the opening sequence of *Ali* and throughout her work in comedy. These aspects of her work have yet to receive due attention.

Charlotte Wynant

Further Reading

Berila, Beth. 2010. "Engaging the Land/Positioning the Spectator: Environmental Justice Documentaries and Robert Redford's The Horse Whisperer and A River Runs Through It." In *Framing the World: Explorations of Ecocriticism and Film*. Edited by Paula Willoquet-Maricondi. Charlottesville: University of Virginia Press.

Blaylock, Sara. 2017. "Bringing the War Home to the United States and East Germany: In the Year of the Pig and Pilots in Pyjamas." *Cinema Journal* 45(4): 26–50.

Grosser, David. 1990. "'We Aren't on the Wrong Side, We Are the Wrong Side': Peter Davis Targets (American) Hearts and Minds." In *From Hanoi to Hollywood: The Vietnam War in American Film*. Edited by Linda Dittmar and Gene Michaud. New Brunswick, NJ: Rutgers University Press.

MacDonald, George B. 1992. "Control by Camera: Milos Forman as Subjective Narrator." In *A Casebook on Ken Kesey's One Flew over the Cuckoo's Nest*. Edited by George J. Searles. Albuquerque: University of New Mexico Press.

Wilder, Carol. 2005. "Separated at Birth: Argument by Irony in Hearts and Minds and Fahrenheit 9/11." *Atlantic Journal of Communication* 13(2): 57–72.

Menke, Sally (1953–2010)

Sally Menke was an American film and television editor best known for her work with American film director Quentin Tarantino. She is known for her unique editing style that took long, slow-cut dialogue scenes and interwove them with bursts of high, intense action and violence. As her work with Tarantino continued, she also introduced an added element of pastiche and mimicry of other film genres to reshape the way traditional Hollywood films were edited. Pastiche is the imitation of the style or character of the work of another artist or collection of artists intended to celebrate these influences. Menke was twice nominated for the Academy Award for Best Film Editing: in 1995 for *Pulp Fiction* (1994) and in 2010 for *Inglourious Basterds* (2009). She was also nominated for the American Cinema Editors Eddie

Award for Best Edited Feature Film for *Pulp Fiction* in 1995 and for Best Edited Feature Film (Dramatic) for *Kill Bill Volume 2* (2004) in 2005. She described film editors as the "the quiet heroes of movies" for their private but crucial relationships with the director (Walters 2010). She also noted, in the documentary *The Cutting Edge: The Magic of Movie Editing*, the additional role that an editor holds with a director: "in giving them support, making them feel like they can look at something that may have trouble or problems and be comfortable enough so that they can approach those problems" (Apple 2005). Menke passed away on September 27, 2010, due to heat-related factors while on a hike in Bronson Canyon, near Los Angeles, California, during an extreme heat wave in the area.

Sally Menke's work with Quentin Tarantino played a key part in the launching of the independent—or "indie"—film boom of American cinema in the 1990s. Their early collaborations *Reservoir Dogs* (1992) and *Pulp Fiction* helped usher in Miramax as one of the premier distributors of independent films, setting off a new wave of successful indies that infiltrated and reinvented mainstream Hollywood cinema. The relationship between Menke and Tarantino was built on the influence that Menke saw between seminal director Martin Scorsese and his editor, Thelma Schoonmaker. After *Reservoir Dogs*, Menke and Tarantino continued to work together on each of his films up until her death in 2010. Sally Menke characterized their relationship as "so intense" that she stated, "I see [Tarantino] more than my husband" (Walters 2010). The pair's seemingly symbiotic relationship created a bond of mutual trust between editor and director, as well as helping them to influence each other in the creation of their distinct style of filmmaking. Menke's editing work is a crucial component in showcasing and augmenting Tarantino's brand of offbeat humor, unique approach to dialogue and character, and predilection for rapid tonal shifts (Colen 2010). Tasked with taking in Tarantino's idiosyncratic approach to the creation of his movies, Menke also developed her own stylistic approach to complement Tarantino's distinct style.

As much as the relationship between Scorsese and Schoonmaker influenced her professional working relationship with Tarantino, Menke was also heavily influenced by Thelma Schoonmaker and her editing style that centralized on building tension, creating a sense of reality, and adding urgency to the scene. Menke stated that she "learned how to collapse time in action but still push characters through a scene" in order to create the "illusion that time is ticking away" by watching Scorsese and Schoonmaker (Menke 2009). For Menke, this manipulation of time adds intensity to even a mundane scene, allowing the audience to follow the emotional shifts of a character, even if he or she is doing something as simple as pouring a glass of milk, as in the opening scene of Menke and Tarantino's project *Inglourious Basterds* (Menke 2009). In addition to collapsing time, Menke's style consisted of prolonged, dialogue-heavy takes that eschews the traditional crosscut technique of editing dialogue. Instead, she would use two-shots and overshots or a restless, roving camera roaming over these long, dialogue-driven scenes. The result of avoiding crosscuts in such scenes allows the audience to become invested in the conversation and the characters when dialogue moves to the forefront—a key trait of Tarantino's style. Moreover, her editing style in these scenes also keys the audience into what is important by shifting the style of cuts in the dialogue throughout the film. As a result, the audience can then begin to differentiate between what is important, what is comedic versus dramatic, in the film's dialogue; thus, Menke allows the dialogue to shine while also not having the audience feel that they are being hit by a wall of words (Colen 2010).

As characteristic as the editing of dialogue, Sally Menke's style interspersed these slow-cut scenes with fast-cut action scenes. Nestled in between Tarantino's long, unique dialogue, Menke cut in bursts of intense and immersive violence as a counterpoint. The effect was the fruition of the urgency she built into the dialogue-heavy scenes, followed by her cutting from the brutal violence back to slow-paced dialogue. This interweaving of violence into the sometimes mundane action intensifies the relationship between the characters while also heightening the viciousness of the action.

Building on these foundations of her editing repertoire, Menke's work on both volumes of Tarantino's *Kill Bill* boasted the added element of pastiche to her style. Along with her established approaches to dialogue and action sequences, Menke emulated the styles from many other film genres: from the "spaghetti Western" style of extreme close-ups, popularized by directors such as Sergio Leone, to the excessive violence and over-the-top action of 1960s and 1970s Hong Kong action–style cinema. In regard to the pastiche element prevalent in *Kill Bill*, Menke stated that "[o]ur [her and Tarantino's] style is to mimic, not homage, but it's all about recontextualizing the film language to make it fresh within the new genre. It's incredibly detailed" (Riley 2010). Menke took the established conventions and language of film editing and manipulated them in a way that redefined Hollywood cinema.

Alexander Lalama

See also: Schoonmaker, Thelma

Further Reading

Apple, Wendy, dir. 2005. *The Cutting Edge: The Magic of Movie Editing,* DVD. Burbank, CA: Warner Home Video.

Colen, Sam. 2010. "Examining the Life and Works of Editor Sally Menke." *Daily Trojan*, November 4. http://dailytrojan.com/2010/11/04/examining-the-life-and-works-of-editor-sally-menke

Menke, Sally. 2009. "Quentin Tarantino and I Clicked." Interviewed by Jason Solomons. *The Guardian*, December 5. http://www.theguardian.com/film/2009/dec/06/sally-menke-quentin-tarantino-editing

Riley, John. 2010. "Sally Menke: Film Editor Whose Cutting Style Was a Crucial Element in the Work of Quentin Tarantino." *The Independent*, October 8. http://www.independent.co.uk/news/obituaries/sally-menke-film-editor-whose-cutting-style-was-a-crucial-element-in-the-work-of-quentin-tarantino-2100864.html

Walters, Ben. 2010. "Sally Menke: The Quiet Heroine of the Quentin Tarantino Success Story." *The Guardian*, September 29. http://www.theguardian.com/film/filmblog/2010/sep/29/sally-menke-quentin-tarantino-editor

Schoonmaker, Thelma (1940–)

Thelma Schoonmaker is an American film editor best known for developing a decisively raw style distinct from conventional Hollywood post-production practices that she has utilized in her lauded work with American film director Martin Scorsese.

Schoonmaker began her editing career in the mid-1960s abridging the runtimes of international arthouse films for the American distribution circuit. During her early career in New York City, Schoonmaker met director-cinematographer Michael Wadleigh and Scorsese when he was a New York University film student. Schoonmaker and Scorsese collaborated as assistant directors and supervising editors on Wadleigh's direct cinema documentary of the 1969 Woodstock Arts and Music Fair titled *Woodstock: Three Days of Peace and Music* (1970). In editing the 120 hours of footage captured at the festival, Schoonmaker "supervised the syncing and logging operations" and coordinated "multiple images for certain sequences," resulting in an assemblage of 16mm Academy ratio footage featuring musical performances and festival happenings that she combined using split-screen techniques into a wide "CinemaScope" frame (Wadleigh 1970, 972–77, 1016–31). Schoonmaker's innovative and meticulous editing of *Woodstock* was recognized with an Academy Award nomination for Best Editing, a rare recognition for a documentary film.

Despite her accomplishments with *Woodstock*, Schoonmaker struggled to acquire post-production employment, as she had not yet completed sufficient apprenticeship hours to enter the male-dominated Motion Picture Editors Guild, to which she was eventually afforded entry in 1980. Schoonmaker reunited with Scorsese in editing *Raging Bull* (1980), for which she won her first Academy Award for Best Film Editing. While Schoonmaker regards her professional relationship with Scorsese as exclusive, she has occasionally edited films in collaboration other directors including co-editing Isabel Coixet's *Learning to Drive* (2014). To date, Schoonmaker has collaborated with Scorsese in editing 18 feature films as well as several short films, music videos, and short and feature documentaries. Among these titles, she has won two additional Academy Awards for editing—for *The Aviator* (2004) and the Best Picture winner *The Departed* (2006)—as well as nominations for *Goodfellas* (1990), *Gangs of New York* (2002), and *Hugo* (2011). More than any other film she has edited, Schoonmaker cites *Goodfellas* as the most influential regarding her reputation in Hollywood, as evinced by the numerous producers who ask Schoonmaker to emulate this previous work in newer Scorsese-directed projects (DP/30 2014). Schoonmaker characterizes her work with Scorsese as deeply collaborative, and she has commented upon the uniqueness of working with a director who appreciates editing as an important filmmaking tool and art form (Eyes on Cinema, 2014).

Schoonmaker's editing style is characterized by her ability to create a raw sense of energy and immediacy, often at the expense of traditional Hollywood post-production techniques of continuity and "invisible" editing. She has described this approach to post-production as informed by the direct cinema documentary filmmakers with whom she and Scorsese collaborated during the 1960s. In Schoonmaker's words, "We like a certain roughness in our film editing style that maybe a Hollywood editor wouldn't like." Schoonmaker has acknowledged that she and Scorsese endeavor to keep in the "bumps" and pursue "a certain grittiness, [a] certain reality" in contrast to the continuity style commonly expected of narrative commercial features in Hollywood (Eyes on Cinema , 2014). While her philosophy of editing is in no way uniformly committed to breaking conventional "rules" of continuity, Schoonmaker's decisions are informed by deliberation over when she and Scorsese want the audience to notice the editing or be affected by it and when they do not. She typically justifies small lapses in continuity (such as an actor's hand placement) not as an intentional stylistic break but in the interest of displaying "the best take for [an actor's] performance" (Pinkerton 2014), as she explained in her approach to *The Wolf of Wall Street* (2013).

In addition to feature film editing, Schoonmaker has been involved in both the technical and promotional aspects of film preservation, an interest that extends from her and Scorsese's cinephilic appreciation for film history evident in the Scorsese-directed film history documentaries she has edited such as *My Voyage to Italy* (2001). Most recently, Schoonmaker has worked toward preserving the filmography of British director Michael Powell, to whom Schoonmaker was married from 1984 until his death. Schoonmaker and Scorsese's promotion of Powell's work as a director has played an important role in revitalizing Powell's cinematic reputation and critical considerations of his historical influence. As of this writing, Schoonmaker has been most recently involved in restoring and publicizing a new print of *The Tales of Hoffman*. Her dedication to film preservation constitutes a deliberate reversal from her first job as an editor, which required her to alter and amend films contrary to their original cuts.

Regarding the role of women editors in Hollywood, Schoonmaker has observed, "There are more women editors than people realize. . . . I think we're more able to keep our eye on what the film needs. Between men sometimes it's a real ego battle, and that's very bad for the film. . . . In the very beginning, women were editors because they were the people in the lab rolling the film before there was editing. Then when people like D. W. Griffith began editing, they needed the women from the lab to come and splice the film together. . . . Then when it became a more lucrative job, men moved into it" (Wood 2015).

Landon Palmer

See also: Menke, Sally

Further Reading

DP/30: The Oral History of Hollywood. 2014. "DP/30: Thelma Schoonmaker Cut the Wolf of Wall Street." YouTube video, 33:39, January 9. https://www.youtube.com/watch?v=KIKRcV4kHzg

Eyes on Cinema. 2014. "Thelma Schoonmaker Talks Scorsese, Editing & Bad Cuts in Rare 17-Minute 1993 Interview." YouTube video, 17:14, December 6. https://www.youtube.com/watch?v=K6hCKyJruJo

Pinkerton, Nick. 2014. "Interview: Thelma Schoonmaker." Film Comment, March 31. http://www.filmcomment.com/blog/interview-thelma-schoonmaker

Robson, Leo. 2014. "Thelma Schoonmaker: The Queen of the Cutting Room." *FT Magazine*, May 9. http://www.ft.com/intl/cms/s/2/b718ca00-d4b5-11e3-bf4e-00144feabdc0.html

Wadleigh, Michael. 1970. "The 'Take One' Challenge of Filming 'Woodstock.'" *American Cinematographer* 51(10): 972–77, 1016–31.

Wood, Gaby. 2015. "Thelma Schoonmaker Interview: 'I Wanted To Kill Myself.'" *The Telegraph*, March 22. http://www.telegraph.co.uk/film/the-tales-of-hoffman/thelma-schoonmaker-interview

Smith, Rose (1897–1962)

Rose Smith (née Richtel) was a film editor, or "cutter," during the silent and early sound eras who is best known for her work with director D. W. Griffith. Working alongside her husband, James (Jimmie) Smith, Rose Smith helped to create the editing techniques that would become the foundation for narrative filmmaking.

Smith began working in the film industry directly out of high school, patching, inspecting, and splicing films at Gaumont and Éclair Studios in New York. During this period, cutting film required nimble hands, and the job of preparing film negatives for editing often fell to young, working-class women. Smith was among a number of women who worked her way from this menial position to that of editor.

In 1914, Smith moved from New York to California to work at Reliance-Majestic, Griffith's new studio. As a director at Biograph, Griffith had been limited to directing one- or two-reel films for nickelodeon theaters. With his new studio, Griffith planned to develop longer, feature-length films for the newly emerging motion picture theaters. Griffith had brought his long-time editor, Jimmie Smith, with him from Biograph, but feature-length films called for more complex editing than was permitted in one- or two-reel films. Working under her maiden name, Richtel, Rose Smith paired with Jimmie to edit several of the director's early feature-length films: *The Battle of the Sexes, The Escape, Home, Sweet Home*, and *The Avenging Conscience*, all of which were released in 1914. That year, she also began working with Jimmie and Raoul Walsh to edit *The Birth of a Nation* (1915).

Rose and Jimmie's most challenging job was editing Griffith's landmark film, *Intolerance* (1916). It took 18 months to edit the film, during which time Rose and Jimmie took a brief break to get married. Coming in at 14 reels, *Intolerance* weaves together four separate stories occurring in different epochs. Rather than present these stories consecutively, as had been done in *Home, Sweet Home, Intolerance* presents the four stories in tandem. Through parallel editing, each story of violence and conflict comments upon the others and on the theme of intolerance, including a thrilling chase in which a racing train parallels a chase on horseback, ending with the nick-of-time rescue of an innocent man from the gallows. The film would inspire filmmakers from around the world, including Vsevolod Pudovkin and other Soviet montage theorists.

In 1918, press reports identify Rose Smith as working under contract with the Pickford Company. However, more research is needed to identify the films Rose worked on there. She was loaned back to Griffith to help Jimmie edit *Hearts of the World* (1918), and in 1919 Griffith brought the couple to New York with him when he opened a production studio on Long Island. Their joint credits from this period include *Way Down East* (1920), *Dream Street* (1921), *Orphans of the Storm* (1921), and *America* (1924). It is difficult to know precisely the extent of Rose's contribution to Griffith's films. Jimmie had been working with the director from the beginning of both men's film careers. However, numerous sources attest to Rose's working as Jimmie's equal in the editing room. *Screenland* described Griffith's films as "not so much written as assembled. Griffith shoots miles of footage, works for months, stages all sorts of fine effects, and then dumps the crude product on the doorstep of Mr. and Mrs. Jimmie Smith. Whereupon Jimmie and the missus rescue the orphan of D. W.'s brainstorm and beat it into submission" (Prophater 1923). Recalling

Griffith's working methods in 1973, Karl Brown wrote that Rose and Jimmie would watch the rushes with Griffith, who would select takes and describe the effect he wanted to produce, leaving it to his editors to work through the details.

Rose Smith's contributions extend beyond realizing Griffith's vision in the editing room. She was also responsible for tinting the films. In the original release prints of *Intolerance*, for instance, each of the four epochs was tinted in a different color. According to Rose, "It is the cutter who decides the intensity of the color effects. Perhaps a certain lighting may have resulted in a tone that is unbecoming to the star. Perhaps it is only a matter of faulty printing. But it is up to the cutter to know just what and why it is" (Copeland 1920). In addition to overseeing the editing and tinting of the films, Rose had the job of cutting down pictures for second-run theaters. Most notably, following the release of *Intolerance*, Rose Smith edited the film down to include just the modern portion of the story, even adding a scene for clarity. The re-edited film was released as *The Mother and the Law* (1919).

In addition to these official duties, Rose played an unofficial role as Griffith's sounding board. Numerous sources report that Griffith relied on Rose's opinion as an indication of how feminine audiences would respond to his films and their stars. Perhaps this is because Rose Smith was the only woman who played a significant role behind the scenes, rather than in front of the camera, in Griffith's films. And it certainly points to the recognition that box-office success relied on female audiences

While Griffith was the most celebrated director of the silent era, he had not managed his businesses wisely, and by 1925 he was working as a contract director with little autonomy. That year, the *Exhibitors Herald* announced that, after working with Griffith for 12 years, Rose Smith would be editing *The Sky Rocket* for Marshall Neilan, whom she is likely to have worked with at Pickford's studio. Over the next decade, Rose edited films for several directors, including Howard Hawks's *Fig Leaves* (1926) and Raoul Walsh's *The Monkey Talks* (1927), both at Fox. Jimmie, on the other hand, continued to work with Griffith; his last film for the director was *Abraham Lincoln* (1930). Rose's career declined significantly after 1930, when the economic Depression prompted a backlash against working women. By the mid-1930s, Rose and Jimmie had divorced and Rose was editing films for Poverty Row Studios. Jimmie continued editing films through the 1940s and moved into television in the 1950s, Rose's last known credit is for *Public Stenographer.*

Kristen Hatch

See also: Booth, Margaret

Further Reading

Brown, Karl. 1973. *Adventures with D. W. Griffith.* New York: Farrar, Straus, and Giroux.

Copeland, Gene. 1920. "The Story of Rosie and Jimmie Smith." *Photoplay*, XVII. 76–78.

Prophater, Anna. 1923. "Hidden Hands of Filmdom." *Screenland*, 8. 100–101.

Svilova, Yelizaveta (1900–1975)

Though many young film scholars, as well as some seasoned veterans, might not recognize Yelizaveta Ignatevna Svilova (alternatively, Elizaveta Svilova) by name, there is more than a decent chance that they are unknowingly aware of at least some of her work. Most known to Western audiences is Svilova's role as editor to Dziga Vertov, both on and off screen, in his 1929 film *Man with a Movie Camera* (*Человек с киноаппаратом*), which is widely held as required viewing for neophyte film theorists and cinephiles alike. In spite of her legacy being overshadowed by her husband Vertov's successes, recent scholarly engagement has vouched for Yelizaveta Svilova's place among the pantheon of Soviet montage filmmakers, which has typically been seen as an all-boys club. Her oeuvre spans several decades, including critical post-war Stalinist Russia, and deals with a variety of subjects, including the liberation of Nazi concentration camps, through the usage of documentary and Soviet montage styles.

For many reasons, the relative dearth of scholarly engagement with Svilova's works is odd. As an editor, Svilova was among the best. What's more, her mind for directing transcended her role as an editor. Christopher Penfold and Jeremy Hicks note that much of her work in the 1920s as editor ought to be considered the work of a co-director rather than simply an editor (Penfold 2013, 69). Since Vertov's films rely on montage, the process of editing and splicing together frames and extended sequences was just as important as the principal photography. Therefore, Svilova's contribution is essential to *Man with a Movie Camera* (1929) and other Vertov films. As such, Penfold, Hicks, and others have begun to isolate Svilova's contributions to these works so that she might receive the credit and admiration she is due beyond her recognition as a dutiful editor and supportive wife.

Could it be that Yelizaveta Svilova is not a household name because of her own modesty? According to Penfold, one of Svilova's autobiographies suggests that she turned down recognition for her work in Vertov's films shortly after her husband's death. Reasons for Svilova's relative obscurity might also include the fact that she is a woman. Thankfully, film scholarship has grown to more fully acknowledge filmmakers and editors of the female persuasion since its inception. As a result, Svilova's works are beginning to come to the fore, allowing academics to glean new information from them about post-war–era Eastern Europe, as well as Soviet montage filmmaking at large.

Among her works, perhaps the most moving and historically important are Svilova's later projects, which revolve around footage of recently freed Holocaust survivors in Poland and Eastern Germany. These wartime documentaries—which include *Atrocities of Fascists on the Soviet Soldiers* (*Зверства фашистов над советскими воинами*) (1943) and *Auschwitz* (*Освенцим*) (1945)—were some of the first recorded images of the atrocities uncovered by the Allies as World War II drew to a close in the European theater (Hicks 2012). Svilova follows up on the topic of the Holocaust and Nazi war criminals with a documentary entitled *Judgment of the Nations* (*Суд народов*) (1946). Although this particular film fails to mention anything about the actual atrocities, it does speak to the Soviet distaste for the Nazi brass and their form of government, according to Hicks. The significance of these wartime documentaries speaks to Svilova's broader oeuvre, which seems to toe the party line in Stalinist Russia, as it were. While Vertov may have fallen out of favor with the Soviet politburo, Svilova continued to produce actionable propaganda in the form of newsreel-style documentary films. Furthermore, these films, *Auschwitz* most readily, demonstrate Svilova's talent in terms of utilizing found footage, or previously recorded images, in her documentary films. Rather than allowing the images alone to speak the film's message, Svilova daringly crafts her film on the editing table to establish the film's voice in the collision of shots and ideas in true Soviet montage form. For example, at one point in Vertov's *Man with a Movie Camera,* Svilova cuts between a working-class woman washing a blanket and a coded-bourgeois woman getting her hair washed. What the collision of these images might intend to demonstrate is class consciousness in Soviet Russia. Even when she directed her films herself, Svilova maintained control over the editing process, imprinting her style on the documentary form as well as in the shape of the number of film series she was a part of, including *Kino-Pravda* (*Кино-Правда*) and *News of the Day* (*Новости дня*), the latter of which ran for several years during and after World War II. A full list of films Svilova contributed to is available with commentary in the filmography appendix of Penfold's thesis.

In the end, Penfold suggests that while Vertov may have had a specific vision regarding how his works would play out, Svilova's editing genius and capacities as a cutting-room-floor director may have been ultimately responsible for the fruition of said vision (Penfold 2013, 38). There can be no doubt, therefore, that Yelizaveta Svilova's legacy is secured, albeit relatively underexplored. Further research and sampling of her works may yet earn her a spot in the pantheon of timeless Russian filmmakers among the likes of Sergei Eisenstein.

Grayson Nowak

Further Reading

Attwood, Lynne, ed. 1993. *Red Women on the Silver Screen: Soviet Women and Cinema from the Beginning to the End of the Communist Era.* London: Pandora Press.

Bordwell, David. 2005. *The Cinema of Eisenstein.* New York: Routledge.

Hicks, Jeremy. 2012. *First Films of the Holocaust: Soviet Cinema and the Genocide of the Jews, 1938–1946.* Pitt Series in Russian and East European Studies. Pittsburgh: University of Pittsburgh Press.

Penfold, Christopher. 2013. "Elizaveta Svilova and Soviet Documentary Film." Doctoral thesis. University of Southampton.

Vertov, Dziga. 1984. *Kino-Eye: The Writings of Dziga Vertov.* Edited by Annette Michelson. Translated by Kevin O'Brien. Berkeley: University of California Press.

Interview with Lynzee Klingman

How did you get your start in editing?

I graduated college in 1965, and I think it was before Betty Friedan's book, which changed everything and started the women's movement. I was a real movie person, but it never occurred to me to work in film. I met someone who worked as an editor for the city of New York, who first got me into it. After knocking on doors for a job, I finally got one with a guy who was looking to hire a girl for the office. They weren't making Hollywood movies; they were making industrials or commercials, just nothing to do with anything anybody would really want to see. And the attitude was that women couldn't do this kind of work. They'd say, "The film is heavy, and you can't carry a lot of cans if you're wearing high heels." That was how I started, and I learned from my really terrible mistakes, because nobody paid any attention to me.

I had no ambition, but the consciousness raising at the time got me involved in the anti-war movement, and that's when I was approached by Emile de Antonio (who had previously done *Point of Order* about the McCarthy hearings), and he was looking for a cheap editor on a feature documentary called *In the Year of the Pig*. It ended up being nominated for an Academy Award! How's that? It's the first one I ever cut.

After I worked on another documentary, *Hearts and Minds* everything changed for me because I really felt that the most painful moments in a person's life in a documentary are the best films, and it made me uncomfortable. My fantasy would be to work on a movie where actors got paid to emulate those emotions but not actually witness someone's pain. I just didn't want to do documentaries anymore. I became friends with the sound editor who had worked on the film, and that's how I got to do *One Flew over the Cuckoo's Nest* in '75.

Is there a long apprenticeship for assistant editors?

I wasn't in the union in New York. They wouldn't let me in. When I came out to California, you had to be an assistant editor for seven years. You had to be an apprentice for three. Then you got to be an assistant. This is longer than neurosurgery. And you had to be on the union industry roster. What is that? It was something that you couldn't get on unless you were in the union, but you couldn't get in the union unless you were on the roster. So you couldn't get into the union, period. It was a closed shop. It was really for the sons, the nephews of the people [who] were in there. It was mostly men.

I was finally in a class action suit with, among others, Haskell Wexler, who was the main DP on *Cuckoo's Nest*. We sued the union (IATSE, International Alliance of Theatrical Stage Employees), and we won. And then, as soon as we got into the union, they let everybody in. I was so pissed. For a while, it was an open union. It was one of those ironies. It was a 12- or 13-year struggle for me. When Steven [Spielberg] called me about *Close Encounters of the Third Kind*, my union status came up, and he said, "I'm going to have so many battles with the studio." So I couldn't do it but I was relieved, because I was scared. I knew how good he was. I knew what drama there had been on *Jaws* because Verna Fields had become a close friend.

How did you manage to balance your personal and work life?

Well the hours were so brutal for me. So when I had my daughter I decided not to work for two years. Because when I work I don't notice the clock. I'm still there working until four in the morning, unless someone stops me.

I didn't get married and have children until I was older, like 36 or 37.

My husband also worked in the film business, which was really difficult and he had become a director. He was always an adventurer. So at the drop of a hat, he would go to Tibet to research a location for a film that he certainly knew as well as I did would never be made, but he'd go. He could never turn down an airplane ticket. So I took two years off with my daughter and then I would only work every other year. If he had a film coming up, I wouldn't work. I also never went on location. I once did and it was kind of a disaster.

I have two of the greatest children. My son was born about seven years after my daughter. I was a very old mother. I had a lot of films done by then. Having a child and having a career is hard, and the people I worked for were just never accommodating to that kind of thing.

It was tough! It was kind of unbelievable. I don't know how I did it. I look back and I don't know. We'd have dinner parties! How did we do that? I can't imagine the life I led now. I just can't imagine. I had a good housekeeper. I don't know how people do it. Today, I think it's a lot easier. I don't know really, because I don't know a lot of young moms. I know a lot of women editors who don't have children, actually.

I did want to mention that when I finally started meeting women who were doing what I was doing, every woman was so supportive of every other woman. Verna Fields was just a cheerleader. She was just the most wonderful, welcoming, warm, friendly, knowledgeable person, and she just loved helping editors. And Dede Allen too—they are two shining beacons of women editors. But there other editors too, I'm friends with a lot of editors. There's a wonderful sisterhood, which is great.

Feature Animation

Introduction

It's critical to recognize that animation is a medium for filmmaking. It is not a film genre. It is also one of the most misunderstood mediums in film, as animation tends to be pigeonholed as a genre only acceptable for children and begrudging parents. The medium has been chronically undervalued and often suffers from the misbelief that animation is easy. But at its core, animation values story just as much as any other narrative-based film, and it demands a mastery of many specialized skills.

The 3D animation pipeline is as follows: idea, pitch, script, concept art, recording, storyboarding (also known as story art), character design, modeling, rigging, texturing, animation, lighting, effects, rendering, and compositing into the final product. For 2D animation the process is somewhat similar, only each frame is painstakingly drawn by hand or posed using a puppet rig. A painstakingly high level of attention to detail goes into development, and the standard animated film takes creators approximately four years to make from start to finish.

Animation perhaps began to be taken more seriously with the nomination of *Beauty and the Beast* for Best Picture at the 1991 Academy Awards. Since then, appreciation for the industry has increasingly grown as films such as *Up* (2009) and *Toy Story 3* (2010) still received nominations for Best Picture despite the creation of a category for Best Animated Feature in 2001.

However, women working in the animation field often struggle to find work, and their history has been long obscured. Animation has been dominated by men since its inception, and women's roles in the industry rarely allowed them to be accepted or encouraged to go further in the field. In the early days of animation women rarely, if ever, received credit for their work, and some had to resort to using male pseudonyms. Despite such challenges, women such as Mary Blair would become one of the most influential artists in Disney's history. There are so many significant women of animation who deserve entries of their own: Reiko Okuyama, Rebecca Sugar, Carole Holiday, Linda Simensky, Brenda Banks, Jennifer Lee, Lillian Friedman, Lauren Faust, LaVerne Harding, Bianca Majolie, Retta Scott, and Kazuko Nakamura, just to name a few. Although women are still underrepresented in this field, they have made some massive gains in recent history. In 2012, Brenda Chapman became the first woman to win an Oscar for Best Animated Feature for *Brave,* and Jennifer Lee won for *Frozen* the following year.

Carrie Tupper

Blair, Mary (1911–1978)

Bold colors, simple shapes, and exaggerated proportions that border on the abstract, Mary Blair's paint-covered hands created memorable scenes from multiple Disney films and parks. A favored artist and friend of Walt Disney himself, Blair's unique twist on playful modern art brought a gradual sea change to the artistic direction of Disney's animated features. Ronald "Rolly" Crump described Mary as able to see the world through a child's eyes, easily relating to and understanding them—a trait she shared with Disney. Ultimately Blair's distinctive style and color work continue to be an influence even in modern highly rendered 3D animated features and series.

Born to a bookkeeper and a seamstress in Oklahoma, Mary had a knack for the arts from an early age. She won a scholarship to the Chouinard School of Art and studied under illustrator Pruett Carter. Blair would later become part of the "California School" of watercolor, a movement of watercolor techniques and styles that grew under the pressure of the Great Depression. After graduating Chouinard in 1933, she struggled to find work before she found a job at Iwerks Studio as a cel painter. After two years at Iwerks, she quit and was hired at Disney Animation Studios as a sketch artist in 1940.

Her earliest work for Disney would later give life to *Dumbo* (1941) and *Lady and the Tramp* (1955). During this time, her job was to work directly with the writers. She described the process as creating "the ideas [of] the picture graphically from its basic beginning" (Johnson 2017, 188). Frustrated with the stifling atmosphere of animation production and eager to move onto "real" art, Blair left the studio to pursue professional painting once again. Two months later she learned that Disney was sending artists to South America. The trip of a lifetime was too good to pass up.

In 1941 she boarded a plane with 18 other Disney artists to participate in a goodwill tour on behalf of the U.S. government's "Good Neighbor Policy," an effort to influence hearts and minds of South America away from Nazism. "El Grupo" as the party called themselves, spent three months traveling through Argentina, Brazil, Bolivia, Ecuador, Guatemala, Mexico, and Peru. At every stop, Blair and her companions were painting, exploring, and enjoying all the continent had to offer. It was on this trip that Blair's famous styling began to solidify into the bold lines, rich color, and modernist minimal abstraction that she became famous for. The paintings Blair produced through the three-month trip became foundational inspiration for some of Disney's more unique feature films, *The Three Caballeros* (1945), *Saludos Amigos* (1943), and parts of *Melody Time* (1948). Colorful images of musicians, children at play, river boats, market scenes, and other forms of daily life enthralled Disney, and he named her artistic supervisor on both *Caballeros* and *Saludos*.

Disney loved the colorful abstract quality of Blair's work and pushed his artists to put her work on screen. This came with pushback from his crew. Disney wanted "realistic" animation that created what he called "the illusion of life," (Johnston and Thomas 1995, 9), but to put Blair's influences on screen meant the animation would look flat in comparison. The interdepartmental compromises made to Blair's work for a finished feature film often meant Blair's ideas were barely visible by completion. This disconnect chaffed Blair. In a letter written to film historian Ross Care she said, "Only on the little train sequence [in *Caballeros*] did I feel that it was really my own artwork and my style" (Canemaker 1996, 124).

After production on *Melody Time*, Blair was assigned a new project, the second princess-based feature, *Cinderella* (1950). The power of her visual design can be seen throughout the *Cinderella* picture. This is especially true in the "So This Is Love" sequence—the soft pastels over dark backgrounds and the organic curving lines of the set elements create an intimate dreamy feeling that fits perfectly with the song. It's no wonder Blair received an Art Direction credit for *Cinderella*. Her artistic impact continued to flourish through production on *Alice in Wonderland* (1951). The extreme angles, repetitive patterns, and mastery of color language took the viewer through an increasingly unsettling world. Blair's guidance on visual development struck a balance between the surreal and unreal. For *Peter Pan* (1953), Blair pulled back from the wild color spaces of *Wonderland* but retained the playfulness. Her color and style bloom throughout the feature, especially in the flight to Neverland, Neverland itself, and the finale's golden flying pirate ship. Disney's post-war return to the big screen wouldn't have been the same without Blair's gentle guidance. *Cinderella*, *Alice in Wonderland,* and *Peter Pan* all benefited from her suggestions on everything from props, settings, mood, costumes, and even character relationships. A few days before the release of *Peter Pan*, Blair resigned from Disney.

While Blair provided a wealth of talent and direction for the projects she worked on, she struggled with jealousies from fellow male artists, including her own husband, Lee Blair. An intense rivalry between Blair and her husband boiled under the surface of their marriage, and it was only exacerbated as Blair grew closer to Disney. This rivalry continued even after her death in 1978. The Walt Disney Company decided to recognize Blair's contributions to their films and parks (Blair designed the iconic It's a Small World ride) with a posthumous Disney Legends Award in 1991. Her husband refused to accept the award on her behalf, frustrated that he was not getting the award when he had worked for the company too, and unlike his wife, was still living.

The legacy of Mary Blair lives on in the world of modern animated storytelling and the concept artists who work in the industry. Her influences on color, shape, or both can be seen in the works of notable contemporary visual development artists Brittney Lee, Lorelay Bové, Victoria Ying, and Mingjue Helen Chen. Elements of her design and color language are lovingly rendered in animated films from a wide variety of studios, not just the Walt Disney Company. John Canemaker, an animation historian, succinctly describes why Mary Blair's artistic prowess continues to inspire today: "One feels good just gazing at Mary Blair's paintings. Like feasting on rainbows" (Canemaker 1996, 142).

Carrie Tupper

See also: Chapman, Brenda; Moberly-Holland, Sylvia; Reiniger, Lotte

Further Reading

Canemaker, John. 1999. *Before the Animation Begins: The Art and Lives of Disney Inspirational Sketch Artists.* .New York: Hyperion, 114–142.

Canemaker, John, and Mary Blair. 2014. *The Art and Flair of Mary Blair: An Appreciation.* New York: Disney Editions.

Gluck, Keith. 2016. "Walt and the Goodwill Tour." The Walt Disney Family Museum, September 8. https://waltdisney.org/blog/walt-and-goodwill-tour

Johnson, Mindy. 2017. *Ink & Paint: The Women of Walt Disney's Animation.* Illustrated ed. New York: Disney Editions.

Walt & El Grupo, DVD. 2008. Directed by Theodore Thomas. Burbank, CA: Theodore Thomas Productions and Walt Disney Studios Motion Pictures.

Chapman, Brenda (1962–)

To appreciate the trials and triumphs of Brenda Chapman one would have to start in a sad place for the world of animation, with the deaths of Walt and Roy O. Disney. The Walt Disney Company was rudderless with their deaths, and during the 18-year period that followed from 1970 to 1988, the studio's feature films had seemingly lost their magic. In the mid-1980s new leadership stepped into the limelight, but elsewhere in the company someone new had just joined the studio's animation department. Chapman would be the woman who would help shape the foundation of the Disney Renaissance, a period beginning with the release of *The Little Mermaid* in 1989 and ending with *Tarzan* in 1999.

Director, writer, and animation story artist Brenda Chapman was the first woman to be hired by a major studio to direct an animated feature, *The Prince of Egypt* (1998). For her work on *Brave* (2012), which she co-directed, she became the first woman to win the Academy Award for Best Animated Feature. (Photo by Mo DeLong)

In 1987, Chapman graduated from CalArts, one of five women in a class of 34. With the help of her short student film, she landed her dream job at Disney Animation. Chapman's first assignment was on *Who Framed Roger Rabbit* (1988) as an inbetweener. The job of an inbetweener is to draw the frames of movement between the lead animators keyframes, or drawings that define the major transition points of a character's or object's movement in animation.

Animation was the gateway to Chapman realizing that her real love was story. When she found out that she would be moving up in the Disney program as a story trainee, she was ecstatic, but the victory was short-lived. Chapman recalls the event in her 2013 TEDx talk: "I was elated for about three seconds, because that was when the executive across from me told me I was hired because I was a woman." The studio was being criticized for their lack of diversity, especially in the story department. Chapman was hired to fill the role of token female. In the story department, Brenda's first project was on *The Little Mermaid.* She contributed ideas for the "Tour of the Kingdom" and the "Part of Your World" reprise sequence from the finale of the film. Token female or not, she proved to the Disney team that she deserved the job for her storytelling skills.

The proverbial training wheels were removed in her story work on *The Rescuers Down Under* (1990). In a film where just about every animal talks, the performance of the character Marahute is unique in that she is a voiceless character. Originally Marahute was supposed to have a voice, but Chapman suggested the idea of letting the bird pantomime her emotions. Chapman's strength in storytelling is put on spectacular display as Cody learns that Marahute's mate was killed by poachers without the eagle having one word of dialogue. Her contribution to this scene provided an emotional bond that carried the film and proved Chapman had the skills to move forward.

She was brought onto *Beauty and the Beast* (1991), partnering with fellow story artist from *The Little Mermaid,* Roger Allers, to create the emotionally resonate sequences that give the movie its solid foundation. One such scene is when Belle is patching up the Beast after her flight from the castle. This sequence of the film provides the emotional turn that sparks the beginning of the film's romance. *Beauty and the Beast* made history as the first animated film nominated for Best Picture at the Academy Awards in 1992. In the background, Chapman was making her own history when she became the first female head of story at Disney. In her new position, she would oversee the story work on *The Lion King* (1994), which at the time was considered a "B" movie in comparison to *Aladdin* (1992) and *Pocahontas* (1995). Chapman's strong story presence is seen throughout the film, and she is responsible for the story sequence where Simba is visited by the ghost of Mufasa. With her leadership in the story department, Chapman's "B" movie became a breakout hit.

In the same year *The Lion King* was released, Jeffrey Katzenberg left Disney to found DreamWorks SKG. Katzenberg brought Chapman onto his team, and she became the first woman to co-direct an animated feature film at a major studio with *The Prince of Egypt* (1998). In 2003, Chapman parted ways with DreamWorks to work at Pixar where she has credits in *Wall-E* (2008), *Ratatouille* (2007), *Up* (2009), and *Toy Story 3* (2010). In 2010, Pixar announced that Brenda would be the first woman to solo direct a feature with *Brave* (2012).

Brave was Pixar's first film with a female lead and was inspired by Chapman's relationship with her daughter and love for old fairy tales. She pitched the idea to Pixar's Chief Creative Officer John Lasseter, and it was greenlit soon after. As production continued, creative friction became a roadblock, and in October 2010,

Chapman was unceremoniously removed from her own project and replaced with Mark Andrews. With her departure, the film changed from a purely mother-daughter storyline to a new take where expectations, betrothal, and marriage provide the main conflict. Having her original project taken from her and given to a male director left Chapman devastated. In an article in *The New York Times* she wrote, "Animation directors are not protected like live-action directors, who have the Directors Guild to go to battle for them." She further goes on to say, "We are replaced on a regular basis—and that was a real issue for me. This was a story that I created, which came from a very personal place, as a woman and a mother. To have it taken away and given to someone else, and a man at that, was truly distressing on so many levels" (Chapman 2012). Though Chapman was removed from the project she still retained a co-director credit. She left Pixar and returned to DreamWorks to develop other projects and has briefly worked for Lucasfilm.

Despite Pixar's efforts to keep her out of publicity for the film, it backfired when *Brave* won an Academy Award for Best Animated Feature. Pixar couldn't stop Brenda Chapman from taking home an Oscar and making history once more. She is the first and only woman to win an Oscar for Best Animated Film. A woman of many firsts, Brenda Chapman's solid understanding of storytelling and the human experience have given life to some of the world's most acclaimed animated films.

Carrie Tupper

See also: Blair, Mary; Moberly-Holland, Sylvia; Reiniger, Lotte

Further Reading

Chapman, Brenda. 2012. "Stand Up for Yourself, and Mentor Others." *The New York Times*, August 14. https://www.nytimes.com/roomfordebate/2012/08/14/how-can-women-gain-influence-in-hollywood/stand-up-for-yourself-and-mentor-others

Johnson, Mindy. 2017. *Ink & Paint: The Women of Walt Disney's Animation.* Illustrated ed. Glendale: Disney Editions.

Lerew, Jenny. 2012. *The Art of Brave.* San Francisco: Chronicle Books.

Mallory, Michael. 2012. "Brenda Chapman and the See-Through Ceiling." *Animation Magazine*, March 1. http://www.animationmagazine.net/top-stories/brenda-chapman-and-the-see-through-ceiling

McNary, Dave. 2013. "Oscars: 'Brave' Wins Tight Animation Race." *Variety*, February 25. http://variety.com/2013/film/awards/oscars-brave-draws-animated-feature-818215

Pallant, Chris. 2013. "The Disney Renaissance." In *Demystifying Disney: A History of Disney Feature Animation.* New York: Bloomsbury, 89–110.

Pershing, Linda, Amanda Lenox, and Melissa Demi Martinez. 2016. "Fortune Favours the Brave: Brenda Chapman's Efforts to Tell a Mother-Daughter Story of Conflict and Love in a Fairy Tale Film." In *Screening Motherhood in Contemporary World Cinema.* Edited by Sayed Asma. Bradford, ON: Demeter Press.

Powers, Lindsay. 2010. "Pixar Announces First Female Director." *The Hollywood Reporter*, September 24. https://www.hollywoodreporter.com/news/pixar-announces-first-female-director-28289

Shepherd, Heather M. 2016. "Interview with Brenda Chapman." Creative Talent Network, March 9. http://creativetalentnetwork.com/blog.php?blogId=26

TEDxTalks. 2013. "Role Model Resilience: Brenda Chapman at TEDxUNPlaza 2013." YouTube video, 15:31, October 2. https://www.youtube.com/watch?v=WDJAImaqwpM.

Jenson, Vicky (1960–)

Director Victoria "Vicky" Jenson is a woman with a skill for creating hilarious scenes and moving moments that not only entertain but charm audiences as well. Quick to crack a joke, Jenson has a style of leadership on film projects that focuses on listening to her team while fostering them to be the best they can. While Jenson rides the line of live action and animation director, her best-known works are found in animation, especially within the DreamWorks SKG film *Shrek* (2001).

Born in Los Angeles, Jenson was a lover of stories and painting from an early age and began painting animation cels at the age of 13. Her love for story and painting continued into adulthood where she studied fine art and literature at the Academy of Art College in San Francisco and Cal State Northridge. After graduating college she found her way into the world of animation through TV animation work. At Filmation Associates she started painting backgrounds for *He-Man and the Masters of the Universe* (1983) animated series. Much like Jennifer Yuh Nelson, she didn't stick to one role. Jenson took her time exploring the different areas of the animation process. On each project she'd had to wear multiple hats, which led her to find her passion for storyboarding. She worked on such television animated shows as *The Smurfs* (1981), *She-Ra: Princess of Power* (1985), *The Original Ghostbusters* (1986), *Jem* (1986), *Animaniacs* (1993), *Ren & Stimpy* (1994), and countless more.

Director and animation story artist Vicky Jenson in her home office in Los Angeles, California. Jenson directed the animated feature *Shrek* (2001), which became the first film to win an Academy Award for Best Animated Feature. Her next animated feature, *Shark Tale* (2004), received a nomination in the same category. Jenson's versatile career spans both animated and live-action films, as well as commercial work. (Photo by Gerard Sandoval)

"I only started planning on becoming a director after working for many years in TV animation," says Jenson (Carrie Tupper, 2018, e-mail message to author, April 26, 2018). In the animation industry the path to directing is often taken through the storyboard or story artist department. With so much time honing her skills in television, Jenson made the leap to film animation with *Ferngully: The Last Rain Forest* (1992) as a storyboard artist. It was around this time that the American Film Institute was hard at work focusing on a program for female directors. "This was a very novel idea at the time . . . women . . . directing . . . gosh, who knew they could? So I wrote my essay, attached my resume and had my backup plan to apply to DreamWorks if I didn't get in." (Carrie Tupper, 2018, e-mail message to author, April 26, 2018).

Unfortunately, the American Film Institute did not accept Jenson into their program (she later ribbed them about it when she was asked to speak there). Thankfully, DreamWorks snapped up the skilled story artist to work on *The Road to El Dorado* (2000). She continued working for the studio, contributing story art on *Chicken Run* (2000) and *Sinbad: Legend of the Seven Seas* (2003). It was just as *El Dorado* was wrapping up that DreamWorks tapped her to work on *Shrek*. "At that point *Shrek* had been through maybe eight producers, four directors, and it had been going on in development for a long time," Jenson says in an interview with *Animation Magazine*. "For a long time, the movie didn't know what it wanted to be" (Mallory 2014). With the death of actor Chris Farley, who was initially hired to voice Shrek, the film went through an upheaval as Jenson and her team worked to find the story without him.

Shrek was almost shelved before the film found its legs, with Jenson working as head of story on the project. After a few months of work, Jeffrey Katzenberg decided it was high time to give Jenson the director role she'd worked so hard for. In partnership with co-director Andrew Adamson, the film began to take shape. "We had some fun twisting fairy tales and turning them on their ear," Jenson told Animation World Network. "The tone of our comedy is a bit irreverent and playful. We were able to play with certain expectations that you have about the characters." (Koseluk 2001). Characters came to life not only through the story but also as Jenson put the best tool in her director's toolbelt to work—listening. When actor Mike Myers came onto the project to give their lead character a new voice, his offhand comments during recordings helped Jenson gain a better understanding of who Shrek was. "Because we were constantly working the sequences, some of his earliest ad-libs helped us find a direction for a particular sequence," Jenson said. "Even after we layered some sequences, he'd say, 'You know what would be a great line right here?' and we'd go back and put it in" (Koseluk 2001).

Her work on *Shrek* is well recognized in a favorite scene of hers: The Gingerbread Interrogation. Created with the help of actor Conrad Vernon, the sequence involved a gingerbread man being questioned by the film's pint-sized antagonist, Lord Farquaad. The riff on, "Do you know the muffin man?" has become one of the film's most quotable lines. In talking on creating effective comedy Jenson told *Variety*, "On *Shrek* we didn't try to figure out how to make adolescents laugh. You have to use yourself as the best judge and use your own instincts. We figured if we laughed at it, chances are good someone else would too" (Atkin 2001). Another sticker of her success on the film was her use of "Hallelujah" as performed by John Cale. She brought the song to the film and fought hard to keep it in, creating a moment of well-needed nuance as Shrek realizes he's lost a dear friend. "The Gingerbread scene I think stands out as defining our unique (at the time) tone of humor and the [use of "Hallelujah"] for showing the depth we could go in telling this story" (Carrie Tupper, 2018, e-mail message to author, April 26, 2018).

Shrek was a breakout hit for DreamWorks, and the film won the coveted first Oscar in the brand-new Best Animated Feature Film category, which beat out

Disney Pixar's film *Monsters, Inc*. The film was a critical sensation, and audiences loved the new twist on tired fairy tales, making *Shrek* rake in $484.4 million at the box office. Jenson's first directorial work in animation became not only one of DreamWorks' highest-grossing films but also laid the groundwork for one of the most successful film franchises in animation history. Over the years since her success on *Shrek*, Jenson continued to direct animation and live-action films, including DreamWorks' *Shark Tale*, *Post Grad*, and multiple shorts. As of this writing she's working with Skydance Media on its very first animated feature called *Split*.

When it comes to working in an industry so lacking in women, Jenson has worked hard to get to where she is today. Her advice to women looking to get into the industry is "learn to take care of yourself. Don't look for limitations, look for opportunities. . . . If you think there is a block in your path it will make you hesitate and that block will become real. Just plow right past as if it doesn't exist and it won't." However, focusing on the up-and-coming creatives is only half the battle. She reminds women already working in the film industry to speak up for themselves. "I think we all need to help each other have a voice. Across gender lines. We need to include to be included" (Carrie Tupper, 2018, e-mail message to author, April 26, 2018).

Carrie Tupper

See also: Nelson, Jennifer Yuh

Further Reading

Atkin, Hillary. 2001. "Vicky Jenson." *Variety*, November 14. http://variety.com/2001/biz/news/vicky-jenson-1117855807

Koseluk, Chris. 2001. "On Co-Directing Shrek: Victoria Jenson." *Animation World Network*, May 10. https://www.awn.com/animationworld/co-directing-shrek-victoria-jenson

Mallory, Michael. 2014. "Firsts among Equals." *Animation Magazine,* March 6. http://www.animationmagazine.net/top-stories/firsts-among-equals

Shada, Samantha. 2015. "Seeking Our Story: An Animated Life: Director Vicky Jenson." IndieWire, December 16. http://www.indiewire.com/2015/12/seeking-our-story-an-animated-life-director-vicky-jenson-210868

Moberly-Holland, Sylvia (1900–1974)

The career of Sylvia Moberly-Holland is a story that starts with music. The daughter of a clergyman who organized an all-women string orchestra, Moberly-Holland was born into a world of music but held a unique passion for art. These skills would serve her well, as later in life she would become a story director for Walt Disney's experimental passion project known in studio as *The Concert Feature*. This project was released in 1940 as *Fantasia*.

Moberly-Holland was a woman of many talents and interests. While growing up in a household of music, her passions for art took her to the Architectural Association School in London, where her draftsmanship was honed to such a fine degree that she became British Columbia's first female architect in 1933. It was in 1936 that Moberly-Holland, a widowed single mother of two, left British Columbia and moved to California. This is where the story of Moberly-Holland's career shifts from architecture to animation.

In 1937, after charming an art director with a drawing of a cat, she was hired as a sketch artist at Universal Studios. With the release of Disney's *Snow White*, Moberly-Holland decided that she was going to work for Disney, regardless of their company-wide policy at the time that prohibited women from doing any creative work. However, she faced a problem: she did not know much about animation. Turning to her job at Universal, she switched departments and worked as a cel inker on Walter Lantz cartoons for three months to learn the ropes. On September 6, 1938, she was hired as a Disney story artist.

With her drafting talents, skill in drawing animals, and ability to communicate movement within her drawings, Disney saw her as a perfect fit for the job. Moberly-Holland became the second female story artist in Disney Animation's history. The first was Bianca Majolie, whose career was short-lived due to creative differences with Disney himself. Moberly-Holland's first assignment was story work on the pastoral sequence of *Fantasia*. She was pivotal to the creation of the centaurettes, fauns, and unicorns that scamper through a pastel landscape of a Greco-Roman myth. Moberly-Holland's daughter, Theo Halladay, explained how her mother was put onto the project when Disney inquired if anyone knew how to draw a horse. Moberly-Holland leaped at the opportunity and drew a horse while walking along with him. She went on to teach her skills to the male animators. With her expertise in drawing animals, Moberly-Holland taught male animators to define the shape and movement of the lithe centaurettes, the heavy built frames of the male centaurs, and the swan-like behaviors and motion used for the Pegasus sequences.

She provided several of the ideas that give the pastoral sequence its relatability and magic. It was Moberly-Holland who suggested introducing the centaurettes by tricking the audience into thinking they were merely human swimmers. This was an idea that Disney enthusiastically ran with. Her perspective came through the work she provided, particularly with the familial, romantic, and childish faun-based scenes. It is unclear whether she had a hand in the creation of racist depictions of black servant centaurs, one of which is named Sunflower. The Walt Disney Company has stayed evasive about the fact these depictions even exist and has erased them from the film entirely.

Based on her outgoing nature, creative energy, and drive, Moberly-Holland was asked to head the "Waltz of the Flowers" and later the "Dance of the Sugar Plum Fairies" (after Majolie was unceremoniously pulled from the project in 1939) sequences in the *Nutcracker Suite*. She poured herself into the work. With Majolie and character designer Ethel Kulsar in tow, she would rummage the fields around Hyperion Studios to find flora that would inspire the tiny dancers in the film. Thistles became Russian dancers; crowds of delicate flowers pirouetted across water, and milkweed seeds floated on air like gentle ballerinas. The problem with leading a team of men in the late 1930s was that men rarely had the patience to take orders from women. That, paired with the rampant homophobia of the time, made many of the men working on "the fairies" feel emasculated. This led some male artists to transfer from Moberly-Holland's team.

When watching *Fantasia* it is easy to notice the sequences Moberly-Holland led, not only for their naturalistic beauty but also for their extraordinary pacing when paired with Tchaikovsky's work. Her understanding of music and timing provided a unique perspective that resulted in animated action that had pinpoint accuracy to each note of the suite. This is especially noticeable in the movements of the dew fairies, the way leaves blow and swirl in the autumn segment, and the whip-fast energy of the frost fairies. Artistically, Disney so enjoyed the look and feel of work created by Moberly-Holland and her peers that the ink and paint department had to invent new techniques for painting cels to retain the soft mood and style. There is also a stark difference in the way Moberly-Holland's art direction represented the female form in the Nutcracker sequence than that of Otto Englander's direction on the pastoral sequence. Moberly-Holland's fairies, though nude, aren't sexualized to the same extent as the centaurettes of Englander's work.

After *Fantasia*'s release in 1940, Moberly-Holland continued to create story concepts and drawings for other features. Many of these were for similar projects to *Fantasia*, but World War II meant the company had to abandon further development on new "Concert Features" of any kind. Most of her continued work was for a Kotex-sponsored educational short film *The Story of Menstruation* (1946), a Goofy short called *How to Play Baseball* (1942), and the war-time animated documentary feature *Victory through Air Power* (1943). There were only three features that she received credit for after this. Two were animated anthology projects: *Make Mine Music* released in 1946 (*Blue Bayou*, a repurpose of her work with *Clair De Lune,* which was a finished piece cut from *Fantasia* and given new modern music) and *Melody Time* released in 1948 (*Bumble Boogie*, also a piece that was repurposed from her development work for the second *Fantasia*). The other was the raindrop sequence from *Bambi* (1942), which reflects her return to naturalistic imagery and the musical prowess seen in her *Fantasia* pieces. She was laid off from the studio in 1941 and only briefly rehired to work on *Victory through Air Power.*

While working for Disney, Moberly-Holland's duties included story direction, writing, preliminary timing, prepping, and illustrating work from camera script to reel and supervising other artists under the eye of a production director. This is the closest any woman ever came to directing a Disney animated feature until Jennifer Lee co-directed *Frozen,* which was released in 2013. As of 2018, The Walt Disney Company has yet to have an animated feature solely directed by a woman. Since the creation of *Fantasia*, the film has inspired multiple creators of renown, including Andy Warhol and Steven Spielberg, and influenced cinematographer Ben Davis on Marvel's 2016 film *Doctor Strange*. Disney adaptations of the *Tinkerbell* film series that ran from 2008 to 2014 are reminiscent of Moberly-Holland's fairies with the occupations fairies have in order to change the seasons. Moberly-Holland's work on *Fantasia* is arguably her magnum opus, showcasing every talent and skill she possessed.

Carrie Tupper

See also: Blair, Mary; Chapman, Brenda

Further Reading

Allan, Robin. 1999. "Walt Disney's Make Mine Music: A Reassessment." *Animation World Network*, April 1. https://www.awn.com/animationworld/walt-disneys-make-mine-music-reassessment

Canemaker, John. 1999. *Before the Animation Begins: The Art and Lives of Disney Inspirational Sketch Artists*. New York: Hyperion, 108–112.

Clague, Mark. 2004. "Playing in 'Toon: Walt Disney's 'Fantasia' (1940) and the Imagineering of Classical Music." *American Music* 22(1): 91–109.

Gabler, Neal. 2015. "Disney's 'Fantasia' Was Initially a Critical and Box-Office Failure." *Smithsonian Magazine*, November. https://www.smithsonianmag.com/arts-culture/disney-fantasia-critical-box-office-failure-180956963

Johnson, Mindy. 2017. *Ink & Paint: The Women of Walt Disney's Animation*. Illustrated ed. New York: Disney Editions.

Nelson, Jennifer Yuh (1972–)

A common idea heard among critics of Hollywood is a director's sense of style. Many attribute style to the way a director will set up a shot or light an actor. Another way to describe a director's style is how they play within their favorite medium. If there is a person within major U.S. animation filmmaking who takes this play to whole new level, it is director Jennifer Yuh Nelson. She has a mastery of composition, an expert eye for action and pacing, and an understanding of what makes a movie lover hold their breath in anticipation of what is coming next. Under her direction, DreamWorks SKG turned a surprisingly successful kung fu–inspired film into a feature franchise that has been incredibly successful.

Nelson's family immigrated to the United States from Korea when she was four. Despite her childhood interests, which resembled storyboarding, the idea of working in animation never occurred to Nelson until a storyboard artist talked to her class at the California State University at Long Beach. While getting her degree in illustration, she landed a summer job at a small animation studio where her sister worked called Jet Lag Productions.

After graduation, she moved on to work for Hanna-Barbera, followed by Bakshi Productions. She then she took a job as a character designer on HBO's *Todd McFarlen's Spawn* (1997–1999). There she got her first director credit and directed three more episodes before she left for DreamWorks SKG. Starting in television animation allowed Nelson to wear the multiple hats required for production. Learning the ropes of every job required to finish a project provided the needed insight for what she wanted to focus on, and it was storyboarding where she flourished. While working at DreamWorks SKG, her first story artist assignments were on *Spirit: Stallion of the Cimarron* (2002). Two years later, she became head of story on *Sinbad: Legend of the Seven Seas* (2003) at the encouragement of friend and mentor, Brenda Chapman. She then took on story work for *Madagascar* (2005).

Nelson's skill in drawing fast-paced action would become key to the success of DreamWorks SKG's next feature film. A fan of kung fu films from a young age, when she heard DreamWorks SKG's next project was called *Kung Fu Panda* (2008), she lit up. "[Other than the title] I didn't know anything about it," she recalled in an interview on the Nick Animation podcast. "If I have to shovel trash to be part of that movie, I'll do whatever" (Navarro 2016). The introverted story artist plucked up the courage to ask to be on the film and was blown away when she was given the job of head of story. On *Panda* it was her job to oversee the story artist department and help the writers, directors, and producers envision the film they wanted to create.

Nelson's geeky side was free to fly on *Panda*, and she took inspiration from favored kung fu films, anime series, comic books, and even video games to bring the action to life. It was *Panda*'s producer Melissa Cobb who suggested Nelson to direct the film's opening dream sequence. Here Nelson's visual style and understanding of fast-paced action came to fruition. Using 2D animation for this dream sequence allowed for a stylistic way of separating the dream world and how Po (the main character) wants to see himself from the reality of the world in which the film takes place. This juxtaposition of 2D dreams and 3D reality was used again in *Kung Fu Panda 2* (2011), as Po's dreams reveal themselves to be memories.

The work Nelson provided on *Kung Fu Panda* impressed animation and live-action filmmakers alike. That year she won Best Storyboarding in an Animated Feature Production at the Annie Awards. When DreamWorks SKG greenlit a sequel, Cobb had to convince Nelson to be the new film's director, as Nelson felt she was too introverted. But when Nelson took the job, she became the first woman in history to solo-direct a major animated feature film.

Paired with Nelson's eye for action and an emotionally resonant story, *Kung Fu Panda 2* was an instant hit. It smashed the box office, earning $665.6 billion worldwide. Nelson's film was the highest-grossing film to be solo-directed by a woman until Patty Jenkins's *Wonder Woman* was released in 2017. At the Academy Awards, Nelson became the first female solo-director to ever be nominated for Best Animated Feature Film. After the success of *Kung Fu Panda 2*, Nelson took the helm of *Kung Fu Panda 3,* earning DreamWorks SKG another $521.1 billion worldwide.

Since the successes of the *Kung Fu Panda* franchise, Nelson has become one of the most powerful women in animation and Hollywood. In 2016, she was appointed to the board of governors for the Academy of Motion Picture Arts and Sciences. While her start has been in animation, she has since left DreamWorks SKG to work on her first live-action film based on a young adult novel called *The Darkest Minds* (2018). Despite all of her skill and success, Nelson never thought she would ever be a director, describing it as something she once thought to be impossible, and yet much like Po in the *Panda* films, she defies the assumptions of her peers, and more notably, herself. Nelson's love for action films, comics, video games, and anime have boiled themselves into a style of directing that is unique among Western feature film animation.

Carrie Tupper

See also: Jenson, Vicky

Further Reading

Academy Originals. 2016. "Creative Spark: Jennifer Yuh Nelson." YouTube video, 5:32, June 20. https://www.youtube.com/watch?v=YQVKyMWhM0A

Bancroft, Tony. 2014. *Directing for Animation: Everything You Didn't Learn in Art School.* Burlington, MA: Focal Press.

Dörr, Luisa. n.d. "The Animator—Jennifer Yuh Nelson." *Time.* Accessed May 10, 2018. http://time.com/collection/firsts/4898583/jennifer-yuh-nelson-firsts

Kit, Borys. 2016. "'Kung Fu Panda' Director Jennifer Yuh Nelson to Make Live Action Debut with 'Darkest Minds.'" *Hollywood Reporter*, July 12. https://www.hollywoodreporter.com/heat-vision/kung-fu-panda-director-jennifer-910193

MacLeod, Jason. 2012. "The Jennifer Yuh Nelson Interview—Part I." The Animation Guild Blog, January 23. http://animationguildblog.blogspot.com/2012/01/jennifer-yuh-nelson-interview-part-i.html

Miller-Zarneke, Tracey. 2008. *The Art of Kung Fu Panda*. London: Titan Books.

Navarro, Hector. 2016. "Episode 15: Jennifer Yuh Nelson." Nick Animation Podcast, August 19. https://www.nickanimation.com/episode-15-jennifer-yuh-nelson

Nelson, Jennifer Yuh. n.d. "Jennifer Yuh Nelson." Women Worth Watching. Accessed. http://www.womenworthwatching.com/jennifer-yuh-nelson

Sperling, Nicole. 2011. "Jennifer Yuh Nelson Is More than Tough Enough for 'Kung Fu Panda 2.'" *Los Angeles Times*, May 25. http://articles.latimes.com/2011/may/25/entertainment/la-et-jennifer-yuh-20110525

Wolfe, Jennifer. 2016. "The Academy Appoints Jennifer Yuh Nelson Governor-At-Large." Animation World Network, July 18. https://www.awn.com/news/academy-appoints-jennifer-yuh-nelson-governor-large

Reiniger, Lotte (1899–1981)

It is often assumed that the first feature-length animated feature produced was Walt Disney's *Snow White and the Seven Dwarfs* (1937). The success of Disney's sound- and color-laden *Snow White* often overshadows the fact that this work was not the first feature-length animated film at all. That honor goes to Charlotte "Lotte" Reiniger and her film *The Adventures of Prince Achmed* (1926). Not only does she hold that laurel, she was also the first woman to ever direct an animated film. A pioneer in silhouette filmmaking, Reiniger's unique style was inspired by the Southeast Asian art of shadow puppetry. Bringing together papercraft and stop-motion animation, Reiniger created beautiful and emotionally resonate retellings of classic fairy tales in a unique style that inspires creatives to this day.

As a child in Germany, Reiniger would entertain family and friends by cutting out paper silhouettes and performing shadow plays with them. These early years of papercutting and performances led to a talent in visual storytelling and an astonishing ability to quickly create paper silhouettes. By holding the scissors steady, she would whip her paper through the blades and create breathtakingly beautiful works of art. Reiniger created these silhouettes by breaking apart her character designs into individual body parts. Before these segments were joined, her characters looked almost grotesque as body parts were laid out in individual pieces (depending on the complexity of movement her character required). The pieces were joined together by wire poked through a hole to create a hinge. These hinges provided the puppet an astonishing degree of movement that made her projects come to life.

When Reiniger began to create her films, she started with a fairly minimal setup: "You take your best dining table, cut a hole into it, put a glass plate over it, and over the glass plate some transparent paper. And then, you put some light on from underneath" (Issacs 1970). Over the course of her career, this simple workspace evolved into a more complex setup: multiple planes of glass were layered under the camera, which allowed an animator to add detail, depth, and further complexity to an otherwise flat animation. She called her invention a "Trick Table" (Esther 2002). This is a technology that Disney later patented as the multiplane camera. As Disney was the first to patent the concept, he is considered its inventor; however, Reiniger has been well documented as the first animation filmmaker to use this technology in her film *The Adventures of Prince Achmed.*

Reiniger started out her career with a desire to be an actress but became famous for her ability to create beautiful silhouettes during downtime on set. Her first credited works were on live-action films. She created accent artwork for dialogue slides on *Rumpelstiltskin's Wedding* (1916) and later created special effects, sets, and costumes for *The Beautiful Chinese Princess* (1917). Her first self-made short film was *The Ornament of the Heart in Love*, released in 1919. In the next three years, Reiniger finished work on six short animated films, with the help of her producer, photographer, and husband, Carl Koch (1892–1963). It was in 1923 that Reiniger started work on *Prince Achmed.* The idea of a feature-length animated picture was a shocking risk for many in the film scene. Since this had never been done before, Reiniger's *Prince Achmed* had trouble finding a distributor, which delayed its first screening until 1926: "This was a never heard of thing. Animated films were supposed to make people roar with laughter, and nobody had dared to entertain an audience with them for more than ten minutes. Everybody to whom we talked in the industry about the proposition was horrified" (Warner 2011, 390–402). Once *Prince Achmed* premiered, it was a hit with critics and audiences alike. Reiniger made history with the film, not only through her success as a feature-length animated picture but also by taking her place as the first woman to ever direct an animated feature. The success of *Prince Achmed* allowed her to create her second feature, *Doctor Doolittle and His Animals* (1928) based on the book by Hugh Lofting (1886–1947).

During WWII, Reiniger and her husband's progressive ideologies clashed with the rising Nazi Party, so they fled Germany, hopping from country to country until they were forced to go back yin 1944. Living under Nazi rule, Reiniger was forced to create films under the strict guidelines of propaganda-focused censorship. In 1949, she moved to London and returned to creating her films freely once more and founded Primrose Productions in 1953. Among her new works, she created over 12 fairy tale shorts for the BBC and Telecasting America. She continued using her unique style to create films and advertisements until her husband died in 1963. At this point, Reiniger did not create any new work for over 10 years. Her last works were *The Rose and the Ring* (1979) and a short called *The Four Seasons* (1980) that was created for the Filmmuseum Düsseldorf. Reiniger was awarded the Filmband in Gold of the Deutscher Filmpreis in 1972. In 1979, she received the Great Cross of the Order of Merit of the Federal Republic of Germany. Reiniger died in 1982.

Reiniger's unique style has influenced everything from movies, to television, and even video games. French animator and filmmaker Michel Ocelot's compilation films *Princes et Princesses* (2000) and *Les Contes de la Nuit* (2011) borrowed heavily from Reiniger's silhouette techniques. The Academy Award–nominated *The Mysterious Geographic Explorations of Jasper Morello* (2005) is an Australian animated short wherein paper-like silhouetted figures are animated amid a three-dimensional steampunk world. Her influences are felt in Joseph Blanc's *Babe's Lair,* a music video produced for Walt & Vervain, Anna Humphries's animated short *Night of the Loving Dead* (2012), and the hit indie game *Limbo* by Playdead ApS. Rebecca Sugar's hit television series *Steven Universe* (2013–) used influences from Reiniger's work for an episode titled "The Answer" (2016). Reiniger's stylization continues to be evident in films today: Ben Hibon, director of the "Tale of Three Brothers" sequence in *Harry Potter and the Deathly Hallows—Part 1* (2010), credits Reiniger for inspiring the visual style of the sequence. Other films that have a touch of Reiniger's influence include the end credits from *Series of Unfortunate Events* (2004) and Disney's *Fantasia* (1940) as Leopold Anthony Stokowski and Mickey Mouse meet briefly in silhouette. On June 2, 2016, Reiniger's 117th birthday was honored with a Google Doodle that featured her silhouetted figure walking through paper-made sets and interacting with characters from her films. As time has progressed, it is clear that Reiniger's legacy continues to bloom across the modern media landscape.

Carrie Tupper

See also: Blair, Mary; Chapman, Brenda; Moberly-Holland, Sylvia

Further Reading

Desowitz, Bill. 2010. "Shadow Play with 'Potter's Tale of Three Brothers." Animation World Network, December 30. https://www.awn.com/animationworld/shadow-play-potters-tale-three-brothers

Eagan, Daniel. 2012. "Five Women Animators Who Shook Up the Industry." Smithsonian, June 13. https://www.smithsonianmag.com/arts-culture/five-women-animators-who-shook-up-the-industry-120442836

Esther, Leslie. 2002. *Hollywood Flatlands: Animation, Critical Theory and the Avant-Garde.* London: Verso.

Gazizova, Karina. 2011. "Biography: Lotte Reiniger." *AnimationResources.org*, December 24. https://animationresources.org/biography-lotte-reineger

Golshan, Tara. 2016. "Lotte Reiniger, Animation Pioneer, Predated Walt Disney by More than a Decade." *Vox*, June 2. https://www.vox.com/2016/6/2/11827922/lotte-reiniger-117th-birthday-google-doodle

Issacs, John, dir. 1970. *The Art of Lotte Reiniger.* Primrose Productions. YouTube video, 8:00, April 12. https://www.youtube.com/watch?v=LvU55CUw5Ck.

Moritz, William. 2009. "Some Critical Perspectives on Lotte Reiniger." In *Animation: Art and Industry.* Edited by Maureen Furniss. Bloomington: Indiana University Press, 13–20.

Ratner, Megan. 2006. "In the Shadows." *Art on Paper* 10(3): 44–49.

Warner, Marina. 2011. In *Stranger Magic.* Cambridge, MA: Harvard University Press, 390–402.

Interview with Brenda Chapman

What does your work schedule look like from day to day or even over the course of a year?

Depending on what type of film I'm on, my day to day can look very different. On a studio film—say DreamWorks or Pixar, I would go from meeting to meeting every hour or two, every day. Depending on what stage of the film, I could be working with the story department for a full day in the beginning—but as time progresses, that shortens to an hour to a quick stop in to make room for layout, editorial, art, lighting, etc.

On an independent film, I spend much of the development and preproduction of the film from home—working with my artists remotely over the Internet. Depending on where the production house is—local or international—dictates whether I continue to work remotely or am able to go in to work directly with the crew.

Any failures or setbacks you're willing to share and, if so, how did you overcome or move past them?

I don't perceive setbacks as failures. You only fail when you give up on something. I've never given up—at least not yet! Being taken off of *Brave* was definitely a setback. But I always say that when a door slams, let the wall fall down and look at the view! I felt vindicated in that most of my vision for Merida and Elinor still made it to the screen and that so many of my colleagues in the industry were and continue to be so incredibly supportive of me. That was so unexpected and so revitalizing—people I had never met before reached out to me—it was a little overwhelming. I had so many more opportunities than I would have if I'd actually stayed on the movie to the end. What I love most that happened is that I realized that I love to share my knowledge with young people getting into animation. I received invitations and started speaking at universities, festivals, and conventions—and it has been wonderfully rejuvenating!

What advice would you give someone trying to break into your field?

1. Don't give up.
2. If you're in school—be true to your own vision—don't try to emulate someone else. It may be the only chance you have for a long while to do your own thing if you go to work for a studio after you graduate.
3. If you're applying or working at a studio that has its own style: Bring yourself (your strengths) to your job. The project(s) may not be your style or choice, but you can have an impact by bringing your own creative and unique self to the table within the parameters of the project.

Did you have a mentor and/or an apprenticeship, or were you on your own?

I relied on my art teachers in high school and community college to help me prepare to apply to CalArts (California Institute of the Arts)—which took me two attempts to be accepted, by the way. Then I relied on my fellow students and teachers at CalArts to help me apply to Disney. When I made it in to Disney, I was a story trainee, and I had a plethora of wonderful mentors (all male—Roger Allers, Ed Gombert, Thom Enriquez, Joe Ranft, Gary Trousdale, Vance Gerry—to name a few) who taught and supported me as I learned to do the job. I was very VERY fortunate.

Were there any women in your field you could look up to?

Not in story—I was the first in decades. There were the legends: Lotte Reiniger and Mary Blair, but they were long gone before I came into the picture. There were women animators who were very inspiring: Sue Kroyer, Kathy Zielinski, and Lorna Cook.

Do you feel you began with any advantages, or did you cultivate them along the way?

I had to put myself through school—my father died when I was 19 and my mother had very limited means. An extra unexpected life insurance policy from my father paid for my first year at CalArts—but it was a loan which I paid back to my mother after I graduated. I had to work summers and part-time during the school year to make it through the next two years. CalArts was definitely an advantage, as it was the primary source for new talent at Disney and the other studios at the time.

There was one "advantage" I would have preferred not to have had when I was hired at Disney. I was told by the executive who interviewed me that I was being hired because I was a woman. Animation was getting "flack from upstairs" (Eisner, Wells, and Katzenberg) that there were no women in creative positions—zero in story. I was the right price, too, because I was a trainee, and if I didn't work out, they wouldn't have spent much on me and could get rid of me in a shorter amount of time. Talk about taking the wind out of my sails. But luckily, the artists I started working with were all very accepting and welcoming and gave me no sign of such discrimination moving forward.

If you have children or dependents, how do you manage career and family?

This is the most difficult question for me. I thought I had it all figured out. We waited to have a child until our careers were established and could hire help. But now that my daughter is grown, I wish that I had taken more time off of work to spend with her. There are even times that I wish that I had been a stay-at-home mom. But at the same time, I know I would have regretted not working and doing what I love to do. It's a Catch-22, and it's up to the individual. I have no real words of wisdom. It's not easy. There will be regrets no matter what you do. But there will be joy, too. Good with the bad. Bad with the good. That's life. It's not perfect.

How nuanced or productive do you find the conversation about sexism in your field (if there is one)?

I feel that it has only recently been acknowledged. I think my being removed from *Brave* began whispers, and now that the subject is so openly discussed industry-wide, it is much more prevalent. It is productive. Change is hard—especially for those who've had it easier without the change. But we need this change—not only across sex, but race as well.

Is there something you feel the current discussion on gender equality lacks?

Due process. I feel that there are some rash decisions being made without looking into the specifics. I would hate to have innocent men or women accused of something they didn't do or intend without being able to prove themselves innocent or make simple amends before losing their jobs. Granted, I know there are plenty who've had enough complaints from many sources that it's obvious they need to be reprimanded. I just think that we need to be careful and not turn into an angry mob with pitchforks and torches.

If your field is male dominated, any thoughts on how to support more women and minorities coming into your field?

Of course it's male dominated! We all should be looking to give the opportunities more evenly. No more excuses about there not being as many women or other races who are as interested in animation. Mentoring. Holding executives accountable for whom they choose to give opportunities. Speak up! No one should expect to be handed their opportunities—they should work for and earn them—but need to be given the opportunity to do so! Nor should we be quiet when we see someone being passed over because of their sex or race.

Does the fact your field is male-dominated prevent solidarity with other women, or do you find women commonly help other women in your field?

To be honest, I've seen both. And I say that about men, too. It's a more competitive field now than ever, so, of course, there is that fear of losing one's job. However, I have seen many women reaching out to mentor, advise, and help other women on their path. I count myself as one of them.

Can inclusion be practiced voluntarily, or do we need quotas?

If we see a change in the voluntary and parity rising, then let's just keep going that way. I think setting a time goal for parity is a good compromise. If that goal is missed and/or there is resistance, then quotas will be a necessary step.

Is there something unique that your gender or identity brings to your field?

Of course there is. Every individual brings something unique to their role by their life experiences, their sex, their race, their temperament. My being a white woman with my own specific personality is definitely going to be creatively unique from a man with his own personality or a Hispanic woman with her own experiences. White men have made films about women and other races for over a century. Women and other races (males included) have not been able to do that as freely. So of course, when women of any race make films about women *and* men, they are going to bring other points of view to the audiences. It can only be refreshing to have more variety!

Interview with Vicky Jenson

What challenges have you experienced working in animation?

The first one I can think of is when I started to work with CGI animation for the first time because I came out of the 2D hands-on animation world. I had never been an animator; I was always a story artist or a background painter or an art director, that kind of thing. I tried animating, but I have no patience.

So when I started on *Shrek*, I found myself in these darkened rooms looking at different iterations of CGI imagery and not knowing much. I'd wonder what I was looking at and who created it because all I could hear were 10 voices behind me in the dark.

It was fun to figure it out, but it was a tricky thing to understand. I'd think: "Okay, so this is a rough model, and here are rough layouts. Then this is lit animation and here's rough animation." The learning curve was steep because it had to be fast, but the artists were really patient. I felt a little like I was in "The Emperor's New Clothes." Like, "Poof, you're a director, so we are all going to listen to you." But I didn't feel like I knew what I was doing.

Do you think it was imposter syndrome?

Yes, and I think that's really common. We all feel like we're going to be found out. I think it goes hand-in-hand with being an artist, because our reaction to art is very subjective. Sometimes you're in the golden light of approval, and other times you aren't and you just don't really know what has changed.

I think we internalize that critical voice, which is important as an artist. You're always going to be the hardest one to please. When others are cool with what you're doing, you've already grown past that, and I think that's probably what leads to that feeling that you'll be found out as a fraud.

Any advice for dealing with imposter syndrome?

It may sound redundant, but I think you need to just listen to yourself. I mean, I hate to say something so cliché as, "believe in yourself," but you got this far for a reason, and it's not like the whole world is conspiring to elevate a fraud. So you have to remember that by simple common sense and the law of averages, if you are there, there's a good reason for it—so at least trust that.

What do you look for in a creative team for animation?

Well, since I'm going through that process right now, I look for people who have the same excitement about the work that I do. That we have a shared language, probably some shared aesthetics, but I do love people to have an opinion. I really look for people with a strong sense of their own artistic voice; I really rely on that. It's important to have people who can surprise you. When you're the storyteller, you're always telling a story and you know how it ends. It can be nice once in a while when somebody comes back to you with something that surprises you.

Then I get to be the audience for a moment. To think: "Wow, I never thought of it that way, that's fantastic." I love that feeling. It's important to me to have artists that really have a strong artistic sense, a strong artistic voice, and one that I think aesthetically, mostly lines up with mine. It doesn't have to be perfectly aligned with mine, but it helps.

How do you get your creative juices flowing again when you've hit a wall?

Get an ice cream sundae! Really, I learned this from Kelly Asbury. I get up and walk around and shake it off. I mean, you usually sort of hit that wall for a couple of hours. Initially, if brainstorms go really well, but if everybody is stuck and you can just tell the energy got sucked out of the room, then you have to change it all up. In the past, we've done all kinds of things. We've done games, we've had contests. We'll just start playing Hangman on a whiteboard. Anything just to shake up your brain a little bit and release the tension and take the pressure off.

What's your process when it comes to working with actors? What's different about working with actors in animation versus live action?

I was initially kind of intimidated to work with actors, then I developed a feeling for it. For instance, I knew right away that you don't tell an actor what to say or how to say it. You can't ask them to parrot you. I found my own way of trying to elicit the performances that I thought would work for a scene. g[Working] with Judith Weston, who's the director's whisperer, helped me to understand through practice, through being an actor for other directors, that there's a set of tools that they need to work with.

The main thing is playable action, giving them playable direction, that you're not eliciting a performance from them that is results oriented, that you're trying to find something that's authentic. Part of that is letting the actor be the author of the emotion. After working with her for a while, I found it was so much fun to work a scene. To me, it's the same as doing rehearsals for theater, or rehearsals for live action. You work the whole scene, and then you break it down into beats.

I really don't like to go line by line, the way some other or at least older, old-school animation direction might have gone. It's like, "Oh, read that line three different ways." You don't get a very honest performance that way, so I would always have another actor in the room, and I would often direct that other actor, who maybe sometimes was one of our more hammy story artists.

I would direct them just as much, because I found if I got them to attack a line a certain way or to approach the actor a certain way, that their response would be what I was looking for, so you get a real reaction responding to one another. I just sort of run a recording session the way I would a rehearsal. I did it when I directed Martin Scorsese and Robert De Niro together.

They'd never, they had done nine movies together, but they had done a movie as both actors, and I had to get them in the room together. It was really fun. Their back and forth, their dialog is really—it was hardly edited in what we put in the movie in a couple of their scenes in *Shark Tale*. It's just the two of them just interacting as their characters. It feels really natural, it feels really good, so that's what you want.

Interview by Carrie Tupper

Makeup and Hairstyling Artists

Introduction

When actresses started to make the transition from the theater to film in the early 1900s, they were surprised to discover their makeup skills (since most actresses applied their own makeup in early cinema) didn't translate to the screen. Early cinema used orthochromatic film, which was blue-sensitive and made their skin appear dark or dirty. In order to look natural on camera, a combination of greasepaint in stick form, eyeliners, and powders had to be applied.

Max Factor, Sr. who immigrated to the United States in 1904, set up a shop in Los Angeles that initially sold makeup and wigs to the theatrical community. However, by 1910 he was selling a modified version of his greasepaint that was suitable for film, which he would perfect by 1914 by inventing a 12-toned cream version to match a wider variety of skin tones. His contemporary, an English wigmaker named George Westmore, also immigrated to the United States and founded the first film makeup department in 1917. Five generations of Westmores would go on to be prominent movie makeup artists in Hollywood. Makeup artists such as Jack P. Pierce, who was the head of Universal's makeup department during the Classical Hollywood era, was a pioneer in special makeup effects (SPMUFX), creating the iconic monsters of *Frankenstein* (1931), *Dracula* (1931), *The Mummy* (1932), and *The Wolf Man* (1941). Foam latex pieces were first used in *The Wizard of Oz* (1939) and were glued on in the morning and removed at night. The further development of prosthetics with different materials would ensure continuity from day to day, since they were reusable and cut down on the preparation time significantly.

Until the 1970s in Hollywood, only men were makeup artists and women were either body makeup artists or hair stylists. One pioneering woman, Dottie Ponadel, was the lone female makeup artist, and she endured discrimination not only by the union, but the studios hid her and she worked out of sight. Dottie constantly fought all-male makeup departments at the studios to get the recognition she deserved. Through a series of events, she evolved into the major female makeup artist in pictures through the 1930s, 1940s, and 1950s—becoming pals with her famous subjects, who included Marlene Dietrich, Helen Hayes, Clark Gable, Gary Cooper, Mae West, Carole Lombard, Paulette Goddard, and Judy Garland—as she gave them the iconic faces that would make them never-forgotten movie stars.

The first female makeup artist in the International Alliance of Theatrical Stage Employees (IATSE) Local 706 was also African American. Bernadine Anderson not only worked in television, but she was also the makeup artist for Eddie Murphy. Christina Smith is known as the first female makeup artist to work in feature films. Most of the women who became makeup artists in the 1970s were proficient with prosthetics, because they were expected to have the same skill levels as men. Oscar winners Ve Neill and Michèle Burke led the way with *Star Trek: The Motion Picture* (1979) and *The Clan of the Cave Bear* (1986) respectively, and were among the earliest women to specialize in prosthetic application. The ladies who didn't mind working in glue, dirt, and fake blood and could realistically produce mind-blowing effects worked tirelessly and were in demand. Originally, the makeup department head designed and oversaw the entire department, from beauty to SPMUFX, but today many shows are compartmentalized, with one group doing beauty and the other SPMUFX. Ongoing advances in technology, such as high definition, have demanded an even higher skill level from makeup and hairstyling artists. What works on the big screen must work equally well on televisions that use 4K or 8K ultra-high-definition, and women today are creating phenomenal special makeup effects across both film and television.

Susan Cabral-Ebert

Burke, Michèle (1959–)

Born in Kildare, Ireland, Michèle Burke has won Academy Awards, BAFTAs, and Emmys as a makeup artist. Acclaimed in both Canada and America, she is also considered in her native Ireland as the "Irish film industry abroad when there was no Irish film industry abroad" (McCarthy 2016). She and Sarah Monzan were the first women to be nominated for and win an Academy Award for Best Makeup for *Quest for Fire* in 1982. A pioneer and innovator of different special effect techniques, Burke's ingenuity was shaped by early years of designing makeup for tightly budgeted horror films in Canada, allowing her to be on the forefront of developing gore, traumatized bodies, and facial transformations via makeup effects, an area of industry lacking women. Transitioning to Hollywood, Burke is popularly known for her work in successful American films *Quest for Fire* (1981), *Bram Stoker's Dracula* (1992), and *Interview with a Vampire* (1994) and modern blockbusters such as *Austin Powers: The Spy Who Shagged Me* (1999) and the *Mission Impossible* series (2006, 2011). These films allowed a diversification of her skills, from aging prosthetics, experience working with leading actors and actresses, managing teams, and, in her own words, "Working on films that had everything, so that if they asked 'Can you do this?' I could say, 'I did it here'" (Essman 2002).

Emigrating from Ireland to Canada in 1973, Burke benefited from local tax breaks, leading to a profusion of film shoots and an abundance of on-the-job training. Often hired for horror films, Burke, still early in her career, recalls, "I was doing work that was way above what was normal to do at that point in your career, but there was really no one else to do it" (Warren 2008). This boon of experience prevented her from realizing that Hollywood women rarely performed makeup effects or lab work with prosthetics; it was not just her techniques and designs that were revolutionary but her gender as well, a fact not currently lost on her as she pushes against Hollywood producers who assume she cannot perform. Burke first earned Hollywood attention for her Oscar-winning *Quest for Fire*, where she developed believable Neanderthal prosthetics for over 50 costumed characters, a task deemed impossible by other effect artists. Burke and Michael Westmore created double-teaming, a system in which two people could apply makeup together, which traveled to Hollywood as she did.

Despite prior successes, Burke spent her early years in Hollywood performing for smaller films to earn union membership and acclimatizing to an industry less accepting of women makeup artists. Burke's reputation for ingenuity and skill were apparent through the diverse projects she took on once recognized by Hollywood: aging characters in her BAFTA-winning *Cyrano de Bergerac* (1990), balancing color palettes for *Interview with a Vampire* (1994), re-creating the character makeup for the second film in the *Austin Powers* (1999) film series, and transforming Tom Cruise for numerous films, including *Vanilla Sky* (2001) and *Tropic Thunder* (2008). *Bram Stoker's Dracula* (1992) earned Burke her second Academy Award win, the first woman to win multiple Oscars in makeup. Though Burke had not fully comprehended the importance of her first Oscar, she notes, "The stakes were higher really. With the second one, I thought: 'If I win, I'd prove to them all that it's not a fluke'" (Essman 2002).

Burke skillfully manages quick transformations for actors who are reluctant to embrace makeup effects. Cognizant of the shifting relationship between actors and makeup artists and the pitfalls of becoming too close and dependent, Burke is not dedicated to a single set of actors. Instead, she focuses on projects that cultivate new skills and inspire her creatively. Her awareness is also apparent in collaborations. Burke recognizes the need to delegate tasks to a carefully selected team, acknowledging that the makeup department head isn't necessarily going to be the most skilled in every makeup effect or specialty. Reflecting on her position in the industry, Burke says, "I see myself as a makeup artist who is capable of spanning the complete spectrum of what is needed, beauty right through to character work, right through to the unreal to the aging to the prosthetic work. I have that ability and I can do most things that are required" and that passion, not gender, is the key to success (Essman 2002).

Renee Ann Drouin

Further Reading

Essman, Scott. 2002. "Profile." Michele Burke. 2002. Accessed February 2018. http://micheleburke.com/profile

Fox, Jordan. 1982. "Who Is Michele Burke?" *Cinefantastique*, 12(2).

McCarthy, Esther. 2016. "How an Oscar-Winning Hollywood Make-Up Artist Turned Her Passion into a Career." *The Gloss*, December 14. http://lookthebusiness.ie/hollywood-make-artist-turned-passion-stellar-career

Warren, Tanya. 2008. "Talking Makeup with Michele Burke." *The Irish Film & Television Network*, July 3. http://www.iftn.ie/crew/?act1=record&aid=73&rid=4281335&tpl=archnews&force=1

Callaghan, Colleen (Unknown–)

Colleen Callaghan is an Academy Award–nominated hair stylist who has worked on over 120 films, television shows, and theater productions ranging from an Oscar-winning film to a Golden Globe–winning miniseries. In 2004, she was honored with a Lifetime Achievement Award from the Hollywood Makeup Artist and Hair Stylist Guild, celebrating her decades worth of contributions to the industry. Callaghan, known for her meticulous and thoughtful creations, remains a highly sought-after hair stylist in the entertainment industry. In addition to her skill, Callaghan holds a reputation for cultivating young talent and building lasting professional relationships with actors.

Callaghan grew up in Texas and was involved in entertainment from an early age. At three years old, she began performing as a singer. She performed in local theater productions and on the radio, and eventually traveled on concert tours. It was during these years of performance that Callaghan realized her passion for behind-the-scenes work. She often did the hair of her friends and fellow performers, and this hobby led her to work as a hair stylist on many theatrical productions. Callaghan eventually earned a cosmetology license in New York City, where she began working on Broadway productions.

Following success in theater, Callaghan turned her attention to the small screen in 1961. Originally focusing on live television, Callaghan styled hair for classic programs like Perry Como's live programming (1948–1967) and *The Ed Sullivan Show* (1948–1971). Callaghan has continued to work in television and to serve as head of the hair department on many notable films throughout her career.

Callaghan's screen credits are impressively diverse. She often works on decorated and well-received projects, such as the Academy Award–winning film *A Beautiful Mind* (2001), Golden Globe–winning miniseries *East of Eden* (1981), popular television series *Blue Bloods* (2010–), and critically acclaimed made-for-television movie *You Don't Know Jack* (2010). Other notable credits include *Steel Magnolias* (1989), *Fried Green Tomatoes* (1991), *Sleepless in Seattle* (1993), *Chicago* (2002), and *Frost/Nixon* (2008).

A true artist, Callaghan is well known for her work and often asked about her craft. In an interview for *Daily Variety*, she explained her work on the 1960s-set film *Down with Love* (2003). Callaghan requested background actors with long hair. She used these actors to create a 1960s feel by styling them with teased updos (Robbins 2004, 14). This attention to detail and expertise at creating atmosphere can be seen throughout her corpus. On the film *Frost/Nixon* (2008), Callaghan used a 1977 cover of *Time* magazine to design a wig that captured the exact wave of Richard

Nixon's hair. She explained how the wig, and its lengthy application, helped actor Frank Langella settle into the intense role. Speaking with *The Los Angeles Times*, she remarked that Langella would "start to pull into Nixon" while donning the $5,000 wig (Day 2008).

For *Monday Night Mayhem* (2002) she re-created sports journalist Howard Cosell's iconic toupees for John Turturro's portrayal. She remarked it was the first time she made a toupee that was meant to look like a toupee. Callaghan was tasked with re-creating more iconic hair for the film *Lovelace* (2013), which chronicles the life of adult film actress turned anti-porn activist Linda Lovelace. Callaghan reproduced the *Deep Throat* (1972) star's frizzy brown locks for actress Amanda Seyfried. Callaghan used the wig to indicate the character's internal state, making it look more frazzled during times of stress or unease.

In addition to her diverse skills, Callaghan is known for fostering young talent within a competitive and challenging industry. When congratulating Callaghan on receiving the 2008 Designing Hollywood Award from New York Women in Film and Television, actress Faye Dunaway remarked on Callaghan's generosity to up-and-coming makeup artists and hair stylists. Dunaway explained that Callaghan trains young people and allows them to assist on projects. According to Dunaway, this type of humanity and care is rare for an artist of Callaghan's caliber, and she lauded the hair stylist for passing on her skills to future artists. Callaghan has also contributed to her profession by serving as the president of her union.

Dunaway has worked with Callaghan on many films and has suggested her to others. Callaghan is skilled at cultivating lasting relationships with actors. She has styled Renee Zellweger on *The Bachelor* (1999), *Nurse Betty* (2000), *Chicago* (2002), *Down with Love* (2003), and *Cinderella Man* (2005). She created several of Meg Ryan's iconic romantic comedy hairdos, and has worked with actress Lucy Liu on multiple occasions, including *Charlie's Angels: Full Throttle* (2003) and *Watching the Detectives* (2007). It was Liu who presented her with the Lifetime Achievement Award from the Hollywood Makeup Artist and Hair Stylist Guild.

Callaghan has been nominated for two Academy Awards for Best Makeup with Greg Cannom and Robert Laden for *Roommates* (1995) and with Greg Cannom for *A Beautiful Mind* (2001). Additionally, when Cannom accepted the Academy Award for Best Makeup for *The Curious Case of Benjamin Button* (2008), he remarked that he shared the award with Callaghan and that she should be beside him on stage. Callaghan's lack of Academy Awards is likely due to the ceremony not containing a hair styling category. However, she boasts many other impressive accolades, including a BAFTA Film Award and Gold Derby Award for Best Makeup and Hair for *The Curious Case of Benjamin Button* (2008).

Steffi Shook

Further Reading

Day, Patrick Kevin. 2008. "Scene Stealer: Turning Frank Langella into Richard Nixon for Front/Nixon." *The Los Angeles Times*, December 10. http://latimesblogs.latimes.com/entertainmentnewsbuzz/2008/12/scene-stealer-1.html

Glass, Katie. 2013. "Under Her Skin." *The Sunday Times,* August 11. https://www.thetimes.co.uk/article/under-her-skin-x0mjzzthh0s

Robbins, Allison. 2004. "Down with Love." *Daily Variety,* January 13. https://variety.com/2004/film/awards/down-with-love-1117898334/

Neill, Ve (1951–)

Since the 1970s, Ve Neill has created some of cinema's most iconic characters. She was one of the first women to break into the field of special effects makeup, and she was the first woman to win an Oscar for Best Makeup. Specializing in what she calls "extreme fantasy," the self-taught Neill has been influential in shaping the field of makeup artistry through her innovative design and commitment to education for new generations of makeup artists.

Three-time Academy Award-winning makeup artist Ve Neill (left) attends a Q&A session at *The Hunger Games: The Exhibition* at the Palace of Fine Arts at Innovation Hangar on June 7, 2016, in San Francisco, California. Neill was one of the first women to break into the male-dominated profession of film makeup in the 1970s. She's known for her work creating iconic characters in films such as *Beetlejuice* (1988), *Edward Scissorhands* (1990), *Mrs. Doubtfire* (1993), and the *Pirates of the Caribbean* film series (2003–2007). (Steve Jennings/WireImage/Getty Images)

Ve Neill was born in Riverside, California, in 1951. Neill's childhood friend and neighbor was the daughter of film and television makeup artist Leo Lotito, Jr. who was then involved with the NBC/ABC television series *Wagon Train*. Neill's fascination with his work and 1930s horror films sparked her interest in creating monsters. However, the lack of women in the field of special effects and makeup hindered her from pursuing it as a career. With no established film makeup education program until 1966, artists learned their trade by apprenticeships, which were rare and usually excluded women. So Neill chose to go to fashion merchandising school where she studied costume design.

When Neill was 18 years old she opened her own vintage clothing shop in Los Angeles, where she specialized in styling local music bands. One of the bands Neill worked with challenged her to create outer space–themed looks for them, so Neill visited a science fiction convention to learn techniques from fans.

By the mid-1970s Neill was working as a makeup artist on low-budget independent films. Neill's first official screen credit for makeup was the 1977 erotic musical *Cinderella* directed by Michael Pataki, where she was also credited as hair stylist.

For the next two years Neill worked steadily, focusing on genre films. In 1979, Fred B. Phillips, head makeup artist for *Star Trek: The Original Series*, asked Neill to join the team for *Star Trek: The Motion Picture* (1979). The film was the first Neill worked on after qualifying to join the California Makeup Artist & Hair Stylists Union (Local 706). Though Neill mainly worked on Klingon prosthetic application, hair application, and painting, the team was also responsible for designing a variety of creatures as background extras. Neill, along with Phillips and makeup artist Janna Phillips, were nominated for a Saturn Award, presented by the Academy of Science Fiction, Fantasy and Horror Films for achievements in those genres. After their work on the film, Fred Phillips mentored Neill, and the two remained close until his death.

In the 1980s and early 1990s, the rise of the big-budget blockbuster put a greater demand on special effects teams in both film and television. The makeup industry grew quickly, and Neill found steady work in both mediums, most notably working on the series *The A-Team* (1983–1987) through 1986.

In 1988, Neill made a career breakthrough when she won an Oscar for Best Makeup for the film *Beetlejuice*, directed by Tim Burton. Neill shared the award with fellow makeup artists Steve LaPorte and Robert Short. Inspired by Burton's sketches of the character, which were deemed too macabre, Neill designed the character's cartoonish style. The film was actor Michael Keaton's breakthrough role and was a huge financial success.

Neill's collaboration with Burton on *Beetlejuice* would be the first in a series of collaborations that earned her acclaim and reputation as a visionary artist. She worked on *Pee-Wee's Playhouse* (1986–1990), which garnered her a Daytime Emmy in 1988. Neill reunited with Burton and Johnny Depp on *Edward Scissorhands* (1990), which earned her a second Oscar nomination. She transformed Danny DeVito into the long-nosed Penguin in *Batman Returns* (1992), earning her an Oscar nomination and her first double nomination in which she was also up for the award for *Hoffa* (1992).

In 1993, Neill won her second Oscar for *Mrs. Doubtfire*. She shared the award with key hair stylist Yolanda Toussieng and Greg Cannom, who (along with Dick Smith) designed and sculpted the prosthetic pieces used to age and transform Robin Williams into the title character. Neill's mastery of transformation earned her a third Oscar win and sixth nomination for her work on *Ed Wood* (1994), wherein she similarly made well-known actor Martin Landau unrecognizable as horror-film star Bela Lugosi.

For the latter half of the 1990s, Neill split her time between film and television work, earning awards and nominations for various projects. She won a 1997 Primetime Emmy for the miniseries *The Shining* (1997) and was nominated the next year for the miniseries *From the Earth to the Moon* (1998). She won her third Saturn award for *Interview with the Vampire* in 1994, and was nominated for two *Batman* sequels, *Batman Forever* and *Batman & Robin*, in 1996 and 1998, respectively.

Though Neill had long been part of the big-budget film landscape, in the 2000s she worked on two of the costliest and well-earning franchises of all time, Disney's *The Pirates of the Caribbean* and the popular *Hunger Games* quadrilogy. Neill was nominated for an Oscar for her work on the *Pirates* franchise in 2004 and 2008, and was nominated for two awards from the British Academy of Film and Television Arts (BAFTA). Neill won a BAFTA for her work on *Pirates of the Caribbean: Curse of the Black Pearl* in 2004.

Neill's commitment to supporting education for young makeup artists is evident in her evolving role as mentor on the *Face-Off* reality series and at formal training schools. In 2011, Ve Neill signed on as a judge for the competition reality series *Face-Off*, which premiered on the American network SyFy (formerly Sci-Fi Channel). The show awards $100,000 to a promising makeup artist. In July 2017, Neill completed her 12th season as judge and was signed to return for season 13.

In 2016, Neill took the position of Director of Education at Cinema Makeup School, one of the most prestigious training schools in the country. That same year, she launched the Ve Neill Masterclass, which is a touring workshop for aspiring and working makeup artists.

Neill was awarded the Lifetime Achievement Award by the Makeup Artists & Hair Stylists Guild Local 706 (the West Coast local of the IATSE) in February 2016. The award is given to one makeup artist and one hair stylist for their exemplary body of work. Neill was the first female makeup artist to ever receive this honor.

Diana E. Martinez

Further Reading

Debreceni, Todd. 2013. *Special Makeup Effect for Stage and Screen: Making and Applying Prosthetics*. Burlington, MA: Focal Press.

Timpone, Anthony. 1996. *Men, Makeup, and Monster: Hollywood's Masters of Illusion and FX*. New York: St. Martin's Press.

Wright, Crystal A. 2004. *The Hair, Makeup & Fashion Styling Career Guide*. Los Angeles: Set the Pace Publishing Group.

Toussieng, Yolanda (1949–)

Yolanda Toussieng is a two-time Oscar-winning hairstylist, and the first hairstylist to win an Oscar. Toussieng has over 75 film and television hair styling credits spanning almost four decades. She is best known for her work on the films *Edward Scissorhands* (1990), *Batman Returns* (1992), *Mrs. Doubtfire* (1993), *Master and Commander: The Far Side of the World* (2003), the film adaptation of the hit musical *Hairspray* (2007), and *Oz, The Great and Powerful* (2013). Toussieng is one of the most sought-after hair stylists working in film and television today for her versatility and outstanding craftsmanship.

Toussieng, who was an artist in her teens and has since considered herself an artist, has an immense body of work that has validated a field that is often overlooked. Proving that hair is as important as makeup and costume to the creation of a character, Toussieng's contributions to the field have been invaluable.

Hair stylist Yolanda Toussieng accepts a Lifetime Achievement Award at the Make-Up Artists and Hair Stylists Guild Awards held at Paramount Studios on February 20, 2016, in Hollywood, California. Toussieng has earned two Academy Awards for Best Makeup and Hairstyling, one for *Ed Wood* (1994) and one for *Mrs. Doubtfire* (1993). (Mathew Imaging/WireImage)

Toussieng was a salon hairdresser for eight years before transitioning to Hollywood. Looking for a challenge, Toussieng looked for work at film and television studios. In 1978, she began working for *The Sunday Show*, co-hosted by Kelly Lange and Pat Sajak.

Soon after, she found work in the wig shop at Universal Studios, which was part of the makeup department. She cleaned, repaired, and styled wigs, as well as found opportunities to learn more about hairstyling and makeup. Toussieng was there for about a year, until Universal (and many other studios) closed their makeup departments in the 1980s.

Throughout that decade, Toussieng found herself nimbly moving from film to television, working on films such as *Sixteen Candles* (1984) and *Revenge of the Nerds* (1984), shifting in 1986 to work on episodes of the miniseries *North and South* (1985–1994) for which she was nominated for a Primetime Emmy Award for Outstanding Achievement in Hairstyling for a Miniseries or a Special, alongside co-hairstylist Shirley Crawford.

In 1988, she joined the hair and makeup team for Tim Burton's *Beetlejuice*. This collaboration with Burton led to work on *Pee-Wee's Playhouse* (1986–1990), which earned her first Daytime Emmy Award for Outstanding Hairstyling in 1989, which she shared with Jerry Masone.

A career highlight for Toussieng was winning the 1993 Oscar for her work on *Mrs. Doubtfire*. The team of Ve Neill, Greg Cannom (both makeup artists), and Toussieng was awarded for the stunning transformation of comedian Robin Williams into the elderly British nanny. Toussieng became the first hairstylist ever awarded an Oscar. Though the Academy had awards for makeup beginning in 1981 (and had awarded a couple of honorary awards for makeup achievement in the 1960s), it was not until 1993 that hairstylists could be nominated as part of the makeup team for their contribution to the overall impact of the character design. Toussieng's win helped highlight the collaborative nature of makeup and hair teams, and affirmed the impact of hairstyling to the film's overall aesthetic. The Oscar also solidified her position as a formidable creative force in Hollywood hair styling.

The next year, Toussieng was nominated and won another Oscar for her work on the film *Ed Wood* (1994), which she shared with Neill and makeup artist Rick Baker. The film, like *Mrs. Doubtfire,* demanded extreme transformations, and Toussieng's wig styling, application, and hairdressing brought back to life iconic stars of the 1950s.

In addition to her Academy Award wins, Toussieng has received two more Oscar nominations: one for the period film *Master and Commander: The Far Side of the World* (2003), and in 2011 she received a nomination for the World War II epic, *The Way Back* (2010). She has been nominated for Best Makeup/Hair three times from the British Academy of Film and Television Arts (BAFTA), won the Daytime Emmy Award for *Pee-Wee's Playhouse* (1986), and received the Lifetime Achievement Award from the Hollywood Makeup Artist and Hair Stylist Guild.

In 2016, Toussieng and Ve Neill received Lifetime Achievement Awards from the Makeup Artists & Hair Stylists Guild, IATSE Local 706, the largest union chapter of makeup and hair stylists. It was fitting that the women should be honored together, as they are longtime collaborators. The two, who together created the Oscar-winning iconic looks for *Mrs. Doubtfire* and *Ed Wood*, as well as the Emmy-winning look for Paul Reubens in *Pee Wee's Playhouse*, were awarded for their contributions to the hair and makeup industries, respectively.

Toussieng's achievements have opened up doors for many hair stylists and women. In an interview, Toussieng addresses her experience as a woman in an industry dominated by men, saying, "Sometimes I feel it's harder to get my voice heard as a woman, but that's mainly in dealing with some crew positions that have less of an impact on my artistic work. With the positions that do affect my art—directors and producers—I don't find that that's an issue. I come from an art world. And if you're good at your art, people are going to listen to you. I feel like the women producers I've worked with have probably faced more challenges with this than me because they're in a different position of power. I can lead with my art, and people either get it or they don't" (Henriques 2013).

Diana E. Martinez

Further Reading

Henriques, Erin. 2013. "Spotlight Interview: Yolanda Toussieng, Academy Award Winning Hairstylist." *Ms. in the Biz*, November 8. http://msinthebiz.com/2013/11/08/spotlight-interview-yolanda-toussieng-academy-award-winning-hairstylist

McGregor, Tom. 2003. *The Making of Master and Commander: The Far Side of the World.* New York: W. W. Norton.

McLean, Adrienne L. 2016. *Costume, Makeup and Hair.* New Brunswick, NJ: Rutgers University Press.

Westcott, Lisa (Unknown–)

Lisa Westcott is an Academy Award–winning makeup artist and hair stylist who has worked on over 30 films and television shows. Nominated for multiple Oscars and a Primetime Emmy, Westcott has received multiple film and television BAFTA Awards from the British Academy of Film and Television Arts. In addition to her professional accolades and highly regarded talent, Westcott is seen as an inspiration to young artists and is renowned for her willingness to stand up for fair working conditions.

Westcott began her career working in television in the late 1970s. She spent the 1980s doing hair and makeup design for British television shows and miniseries, collecting many awards and nominations along the way. Her work included the BAFTA-winning television miniseries *Portrait of a Marriage* (1990), the long-running, BAFTA-winning television series *Grange Hill* (1978–2008), and the miniseries *Masterpiece Theater: Bleak House* (1985) for which she received a BAFTA TV Award for Best Makeup.

Westcott's film credits demonstrate her diversity in design. From dramatic period piece films like *Shakespeare in Love* (1998), to comedies like *Fred Claus* (2007), Westcott is known for achieving verisimilitude through character design. Additionally, her work on *Captain America: The First Avenger* (2011) demonstrates her ability to create looks that hold up in action scenarios.

For the film *Iris* (2001), Westcott brought the novelist Iris Murdoch's decline into Alzheimer's disease to life through the use of three separate wigs. Westcott fashioned multiple hair pieces for actress Judi Dench to communicate the severity of the character's disease. When the character is driven to a nursing home, Wescott made Dench's hair thin and unruly. She also had the actress wear opaque contact lenses to stress the psychological distance between Murdoch and her surroundings (Kellaway 2002).

In addition to bringing real-life characters to the screen, Westcott has been lauded for her ability to bring historical moments to life through detail-oriented hair and makeup design. For the film *Shakespeare in Love* (1998), Westcott again worked with actress Judi Dench to resurrect a figure from the past. To communicate Queen Elizabeth's age and status, Westcott weathered Dench's skin, a decision based on historical research. Westcott explained that the queen likely had damaged skin due to mercury poisoning, inspiring Westcott to use heavy makeup to achieve the appropriate texture. Queen Elizabeth was also known to have multiple wigs, so Westcott gave Dench a receding hairline to indicate heavy wig use. Westcott's research and skill paid off. Reportedly, the set went silent when Dench made her debut in the strikingly regal look (Milner 2016).

Westcott's aptitude for historical re-creations is most clearly demonstrated in the film that won her an Academy Award for Best Achievement in Makeup and Hairstyling, the musical adaptation *Les Misérables* (2012). Director Tom Hooper praised Westcott's ability to take characters through a journey. The film portrays Jean Valjean's long and difficult life. Westcott painted this struggle onto actor Hugh Jackman through manufactured dirt, scars, and damaged teeth. Teeth were of particular concern to Hooper, as the film required close-ups of the actors singing. Westcott was able to portray strife and hardship by creating prosthetic teeth and painting sores in the actors' mouths (Ryzik 2012). The character Fantine goes through a dramatic journey as well, and Westcott explained that the actress Anne Hathaway's beauty became a challenge. Westcott was able to turn the young actress into a disease-ridden prostitute through crude makeup and bloody sores (Weisman 2012).

Westcott received the Academy Award for Best Achievement in Makeup and Hairstyling with Julie Dartnell for their work on *Les Misérables*. She was also nominated for her work on *Shakespeare in Love* and *Mrs. Brown* (1997). Westcott was nominated for a Primetime Emmy for her work on the television movie *The Last of the Blonde Bombshells* (2000). Additionally, she has won five BAFTA Awards and was nominated for three others.

Steffi Shook

Further Reading

Kellaway, Kate. 2002. "Iris through the Looking Glass." *The Guardian*, January 13. https://www.theguardian.com/film/2002/jan/13/biography.irismurdoch

Milner, Ali. 2016. "A Queenie Moment." *Warpaint Magazine*, November 15. http://www.warpaintmag.com/2016/11/15/a-queenie-moment

Ryzik, Melena. 2012. "Hugh Jackman, All Muscles and Fake Teeth." *The New York Times*, December 11. https://carpetbagger.blogs.nytimes.com/2012/12/11/hugh-jackman-all-muscles-and-fake-teeth

Weisman, Aly. 2012. "'Les Mis' Makeup Artist Reveals How She Transformed Anne Hathaway into a 'Diseased Prostitute.'" *Business Insider*, December 10. http://www.businessinsider.com/les-mis-makeup-artist-reveals-how-she-transformed-anne-hathaway-into-a-diseased-prostitute-2012-12

Interview with Ve Neill

What was your profession like when you started?

Back before the 1970s, there was a man in charge of both the makeup and hair department. It would be one giant department. There was more or less a female who was in charge of the hair styling department, and she did run it, but it was still all under the umbrella of the one person that ran the makeup department. And it was definitely a male-dominated field when I started. The few department heads that were left at the studios were all men.

In fact, I was on a TV show for three or four seasons and in the middle of it, the creators decided they were going to replace the department head. When they came to me for suggestions on what other guy to replace him with, I said, "Uh, hello, I'm here! I've been on the show since season one." They were like, "But you're a woman!?!" and I smiled and said, "I know, isn't that cool?" It was so obvious that they should hire me. I knew the show, I did prosthetics—why couldn't I be department head?" The mentality for a long time was, "Oh, she's a woman, she can't be the department head." That has changed obviously.

The credits for hair and makeup artists are inconsistent; are the credits a designation of who's in charge?

People can basically call themselves whatever they want. A makeup designer is like a whole new thing that's come into play in the last probably 10 years. People like to call themselves makeup designers. Especially a big show that has involved a lot of different types of makeup. You can be the makeup designer and the department head, or you might actually just be somebody who designed the makeup and the prosthetics and did not do any application. Sometimes, a whole shop will receive credit. Like, in *The Hunger Games*, I was the makeup designer and the department head. So it's not so much a matter of a hierarchy as it is "what do I want to couch myself as?"

How big is the makeup department on a large film such as *The Hunger Games*?

It was huge. I had upwards of sometimes 50 makeup artists with me because we had enormous crowd scenes. We had a big cast too. Our cast was probably at least 15 principals almost all the time, and then we had huge background days. I always had at least 3 to 4 makeup artists with me doing regular cast as well as 40 to 50 makeup artists doing background dependent on how many extras would work that day.

How did you know you wanted to become a makeup artist?

I wanted to do it ever since I was a little girl, but was told, "No, you can't do it because you're not a guy. You don't know anybody. You have to be born into it." I was given many reasons for why I couldn't do it, but the most common one was because I was a woman.

I thought, "Well that's just stupid so I'm going to figure this out on my own," and eventually I did. I started out working for some rock bands, and this one little quirky band in particular wanted to look like aliens with big heads and pointed ears. I hadn't done that before so I said, "Okay, well I'll go find out how to do that." So I went to a science fiction convention and met these guys who were doing wild makeup, and I said, "Hey, can you show me how to do that? Can you teach me how to do that?" That was how it started. From there on out I just said, "Okay, this is what I'm doing now."

How would you explain what your profession is and how it contributes to a film?

Well, I think that makeup tells the story, and it can help the actors tell theirs. It brings their character to life. A lot of times an actress or actor doesn't really feel the part until they look right. For me, that is really special. I love the fact that we can give the actors a tool to use. Plus, I like working with the directors because we also help bring their vision to life. Makeup is a tool that helps to tell a story; it enables us to create these fantastic characters.

We all have to work together as a symbiotic group. As you work closely with an actress or actor, you have to remember he or she is going to be wearing this. So it has to be comfortable for them, it has to feel like they are their character. You kind of have to have this sort of symbiotic relationship between the director [and] the costume designer. Sometimes even the art director has input, because they're creating the world that this person is living in.

Did you have a mentor or an apprenticeship? Do you mentor others?

I didn't really have an apprenticeship, but I did have a mentor, and his name was Fred Phillips. Fred was very kind to me as I was coming up. He was one of the older makeup artists that I met when I was first starting out. Fred was the makeup artist who did the original *Star Trek* TV series. Fred actually gave me my first big job in a motion picture; he called and asked me to do *Star Trek: The Motion Picture* with him. *Star Trek* was my first really big union movie job. Monty Westmore and Nick Smith were always incredible inspirations too. Yeah, we all had mentors growing up in this business.

I feel that I'm a mentor to just about every young woman in this business. Every time I meet them, they freak out, and some of them cry and stuff. I'm going, "Oh my God, I feel so weird. It's just me." I just feel happy that I can share everything that I've learned and everything that I'm still learning with students, because now I'm also the director of education at Cinema Makeup School. So when I'm not on film sets, I am at school being what I wish I could have had when I was learning.

How have you stayed relevant in your career as technology has evolved?

Technology is advancing so rapidly in every field, not just in makeup effects. It's visual effects and everything else even connected with them. Now we're building and designing characters that are specifically made to work with CGI. We all have to have a knowledge of all these different things to stay on top of everything that's happening. I don't think CGI will replace makeup, but it's certainly going to enhance makeup.

For instance, when we did the first *Pirates of the Caribbean* film, Davy Jones was going to originally be in makeup. Then I started talking to ILM [Industrial Light and Magic] and said, "Well, maybe we should just work together and make him look like he's wearing a makeup? Let's figure this out." So John Knoll and I worked together very closely, and they actually fashioned the CGI characters after our makeup. They had the same textures and movements. You really didn't know what you were looking at. So that was really fantastic because for the longest time people asked, "How did you get those tentacles to move on Davy Jones like that?" and I would say, "Davy Jones was a CGI character." They couldn't believe how good it looked.

You couldn't tell the difference between the CGI characters and the living characters in that movie, which is exactly what we wanted. Bootstrap Bill, played by Stellan Skarsgård, for example, was in makeup all the way through and went through like eight different phases. After the third phase, Bootstrap Bill was initially supposed to become a CGI character, but he liked wearing the makeup so much he continued to wear it live. I warned him that it would get heavier from that point on, but he said it would only make him act better.

Do you feel there's ageism in your field?

I don't think you do get penalized for being old in this field, because I keep threatening to retire and everybody goes, "No, no, don't retire!" But I don't want to be on a set for 16 hours a day for nine months of the year. Definitely I want to retire. I just want to maybe do one, a couple of six-week-long movies or something. After a while you just get tired of being gone all the time, because we're never at home. Recently I've [done] smaller movies where I either like the actors or I think the project is really cool. That's kind of where I am right now.

Music

Introduction

Film music is hardly ancillary to film production. While it is rare that music teams are involved with or even privy to the actual scripting, filming, or editing of a production, they nonetheless play a substantial creative role in any final product. At its simplest, film music amplifies narrative setting and tone and provides a sonic glue that facilitates seamless transitions between even the most diverging sequences. More subtly, film music provides an ongoing, deeply nuanced psychological commentary which the lay viewer senses and responds to in emotional and physiological ways, even if not wholly aware that music is actually playing. Themes and leitmotifs define and transform alongside characters as they develop through different events and situations. Music communicates the unseen thoughts, intentions, and emotional states of characters even before action and dialogue reveal them. And music provides both the tapestry and the emotional hue for montage sequences, encasing a collage of scenes featuring different events, times, locations, and characters within a single musical cue.

For all of these reasons, film productions frequently feature a headline composer in the title credits. Yet viewers should rid themselves of the romantic conception of a single composer working in an isolated studio, setting pencil directly to musical parchment as she views a film. Film music is collaborative, and it is digital. Thus, the musicians featured in the following profiles represent a host of musical disciplines not limited to traditional composition but also including synthesized musical production, orchestration and arranging, performance, music supervision and editing, sound design, and song writing—and it is not uncommon for a single musician to fulfill more than one of these roles on a single film. While several significant women in the film music industry by necessity of space are omitted from this collection (Wendy Carlos, Debbie Wiseman, and Deborah Lurie, to name just a few), it nonetheless attempts to feature a range of musical artists representing different time periods in film and different music specializations.

Stylistically, the artists profiled represent the breadth of musical traditions and approaches, from traditional acoustic scoring and orchestration (Rachel Portman and Shirley Walker) to world-music traditions (Lisa Gerrard) and song writing (Marilyn Bergman), with several artists navigating traditional and popular music styles adeptly (Angela Morley and Anne Dudley). Portman, Dudley, and Bergman stand out as winners of the Academy Award, though the entire collection of artists has garnered countless additional nominations and accolades. Significantly, some of film music's most iconic scores are underpinned by women working in uncredited roles as orchestrators or advisors: enter both Morley and Walker, who worked closely with scoring giants John Williams and Hans Zimmer, respectively. Not least, most of these artists create film music in myriad ways: Dudley as a composer, performer, and producer; Gerrard as a composer, orchestrator, singer, and instrumentalist; Yvonne Moriarty as a multi-instrumentalist and orchestrator; and Walker as a composer, orchestrator, and conductor. This sampling of workers in film music exemplifies the diverse, creative talents women bring to the industry.

Scott M. Strovas

Bergman, Marilyn (1929–)

Marilyn Bergman's name seems inextricably linked to her husband Alan's name. For more than half a century, this husband-and-wife songwriting team has contributed lyrics for music composed for television, film, theater, and albums. Although widely known for their work on theme songs for television shows, such as *Maude*, *Good Times*, *Alice*, and *In the Heat of the Night*, the duo is perhaps best known for their work in film, including songs for *The Thomas Crown Affair* (1968), *The Way We Were* (1973), *Tootsie* (1982), and *Yentl* (1983). The Bergmans have often collaborated with notable composers, including Michel Legrand, Marvin Hamlisch, Henry Mancini, John Williams, and Quincy Jones, and their hit songs have been performed by major recording artists, including Frank Sinatra, Fred Astaire, Barbra Streisand, and Tony Bennett. Independent of her husband, Marilyn has left her own mark on the industry. In 1985, she became the first woman to serve on the board of directors of the American Society of Composers, Authors and Publishers (ASCAP), and in 1994, she became the first woman to serve as president and chair of the board. During her 15-year tenure as president of ASCAP, Marilyn advocated for the rights of songwriters, proved essential in the upholding or passing of legislation related to copyright protection, and established educational programs. She also held two terms as president of the International Confederation of Societies of Authors and Composers (CISAC) and served as the first chair of the National Recorded Sound Preservation Board of the Library of Congress. Marilyn received honorary doctorates from Berklee College of Music, Trinity College (Hartford, Connecticut), and the University of Massachusetts Amherst. She and her husband have also served on the executive committee of the Music Branch of the Academy of Motion Picture Arts and Sciences.

Marilyn and Alan Bergman were born in the same hospital in Brooklyn, New York, although they would not meet until the 1950s, subsequent to relocations to Los Angeles, California. Marilyn Bergman (née Keith) attended the High School of Music & Art in New York, where she became friends with the niece of lyricist Bob Russell, known for hit songs including "Don't Get around Much Anymore." During afternoons after school, Marilyn played piano for Russell as he experimented with ideas for songs. After graduating from high school in 1945, Marilyn studied English and psychology at New York University. In the early 1950s, she fell down some stairs, breaking one shoulder and dislocating the other. Seeking the help of her parents as she recovered, she moved to Los Angeles, where her family had relocated in 1949. Russell, who had also moved to Los Angeles, encouraged her to write lyrics while she recuperated, since she would not be able to play the piano. Marilyn commented, "I often thought that if I had broken my legs, I would have been a composer!" (Lumme 2002, 105).

When Marilyn presented a lyric to Russell, he introduced her to songwriter Lew Spence, and she became his lyricist. While working with Spence, Marilyn finally met Bergman, Spence's other lyricist, and their professional and romantic partnership blossomed. In 1957, the team enjoyed their first hit, "Yellow Bird," and in 1958, the couple married. In 1961, they provided lyrics for *The Marriage-Go-Round*, the first of many motion picture projects. While the Bergmans had written various types of songs just to get by, their goal was always to write songs for film. The combination of music, narrative, and image attracted the couple. Although sometimes an idea or phrase sparked the melody for the composer with whom the team was collaborating, the two generally liked the music to come before the words, since they drew inspiration from rhythmic and structural elements. For Marilyn, songs for film should serve a purpose beyond merely building a soundtrack. She states that a song "should either underline a mood or add another level to what the characters are experiencing. We always try to fly at a different altitude than the images" (Lumme 2002, 105). Marilyn believes their key to success was realizing that songs are not written, but, instead, rewritten.

Marilyn cites George and Ira Gershwin, Irving Berlin, Cole Porter, Johnny Mercer, and Jerome Kern, among others, as influences. While stylistic characteristics of these models are identifiable in the couple's songs, the two have demonstrated incredible versatility, producing a body of work spanning styles, topics, and points of view. The Bergmans have amassed a number of accolades, including 16 Academy Award nominations and 3 wins (for "The Windmills of Your Mind" in 1968, "The Way We Were" in 1973, and the score for *Yentl* in 1983), 2 Grammy Awards, 2 Golden Globe Awards, and 4 Emmy Awards. They were inducted into the Songwriters Hall of Fame in 1980 and received the Johnny Mercer Award from the organization in 1997. At the 2009 Motion Picture Academy Tribute to the Bergmans, John Williams said the couple should be "on anyone's list of the greatest lyricists of all time" (Burlingame 2009).

Breena L. Loraine

See also: Dunaway, Faye

Further Reading

American Society of Composers, Authors and Publishers. n.d. "Board of Directors: Marilyn Bergman." Accessed December 30, 2017. https://www.ascap.com/about/board-intro/bergman-bio.aspx.

Burlingame, Jon. 2009. "Motion Picture Academy Tribute to Alan and Marilyn Bergman: Host Quincy Jones Joined by Streisand, Legrand, Grusin and Others." *The Film Music Society*, June 4. http://www.filmmusicsociety.org/news_events/features/2009/060409.html?isArchive=060409

Ewen, David. 1987. *American Songwriters: An H. W. Wilson Biographical Dictionary*. New York: The H. W. Wilson Company.

Lumme, Helena. 2002. *Great Women of Film*. New York: Billboard Books.

National Public Radio. 2011. "The Couple Behind Some of Hollywood's Classic Tunes." *NPR*, September 2. https://www.npr.org/2011/09/02/140089584/the-couple-behind-some-of-hollywoods-classic-tunes

Pogrebin, Abigail. 2005. *Stars of David: Prominent Jews Talk about Being Jewish*. New York: Broadway Books.

Songwriters Hall of Fame. n.d. "Marilyn Bergman." Accessed December 30, 2017. https://www.songhall.org/profile/Marilyn_Bergman

Dudley, Anne (1956–)

Music producer, pianist, British popular music icon, and Academy Award–winning composer of over 30 film scores, Anne Dudley personifies the creative quality and agile musicianship demanded of contemporary film composers. Her wide-ranging educational and professional experiences inform her almost three-decade tenure composing for film and television. While Dudley has proven to be a composer adept at providing archetypal music to support a film or scene's dramatic tone and onscreen action, she demonstrates the extent of her introspective resourcefulness in films such as *The Full Monty* (1997) and *American History X* (1998), in which her music reinforces the psychology behind the characters' actions.

Dudley's career in music is as diverse as it is accomplished. Classically trained at the Royal College of Music and King's College, she has composed two operas and, among other more traditional works, two orchestral compositions, which she completed as part of her illustrious residency with the BBC Concert Orchestra. Yet Dudley experienced her first professional and commercial success in the 1980s as a founding member of the Grammy Award–winning electronic ensemble, Art of Noise. The impact of the group's explorations into sound production, audio sampling, and synthetic music on Dudley's career cannot be understated. Her ability to craft primarily synthetic scores undoubtedly bolstered her opportunities in the film music industry, informing efforts across the span of her career, from *Hiding Out* (1987) and *Knight Moves* (1992) to *Pushing Tin* (1999) and *The Walker* (2007), and providing end-credit music to such films as *The Gathering* (2003) and *Perfect Creature* (2006), for which she otherwise composed more acoustic instrumental underscores. Dudley's work with Art of Noise also positioned her as a capable producer both of popular musicians—including prominent artists Tom Jones, Seal, Phil Collins, and The Spice Girls (Vickers 1998, 33)—and of music for film, most notably the orchestra recording sessions for *Les Misérables* (2012).

Limited musical resources and short transitional music cues broadly characterize Dudley's approach to film scoring. Even when working within the medium of orchestra, she prefers the reduced instrumentation of strings alone to provide a consistent textural and atmospheric backdrop, while supporting setting and onscreen action with archetypal solo wind instruments and percussion. For instance, the brief cues that comprise Dudley's score to *The Crying Game* (1992) are "reserved largely for the poignant and tender moments, emphasizing the essentially gentle nature of this story," writes composer-scholar David Burnand. Dudley colors her primarily string underscore with militaristic snare drum in scenes featuring the Irish Republican Army. Music-literate audiences might also recognize in the film's brief, but oft-repeated solo trumpet call a possible allusion to composer Charles Ives's *The Unanswered Question* (1906), which might reflect the crises of war and identity depicted in the film. Much longer film music cues comprise *Tristan and Isolde* (2006), for which Dudley layers solo flute and oboe above string orchestra to enhance the film's medieval Anglo-Irish setting. The addition of drums accentuates the film's action and battle sequences, a technique she repeats in her primarily string orchestra score to *Perfect Creature*.

In a year in which *Titanic* (1997) garnered 11 Oscars, Dudley's Academy Award–winning score to *The Full Monty* perhaps benefitted from a brief period during which the Academy distinguished between comedic and dramatic scores. Still, Dudley's limited instrumentation and characteristically short cues complement *The Full Monty* as skillfully as does James Horner's complex score to *Titanic*. *The Full Monty* follows Gaz and Dave, who organize a strip show featuring themselves and four other blue-collar workers, most of whom have been unemployed since Sheffield's (England) steel factory closed six months earlier. Gaz's idea for the strip show is but one of many juvenile schemes he conspires throughout the film, and Dudley crafts the film's main musical groove—which she describes as "sort of loping, slightly reggae-ish, slightly sort-of-innocent optimistic atmosphere"—in the spirit of his quirky scams (Kermode 2015). A rhythm band of alto saxophone, trumpet, baritone saxophone, guitar, and drums reenters each time Gaz's schemes are discussed or in motion. His delinquency is matched by Dudley's adoption of the surly tone of the baritone saxophone for the bass line, rather than electric string bass, above which alto saxophone sounds a bouncy, repeated melodic idea accompanied by the guitar's offbeat block chords.

While Dudley's music befits the situational comedy inherent in *The Fully Monty*'s portrayal of the very un-Chippendale-ish gents as they muster the courage to learn and perform the routine, it more subtly expresses the duality between Gaz's degenerate guile and the economic hardships confronting the group. Recognizing that "the best comedies always have these really heartbreaking moments, . . . and the music has to take that all seriously," Dudley discreetly manipulates the tone of her groovy theme to reiterate the psychological turmoil the men endure without the prospect of gratifying job opportunities and affirmation of their roles as bread-earners (Kermode 2015). By replacing the playful saxophones with the desperate long tones of solo harmonica above smoother-sounding electric bass, Dudley captures Gaz's despair upon realizing that he is losing the affection of his son; similarly, she reinforces Dave's insecurities about his wife's possible infidelity through broken guitar chords and limited drum set.

Dudley puts her insight to use again in her score to *American History X*, a film in which the protagonists' psychological struggles manifest as a kind of sick religion. Derek and his younger brother Danny have turned to the Neo-Nazi movement as a means of coping with the loss of their father, their perverted devotion to the white-power cause manifested most tragically in Derek's murder of two young black men. In a masterful touch of religious musical pastiche, Dudley prefigures and emphasizes the religiosity of Derek's fanaticism. The film opens with imagery of the Venice Beach beachfront accompanied by mournful solo French horn. The horn has a chant-like quality, in imitation of the earliest notated Christian music, as well as an American-ness in its broad melody which harks back to Aaron Copland's 1930s' and 1940s' orchestral soundscapes of the American frontier, only graver. The horn's solemnity does not simply establish the tone of the film; it also reinterprets Copland's nationalistic optimism as a sort of requiem for the unfulfilled promise of America. Dudley solidifies the religious nature of her title theme with the inclusion of a boys choir singing *Kyrie eleison* ("Lord have mercy"), the first words of the Roman Catholic Mass Ordinary. And it is this music of the boys chorus, which Dudley conceives as "Aryan [in] sound," to which she returns as police arrest Derek shortly after he brutally stomps to death one of his victims (Dudley 2010). Wide-eyed, Derek plummets into zealous madness. He locks eyes with Danny, gives him a smirk, and raises his eyebrows in alarming indifference toward his horrific actions. As intelligent, funny, and dedicated to his family as Derek is previously portrayed, audiences may perceive his actions, at best, as incomprehensible and, at worst, contrived, save Dudley's contribution. Her juxtaposition of the *Kyrie* with Derek's expressions affirms his blind faith in the Neo-Nazi movement, for which he commits acts of terrorism, domestic violence, and murder.

As a composer, Dudley avoids stylistic classification. Her compositional path balances the small rhythm bands and cabaret ensembles of *The Full Monty* and the television series *Jeeves and Wooster* (1990–1993) with the sweeping, multicultural, fully orchestrated soundscapes of epics such as *Miracle Maker* (2000). What's more, she remains an adaptable musician who cannot simply be addressed as a composer. Her work on *Bright Young Things* (2003) represents the best of the multifaceted, 21st-century working musician—an artist facile, creative, and sensitive enough to craft a Gershwin-inspired, symphonic jazz underscore for a film set in Jazz-Age London, produce the recording sessions for new jazz arrangements of 1930s' big-band hits used throughout the film, and perform as keyboardist on those arrangements.

Scott M. Strovas

Further Reading

Burnand, David. "Dudley, Anne." *Oxford Music Online*. Accessed August 11, 2015. http://www.oxfordmusiconline.com/subscriber/article/grove/music/48846

Cool Music. "Anne Dudley—Composer Profile." Accessed August 10, 2015. http://coolmusicltd.com/composers/anne-dudley

Dudley, Anne. 2010. "American History X." Accessed August 10, 2015. http://www.annedudley.co.uk/Default.aspx?page=64&node=75

Hodgkinson, Will. 2003. "Soundtrack of Her Life." *The Guardian*, August 15. http://www.theguardian.com/music/2003/aug/15/2

Kermode, Mark. 2015. "The Mystery of Composing." Narrated by Mark Kermode. Mark Kermode: The Soundtrack of My Life. *BBC Radio 2*, May 27. http://www.bbc.co.uk/programmes/b05vy9w0

Vickers, Graham. 1998. "The Full Dudley." *Creative Review*, May. https://www.zttaat.com/article.php?title=625.

Gerrard, Lisa (1961–)

Australian vocalist, instrumentalist, and composer Lisa Gerrard first came to public notice as a member of the world fusion/ambient pop group Dead Can Dance, but she is probably more widely known for her work as a composer and performer of music for film. Her unique singing style and technique, as well as her trademark ambient keyboard textures and her playing of the *yangqin,* a Chinese hammered dulcimer, lend the scores to which she has contributed a distinctive air that avoids the usual romantic orchestral gestures so familiar to Hollywood film music. Drawing on a broad range of world music traditions, she combines culturally and temporally disparate elements into a synthesis that is at once seamless and natural sounding, while expressing the film's emotional core.

Australian musician, singer, and composer Lisa Gerrard of the music group Dead Can Dance performs live during a concert at the Zitadelle Spandau on June 17, 2013, in Berlin, Germany. Gerrard received a Golden Globe Award for Best Original Score for *Gladiator* (2000), which she composed with Hans Zimmer. (Frank Hoensch/Redferns via Getty Images)

Gerrard's first involvement with film was composing, with Dead Can Dance, the score for *El Niño de la Luna* (1989), a film by Spanish director Agustí Villaronga in which she also acted. Also with Dead Can Dance she contributed to Michael Stearn's soundtrack for Ron Fricke's film *Baraka* (1992). Since then she has contributed music to many films as performer, writer, and composer, while gaining a reputation as an ace collaborator. Her numerous commercially released recordings with Dead Can Dance have also been used in many scores for film and television.

Continuing an approach developed with Dead Can Dance, Gerrard's music for films draws on many cultures and time periods: Western and Eastern, medieval and modern, acoustic and electronic. Her distinctive singing voice is in the exceedingly rare dramatic contralto range, which is very low for a female voice, and she often integrates it into instrumental textures as an additional instrumental voice. She often sings in a language other than English, such as Latin or Irish Gaelic, but she frequently sings in a language of her own creation, one that she has used since she was a child, through which she "believed that [she] was speaking to God" (IMDb 2015).

Gerrard's compositional style could be described as ambient, frequently drone-based, often with simple triadic harmonies suspended above a ground or drone. Her melodies tend to be in minor keys and at moderate tempo. Sometimes a kinetic energy is built against such melodies with faster moving figures in percussion or plucked strings. Gerrard often utilizes vocal inflections and ornamentations inspired by Balkan and Middle Eastern music but without sounding too much like her sources of inspiration. Thus she avoids obvious cultural appropriations while sounding rather exotic, timeless, and spiritual.

Gerrard contributed to Elliot Goldenthal's score for Michael Mann's *Heat* (1995). She and Dead Can Dance alumnus Pieter Bourke were subsequently hired by Mann to score his film *The Insider* (1999). A major breakthrough for Gerrard was her collaboration with composer Hans Zimmer on the soundtrack for Ridley Scott's blockbuster *Gladiator* (2000), for which she and Zimmer shared a Golden Globe award for Best Original Score and a nomination for the British Academy Film Awards. They also earned an Oscar nomination, but the Academy of Motion Picture Arts & Sciences deemed Gerrard's contribution not significant enough in terms of actual screen minutes (she composed and performed 6 out of the 17 pieces) for recognition (Kendall 2001). She continued working with Zimmer on several projects over the next few years that brought her music to the attention of millions of cinemagoers.

Gerrard again collaborated with Bourke on Mann's *Ali* (2001). Both her scores with Bourke garnered Golden Globe nominations for Best Original Score. She also contributed to Hans Zimmer's scores for *Mission Impossible 2* (2000), *Black Hawk Down* (2001), and *Tears of the Sun* (2003). Gerrard's first solo soundtrack was composed for New Zealand director Niki Caro's *Whale Rider* (2002). In 2004 she collaborated with Irish composer Patrick Cassidy on a score for Mel Gibson's *The Passion of the Christ,* but the score was withdrawn. She has well over 60 credits as composer and soloist on the Internet Movie Database, most of them since 1999.

Collaboration has been a hallmark of Gerrard's artistic and professional life, from working in Dead Can Dance with Brendan Perry to her multiple collaborations with Michael Stearns, Pieter Bourke, Patrick Cassidy, and Hans Zimmer. It is worth noting that when working with these other composers Gerrard seems to inhabit a sonic territory that contrasts sharply with that of her collaborators.

One case in point is the *Gladiator* score. All of Gerrard's more conspicuous contributions to that work, her characteristic vocals and *yangqin* playing, sound especially exotic in the context of Zimmer's orchestral score, which has the Western classical tradition as its orientation, at times closely imitating the music of Wagner. One exception to the overt Europeanism of most of Zimmer's writing for *Gladiator* is Djivan Gasparyan's Armenian *duduk* playing for one scene, "To Zucchabar," which he and Zimmer co-wrote. But most of the film's musical exoticism comes from Gerrard, a collaborative model that she and Zimmer tend to adhere to across projects.

One of the reasons for the effectiveness of the *Gladiator* score is the use of Gerrard's unique voice to represent the emotional core of the protagonist Maximus, played by Russell Crowe. Her voice is sometimes overlaid on Zimmer's orchestral foundation but at other times it is accompanied by sparse instrumentation. In these instances the compositional style is recognizable as Gerrard's, the instrumental background being more ambient, with less development and simpler harmony than the heavy orchestral writing.

Throughout the score these exotic and familiar elements are played off one another as if to represent the protagonist's isolation in his struggle with Rome, but they come together for the end titles theme, credited to Zimmer, Gerrard, and score producer Klaus Badelt. "Now We Are Free" has Gerrard's multitracked voice (in one of her invented languages) harmonizing with itself over Zimmer's orchestra accompanied by multiple ethnic percussion instruments. The tension of this dichotomy between exotic and familiar elements is resolved in a fusion of styles that effectively mirrors the resolution of the film's plot.

However, Gerrard's solo score for *Whale Rider* is remarkably different. Consisting of her trademark ambient keyboards, infrequent but very subtle use of her voice, and some tribal-sounding percussion, the textures are much more sparse than *Gladiator's* and there is hardly any development at all. Yet this understated work underpins the simple story of New Zealand director Niki Caro's film very effectively, its restraint adding force to the emotion on the screen, the quiet dignity of the film's Maori characters and their relationship to the natural world, and reflecting the marine environment which is the setting for most of the film's action.

Roger W. Landes

Further Reading

Internet Movie Database. 2015. "Lisa Gerrard." Accessed August 1, 2015. http://www.imdb.com/name/nm0314713/bio?ref_=nm_ov_bio_sm.

Kendall, Lukas. 2001. "Film Score Friday 2/23/01." *Film Score Monthly*, February 22. Accessed August 1, 2015. http://www.filmscoremonthly.com/daily/article.cfm?articleID=3516

Reesman, Bryan. 2003. "Lisa Gerrard: The Colour of Sound." *Mix Magazine,* February. https://www.mixonline.com/sfp/lisa-gerrard-color-sound-369020

Robertson, Rowena. 2008. "From the Music Studio to the Silver Screen: Lisa Gerrard, Warren Ellis and Paul Kelly on Making Music for Film." *Metro Magazine: Media & Education Magazine,* 15: 76–80.

Moriarty, Yvonne Suzette (Unknown–)

With a career spanning over 22 years, primarily as an orchestrator, but also as a performer on French horn, trombone, and flugelhorn, Yvonne Moriarty has had an undeniable influence within the film music profession. During her years within this industry, she has averaged more than four projects a year, and a peak of eight in 2003. Her work largely encompasses movie soundtracks, with the exception of a number of TV miniseries episodes of *The Pacific* (2010). Her job as an orchestrator is to take music that has been already composed and arrange (or orchestrate) that music for the previously delineated instrumentation depending on the mood the music is trying to convey. As would be expected, this may change based upon the composer's or director's desire for the final production of the scene.

Moriarty has collaborated with several well-known and respected soundtrack composers. Some of these names include Steve Jablonsky and John Powell, both on 3 projects; Junkie XL on 6 projects; and most notably Hans Zimmer on an astounding 21 projects. Every project that included Junkie XL also included Hans Zimmer. Her most noted collaborations involving Steve Jablonsky are two movies from the *Transformers* franchise. These movies, the second and fourth movies in the franchise, are *Transformers: Revenge of the Fallen* (2009) and *Transformers: Age of Extinction* (2014). Moriarty worked with John Powell on *Evolution* (2001), *Paycheck* (2003), and *Robots* (2005). Although these titles were somewhat successful in the box office, none of these movies received much critical acclaim for their scores.

In 1994, on just her second project, Moriarty was part of a music production team whose work on *The Lion King* garnered critical acclaim for both its original songs and underscore. Hans Zimmer earned an Academy Award for Best Original Score, and Moriarty likely played a role in orchestrating his four credited titles: "This Land," "To Die For," "Under the Stars," and "King of Pride Rock." In terms of orchestration, these tracks seem distinctive for several reasons such as the use of ethnic percussion, driving rhythms, use of chorus in a rhythmic way, and fluidity within diverse styles yet seamless integration from one track to another.

Distinguishing the prevailing stylistic trends of an orchestrator requires broad listening and informed speculation, but there are some shared characteristics between Moriarty's orchestrations that seem to stand out. She is quite skilled at using choral texture as a means of creating a more folk-like soundscape. The two scores of *The Lion King* (1994) and *Gladiator* (2001) in some ways employ similar sound-sets to evoke comparable moods and aural impressions. For example, in both *The Lion King* track, "To Die For," and "Honor Him" from *Gladiator*, Zimmer and Moriarty craft the music in a brooding, pensive style, developing slowly as the texture builds and helping to give the music an overall feeling of nonresolution. Both of these tracks eventually give way to the use of more ethnic sounds like that of percussion, drums, and choral chanting, establishing a dance-like natural feel. These choral textures return consistently in work throughout the breadth of Moriarty's career and with different collaborators. They appear again in *Gladiator*, "Now We Are Free," as well as in Jablonsky's "Matrix" from *Transformers: Revenge of the Fallen*, which, interestingly, seems to hint at the later Zimmer/Moriarty soundtrack, *Man of Steel* (2013).

With the release of *Batman v. Superman: Dawn of Justice* (2016), the sequel to *Man of Steel,* a more obvious connection with the sounds and style of Moriarty can be easily discerned. There is a bit of irony in this project because Zimmer and Moriarty were involved with the soundtrack production of the Grammy Award–winning soundtrack of *The Dark Knight* (2008). Hans Zimmer, who had already composed a musical theme for the character of Batman (albeit for a different movie franchise) decided to hand the "Batman theme" responsibility over to a different composer named Junkie XL.

In her years working as a soundtrack orchestrator, Moriarty has worked with several prominent composers on many critically acclaimed productions. When taking into account the number of these projects with which she has been involved, the volume of projects that were nominated for Grammys is indeed impressive. These projects include *The Lion King, Gladiator, Pirates of the Caribbean: Dead Man's Chest* (2007), *The Dark Knight* (2008), and *Inception* (2010). Of these films, *The Lion King* and *The Dark Knight* were Grammy Award–winning soundtracks. No matter what future endeavors she decides to embark upon, it is clear based upon her outstanding output, exceptional quality, and consistent success that Yvonne Moriarty will continue to be a recognizable standard of excellence for female musicians within today's film music industry.

Anthony J. King

Further Reading

All Music. "Moriarty, Yvonne S." Accessed June 30, 2016. http://www.allmusic.com/artist/yvonne-s-moriarty-mn0001201136/credits

Cinema Blend. "Justice League Part One." Accessed June 30, 2016. www.cinemablend.com/Justice-League-Part-One-6888.html

Internet Movie Database. 2016a. "John Powell" Accessed June 30, 2016. www.imdb.com/name/nm0694173/?ref_=nv_sr_2

Internet Movie Database. 2016b. "Junkie XL" Accessed June 30, 2016. www.imdb.com/name/nm0432725

Internet Movie Database. 2016c. "Steve Jablonsky" Accessed June 30, 2016. www.imdb.com/name/nm0413011/?ref_=nv_sr_1

Internet Movie Database. 2016d. "Yvonne S. Moriarty." Accessed June 30, 2016. www.imdb.com/name/nm0605372

Morley, Angela (1924–2009)

Angela Morley is not one of the most immediately recognizable names in 20th-century film music. Though she was an Academy Award–nominated and Emmy Award–winning arranger, an Ivor Novello Award–nominated composer, and an orchestrator for a large volume of award-winning film scores, her contribution to film music, though varied and extensive, is often unrecognized. In order to appreciate the full breadth of Morley's work, one must first seek out compositions and film music contributions under two separate names: "Wally Stott" (Angela Morley's birth name) and "Angela Morley" (her name following her 1972 gender reassignment).

Next, though Morley had quite a widespread credited film music résumé, the works for which she was uncredited are plentiful. Fuller consideration of Angela Morley's career reveals that her contribution to film music was both far-reaching and important.

Born in Leeds, Yorkshire, England, Morley began her musical career playing in and arranging for dance bands at a very young age. This influence would carry into her compositional style for the rest of her career. Morley's musical voice may be broadly defined as *light music*. Light music is a British musical style that is orchestrated like classical music but is more centered upon melody and possesses a purposeful easy-listening quality.

Morley was the primary composer for roughly 15 motion pictures between 1952 and 1978. The most noted film for which Morley served as the credited composer was the animated film *Watership Down* (1978). The score was nominated for an Ivor Novello Award (an esteemed British award for songwriting and composing) and named one of the 10 best film scores of 1978 by the Academy of Motion Picture Arts and Sciences. Morley accepted the commission to compose the music for *Watership Down* after its original commissioned composer, Malcolm Williamson, was unable to compose more than roughly six minutes of the score due to ill health. The prologue and the four-minute cue in the opening scene were sketched by Williamson, while the remainder of the score is completely Morley's. Morley's musical atmosphere of the film score complements the English countryside setting of *Watership Down*. Many of her calm and peaceful moments of the score feature mellow woodwind solos embellished by harps and strings, underscoring the pastoral landscape upon which the rabbits travel. "Kaheer's Theme" is purposefully contrasting. Kaheer is a foreign seagull from across the "big water." On her website, Morley described Kaheer's theme as follows: "I put aside my English pastoral instrumental vocabulary in favour of a Belgian invention, the alto saxophone, and composed for ["Kaheer's Theme"] a Viennese novelty waltz" (Morley 2001–2008). The theme features a lilting, chromatic alto saxophone solo (incidentally Morley's primary instrument) accompanied by orchestra. During the injured seagull's introduction into the film, Morley fragments the theme. However, when Kaheer flies for the first time since his injury, she resolves Kaheer's motif as a brilliant, fanciful waltz, seemingly signifying that Kaheer is made complete again by the ability to fly. Although Morley creates an atmosphere of splendor and importance in Kaheer's flight music, the quirky nature of the composition makes it clear that even during his finest moment, Kaheer is not a graceful bird but one with great uniqueness of character.

Morley's collaborative film scores were highly acclaimed. Following her Academy Award–nominated collaboration with the lyricist/librettist team Alan J. Lerner and Frederick Loewe for the film score, *The Little Prince* (1974), she received her second Academy Award nomination for her work on the 1976 film score, *The Slipper and the Rose*, a musical retelling of the classic fairy tale, *Cinderella*. Alongside the famous musical film songwriting brothers Robert B. Sherman and Richard M. Sherman, Morley arranged, adapted, and underscored music for *The Slipper and the Rose*. The musical arrangements of the dance music during the prince's royal ball are Morley's. During a succession of courtly dances, a series of princesses is imposed upon the unhappy prince in hopes of finding him a wife. Morley's first ballroom dance, a polonaise, introduces a stately musical motif. Though she changes the style and type of dance as the prince is brought different partners, the motif never changes, seemingly signifying that the prince remains in the same unhappy state with each princess he meets. However, when Cinderella enters the ballroom, everything stops. Morley strips away the courtly formality of the dance music. As Cinderella and the prince begin to dance, entranced by one another, Morley replaces haughty propriety with a slow, quiet waltz. She borrowed the theme of the slow waltz from a song from later in the film, "He Danced with Me." Morley introduces woodwind solos into the waltz as the prince's emotions and feelings mount for Cinderella. Slowly, she builds upon the waltz's tempo and orchestration until a smile lights the faces of Cinderella and her prince, prompting others to join in dancing the waltz.

Morley's uncredited contributions to film scores are extensive. She served in some capacity for scores by film music giants such as John Williams, Miklós Rózsa, and James Horner (Morley 2001–2008). Of Morley, John Williams recalled, "She was certainly one of the finest musicians I've ever known or worked with. As an orchestrator, her skill was unsurpassed" (Burlingame 2009). A few on the list of many film scores for which Morley played some supporting role are *The Empire Strikes Back* (1980), *E.T. the Extra-terrestrial* (1982), *Hook* (1991), *The Right Stuff* (1983), and *The Karate Kid* (1984). Among the most famous uncredited film cues Morley orchestrated is the scene in *Star Wars* (1977) during which Obi-Wan Kenobi's voice instructs, "Use the Force, Luke." The militaristic brass and percussion music that is heard as the chase ensues within the trenches of the Death Star is overtaken by a sudden shift to the purity of stringed instruments, projecting a peaceful moment of clarity over Obi-Wan's spiritual guidance. Other recognizable musical film moments that Morley claimed as her own are orchestrations for *Superman*'s (1978) Ice Palace music, arrangements for Viennese Waltz music in *Schindler's List* (1993), and arrangements of Christmas songs in *Home Alone* (1990) (LaFave 1997).

Kimberly Mullendore Brown

Further Reading

Burlingame, Jon. 2009. "Angela Morley Dies at 84: Respected British Composer-Arranger Wrote for Film, TV, Records, Concerts." *The Film Music Society*, January 19. http://www.filmmusicsociety.org/news_events/features/2009/011909.html?isArchive=011909

LaFave, Kenneth. 1997. "Arranger Has Scored Many Successes." *The Arizona Republic*, Accessed June 6, 2015. http://jazzpro.nationaljazzarchive.org.uk/profiles/morley.htm

"Morley, Angela. 2001–2008." Accessed June 26, 2015. http://www.angelamorley.com

Patsavas, Alexandra (1968–)

Music supervisors, responsible for tasks as wide-ranging as collaborating with directors and creative teams to recommending or selecting music, securing copyright, clearing licensing, managing budgets, negotiating costs, and supervising the technical aspects of synchronizing music with visual and narrative elements, have become key players in the artistic, legal, and business facets of the entertainment industry. In the 1980s and 1990s, music supervisors were primarily concerned with the administrative tasks related to copyright and licenses, but since the early 2000s, they have moved into a more creative position and have accrued additional power in the production and creative decision-making processes. With a music supervision career spanning more than 20 years, Alexandra Patsavas has been at the forefront of this transition. She has worked on dozens of projects, including films such as *Wonder* (2017), *The Hunger Games: Catching Fire* (2013), *The Perks of Being a Wallflower* (2012), *Water for Elephants* (2011), *The Dilemma* (2011), and *The Twilight Saga* series, as well as television series, including *How to Get Away with Murder*, *Grey's Anatomy*, *Scandal*, *Mad Men*, *Gossip Girl*, and *The O.C.* Patsavas has demonstrated diverse musical tastes, has brought undiscovered artists and independent "indie" music to the attention of general audiences, and has been nominated for three Grammy Awards in the category of Best Compilation Soundtrack Album for Motion Picture, Television or Other Visual Media.

Patsavas grew up in the suburbs of Chicago, Illinois, where she immersed herself in the local music scene of the 1980s, drawing inspiration from record stores, live performances at clubs, radio, and the films of John Hughes, such as *The Breakfast Club* (1984) and *Pretty in Pink* (1986). While studying politics at the University of Illinois at Urbana-Champaign, she participated in the organization responsible for inviting bands to campus. She then started her own business promoting clubs, and she invited bands like Nirvana and Smashing Pumpkins to appear on campus. Patsavas decided to quit school, and, in 1999, relocated to Los Angeles where she started her career as what she calls "a classic huge agency mailroom employee" at Triad Artists (thereafter acquired by the William Morris Agency) (Price n.d.). She then worked at BMI, where she first encountered and learned about music supervision. Patsavas was soon recruited to serve as a music coordinator at Concorde Films. The first movie for which she provided music supervision services was *Caged Heat 3000* (1995), followed by 50 other movies over the subsequent three years.

In 1998, Patsavas founded Chop Shop Music Supervision, which she initially operated out of her apartment. Her creative choices and ability to clear licenses efficiently placed her in high demand, and she has since worked on many film and television projects. While she has provided supervision services for numerous adaptations of young adult literature, and much of her work falls into the genre of teen drama, she has proven to be versatile and adept at choosing music appropriately suited for diverse genres. Patsavas's creative process is rooted in collaboration. She typically begins work on a project by discussing the "feel and vibe of the songs and the movie" with the director (IFC 2011). She then either pitches music prior to filming or, once editing is complete, she pitches music synched with the moving image. She recognizes the artistic aspect of her job as working with creatives to identify and achieve "a signature sound for a project" (Neumann 2017).

For Patsavas, music chosen must be an appropriate fit for the film's corresponding dialogue or emotion. Sometimes the first song she pitches is selected, but other times, it might take hundreds of songs to arrive at the "right" song. She stresses the importance of having "a really good understanding of drama and storytelling, how an episode of television or a film unfolds and of how musical components can help enhance the drama," as well as understanding "how music tells the story by itself" (Medd 2010, 42). She also emphasizes the importance of recognizing the difference between music emanating from a source onscreen as opposed to the score. One consideration that helps Patsavas determine if she should seek new music or request a cover of a preexisting song to be recorded is whether or not the band will perform live onscreen. For some films, though, her work involves supervising the creation of entirely new music. Many bands wanted to contribute original music for *The Twilight Saga: Eclipse* (2010), for instance, following the immense success of the first film in the series.

Through her musical choices, Patsavas adds depth and layers of meaning to moods, atmospheres, and characterizations simultaneously evoked onscreen and in narrative. In essence, music becomes a character for Patsavas, and she contemplates "musical personality" (IFC 2011). She generally has little difficulty eliminating songs that neither satisfy her taste nor seem to fit the story, characters, or setting of the project. Although there are exceptions, she can almost instantly discern the suitability of a song based on the vocal quality of the singer. For example, she likes "how Thom Yorke's voice works as an instrument rather than a voice, how Mark Lanegan's sounds like the most weary and timeworn ever" (Medd 2010, 43). For Patsavas, choosing the right song is paramount, so she is open to selecting music from well-known bands. However, she also believes "there's nothing more compelling than an audience or a viewer hearing a song for the first time while watching a show that's very dear to them" (Channick 2016). She enjoys the fact that when viewers hear the song again, they will think of the story, the characters, and the visuals, and vice versa.

Patsavas's penchant for undiscovered and "indie" music is apparent in many of her projects. In fact, she has played a significant role in positioning the music supervisor in a stance of power through the sheer ability to "break" artists by including their music in film or television. In an interview, she explained, "Showcasing talent and premiering new songs is one of my favorite aspects of music supervision" (Neumann 2017). She has proved pivotal to the careers of many "indie" bands, including Death Cab for Cutie, The Killers, The Fray, Florence + the Machine, The Black Keys, and Muse, among others. With such a keen ear for new talent, Patsavas launched a record label in order to sign artists that captivated her attention. In 2007, she founded Chop Shop Records. The label has a relatively small roster, which she strives to keep small in order to devote sufficient focus to each artist. Although there are synergistic advantages for a music supervisor who owns a label—she can pitch the label's music for specific projects—the purpose behind starting the label was geared toward artistic development.

Patsavas has been nominated for the Grammy Award three times in the category of Best Compilation Soundtrack Album for Motion Picture, Television or Other Visual Media, first in 2006, for *Grey's Anatomy Original Soundtrack, Volume 2* (2006), then in 2009, for *Twilight (Original Motion Picture Soundtrack)* (2008), and in 2010, for *The Twilight Saga: Eclipse (Original Motion Picture Soundtrack)* (2010). She was a founding member of the Guild of Music Supervisors, which officially launched in 2010 as the nonprofit organization dedicated to the promotion and expansion of the profession. Patsavas has earned nominations for the Guild of Music Supervisors Award in multiple categories, has become a trendsetter in musical tastes among audiences and fellow music supervisors, and has amassed critical acclaim as perhaps the foremost music supervisor in the contemporary film and television industries.

Breena L. Loraine

Further Reading

Anderson, Tim J. 2013. "From Background Music to Above-the-Line Actor: The Rise of the Music Supervisor in Converging Televisual." *Journal of Popular Music Studies* 25(3): 371–388.

Channick, Robert. 2016. "Hollywood Music Supervisor Looks to Chicago Roots for New Talent." *Chicago Tribune*, October 21. http://www.chicagotribune.com/business/ct-chop-shop-music-patsavas-exec-qa-1023-biz-20161021-story.html

Grammy Awards. n.d. "Alexandra Patsavas." Accessed January 15, 2018. https://www.grammy.com/grammys/artists/alexandra-patsavas

Guild of Music Supervisors. n.d. "The Role." Accessed January 15, 2018. http://www.guildofmusicsupervisors.com/the-role

IFC. 2011. "*Twilight* Music Supervisor Alexandra Patsavas Discusses the Art of the Soundtrack." January 15. http://www.ifc.com/2011/11/alexandra-patsavas-twilight-music-supervisor

LeBlanc, Larry. 2018. "Industry Profile: Alexandra Patsavas." January 15. http://members.celebrityaccess.com/members/profile.html?id=586&PHPSESSID=

Maximum Fun Intern. 2009. "Music Director Alex Patsavas: Interview on *The Sound of Young America*." *Bullseye with Jesse Thorne*, November 30. http://www.maximumfun.org/sound-young-america/music-director-alex-patsavas-interview-sound-young-america

Medd, James. 2010. "The Rules: Alexandra Patsavas on Picking Music for Screen Dramas." *The Word* 11: 42–43. ProQuest Performing Arts Periodicals Database.

Neumann, Sean. 2017. "How the Music Supervisor for 'The O.C.' and 'Gossip Girl' Changed the Game for Indie Rock." *Noisey*, October 20. https://noisey.vice.com/en_us/article/ne3w38/music-supervisor-alexandra-patsavas-interview-2017-the-oc-gossip-girl-tvweek

Price, Nancy J. n.d. "10 Questions with Music Supervisor Alexandra Patsavas." *Myria*. https://myria.com/10-questions-with-music-supervisor-alexandra-patsavas

Trakin, Roy. 2006. "Alexandra Patsavas, Music Supervisor: Indie-Music Fans Are All Ears for Uncanny Touch of Patsavas with Soundtracks Almost as Popular as Hit Show." *Adage*, May 16. http://adage.com/article/special-report-entertainment-marketers-of-the-year/alexandra-patsavas-music-supervisor/109170

Portman, Rachel (1960–)

British composer Rachel Portman is one of the most prolific and highly decorated female composers of film music. She has established a firm reputation in the film music industry for her characteristically lush, introspective scores, and was the first woman to receive an Academy Award for an original film score for *Emma* (1996). Portman was nominated for two more Academy Awards and Grammy Awards (for

The Cider House Rules in 1999 and *Chocolat* in 2000), and was appointed Officer of the Order of the British Empire in 2010 for service to music.

Portman studied traditional classical composition and orchestration at Oxford, but quickly found herself drawn to film music. Largely this was a reaction against the criticism she received from her professors, whose 20th-century compositional philosophies discouraged her from writing music that has both a melody and a harmony. After working on student films at Oxford, Portman worked in British television for much of the 1980s before transitioning mostly to film music by the mid-1990s. Portman's work mainly consists of independent films and television series rather than major-studio releases. *The Manchurian Candidate* (2004) features the largest budget of any of Portman's films, at $80 million. She does much of her own orchestration while often collaborating with Jeff Atmajian, but prefers not to conduct her own music, frequently working with conductor David Snell. Her scores cover a full range of emotional colors, from lush, light, and witty (*Emma*)

Film score composer Rachel Portman shown holding her OBE (Order of the British Empire) badge, awarded to her by the Prince of Wales at an investiture ceremony at Buckingham Palace, London, on June 9, 2010. Portman was the first female composer to win an Academy Award for Best Musical or Comedy Score for composing *Emma* (1996). She has received two additional Academy Award nominations for Best Musical Original Score: one for *The Cider House Rules* (1999) and the other for *Chocolat* (2000). (Dominic Lipinski/PA Images via Getty Images)

to dark, tense, and sinister (*The Manchurian Candidate* and much of *The Duchess* [2008]). Besides her famous scores for *Emma*, *The Cider House Rules*, and *Chocolat,* Portman has scored many romantic comedies and dramas—*Addicted to Love* (1997), *The Right Kind of Wrong* (2013), *Only You* (1994)—as well as a number of family films—*The Adventures of Pinocchio* (1996), *Beauty and the Beast: The Enchanted Christmas* (1997), *Because of Winn-Dixie* (2005)—and war films (*Hart's War* (2002), *The Manchurian Candidate,* and *Private Peaceful* (2012).

Her training manifests itself in her orchestrations, which use acoustic instruments in the traditional symphonic vein. In an age where many movie scores feature electronic sounds, synthesized instruments, and pop/rock idioms, Portman places herself firmly within the idiom of acoustic orchestral music. Indeed, when asked about her musical influences, Portman has mentioned that she listens almost exclusively to classical music, particularly Bach, Mozart, Schubert, Ravel, and Debussy. Rather than using digital music notation software, she composes and orchestrates from the piano, using pencil and paper, while watching the film on a screen to the side of her instrument.

Many of Portman's scores produce an understated effect, subtly illuminating the atmosphere of a scene or the attitude of a character. Her instrumentations generally feature piano, harp, or upper wind instruments over strings. The main titles from *Chocolat,* for instance, showcase harp and thinly spaced strings at the outset, with flute and piano entering shortly thereafter with the main melodic figure of the film. The main titles from *The Cider House Rules* feature very similar orchestration but with thicker strings and a French horn added at the climax of the cue, producing an overwhelming sense of nostalgia. This nostalgia is exemplified by a melodic line that remains unsettled throughout the opening gestures, creating a sense of unresolved longing. This particular cue happens to be an excellent example of an earworm, as the main theme features a repeated pattern of one long note and three short notes over a similar melodic gesture, which remains in the listener's consciousness long after even an initial hearing.

Portman maintains an understated aesthetic even across contrasting moods. In scenes portraying conflict or tension, Portman lets a change of articulation or a carefully chosen dissonance illustrate the negative emotions, rather than abruptly changing the tempo or introducing brash sounds into the score. In "Ashes to the Wind/Roux Returns" from *Chocolat,* Portman uses a primitive flute over harmonically static strings to evoke the main character Vianne's poignant memory of her Central American mother. In "Fire" from the same film, thinly scored but powerful dissonances in the strings combine with harp and piano to create a compelling sense of foreboding. "Gypsies" from *Emma* is a particularly haunting example, with tightly scored dissonances in the strings underpinning a threatening situation onscreen. The opening of "Passage of Time" from *Chocolat,* with its light character and steady harmonic progression within a persistent minor-key environment, is an excellent example of musical irony. This cue captures Vianne's struggle to maintain a cheerful demeanor and optimistic spirit despite being faced with systematic negative pressure from town authorities.

Brighter emotions tend to feature shorter articulations or somewhat faster tempos, without changing the basic fabric of the instrumentation. About a third of the way through "Homer's Lessons" from *The Cider House Rules,* a bouncy combination of strings and bassoon immediately recalls sections from Aaron Copland's ballet *Appalachian Spring* (1944) with its quintessentially American driving rhythms providing a sense of forward momentum while subtly reminding the listener of the film's placement in rural New England. Portman's understated scoring is particularly effective in humorous moments, such as "Sewing and Archery" and "Mrs. Elton's Visit" from *Emma,* where the music punctuates the characters' conversation and hints at subtext by abruptly shifting tempi and articulation to match unexpected twists or ripostes in the scene. Portman uses pizzicato strings, bassoon, and clarinet to great effect.

Portman consistently finds ways to introduce musical sounds unique to a film's context while remaining true to her basically introspective approach. "Party Preparations" from *Chocolat* includes harmonium and clarinet, producing a timbre stereotypical of music in a "French" cafe. "Vianne Sets Up Shop" includes guitar and native flute as well as harmonium.

Portman's penchant for simple, folk-like melodies over uncomplicated harmonies, and her use of strings in particular, often evoke a peculiarly British character, placing her within a heritage including Percy Grainger and Ralph Vaughan Williams. Portman's score for *Emma,* appropriately enough, contains perhaps the best-known examples of a "British" sound in her work. The second half of the main titles from *Emma* features a quick dance in 6/8 time, combining an energy and contrapuntal style reminiscent of George Frederick Handel with a flowing melodic character. Traditional British tunes appear throughout the film as well, such as the country dance tune *Auretti's Dutch Skipper* in "Dance," giving an even more authentic flavor to the music. "Emma Dreams of Frank Churchill" opens with a melodic passage that would certainly not be out of place in a Grainger suite.

Melodic unity is a hallmark of Portman's style. In each film, one can trace the main theme and one or two complementary themes throughout the score, each varying to fit the emotion present in the scene. In "Burying Fuzzy" and "Dr. Larch Dies" from *The Cider House Rules,* the main theme of the film is played very slowly by the piano and oboe, respectively. The extremely slow tempo illustrates the grief in each scene. However, by retaining the major tonality Portman captures a poignant emotion of long-awaited resolution. The characters' simple faith that the deceased have indeed gone "home" is a powerful image seen repeatedly throughout the film. In *Chocolat,* both the melodic material and the underlying texture from "Vianne Confronts the Comte" recur in "Taste of Chocolate," symbolizing the downfall of the Comte's pride by way of Vianne's wares.

Rachel Portman has a unique gift for subtlety, helping her audience subconsciously experience the emotional content of each film she scores. While having developed a singularly recognizable voice as a composer, Portman moves easily between genres in her work. She is as comfortable scoring a romantic comedy or a dark drama as she is at home in a British period piece or an emotionally understated independent film. She enjoys a deserved reputation as one of the leading film composers of the early 21st century.

Richard Fountain

Further Reading

British Academy of Film and Television Arts. "Rachel Portman: Conversations with Composers." Accessed August 4, 2015. http://guru.bafta.org/rachel-portman-conversations-composers

Grammy Awards. 2014. "5 Questions with . . . Rachel Portman." Grammy Awards, December 2. http://www.grammy.com/news/5-questions-with-rachel-portman

Greiving, Tim. 2010. "Rachel Portman." Projector & Orchestra, September 3. http://projectorandorchestra.com/rachel-portman

Holleran, Scott. 2003. "Interview with Rachel Portman." Box Office Mojo, October 30. http://www.boxofficemojo.com/features/?id=1259

Larson, Randall D. 2013. "Rachel Portman on The Legend of Bagger Vance." *Soundtrack Magazine,* November 11. http://www.runmovies.eu/?p=5870

Portman, Rachel. 2009. "Rachel Portman: The Official Website of the Film Composer Rachel Portman." Accessed August 4, 2015. http://www.rachelportman.co.uk

Walker, Shirley (1945–2006)

Though the film business is male dominated, and has historically been so, a select few women have led lucrative careers writing music for Hollywood feature films. Among the most active and respected talents in the industry was Shirley Walker. Remembered as a "trailblazer," Walker's 40-year tenure as composer, orchestrator, arranger, performer, and conductor rendered her a formidable force in the historically male-dominated film music business. In 1979, Walker received her first major film credits in collaboration with Carmine Coppola as a synth-keyboardist for *Apocalypse Now* (1979) and co-composer for the Golden Globe Award–winning score to *The Black Stallion* (1979). Walker's subsequent film work included scores for *The Dungeon Master* (1984), *Ghoulies* (1984), John Carpenter's *Memoirs of an Invisible Man* (1992), *Escape from L.A.* (1996), *Turbulence* (1997), *Mystery Men* (1999), *Willard* (2003), the first three installments of the *Final Destination* film series, and *Black Christmas* (2006). According to Jon Burlingame, Walker held the "record for composing more original scores for major-studio feature films than any other American woman" (Burlingame 2006). Her influence on an entire generation of film composers serves as testament to her legacy.

Several of Walker's most notable projects are associated with DC Comics superheroes, including *The Flash* live-action TV series (1990–1991), the animated *Superman* series (1996–2000), *Batman: The Animated Series* (1992–1995), *Batman Beyond* (1999–2000), and the animated feature-length film *Batman: Mask of the Phantasm* (1993). She was awarded Daytime Emmys for her work on both *Batman: The Animated Series* and *Batman Beyond.* Unusual for TV scoring at the time, many of Walker's scores for TV were recorded by full studio orchestras, as opposed to synthesizers. In a business dependent on technology to create music, Walker often wrote music by hand with a pencil and paper, akin to many of film music's luminaries, including Bernard Herrmann and John Williams.

Apart from her solo writing credits, Walker also spent considerable time in her career selflessly helping colleagues, at times going uncredited for her work. An early portion of Walker's career was spent ghostwriting for other major film composers.

Some of Walker's work will unfortunately remain anonymous, as the composer herself respectfully never disclosed any of the composers for whom she wrote.

Many of Walker's film credits spawn from her selfless "determination to open doors of opportunity for aspiring composers," remarks fellow female composer Lolita Ritmanis (Burlingame 2006). Many currently active, prominent composers, including Danny Elfman and Hans Zimmer, began their film scoring careers under Walker's tutelage. Elfman and Zimmer are both currently among Hollywood's successful, in-demand film composers. Many of Elfman's earliest big-budget efforts were conducted and/or orchestrated by Walker, including *Scrooged!* (1988), *Batman* (1989), *Dick Tracy* (1990), and *Edward Scissorhands* (1990). Elfman's own iconic Batman theme was later reused as the opening and closing titles of *Batman: The Animated Series*, for which Walker scored numerous episodes. She enjoyed a similar relationship with Zimmer, who called her "truly one of the most incredible composers I've ever met" (Burlingame 2006). Walker aided Zimmer as conductor and orchestrator for such scores as *Black Rain* (1989), *Days of Thunder* (1990), and *Backdraft* (1991). The electronically backed, orchestrally centered aesthetic of these scores set the standard for action-oriented film scoring throughout the 1990s. Walker often refused credit for such projects in her dedication to "making the actual composers' work shine" (Burlingame 2006). Apart from orchestrating for other composers, she also conducted recording sessions for such films as *Cujo* (1983), *Arachnophobia* (1990), and *True Lies* (1994).

While Walker aided others in finding their voice, she was, as Danny Elfman proclaimed, "a fine composer in her own right" (Elfman 1990, 54). Her versatile career encompassed a multitude of genres from the lighter fare of *The Love Bug* (1997; TV movie) and episodes of Steven Spielberg's *Tiny Toon Adventures*, to the drama of *Falcon Crest* (1981–1990), to the symphonic brawn of *Turbulence* and *Asteroid* (1997; TV movie). Walker's artistic touchstone was her Gothic orchestral sound as heard in the *Final Destination* film series and *Willard*. Her bold, nuanced sound managed to add dramatic weight to otherwise outlandish, sometimes outright ridiculous, film premises. The haunting lower tones of her main theme of the *Final Destination* series suggests the forthcoming terrors surrounding the film series' hapless central characters while also adding a general sense of horror to the levity of said characters' macabre deaths.

Walker's offbeat score for the 2003 remake of *Willard* utilizes a large accordion section (in tandem with a full orchestra) to accentuate the socially awkward demeanor of the film's titular, rat-obsessed character. The inherent out-of-tune nature of an accordion section juxtaposed with traditional orchestral instruments creates a queasy, unsettling feeling that accents the inherent camp value of a film about a grown man whose only friends are his multitude of pet rats.

Walker's stylistic versatility permeates the score to *Batman: Mask of the Phantasm*. Though the animated Batman feature failed to achieve box office success, it was warmly received by critics, some of whom praised Walker's "powerful" score (Harrington 1993). As a continuation of *Batman: The Animated Series*, *Mask of the Phantasm* features an array of leitmotifs, short melodic ideas associated with specific characters, locales, or ideas, lifted from the TV show. Such musical gestures include Walker's themes for Batman and the Joker, as well as new musical ideas for the *Phantasm* villain and a love theme for Bruce Wayne and his romantic interest. The opening titles introduce Walker's stirring Batman theme in a barrage of blazing horns, soaring strings, and full chorus in a musical setting reminiscent of Carl Orff's "O Fortuna" from *Carmina Burana*. Serving as the hero's and film's musical identity, this theme functions as an overture as well as a means of accentuating the Dark Knight's brooding yet heroic characterization, much like Danny Elfman accomplished with his own *Batman* theme. Walker's circus-tinged music for the Joker also receives its fair share of variations, such as a lounge piano rendition which underscores the demented villain's lair. When separated from the film, the uninitiated listener may infer that he is listening to music written for a Hollywood epic, and this in turn makes the film *feel* bigger than mere animated fare.

Bryce N. Biffle

Further Reading

Burlingame, Jon. 2006. "Shirley Walker: An Appreciation." *The Film Music Society*, December 7. http://www.filmmusicsociety.org/news_events/features/2006/120706.html?isArchive=12070

Carpenter, John. 1992. "Memoirs of an Invisible Man." *ShirleyWalker.filmmusic.com: The Film and Television Music of Shirley Walker*. Accessed July 29, 2015. http://walker.cinemusic.net/memoirs_of_an_invisible_man.html

Davis, Richard. 1999. *Complete Guide to Film Scoring*. Boston: Berklee Press.

Elfman, Danny. 1990. "An Open Letter from Danny Elfman." *Keyboard Magazine*, March 1, 64.

Harrington, Richard. 1993. "Review: Batman: Mask of the Phantasm." *The Washington Post*, December 27. http://www.washingtonpost.com/wp-srv/style/longterm/movies/videos/batmanmaskofthephantasmpgharrington_a0aba0.htm

Schelle, Michael. 1999. *In the Score: Interviews with Film Composers*. Beverly Hills, CA: Silman-James Press.

Producers

Introduction

Perhaps no other job in filmmaking has been as difficult to define as that of the film producer. Not only is the term a vague one, it is also commonplace to have multiple producers working on a single project because producers cannot always supervise everything on a large production and movies are an expensive and collaborative endeavor.

There are several different types of producers; however, the primary credit position of "Produced by" goes to the individual with the most responsibility for all business and creative aspects of the production. This producer guides a project from beginning to end and rarely, if ever, finances their own films. They must be familiar with the business side of Hollywood, as they are typically in charge of putting deals together by locating the principal talents (actresses and actors), the funding, and the material (script) for a film project. Once the film is complete, the producer is still beholden to guide it through its distribution and marketing.

The executive producer has either secured at least 25 percent of the financing and/or owns the rights to the material (or significantly contributed to obtaining the rights) and is not usually involved technically or creatively in the project. Co-producers and line producers are hired by the producer once a project is given a green light and handle the logistics from pre-production through production. Co-producers may assist the producer with financing, casting, and post-production, whereas a line producer supervises the budget on set throughout production. An associate producer is sometimes designated by the producer to handle one or more specified production tasks or is sometimes just an honorary designation that is up to the producer's discretion. In an effort to solidify these classifications, the major studios decided to implement the Producers Mark on their releases in an agreement with The Producers Guild of America (PGA) in 2013. It is a certification mark that appears following the names of producers receiving the "Produced by" credit in lowercase letters separated by periods: p.g.a.

Julia Phillips was the first female producer to win the Academy Award for Best Picture in 1973 for *The Sting,* which she co-produced with her husband, Michael Phillips, and producer Tony Bill.

Laura L. S. Bauer

Alonso, Victoria (1965–)

Consisting of films like *Iron Man* (2008), *Guardians of the Galaxy* (2014), *The Avengers* (2012), and *Black Panther* (2018), the Marvel Cinematic Universe (MCU) has broken box office records, revitalized the Marvel brand under its new owner Disney, and arguably spearheaded the golden era of comic book movies in Hollywood. The architects behind the success of the MCU have been Marvel Studio's President Kevin Feige, Co-President Louis D'Esposito, and significantly, Victoria Alonso, Marvel Studios' executive vice president (EVP) of visual effects (VFX) and post-production. In her role, Alonso has helped direct the creation of the MCU's bombastic visual worlds and fantastic creatures, from the giant green rage monster Hulk to the fast-talking Rocket Raccoon.

Born on December 22, 1965, in Buenos Aires, Argentina, Alonso moved to Los Angeles at the age of 19. Starting out as a production assistant, like many people in the film industry, Alonso eventually worked her way up to an executive position at leading VFX studios like Digital Domain, Rhythm and Hues, DreamWorks, and Sony Imageworks. She then joined Marvel Studios as EVP of visual effects and post-production on the ground floor during the production of the first MCU film *Iron Man.* She received two Visual Effects Society (VES) award nominations for work on *Iron Man* and won the VES award for Outstanding Supporting Visual Effects in a Motion Picture for 2005's *Kingdom of Heaven.* With a career spanning well over 20 years, Alonso regularly speaks at industry conferences and events, including SIGGRAPH (Special Interest Group on Graphics and Interactive Techniques), where she shares her vast experience and knowledge with seasoned and emerging talent.

In her senior executive role at Marvel Studios, Alonso provides creative leadership for the biggest franchise in Hollywood history. With the release of 2014's *Captain America: The Winter Soldier,* the MCU became the highest-grossing movie franchise, topping the Harry Potter franchise in total box office revenue. With multiple films releasing every year, the MCU only looks to increase its dominance in the decade to come. Not surprisingly, Marvel's *The Avengers* and *Iron Man 3* hold the records for the first and sixth highest opening weekend box office, at $270 and $212 million, respectively. Her latest film, *Black Panther,* broke several box office records that include (but are not limited to) having the highest-grossing film to ever be directed by a black director. Under Alonso's stewardship, the MCU films have collectively been nominated six times for Academy Awards for visual effects.

Notably, Alonso has risen to prominence in the Hollywood system despite many challenges, including the sexism endemic to Hollywood and the VFX industry, and the VFX industry's own existential problems. The gender gap in the VFX industry affects every level of employment, from management down to individual artists. A 2013 study found that among the top 250 grossing films in the United States that year, only 5 percent had women VFX supervisors. Moreover, of the 322 active visual effects members in the Academy of Motion Picture Arts and Sciences (AMPAS) in 2014, only 3 percent were estimated to be women. Accordingly, Alonso constantly challenges the industry's gender makeup at industry events by publicly demanding, "Where are the women?" (Milliken 2014). By repeating this refrain and making appearances at live-streamed industry events, Alonso tries to inspire young girls around the world to enter the field of visual effects.

Of course, Victoria Alonso is not only a powerful woman in an industry dominated by men, she is also a Latina in a decidedly white industry. While Alonso rarely comments on her Latina identity, in 2013 the National Latino Media Council applauded Alonso's inclusion, among 21 other Latinos, in AMPAS. This is especially significant given that the Academy is over 90 percent white and over 70 percent male, according to recent numbers.

Fearless to engage in controversial topics, Alonso has been a powerful voice in debates concerning the future of the VFX industry as it wrestles with a broken business model, the forces of globalization, and competition between national governments trying to lure Hollywood spending. Given her role in keeping the Marvel Studio machine running, Alonso advocates for spreading post-production work on a film across several specialized VFX studios around the world, often chasing tax rebates and incentives offered by local governments to keep costs down. These opportunistic practices ultimately cause studios to underbid each other—or risk losing work—resulting in a wave of VFX studio closures and bankruptcies in the last several years. Despite perpetuating some of these problems in her leadership role, Alonso has been sympathetic to rank-and-file artists dealing with precarious employment conditions and a mobile lifestyle that forces them to move for work—sometimes across the world. Moreover, when the prominent VFX firm Digital Domain, where Alonso got her start in the industry, went bankrupt in 2012, Alonso urged Hollywood studios to support the financially struggling company by bringing work to them.

As a visual effects shepherd for the world's most successful film franchise, Victoria Alonso commands more influence, power, and respect than many women in Hollywood, let alone the visual effects industry. If Marvel is the "House of Ideas," as its classic company slogan suggests, Alonso is a woman who lives up to the rhetoric. From a man in an iron suit to a talking tree, she has expertly guided the expansive yet cohesive visual design of the MCU while also cementing her place in Hollywood history.

John Vanderhoef

Further Reading

Cohen, David. 2014. "Marvel's Victoria Alonso Wants a Female Superhero Movie, Calls for More Women in VFX." *Variety*, October 18. http://variety.com/2014/film/news/marvels-alonso-calls-for-more-women-in-vfx-and-female-superhero-pic-1201333443

Hunt, Darnell. 2015. "Behind the Oscars, an Academy Lacking Variety." *All Things Considered. National Public Radio*, January 25. http://www.npr.org/2015/01/25/379843765/behind-the-oscars-an-academy-lacking-variety

Johnson, Ted, and Karen Idelson. 2012. "Marvel's Alonso to Studios: Support Digital Domain." *Variety*, September 13. http://variety.com/2012/film/news/marvel-s-alonso-to-studios-support-digital-domain-1118059222

Kilday, Gregg. 2013. "Latinos Applaud Their Inclusion among New Academy Members." *Hollywood Reporter*, June 28. http://www.hollywoodreporter.com/news/latinos-applaud-inclusion-new-academy-577377

Milliken, Mark. 2014. "State of the Art: Women Call Few of Film's Digital Shots." *Reuters*, May 29. http://www.reuters.com/article/2014/05/29/us-film-women-idUSKBN0E910L20140529

Nicholson, Max. 2014. "Marvel Now the Biggest Movie Franchise Ever." *IGN*, April 9. http://www.ign.com/articles/2014/04/09/marvel-now-the-biggest-movie-franchise-ever.

Sarto, Dan. 2012. "Victoria Alonso Talks VFX Production, Marvel and 'The Avengers.'" *Animation World Network*, April 9. http://www.awn.com/vfxworld/victoria-alonso-talks-vfx-production-marvel-and-avengers.

Donner, Lauren Shuler (1949–)

Lauren Shuler Donner has a nearly 40-year history of producing blockbuster movies. From her first film producer credit on the comedy hit *Mr. Mom* (1983), to her current slate of Marvel superhero films and spinoffs, she has crossed not only genres but also gender barriers along the way. In an industry where success is often fleeting, she has maintained her position as one of the biggest producers in Hollywood, recently adding two hit television shows to an already full filmmaking slate. She has had producer deals at Disney, Warner Bros., and Fox, served on the board of the Directors Guild of America (DGA), and represented the Producers Branch while serving on the board of governors for the Academy of Motion Picture Arts and Sciences (AMPAS) for eight years. Honored by the prominent entertainment trade publication *Variety* in 2003 as a "billion dollar producer," Donner's projects continue to find success on both the large and small screen.

Donner found her passion while attending Boston University, where she earned a bachelor's of science in film and communication before heading to Los Angeles in 1972. Her first industry job was as an assistant editor for medical and educational films. From this unglamorous beginning, she was able to work her way to a cameraperson position in TV production and earned the distinction of being the first woman voted into the International Cinematographers Guild IATSE Local 600 (known as IATSE Local 659 at the time of her inclusion). Her first foray into producing came in 1979, with an associate producer credit on a well-received NBC TV movie. She found she enjoyed developing scripts and had a good sense of story, so in the 1980s she began producing on her own.

Donner has stood out due to her ability to consistently produce box office successes in multiple genres. Her first dozen films included several comedies, 1980s "Brat Pack" classics *Pretty in Pink* (1986) and *St. Elmo's Fire* (1985), and *Ladyhawke* (1985), a medieval fantasy/adventure film. She went into the 1990s producing such hits as the *Free Willy* franchise, the savvy political comedy *Dave* (1993), and the romantic comedy *You've Got Mail* (1998). However, it was her foray into the X-Men universe where she showed that her producing skills easily extended into the typically male-dominated worlds of action and superhero films. Starting in 2000 with the original *X-Men* film (where she was responsible for casting a then-unknown Hugh Jackman), she has shepherded the franchise through 10 films, with more still in development (Robinson 2017). In 2003, *Variety* published a special issue on Donner, honoring her achievement as "Billion Dollar Producer"—to date, the films she has produced have grossed over $5 billion worldwide.

Her influence on the industry extends well beyond the list of projects she has shepherded to the screen. Perhaps because she herself did not have anyone to mentor her, Donner, along with her director-husband Richard Donner, has for years given industry newcomers a chance to excel. More than one current Hollywood power player owes a part of their success to the mentorship and opportunities the Donners provided to them. Nina Jacobson, former Buena Vista Motion Pictures president and current blockbuster producer in her own right (see *The Hunger Games* franchise), had her start as a reader-researcher with Donner's production company. Julie Durk began her career as Donner's assistant and went on to become president of Deep River Productions. Kevin Feige, current president of Marvel Studios, got his first post-college internship with the Donner Company, where he credits Lauren with teaching him the "art of storytelling" (Maynard 2003). She has also taught producing at UCLA Extension, passing her knowledge to the next generation of filmmakers, as well as served on the boards of multiple film schools.

Outside of motion pictures, Donner has a long and prominent history of philanthropy, focusing especially on animal rights, cancer research, and women's issues. Notably, but not surprisingly for the producer of *Free Willy*, she and her husband donated a fleet of boats to the Whale Rescue Team to protect dolphins off the coast of Southern California. She is an animal activist, championing the passage of laws to ensure humane treatment of farm animals in California, promoting animal rescues and anti-fur campaigns, and supporting causes that protect wild animals and their habitats. Using her personal struggles to empower others, Donner has become an advocate for women's health, raising funds and awareness for breast cancer research, lupus, and serving on the board of Planned Parenthood. She was honored by the American Cancer Society in 2006, after talking publicly about her battle with breast cancer. Similarly, after suffering from lupus since her twenties, she decided to go public with her illness, becoming a voice for awareness and treatment. She sought to fight the stigma of chronic illness, especially in Hollywood, where the necessity of ensuring film productions means that someone with a known health issue is often seen as a risky hire. Through a prolific body of work, she has shown that people suffering from illness need not lead a less productive life.

Donner's achievements received accolades both inside and outside of the film industry. In 2000, *Elle* magazine gave her its Women in Hollywood Icon award. She and her husband both received stars on the Hollywood Walk of Fame in 2008, the same year she was given a lifetime achievement award from the Ojai Film Festival. In 2010, she received the Producer's Showcase award at the 36th annual Saturn Awards for her work on the *X-Men* franchise. She was awarded Women in Film's prestigious Crystal Award for Excellence in Film in both 2006 and 2016, becoming one of only three women to ever receive this honor twice. Her films have been nominated for both Golden Globes and Academy Awards, and her current list of projects in development will continue to cement her reputation as one of Hollywood's preeminent producers.

Rachel Rohac Bernstein

See also: Jacobson, Nina

Further Reading

Daunt, Tina. 2008. "No Need to Whisper: It's Lupus." *Los Angeles Times*, June 13. http://www.latimes.com/entertainment/la-et-cause13-2008jun13-story.html

Macnab, Geoffrey, and Sharon Swart. 2013. *Filmcraft: Producing.* New York: Focal Press.

Maynard, Kevin. 2003. "Mentor Mentality Radiates Down the Line." *Variety*, November 21, A4.

Robinson, Joanna. 2017. "The Woman behind the X-Men Reveals How the Mutants Got Their Groove Back." *Vanity Fair*, March 3. https://www.vanityfair.com/hollywood/2017/03/logan-legion-deadpool-x-men-renaissance-lauren-shuler-donner-interview

Ellison, Megan (1986–)

Margaret Elizabeth "Megan" Ellison started her career in Hollywood as an independent producer and founded the production company Annapurna Pictures in 2011. The Annapurna logo serves as an accessory to Ellison's persona: minimalist in basic black, with the pixelated white "A" gesturing to Hollywood's analog or video past. Annapurna's Tumblr, similarly, is a catalog of hip artifacts old and new, from *Twilight Zone* screenshots and vintage toys to a *Back to the Future/Wolf of Wall Street* YouTube mash-up. Annapurna itself has been a prolific company, co-producing four films in its first year alone. Furthermore, many titles have received critical acclaim such as *Zero Dark Thirty* (2012), *American Hustle* (2013), *Her* (2013), *Foxcatcher* (2014), *Spring Breakers* (2012), and *Joy* (2015). This sampling of Annapurna titles illustrates Ellison's commitment to making highbrow commercial films that are in line with the 1970s New Hollywood style she favors. The films coming out of Annapurna are not representative of the current Hollywood climate, dominated as it is by money-making franchises; as producer Ted Hope puts it: "[Ellison is] the only one out there putting reasonable budgets behind adventurous movies for adults that are 100% their directors' visions" (Leigh 2013).

Despite having produced such a fine body of work in such a short amount of time, the press hasn't always been kind. Ellison refuses to give interviews and, as a result, has become a somewhat mysterious public figure. Daughter of software mogul Larry Ellison and sister of Skydance Productions' David Ellison, she is often referred to in the press as a "trust fund baby"; she is also said to count David Geffen as a professional mentor as well as a personal family friend. One *Vanity Fair* article on Ellison, entitled "Caution: Heiress at Work," describes her as "pretty but a bit overweight," "partial to butch, grunge chic" and giving off a "slacker vibe." In response to Ellison's detractors, former Sony chairperson and producer Amy Pascal has been quoted as saying: "Sometimes when you're a woman, people judge you a little more harshly. I think that if Megan was a guy people wouldn't be jumping on her as much" (Grigoriadis 2013).

Ellison began producing films after dropping out of the University of Southern California's School of Cinematic Arts and earned her first producer credit with director Katherine Brooks's *Waking Madison* (2010). That same year she also co-produced the Coen Brothers' remake of *True Grit.* The body of films coming from Annapurna Pictures has been eclectic from its origins: in the year 2012, Annapurna Pictures co-produced and released *Zero Dark Thirty, The Master,* and *Spring Breakers*—all three movies directed by established auteurs but which are otherwise disparate in tone, theme, and genre. Annapurna Pictures' mission statement articulates the company's objective to "creat[e] sophisticated, high-quality films that might otherwise be deemed risky by contemporary Hollywood studios." In a historical moment where many look to television for "serious" entertainment, Annapurna broadcasts its sustained commitment to "mature, adult dramas" for the cinema (Annapurna Pictures n.d.). Annapurna's partners on such endeavors toggle between Hollywood's old-guard establishments, like Sony and the Creative Artists Agency, and smaller entertainment companies with edgier brands, like Vice Media and VRSE.farm. For example, Ellison's collaboration with Vice is the upcoming *The Bad Batch,* to be directed by Ana Lily Amanpour. Ellison's approach to producing has been described as "creative [and] hands-on," going beyond simply funding the films to taking an active interest in the productions and traveling to visit the sets of Annapurna films (Foundas 2014).

Ellison's films have a decidedly mixed track record, with some of her earliest producing credits, including *Passion Play* (2010) and *Killing Them Softly* (2012), proving unsuccessful both critically and commercially. That said, the majority of Annapurna's films have won much favorable attention, especially during awards' season—*Zero Dark Thirty* (2012), *American Hustle* (2013), and *Her* (2013) were all nominated for Best Picture at the Academy Awards. In fact, Ellison is the first woman to get two nominations for Oscars' Best Picture in one year (for *American Hustle* and *Her* in 2014). These titles, together with *Foxcatcher* (2014) and *The Master* (2012), garnered nods from BAFTA, the Independent Spirit Awards, and the Los Angeles Film Critics Association Awards, as well as Oscar nominations in the top categories. And with upcoming projects from such directors as Richard Linklater (*That's What I'm Talking About*), Todd Solondz (*Wiener-Dog*), and David O. Russell (*Joy*), we can only expect the accolades will continue.

Two recent anecdotes about Ellison from January 2015 gesture to Ellison's passions and her future in the industry. In the first instance, Ellison was named one of a group of benefactors for Santa Monica's failing video shop, Vidiots. Vidiots was set to close its doors when a band of patrons, including Ellison, donated an undisclosed amount to keep the landmark afloat. Ellison's spokesperson told the press: "A lot of people in the film industry got their education in the video aisles. They went there to learn about movies," while Ellison tweeted only: "Be Kind Rewind" (Rainey 2015). In the second news item, Annapurna Pictures announced the opening of its virtual reality division, a joint venture with mobile app VRSE.farm and music video directing veteran Chris Milk. The first product of this collaboration, a "'photo-realistic CGI-rendered 3-D virtual reality film'" called *Evolution of Verse,* premiered at the 2015 Sundance Film Festival (Beigelman 2015). What Megan Ellison's career demonstrates is how a Hollywood producer—and perhaps how the industry at large—can be forward-looking while always keeping Hollywood's grand history and legacy in sight.

Annie Berke

See also: Bigelow, Kathryn; Pascal, Amy

Further Reading

Annapurna Pictures. n.d. "About." Accessed March 17, 2015. http://annapurnapics.com/main/#about.

Beigelman, Victor. 2015. "Cool Producer Megan Ellison Is Getting into Virtual Reality." *AV Club*, January 23. http://www.avclub.com/article/cool-producer-megan-ellison-getting-virtual-realit-214266.

Foundas, James. 2014. "Three Game-Changing Female Producers Make Sure Passion-Driven Films Hit the Screen." *Variety*, October 7. http://variety.com/2014/film/news/megan-ellison-gigi-pritzker-molly-smith-1201322765.

Grigoriadis, Vanessa. 2013. "Caution: Heiress at Work." *Vanity Fair,* March. http://www.vanityfair.com/hollywood/2013/03/megan-ellison-27-producer-zero-dark-thirty

Leigh, Danny. 2013. "Megan Ellison, the Most Powerful New Force in Hollywood." *The Guardian*, February 18. http://www.theguardian.com/theguardian/2013/feb/18/megan-ellison-producer-the-master

Lyons, James. Forthcoming. "'A Woman with an Endgame': Megan Ellison, Annapurna Pictures, and American Independent Film Production." In *Indie Reframed: Women Filmmakers and Contemporary American Cinema.* Edited by Michele Schreiber, Linda Badley, and Claire Perkins. Edinburgh: Edinburgh University Press.

Rainey, James. 2015. "Megan Ellison's Annapurna Gives to Save Santa Monica's Vidiots." *Variety*, January 30. http://variety.com/2015/film/news/megan-ellisons-annapurna-gives-to-save-santa-monicas-vidiots-1201420018.

Gardner, Dede (1967–)

Dede Gardner was the senior vice president of production at Paramount Pictures before she became president of actor Brad Pitt's boutique production company, Plan B Entertainment, in 2003. In this current position, she has successfully brought to the screen some of the most critically acclaimed films of the 21st century, including Terrence Malick's *The Tree of Life* (2011) and Steve McQueen's *12 Years a Slave* (2013). The latter earned her a 2014 Academy Award for Best Picture. She received a 2015 Producers Guild of America Visionary Award on the heels of releasing Ava DuVernay's civil rights movement film, *Selma*. The Visionary Award speaks to the integral labor of the producer as the Hollywood player that is able to cultivate important film projects that inspire and uplift through storytelling. Specifically, Gardner's commitment to taking aesthetic and political risks with the projects she invests in brings those images and figures that exist on the margins of Hollywood to the forefront of the entertainment media industry.

Born Dorcas Wright Gardner, the accomplished female producer is no stranger to the importance of storytelling. Gardner graduated from Columbia University in 1990 with a bachelor's degree in English literature. After a stint as an NYC location scout and equipped with a knowledge of, as well as appreciation for, the concept of narrative, she began to work with renowned book publisher Joni Evans in the literary department at William Morris Agency in 1994. This led to her position as director of creative affairs at Paramount in 1996 before she was named vice president in 1997.

During the studio system era of the 1920s to 1940s, producers were known to be at the helm of the motion picture industry. They took on the role of supervisor and singularly controlled all facets of the production of a movie. The producer's status became less rigid during the independent film movement of the 1990s. More freedom was given to screenwriters and directors, allowing film projects to emerge in the spirit of collaboration. Gardner maintains this flexible ethos in her career with Plan B. The company identifies, obtains, and develops pieces, providing financial support and other creative resources, with Gardner as facilitator of the deals. The network of talent she finds and unites for each project results in unique films that, taken together, promotes a brand of production that opens up possibilities for the merging of art and commercial cinema.

The films that Gardner produces are stylistic tour de forces across a wide range of genres. Many of the projects are adaptations of literary material such as memoirs and fiction novels. Her first projects with Plan B include *A Mighty Heart* (2007), *The Time Traveler's Wife* (2009), *The Private Lives of Pippa Lee* (2009), and *Eat Pray Love* (2010). While these movies exhibited varying degrees of mainstream popularity, they all center on the lives of women on journeys of personal discovery amidst joy and trauma. Reflecting on her work as producer and her own exploratory process, Gardner comments: "The truth is that you embark on this, making movies, and you just watch it happen" (The Film Stage 2014).

This adventure involves a certain amount of unpredictability in terms of film production, distribution, and exhibition. Andrew Dominik's *The Assassination of Jesse James by the Coward Robert Ford* (2007), though receiving highly favorable reviews from critics, performed poorly at the box office. Yet a revival campaign launched for the movie has solidified its status as a cult classic. *The Tree of Life*, winner of the 2011 Cannes Film Festival Palme d'Or prize, also earned Gardner her first Best Picture Academy Award nomination. The project emerged through conversations with Malick, known for his nontraditional approach to narrative filmmaking. The experiential story portrays the existence of a family interspersed with images of the universe and the origins of life on earth. A highly experimental piece of work, Gardner and Plan B dealt with two years of post-production, allowing the eclectic film to organically evolve in its development and editing process. Outside of art-house projects, Gardner also brought the Brad Pitt star vehicle *World War Z* (2013) to theaters. Before its release, her first blockbuster movie was fraught with media reports of its impending failure due to various financial issues and alleged behind-the-scenes drama during production. Though it ultimately became a commercial success, the project reflects the precariousness of the producer, who becomes responsible for a film in a profit-driven industry.

Uncertainty is a salient feature of the production process whether the project is big or low budget. Gardner's simultaneous patience and persistence allow her to see projects that she believes in to fruition and especially those that are socially relevant. One such project was *12 Years a Slave*, the story of African American freeman Solomon Northup who was kidnapped and sold into slavery. Gardner brought together a formidable team: black British video artist and director Steve McQueen, screenwriter John Ridley, and actors such as Lupita Nyong'o. They were able to treat the heavy source material concerning the violence of racial subjugation with subtlety and honesty. Gardner's engaged presence for the entirety of a project and trust in the creative ensemble reflect her respect for the craft and desire to create spaces of opportunity for filmmakers to tell rich and complex stories. Gardner continued to develop projects that concern the history of U.S. race relations with 2014's *Selma*. In development for years, the project found its voice when Gardner saw potential in black female filmmaker DuVernay and asked her to direct. Receiving another Academy Award nomination for Best Picture in 2015, the film came at a time in U.S. national culture when such images of anti-black violence and protest do not only belong to the past but also pervade the present in the aftermath of the events occurring in Ferguson, Missouri, in 2014. Bringing these representations to mainstream audiences and stressing the importance of intellectual dialogue about film, she states: "It's always interesting to me to see how art factors in these moments. I can't quite understand it except to believe a little bit in energy" (The Film Stage 2014). In this way, Gardner's productions attest to how Hollywood can not only entertain but also educate.

Brandeise Monk-Payton

See also: DuVernay, Ava

Further Reading

Galloway, Stephen. 2013. "How a Brad Pitt Mantra, 'Game On, F—ers!,' Fueled His Oscar Contender '12 Years a Slave.'" *Hollywood Reporter,* October 11. http://www.hollywoodreporter.com/news/brad-pitt-12-years-a-639856?page=1&template=cap

Goldwyn, Liz. 2014. "The Girls Club: Dede Gardner and Ann Philbin." *Town and Country Magazine*, August 6. http://www.townandcountrymag.com/leisure/arts-and-culture/reviews/a1645/dede-gardner-ann-philbin

Holson, Laura M. 2013. "Brad's War." *Vanity Fair*, June. http://www.vanityfair.com/hollywood/2013/06/brad-pitt-world-war-z-drama

Raup, Jordan. 2014. "Producer Dede Gardner Talks Bringing 'Selma' to Life, the Legacy of 'Jesse James,' and More." *The Film Stage*, December 26. http://thefilmstage.com/features/producer-dede-gardner-talks-bringing-selma-to-life-the-legacy-of-jesse-james-and-more

Thompson, Anne. 2013. "Plan B Producer Dede Gardner Talks '12 Years a Slave,' 'World War Z,' and Partner Brad Pitt." *Indiewire*, October 15. http://blogs.indiewire.com/thompsononhollywood/plan-b-producer-dede-gardner-talks-12-years-a-slave-world-war-z-and-partner-brad-pitt?page=3

Gigliotti, Donna (1955–)

After nearly 40 years in Hollywood and a cumulative worldwide box office of $633 million, Donna Gigliotti's impressive career solidifies her as one of the most influential women in 20th-century filmmaking. Her steadfast, unprecedented navigation of the entertainment industry has paved the way for numerous women to follow. As a producer, she oversees the film's development from the script to the film's release and has helped bring some of the most unforgettable female-centric narratives in modern filmmaking to the screen. As one of the first female studio executives, one of only eight women to win the Academy Award for Best Picture, and now president of her own production company, Donna Gigliotti has made momentous strides for women in a notoriously male-dominated field.

Film producer Donna Gigliotti attends the 28th Annual Producers Guild Awards Nominees Breakfast at Saban Theatre on January 28, 2017, in Beverly Hills, California. Gigliotti produced *Shakespeare in Love* (1998), which won the Oscar for Best Picture. Three of her subsequent films received nominations for Best Picture as well. Gigliotti began her career as Martin Scorsese's assistant on the production of *Raging Bull* (1980). (Todd Williamson/Getty Images)

The secret to her success seems to be telling women's stories, as it is rare that a Hollywood producer consistently positions a woman's point of view at the center of a film's narrative. Disregarding the notion that female-driven stories do not sell, Donna Gigliotti has produced—among more than a dozen other productions—three Oscar-nominated films featuring strong female leads: *Silver Linings Playbook* (2012), *The Reader* (2008), and *Shakespeare in Love* (1998) (for which she won the Academy Award). Each of these films also received Golden Globe nominations in their respective years (which *Shakespeare in Love* also won), among numerous other industry accolades. Moreover, each leading lady was not only nominated for the Best Actress Academy Award but also won the top prize. These achievements emphasize Gigliotti's talent for developing exceptional female stories and characters. When asked during a panel at the Produced By: NYC 2015 conference—hosted by the Producers Guild of America, of which Gigliotti serves as a vice chair for the eastern division—what inspires her creations, she replied: "I think about strong women all the time. . . . Men who run studios don't think there's a market for women-driven projects, but that's not true" (Kouguell 2015). The success of her films that depict strong women has certainly proven her insights to be correct.

After graduating from college in 1976—and a chance run-in with actor Robert De Niro—Donna Gigliotti found herself in Martin Scorsese's office and officially launched her career as his assistant on the production of *Raging Bull* (1980). Scorsese became her first mentor and formal introduction to Hollywood. Industrious and determined, Gigliotti later co-founded Orion Classics, which became a top distributor for independent film. At the time of its founding, no other studio had a classics or specialty division; today, nearly every major studio has one. Donna Gigliotti possessed incredible foresight, knew great content when she encountered it, and became a trailblazer in every sense, particularly at a time when influential businesswomen in Hollywood were scarce and voices that advocated for women's stories were meager. After leaving Orion Classics, she became one of the first women to be hired at a major Hollywood studio when she served as executive vice president (EVP) at Miramax Films from 1993 to 1996, where she worked for now-disgraced executive Harvey Weinstein. Gigliotti was one of the few producers during that time to entertain the idea that well-developed films about women could, in fact, sell in an industry saturated with mostly men telling mostly men's stories; today, that prescience has manifested throughout the studios, as increasingly more female-driven projects materialize each year.

Film producing is a complex job, entailing nearly every moviemaking responsibility from optioning scripts to casting actors, managing budgets and hiring screenwriters, to considering marketing strategies—never forgetting the importance of story and character development along the way. Donna Gigliotti considers herself a hands-on producer who enjoys being on set and becoming intimately involved with every part of the process; she also tends to be somewhat unorthodox in her approach to a film's budget. While many Hollywood producers do not hesitate to spend any necessary amount of money to reach as wide an audience as possible, Gigliotti suggests a different equation: "What it is you want to do creatively, can you see the market, and what's the price for it" (Leahey 2015). Her approach is not dependent on overspending in order to attain a larger audience, and this personal equation and emphasis on storytelling above all else have ultimately set her films apart in 20th-century filmmaking. After many successful years of working for some of Hollywood's most influential men, and in an effort to control not only her creative fate but her financial fate as well, Donna Gigliotti recently started her own production company—Levantine Films—with business partner Renee Witt, placing an emphasis on the over-25 moviegoer market. Their mission (found on the company's website) reflects Gigliotti's dedication to telling stories that are often deemed "unworthy" or incapable of blockbuster success by many Hollywood studio producers: "aiming to promote understanding and inspire dialogue across cultures, captivating audiences, and challenging stereotypes through the power of great storytelling" (McNary 2014).

In 2014, *The Daily Beast* deemed Donna Gigliotti one of "Hollywood's 50 Greatest Producers of All Time," determined by Oscar nominations and wins, box office data, and prolificacy. It is a title she has indisputably earned. When Gigliotti first began her career, there were few female producers and even fewer female studio executives; fewer still were the number of films produced that featured a woman's point of view. Her exceptional films, advocacy for women's stories, and success as a woman in Hollywood herself make up her significant contributions to 20th-century film history—and will undoubtedly continue to inspire generations of women in Hollywood to come.

Sarah Dawson

Further Reading

Deadline Staff. 2010. "Donna Gigliotti Named President of Production for The Weinstein Company." *Deadline Hollywood*, October 17. http://deadline.com/2010/10/donna-gigliotti-named-president-of-production-for-the-weinstein-company-76362.

Kouguell, Susan. 2015. "What Producers Are Really Thinking and Talking About." *Su-City Pictures East*, November 4. http://su-city-pictures.com/what-producers-are-really-thinking-and-talking-about.

Leahey, Colleen. 2014. "Hollywood's Sexism Is Hurting its Bottom Line." *Fortune*, May 21. http://fortune.com/2014/05/21/hollywoods-sexism-is-hurting-its-bottom-line.

McNary, Dave. 2014. "*Silver Linings Playbook* Producers Teaming at Levantine Films." *Variety*, March 25. http://variety.com/2014/film/news/silver-linings-playbook-producers-teaming-at-levantine-films-exclusive-1201146217.

Siegel, Tatiana. 2011. "Gigliotti & Poster: The Weinstein's Dynamic Duo." *Variety*, September 22. http://variety.com/2011/film/markets-festivals/gigliotti-poster-the-weinsteins-dynamic-duo-1118042754.

Kennedy, Kathleen (1953–)

Since the inception of cinema, male executives have dominated the film industry, and consequently women have been significantly underrepresented in the executive production role. In particular, there is a pervasive dearth of female producers on large-budget studio pictures; instead, female producers are recurrently sequestered to associate or assistant positions. According to Martha M. Lauzen's study, in 2012 only 17 percent of executive producers on the top 250 box office films were women. With the odds recurrently against her, Kathleen Kennedy—with 28 producer credits and eight Academy Award nominations—is distinguished as one of the most prolific and financially lucrative film producers in history. After serving as a leading producer on some of the most popular films of the 1980s, 1990s, and the 2000s, George Lucas, creator of the Star Wars franchise, named Kennedy co-chair and successor of the Lucasfilm enterprise in 2012. In addition to her box office receipts totaling over $5 billion, she has produced seminal Academy Award–winning motion pictures that have captured the zeitgeist and infiltrated the global consciousness in the postmodern Hollywood era.

A California native, Kathleen Kennedy was born and raised in Berkeley. Earning a degree in telecommunications and film from San Diego State University, she began her entertainment career in television at KCST, a local TV station. Her first jobs included serving as a camera operator and video editor. Soon, she moved up the ladder and was hired as a floor director and news production coordinator. In these positions, she exercised creative energy and strengthened her skills as a production manager. After her time with KCST, she moved to Los Angeles and transitioned into the film; she first served as a production assistant for John Milius's company responsible for making Steven Spielberg's World War II comedy *1941* (1979). Spielberg, who garnered public attention after *Jaws* in 1975 and *Close Encounters of the Third Kind* in 1977, was so thoroughly impressed with Kennedy's performance as a production assistant on *1941* that he hired her as his assistant.

Producer Kathleen Kennedy speaking onstage during Star Wars Celebration on April 16, 2015, in Anaheim, California. Kennedy is the co-founder of Amblin Entertainment with her husband, Frank Marshall, and Steven Spielberg, and became president of Lucasfilm after its acquisition by The Walt Disney Company in 2012. Kennedy was involved in producing some of the largest blockbusters in Hollywood history, ranging from *E.T. the Extra-Terrestrial* (1982) to the *Indiana Jones* and *Star Wars* film franchises. (Alberto E. Rodriguez/Getty Images for Disney)

Kennedy's first associate producer credit came in 1981 with the Spielberg's first Indiana Jones installment *Raiders of the Ark*, produced by George Lucas and future business partner and husband Frank Marshall. This collaboration commenced the enduring partnership between her and Marshall and Spielberg. Following the success of *Raiders*, Kennedy, Marshall, and Spielberg formed their first independent film company, Amblin Entertainment. The year 1982 brought success for her new co-production company: she was a co-producer for Amblin's horror film *Poltergeist* and received full producer credit for Spielberg's. *E.T.: The Extra-terrestrial*. The film was nominated for nine Academy Awards and won four awards for Best Score, Editing, Sound, and Visual Effects. Kennedy received her first of eight Oscar nominations for Best Picture as producer of the film. *E.T.* became the highest-grossing film of the 1980s and is now recognized as a masterpiece of American cinema, appearing on several best-of lists.

During Kennedy's tenure as president of Amblin Entertainment she oversaw the development some of the most popular films of the 1980s and early 1990s. Along with Spielberg, Marshall, and Quincy Adams, she co-produced the film adaptation of Alice Walker's Pulitzer Prize–winning novel *The Color Purple* in 1985. She was nominated for her second Oscar for Best Picture as one of the co-producers. Continuing in the 1980s and early 1990s, Kennedy made her mark as Hollywood's primary financier on unabashedly sentimental, high-concept movies marketed for mass appeal. As president of Amblin, she executive-produced blockbuster hits, including *Gremlins* (1985) and Robert Zemeckis's *Back to the Future* (1985) and *Who Framed Roger Rabbit* (1988). In 1993, she produced Spielberg's *Jurassic Park*—which became the top-grossing film of the year—and executive-produced Spielberg's Holocaust drama *Schindler's List*.

Kennedy and Marshall launched their own banner, The Kennedy/Marshall Company, in 1991. As co-founder and chair of the company, Kennedy increased the company's pedigree with films such as the sleeper hit of 1999 *The Sixth Sense*, *Seabiscuit* (2003), *Munich* (2005), *The Curious Case of Benjamin Button* (2008), *War Horse* (2011), and *Lincoln* (2012). These films proved to be commercially profitable, and Kennedy received six more Oscar nominations for Best Picture. During her streak of sustained triumphs, she served as the co-president of the Producers Guild of America and is a sitting member of the board of governors of the Academy of Motion Picture Arts and Sciences. In October 2012, after The Walt Disney Company purchased Lucasfilm, George Lucas selected Kennedy to be the co-chair of the company. When Lucas stepped down, he named Kennedy the president of the company. Under her leadership, Lucasfilm announced their plans to release three additional *Star Wars* sequels, beginning with *The Force Awakens* at the end of 2015. For nearly 30 years, Kennedy has been committed to advocating for female filmmakers while increasing the visibility of women in executive roles in the industry.

Robert Sevenich

Further Reading

The Kennedy/Marshall Company. 2015. "About: The Kennedy/Marshall Company." Accessed June 1, 2015. http://kennedymarshall.com

"Kathleen Kennedy." 2005. In *The Palgrave Macmillan Dictionary of Women's Biography*. Edited by Jennifer S. Uglow and Maggy Hendry. Basingstoke, UK: Macmillan Publishers.

Lauzen, Martha M. 2013. "The Celluloid Ceiling: Behind-the-Scene Employment of Women on the Top 250 Films of 2012." http://womenintvfilm.sdsu.edu/files/2012_Celluloid_Ceiling_Exec_Summ.pdf

Spielberg, Steven, Dee Wallace, Drew Barrymore, and Kathleen Kennedy. 2002. *The Evolution and Creation of E.T.*, Bonus Features. DVD. Directed by Laurent Bouzereau. Los Angeles, CA: Universal Home Entertainment..

Spielberg, Steven, Frank Marshall, and Kathleen Kennedy. 2003. *"Indiana Jones": Making the Trilogy*. Bonus Material. DVD. Directed by Laurent Bouzereau. Tarzana, CA: Paramount Home Video.

Meyers, Nancy (1949–)

Nancy Meyers is a prominent Hollywood screenwriter, director, and producer, best known for her work in contemporary screwball comedies. Along with partner and former husband Charles Shyer, she worked on *Private Benjamin* (1980), *Baby Boom* (1987), *Father of the Bride* (1991), *Father of the Bride Part II* (1995), and *The Parent Trap* (1998)—producing and writing all of them, as well as directing the last. Following her split from Shyer, Meyers moved more solidly into directing, including the films *What Women Want* (2000), *Something's Gotta Give* (2003), *The Holiday* (2006), *It's Complicated* (2009), and *The Intern* (2015), all of which she also wrote, save for *What Women Want*. Her films have been tremendously successful at the box office, though she has been less critically acclaimed, receiving only one Oscar nomination for *Private Benjamin* (Best Screenplay).

Heavily influenced by classical films made during the Hollywood studio era, Meyers demonstrates a thorough knowledge of screwball comedies. Her production company, Waverly Films, is named after her childhood movie theater, where like other, more recognized auteurs, she studied classic films and mined them for inspiration. Like the screwball comedies of the 1930s and 1940s, her films showcase elite settings and romantic getaways, physical comedy, verbal sparring, and love and marriage. Her collected works demonstrate her deep love of the screwball comedy, and she has included many direct homages to the genre in her films. Though not always as conspicuous as other popular Hollywood filmmakers, she re-creates scenes directly from some of her favorite films. For example, the scene in which the two divorced parents meet in the hotel lobby in *The Parent Trap* is nearly a direct shot-for-shot tribute to *My Favorite Wife* (1940). She similarly borrowed heavily from Billy Wilder's *The Apartment* (1960) when envisioning *The Holiday*. Her films, all of which are released through the Hollywood studio system, acknowledge classical Hollywood's legacy in establishing generic tropes.

Though contemporary Hollywood will often classify a film as being a romantic comedy if it features any type of love story, classic screwball comedies were considered to be suitable entertainment for both men and women. Additionally, although her commercial success is often strictly attributed to her appeal to older, middle-class female audiences, Meyers's box office success demonstrates that she is able to attract a far greater spectatorship than this narrow demographic.

Since 2003, Meyers has garnered attention for her comedies featuring atypical romantic leads. Though her protagonists are universally white and wealthy, she employs actors in the later stages of their careers and highlights middle-age romance. *Something's Gotta Give*, which was the first film in which she both wrote her own story and directed, starred Jack Nicholson (who was 66 years old at the time) and Diane Keaton (who was 57) as romantic leads. She did not shy away from sex scenes or later-life nudity, which is at odds with what is normally deemed a selling point to potential romantic comedy audiences. She has frequently collaborated with Diane Keaton, who has appeared in four of her films, and with Steve Martin, who has appeared in three. Hans Zimmer scored three of her films, Alan Silvestri also scored three, and Bill Conti scored two.

In all of her work, Meyers provides beautiful landscapes and domestic settings. The kitchen as a space of work and beauty is particularly highlighted in both the opening credits of *Father of the Bride Part II* and in the narrative of *It's Complicated*. In these and other of her films, food and drink serve as both conduits to and metaphors for sexual desire.

The domestic spaces are heavily stylized and are usually situated either in California (as in *Father of the Bride Parts I and II, The Parent Trap, The Holiday,* and *It's Complicated*) or in New York (as in *Something's Gotta Give* and the upcoming *The Intern*). These settings are at once approachable, as they are familiar spaces, while also distinct in their simplistic elegance. Film scholar Robert Alpert connects her obsession with sets to that of another prolific director of comedies featuring romance, Ernst Lubitsch, and makes clear that Meyers acknowledges her predecessor by including him as an aside in the film *Irreconcilable Differences* (1984), which she wrote. Her costuming choices similarly reflect a refined, high-street sensibility evoked through a soft color palette. Many of her film's climactic scenes occur outdoors, and throughout she demonstrates a keen awareness of how to best harness natural light for her narrative arcs.

As Darryl Wiggers exhaustively catalogues in his piece, "Enough Already: The Wonderful, Horrible Reception of Nancy Meyers," her top films consistently outsell more tickets than Woody Allen and Richard Curtis—two male directors who frequently focus on romantic relationships in their works—as well as other notable and critically acclaimed male directors (Wiggers 2010, 67). Despite the fact that Meyers's second directorial effort, *What Women Want*, was at the time of its release the most commercially successful film ever directed by a woman, she is rarely acknowledged as important or crucial to the Hollywood studio system.

Unfortunately, though her films are extraordinarily successful at the box office, there is a dearth of academic and critical literature about this female filmmaker. Like Nora Ephron, she is frequently cast aside as an unimportant maker of romantic comedies. This criticism, popularized by the press's obsession with her mature love story narratives, fails to account for her films' appeal to both male and female audiences. Due to the fact that her films are not labeled as art films, like Sofia Coppola's, or as hard-hitting war pieces, like Kathryn Bigelow's, her work remains unstudied.

Eleanor M. Huntington

See also: Bigelow, Kathryn; Coppola, Sofia; Ephron, Nora; Pascal, Amy

Further Reading

Alpert, Robert. 2012. "Ernst Lubitsch and Nancy Meyers: A Study on Movie Love in the Classic and Post-Modernist Traditions." *Senses of Cinema*, 62. http://sensesofcinema.com/2012/feature-articles/ernst-lubitsch-and-nancy-meyers-a-study-on-movie-love-in-the-classic-and-post-modernist-traditions

Marshall, Kelli. 2009. "*Something's Gotta Give* and the Classical Screwball Comedy." *Journal of Popular Film and Television* 37(1): 9–15.

Merkin, Daphne. 2009. "Can Anybody Make a Movie for Women?" *New York Times*, December 15. https://www.nytimes.com/2009/12/20/magazine/20Meyers-t.html

Wiggers, Darryl. 2010. "Enough Already: The Wonderful, Horrible Reception of Nancy Meyers." *CineAction* 81: 65–72.

Phillips, Julia (1944–2002)

Julia Phillips was a controversial and fascinating producer. Graduating from Mt. Holyoke College in the spring of 1965 with a degree in political science, Phillips knew that she sought a different path than what was normally expected or available for young women in the mid-1960s. As she reminisced, "I have no inclination to pick a secretarial job, no other skills, I think it best to get a college degree" (Phillips 1991). While political science might seem a strange degree for someone in the film industry to have, for Phillips this education would pay off immensely. Political science involves understanding situations that require tact and diplomacy but with an understanding that chaos is ever present in business and one can use that to an advantage. In her job as producer, Phillips had a knack for brash negotiation and skillfully navigated the ins and outs of the film industry.

With her husband and producing partner Michael Phillips (sharing the latter title throughout their film career and the former title until 1974), the film landscape of the 1970s would prove a fertile land for the duo. With their producing partner Tony Bill, they produced some of the most successful and critically acclaimed films of the 1970s, including George Roy Hill's *The Sting* (1973), Martin Scorsese's *Taxi Driver* (1976), and Steven Spielberg's *Close Encounters of the Third Kind* (1977). *The Sting* would earn her, her husband Michael, and Bill Academy Awards for Best Picture. Phillips would be the first woman in history to win this honor. However, Phillips's penchant for confrontation, fueled by excessive vices, derailed her career and earned her an exile from the business she fought so hard to break into. After many years removed from the film business, Phillips, whether seeking a potential return or fatalistically set on destroying the remaining goodwill she had in the business, wrote a tell-all book about her experiences in the industry. In her book, acerbically titled *You'll Never Eat Lunch in This Town Again,* Phillips named names, events, and excesses, both hers and others, that rattled the Hollywood elite. The book and the revelations in it earned her the enmity of the film community she was once a part of.

In his review for *The New York Times*, Steven Bach noted the book's audacity and had no problem praising Phillips, while simultaneously taking her to task for the excesses that brought her to this point. Bach remarked that "[o]ne cheers for her intelligence, for her gallows humor and mostly for her conquering freebase with nothing worse than scorched furniture and a depleted bank account to show for it" (Bach 1991). The book's editor, Joni Evans, mused that the book's attitude mirrored its author's, noting "its mix of fearlessness and recklessness was pure Phillips. Where some of us glow, she burned" (Gliatto 2002).

After the book, Phillips would continue to make waves and her presence in the industry known. Attempting a comeback into the film industry, Phillips, along with ex-husband Michael, were producers of the 1992 teen film *Don't Tell Mom . . . The Babysitter's Dead.* However, the film failed to earn at the box office and received tepid reviews. Julia Phillips remained persona non grata in Hollywood and in 1995 released a follow-up book called *Driving under the Affluence.* While still telling her story and those of others with the same acerbic wit, Phillips gained understanding that while she had no problem setting her own career ablaze, others connected to her did not need to have theirs destroyed. In the book's acknowledgements, she chose to not name names, remarking that "just because I'll never eat lunch in this town again, doesn't mean you shouldn't" (Phillips 1997).

Hollywood is full of those who were granted a third act, a renaissance of sorts. Tragically, Julia Phillips had no chance to fully return to her previous, well-earned place in the world of film. Diagnosed with cancer, Phillips passed away on January 1, 2002. It was not disclosed what type of cancer it was that Phillips suffered from. Even though she may have burned all her bridges or as writer and producer Lynda Obst remarked, "fatally rode the horse backwards" (Obst 1997), Phillips left Hollywood on her terms and with her place in cinema history fully entrenched. In a business full of tough uncompromising players, she showed that a woman could build a reputation for producing big-budget films with top-name actors. No matter what tumult surrounded her or that emanated from her, she was the first women to ever win an Academy Award for Producing, cementing her name and her talent into Hollywood. Steven Bach aptly describes the short but memorable life of Julia Phillips: "Ms. Phillips is a smart woman who did some very dumb things with the millions she earned from the smart things she did" (Bach 1991).

Shawn Driscoll

Further Reading

Bach, Steven. 1991. "Hollywood Chainsaw Massacre." *The New York Times,* March 17. http://www.nytimes.com/1991/03/17/books/hollywood-chainsaw-massacre.html?pagewanted=all

Biskind, Peter. 1998. *Easy Riders, Raging Bulls: How the Sex Drugs and Rock 'n' Roll Generation Saved Hollywood.* New York: Simon & Schuster.

Citron, Alan. 1992. "Hard Times for 'Sting' Producer: Phillips Wants to Take His Ailing Production Company Private." *Los Angeles Times,* January 17. http://articles.latimes.com/1992-01-17/business/fi-318_1_michael-phillips-productions

Gliatto, Tom. 2002. "On Her Terms." *People,* January 21. http://people.com/archive/on-her-terms-vol-57-no-2/

Obst, Lynda Rosen. 1997. *Hello, He Lied: And Other Truths from the Hollywood Trenches.* New York: Broadway Books.

Phillips, Julia. 1991. *You'll Never Eat Lunch in This Town Again.* New York: Random House.

Phillips, Julia. 1997. *Driving under the Affluence.* New York: Harper Paperbacks.

Weinraub, Bernard. 2002. "Julia Phillips, 57, Producer Who Assailed Hollywood, Dies." *The New York Times,* January 3. https://www.nytimes.com/2002/01/03/arts/julia-phillips-57-producer-who-assailed-hollywood-dies.html

Thomas, Emma (1968–)

A key player in the "smart" blockbuster trend, producer Emma Thomas has a filmography that has garnered praise from critics and grossed more than $5.5 billion at the box office worldwide. Since her humble beginnings producing *Following* (1998) for just thousands of dollars to helping launch a multibillion-dollar cinematic universe with *Man of Steel* (2013), Thomas, like many producers, is often the unsung filmmaker behind the intelligent and crowd-pleasing films of director Christopher Nolan, her producing partner and husband since 1997.

Thomas grew up with plans to follow in her diplomat/civil servant father's footsteps and enter the Foreign Service but decided to attend University College London. There she studied English literature and ran the university's film society, which is how she met Nolan. Together, they organized film screenings and used the funds from ticket sales to finance their filmmaking endeavors, with Nolan directing and Thomas performing producing and other duties. Shooting on weekends, the pair produced their first feature film, the black-and-white neo-noir crime drama *Following,* for approximately $6,000. The film premiered at the 1998 Toronto International Film Festival and screened at various other festivals as well. It picked up numerous awards, including Best First Feature at the San Francisco International

Film Festival, the Tiger Award at the International Film Festival Rotterdam, and the Black & White Award at the Slamdance Film Festival.

After completing her degree, Thomas interned with Working Title Films, learning the ins and outs of filmmaking. According to Thomas: "I was working in the production department as in-house production coordinator; it was a fantastic experience and I learned an enormous amount about the way movies are made" (Morrow 2017). Thomas applied her experiences at Working Title to forge ahead as a film producer, working almost exclusively with Nolan. In fact, since their initial collaboration on *Following*, Thomas has produced less than a handful of films not directed by Nolan.

Her near-exclusive partnership with Nolan allows Thomas to be an integral and ever-present part of the entire filmmaking process, from hearing the initial idea proposed by the director to reading drafts of the screenplay, and from principal photography to the advertising and marketing of the finished film. In all their filmmaking, Thomas is the first person to read and provide feedback on Nolan's screenplays, which has led her to describe her job as a facilitator helping Nolan achieve his cinematic vision for the script. She's the first party responsible to bring life to Nolan's ideas, whether finding a suitable Gotham City, understanding interstellar space and black holes, or brainstorming methods to portray dreams within dreams within dreams within dreams: "Every film has a new set of challenges . . . and I think that's massively exciting" (Green 2017).

Following the release of the cerebral noir *Memento* (2000), Thomas and Nolan founded their production company Syncopy Films. in London. Beginning with the gritty noir comic book adaptation *Batman Begins* (2005) up to and including the historic war drama *Dunkirk* (2017), every Nolan-directed film has been produced by Syncopy, with Warner Bros. serving as distributor.

On the heels of the critical success of *Memento* and *Insomnia* (2002), Thomas and Nolan were hired to reboot the Batman franchise at Warner Bros. *Batman Begins*, a gritty, realistic take on the iconic comic book character, helped usher in a new wave of superhero movies that continues today. Thomas and Nolan returned to Batman with the critically acclaimed and box office record breaker *The Dark Knight* (2008) and closed out their saga with *The Dark Knight Rises* (2012). In between those epic blockbusters, the duo brought to the screen a twisty tale of dueling magicians in *The Prestige* (2006) and the mindbender *Inception* (2010), which garnered four Academy Awards from its eight nominations (including a Best Picture nomination for Thomas and Nolan).

Since 2014, Thomas has brought to life Nolan's vision of the vastness of outer space, black holes, and interdimensional time travel with *Interstellar* (2014) and put audiences on the beach, in the air, and on the sea in the intimate World War II epic *Dunkirk* (2017). Both, like many of the producer's other films, were box office hits and received critical acclaim. As Thomas stated: "There are different types of movies. Some are pure entertainment, and others strive to be something beyond that. I like to think our films will stay with people beyond those two or two-and-a-half hours they are watching them, and make an impact on how they think and feel about things" (ICG Editor 2010).

Zach Jansen

Further Reading

Box Office Mojo. 2017. "Emma Thomas." Accessed April 18, 2018. http://www.boxofficemojo.com/people/chart/?id=emmathomas.htm

Green, Chris. 2017. "Emma Thomas." *Produced By* 10(4): 22–30.

ICG Editor. 2010. "Emma Thomas—Inception." *International Cinematographers Guild Magazine*, August 11. http://www.icgmagazine.com/web/exposure-emma-thomas

IMDb. 2017. "Emma Thomas." Accessed April 18, 2018. http://www.imdb.com/name/nm0858799/awards?ref_=nm_awd

Morrow, Brendan. 2017. "Emma Thomas, Christopher Nolan's Wife: 5 Fast Facts You Need to Know." Heavy, July 20. http://heavy.com/entertainment/2017/07/emma-thomas-christopher-nolan-wife-kids-children-family

Interview with Donna Gigliotti

How would you explain your profession and its contribution to a film? What does your work schedule look like from day to day or even over the course of a year? What makes you good at what you do?

There are lots of definitions of film producers. The way I do the job is very comprehensive. I identify a book, idea, or newspaper article that I believe has commercial cinematic possibilities. Next, I select a screenwriter and commission a screenplay. I enjoy working with writers, and I have a lot of input into the script. Once the script is in good shape, it's submitted to talent agencies who suggest directors. With the director, I start to put together cast and crew while creating a production plan and a budget. Finding the financing happens simultaneously—the choices are a studio or independent financing. Either way, with the money in place, we embark on pre-production.

The planning phase is probably my favorite part of the process. Location scouting, production design, costume design—it's great because you have nothing but a world of possibilities in front of you. Then, the penny drops and you start the actual filming, probably my least favorite part of the process. Unforeseen problems always crop up no matter how thorough you've been: an actor gets kidney stones and is writhing in pain during the shoot, it snows in Georgia in March, the star of the film goes AWOL the night before shooting. It's all happened to me and it's not fun. The peace of the editing room comes as a welcome relief after principal photography.

Cutting a film is always interesting. You have the ability to shape the narrative in completely different ways than you might have thought. Getting it right is usually a process that involves testing the film in front of recruited audiences. Once picture is locked, I step away from the final phases of postproduction. I'm a little tone deaf so the best I can do is trust the composer and the sound designer. When the film is completed and delivered, I consider most of my job done. If required, I'll do press interviews. If lucky, I'll go to award shows!

In order to do [all of this], you have to be a self-starter. In any given year, I am juggling five or six projects in various stages of development and production. My days consist of talking, talking, talking—to writers, directors, agents. Finding time to read scripts and books is very difficult to do during the work week. Which is ironic because I think what makes me good at my job is the material I [choose] to develop.

I've got a pretty good sense of what's in the zeitgeist. I think it comes from reading *The New York Times* every day of my life since the age of 17. If you can understand the prevailing mood of the times, it's not that hard to understand what audiences might find interesting and entertaining in a film. *Hidden Figures* is a good example. When I read the book proposal, I was surprised to learn about the NASA female computers. No one had ever heard of them. I read the proposal around the same time that Google revealed the makeup of their work force, which was overwhelmingly white and male. That, coupled with the brewing controversy of #OscarSoWhite, made me believe that *Hidden Figures* could be made into a commercially viable film. The film took on a life of its own; it almost became a movement. If one young girl becomes a mathematician or an engineer because of the women portrayed in the film, that's a job well done. Positive, inclusive images of women in all forms of media can be empowering, so I am proud of *Hidden Figures.*

How did you know you wanted to do this? What advice would you give someone trying to break into your field?

From a fairly young age, I knew I wanted to be connected to movies. I remember seeing *The Sound of Music* when I was eight or nine years old. The opening helicopter shot of Julie Andrews brought me into another world. For a while, after seeing the film, I thought I wanted to be a nun!

For anyone who wants to become a film producer, my best advice is watch movies—old movies, new ones, foreign movies, good ones, bad ones. You can learn a lot from what others have done before you.

Did you have a mentor? Do you feel you began with any advantages?

I didn't have a mentor when I got started but I had some terrific bosses who were generous with their knowledge, especially Marty Scorsese and Arthur Krim. I didn't have any industry connections initially but I had a good liberal arts education from Sarah Lawrence College. My father tried hard to be supportive but really, down deep, he thought I should have become a lawyer. My mother was more gung-ho. It's a great regret that she didn't live long enough to watch me win a Best Picture Oscar.

How have you had to adapt over the course of your career to stay relevant?

In order to stay relevant you have to stay curious.

Have you ever felt discriminated against in your field simply because of your gender or identity?

I haven't particularly felt discriminated against even though sexism is fairly rampant in the motion picture industry. In order to be an effective film producer you have to adopt a pretty tough attitude. I'm sure I put out a "Don't Mess with Me" vibe. Once, a New York teamster captain told me he was afraid of me. I took that as a compliment.

Any thoughts on how to support more women and minorities coming into your field? Can inclusion be practiced voluntarily, or do we need quotas?

To me, diversity and inclusion in the movie business is an employment issue. Producers have the power to hire more diverse casts and crews. No one is stopping us from hiring a woman gaffer! But you have to make an effort to do it. In the short term, quotas may be the answer. Making diversity a condition of film tax incentive programs could be an effective means of legislating inclusion. In my experience, money talks!

Production Design

Introduction

Producer David O. Selznick was the first to coin the term "production designer" for William Cameron Menzies for his visual contribution to the sets of *Gone with the Wind* (1939). But what does it mean to create the overall visual look of a film? A production designer guides the art departments on a film and works closely with the director, costume designer, cinematographer, makeup artist, and set builders to create the world of the film starting in pre-production. Perhaps it's obvious that visually memorable films have great production designers and set decorators who carefully select items for the backdrop such as furniture and props. However, another hallmark of good production design is when the production designers have done such a fine job that their contributions go unnoticed—the environment they've fabricated is so convincing that audiences are unaware of its creation.

In order to create a believable world, a production designer helps translate the script into images. A color palette is usually agreed upon between the production designer and the director, cinematographer, and costume designer in order to create a distinct atmosphere and visual tone for the film. Many production designers are trained in the visual arts and come from a theatrical background.

The duties of a production designer vary from film to film based on its size as well as its director. They have less of a creative role in instances when the director has a distinct visual style, for example. On a smaller production, they may take on more duties (such as art director and set decorator), whereas on big-budget films, they may be in charge of a department that has an art director handling logistics and set decorators to find, purchase, or rent props. Production designers are often called upon to reconstruct actual locations, which can take a lot of time and careful research. Needless to say, production designers play a key creative role in the creation of the believability of a film and its story.

Laura L. S. Bauer

Arrighi, Luciana (1940–)

Luciana Arrighi is an Australian production designer, best known for her work with directors Gillian Armstrong and John Schlesinger, and for the production company Merchant Ivory. Most of Arrighi's designs have been for period movies; her visual style blends historically correct details with a degree of stylization in décor and color that echoes the structural patterns and emotional rhythms of the screenplay. By creating visual contrasts to emphasize thematic pairings or juxtapositions, Arrighi's designs emphasize the ways in which a film's visual world becomes symbolic of characters' emotional journeys.

Arrighi's early work was in television. She was a member of the British Broadcasting Corporation's (BBC) design staff managed by Richard Levin. Levin's approach to nonrepresentational design emphasized the creation of "a significant visual pattern to which an audience can respond" (Ede 2012). While at the BBC, Arrighi worked with the director Ken Russell on the series *Omnibus*. Russell's directorial approach also privileged the symbolic potential of design; actors are placed significantly within landscape and décor so that the décor works as another performer. This approach to movie-making requires that the production designer be closely involved with a piece from its inception so that all elements of storytelling blend seamlessly. Arrighi's feature film debut came as the set designer on Russell's *Women in Love* (1969), for which she was nominated for a British Association of Film and Television Award (BAFTA) for Best Art Direction.

Arrighi was set decorator for John Schlesinger's *Sunday, Bloody Sunday* (1971) and then returned to Australia as production designer for Gillian Armstrong's *My Brilliant Career* (1979), which won the Australian Film Institute's (AFI) Award for Best Achievement in Production Design. Arrighi's philosophical approach to production design, influenced by Levin and Russell, was clearly apparent this early in her career. In 1979, Arrighi asserted, "Ideally, a production designer . . . starts at the embryonic stage, when the script is being written; it is then that visual ideas can be formed before the production begins. [. . .] With a period film like *My Brilliant Career* the first task is to get to the essence of the period. . . . Then it's a matter of detail; layer after layer of immaculate detail" (Adler 1979). Arrighi's work on the film visually charted the growing rebellion of the heroine as spaces expand and contract around her. Arrighi returned to England as production designer for her second collaboration with Schlesinger, 1988's *Madame Sousatzka*, a character-driven film that "honed her skills for creating symbolic, evocative sets that add to rather than overwhelm a film's focus" (TCM 2017).

In 1992, Arrighi began an association with producer Ismail Merchant and director James Ivory as production designer on *Howards End*. Their combined production endeavor, Merchant Ivory, is renowned for visually stunning period films concerned with the tensions within and between social classes, often adapted by screenwriter Ruth Prawer-Jhabvala from historical novels. The plot of *Howards End* (1992) traces the interactions of three families in Edwardian England: the wealthy Wilcoxes, the intellectual Schlegels, and the working-class Basts. Arrighi's designs, for which she won an Academy Award for Best Art Direction/Set Decoration (shared with Ian Whittaker) and was nominated for a BAFTA for Best Production Design, allow each family's home to "depict their own unique style and [offer] clues to their class standing in English society. For the self-important, aristocratic Wilcox family, [she] went for a 'claustrophobic, Edwardian opulence,' while the philanthropic Schlegels' interiors received cool gray and green tones. [. . .] For Leonard Bast's cramped dwelling, she used dark, depressing colors" (Whitlock 2010).

In 1993, Arrighi again collaborated with Merchant Ivory on *The Remains of the Day*, for which she received her second Oscar nomination. Once again, her designs visually delineate the contrasting worlds of the film: as the butler Mr. Stevens comes to realize that he has chosen service and sterility rather than an emotional and physical life with the housekeeper Miss Kenton, the warmth of the servants' hall and the English countryside are gradually replaced with the lavish but cold world of the aristocracy. Arrighi's third film with Merchant Ivory was 1996's *Surviving Picasso*, for which she re-created the artist's two-story Parisian home and workshop, the intricacy of which allowed for filmic compositions evocative of Picasso's artistic compositions.

Much of Arrighi's work in the 1990s emphasized the visual distinctions between the worlds contained within a film. She received a BAFTA nomination for her design of Ang Lee's *Sense and Sensibility* (1995). Calm, ordered interiors and landscapes equated with the sense of level-headed Eleanor, while lavish London residences and stormy landscapes evoked her sister Marianne's emotion-driven sensibility. In 1997 *Oscar and Lucinda* was Arrighi's second film with Gillian Armstrong and earned her a second AFI Award for Best Achievement in Production Design. For the film, Arrighi created a dark, sparse English space for Oscar, seen in comparison to Lucinda's bright and lively Australian world; a glass church provided the centerpiece of her design. Arrighi received a third Oscar nomination, and a nomination from the Art Directors Guild for Excellence in Production Design, for 1999's *Anna and the King*, in which Anna Leonowens's English trappings are distinctly out of place within the epic visual scope and vibrant colors and textures of Siam.

Arrighi's career has continued into the 21st century with *The Importance of Being Earnest* (2002), *Being Julia* (2004), *Time Traveller* (2009), and *The Man Who Knew Infinity* (2015), among others, all period pieces concerned with examining the contrasts between dissimilar worlds.

Sarah McCarroll

See also: Foster, Jodie

Further Reading

Adler, Sue. 1979. "Luciana Arrighi: An Interview." *Cinema Papers* 22: 421–424.

Ede, Laurie N. 2012. "British Film Design in the 1970s." In *British Film Culture in the 1970s: The Boundaries of Pleasure*. Edited by Sue Harper and Justin Smith. Edinburgh: Edinburgh University Press, 50–61.

Harper, Sue. 2000. *Women in British Cinema: Mad, Bad, and Dangerous to Know*. London: Continuum.

TCM (Turner Classic Movies). 2017. "Luciana Arrighi Biography." Accessed November 11, 2017. http://www.tcm.com/tcmdb/person/5962%7C101844/Luciana-Arrighi/biography.html

Whitlock, Cathy and the Art Directors Guild. 2010. *Designs on Film: A Century of Hollywood Art Direction*. New York: Harper Collins.

Brandenstein, Patrizia von (1943–)

Production designer Patrizia von Brandenstein values collaboration as part of her job description. It has been her desire to have fruitful collaboration with filmmakers, coupled with the many film directors whom have sought out *her* talent, that has cemented her reputation as one of the best in the business.

Born in Arizona, Brandenstein apprenticed abroad, most notably with the Comédie Française, which was founded in 1680, and today remains one of the oldest active theaters in the world. Returning stateside, she worked on off-Broadway productions and with the Famed New York Actors Studio. Toward the late 1960s Brandenstein worked exclusively with San Francisco's American Conservatory Theater. Her work in the theater world, most notably with costuming and set design, prepared her for the transition to motion pictures. Brandenstein entered the world of movies at a time where writers and directors not only had more creative control but also began to build new creative collaborations with artists such as Brandenstein. Notably, one of Brandenstein's earliest contributions to cinema was her work as costume designer for John Badham's 1977 film *Saturday Night Fever.* The film was a major hit, making a star out of the film's lead, John Travolta, and Brandenstein's costuming. Notably, Travolta's character's white polyester suit helped propel, and in many ways define, disco culture in the 1970s and 1980s. The film, but most assuredly Travolta in this suit, became the personification of cool and remains a symbol of both the disco scene and film history today.

High praise for Brandenstein's craft came in 1985 when she won the Academy Award for her production design work on the Milos Forman film *Amadeus* (1984), about the life of composer Wolfgang Amadeus Mozart. Not only did she earn this high honor, she also was the first female to win an Academy Award for Art Direction. But the awards and praise did not mean Brandenstein rested on her laurels. If anything, it propelled her creatively into new projects, giving her new challenges in her craft. Her win for *Amadeus* was bookended by Best Art Direction nominations for 1981's *Ragtime* (also directed by Forman) and Brian De Palma's 1987 film adaptation of the television show, *The Untouchables.* Consequently, the ensuing years would draw directors to actively seek out Brandenstein and her work, and this would set up long-lasting collaborations with specific directors. Remarking on her role in the creative process, Brandenstein plainly states, "The production designer translates the film visually; cooperates with the director of photography, and with the director" (Schwartz 1994).

Two directors whom Brandenstein has had long-standing fruitful collaborations with are directors Mike Nichols and Milos Forman. Nichols's films, including the 1983 drama *Silkwood* and comedies *Working Girl* (1988) and *Postcards from the Edge* (1990), and Forman's works such as *Amadeus* and *The People vs. Larry Flynt* (1996) show Brandenstein's ability to create distinct worlds for strong characters. Whether it is the world of big business, or the frantic Los Angeles world of filmmaking, or the debauched world of *Hustler* creator Larry Flynt, Brandenstein makes sure that each production design is distinct and collaborative with all parts of the production team. Speaking on her ability to create these dissimilar sets, Author Beverly Heisner remarks that "[Brandenstein's] film designs are in agreement with her dictum that each film prompts its own unique visual treatment" (Heisner 2004, 157).

Brandenstein's work in film is widespread, eclectic, and well respected. The work of a production designer serves as both an amplifier of their own visions and a projector of others (director, writer, and cinematographer). Commenting on this process, Brandenstein remarked, "The responsibility is translating the story in visual terms, so the vision of the director and cinematographer can coalesce and the dream can come true" (Giardina 2016). Brandenstein recognizes that her role as production designer "represents the film visually, represents the film artistically, and that is your main responsibility" (Schwartz 1994).

These examples speak to the artistry and demand of Brandenstein and her work. As Heisner notes, "[H]er popularity as a production designer would seem to be tied to pinpoint accuracy of her definition of character through their surroundings and her ability to emotionally charge the film's action with sets that are able to comment on and enhance it" (Heisner 2004, 157). In recent years, Brandenstein has brought her artistic talent and vision to the medium of television. This change in venue has earned her similar praise and awards as in her film career. Her work on the 2013 HBO film *Phil Spector* earned her an Emmy Award nomination for Best Art Direction. She also garnered Art Directors Guild nominations for *Phil Spector*, the 2015 miniseries *Houdini*, and the HBO limited series *The Night Of* (2016). The latter earned her the ADG award for Excellence in Production Design.

In 2015, von Brandenstein was honored with the Art Directors Guild's Lifetime Achievement Award. Looking back on many years of artistic endeavors and triumphs, she humbly remarked on her place in the world of film, "I'd want to be remembered as somebody who worked! Who kept on working! And not burn out, and not get hateful, and not get mean, and still believe that anything was possible" (Schwartz 1994).

Shawn Driscoll

Further Reading

Giardina, Carolyn. 2016. "Meet the Production Designer Who Created Mozart's Bedroom." *The Hollywood Reporter*, January 31. https://www.hollywoodreporter.com/behind-screen/meet-production-designer-who-created-859253

Heisner, Beverly. 2004. *Production Design in the Contemporary American Film: A Critical Study of 23 Movies and Their Designers*. Jefferson, NC: McFarland.

LaMotte, Richard. 2011. *Costume Design 101. The Business and Art of Creating Costumes for Film and Television: The Business and Art of Creating Costumes for Film and Television*. Studio City: Michael Wiese Productions.

Schwartz, David (moderator), and Museum of the Moving Image. 1994. "Moving Image Pinewood Dialogues: Patrizia von Brandenstein." *Moving Image Source*, October 15. http://www.movingimagesource.us/files/dialogues/2/12861_programs_transcript_html_211.htm

DeScenna, Linda (1949–)

Linda DeScenna is a five-time Academy Award–nominated set director and production designer. DeScenna worked actively between 1977 and 2008, focusing primarily on science fiction, fantasy, and comedy films. Her work is defined by color and texture, with attention to lighting and historical significance. In her home life, DeScenna lives in a house painted completely white and has a wardrobe made mostly of blacks and whites. She cites these muted tones as her sanctuary, free from all the color and props that crowd her work (Mancini 1991, 35). Despite this reprieve in her personal life, DeScenna's work is defined by the unique vision she brings to sets. Her projects are intricate and involved, leaving a lasting impression on Hollywood as well as the science fiction and fantasy genres.

Linda DeScenna was born in Warren, Ohio, on November 14, 1949, to Jack Loveless and Dorothy DeScenna. She attended Kent State University from 1967 to 1971, where she majored in cinematography and minored in painting and art history. After graduation, DeScenna moved to Hollywood to begin her career, but she was not immediately welcomed into the industry. DeScenna spent several years working and saving money, both as a studio secretary and as a cocktail waitress at Beverly Wilshire Hotel. For her first Hollywood job, she worked as a set dresser on the television series *The Fantastic Journey* (1977) as well as *Logan's Run* (1977–1978). These two shows gave her a foot into the door and help her land work as a set decorator for *Star Trek: The Motion Picture* (1979).

Star Trek: The Motion Picture was a major success, earning DeScenna and her team her first Academy Nomination for Best Art Direction—Set Direction (now called Production Design). Most notably, DeScenna redesigned the chairs that were seen on the bridge of the USS *Enterprise*. These chairs were unique and vertebrae-like, and supposedly provided massage functions. This film served as DeScenna's venture into the American "New Wave." The 1970s also served as the advent of the blockbuster hit and awakening interest in science fiction. DeScenna's work on *Star Trek* made her a recognizable name in the science fiction genre, and she jokingly cites her Academy nomination for *Star Trek* as what helped her land her next major job, on Ridley's Scott's *Blade Runner* (1982) (BladeZone 2001).

Her work on *Blade Runner* was interesting because DeScenna was not originally hired as set director. The set director position initially went to Tom Roysden, while DeScenna was hired as exterior set dresser. After a few weeks, she was moved to interiors and someone new was hired for exteriors. When that person was let go and Tom Roysden had to leave, DeScenna was contracted to take over all previously listed jobs, thus becoming primary the set decorator for *Blade Runner.* Many of the projects for *Blade Runner* included building entire sets, making props, and retrofitting and modifying pieces in short periods of time. Ridley Scott had a very specific vision for the film, and often left DeScenna and other teams drawings to work with for inspiration. To flesh out Ridley's vision, DeScenna worked with her instincts, and in the end, her work on *Blade Runner* earned her a second Academy Award nomination for Best Art Direction—Set Direction.

Over the next several years, DeScenna had consistent work as both as a set director and production design. Between 1982 and 1992, she worked on 25, primarily within the science fiction, fantasy, and comedy genres. These included *The Color Purple* (1985), *Rain Man* (1988), and *Toys* (1992), all of which earned her Academy Award nominations for Best Art Direction—Set Direction. However, although DeScenna has been nominated five times, she has never won an Academy Award.

DeScenna continued to work after 1992, although no film has earned her an Academy Award nomination since *Toys*. DeScenna seemingly retired in 2008 and has produced no public work since *Bedtime Stories* (2008).

Throughout her career, DeScenna was credited as both "Linda DeScenna" and "Linda De Scenna." She also has a single acting credit, appearing as a guest at a baby shower in *Father of the Bride Part II* (1995). Notable projects throughout her career included matching the four seasons to five different time periods in *The Color Purple* (1985), dressing over 200 sets for *Avalon* (1990), reupholstering hundreds of chairs for *The Rockateer* (1991), and building a 200,000-square-foot hospital set from scratch for *Patch Adams* (1998).

She was applauded for her work on *Evan Almighty* (2007), which included construction of a complete replica of Noah's Ark. DeScenna built the bottom of the ark from steel-reinforced wood and made the bow out of Styrofoam. When completed, the ark was 250 feet long, 80 feet wide, and a little more than 50 feet tall. It also included interior work that was nearly three stories tall. It was an intricate and involved process that became a notable example of the work that DeScenna has done throughout her career.

From the start, DeScenna's career has been a practice of intricate and involved work. Her style is defined by attention to color, light, and details that breathe life into still sets. From *Star Trek: The Motion Picture* onward, she has worked on set dressing, building, creation and consolidation of props, and bringing the visions of directors and designers into reality. She has been noted for having an imagination that explodes with color and has created some of Hollywood's most visually textured films. She has a unique understanding of the dramatic and historical significance of moments; she knows how to use this to enhance cinematography.

Keshia L. McClantoc

Further Reading

BladeZone. 2001. "Dressing Blade Runner: A Candid Interview with Linda DeScenna." *BladeZone*, July 11. http://media.bladezone.com/contents/film/production/Linda-DeScenna/index.html

Dunkleberger, Amy, and Torene Svitile. 2008. *So You Want to Work in Set Design, Costume, or Make-up?.* Berkeley Heights, NJ: Enslow Publishing.

IMDb. 2017. "Linda DeScenna." Accessed December 13, 2017. http://www.imdb.com/name/nm0220984/

Mancini, Marc. 1991. "Linda DeScenna." *Premiere* 4:35–38.

Reeves-Steven, Judith, and Garfield Reeves-Steven. 1997. *The Arts of Star Trek.* New York: Simon & Schuster.

Wloszczyna, Susan. 2007. "The Ark and Other Structures." *USA Today,* June 22.

Heron, Julia (1897–1977)

As a set decorator whose career spanned almost 40 years, Julia Heron worked with some of the greatest directors of classic films from Hollywood's golden age (1917–1960s). Her set designs provided the practical backdrops for a number of films, including those by John Ford, Alfred Hitchcock, William Wyler, and Stanley

Kubrick, and became characters themselves in many of Douglas Sirk's lavish Technicolor melodramas of the 1950s. Not one to back away from a challenge, Heron also made her mark in broad comedies, sci-fi B flicks, and combinations of the two—*The Groom Wore Spurs* (1951), *This Island Earth* (1955), and *Abbott and Costello Go to Mars* (1953), respectively. Before retiring from filmmaking in the late 1960s, Heron made history twice over by being the first woman nominated for Best Art Direction at the Academy Awards for *That Hamilton Woman* (1941) and the first to win in the same category 19 years later for *Spartacus* (1960).

Born in Montana, Heron didn't work on her first film until 1930, going uncredited for handling props in the early noir film *Blood Money* (1930). Throughout much of the 1930s, Heron went uncredited for her work, although studio records indicate her contributions for popular and critically acclaimed films of the time such as *Les Misérables* (1935), *The Informer* (1935), *The Hurricane* (1937), and *Dead End* (1937). Her first onscreen credit—for which she was listed as "Julie Heron"—was for *They Shall Have Music* (1939).

In 1940, Heron wrote an essay for the book *Plan Your Own Home*, offering advice to homemakers about how to tell the story of their families through their choices of interior decorations. In her essay, Heron wrote, "No matter how much you spend on your home, if it is not decorated correctly to match your personality, size, shape and coloring, then you can look like nothing in a $100,000 mansion," and further suggested that anyone can look out of place in their surroundings if the decoration appears off (Lawrence 1999). Looking at her various set designs and ability to decorate those sets, Heron took her own advice to create settings that emphasized characters' connections or disconnections to their films' settings.

Following her first Academy Award nomination for *That Hamilton Woman*, Heron began an 18-year working relationship that covered more than 100 films with fellow art director Russell A. Gausman. Their collaborations culminated at the 33rd Academy Awards when, along with Alexander Golitzen and Eric Orbom, they were awarded Best Art Direction (Color) for Stanley Kubrick's *Spartacus*. Heron was the first woman to win in the category and would remain the only woman to receive an Oscar in this category until the 56th Academy Awards, when Anna Asp and Susanne Lingheim won for *Fanny and Alexander* (1982 [released in the United States in 1983]).

Heron would finish the final decade of her career working mostly in television, usually in noir-ish series that included *Thriller* (1960–1962), *Alfred Hitchcock Presents* (1955–1962), and *The Alfred Hitchcock Hour* (1962–1965). After working on a handful of films in the late 1960s, Heron retired in 1969. She died in Los Angeles in 1977.

Zach Jansen

Further Reading

IMDb. 2018. "Julia Heron." Accessed May 9, 2018. http://www.imdb.com/name/nm0380243

Lawrence, Amy. 1999. "Trapped in a Tomb of Their Own Making: Max Ophuls's *The Reckless Moment* and Douglas Sirk's *There's Always Tomorrow*." *Film Criticism* 23(2/3): 150–166.

Official Academy Awards Database. 2018. Accessed May 9, 2018. http://awardsdatabase.oscars.org

Martin, Catherine (1965–)

Catherine Martin is one the most influential craftspeople in modern filmmaking, creating some of the most unforgettable Hollywood costumes of the last two decades, from *Romeo + Juliet*'s (1996) angel wings and Hawaiian t-shirts, to Nicole Kidman's tailored red dress in *Moulin Rouge!* (2001), as well as the flapper opulence of *The Great Gatsby* (2013). Her four Oscars make her the most awarded Australian in Oscar history, surpassing 1950s costume designer Orry-Kelly.

From an early age, Catherine Martin was intrigued by fashion and costuming, and *Dumbo* (1941), *The Wizard of Oz* (1939), and *Gone with the Wind* (1939) were some of her early cinematic inspirations when it came to her love of film and design. She studied design at the National Institute of Dramatic Art (NIDA), where she began a collaboration with fellow Australian Baz Luhrmann, her now husband, that has lasted until today, working on all of Luhrmann's projects—from theater and film to opera and television. There are conflicting reports regarding whether Martin did early work on the theater production of *Strictly Ballroom*, which Baz Luhrmann staged in 1984; however, their first official collaboration was in 1988, according to Catherine Martin herself (Karan 2002, 147), who designed the set and costumes for his production of *Lake Lost*, and subsequently for *La Bohème* (1990) and *A Midsummer Night's Dream* (1993). For the film production of *Strictly Ballroom* (1992)—which returned to the stage as a musical in 2014—she worked as a costume and production designer. Later, she worked as an art director and production designer in *William Shakespeare's Romeo + Juliet* (1996), and as costume and production designer in *Moulin Rouge!* (2001), *Australia* (2008), and *The Great Gatsby* (2013), all directed by Luhrmann—as well as the Netflix series *The Get Down* (2016). Given that Martin and Luhrmann have worked on only a handful of films, Laleen Jayamanee admires how they were able to create "a globally marketable brand" (Jayamanee 2014, 226).

Costume and production designer Catherine Martin (left) and American *Vogue* Editor-in-Chief Anna Wintour attend the ribbon-cutting ceremony for the Anna Wintour Costume Center grand opening at the Metropolitan Museum of Art on May 5, 2014, in New York City. Martin won Academy Awards for Best Art Direction and for Best Costume Design for both *Moulin Rouge!* (2001) and *The Great Gatsby* (2013). She has collaborated almost exclusively with Australian film director and husband Baz Luhrmann. (Dwong19/Dreamstime.com)

Baz Luhrmann has described the creative collaboration with Catherine Martin as a "conversation" that started from the moment they met (Karan 2002, 147). The centrality of their partnership is crucial to their work. Alongside one another, Martin and Luhrmann have created a bold aesthetic that borrows heavily from opera and musical theater. Their signature style is characterized by a heightened reality, often in excessive, luxurious, and camp ways. Pam Cook argues that theirs is an aesthetic of artifice, where the decorative accouterments and visual sensuality on display function as a means to an end: revealing an emotional truth through patent theatricality and, sometimes, excess. Their worked is ensconced in the tradition of the Hollywood narrative cinema. While they work within a contemporary historical context, their films borrow heavily from the Classical Hollywood period (1920s–1960s). Nonetheless, their modus operandi is to update it with a modern and camp sensibility that is seldom seen in either blockbuster or independent cinema. Martin's particular style and work, to the extent that it can be singled out, is outlined by Jayamanee as "dandyesque-camp-couture," which she describes as "unique to Catherine Martin's costume and production design aesthetic and ethos" (Jayamanee 2014, 159). Martin is known for the historical authenticity of her designs, through intense research, but there is also an exuberant sense of fantasy and indulgence when designing period pieces. Her core principle of appropriation instead of mindless reverence, however, never allows for nostalgia. Martin values pursuing feelings and moods—which need to be properly translated in order to be exciting—over slavishly faithful historical portrayals, which sometimes leads to anachronistic period costuming, such as the slimmer suits and heels used in *The Great Gatsby.*

Catherine Martin's accolades include two Academy Awards for *Moulin Rouge!* in 2002, for Best Art Direction and Best Costume Design, and another two for *The Great Gatsby* in 2014, for Best Costume Design and Best Production Design. She has five awards from the British Academy of Film and Television Arts (BAFTA), having won for *Strictly Ballroom* in 1993 and *The Great Gatsby* in 2014, both for Best Production Design and Best Costume Design, and Best Production Design for *Romeo + Juliet* in 1998. Martin also won two Art Directors Guild awards: one in 2002 for *Moulin Rouge!* in the category of Period or Fantasy Film, and another in 2014 for *The Great Gatsby* in the category of Period Film. As a producer, she also won Best Film along with the awards for Best Production Design and Best Costume Design at the Australian Academy of Cinema and Television Arts Awards for *The Great Gatsby* in 2014, The Australian Film Institute awarded her for Best Production Design for *Strictly Ballroom* in 1992, as well as Best Costume Design and Best Production Design for *Moulin Rouge!* in 2001 and for *Australia* in 2009. Martin also won, along with Luhrmann, the Byron Kennedy Award in 1999, awarded by the AFI, which recognizes outstanding creative initiative, innovation, and the pursuit of excellence. According to the AFI, they won for their process of "total filmmaking," meaning the unconventional immersion of their whole crew in experimentation and pre-visualization, thereby achieving a comprehensive aesthetic from concept to poster. Martin also received a Tony Award for Best Scenic Design for the updated version of a production of Puccini's classic *La Bohème* that Luhrmann and Martin first staged in 1990. This updated version ran from December 8, 2002, to June 29, 2003.

Ana Cabral Martins

Further Reading

Bullock, Maggie. 2013. "Baz Luhrmann's Leading Lady." *Elle*, May 3. http://www.elle.com/fashion/spotlight/great-gatsby-costume-designer-catherine-martin-profile.

Cook, Pam. 2010. *Baz Luhrmann*. London: Palgrave Macmillan.

Jayamanee, Laleen. 2014. *The Epic Cinema of Kumar Shahani*. Bloomington: Indiana University Press.

Karan, Donna. 2002. "Catherine Martin." *Interview*: 146–149.

Landis, Deborah Nadoolman. 2013. *Hollywood Costume*. New York: Harry N. Abrams.

Ryan, Tom, ed. 2014. *Baz Luhrmann: Interviews*. Jackson: University Press of Mississippi.

McMillan, Stephenie (1942–2013)

Stephenie McMillan is an English set decorator best known for her collaborations with production designer/art director Stuart Craig. The interiors McMillan dressed were "characterized by technical finesse, elegance and wit" (Craig 2013). She grounded her approach to set decoration in close observation to detail and an understanding of how those details influenced a storyline, telling the British Academy of Film and Television Arts (BAFTA) in a 2012 interview: "You learn through observation. Look around and see what's in a person's room. I always look to see what books people have sitting behind them in interviews" (Denham 2012). This attention to detail was applied to her decoration of large sets, at which she excelled, particularly in her work on the *Harry Potter* movie franchise.

McMillan's career began at the architectural firm Stillman and Eastwick-Field; it was here that she claimed to have learned her appreciation for space and design. In her early working years, McMillan also served as a freelance stylist for photographers and on television commercials. Her first film credit was as set decorator on Paul McCartney's concept movie *Give My Regards to Broad Street* (1984).

As a set decorator, McMillan was responsible for acquiring and arranging the furnishings and decorations that fleshed out the interior locations of the films she worked on. If a production designer is responsible for creating the visual narrative of the film, in collaboration with the director and cinematographer, it is the set decorator who brings the visual concepts to life. Set decorators "establish a character's personality through the use of interior decoration . . . they provide a true narrative backstory by bringing environments to life through detail and decoration" (Whitlock 2010). Set decorators are also responsible for supervising the artisans who create specific pieces and for sourcing and purchasing items that are not being specifically constructed for a film. McMillan believed that "[s]et decorating should never steal thunder from actors, nor should it ever be so showy that you're looking at the furniture rather than the action" (Denham 2012).

McMillan began her artistic partnership with Stuart Craig on *Chaplin* (1992). Craig and McMillan again collaborated on *The Secret Garden* (1993), *Shadowlands* (1993), and *Mary Reilly* (1996). Also in 1996, the pair worked together on *The English Patient* (1996), for which they won an Academy Award for Best Art Direction/Set Decoration. For *The English Patient*, Craig and McMillan created exotic, colonialized settings in North Africa, juxtaposed with war-torn Italy; both locations, however, rely on texture to enliven spaces and advance the tonal narrative of the

Set decorator Stephenie McMillan poses on the re-created set of *Harry Potter and the Prisoner of Azkaban* during the opening of *The Secret Life of Sets: Set Decorators at Work* at the Academy of Motion Picture Arts and Sciences, on May 13, 2004, in Beverly Hills, California. She won the Academy Award for Best Art Direction-Set Decoration for her work on *The English Patient* (1996), and has received nominations for the first, fourth, seventh, and eighth *Harry Potter* films. Throughout her career she has collaborated closely with acclaimed production designer Stuart Craig. (Stephen Shugerman/Getty Images)

film. Craig has said that McMillan "instinctively preferred understatement," so that in a sparse setting, each piece included by the set decorator becomes heavy with the weight of its meaning to the mood or tone of the whole (Craig 2013).

Craig and McMillan's other films together include *The Avengers* (1998), *Notting Hill* (1999), and *Gambit* (2012). Their work together includes both major studio releases and smaller independent film projects, but the most sustained collaboration between the two was between 2001 and 2011; over this decade Craig and McMillan were responsible for the art direction and set decoration for all eight of the *Harry Potter* films in the franchise, providing a sense of visual continuity to the series even as directors and cinematographers varied between films. They relied on the vast amount of detail provided by author J. K. Rowling in the original books as the basis for the films' designs and décor.

Fantasy films represent "one of the most creatively challenging genres" for an art department, as, even when working on adaptations, as with the *Harry Potter* films, the world of the film must be created as a wholly original environment designed to take audiences "into another world that usually involves magic and myth, imagination and illusion, and the ultimate escape" (Whitlock 2010). McMillan and Craig's success in creating the locations central to the *Potter* films was recognized by their peers: they were nominated for Academy Awards for *Harry Potter and the Sorcerer's Stone* (2001), *Harry Potter and the Goblet of Fire* (2005), *Harry Potter and the Deathly Hallows—Part 1* (2010), and *Harry Potter and the Deathly Hallows—Part 2* (2011). The pair were nominated for Art Directors Guild Awards for Excellence in Production Design for *Harry Potter and the Half-Blood Prince* (2009), *Harry Potter and the Deathly Hallows—Part 1*, and *Harry Potter and the Deathly Hallows—Part 2*, winning the award for the third film. McMillan and Craig also shared in the award when the entire series was also honored by the guild for Contribution to Cinematic Imagery in 2012. In addition, McMillan and Craig were nominated for BAFTA Awards for *Harry Potter and the Order of the Phoenix* (2007), *Harry Potter and the Half-Blood Prince*, and *Harry Potter and the Deathly Hallows—Part 2*.

McMillan and Craig also collaborated on the designs for the Harry Potter theme park in Orlando, Florida, and on "The Magical World of Harry Potter" at the Warner Bros. Leavesden, England studios, where much of the sound-stage work on the series had been filmed. For these spaces, they re-created many of the spaces originally seen in the films, including the Great Hall of Hogwarts, and Diagon Alley.

McMillan's other film credits include *A Fish Called Wanda* (1988) and *Chocolat* (2000), for which she decorated the interior of the film's chocolaterie as it shifts from rundown to redecorated and vital, and supervised the creation of plaster-of-Paris chocolate creations for window and counter displays. Stephenie McMillan died in 2013 of ovarian cancer.

Sarah McCarroll

Further Reading

Craig, Stuart. 2013. "Stephenie McMillan Obituary," *The Guardian*, August 27. https://www.theguardian.com/film/2013/aug/27/stephenie-mcmillan

Denham, Lucy. 2012. "Stephenie McMillan: Interview," *Guru: Inspiring Minds in Film, Games and TV: British Academy of Film and Television Arts*, November 21. http://guru.bafta.org/stephenie-mcmillan-interview

Whitlock, Cathy, and the Art Directors Guild. 2010. *Designs on Film: A Century of Hollywood Art Direction*. New York: Harper Collins.

Platt, Polly (1939–2011)

The versatile and resilient Hollywood production designer Polly Platt is quoted as saying, "[Y]our [design] work should be invisible" (Platt 1983). However, Platt's extensive and illustrious career (lasting from the late 1960s until her death in 2011) in a predominately male industry is anything but "invisible." Platt is what one could consider a "trailblazer" for women in the film industry in a multitude of ways. Platt is arguably most well known her work as a Hollywood production designer and art director in the 1970s to 1980s. However, it is important to discuss Platt's life before filmmaking and the direct influence her personal life often seemed to have on her work.

Born Mary Marr Platt (later adopting the name "Polly"), Platt's upbringing was somewhat unconventional. Platt and her family moved to Germany at age six, where her father John, a colonel in the army, served as a judge in the Dachau Trials of Nazi war criminals. According to her daughter Antonia, it was Platt's time in Europe that most contributed to her unique artistic taste and cultural point of view (Keegan 2011). Interestingly, Platt's mother Vivian worked as an advertising executive, which could partly explain where Platt's affinity for production design came from.

Advertising is comparable to production design and art direction, in that both involve the development and execution of visual ideas. According to the visual consultant Bruce Block, "[A] production designer has to understand the characters and the story from an emotional point of view. They have to have great taste and they have to understand what happens to things when you photograph them," which is one way of describing what made Platt such a unique production designer (Olson 1999, 11). Her production design work often reflects a heightened attention to the emotional motivation of the characters as well as an absorbing and authentic "look," with a focus on re-creating realistic details to establish the particular time period and setting for each film, such as her efforts to re-create of Depression-era America in *Paper Moon* (1973).

After moving back to America and attending Carnegie Mellon University, Platt's work and personal life once again merged when she met her second husband, film director Peter Bogdanovich, whom she worked with on several of her first films. It is interesting to note that Platt began her career in a time of change in Hollywood (the era now often referred to as "New Hollywood"), when the MPAA Ratings System replaced the Motion Picture Production Code in 1968. This change led to films with more liberal and challenging subject matter being more commonly produced, such as Platt's first film *Targets* (1968). Much like the "New Hollywood" films of Martin Scorsese and Francis Ford Coppola, *Targets* directly comments on anxieties surrounding the Vietnam War. The plot revolves around a disgruntled Vietnam War veteran/sniper (Tim O'Kelly), who is planning a mass shooting at a drive-in. It was *Targets* that first gave Platt experience in a variety of roles behind the camera: production designer, costume designer, and writer. That was an experience that very few women were getting at the time, even though she was only credited as the production designer. She continued to expand on that throughout the decades that followed.

While many scholars and critics cite *Paper Moon* (1968) and *The Last Picture Show* (1971) as two of Platt's most notable works (both directed by her then husband Peter Bogdanovich), it is the work that Platt did independent of her husband (which came after their divorce) that could be considered to be more representative of her own personal style and artistic sensibility. This may also partly be attributed to the effects her tragic and highly publicized divorce had on her work.

The kinds of stories Platt chose to invest her time (as a writer) and money in (as a producer) suggest that she was focused on telling stories for and about women, as well as films that were attempting to provide audiences insight into the changing attitudes and ideas of the time, rather than simply reinforce them. The films listed in this entry are a small sample of her work, which can also be discussed in relation to their more challenging explorations of gender, sexuality, and life in contemporary society. For example, Platt's first film as a screenwriter, *Pretty Baby* (1978), focuses on the complex and convoluted (sexual-familial) relationship between a prostitute, her daughter, and a photographer in a brothel in 1917 New Orleans. Much like *Targets* and *Pretty Baby*, Platt's work continually attempted to challenge the status quo and tell stories that focus on dysfunctional families, issues around gender/identity, sexual politics, and women's agency. Most notable in this regard are *Terms of Endearment* (1983) (which also earned her an Oscar nomination for Best Art Decoration—Set Decoration) and *The Witches of Eastwick* (1988). Both films focus on fractured familial relationships and the struggle of women in different phases of life as they try to find their way in the world. The women ultimately persevere, despite the various hardships they face, much like Platt's perseverance throughout her career. In the late 1980s, Platt started producing films, including *Broadcast News* (1987) and *Say Anything . . .* (1989), which also explore stories about the struggle for women (as well as men) to find their place in the world. Against the backdrop of the right-wing Reagan era and the backlash against second-wave feminism, it is important to recognize that Platt was one of the few Hollywood filmmakers who actively wanted to produce work that attempted to challenge the dominant, conservative, and reactionary sociocultural attitudes of the time.

In a career as long and wide-ranging as Platt's, it is somewhat reductive to suggest that there is just one aspect of her career (such as production design), which makes her an important and influential woman in film history. Platt's significant place in film history can be seen in her diverse repertoire of films, as well as in the various relationships and collaborations she fostered throughout her career, which are still present within the industry today. For example, along with being the first female art director in the Art Directors Guild, Platt was also the executive vice president of Gracie Films (writer-director James L. Brooks's production company) from 1985 to 1995, where she was instrumental in bringing on *The Simpson*'s creator Matt Groening. In addition to Groening, Platt helped launch the careers of Cameron Crowe and Wes Anderson. She produced both of their directorial-debut films (*Say Anything . . .* in 1989 and *Bottle Rocket* in 1996, respectively), and they are both still actively working in film and television today. Therefore, Platt's work as a production designer and screenwriter is just as important to consider when discussing her "Heroine-like" qualities as her work as producer and executive vice president.

To further demonstrate how and why Platt can be considered a "Hollywood Heroine," one could look to her final project, *Corman's World: Exploits of a Hollywood Rebel* (2011), on which she was working as an executive producer at the time of her death. The subject of the documentary, Roger Corman, was one of the first producers of independent horror films/low-budget teen films (also known as B-movies) beginning in the 1950s and 1960s. Corman was a significant figure in Platt's life, in that he gave her (and her ex-husband Bogdanovich) her first "real job" in the film industry (they both reportedly served as Corman's assistants on his 1967 film *The Wild Angels*). As a way of bringing her career full circle (and paying homage to the man who helped galvanize her career), Platt spent her final days contributing to a project aimed at telling the story of a man whom she admired and respected as an important part of film history in his own right.

Stephanie Oliver

Further Reading

Keegan, Rebecca. 2011. "Polly Platt Dies at 72; Oscar-Nominated Art Director." *Los Angeles Times*, July 28. http://articles.latimes.com/2011/jul/28/local/la-me-polly-platt-20110728

Olson, Robert. 1999. "What Does an Art Director Need to Know?." In *Art Direction for Film and Video*. Waltham: Focal Press.

Platt, Polly. 1983. *Filmmakers on Filmmaking: The American Film Institute Seminars on Motion Pictures and Television*. Edited by Joseph McBride. Boston: Houghton Mifflin.

Schiavo, Francesca Lo (1948–)

As a multiple Academy Award winner, Francesca Lo Schiavo has been recognized for excellence in set decoration. Born in Italy, Lo Schiavo began her film career working on Italian and French films but soon crossed over to English and American films. She is known for her partnership with her husband, production designer Dante Ferretti. The collaboration between the pair has won them three Academy Awards for Best Art Direction out of a total seven nominations. The long span of Lo Schiavo's career has seen her move between the film industries of different countries and between the film and digital eras, as well as stand out in Hollywood both in her field and as a woman working in a production role.

Lo Schiavo cites her lifelong appreciation of art as the foundation of her first career as an interior decorator. When she met Ferretti, he suggested that Lo Schiavo use this skill set to try a career in film. A set decorator fills the space of an interior or exterior set by choosing and arranging furniture and other decorative objects, creating a sense of reality. Different types of films necessitate a rethinking of perspective such as when, while working on her first 3D film *Hugo* (2011), Lo Schiavo discovered the need to place more objects in the foreground. The profession also requires budget management and research into the historical context of the film. Another important aspect is working in collaboration with the rest of the art department to ensure cohesive use of color and style and any other necessary specifications, like space for action sequences or the integration of props.

Beginning her career in the late 20th century and continuing through to the 21st means that Lo Schiavo has worked through a changing industry with the rise of the digital era. This change has had ramifications for all crew involved in production design as visual effects, able to create more expansive scenes at less expense, have become the norm across the industry, particularly in the past two decades. The prevalence of digital effects has influenced one of the most important parts of the set decorator's role: the negotiation of the budget. Lo Schiavo faced this challenge when she fought for real chandeliers over computer-generated ones on *Cinderella* (2015) and ended up simplifying the set and buying smaller, less expensive chandeliers.

Lo Schiavo's film career began as an assistant set decorator on the Italian film *La Pelle* (1981). She then progressed to the role of set decorator on several other Italian films over the following years, including the influential director Federico Fellini's *And the Ship Sails On* (1983) before her Oscar-nominated work for the

British film *The Adventures of Baron Munchausen* in 1988. From there, Lo Schiavo and Ferretti continued to work on English-language films and garner Oscar nominations, including one for *Hamlet* (1990) and *Interview with the Vampire* (1995). She found it difficult to get work before becoming a U.S. resident and so she did not decorate the set of Martin Scorsese's *Age of Innocence* (1993) for which Ferretti was also Oscar nominated. Both Lo Schiavo and Ferretti, however, would go on to receive four Oscar nominations on the Scorsese films *Kundun* (1997), *Gangs of New York* (2002), *The Aviator* (2004), and *Hugo* (2011), the latter two for which they won the award. For *Hugo*, they also received a BAFTA award. The pair's third Academy Award was awarded for *Sweeney Todd: The Demon Barber of Fleet Street* in 2007.

With an impressive amount of Oscar awards and nominations, Lo Schiavo has successfully established herself in the Hollywood film industry. The very same industry has, particularly in recent years, been under critique for its low percentage of women in "behind-the-scenes" roles and particularly women in power in roles such as director or producer. Lo Schiavo's career can exemplify this as, over her nearly 40-year career, she has worked with only two female directors, both of whom were the directors of Italian films in the 1980s. Similarly, outside of acting, the Academy Awards and other award shows have been under scrutiny for a lack of female nominees and winners. However, in addition to Lo Schiavo's three wins, over the past 20 years there has been a roughly equal ratio of female and male set decoration winners, with women dominating the nominations. The same cannot be said for most other production categories, including the other half of the award for art direction, which goes to the production designers. Though prior to the 1990s, the award for set decoration had a small proportion of female nominees and only two winners, the category now stands out from other production roles as one in which women are very successful.

A cultural uneasiness with women in power leads the film industry to consider women in leadership roles a financial risk, accounting for the lack of women in the most powerful production roles. The success of women in set decoration is possibly the result of its distance from the top positions of power. Even so, the set decorator is an important aspect of the art direction of the film, as this role oversees part of the art department and is largely responsible for the look, perspective, and details of a film. Lo Schiavo is also exemplary in this field, as the only female set decorator to receive more than one Academy Award, the only set decorator since 2000 to receive more than one Academy Award, and the only set decorator to have received three or more Academy Awards since 1975.

Jess Donohoe

Further Reading

Ackland-Snow, Terry, and Layburn, Wendy. 2017. *The Art of Illusion: Production Design for Film and Television*. Ramsbury, Wiltshire, UK: The Crowood Press.

Garcia, Maria. 2013. "Designing and Dressing Imagined Worlds: An Interview with Dante Ferretti and Francesca Lo Schiavo." *Cinéaste* 39(1): 30–34.

Rizzo, Michael. 2005 *The Art Direction Handbook for Film*. Abingdon, UK: Focal Press.

Screenwriters

Introduction

The development of the modern screenplay follows the technological advances in filmmaking since the dawn of cinema. Early film did not start out in narrative form, and so the scripting practices were in their infancy, appearing as brief descriptions of a scenario. The earliest version of a screenplay is attributed to Georges Méliès's *A Trip to the Moon* (*Le Voyage Dans la Lune,* 1902). Although it hardly resembles what we would consider a screenplay today, it is the first example of narrative being introduced to filmmaking, and therefore his written list of ordered scenes and shots can be considered a primitive version of a script.

Women played a pivotal role in legitimizing and forming the craft of screenwriting during the silent era of Hollywood and were present in all areas of screenwriting across the major studios. One of their biggest contributions was the early development of the "blueprint," or continuity, screenplays that we are familiar with today. In 1920, Anita Loos co-wrote one of the earliest books on screenwriting with her husband, John Emerson, entitled "How to Write Photoplays." Despite the large female presence in the profession, many women writers went uncredited during this time due to the lack of a standardized crediting system. The rise of the studio system in the 1930s marked a decline of power for women writers in Hollywood. Although some successfully made the transition to sound, all personnel worked within a contract system where they were no longer given the creative freedoms they once enjoyed. The continuity script was further developed, becoming vital to the assembly line of production practiced by the studios during that time. An original speculative screenplay (a "spec script," written by a writer who isn't commissioned) was not very popular until the 1970s, after the decline of the studio system when directors and actresses, free of studio control, gained the power and freedom to be more selective about the projects they wanted to develop.

Screenplays are an unusual literary form, as they are essentially an unfinished product and there are an abundance of methods and theories on what makes a good screenplay. Although a script itself is in written form, its goal is to tell a story visually, which is enormously challenging. In general, the stories are well structured, and a professional screenwriter keeps stage directions and exposition to a minimum. Usually, the more text there is on the page, the more inexperienced the writer. Selling a spec script today is extremely difficult and competitive. Most writers covet being given an assignment where they are under contract to write. On a film, a script is usually altered to varying degrees several times during development. Often, the original screenplay will look unrecognizable by the time it is ready to be shot, and typically none of the writers hired to make changes will receive screen credit unless they made significant changes to at least half the script.

Laura L. S. Bauer

Allen, Jay Presson (1923–2010)

The first person to earn a solo editing credit during the opening titles of a film (*Bonnie and Clyde* 1967), Jay Presson Allen is one of the most famous and innovative film editors in Hollywood history. After 14 years in the filmmaking business performing a variety of tasks, Allen became a film editor, one who some deem an auteur, whose career spanned more than 30 films over 50 years. She was a natural with the mechanics of film, and her approach to film editing was less intellectual and more visceral. She famously and repeatedly claimed, "You have to cut with your gut," offering that advice when mentoring the younger generation of film editors who would follow her (Block and McKay 2010).

Born in Cleveland, Ohio, as Dorothea Carothers Allen (or "Dede" as she was affectionately known), always enjoyed the movies growing up. Never having much homework growing up during the Depression and influenced by her mother's own love for film, Allen would go to the movies almost every day. Allen worked in many departments during her early years in Hollywood, which helped her develop a rich background that aided her understanding of every phase of film production. In 1943, an 18-year-old Allen worked as one of the first female messengers at Columbia Pictures during the summer while attending Scripps College, to which she never returned. She made her way into the cutting room and would go on to work as a script supervisor and sound librarian far before her work as a feature film editor began in the late 1950s. In interviews, Allen talked about how her beginning career work in sound ingrained in her the rhythm necessary to edit visuals. Indeed, she became one of the first film editors to suggest that the audio and the visuals hold equal importance.

Robert Wise, the film editor for Orson Welles's *Citizen Kane* (1941) and director of films like *The Sound of Music* (1965), mentored Allen and encouraged her to experiment with the craft on her first major film-editing job, *Odds Against Tomorrow* (1959). In this early film, Allen developed the revolutionary technique of the "audio shift," overlapping sound from the end of the last shot into the beginning of the next one, thus causing an increase in the film's pacing. Other directors in Hollywood soon recognized her prodigious talent, such as Robert Rossen, who hired her to edit *The Hustler* (1961), and Arthur Penn, with whom she worked on six films, most notably her greatest and most masterful enterprise in editing, *Bonnie and Clyde* (1967).

In *Bonnie and Clyde*, Allen acted directly against the principles of classical editing structure in order to better nurture Penn's desire for faster-paced images. The film's climactic scene features 60 individual shots edited into 63 seconds, a showcase of "the era's fastest cutting" (Keil and Whissel 2016, 111). Her overall "shock-cutting," as Andrew Sarris called it, in the film gives it "a jagged, menacing quality and creates a sort of syncopated rhythm" (Garga 2005). Warren Beatty praised how "her use of image and sound in counterpoint both embellish and enlarge the poetic context of the drama" (Gentry 1992, 12). Her innovative editing of the film countered the classical paradigm, causing *Bonnie and Clyde* to become a foundational film text in the era of "New Cinema" and cementing her reputation as a revolutionary in Hollywood.

While editing feature films through the 1960s and 1970s, Allen would amass a set of radical editing techniques, including the previously discussed audio shift, also known as pre-lapping, and rapid cutting using a variety of shots to quicken movement. In addition to her bold use of pacing and transitions, she would often mix regular-speed and slow-motion shots and fracture time with a shifting of scene sequence. During this period, Allen also mentored a number of novice editors, some of whom would become Oscar-nominated editors, including Barry Malkin (*The Godfather: Part II* 1974) and Jerry Greenberg, her apprentice on Elia Kazan's *America, America* (1963), who would go on to edit *Apocalypse Now* (1979) and *The Untouchables* (1987). Through her teaching, Allen established what came to be known as the New York School of Editing.

Allen's career as a film editor in Hollywood spanned 60 years, and her credits include *Rachel, Rachel* (1968), *Serpico* (1973), *Slap Shot* (1977), *The Breakfast Club* (1984), and *The Addams Family* (1991). She was nominated for an Academy Award in Film Editing three times in three different decades, for *Dog Day Afternoon* (1975), *Reds* (1981), and *Wonder Boys* (2000). Though she never earned an Oscar, she did receive a BAFTA for *Dog Day Afternoon* (1976) and a Women in Film Crystal Award (1982), honoring outstanding women who have helped to expand the influence of women in the entertainment industry. In addition, she was awarded career achievement awards from the American Cinema Editors in 1994 and another from the Los Angeles Film Critics Association in 1999. By this time in the early 1990s, Allen had become the head of post-production at Warner Bros., but she continued to edit films until her last in 2008, the domestic drama *Fireflies in the Garden*. In 2012, the Motion Picture Editors Guild released a list of 75 of the best edited films, on which three done by Dede Allen appear, putting her a close second to George Tomasini's four.

Jay Presson Allen died in 2010, leaving behind her husband of 63 years, Stephen, and her children, Tom Fleischman and Ramey Ward, who have both worked in Hollywood as well.

Christina Parker-Flynn

See also: Dunaway, Faye

Further Reading

Acker, A. 1993. *Reel Women: Pioneers of the Cinema 1896 to the Present.* New York: Continuum.

Apple, W, dir. 2004. *The Cutting Edge: The Magic of Movie Editing.* Meridian: Starz Encore Entertainment.

Block, M., and C. McKay. 2010. "The Legacy of Film Editor Dede Allen." *NPR*, April 19. https://www.npr.org/templates/story/story.php?storyId=126115019

Dimare, P, ed. 2011. *Movies in American History: An Encyclopedia, Volume 1.* Santa Barbara, CA: ABC-CLIO.

Gentry, R. 1999. "An Interview with Dede Allen." *Film Quarterly* 46(1): 12–22.

Keil, C., and K. Whissel, eds. 2016. *Editing and Special/Visual Effects.* New Brunswick, NJ: Rutgers University Press.

Lumme, H. 2002. *Great Women of Film.* New York: Billboard Books.

Garga, B. D. 2005. *The Art of Cinema: An Insider's Journey Through Fifty Years of Film History.* London, England: Penguin.

Brackett, Leigh (1915–1978)

A prolific writer in multiple genres and forms, Leigh Brackett's greatest love was science fiction. Over the course of her life, Brackett published over 50 stories, more than a dozen novels, and wrote 11 produced screenplays before succumbing to cancer at the age of 62. She began her career in film as co-writer of *The Big Sleep* (1946) and finished with the first draft of *The Empire Strikes Back* (1980), which she handed in weeks before her death. The latter film is dedicated to her memory.

Brackett's writing style made famed director Howard Hawks mistake her for a man. In 1944, while looking for a scenarist (as screenwriters were called at the time) to join the formidable William Faulkner in writing the screen adaptation of Raymond Chandler's *The Big Sleep*, Hawks remembered reading a hard-boiled crime novel titled *No Good from a Corpse* written by Brackett. Hawks told an assistant to get him "that Brackett guy" and was stunned when a young woman in her twenties showed up at his office. Hawks hired her, later recalling, "She looked as if she wrote poetry. But she wrote like a man" (Rule 1995).

Brackett went to work on the script, writing in cooperation with Faulkner. In a 1965 interview she remembered, "We blocked out the story in sections; then he took some and I took the others. We worked in adjoining offices. . . . But he had built a wall around himself and one didn't penetrate it" (Hopper 1965). Brackett and Faulkner wrote the script in eight days, including three days that Faulkner didn't show up to work. When lead actor Humphrey Bogart got his script, he went to Brackett complaining that the dialogue she'd written for him was too soft, and she politely informed Bogart that the dialogue he was complaining about had actually been written by Faulkner.

Brackett gained her knack for dialogue by reading Dashiell Hammett, John Steinbeck, Ernest Hemingway, and Rudyard Kipling "to crisp and compress her style" (Rule 1995). Her youth had been spent reading the works of Edgar Rice Burroughs, beginning with *The Gods of Mars*. In that book, Brackett found her calling. She began writing science fiction stories at the age of 13 and wrote for 10 years before selling two stories in a single week to *Astounding Stories* magazine in 1939. Brackett was always a writer of pulp fiction first and foremost, but she enjoyed her time in film as well.

"When the job on *The Big Sleep* fell into my lap, out of the blue, and I was signed to a seven-year contract," Brackett wrote, "everybody told me I had it made. . . . After two-and-a-half years the independent company which had signed me was dissolved for tax purposes, and I was dissolved with it, still somewhat short of my million" (Brackett 1977, 361). Afterwards, Brackett was able to effortlessly return to writing her own stories. Her husband, Edmond Hamilton, remarked on Brackett's unique ability to fluidly move between genres: "In eighteen months, in 1956–57, she wrote not only *The Long Tomorrow* [her most popular science fiction novel] but also two novels of crime and suspense, *The Tiger Among Us*, which became an Alan Ladd movie, and *An Eye for an Eye*, which formed the pilot for the 'Markham' series on television" (Brackett 1977, x).

Through the years Hawks remained in touch with Brackett and hired her to write three Westerns: *Rio Bravo* (1959), *El Dorado* (1966), and *Rio Lobo* (1970), as well as an African safari film, *Hatari!* (1962)—all starring John Wayne. When Robert Altman wanted to do an update of Raymond Chandler's *The Long Goodbye* (1973), Brackett was his first and only choice for screenwriter.

In her films, as in her fiction writing, Brackett's favored theme is of "a strong man's quest for a dream and of his final failure when it turns to smoke and ashes in his hands. . . . Her heroes seek something they can never quite attain, yet their failure is not really defeat" (Brackett 1977, viii). Regardless of genre, her characters "are the people who make up a frontier: outcasts, renegades, petty criminals and rebels, men with too much past and too little future" (Brackett 2003, 30). Brackett thus seemed a natural choice to pen *The Empire Strikes Back* (1978). George Lucas had been a long admirer of Brackett's work. Beyond her crisp dialogue, Brackett was known for exceptional detail and creativity. Fellow science fiction writer Mike Moorcock reportedly said, "With Brackett, it's the atmosphere that gets you; the visuality and sheer physicality of her writing, the reflective landscapes that become, themselves, a species of narrative" (Brackett 2003, 33). Brackett brought this skill to her story conferences with George Lucas and to her first draft of the script. Though Brackett was suffering from cancer, she turned the screenplay in ahead of schedule. She passed away two weeks later.

Lawrence Kasdan was later hired to continue writing *Empire*. The story was still in substantial flux at the time of Brackett's death (for example, George Lucas had not yet determined that Vader would be Luke's father), and little of Brackett's first draft remains in the final film. Despite that fact, Lucas gave Brackett a writing credit on the film and *The Empire Strikes Back* is dedicated to her memory.

Angela Bourassa

Further Reading

Brackett, Leigh. 1977. *The Best of Leigh Brackett*. Edited by Edmond Hamilton. New York: Nelson Doubleday.

Brackett, Leigh. 2003. *Martian Quest: The Early Brackett*. Edited by James Sallis. Hoboken, NJ: Spilogale.

Hopper, Hedda. 1965. "They Call Her for Salty Dialogue." *Los Angeles Times,* December 28. https://www.newspapers.com/newspage/161750364/

Rule, Vera. 1995. "Woman Who Nixed the Mimsy." *The Guardian*, August 3. http://www.reelclassics.com/Movies/BigSleep/bigsleep-article.htm

Sallis, James. 2003. "The Unclassifiable Leigh Brackett." *Boston Globe,* May 11. http://www.grasslimb.com/sallis/GlobeColumns/globe.09.brackett.html

Comden, Betty (1917–2006)

As one half of Comden and Green, the longest-running screenwriting partnership in Hollywood and Broadway history, Betty Comden helped create some of the most beloved movies and plays of all time. Known for her wit, eye for dialogue, and New York sensibility, she and Adolph Green wrote such hits as *On the Town* (1949), *Peter Pan* (the 1954 musical), and, most notably, *Singin' in the Rain* (1952). Throughout their luminous career, they were nominated for two Oscars, though they never won. They did, however, win 7 of the 12 Tony Awards for which they were nominated.

Though she eventually became a sought-after Hollywood and Broadway screenwriter, even being awarded the Kennedy Center Honors in 1991, Betty Comden was not born into a life of glamour. She was born Basya Cohen to Russian Jewish immigrants in Brooklyn in 1917. She met Green while studying drama at New York University, and they became friends while trying to find work onstage. Frustrated by their failed attempts to get cast in anything, they joined with their friends, including Judy Holliday and occasionally Leonard Bernstein, to form the Revuers. They wrote their own skits and songs, and they got a steady gig in Greenwich Village. The Revuers gained local success and almost led to Comden's big break. The group appeared in a 20th Century Fox production, but Comden's part was cut almost entirely.

One member of the group, however, was quickly gaining fame as a conductor and composer. Bernstein wrote the score to a ballet, and when he wanted to turn it into a musical, he called in Comden and Green. In 1944, the ballet *Fancy Free* became the hit musical *On the Town,* and the writing pair began their careers in earnest.

For the next two decades, Comden and Green saw steady success writing for both film and stage. It was the golden age of the Hollywood musical, and they played a big part in that era. Their credits during this time include *The Barkleys of Broadway* starring Fred Astaire and Ginger Rogers, the film adaptation of *On the Town* starring Frank Sinatra and Gene Kelly, and *Auntie Mame,* the highest-grossing film of 1959. Comden and Green were nominated for Academy Awards in the Best Writing, Story, and Screenplay category for *The Band Wagon* and *It's Always Fair Weather.* They were also nominated for a Best Soundtrack Grammy for their work on *Bells Are Ringing.*

However, their most famous movie is the 1952 classic *Singin' in the Rain.* While the movie is appreciated by many for its romance, humor, and enthusiasm, it actually began as a vanity project by Arthur Freed. Freed was the head of the musical unit at Metro-Goldwyn-Mayer (MGM), and he decided that he wanted to make a new musical out of songs he and his writing partner, Nacio Herb Brown, had written for older MGM musicals. At first, Comden and Green refused to work on the project, but they eventually relented once they realized that they were under contract to MGM and therefore did not have a choice. Freed told them that the movie should focus on the early days of Hollywood and feature songs from his catalogue. With no more information to go on, Comden and Green rented a house in Beverly Hills and spent the summer of 1950 writing.

With Gene Kelly directing and starring, the movie was expected to be a hit, but although successful it was unable to garner the expected attention. While Comden and Green won the Writers Guild of America award for Best Written American

Musical, the film was largely forgotten until a theatrical re-release in 1975. Since then, *Singin' in the Rain* has gone on to become both critically acclaimed and beloved by many. The American Film Institute lists it as the greatest American movie musical, and the song "Singin' in the Rain" is ranked third in the institute's list of best songs from movies.

Eventually, however, all things must come to an end, and, in the mid-1960s, the movie musical faded from popularity. During this time, the writing partners continued to work on Broadway, earning quite a few Tony Awards along the way. While they did win a Tony in 1953 for *Wonderful Town,* their other six wins all occurred after their long career in Hollywood had petered out.

After their primary writing years were over, Comden and Green continued to receive accolades for their body of work. In addition to the Kennedy Center Honors, they were awarded the National Board of Review Award for Distinction in Screen Writing in 1995 and the Writers Guild of America Laurel Award for Screen Writing Achievement in 2001.

Betty Comden and Adolph Green made an interesting pair. She was the more reserved of the two, and she was responsible for the basic form and structure of their work. The overall style also came from her, and the sheer joy and inherently New York feel of their work can therefore be attributed to Comden. What Green brought to the table was intensity and madness. He took her ideas and turned up the volume. They were opposite personalities who blended their styles to make energetic, witty, relatable, exciting stories.

Despite the fact that they were never romantic, their exclusive professional partnership lasting nearly six decades did raise some eyebrows. Though their relationship was unusual, especially for mid-20th-century America, Comden always insisted they never viewed each other as anything more than friends.

In fact, Comden married designer and businessman Steven Kyle in 1942, and he was incredibly supportive of her career. He even helped her brainstorm scenes for *Singin' in the Rain,* and his idea of blending their three possible opening scenes into one made it into the movie. After Kyle died in 1979, Comden never remarried.

Even though Comden herself passed away in 2006, her legacy continues. She and Green wrote some of Broadway's most memorable songs, and their work still appears in movies, television shows, revues, and revivals regularly. Her work may be done, but her list of credits continues to grow.

Audrey Curtis

Further Reading

Barrios, Richard. 2014. *Dangerous Rhythm: Why Movie Musicals Matter.* Oxford, UK: Oxford University Press.

Comden, Betty. 1995. *Off Stage.* New York: Simon and Schuster.

Ewen, David. 1987. *American Songwriters: An H. W. Wilson Biographical Dictionary.* New York: H. W. Wilson.

Hess, Earl J., and Pratibha A. Dabholkar. 2009. *Singin' in the Rain: The Making of an American Masterpiece.* Lawrence: University Press of Kansas.

McGilligan, Pat, ed. 1997. *Backstory 2: Interviews with Screenwriters of the 1940s and 1950s.* Berkeley: University of California Press

Coppola, Sofia (1971–)

Sofia Carmina Coppola was born May 14, 1971, in New York City. As a child, she went by "Domino," and is credited as an actor by the nickname, but transitioned back to "Sofia" before her directorial debut. Her mother, Eleanor Coppola (born Eleanor Jessie Neil), is an American filmmaker and artist, and her father, Francis Ford Coppola, is an Academy Award–winning filmmaker and a staple of the New Hollywood film era. Her paternal grandfather was composer Carmine Coppola. Descended from a notable Italian American Hollywood filmmaking family, Sofia Coppola began her career as an infant, appearing in films directed by her father, including *The Godfather* (1972), *The Godfather Part II* (1974), *The Outsiders* (1983), and *Rumble Fish* (1983). As a teenager, she appeared in a small supporting role in *Peggy Sue Got Married* (1986), another film directed by Francis Ford Coppola. In 1990, she took on one of her largest roles as an actress, portraying the character of Mary Corleone in *The Godfather Part III* (1990). Despite appearing in music videos throughout the 1990s and early 2000s, her performance in *The Godfather Part III* was not well received by critics, and in 1998 Coppola began her transition from actress to director and screenwriter with a short film titled *Lick the Star* (1998). Her feature film debut, *The Virgin Suicides* (1999), officially launched her directing career, and it was well received among the indie movie circuit after its 2000 premiere at the Sundance Film Festival. Coppola's second feature film, *Lost in Translation* (2003), starring Scarlett Johansson and Bill Murray, was also critically acclaimed, earning her an Academy Award for Best Original Screenplay. She has directed eight films and won one Academy Award and two Golden Globes. In 2016, Coppola began directing a production of the opera *La Traviata* in Rome, Italy. She has two daughters with her husband, French musician Thomas Mars.

Influenced by Jean-Luc Godard, father Francis Ford Coppola, Wes Anderson and Tamara Jenkins, Sofia Coppola's style descends from the New Hollywood films of the 1960s and 1970s (aka American New Wave), characterized by their subversion of Classical Hollywood narratives and aesthetics. The directorial continuity of Coppola's first three films lends to the development of her own auteurism and has solidified her presence as a central figure of independent American filmmaking in the 21st century.

Adapted from Jeffrey Eugenides's novel of the same name, Coppola's first feature film, *The Virgin Suicides,* chronicles the lives of an upper-middle-class group of sisters living in Michigan. Coppola's follow-up to *The Virgin Suicides* came nearly four years later, with her Academy Award–winning feature, *Lost in Translation. Lost in Translation* follows a young woman (Johansson) who forms an unlikely friendship with an actor (Murray) while traveling with her photographer husband (based loosely on Spike Jonze, Coppola's first husband). Both films received critical acclaim and recognition for Coppola's screenwriting and directing.

Coppola's third feature film, *Marie Antoinette* (2006), is a biographical film about the queen of France adapted from Antonia Fraser's 2001 biography *Marie Antoinette: The Journey. Marie Antoinette* debuted at the 2006 Cannes Film Festival and received mixed reviews from critics and audiences. Kirsten Dunst, in a continuation of her relationship with Coppola after starring in *The Virgin Suicides*, portrays the titular figure, and Coppola's cousin, actor Jason Schwartzman, stars as King Louis XVI. Filmed on location at the Palace of Versailles, the film provides a colorful, stylized, and sympathetic interpretation of the life of Marie Antoinette, rather than providing a completely factual historical representation of the "ancien régime" (Dargis and Scott 2006).

While Coppola's first three feature films are not necessarily related in terms of their plots, they do hold a level of interconnectivity with each another. Whether adapted or based on an original screenplay by Sofia Coppola, her early films are characterized by their focus on the lives of upper- and upper-middle-class women and the "complex variations on a theme with deep personal, even autobiographical, meaning for their screenwriter/director" (Palmer 2012, 41). Coppola's films are also characterized by their focus on the complications of domesticity and the transitions from adolescence to maturity among the female protagonists of each film. Taking their thematic similarities into account, the films can be read as a trilogy of sorts. R. Barton Palmer writes of Coppola's first three feature films:

> A product more of reception than production and distribution, this is a trilogy that responds interestingly to the ways in which the classic studio model, with its industrially determined forms of multiplicity, has been transformed, even as its appeal persists into the contemporary phase of the New Hollywood era (at least among the cognoscenti). (Palmer 2012, 42)

Coppola followed *Marie Antoinette* with *Somewhere* (2010), filmed on location at the luxury Hollywood hotel, Chateau Marmont. The film follows a Hollywood actor whose young daughter re-enters his life. To describe her motivation for directing *Somewhere,* Coppola is quoted in *Entertainment Weekly* as saying, "*Marie Antoinette* was so decorative, and girly, and frilly, that after that, I wanted to do something as minimal as possible. Just something different after being in that crazy macaroon world for so long" (Staskiewicz 2010).

After *Somewhere*, Coppola directed *The Bling Ring* (2013), a film that satirized the infamous robberies of the homes of several Hollywood actors and celebrities. From late 2008 to late 2009, a group of teens known as the "Bling Ring" burgled the homes of actors Paris Hilton (who appears as herself in the film), Lindsay Lohan, and Orlando Bloom, as well as the Hollywood homes of several other notable celebrities. Many critics positively favored the film. In 2015, Coppola made a Netflix Christmas special with Bill Murray, titled *A Very Murray Christmas* (2015), and in 2016 began pre-production on a forthcoming remake of the 1971 Clint Eastwood film, *The Beguiled* (2017). Her direction of the opera *La Traviata* at the Teatro Nazionale in Rome, Italy, began in 2016 and was met with mixed reviews.

Coppola's *Lost in Translation* was nominated for three Academy Awards, including Best Picture, Best Director, and Best Original Screenplay. Coppola won the Academy Award for Best Original Screenplay, making her part of a three-generation Academy Award–winning family (her father and grandfather both won Oscars), and was the first American woman and youngest woman nominated for the Best Director Academy Award. *Lost in Translation* also earned her two Golden Globe awards for Best Motion Picture and Best Screenplay, and was nominated for three British Academy Film Awards (BAFTA). *Marie Antoinette* was nominated for the

Palme d'Or at Festival de Cannes, and Coppola was the first American woman to win the Golden Lion award at the Venice International Film Festival, which she earned for her fourth feature film, *Somewhere.*

Brooke A. Marine

See also: Canonero, Milena; Meyers, Nancy

Further Reading

Belton, John. 1993. *American Cinema/American Culture.* New York: McGraw-Hill.

Dargis, Manohla, and A. O. Scott. 2006. "'Marie Antoinette': Best or Worst of Times?" *The New York Times*, May 25. http://www.nytimes.com/2006/05/25/movies/25fest.html?_r=0

Palmer, R. Barton. 2012. "Some Thoughts on New Hollywood Multiplicity: Sofia Coppola's Young Girls Trilogy." In *Film Trilogies: New Critical Approaches.* Gordonsville, UK: Palgrave Macmillan.

Smail, Belinda. 2013. "Sofia Coppola: Reading the Director." *Feminist Media Studies* 13: 148–162.

Staskiewicz, Katie. 2010. "Sofia Coppola and a Coen Brother Talk 'Somewhere' at DGA Screening." *Entertainment Weekly*, November 20. http://www.ew.com/article/2010/11/20/sofia-coppola-joel-cohen-somewhere-dga

Vidal, Belén, and Tom Brown. 2013. *The Biopic in Contemporary Film Culture.* New York: Routledge, 2013.

Ephron, Nora (1941–2012)

As she learned from her famous screenwriter parents, everything is copy, and Ephron drew from the lessons learned through both heartbreak and laughter for her own creative fuel. As a screenwriter she earned three Academy Award nominations for best writing in a screenplay for *Silkwood* (1983), *When Harry Met Sally* (1989), and *Sleepless in Seattle* (1993), leaving a high bar for writing relatable characters.

Ephron was in her twenties in 1960s America—where nearly every tradition, belief, and institution was re-examined and challenged. Her works in each field show she embraced some of these changes and challenged the status quo through her coverage as a journalist and in her works. Ephron said she picked what topics she covered and particularly focused on the treatment of women and their roles in both society and the home. As a reporter she offered up facts to consider, what she called "equal conversation," and she incorporated that factual accuracy into her work.

Her attention to every angle and detail translated perfectly to working in Hollywood. From lines of main characters to a little detail in the setting, Ephron's works all had connections to herself. They had pieces of her in them: her love of New York, a frequent setting; characters' lines and career choices; and any subject she was fascinated with.

One of her final works was the award-winning picture *Julie and Julia* (2009). Ephron worked on it in the capacity of its screenwriter, producer, and director. Ephron loved recipes, kitchens, restaurants, and entertaining, having earlier covered food from recipe changes to food competitions. In her more personal essays, she even talked of looking for ways to incorporate in Cuisinarts because this new technology in the kitchen fascinated her. Food critics as dinner guests thrilled her as a subject, and a dream of hers was to get at least one recipe of her own published. A film about a modern woman, Julie, finding solace through cooking based off of Julia Child's famous kitchen teachings in Ephron's hands was all it should be. Ephron perfectly intertwined the cooking part of these women's lives with their personal lives, both filled with love, laughs, trouble, and some heartbreak.

She used her skills in other genres too. Her third film project, and first movie she wrote, was *Silkwood.* Karen Silkwood was a worker in a plutonium plant who suspected and started investigating illegal corner-cutting at her job and died under mysterious circumstances. Ephron goes beyond a basic biography about an important person; she *covers* Silkwood in the time surrounding her investigation until her death. The true triumph, as in all of Ephron's works, is to give as much value and interest to rendering her subject faithfully as she does to developing the strong and relatable female characters who have made her famous.

Every film written by Ephron had a strong female character, no matter the genre. Two of her most well-received and awarded films were in the romantic comedy category: *When Harry Met Sally* and *Sleepless in Seattle.* She made both with in-depth looks at both women and men who were relatable as well as lovers. At the time *When Harry Met Sally* was being discussed as a possible project, it began with one of the most honest conversations between a man and woman—Ephron and the director, Rob Reiner—about assumptions and truths in relationships. Both were surprised at the others' answers on things they thought they were sure of, and the notes the two took in this meeting made their way to the screenplay Ephron wrote. Both saw themselves in the respective roles of Sally and Harry, and their similarities were purposefully written, as well as the discussions they had, into the surprisingly thought-provoking movie. It is hard to pinpoint what makes these, and another favorite, *You've Got Mail* (1998), so timeless, but her focus on depth of character and not just the romantic relationships is certainly a part of it.

One of the many subjects discussed in the history of film since the 1960s has been the portrayal of women. For a woman, there are sad numbers regarding their representation in Hollywood leadership, and the question has been asked: If men are in the top roles of films, are all female roles and heroines being portrayed to the fullest potential? Ephron gracefully shows women's roles have the potential to be much richer, in any genre. She shows this through research, for male and female roles, and using her journalistic skills to write beautifully complex stories about people. The results include her classic movies.

These huge successes hopefully do her, and women, credit and allow for fuller and more relatable female characters to be written, and for any genre to not be afraid to add more depth to their characters. It always came down to the writing with Ephron. Even as she progressed from a screenwriter to taking on production and director roles, she always kept a writer she trusted nearby.

The table of contents of the posthumous collection of some of Nora Ephron's work, *The Most of Nora Ephron*, clearly shows the various areas of the world she also touched, changed, and opened up to both further conversation and change in similar ways. Journalist. Advocate. Profiler of women. Novelist. Playwright. Screenwriter. Foodie. Blogger. The book ends with a section of personal entries and essays but also speaks to how she always kept a little bit of herself in all of her works. Tom Brokaw, the legendary night news anchor, praised, "She was able to pull off the journalistic hat trick of reporting the big picture, commenting on the telling details, and leaving just enough of herself in the piece so the reader knew that the writer had a personal stake in the story" (Brokaw 2007, 200). This praise was certainly not limited to just the articles she wrote, however.

Alaina Pangelina

See also: Meyers, Nancy; Pascal, Amy

Further Reading

Brokaw, Tom. 2007. *Boom!: Talking about the Sixties: What Happened, How It Shaped Today, Lessons for Tomorrow.* New York: Random House.

Ephron, Nora, dir. 2009. *Julie and Julia,* DVD. Los Angeles: Columbia Pictures.

Ephron, Nora. 2013. *The Most of Nora Ephron.* New York: Knopf.

Reiner, Rob, dir. 1989. *When Harry Met Sally,* DVD. Los Angeles: Columbia Pictures.

Hellman, Lillian (1905–1984)

Lillian "Lilly" Hellman, renowned for her work as a playwright, was also an accomplished screenwriter working primarily in the first decades of talking films. She gained notoriety for her deft skill at crafting screenplays with meaningful dialogue, motivated action, and well-wrought characters. Perhaps her most enduring legacy as a writer in Hollywood is her principled arguments for writers' creative control and the need to fight for the civil liberties guaranteed by the Constitution. Both in her writing and her life, Hellman focused on social responsibility and the importance of action.

Lillian Florence Hellman was born in New Orleans, Louisiana, on June 20, 1905. Her family moved to New York in 1910, where Hellman spent the majority of her childhood. After attending New York University for two years, she dropped out of college and managed to secure a position as a manuscript reader for Boni and Liveright, a young publishing house with a reputation for taking risks on new authorial voices, such as William Faulkner and Nathanael West. Hellman encountered first-rate authors' writing and met many in person. The position at Boni and Liveright was equally important because it made the practical decisions of publishing plain to see. This first foray into the literary world was short-lived but formative.

On December 31, 1925, Hellman married Arthur Kober, an aspiring writer working as a theatrical press agent at the time. In February 1930, Kober accepted a position as a junior writer for Paramount Pictures in Hollywood. Hellman joined her husband in Hollywood in the fall of that year, but found herself unhappy at home. Through a connection to Samuel Marx at Metro-Goldwyn-Mayer, Hellman started working as a manuscript reader for $50 a week. Hellman found the low pay and rigid hierarchy at MGM demeaning and attempted to organize her fellow readers to demand for higher pay and better work. Hellman was let go because of her efforts.

In November 1930, Hellman met Dashiell Hammett, a fellow author who would remain an important part of Hellman's professional and personal life until his death. Shortly after, Hellman would leave Hollywood and Kober for New York, living with Hammett. *The Children's Hour*, her first play, opened on November 20, 1934, and launched Hellman's writing career.

Based on the response to *The Children's Hour*, Samuel Goldwyn brought Hellman back to Hollywood in 1935 as a screenwriter for a remarkable $2,500 a week. Hellman's first project back in Hollywood was to work with fellow playwright Mordaunt Shairp on a screenplay of *The Dark Angel* (1935), based on a play that Goldwyn had bought the rights to and produced as a silent film in 1925. Hellman's skill as a writer and prior experiences as a manuscript reader enabled her to excel as a screenwriter and produce a product that satisfied Goldwyn and critics alike.

Goldwyn went on to purchase the rights to *The Children's Hour*, which Hellman would adapt for the screen. This screenplay would prove Hellman's adept ability to negotiate the demands occasioned by the change in medium from stage to film. The screenplay required Hellman to work within the Motion Picture Production Code. In the play version of *The Children's Hour*, the central action focuses on a student's allegation that two of her teachers are lesbians. According to the Production Code, homosexuality could not be depicted or insinuated on screen, so Hellman reworked her story, shifting the child's charge from lesbianism to a love triangle in which the two teachers loved the same man. The final product of these changes was *These Three* (1936).

While Hellman was willing to acknowledge the commercial needs and practical limitations of working in Hollywood, one of her enduring legacies is her outspoken advocacy for the Screen Writers Guild. In 1933, studios had cut writers' wages to stay in operation during the Great Depression (1929–1939). As the 1930s progressed, screen writers had virtually no control over their work, continued to be underpaid, and had little, if any, job security. Hellman had already lost one job in Hollywood for her labor sympathies at MGM, and her relationship with Hammett seems to have only encouraged her to be more politically active. Her accomplishments as a playwright afforded Hellman the opportunity to speak out on behalf of her fellow screenwriters because she was not financially dependent on her work in Hollywood. Studios would not recognize the guild until the end of the decade, but Hellman is recognized as an indispensable voice for writers' creative control and right to fair compensation.

Hellman's next screenplay, the *Dead End* (1937), showcased her ability to distill the essential elements from a text—in this case, the 1935 play of the same name by Sidney Kingsley. Hellman altered characters, their names, and their priority in the story to accommodate various forces ranging from audience expectations to casting decisions, or her own sensibilities. *Dead End* went on to be nominated for four Academy Awards. Hellman maintained her dominant position in Hollywood with an adaptation of her play *The Little Foxes* (1939). The film, released in the summer of 1941 under the same name, earned nine Academy nominations, including Hellman's first for Best Adapted Screenplay.

In 1942, Goldwyn proposed what would be Hellman's final screenplay for him. With America entrenched in the Second World War and allied with the Soviet

Union, the Roosevelt administration looked to Hollywood to bring a new, positive depiction of Russians that would promote the alliance to the public. Goldwyn tasked Hellman with this political project. *The North Star* (1943) was intended to be a documentary before the film's producers determined it should be a commercial film that would be shot entirely on the studio lot. After receiving some 50 pages of revisions from the film's director, Lewis Milestone, and further losing artistic control of a film that would ultimately have four musical numbers, Hellman opted to buy back the rest of her contract with Goldwyn for $30,000. Before the film was released in the fall of 1943, Hellman published her original script to clearly establish the changes that had been made to her work. Hellman made a principled stand for her rights as a writer and never worked with Goldwyn again, though *North Star* would go on to be nominated for six Academy Awards, including for Hellman's writing of an original screenplay.

As World War II came to an end and the Soviet Union reemerged as a national enemy, Hellman began to fall out of popular favor. In 1949 she refused to sign a loyalty oath at the behest of Hollywood producers and was subsequently blacklisted. Hellman came under even greater scrutiny when she was called before the House Committee on Un-American Activities in May 1952. She sent the committee a letter advising that she would answer any questions regarding her involvement in the Communist Party and her own beliefs but refused to speak regarding other people, citing American values of honor and decency. The letter only served to enhance Hellman's reputation as a proponent of civil rights. Hellman would not work in Hollywood again until she was brought on to adapt Horton Foote's play *The Chase* (1952) for film in 1966. *The Chase* was a letdown for Hellman who, disillusioned with both Hollywood and the theater, spent the finals years of her life writing her memoirs and teaching.

Lauren Morrison

See also: Allen, Jay Presson; Davis, Bette

Further Reading

Dick, Bernard F. 1982. *Hellman in Hollywood.* Teaneck, NJ: Farleigh Dickinson University Press.

Kessler-Harris, Alice. 2012. *A Difficult Woman: The Challenging Life and Times of Lillian Hellman.* New York: Bloomsbury Press.

Rollyson, Carl. 1988. *Lillian Hellman: Her Legend and Her Legacy.* New York: St. Martin's Press.

Wright, William. 1986. *Lillian Hellman: The Image, the Woman.* New York: Simon and Schuster.

Jhabvala, Ruth Prawer (1927–2013)

"I was never interested in film. Never. I never even thought of it," said novelist Ruth Prawer Jhabvala (Horne 2012, 136). She never thought of it, of course, until James Ivory and Ismail Merchant, the director and producer pair comprising the now-household name of Merchant Ivory Productions, came literally knocking on her door in India in 1963 to ask if she would consider writing the screenplay for her novel *The Householder* (1960), to which they purchased the rights. Her response: "Well, I've never written a screenplay," was met with "Well, try. We haven't made a feature film before" (Horne 2012, 136). Thus began the threesome's more than four-decade working partnership that boasts over 20 films exploring clashes of culture and class. During her lifetime, Jhabvala considered herself "primarily a novelist, and not a screenwriter" (Horne 2012, 135); nonetheless, within her comfortable role at Merchant Ivory, rarely working with another director, she rose to accomplishment and respectability in the film industry. She wrote and published 12 novels, eight collections of short stories, and 23 screenplays, 14 of which were adaptations of classic or contemporary novels, including two of her own.

Jhabvala's self-taught process in transforming a book into a script was not a science, but it nevertheless engineered organic and cohesive screenplays despite her lack of formal training in any area of film. When adapting for screen, Jhabvala read the chosen novel "once, twice, three times" after already having "read it in the past," and then created scene-by-scene synopses of the entire book (Katz 2000, 4). Then, she set aside the book to rework and reshape the synopses to better fit the narrative conventions of film. Preparing the script, she would "rewrite, strengthen some scenes, throw out a lot that [she had] written" (Katz 2000, 4). Her process involved constant rewriting to work "through many different versions" all the way up to and even during the film shooting; in fact, she thought of viewing the rough cuts "in the editing room as one more chance—the last—to improve the screenplay" and to work the "magic" of revision (McGrath and MacDermott, 2012, 159, 162).

Novelist and screenwriter Ruth Prawer Jhabvala at the home of director James Ivory in Claverack, New York, September 1981. Jhabvala was a Booker Prize–winning novelist and won two Academy Awards as a screenwriter for adaptions of the E. M. Forster novels *A Room with a View* (1985) and *Howards End* (1992). She is noted for her long-time collaboration with Merchant Ivory Productions. (Mikki Ansin/Getty Images)

Turning literary dialogue into film dialogue proved to be tricky, according to Jhabvala, and the hardest part of adapting. To create strong dialogue, she strove to know the characters inside and out; therefore, while re-reading the book she would chart every instance of every quality of every character, such as appearance, turns of speech, integrity, deviousness, and other attributes, "running the whole gamut of human personality and passions" (McGrath and MacDermott 2012, 159). Then, she would chart relationships in the same way, tracing every link between every character. Analyzing these attributes and connections allowed her to write efficient dialogue—conversations that were brief but packed with meaning. She learned that dialogue "can't be the same as on the page in a novel—it must be much more direct and the language has to be simpler" (Katz 2000, 3). She explained what simplifying the dialogue looked like in practice, saying, "I write down what I want my characters to say and then compress that as much as possible into what they need to say" (McGrath and MacDermott, 2012, 161). In other words, Jhabvala always looked for ways to streamline a script down to its necessary components.

Jhabvala's method of scripting was to be "spare in terms of everything but dialogue" (Katz, 2000, 6), though a film dialogue is much thinner than a novel's. She omitted direction in her scripts, arguing, "an actor doesn't want that sort of thing," and gladly left the directing to Ivory (Katz 2000, 6). She focused instead on creating "authentic" reactions, "as though [they] could have happened to me, [as] if my responses had been those of the character in the story" (McDonough 2012, 95). She supplied "the characters, the situations, and the dialogue [. . .] perfectly content to leave everything else to other people" (Pym 2012, 62). That "everything else," she told Susan Bullington Katz (2000), includes "mannerisms and inflections and all sorts of things" that living, breathing actors can do that fictional characters in books cannot; Jhabvala believed that "the actors are in fact doing 50 percent of the work for you" (6). Thus, while she rarely visited the set during a film shooting, she made a habit of consulting actors and considering their suggestions for the script. Though she invited feedback from the cast and crew, Jhabvala avoided reading any literary criticism while creating her own analyses and versions of the story and characters, saying that it was not her business and that it was a distraction from her efforts at authenticity.

Jhabvala earned notoriety, respect, and critical acclaim across communities of both literature and film. To date, she is the only person ever to have received both an Academy Award and a Man Booker Prize. Most of her works did not win awards—her prolific and diverse bibliography nearly makes this impossible—but when a work did attract critical praise, it monopolized many of that year's major awards in the field. Much of Jhabvala's dual acclaim in literature and film arose from her publication of the postcolonial novel *Heat and Dust,* which won the 1975 Booker Prize for the year's best English-language work of fiction published in the UK, as well as two film awards in 1984 for the *Heat and Dust* screenplay: a London Critics Circle Film Award (for Screenwriter of the Year) and British Academy of Film and Television Arts (BAFTA) Award (for Best Adapted Screenplay).

Critical acclaim also came to Jhabvala's screenplay adaptations of a few select 20th-century novels of manners. For example, Jhabvala's screenplay adaptations of Forster's *A Room with a View* (1985) and *Howards End* (1992) led to two Academy Awards for Best Adapted Screenplay and two nominations for the BAFTA Award for Best Adapted Screenplay. Garnering further accolades, *A Room with a View* won the Writers Guild of America award for Best Screenplay Based on Material from Another Medium (1987), and *Howards End* was nominated for a Golden Globe Award for Best Screenplay (1992). In addition, Jhabvala's screenplay of

Ishiguro's *The Remains of the Day* (1993) was enormously successful with critics, being nominated for all three major screenplay awards in 1993—Academy Award, Golden Globe, and BAFTA—but falling short against Steven Zaillian's adaptation of *Schindler's List*. In 1990, Jhabvala's screenplay for *Mr. & Mrs. Bridge* won the Best Screenplay Award from the New York Film Critics Circle. Adapted from two separate novels, *Mr. Bridge* and *Mrs. Bridge*, by Evan S. Connell, *Mr. & Mrs. Bridge* was one of two—the other being *The Golden Bowl*—that she called her favorite and "equally difficult and equally rewarding" (Horne 2012, 139). Jhabvala's accomplishments in screenwriting culminated in a lifetime achievement award, the Laurel Award for Screenwriting Achievement, in 1994, for her outstanding contributions to the profession and industry.

Jhabvala spoke humbly of her scripts, believing them to be "essential" components of films but not having any isolated value; she says of scripts, "It is as though they are waiting for something more, someone else to breathe life into them, as a composer breathes life into a libretto" (McGrath and MacDermott 2012, 162). Consequently, she encouraged the crew and actors to "feel as free with the script as I was with the original novel . . . I want them to take possession of it for themselves" and be liberally creative, to awaken the potential she embedded in her notably stark scripts (McGrath and MacDermott 2012, 162).

She may be best remembered in the screenwriting industry as a woman of prolific talent demonstrated by her four-decades-long relationship as an indispensable third component to the Merchant-Ivory duo. Ultimately, though, her loyal readers and viewers recall her ability to depict conflict and diversity of class and heritage, all within relatable narratives of travel, morality, and marriage.

Karen Beth Strovas

See also: Marion, Frances

Further Reading

Bailur, Jayanti. 1992. *Ruth Prawer Jhabvala: Fiction and Film*. New Delhi: Arnold Publishers.

Crane, Ralph J. 1992. *Ruth Prawer Jhabvala*. New York: Twayne Publishers.

The Golden Bowl, DVD. 2001. Directed by James Ivory. Produced by Ismail Merchant. London: Merchant Ivory Productions.

Heat and Dust, DVD. 1983. Directed by James Ivory. Produced by Ismail Merchant. London, England: Merchant Ivory Productions.

Horne, Philip. 2012. "Conversation with Ruth Prawer Jhabvala (2000)." In *Merchant-Ivory: Interviews*. Edited by Laurence Raw. Jackson: University Press of Mississippi, 135–145.

Jhabvala, Ruth Prawer. *Heat and Dust*. 1975. London: Murray.

Katz, Susan Bullington, ed. 2000. "Ruth Prawer Jhabvala." *Conversations with Screenwriters*. Portsmouth, NH: Heinemann, 1–8.

McDonough, Michael. 2012. "Interview with Ruth Prawer Jhabvala (1986)." In *Merchant-Ivory: Interviews*. Edited by Laurence Raw. Jackson: University Press of Mississippi, 94–100.

McGrath, Declan, and Felim MacDermott. 2012. "Interview with Ruth Prawer Jhabvala (2003)." In *Merchant-Ivory: Interviews*. Edited by Laurence Raw. Jackson: University Press of Mississippi, 158–163.

Pym, John. 2012. "Where Could I Meet Other Screenwriters? A Conversation with Ruth Prawer Jhabvala (1978)." In *Merchant-Ivory: Interviews*. Edited by Laurence Raw. Jackson: University Press of Mississippi, 61–70.

Raw, Laurence. 2012. *Merchant-Ivory: Interviews*.. Jackson: University Press of Mississippi.

Khouri, Callie (1957–)

Carolyn Ann "Callie" Khouri has penned a handful of films, including *Something to Talk About* (1995) and *Divine Secrets of the Ya-Ya Sisterhood* (2002). She served as creator and executive producer of the critically acclaimed television show *Nashville* (2012–). She is also an accomplished director, but history is likely to remember Callie Khouri primarily as the woman behind *Thelma & Louise* (1991), the screenplay which was the first she ever wrote and which won her an Oscar.

Nearly 25 years have passed since *Thelma & Louise* first appeared on the big screen, but the movie continues to strike a chord with critics and audiences alike. It fared well at the box office, but the nation was—and remains—divided as to whether the film is a triumph for women or a dangerous feminist manifesto. Directed by Ridley Scott, *Thelma & Louise* was positively featured on the cover of *Time*, but a *Newsweek* article questioned whether the film was "feminism or fascism?" Rush Limbaugh went so far as to call Khouri a "feminazi" (Konow 2014).

Two moments in the film are at the heart of the controversy. Near the end of the first act, Thelma (Geena Davis) is attacked by a man in a parking lot that she had been dancing and flirting with earlier in the evening. The man attempts to rape her, but he is stopped by Louise (Susan Sarandon) pressing a gun against his neck. The two women are walking away when the man calls after them, saying lewd things. Louise shoots the man in the chest, killing him.

The other highly controversial moment in the film is its iconic ending: Thelma and Louise barreling over the edge of the Grand Canyon together instead of turning themselves in to the cops, who have them surrounded.

At the beginning of the film, Thelma defies her deadbeat husband's wishes and leaves for a two-day vacation with Louise. Khouri's script firmly establishes that both of these women feel caged in their lives and need an escape. They intend for that escape to be temporary, but when Louise pulls the trigger, they begin new lives, and nothing can convince them to return to their former existences.

As Louise says to Thelma late in the film, "You've always been crazy. This is just the first chance you've had to express yourself."

Indeed, the expression of women is at the core of *Thelma & Louise*, and the title characters ultimately express themselves through crime and destruction, as well as their devotion to one another above all else. Male characters as fully realized as Thelma and Louise influence the women's lives—namely Jimmy (Michael Madsen), Louise's boyfriend; J. D. (Brad Pitt), a hitchhiker who has a fling with Thelma; and Hal (Harvey Keitel), the detective who wants to protect both women. But Thelma and Louise repeatedly choose each other—and simultaneously freedom—over these men.

Khouri felt strongly about the ending and insisted that it not change. She never intended for the ending to be seen as a suicide, but rather as a triumph. That is why audiences do not see the car crash into the canyon, but instead see it freeze in midair before being thrown into a montage of happy moments from earlier in the film. As Khouri puts it, "All the way through I was really writing towards the ending—I remember knowing that the image was going to be really spectacular. Thelma and Louise have outgrown the world, they are two women who have no place in it" (Francke 1994, 131).

Whether or not audiences approved of or were threatened by Thelma and Louise's choices, they were certainly stunned to see a crime film and, by many measures, a comedy with two female leads. Geena Davis told *The New York Times* that she was thrilled to be cast because, "It's not often you see parts for two fully realized women characters" (Konow 2014).

Indeed, to this day, only a fraction of studio films each year feature strong female characters and even fewer pass the infamous Bechdel test, which requires that a film feature (1) at least two female characters who (2) talk to each other about (3) something other than a man.

That is part of the reason Khouri wrote the script. At the time, she was working as a producer on music videos, which frequently featured women as props. Khouri reportedly felt that writing the script might help balance her karma.

The idea for *Thelma & Louise* came to Khouri all at once. She knew she wanted to write a movie about two women who go on a crime spree. Over the following four months, she mulled over the idea and figured out how two ordinary women might find themselves in such an extraordinary situation. She then wrote the script longhand, sticking closely to the standard three-act structure found in most feature films. While many screenwriters find the writing process stressful, Khouri claims that writing *Thelma & Louise* was the most fun she ever had in her life.

When the movie was ultimately made, she won the Academy Award for Best Original Screenplay. At the time of writing, only two other women have won the award since.

Khouri realizes that her fast success has given aspiring screenwriters false hope that they can achieve the same accolades on their first attempt. Khouri once said,

> I feel like I owe [aspiring writers] at least the warning that they are picking maybe the hardest thing there is to do in the business. . . . It doesn't matter anymore how good you are. In some ways, it never really did. Bad movies get made as often as good ones, but so few movies get made now, period. . . . I was very lucky because Ridley really wanted to tell [*Thelma & Louise*]. He wanted to make the movie I wanted to make. But oftentimes that's not the case at all. (Rudder 2011)

Angela Bourassa

Further Reading

Francke, Lizzie. 1994. *Script Girls: Women Screenwriters in Hollywood.* London: British Film Institute.

Khouri, Callie. 1990. "Thelma & Louise—Shooting Script." *Daily Script*, June 15. http://www.dailyscript.com/scripts/thelmaandlouise.html

Konow, David. 2014. "I Wouldn't Send Any Impressionable Young Woman I Know to See Thelma and Louise." *Creative Screenwriting Magazine*, December 26. https://creativescreenwriting.com/i-wouldnt-send-any-impressionable-young-woman-i-know-to-see-thelma-and-louise

Lanouette, Jennine. 2012. "An In-Depth Look at the Screenplay Structure of Thelma & Louise." *Screentakes*. https://www.screentakes.com/thelma-louise-sample-chapter

Rudder, Randy. 2011. "20th Anniversary Edition: Callie Khouri Looks Back on Thelma & Louise" *Script Magazine*, July 22. http://www.scriptmag.com/features/20th-anniversary-edition-callie-khouri-looks-back-on-thelma-louise

Loos, Anita (1888–1981)

Anita Loos wrote more than 150 screenplays in over 30 years, spanning both the silent film era and the golden age of Hollywood in the 1930s and 1940s, and was considered one of the most productive and esteemed film writers of her day. In recalling her work, Loos remembered that she viewed screenplays "as crossword puzzles—frustrating when they failed, but rewarding when dramatic unities began to unfold which indicated they were going to work out" (Loos 1966, 237). Loos also pushed the use of intertitles (also known as title cards), arguing that they could be used "to furnish not just expository information, but also more poetic musings" (Stamp 2015, 25).

Born Corinne Anita Loos in Sissons, California, Loos was a child actress before beginning to write story ideas—or "scenarios," as they were known at the time—for films in 1912. For the first two years of her career, Loos, like many early screenwriters, worked from home, selling more than 50 stories to Hollywood studios. Her first screenplay to be made into a movie was *The New York Hat* (1912), starring Mary Pickford and Lionel Barrymore. By 1914, Loos was living in Hollywood and writing scenarios, eager to impress film director D. W. (David Wark) Griffith. Her scenarios from this period are written as three- to five-page stories; they were filed away at the studio, waiting to be used for films. Loos also provided intertitles for a few Griffith projects, including *Intolerance: Love's Struggle throughout the Ages* (1916).

Loos began making films with Broadway director John Emerson and stage actor Douglas Fairbanks during this period. Their first film together, *His Picture in the Papers* (1916), began a prolific and successful partnership. This film demonstrated Loos's interest in utilizing intertitles. In all of their films with Fairbanks, Emerson shared Loos's writing credit; however, his name appears first. By the mid-1910s, Loos already had established the work pattern she continued throughout her life, rising at five o'clock in the morning to write for several hours on a legal pad, while lying on her chaise lounge at the Hollywood Hotel. In the afternoons, she would meet with Fairbanks in his dressing room and read her script aloud to the rest of the team. Emerson and Loos became celebrities in their own right, alongside their handsome star, thanks to Emerson's publicity work, including multipage spreads in trade magazines with staged photographs.

After splitting with Fairbanks, Emerson and Loos, now romantically involved, moved to New York to create "John Emerson-Anita Loos Productions." Loos's screenplays during this period, like others being written at the same time, changed from short stories to detailed scenarios of about 100 pages, containing script, scenery, costume ideas, and stage directions. As studios became more organized and professionalized, scenario writing did too. Trade publications and books gave advice to would-be screenwriters. Emerson and Loos capitalized on this interest by publishing two works of their own, although some experts argue that *How to Write Photoplays* (1919) and *Breaking into the Movies* (1921) must have been ghostwritten because their style does not match anything else written by Loos and because Emerson was a writer in name only. Early in the 1920s, Associated First National Pictures head Joseph M. Schenck hired Loos and Emerson to make six films for actress Constance Talmadge. Later that decade, Loos stopped creating screenplays; however, she continued writing, including the novel that became her signature: *Gentlemen Prefer Blondes* (1925).

Loos returned to Hollywood and screenwriting in 1931 to work at Metro-Goldwyn-Mayer (MGM) on *The Redheaded Woman*, starring Jean Harlow. During Loos's time away from the film industry, the advent of sound arrived, and there was no more call for Loos's witty intertitles. Now she could fully develop her scripts, replete with double entendres designed to sneak by the censors. *Redheaded Woman* (1932) is a great example of Loos's successful transition to sound. Irving Thalberg, MGM's production chief, held Loos in such high regard that he encouraged her to follow her script for *Redheaded Woman* through production, which was highly unusual at the time. Thalberg made MGM an especially welcoming place for women screenwriters making "women's films" during that decade due to his belief that women wrote better for female actors and would provide more authentic scripts (Francke 1994, 34–35). Following the film's highly successful release in 1932, Emerson followed Loos west and demanded a job of his own. Thalberg was not interested in hiring Emerson, so Loos arranged for her salary, $2,000 a week, to be split between them so he could direct the films she wrote. In addition to writing her own scripts, she worked on other scripts and served as line producer, with very little credit or pay for either. A few years later, Loos collaborated with Robert "Hoppy" Hopkins on *San Francisco* (1936). The film received Academy Award nominations for both Best Picture and Best Original Story in 1936. While there is no doubt that Loos wrote the screenplay, only Hopkins appeared in the credits and, ultimately, took home the Oscar.

When Thalberg died in September 1938, Loos and Emerson left MGM and went to work for Sam Goldwyn. Much to Loos's dismay, she learned that per the contract Emerson signed on her behalf, she now made half the salary she received previously and that her husband both pocketed the $100,000 signing bonus and arranged for annuities to flow directly to him.

By February 1938, Loos had gotten herself out of her contract with Sam Goldwyn and returned to MGM, where she happily began work on *The Women* (1939). The original play, written by Clare Booth, contained more than 100 lines that could not pass the censors. Not only did Loos adjust the dialogue to allow the movie to be released, she also shifted the slant of the film, making it less bitter and more a celebration of women. The film, directed by another of Loos's favorites, George Cukor, starred a veritable who's who of Hollywood leading ladies: Norma Shearer,

Joan Crawford, Rosalind Russell, and Paulette Goddard. Cukor insisted Loos attend the filming; she also wrote and edited the trailers for the film.

In August 1943, MGM told Loos that they would not be renewing her contract. She continued to do some freelance work, but her career as a screenwriter was virtually over. Loos came back to adapt her best-selling novel for both the stage and screen. She remained a Hollywood icon for the rest of her life, celebrated on both coasts for her writing talent, ready wit, and fashion sense.

Rebekah A. Crowe

See also: Mathis, June; Pickford, Mary

Further Reading

Beauchamp, Cari. 1998. *Without Lying Down: Frances Marion and the Powerful Women of Early Hollywood.* Berkeley: University of California Press.

Francke, Lizzie. 1994. *Script Girls: Women Screenwriters in Hollywood.* London: British Film Institute.

Loos, Anita. 1966. *A Girl Like I.* New York: Viking Press.

Ruvoli, JoAnne. 2013. "Anita Loos." In *Women Film Pioneers Project.* Edited by Jane Gaines, Radha Vatsal, and Monica Dall'Asta. Center for Digital Research and Scholarship. New York: Columbia University Libraries. https://wfpp.cdrs.columbia.edu/pioneer/ccp-anita-loos

Stamp, Shelley. 2015. *Lois Weber in Early Hollywood.* Berkeley: University of California Press.

Marion, Frances (1888–1973)

Frances Marion (birth name Marion Benson Owens) was born in San Francisco to Len Douglas Owens and Minnie Benson Hall. She is one of the first and most renowned Hollywood screenwriters—male or female—of the 20th century. Marion broke multiple barriers for women working in film, and for women in general. Her work also accomplished many "firsts" for a screenwriter in the industry. Marion was one of the first (and still one of the only) screenwriters to write over 300 film scripts over the course of her career. Additionally, she was the first screenwriter to win two Oscars; only 16 women have won Oscars for screenwriting, and the only other female screenwriter to win two Oscars is Ruth Prawer Jhabvala, who won for *Howards End* in 1993 and *A Room with a View* in 1987. Marion's Oscars were for *The Big House* in 1930 and for *The Champ* in 1932. She was also nominated for *The Prize Fighter and the Lady* in 1933. Marion served as the vice president and only woman on the first board of directors of the Screen Writers Guild. She was also the first woman to be paid $3,000 per week (starting in 1925) for her work as a screenwriter for MGM. While her accomplishments in Hollywood are numerous and varied, it is important to note that Marion's life was dedicated to her craft, and it is her significant contributions to the film industry that make her one of the most important figures in American film history.

Marion wrote both adapted and original screenplays, and her career can be broken up into four relatively distinct periods. Based on chronology and the focus of her work at a given time, she was active in Hollywood from roughly 1915 to 1946.

Film director and screenwriter Frances Marion (right), pictured next to actress Mary Pickford on the set of the United Artists war drama *The Love Light* (1921), on December 28, 1920. Marion won two Academy Awards for screenwriting and is considered one of the most renowned female screenwriters of the 20th century. She was both prolific and skilled as a writer, noted for defining the careers of many star actors and contributing substantially to the success of MGM at the time. (General Photographic Agency/Getty Images)

Each "period" of Marion's career will be briefly discussed to give a more complex and comprehensive examination of her work and highlight her unique place in film history.

The first period of Marion's career could be considered her time spent as a journalist (she covered women's contributions to the war effort on the front lines of World War I) and photographer, as well as her work in the early years of silent cinema. In 1915, Marion began her career in film as an actress and apprentice screenwriter/general assistant under the pioneer film director-producer Lois Weber. Under Weber, Marion worked on/acted in *A Girl of Yesterday* (1915). Marion was often remarked as being an attractive women—she even worked as print model for the photographer Arnold Genthe—where she learned about the art of layouts and experimented with color film. After several years of training under Weber, Marion was soon under contract with MGM.

The second period of Marion's career could be considered her "golden age" in Hollywood. This partly coincided with Hollywood's golden age, often remarked as the late 1920s to the early 1960s with the creation and implementation of the Motion Picture Production Code. During this period, Marion was particularly adept at adapting novels and plays for the screen, such as *Stella Dallas* (1925) and *The Scarlet Letter* (1926). Both of these films feature strong female leads and target female viewers, a trend that can be seen in many of the films across her body of work. While Marion's films covered a wide range of genres and topics, the majority of Marion's films were "star vehicles" (films written or produced for a specific star) written for her litany of friends, a countless list of silent film era and Classical Hollywood era A-list stars. For example, Marion wrote films for stars including Gary Cooper, Rudolph Valentino, Clark Gable, and Marie Dressler. As many scholars and critics have pointed out, Marion's friends and close personal relationships with other stars and women in the industry in particular are part of what makes her career so unique and what primarily contributed to her long-term success as a screenwriter.

Perhaps most notably, scholars and critics have often discussed the relationship between Marion and Mary Pickford, as they developed a strong and lucrative partnership for nearly two decades. Marion wrote films for Pickford throughout the late 1910s and early 1920s, including *The Poor Little Rich Girl* (1917), *Rebecca of Sunnybrook Farm* (1917), *The Little Princess* (1917), *Stella Marris* (1918), and *Pollyanna* (1920). Marion and Pickford's partnership initiated a new generic "formula" within these films, which can be described as adding slapstick comedy to drama. These films also cultivated Pickford's star image as the eternally "spunky little girl . . . despite the fact that she was in her late twenties" when the two of them were working together (Benjamin 2017). Marion also directed several films during this period. Marion's three directing credits are *The Love Light* (which also starred Pickford), *Just around the Corner* (both were released in 1921), and *The Song of Love* in 1923 (co-directed by Chester M. Franklin).

With the development of sound in the late 1920s, Pickford's career began to decline, and Marion began to work on projects for other stars such as Greta Garbo and Marion Davies. During this period, Marion penned the screenplay for *Anna Christie* (1930), which earned Garbo an Oscar nomination for Best Actress and fundamentally launched her career in the sound era.

The "third period" of Marion's career could be considered her final years in Hollywood. After the untimely death of her close friend and boss, MGM producer Irving Thalberg, in 1936, Marion's influence and career as a screenwriter began to wane. As times continued to develop and change in Hollywood, Marion's interest in screenwriting also began to diminish, and she decided to leave Hollywood in 1946. One of Marion's final film credits during this period is 1945's *Molly and Me*, which was based on her 1937 novel, *Molly, Bless Her.*

This leads to the "fourth period" of Marion's career, post-Hollywood (1946–1973 and beyond). After spending three decades as one of the highest-paid screenwriters in Hollywood, Marion went on to have success as an author of several stage plays and novels, including her memoir, *Off with Their Heads*! (1972), her final work before her death. This period could also be considered her "rebirth" in the work of screenwriters and filmmakers who came after her. Several films, such as *The Clown* in 1956 and the remake of *The Champ* in 1979, can be seen as Marion's work being adapted and shared with new generations of audiences, even though she had no direct involvement with such projects. Perhaps writers will continue to revitalize Marion's work by adapting and evolving her scripts/stories in infinitely new and interesting ways.

Marion worked in nearly every facet of Hollywood—she was as an actress, writer, director, and producer (Marion is credited with producing *The Ten Commandments* in 1923 and *Simon the Jester* in 1925). While this level of involvement in production for women in Hollywood is somewhat rarer today, Marion was working in Hollywood at a time when women were not only allowed but welcomed in the industry, and it was their collaboration and solidarity that led to such long and prosperous careers (Beauchamp 1998, 12). Marion began her career in Hollywood over 100 years ago, and very few women (arguably no woman) in the industry have been able to match the achievements of her work. For all of her accomplishments as a writer, Marion is a reminder (or proof) of what is possible for future female screenwriters in the industry.

Stephanie Oliver

See also: Garbo, Greta; Jhabvala, Ruth Prawer; Pickford, Mary; Weber, Lois

Further Reading

Beauchamp, Cari. 1998. *Without Lying Down: Frances Marion and the Powerful Women of Early Hollywood.* Berkeley: University of California Press.

Benjamin, Melanie. 2017. "How Frances Marion and Mary Pickford Conquered Hollywood." *Literary Hub*, December 13. https://lithub.com/how-frances-marion-and-mary-pickford-conquered-hollywood

Bowerman, Jeanne Veillette. 2018. "International Women's Day: Frances Marion—The Original Power-Woman of Hollywood." *Script*, March 8. http://www.scriptmag.com/features/writer-profiles/international-womens-day-frances-marion-the-original-power-woman-of-hollywood

Mathis, June (1887–1927)

In the 1920s, June Mathis was one of the most powerful and prolific women in the American film industry. As a screenwriter behind 114 films and the first female executive for Metro/MGM studios, Mathis notably shaped the career of Rudolph Valentino, among others, and was part of a small cohort of women, like Frances Marion and Anita Loos, who wielded unprecedented power during the silent film era.

June Mathis (born June Beulah Hughes) was born in Leadville, Colorado. She attended school in Salt Lake City and San Francisco. Though early biographies claimed that she had a performance lineage, scholar Thomas J. Slater discovered that her parents were not associated with entertainment. Slater is also responsible for confirming Mathis's birth year. Her birth year has been published as 1892 and 1889. However, Slater asserts her date of birth was January 23, 1887. As a teen in San Francisco, Mathis began performing, first in vaudeville and then in Broadway for a total of 13 years. Most notably, she toured with actor and female impersonator, Julian Eltinge.

To pursue her dream of being a screenwriter, Mathis and her widowed mother moved to New York City. There, she entered screenwriting competitions that led to job offers. Her first script was for a film called *House of Tears* (1915), which was directed by Edwin Carewe. According to Thomas J. Slater, Mathis was one of the first scenarists to include stage directions and setting descriptions in her scripts—a true screenwriter who not only envisioned the plot and dialogue of the film but the style and look of it as well.

By 1918, Mathis had a contract with Metro Studios, and shortly thereafter she moved to Hollywood. After a year, Mathis was promoted to chief of Metro's Scenario Department—the first female film executive ever. Mathis had control and wielded great influence over casting, director choices, script preparation and edits, and many other aspects of production. Mathis was 27 at the time.

Mathis is best known for her collaborations with actor Rudolph Valentino. In 1921, Mathis adapted the Vicente Blasco Ibáñez novel *The Four Horsemen of the Apocalypse*. She was pivotal in casting then-unknown actor Rudolph Valentino in the starring role. In the film, Mathis presents Valentino as a melodramatic, sensitive hero, whose persona matched the post-war period. The Rex Ingram–directed film was a hit, grossing $4.5 million domestically in its initial run in theaters, and Mathis became highly sought after. Though Valentino was courted by several other studios after the film, Mathis convinced him to stay at Metro. Eventually, when Valentino became unhappy with his salary for his follow-up, *The Conquering Power* (1921), and he was upset by how much of his role had ended up on the cutting room floor, he moved studios to Famous Players-Lasky. Mathis soon followed.

In 1922, Mathis penned another Valentino hit, *Blood and Sand*. The film (along with smaller Valentino vehicles *Camille* [1921] and *The Conquering Power*) proved Valentino's star power. Mathis wrote roles that not only took advantage of Valentino's exotic good looks but also softened his sexuality with backstories filled with loss and loneliness. In this way, she was able to craft a male star persona that was not only sympathetic for women but seemingly understood what appealed to women. Mathis's scripts redefined masculinity and exposed patriarchy's fragility.

Mathis soon moved to Goldwyn, where she also had a great degree of creative agency. At Goldwyn, Mathis was involved in two large-scale productions. First, Mathis supervised the making of Erich von Stroheim's *Greed* (1924), an adaptation of Frank Norris's *McTeague*. Stroheim was incredibly ambitious, opting to film on location in the desert and shooting over 85 hours of footage. In an effort to appease the studio, Stroheim cut down the originally 10-hour-long movie to 6 hours. Goldwyn was not pleased, and Ingram stepped in and cut the film down to 4.5 hours. The film was cut further. Though eventually the final cut came in at 2.5 hours, the film was sorely lacking in continuity and narrative coherence. Though Mathis is credited as the editor of the film (alongside Joseph W. Farnham), it is unclear how much creative control Mathis had in that final cut. However, she was largely blamed for tarnishing von Stroheim's potential epic masterpiece.

That same year, Mathis was also involved in the making of *Ben-Hur* (1925). Mathis lobbied for George Walsh to play the lead and Charles Brabin to direct. She was also responsible for the film shooting on location in Italy. Despite championing Brabin, when Mathis arrived on set, Brabin refused to collaborate and only allowed her superficial script approvals (regardless of the fact that she was the mediator between the production and the studio). Furthermore, production slowed due to Italian labor disputes and political turmoil. There were also issues in the cast and crew, and in one particularly harrowing incident, a stuntperson was killed while filming a chariot race after one of the wheels came apart.

During this time, Metro, Goldwyn, and producer Louis B. Mayer were making plans to merge their studios. The newly formed Metro-Goldwyn-Mayer (MGM) did not want their first feature to be a disaster. The studio moved production back to California and appointed studio head, Louis B. Mayer, promptly fired Mathis, Brabin, and Walsh. Ramon Novarro eventually earned the titular role, and Fred Niblo took over as director. The film was plagued with unforeseen circumstances such as these, which also added to the costliness of the production. Mathis was blamed directly for the lackluster cast and the production issues, and eventually attempted to disassociate herself from the film altogether. Despite the professional setbacks in Italy, while filming Mathis met Italian cameraman, Sylvano Balboni. The two fell in love, returned to America, and were married in December 1924.

Mathis was not unemployed for long. She was quickly hired by First National as editorial director, where she worked on several films for actress Colleen Moore such as *Sally* (1925), *The Desert Flower* (1925), and *Irene* (1926). She remained at First National for two years.

In 1926, Mathis was voted the third most important woman in the film industry by the Western Association of Motion Picture Advertisers (WAMPAS), behind only Mary Pickford and Norma Talmadge. This was a great achievement, especially in light of how the studios attempted to blame her for the failures of *Greed* and *Ben-Hur*.

In 1927, Mathis signed with United Artists and made *The Masked Woman*, directed by her husband and for which she earned her final credit as screenwriter. It is unclear under what circumstances or reasons she had for leaving United Artists, but she returned to MGM as a freelancer in 1927. She is credited as continuity editor for *The Magic Flame* (1927), directed by Henry King and starring Ronald Colman. The five-reel film earned cinematographer George Barnes the first ever nomination for Best Cinematography. Both films are assumed lost.

Mathis died July 26, 1927, at the age of 40 of a heart attack, following health complications. Her dramatic death, which took place while attending a performance of *The Squall*, was covered by trade papers and newspapers. Her final words were reported to be "Mother, I'm dying!" Mathis's remains are in a crypt near Rudolph Valentino at the Hollywood Forever Cemetery.

Mathis, like many women contributing to film of this era, remains under-researched. Furthermore, it is difficult to assess the totality of her contributions to films since she (and several writers) is credited under "story by," "adaptation by," "continuity by," or "editorial supervision by" and variations of such. According to the Women Pioneers Project, correspondence found in the Warner Bros. Archive at the University of Southern California suggests there may be many more unproduced scripts and script drafts by Mathis that have not yet been found.

Diana E. Martinez

See also: Loos, Anita; Pickford, Mary; Talmadge, Norma

Further Reading

Hall, Gladys, and Adele Whitely Fletcher. 1923. "We Discovered Who Discovered Valentino." *Motion Picture Magazine*, April 25: 20–22, 93–95.

Slater, Thomas J. 1998. "June Mathis's Classified: One Woman's Response to Modernism," *Journal of Film and Video* 50(2): 3–14.

Slater, Thomas J. 2008. "June Mathis's The Legion of Death (1918): Melodrama and the Realities of Women in World War I," *Women's Studies* 37(1): 833–844.

Slater, Thomas J. 2010. "June Mathis's Valentino Scripts: Images of Male 'Becoming' after the Great War," *Cinema Journal* 50(1): 99–120.

Sound

Introduction

Audiences automatically tend to privilege the visuals of cinema over the auditory experience it offers, which is understandable since our sense of sound often takes a backseat to our visual attentions in everyday life. Film sound can be difficult to study and analyze because it is not easily observable. It can feel natural to think of it as a secondary component to a movie when, in fact, it is an absolutely essential part of what makes a film, a film.

The movies have never truly been without sound. The label given to the film movement known as the silent era (i.e., before synchronous sound) is perhaps misleading, since films of that time were always screened with either a phonograph or live musical accompaniment. Title cards (or intertitles) were used in lieu of spoken dialogue, and expository intertitles were used to supplement the narrative when the visuals were not able to fully communicate the narrative. The great transition from silent cinema to the "talkies" is attributed to *The Jazz Singer* in 1927, which contained instances of synchronized sound that was recorded on set. Although the transition was gradual, it necessitated the rapid advancement of many film technologies, and no part of the industry was left unaffected. It ended the careers of many famous silent movie stars who had thick accents that were easily concealed (such as Norma Talmadge) and ushered in major literary figures such as William Faulkner and Nathanael West, who knew how to write dialogue.

Great sound design is an incredibly powerful film technique that shapes how we interpret the images and story by creating atmosphere and providing audiences with emotional cues. Soundtracks can be as complicated as the carefully fabricated images that appear on screen, and audiences have come to recognize sound conventions such as the classic "Wilhelm scream" just as readily as they do visual conventions. A soundtrack is constructed separately from the film's visuals, and is generally composed of three parts: the dialogue, sound effects, and music. There is a very long list of specific jobs involving sound on a feature film, but in general the sound editor is responsible for gathering all the sound created and recorded for the film (some sounds are recorded on set, but others must be created from scratch by technicians in post-production). The sound mixer then combines and balances the levels for all the sounds in preparation for the final soundtrack. The sound editing and mixing categories can incorporate several distinct jobs depending on how large a production is. There is an art to crafting film sound, and nothing you hear in a film should be thought of as "accidental."

Although Kay Rose was the first woman to receive a Special Achievement Academy Award in the category of Best Sound Editing for *The River* in 1984, it wasn't until 2016 that sound editor Mildred Iatrou Morgan and sound mixer Ai-Ling Lee became the first female team ever Oscar-nominated for Best Sound for their work on *La La Land* (2016).

Laura L. S. Bauer

Adair, Deb (1966–)

The sound mixer Deb Adair has significantly shaped the characteristic audio track of animated television series of the 1990s and blockbuster movies since the 2000s. While superheroes and animation dominate her repertoire, she is also the re-recording mixer of short films and remains open to style and genre.

Sound mixer Deb Adair sitting in the Howard Hawks Dubbing Theatre at Fox Studios. Adair was nominated for an Academy Award for Best Achievement in Sound Mixing for the film *Moneyball* (2011), and has won three Daytime Emmy Awards for Outstanding Sound Mixing—Special Class for her work on the *Aladdin* franchise (1995–1996) and the television series *Timon & Pumbaa* (1997). (Photo by Luke Schwarzweller)

Deb Adair received her bachelor's degree in film production from Syracuse University and began her work in the music recording industry in Nashville before moving to Los Angeles where she is in charge of sound mixing and editing for the film industry.

As a re-recording mixer she is responsible for working with all the sound elements of a film in order to create the final soundtrack. The sonic information is recorded separately and contributes considerably to the way audiences understand the images. This involves a range of tasks from the first recording of dialogues and sounds to the editing and mixing of the sounds to achieve a smooth effect with the visual images. Often a number of sounds need to be played simultaneously, voices and background sounds, for example, or music and weather sounds. Each sound has to be measured and included in exactly the right doses to achieve the desired (emotional) effects. Sound is also crucial in linking scenes and events and thus requires beside the technical know-how artistic understanding and creativity.

During the 1990s, the beginning of the digital age for sound effects, Deb Adair recorded and edited the dialogue for three episodes of the animated television series *The Legend of Prince Valiant* (1992) and for multiple episodes between 1991 and 1994 of the long-running series *Teenage Mutant Ninja Turtles* (1987–1996). In the early years of her career, she had been responsible for recording the sound in the best possible quality to be used later in the post-production mixing process. While sticking with the genre of animated television series, Adair was increasingly assigned the position of re-recording mixer. When creating the final version of a soundtrack for film and television, the provided noises and voices have to be adjusted, cut, and edited to create the desired final effect for sonic balance. With its magical setting, flying carpets and frequent monster/ghost invasions, the soundscape of the animated Disney television series *Aladdin* (1994–1995) offered a larger variety and interesting complexity that extended Adair's expertise beyond the superhero genre. Superhero and fantasy genres allow for more creativity when it comes to sound. As the narratives play with superpowers and surreal twists, characters, and effects, sound more than vision, has to draw the viewer convincingly into the strange worlds of the imagination.

Her work for *Aladdin* earned her two Emmy Awards for Outstanding Sound Mixing (1994 and 1995). After *Aladdin*, Adair worked as the sound mixer for the Disney series *Timon and Pumbaa* (1995–1996), for which she achieved another Emmy Award in 1995. More animated Disney and superhero programs followed (such as *Spawn* and *101 Dalmatians: The Series* in 1997) before Adair finished the decade with the blockbuster animated movie *South Park: Bigger, Longer & Uncut* (1999) for which she supervised the sound editing and appears in a small voice role (the woman in the theater). The film was nominated for the Golden Reel Award for the best sound editing.

During the 2000s, Adair focused on blockbuster movies instead of television series. In 2004 she mixed the sound for *The Bourne Supremacy,* and in 2011 her work for *Moneyball* earned her a nomination for an Academy Award for the Best Achievement in Sound Mixing (while *Moneyball* did not win the Oscar, the Cinema Audio Society rewarded the movie with its CAS Award for the Best Sound Editing). Also in the blockbuster category, Adair remained faithful to the superhero genre doing the re-recording mixing of *The Amazing Spider-Man* (2012) and

The Amazing Spider-Man 2 (2014), as well as to the category of animation working as the re-recording mixer for *The Emoji Movie* (2017) and *Smurfs: The Lost Village* (2017), which allowed her to draw on her animation career establishing a repertoire of characteristic sounds that link those works to the tradition of comic book onomatopoetic art.

Andrea Zittlau

Further Reading

David Bordwell, Jeff Smith, and Kristin Thompson, eds. 2017. "Sound in the Cinema." In *Film Art. An Introduction*. 11th ed. New York: McGraw-Hill.

Baker Landers, Karen (Unknown–)

Southern California native Karen Baker Landers is one of the foremost sound editors in the entertainment industry. She has worked on such notable films as *Hannibal* (2001), *The Bourne Identity* (2002), *The Bourne Supremacy* (2004), and *The Bourne Ultimatum* (2007), for which she and her collaborators won the Academy Award for Best Sound Editing, the British Academy of Film and Television Arts (BAFTA) Award for Best Sound, and the Hollywood Professional Association (HPA) Award for Outstanding Audio Post in a Feature Film, as well as *Green Lantern* (2011), for which she won the HPA Award for Outstanding Sound in a Feature Film, *The Bourne Legacy* (2012), *Skyfall* (2012), for which she won her second Academy Award, *Spectre* (2015), and *xXx: Return of Xander Cage* (2017), among others. Baker Landers's interest in sound started early in her childhood when she began telling stories solely with the use of sound effects. Her emphasis on storytelling and the ability of sound to connect with the emotions of listeners has continued as a fundamental drive in her creative process. While she often works alone on major projects, she has collaborated with fellow sound editor Per Hallberg for more than three decades. The pair shared the aforementioned Academy Awards, making Baker Landers the first woman in history to win two Academy Awards for Best Sound Editing.

Baker Landers's fascination with sound first emerged when she was just 11 years old. She explains, "When I was very young, my parents bought me a handheld tape recorder, and I would walk around the house and record sounds and try to tell stories with just sound. I'd see if anybody in my family could figure out what story I was telling" (Variety Staff 2008). This penchant for sound editing grew when sound in films caught her attention. Watching *Rocky* (1976) proved pivotal; it was "the first and last film where [she] ever stood up in the theater and cheered," and it urged her to think about pursuing sound editing professionally (Variety Staff 2008). Baker Landers went on to study film at California State University, Long Beach (CSULB). While still a student, she stood out to sound designers Richard Anderson and Mark Mangini, and they invited her onto their team as an intern. Her originality and innovative spirit were already apparent during these years. In a recent interview, Baker Landers recounts, "For my first task, Richard asked me to find a ratchety sound, for hoisting a bucket out of the water on a pulley, for *Goonies* (1985). I went to a junk store and found an old eggbeater and brought it back to them" (Kaufman n.d.).

In the early years of her career, Baker Landers met Per Hallberg when they were both working as assistants, and they began a professional collaboration that would continue for more than 30 years. One of her favorite films the two worked on together was *Ray* (2004), for which they won the BAFTA Award for Best Sound. She explains how the project required a subtler touch than films with explosions or fight scenes, and it seemed to call for closer attention to what one would hear, as opposed to what one would see (Kaufman n.d.). In order to more accurately depict soundscapes that would highlight how Ray Charles, a blind man, might have perceived sound, Baker Landers sought to develop a deeper understanding of his personal experience. She would close her eyes and walk down streets with her husband as her guide. This influenced her creative process and resulted in soundscapes that suggested distinct points of view.

Supervising sound editor Karen Baker Landers attends the Academy of Motion Picture Arts and Sciences's celebration of the art of motion picture sound at the Samuel Goldwyn Theater on March 8, 2008, in Beverly Hills, California. Baker Landers is a two-time Academy Award-winning sound editor, a two-time British Academy of Film and Television Arts (BAFTA) winner, and has won three Golden Reel Awards for sound editing from the Motion Picture Sound Editors. She collaborates frequently with award-winning sound editor Per Hallberg. (Charley Gallay/Getty Images)

Although she often supervises sound editing alone, Baker Landers continues to collaborate with Hallberg as opportunities arise. Hallberg believes one important factor that has led to their success is that they "fight more than most people" (Variety Staff 2017). Baker Landers agrees, saying, "We have similarities, but we're really opposite in a lot of areas, which is good." And, whereas Hallberg seems to emphasize practicality, Baker Landers focuses more on eliciting emotional responses. She explains, "We read the script and try to tell the story of the film through sound. It's painting with sound. It's finding that emotion." In fact, one of the reasons she is so interested in sound editing is because sound connects to emotions. When watching scenes and considering sound, she often asks, "How can we get the most emotion out of this?" (Variety 2017). Baker Landers also believes she and Hallberg are successful as a team because of their friendship and honest communication (Kaufman 2011). She states, "There's complete trust. If I'm questioning how something sounds, Per will be honest, and I need that. I may disagree with him, but it's a relationship that's built on trust and respect" (Farinella 2008). Baker Landers now serves as supervising sound editor at Formosa Group. In 2014, she established the Karen Baker Landers Endowment at her alma mater, CSULB, to offer scholarship opportunities to students in the Department of Film and Electronic Arts.

Breena L. Loraine

Further Reading

Beach Scholarships. n.d. "Karen Baker Landers." Accessed March 18, 2018. https://csulb.academicworks.com/donors/karen-baker-landers

Daley, Dan. 2004. "Sound Design Reveals a Blind Man's POV." *Studio Daily*, November 1. http://www.studiodaily.com/2004/11/sound-design-reveals-a-blind-mana%C2%A2aeas-pov

Farinella, David John. 2008. "Karen Baker Landers & Per Hallberg: Sound Editing Partners Powered by Big Year." *Variety*, January 7. http://variety.com/2008/film/awards/karen-baker-landers-per-hallberg-1117978603

Formosa Group. n.d. "Karen Baker Landers: Supervising Sound Editor." Accessed March 18, 2018. http://formosagroup.com/features/karen-baker-landers-profile

Giardina, Carolyn. 2013. "Oscar-Winning Sound Editors Per Hallberg, Karen Baker Landers Joining Formosa Group." *Hollywood Reporter*, October 16. https://www.hollywoodreporter.com/behind-screen/oscar-winning-sound-editors-hallberg-649052

Goldman, Michael. 2015. "Podcast: Supervising Sound Editors Per Hallberg and Karen Baker Landers on *Spectre*." Studio Daily, December 2. http://www.studiodaily.com/2015/12/sound-editors-per-hallberg-karen-baker-landers-spectre

Kaufman, Debra. 2011. "Karen Baker Landers and Per Hallberg: Supervising Sound Editors." Creative Cow. https://library.creativecow.net/article.php?author_folder=kaufman_debra&article_folder=Soundelux-Karen-Baker-Landers-Per-Hallberg&page=1

Variety Staff. 2008. "Karen Baker Landers—Women's Impact Report: Specialists." *Variety*, July 30. http://variety.com/2008/scene/markets-festivals/karen-baker-landers-1117989787

Variety Staff. 2017. "Karen Baker Landers and Per Hallberg: Sound Editors Argue Their Way to Their Art." *Variety*. Accessed March 18, 2018. http://variety.com/video/karen-baker-landers-per-hallberg-art-of-sound

Behlmer, Anna (1961–)

During her career, sound mixer Anna Behlmer has worked on over 150 projects. Her contributions span across multiple genres. She can capture the action of films like *Mission Impossible 2* (2000) and the quieter intensity of dramatic films like *Marshall* (2017). She has seen the sound industry move from analog to digital and has worked on all aspects of mixing. Behlmer still prefers working on action sequences, primarily as an effects mixer. During her partnerships with other mixers, she created the effects while another mixer works on music and dialogue. Her affection for reverb and boom comes through when listening to her work for car chases or helicopter sequences. In the work she has done for both live-action films and animations, she is known for creating a sense of space through her mixing. For Behlmer, sound mixing is a collaborative art form that relies on an understanding of emotion and storytelling. The mentorships and collaborations Behlmer experienced throughout her career have been important for her growth, and she now gives back by mentoring three other women mixers at the Technicolor facility. In Behlmer's own words, she never aimed to break barriers, "I felt like I had to work harder and be better. It was a boy's club and I just wanted to be accepted; that was my main focus. I wasn't thinking about breaking ceilings or being a role model" (Urban 2018, 15). While Behlmer did not start out in the industry to set an example, she has done just that.

As the daughter of Italian immigrants, Behlmer grew up as a first-generation American in Los Angeles. Even though Behlmer grew up in Hollywood, she did not originally believe she would go into the film industry. While helping her sound-engineer boyfriend load dubbers at Ryder Sound, sound mixer Gary Bourgeois said she was there so often she should get a union card. Unsure of what to major in at college and feeling bored, Behlmer decided to take his advice and got her union card. After receiving her union card, she went to Glen Glenn Sound because it was said that women could actually get a job there, which already had two women working there at the time.

She began her career as a Y-15 loader at Paramount. When Bourgeois joined Glen Glenn, he promoted Behlmer to sound recordist. She worked on such films as *Three Men and a Baby* (1987) and *Earth Girls Are Easy* (1988). Glen Glenn eventually merged with Todd-AO, which developed a mixer training program. With encouragement, Behlmer decided to join the 90-day training program in 1989.

When Behlmer completed the program, there were very few women working in the sound industry. She became one of first women to work as a re-recording mixer for feature-length films. The first feature-length film she was the re-recordist mixer for was *Kindergarten Cop* (1990). Most other women working in sound at the time were working on television.

Due to the lack of women working in mixing for feature-length films, her presence at the mixing console was questioned. While working on *The Hand that Rocks the Cradle* (1992), a member of the editorial staff tried to get her removed from the project (Lang 2014). Criticism regarding her abilities as a female sound mixer lessened as the award nominations began to accumulate.

Throughout her career she has worked with various other mixers, including famed Richard Portman, with whom she learned to value the importance of story and understand what the image needs. After Portman, Behlmer began a nearly 20-year collaboration with Andy Nelson. In 1998, Behlmer moved to Fox Studios, where she mixed for 14 years. During this time, she forged a long-time collaboration with Terry Porter. Behlmer returned to the Paramount lot in 2012 when she began working at the Technicolor facility.

During her career, Behlmer continues to break new ground for women working in the sound industry. In 1996, Behlmer became the first woman nominated for the Best Sound Mixing category at the Academy Awards for her work in *Braveheart*

(1995). The following year she was nominated again for an Oscar for her work in *Evita* (1996). She would go on to be nominated several more times for her work in *L.A. Confidential* (1997), *The Thin Red Line* (1998), *Moulin Rouge!* (2001), *Seabiscuit* (2003), *The Last Samurai* (2003), *War of the Worlds* (2005), *Blood Diamond* (2006), and *Star Trek* (2009). Seventeen years after Behlmer's watershed nomination for *Braveheart* (1995), Lora Hirschberg became the first woman to win an Oscar for *Inception* (2010). Behlmer has also been nominated for 12 CAS (Cinema Audio Society) awards and six BAFTA (British Academy Film Awards) awards. Of those six BAFTA nominations, she has won three awards. She has also been nominated five times for the Satellite Award. While the award nominations are an important testament to her career, they are also a testament to the lack of women in the industry, as Behlmer is frequently the only woman nominated in these categories. Behlmer broke barriers again by being the first woman to receive the CAS Career Achievement Honor in 2018.

Celeste Reeb

See also: Hirschberg, Lora (Sound Mixer)

Further Reading

"Analog Hero in a Digital World: Making of 'Live Free or Die Hard.'" 2007. *Live Free or Die Hard*, collectors ed., DVD. Directed by Len Wisemen. Beverly Hills, CA: 20th Century Fox Home Entertainment.

Coleman, Michael. 2015. "The Art of Sound Mixing (feat. Anna Behlmer)." Produced by Colemanfilm Media Group. *Soundworks Collection*, September 15. Podcast, MP3 audio. Accessed March 4, 2018. https://soundcloud.com/soundworkscollection/the-art-of-sound-mixing-anna

Lang, Brent. 2014. "Women Prevailing Despite Sexism in Slowly-Changing-Below-the-Line Industry." *Variety*, July 29. http://variety.com/2014/artisans/news/women-prevailing-despite-sexism-in-slowly-changing-below-the-line-industry-1201270573/anna

Urban, Karol. 2018. "CAS Career Achievement Recipient: An Interview with Re-Recording Mizer Anna Behlmer." *CAS Quarterly*, Winter 2018. http://cinemaaudiosociety.org/cas-quarterly

Hall, Cecelia (Unknown–)

Cecelia Hall has played a pivotal role in paving the way for women seeking to establish careers in the field of sound editing. She was the first woman to be elected president of the board of governors of Motion Picture Sound Editors in 1984, and in 1987, she became the first woman to be nominated for an Academy Award for Best Sound Editing for her work on *Top Gun* (1986). She was also the first woman to be employed in the sound editing department at Paramount Pictures, where she ultimately rose to an executive position. Hall has worked on a number of films, including *Star Trek: The Motion Picture* (1979), *Star Trek II: The Wrath of Khan* (1982), *Flashdance* (1983), *Beverly Hills Cop* (1984), *Witness* (1985), *Beverly Hills Cop II* (1987), *The Hunt for Red October* (1990), for which she won the Academy Award for Best Sound Editing, *The Addams Family* (1991), *Addams Family Values*

(1993), *Lassie* (1994), and *A Small Act* (2010), among others. Hall won the Motion Picture Sound Editors (MPSE) Golden Reel Award for *Something So Right* (1982) and *Top Gun* (1986), and she has been nominated for numerous MPSE Golden Reel Awards for other projects. She has served on the executive branch of the Academy of Motion Picture Arts and Sciences, and, since 1995, she has held several teaching positions at academic institutions.

Hall realized she wanted to pursue a career in film editing after seeing *Bonnie and Clyde* (1967) when she was 14 years old. She first worked as a trailer editor and negative cutter before becoming interested in sound and starting a career as an independent sound editor. She later worked in the sound editing department at Paramount Pictures, where, after overseeing many films, she became senior vice president of post-production sound, a role she held from 1978 to 1992. Hall supervised an array of feature films, including *Clear and Present Danger* (1994), *The Hours* (2002), and *The Italian Job* (2003), as well as other projects. She also contributed to the sound design for films produced by Nickelodeon, Vantage, and MTV, including *Nacho Libre* (2006) and *Hustle & Flow* (2005). Over the years, Hall developed several professional partnerships, such as collaborations with sound editor George Watters II, with whom she shared her Academy Award nominations and win, director Peter Weir, and producers Scott Rudin and Jerry Bruckheimer.

From the early stages of her career, Hall recognized the significant role she played as one of the few women working in sound editing, and she was determined to become a pioneer for others. She says, "If there had been even a few other women working, I probably wouldn't have been as worried, but for women at that time, we were concerned about the women coming up. We were extremely conscious of our responsibility to set an example, to show everyone that women could do this work and do it well" (Gregory 2002, 265). From the late 1970s to the late 1980s, Hall felt men were waiting for her to become a disappointment, but after her success with *Top Gun*, she felt empowered. She says, "I felt they couldn't touch me . . . I had proven myself to them and, more important, to myself" (Gregory 2002, 263). Hall became known for employing and offering promotions to women, even though it often proved difficult because there simply weren't many women seeking to establish themselves in the field yet.

Hall's reputation was not only based on inclusivity but also hard work and creativity. Stylistically, Hall has been drawn to juxtaposition. She states, "If I have a particular style, I would have to say that I prefer a lot of contrast" (LoBrutto 1994, 195). The inspiration for her creative choices related to sound design and sound effects has seemed to emerge from a diverse set of factors and individuals. For instance, in *Sound-on-Film: Interviews with Creators of Film Sound*, she explains that production design informs sound design in that it is "the map with all the clues" (LoBrutto 1994, 189). But she also draws influence directly from the script, the director, and the editor. She says, "It's a collaborative effort; you can't fly blind on any of this. You're getting input all the time from the director or the picture editor. The picture editor is usually our greatest source because they've spent an intense six months with the director, so they have a sense of the atmosphere he or she wants to create" (LoBrutto 1994, 190). This notion of "atmosphere" is fundamentally important to Hall. In fact, she believes "the single most important element to sound design is making your audience believe they're in that environment" (Gregory 2002, 264).

Employing sound to create an atmosphere has become one of the key aspects Hall stresses when instructing her students. For years, she has taught sound design in the School of Theater, Film and Television at the University of California, Los Angeles, and she has held visiting sound design instructor positions in the School of Entertainment Arts at the Savannah College of Art and Design and at California State University, Monterey Bay. She also appears on panels and serves as a sound consultant, a capacity in which her tasks vary but range from offering creative ideas and insights to choosing and overseeing sound editing collaborators.

Breena L. Loraine

Further Reading

Gregory, Mollie. 2002. *Women Who Run the Show: How a Brilliant and Creative New Generation of Women Stormed Hollywood.* New York: St. Martin's Press.

Internet Movie Database. n.d. "Cecelia Hall Biography." Accessed March 18, 2018. http://www.imdb.com/name/nm0355398/bio

LoBrutto, Vincent. 1994. *Sound-on-Film: Interviews with Creators of Film Sound.* Westport, CT: Praeger Publishers.

Savannah College of Art and Design. n.d. "Cecelia Hall." Accessed March 18, 2018. http://www.scad.edu/academics/faculty/cecelia-hall

Hirschberg, Lora (1963–)

When Lora Hirschberg began film school at New York University (NYU), she thought she wanted to become a director. She enjoyed the mechanical and technical aspects of filmmaking. At the same time, she was studying music. These interests eventually combined and led her to a career as a sound mixer, a career in which she became the first woman to win the Academy Award for Best Achievement in Sound Mixing, shared with Gary A. Rizzo and Ed Novick, for her work on *Inception* (2010). Her work on this film also won her the 2011 BAFTA for Best Sound, the Critics' Choice Award, a Cinema Audio Society (CAS) nomination, a Golden Derby Award, a Hollywood Post Alliance nomination for Outstanding Sound in a Feature Film, a win for the International Online Cinema Award (INOCA), a win for the Online Film and Television Association (OFTA), and a Satellite Award nomination.

After NYU, Hirschberg moved to San Francisco in 1989 to work at Francis Ford Coppola's Zoetrope Studio, where she worked in the machine room. One of her first projects there was the 1984 documentary *The Times of Harvey Milk*. Hirschberg has continued to work on documentaries throughout her career. As a sound mixer, she won her first Emmy nomination for the HBO documentary *The Celluloid Closet* (1985). One of her personal documentaries she has worked on is *Paragraph 175* (2010). One theme both *The Celluloid Closet* and *Paragraph 175* share is their examination of queerness. Hirschberg is married to Dr. Laura Norrell, with whom she has two daughters. Despite being a woman in a heavily male-dominated field and a lesbian, Hirschberg says she has faced very little discrimination. In a

2009 interview with *The Advocate*, Hirschberg states that while perhaps a hundred people in the whole country do her job for feature films, only about two of those people are women. She is already a special case whenever an issue based around stereotypes comes up at work; she says, "I get to say what other people don't" (Marler 2009). She enjoys shattering the myth that sound mixers need to be a certain way. This ability to face any criticism head on and work hard at her craft has made Hirschberg into an inspiration for many young women looking to enter the field. One of the ways Hirschberg has embraced this role as a mentor is through educational programs. Hirschberg, along with another mixer, Leslie Jones, created a two-week program where film and recording school students could shadow people at Skywalker Studios. She also encourages young girls in high school to visit her at Skywalker Studios to see what a career in audio entails.

While working at Skywalker Studios, Hirschberg has worked on some of the biggest blockbusters such as *Guardians of the Galaxy Vol. 2* (2017), *The Avengers* (2012), *The Dark Knight* (2008), *Iron Man* (2008), and *Pirates of the Caribbean: At the World's End* (2007). *The Dark Knight* won Hirschberg her first Academy Award nomination, her first BAFTA nomination, a CAS nomination, a Golden Derby nomination, a INOCA win, an OFTA nomination, and a Satellite Award win. The first *Guardians of the Galaxy* (2014) received a CAS nomination, and *Guardians of the Galaxy Vol. 2* won her a Hollywood Professional Association Award. *Iron Man* received a CAS nomination and an INOCA nomination, while *Iron Man 2* (2010) won her a Satellite Award. For her work on *Batman Begins* (2005), she received both an OFTA and INOCA nomination. While her work on the action-packed blockbusters and comic book movies have earned her recognition, she still enjoys working on smaller independent films. Some of her favorites include *Shortbus* (2006) and *Please Give* (2010). No matter the film, her favorite part of being in the film industry is watching the films over and over again.

Whether working on big-budget or low-budget films, certain trends continue throughout Hirschberg's work. She often thinks about how the sounds relate in terms of editing. Oftentimes, music can lead to a cut. When thinking about music, she will try to capture the emotions of a scene, which means working closely with a director. In fact, she often seeks out directors she wants to work with rather than waiting for them to contact her. For the film *Finding Neverland* (2004), Hirschberg collaborated with director Marc Foster to achieve the emotional aspects as well as ensuring the film did not sound like it was filmed in modern-day London. Hirschberg helped ensure that the sounds of airplanes and traffic were removed. She also made sure that the fabric from the costume is not heard on the dialogue track. She was also able to build music around birds flapping their wings. She achieves this level of detail because she spends a great deal of time listening to the world in her everyday life. She tries to understand the sounds that are usually tuned out so she can consider when they might want to be added to a film. From the technical aspects to the creative ones, Hirschberg's attention to detail continues to shape the films she works on.

Celeste Reeb

See also: Behlmer, Anna (Sound Mixer)

Further Reading

Keating, Carolyn. 2010. "Breaking the Sound Barrier." Feat. Lora Hirschberg. *Women Tech World.* http://www.womentechworld.org/bios/electron/articles/breaking_old.htm

King, Susan. 2004. "In a Largely Male Domain, She Mans the Soundboard." *Los Angeles Times*, December 5. http://articles.latimes.com/2004/dec/05/entertainment/ca-wkhollywood

Marler, Regina. 2009. "Go for the Gold." *The Advocate*, February 19. https://www.advocate.com/arts-entertainment/film/2009/02/19/grabbing-gold

Rose, Kay (1922–2002)

During a career spanning over 50 years, Kay Rose edited the sound for a diverse range of films, including B-horror movies, action blockbusters, and critically acclaimed dramas. In 1985, she became the first woman to receive an Academy Award for Sound Editing. In addition to the Academy Award, Rose was presented with a Lifetime Achievement Award from the Motion Picture Sound Editors in 1993 and the Career Achievement Award from the Cinema Audio Society in 2002.

Rose was born Catherine Theresa Gaffney on February 12, 1922, in Bronx, New York. She began her career as a film apprentice in the Editorial Department of the Signal Corps Photographic Center (SCPC) in 1942. Located in Astoria, Queens in the former Paramount Studios lot, the SCPC was under the supervision of the Army during World War II and produced training films, newsreels, and a library of still images taken during the war. Rose worked on training films and on John Huston's wartime documentary *Report from the Aleutians* (1943).

In 1944, she moved to Hollywood with recommendation letters from her supervisors in New York. After waiting for weeks with no replies from the studios' editorial departments, she ran out of money. Before wiring her mother to ask for the funds to return home, she decided to visit Universal Studios and ask for a job in person. In a 2001 interview with the *Motion Picture Editors Guild Magazine*, she described her efforts: "I went up to the gate and asked the guard if I could call Editorial. He said, 'What for?' and I said, 'I want to apply for a job.' He got hysterical with laughter and said, 'That's not how you get a job—but because you're here, I'll let you do it.' So I called Editorial and a man answered. He said 'Are you any good?' Well, what do you say when someone asks you that? You say, 'Yes.' And he said, 'You're hired!'" (Shatz 2001a). Unbeknownst to Rose, an editor's assistant had just quit and there was a shortage of experienced film assistants due to the war. Rose worked as a picture assistant at Universal for two years until World War II ended and the servicemen returned to their jobs.

Rose continued to work as a film assistant in Hollywood and married film editor Sherman Rose in 1951. The couple worked together on the low-budget science fiction film *Target Earth* in 1954 with Kay as the sound effects editor, credited as Kathleen Rose, and Sherman Rose as director and editor. The film, which was made for less than $100,000, later became a cult classic. Kay Rose continued to work on low-budget horror films, such as *Blood of Dracula* (1957) and *I Was a Teenage Frankenstein* (1957) and pulp Westerns like *A Lust to Kill* (1958). During the 1960s, Rose edited the sound on more than 14 different television shows, including the Westerns *The Rifleman* (1958–1963) and *The Big Valley* (1965–1969) and anthologies such as *The Lloyd Bridges Show* (1962–1963) and *The DuPont Show with June Allyson* (1959–1961).

In 1966, Rose worked on her first big-budget film, *The Professional*, a Western starring Burt Lancaster and directed by Robert Brooks. In 1969, Rose left television and worked as sound editor for legendary directors Mark Rydell, Sydney Pollack, Robert Altman, and Martin Scorsese, among others. In 1985, Rose won the Academy Award's Special Achievement Award for her sound editing on Mark Rydell's *The River* (1984). This honorary award was created in 1972 for contributions to films that were not covered by the competitive annual categories. According to then Academy President Gene Allen, Rose was awarded for her superior sound effects accomplishment. Prior to winning her Oscar, Rose was nominated for a British Award for her work on *New York, New York* (1977) in 1978 and again in 1980 for *The Rose* (1979). In 1987, Rose was appointed the governor of the Sound branch of the Academy Awards. She retired from film in 1999.

In October 2002, the University of Southern California's School of Cinema-Television created the Kay Rose Chair in the Art of Sound and Dialogue Editing through an endowment from directors George Lucas and Stephen Spielberg. During the endowment ceremony, composer John Williams, with whom Rose worked on *The River*, surprised Rose by directing the USC student orchestra in her honor. She was accompanied by her daughter, Victoria Rose Sampson, a film editor and director, whom Rose often brought to set as a child. In a 2017 interview with Ball State University's student newspaper *The Ball State Daily News* regarding her own 40-year career in Hollywood, Sampson stated that Rose viewed sound designing as a creative endeavor and encouraged sound editors "to think of themselves as filmmakers not technicians" (Rogers 2017). Kay Rose died on December 11, 2002, at the age of 80.

Megan Heatherly

Further Reading

McGee, Marty. 2010. *Encyclopedia of Motion Picture Sound.* Jefferson, NC: McFarland.

Movie Magic. 1994. "Sound Effects: Audio Awareness." Season 1, Episode 15. Created by Benz, Gary R, Stephen Rocha, and Lise Romanoff. Silver Spring, MD: Discovery Channel.

Shatz, Leslie. 2001a. "An Interview with Legendary Sound Editor Kay Rose (Part 1)." *The Motion Picture Editors Guild Magazine* 22(1). http://cinemontage.org/2001/03/interview-kay-rose-part-1/

Shatz, Leslie. 2001b. "An Interview with Legendary Sound Editor Kay Rose (Part 2)." *The Motion Picture Editors Guild Magazine* 22(2). http://cinemontage.org/2001/05/interview-kay-rose-part-2/

Rogers, Jeremy. 2017. "Vickie Sampson Reflects on a 40-Year Sound Editing Career." *The Ball State Daily News,* November 30. http://www.ballstatedaily.com/article/2017/11/vickie-sampson-reflects-on-a-40-year-sound-editing-career

Whittle, Gwendolyn Yates (1961–)

Gwendolyn Yates Whittle has worked as a supervising sound editor and with automatic dialog replacement (ADR) as an editor and supervisor for the majority of her career. A Buffalo, New York native, Whittle graduated from Buffalo Seminary school

Sound editor Gwendolyn Yates Whittle driving an off-road vehicle while on a sound effects recording trip in Hawaii for *Jurassic World: Fallen Kingdom* (2018). She received Academy Award nominations for Best Achievement in Sound Editing for *Avatar* (2009) and *Tron: Legacy* (2010). As of 2018, Whittle has been awarded six Golden Reel Awards by the Motion Picture Sound Editors and is a supervising sound editor at Skywalker Sound, a division of Lucasfilm. (Photo by Gwendolyn Whittle)

in 1979. She graduated with her BFA in Film and Television from New York University in 1984. She and her sister moved to San Francisco, where she landed her first job as an assistant editor for an independent film *Smooth Talk* (1985). With a staff of only two (including Whittle), she had to learn everything it takes to run an editing room. Beginning in the late 1980s, Whittle began working as an assistant dialog editor.

While she has worked with such Hollywood directors as David Fincher, Steven Spielberg, and J. J. Abrams, she enjoys working on smaller independent films since they are often dialog driven. She worked on several major films during the early 1990s, such as *Terminator 2* (1991) and *Mission: Impossible* (1996). Then in 1998 she won her first Golden Reel Award for her work on *Titanic* (1997). Her work with James Cameron would eventually land her more nominations, including her first Academy Award Nomination for her work on *Avatar* (2009). She also won awards with OFTA (Online Film & Television Association) and INOCA (International Online Cinema Awards) and a Golden Derby Award. Her work on *Avatar* was the first time that she worked with an alien language, Na'vi. She layered the Na'vi language, creating a sense of the environment and everyday life. While Na'vi was her first galactic language, Whittle has worked on films in various languages, including German in *Munich* (2005) and Urdu and Pashai in *Lions for Lambs* (2007). Her work on the English/Spanish short film *Carne y Arena* (2017) won her a Golden Reel award in 2018.

Whittle enjoys working with people, and often cites this as her reason for working in dialog rather than other areas of sound editing. Her attention to detail requires her to understand the nuances of performance and hearing the musicality in an actor's voice. She must also understand and keep track of the technical details, such as what microphones were used during production so she can match them in recording sessions. It is not only the dialog and performance she must match but also air flow. In an interview with Glenn Kiser of the Dolby Institute, Whittle jokes that she is the "keeper of the air," meaning she ensures that the automated dialog replacement (ADR) sounds as if it was recorded under the same conditions as the rest of the dialog. She understands the importance of pauses, silence, and breaths. Her attention to detail resulted in another round of nominations for her work on *Tron* (2010). She worked with the sound department and the director Joseph Kosinski to achieve characters whose voices reflected important character details. The closer a character is to human determines the amount of processing done on an actor's voice. Her work on the film earned a second Academy Award nomination, a Golden Derby nomination, two Golden Reel nominations, and an OFTA nomination.

Not only has she been recognized for her work on live-action films, she was nominated for an HPA (Hollywood Post Alliance) Award for her work on *Brave* (2012). She also won a Golden Reel for her work on *Ferdinand* (2017) and *Epic* (2013). She enjoys working on animated films because the recordings are done in pristine conditions. Rather than focusing on fixing issues or removing unwanted sounds, animated films allow her to focus on the performance aspects and creating the world. In total, Whittle has been nominated for 13 Golden Reel Awards for her work and has won 7 for films including, *Super 8* (2011), *The Curious Case of Benjamin Button* (2008), and *Saving Private Ryan*. She has also been nominated three times for the OFTA award and once for the Satellite Award. Whittle's work specializing in dialog is impressive, not only because so few women work within sound departments but also because within the sound editing world, many sound editors and mixers try to avoid dialog. She embraced dialog, and is now a supervising sound editor at Skywalker Ranch.

Celeste Reeb

Further Reading

Farinella, David John. 2010. "Loop-Group Troupe Lassoes Lingo: Post-Production Challenge Proves Out-of-This-World." *Variety*, February. http://variety.com/2010/digital/news/loop-group-troupe-lassoes-lingo-1118015468

Kiser, Glenn. 2015 "Dialog Editing & ADR Feature Gwen Yates Whittles." Produced by Colemanfilm Media Group. *Soundworks Collection.* September 21. Podcast, MP3 audio. Accessed March 25, 2018. https://soundcloud.com/soundworkscollection/dialog-editing-adr-gwen

Soundworks Collection. *The Sound of Brave.* Online Video, 12:26. http://soundworkscollection.com/videos/brave

Soundworks Collection. *The Sound of Tron Legacy.* Online Video, 9:05. http://soundworkscollection.com/videos/tronlegacy

Interview with Deb Adair

What's your story as a sound mixer?

After I graduated Syracuse, I packed my bags and headed to Los Angeles in hopes of starting my career in the movie industry. I drove an old car across the country with nothing more than my clothes and $500. When I first arrived in Los Angeles, I took whatever job I could find just to make ends meet. I worked as a waitress at a diner and handled payroll at a hardwood flooring company. I was finally hired to do phone sales for a small post-production facility. At the end of each day, I would hang out with the mixers and engineers who worked there and would ask a lot of questions. Eventually, I learned the console on my own time and was hired by a post-production facility as an ADR mixer.

I started off recording numerous animation and television shows. I stayed at this post-production facility for about 10 years, and I was very successful with what I was doing at the time, earning three Emmys and two Golden Reel awards, but my true passion was to work on feature films. I was offered the position of sound supervisor for *South Park: Bigger, Longer & Uncut*. Leaving the security of this studio was a big risk that left me with the uncertainty of whether it would be good for my career. After some careful thought and discussion with my husband, I decided to make the move. After 11 months, the South Park movie was finished and I received the opportunity to work as a TV mixer at Sony.

There were several people at Sony [who] took me under their wing and told me what I needed to do if I wanted a career as a sound mixer. There were only three female sound mixers for features in the entire industry and none at Sony. My mentors advised me that it would be a struggle because the people in the mixing positions were going to be very reluctant to share any kind work with another mixer. I started at Sony working on television shows, but this gave me the opportunity to meet and get to know the established mixers. Eventually I earned enough trust from some of the other mixers that they started letting me assist with some of the feature films. I still remember what the first film was today and how excited I was to be part of such a creative process.

The more I was able to work with the established mixers, the more trust and respect I gained from them. It was not a fast or easy process. It took many years of hard work and setbacks to overcome the obstacles that I had to face. Looking back, though, the hard work it took to break through made me a better mixer. I wanted to be the best mixer I could possibly be, and that drove me to learn as much as possible.

I love my job and can't think of anything else that I would want to do for a career. I feel very lucky and grateful to be in my profession and enjoy every minute of my day.

Interview with Gwendolyn Yates Whittle

How would you explain your profession and its contribution to a film?

I am a supervising sound editor, specializing in words. I usually partner with a sound designer whose specialty is sound effects. At the beginning of a show we choose the crew and make a budget. I keep track of the money flow and communicate with the post supervisor if changes need to be made. I make sure all the production sound is edited and prepped well for the mix. To fix any technical problems with the production sound, or added lines, I supervise the automated dialog replacement (ADR) with the actors and the extra voices (called "loop group") recordings. My work helps bring the spoken part of the film to life. My work should feel invisible. The dialogue track should be as perfectly integrated with the image as possible.

What does your work schedule look like from day to day or even over the course of a year?

My typical workday changes over the course of a job, which lasts on average 24 weeks per show. We usually work a 45- or 50-hour week. At the beginning of a show, we meet with the picture editor and director to hear how they feel sound can help tell the story. The sound editors start cutting, we divvy up the reels, I cue the ADR and loop group (LG), the Foley gets cued and walked, the sound effects get recorded and edited. We usually have at least one temp mix. These mixes are very useful in making sure the music, the special effects (FX), and the dialogue are all working in concert with one another, and in line with the director's vision. I travel to record the ADR, sometimes to fun exotic places like Tel Aviv, Paris, and London, but most often to Los Angeles or New York. Once we have all the elements edited, we premix them into their "food groups"—production dialogue, ADR, LG, Foley footsteps, Foley props, ambience, crowds, hard FX, vehicles, creatures, etc., depending on the film. After the premix, we combine and balance all the edited sounds with the director and picture editor on the final mix stage. We hope to create a track that is beautifully balanced and best tells the story, sometimes letting the words take the lead, sometimes the sound effects, and sometimes the music. Once the last note has been addressed we make all the different formats of the film, including the music and effects (M&E). The M&E is where you take all the English out of the film but leave all the rest so it can be dubbed in different languages. Atmos, Auro, DTSx, home video, 7.1, 5.1 (and I am sure more formats in the future) also get made. Then we take a weekend off.

How did you know you wanted to do this?

I didn't start off wanting to be a sound editor. I just wanted to work in film, doing anything. I graduated from NYU and moved to San Francisco with my sister. Clearly we were thinking adventure, not practicality, as most film graduates would have chosen to move to L.A. I got a job as an unpaid PA (production assistant) on a Sundance project, *Smooth Talk* starring Laura Dern. I overheard in the production office that they needed an assistant editor. I piped up that I was interested. I met with Patrick Dodd, the picture editor, and was hired. I realized instantly how little I knew and how patient a teacher he was. We were a crew of two that expanded to a crew of four when sound started. I learned so much on that job because there were so few of us. Unlike most post crews, the picture department and sound department were interchangeable. It was so much fun. The downside of a crew so small was that the next job was not instantly in sight. This was all in the Jurassic years before the Internet, but we did have answering machines! I got the *Hollywood Reporter* and sent off hundreds of resumes to films in production. And I waited. And waited. Finally I decided that I was not going to stare at the answering machine anymore and I left the apartment for four hours. I came back to three messages. The first two were for picture jobs in L.A., the last one was to work at Skywalker Sound on *Willow*. I chose the one close to where I lived. If I had been home, I would have taken that first L.A. job in a heartbeat. I became a sound editor because I liked my apartment in San Francisco!

The business is so different now than when I started working with splicers and Mag. The digital workforce is much smaller. Being workflow savvy is as important, as [is] knowing how to edit out a lip smack. Mixing and editing are no longer so separate. Editors mix; mixers edit. The editing platform, Pro-Tools, is often the mixing platform. The evolution is not bad. It's just different.

Did you have any advantages or connections, or were you on your own?

I knew no one in the business, nor did I have funding. Graduating from NYU film school gave me some credibility. My grandfather lent me his car to go to the interview for *Smooth Talk*. I was audacious in taking chances and saying yes to things. I watched the people I admired. I saw which editors got steady work and learned what made them good at what they did. I am lucky to work with some brilliant editors. C. J. Appel taught me the intricacies of ADR. Michael Silvers inspired my dialogue editing. Supervisors Tom Bellfort, Richard Hymns, Gary Rydstrom, Chris Boyes, and Randy Thom taught me the importance of balance and integration in the soundtrack and also within the crew. Lora Hirschberg gave me confidence by her example. She showed me that I was also qualified to work alongside, not just for, these talented men.

If you have children or dependents, how do you manage career and family?

I cannot do any of this without my husband. He has been supportive and flexible with the demands of my career from the start. He somehow always made his work schedule work with mine so the kids were well taken care of. When I would go out of town for long stretches of ADR or mixing work, our family members would come and help. The upside is that our kids are very close with family who live far away. I was also lucky when the kids were tiny, Skywalker Ranch had an onsite daycare, so when I was still nursing them, the daycare would call me up and I could pop down the road, feed them, and give them some loving. When they got older I got to have lunch with them. The daycare is no longer on site any more, but it is close by.

Is there ageism in your field, or is growing older positively correlated with skill and experience?

Ageism is definitely a factor in our work. Hearing loss can be a serious consequence for a sound editor! Luckily it does not affect everyone. Age equates with experience for sure, but the film industry thrives on new, different, fresh. There are only so many movies made, only so many jobs, and competition is intense. The relationships people build with picture editors, producers, and directors are as important as doing stellar work. Winning and being nominated for awards helps too!

Interview with Karen Baker Landers

How would you explain your profession and its contribution to a film?

My title is supervising sound editor. However, I think that description is hard for most people to understand. I prefer sound designer, because that's what we do—we help create and design the sound of a film.

Basically, sound editors or sound designers create everything you hear when you're watching a movie. From backgrounds or atmospheres (like winds, birds, thunderstorms, city environments, etc.) to vehicles, weapons, creature vocals, or the sound of undiscovered planets or magical worlds.

There is so much detail and thought that goes into supporting the story the director is trying to tell; we will prepare literally thousands and thousands of tracks before the sound on a film is finished.

How did you know you wanted to do this?

I was always interested in the way things sounded: the sound of daily life, of nature, things in the world.

When I was about 10 years old, my parents bought me a tape recorder. I would walk around the house and record "stories." No dialogue, just sound. I'd try to create a story and see if my family could figure out what it was. I'd usually do murders . . . the sound of someone's feet walking down a street, then a big thud, a scream, and a big splash, then feet running away. So basically, someone got hit in the head, tossed in a body of water, and the murderer ran away. Really simple stories, and I was obsessed with making them.

It wasn't until going to college that I discovered you could have a career working with sound. Once I realized I could make a living doing something I loved, I never looked back. I just kinda figured things out as I went. I didn't know what I didn't know. In hindsight, that was a blessing. I just kept moving forward.

How did you get your start as a sound editor?

One of my film professors at Long Beach State, Stephen Hubbert, invited two sound designers to come speak to our class. Richard Anderson and Mark Mangini had designed the sound for some amazing films. After the lecture, I asked Richard if I could come and work at his studio for free. He said yes and I dropped out of school and went right to work. I started as a driver/gopher. I did a little bit of everything and got to meet some incredibly talented people, many of whom I'm still friends with today.

I watched, listened, and learned from the best. I learned sound was about storytelling and supporting the director's vision for his or her film. It was a stressful time, but again, ignorance is bliss. Although I didn't really have a plan, I just kept working, meeting people, and moving forward.

What supports have been the most helpful as your has career developed?

Staying relevant in a highly competitive industry is important. You find yourself hanging out with some pretty interesting people, and it's good to have something to say. I believe travel, reading, going to movies, spending time in nature, going to museums, and more travel is crucial to staying relevant and creative.

I also believe that surrounding yourself with people you genuinely like and trust is one of the most important things you can do for yourself. You need a safe place to do your best work, to create, to feel free, and to have a not-so-great idea and not be judged by it. I work with some wonderful and talented people [who] feel more like family then co-workers. I wouldn't want to do this without them.

I also have an amazing support system of friends and family. My husband, Chad, loves me and takes care of me when I'm busy working long hours. He's genuinely my biggest fan. His strength and sense of humor have gotten me through some very hard times. I honestly could not do this without him.

Have you ever felt discriminated against in your field simply because of your gender or identity?

I've definitely had moments where I felt like being a woman has worked against me. But I've also had the privilege to work with some pretty amazing men—men on my crew, mixers, directors, producers, etc.; there are certainly far, far more good than bad.

I've had a male work partner, Per Hallberg, for almost 30 years. We've had big highs and big lows. We fight, we laugh ,and we both bring something completely different to the creative process. We have total trust and respect for one another.

As I've gotten older, many of the problems I thought I had with men were really because I lacked confidence in myself and my own worth. It has always mattered to me what people thought of me, maybe a little too much, and I let that control me for a lot of years. I thought I had to be a certain way to be taken seriously.

However, over many years of trying to "figure it out," I've finally learned that being me IS my biggest strength. I can be kind and direct, immature and serious, insecure and confident, weak and strong, have major creative blocks and complete creative highs. I can feel and be all these things. I am all these things . . . and that's enough.

Studio Heads and Executives

Introduction

Cinema in the United States, as well as the global film industry, has always been dominated by the major film studios, and there is a reason why Hollywood is also commonly referred to as "the movie business." The Hollywood industry, like any business, has at its core always been about turning a profit. As a business, films are products that need to make money so the industry thrives. Although it is certainly possible for the occasional Hollywood film to transcend the boundaries of commercialism into a work of art, that has never been the primary goal—at least not where the studios' bottom lines are concerned.

The business of creating commercially viable films should not itself be considered a criticism. Films are an extremely expensive undertaking and are always a risk to make because their financial success can be difficult to predict. Sometimes a studio will pour an enormous amount of resources, talent, money, time, and energy into a project that ends up doing poorly at the box office such as Disney's *John Carter* (2012), whereas other times a film with low expectations can prove a wild success like *Mamma Mia!* (2008). Not only is it difficult to determine which property or idea will sell to the public, but a movie is always in danger of falling apart due to the unexpected, no matter how grand or modest its budget may be. Historically speaking, the volatility of the business and marketplace, combined with changing viewer habits, has always placed enormous pressures on the executives at the top.

High-level studio executives have to contend with major changes, and their day-to-day responsibilities can be numerous—from development to marketing, distribution, and merchandising. They are the decision makers who determine what gets made and what gets passed on, which makes them enormously powerful not just in terms of who will get work but more importantly in terms of the impact their decisions will have in shaping popular culture. The primary responsibilities of an effective studio head are to both identify a compelling story or property and then determine whether the financial risk to make the film is acceptable. Due to the expense and collaborative nature of filmmaking, it is not uncommon for a potentially lucrative script to have to wait several years before the right confluence of events makes it possible for the studio to greenlight the project. Women did not start to enter into key positions of power at the studios until the 1970s, and it was not until the 1980s with pioneers such as Sherry Lansing and Dawn Steel that the first women in history would run a studio.

Laura L. S. Bauer

Jacobson, Nina (1965–)

In 2006, Nina Jacobson was one of the top movie studio executives in Hollywood. She was in her 10th year as president of Walt Disney's motion picture group with box office triumphs such as *The Sixth Sense* (1999), *Pearl Harbor* (2001), and *Pirates of the Caribbean* (2003) to her credit. While she was in the hospital waiting for her wife, Jen Bleakley, to give birth to their third child, Jacobson got a call that would change the course of her career. Disney unexpectedly fired her. Rather than let that setback stall her career, Jacobson formed her own production company, Color Force, in 2007. This was the first step toward Jacobson becoming one of Hollywood's most successful independent producers.

Producing is one of the riskiest jobs in Hollywood. With big-budget movies often costing $20 million or more, studios are always looking for the next runaway hit, yet are wary of risk. Producers walk a fine line between making an artistic choice and a financial one. Choosing the best story does not always result in the highest box office earnings. Finding and optioning the right material is no easy task. Creative properties can often spend years lingering in development before getting to the big screen. Instinct, luck, and timing are all part of a hit-or-miss method of finding and developing a successful property. Nina Jacobson has built a thriving Hollywood producing career with a combination of those three ingredients.

After producing the popular film *Diary of a Wimpy Kid* in 2010, which grossed over $118 million, Jacobson searched for her next property. Jacobson explains how she decides what type of projects to pursue as a producer: "I'm always looking for the page-turner, the thing I can't put down, that you can't stop thinking about—the book, the script that you don't want to be interrupted while you're reading" (Karpel 2013). Jacobson discovered that page-turner in author Suzanne Collins's YA (young adult) book series, *The Hunger Games*. She pursued an option to translate the series to film and rose above the competition by convincing Collins how passionate she was about the books and that she would make a movie that would remain true to the vision of the story.

Jacobson pitched the idea of a lead action heroine in *The Hunger Games* to several Hollywood studios until she found the right partner in Lionsgate. Until *The Hunger Games*, Hollywood generally steered clear from gambling on a female-led multifilm franchise. Lionsgate's belief in Jacobson's vision for the films turned out to be a very wise choice. In the end, the series of four *The Hunger Games* movies (*The Hunger Games* [2012], *The Hunger Games: Catching Fire* [2013], *The Hunger Games: Mockingjay Part I* [2014], and *The Hunger Games: Mockingjay Part II* [2015]) grossed a combined worldwide total of over $2.9 billion. (The Numbers 2017). Because of the success of these films, Hollywood greenlit several other YA film adaptations, including the *Maze Runner* and *Divergent* series.

Jacobson has been a pioneer in bringing new types of entertainment first to the big screen and, now, television. She had never produced TV when she and her producing partner from Color Force, Brad Simpson, brought the dramatized short-run television series *The People v. O.J. Simpson: American Crime Story* to the FX network in 2016. At the time of development, there were very few limited series (also known as anthologies) on the air (Thompson 2016).

The critically acclaimed series was nominated for 22 awards and won in multiple categories, including both a 2016 Golden Globe Award for Best Miniseries or Television Film and 2016 Emmy Award for Outstanding Limited Series. Focusing on a deep connection to characters and story is what has led to much of Jacobson's success.

One part of Nina Jacobson's legacy is being the highest-level out-lesbian studio executive in Hollywood during her tenure at Disney. She has championed for LGBT visibility in media throughout her career. She began an organization in the mid-1990s called Out There with co-founder and *American Horror Story* writer/director/producer Ryan Murphy, which focused on increasing female and LGBT representation in media, particularly in production roles behind the camera. She is helping change the face of Hollywood through involvement with multiple initiatives. Not only does she do this with the stories she champions but also with the organizations she supports.

Nina Jacobson helped develop one of the most successful film franchises of all time. She helped revitalize short-form television storytelling. As she moves forward with more projects, Jacobson continues to focus on finding stories that need to be told and the audience that wants to see them. Her instincts about story continue to pay off. As Hollywood moves more toward inclusivity, both in the stories it tells and in the talent in front of and behind the camera, Nina Jacobson will be leading the pack.

Micky Small

See also: Donner, Lauren Shuler

Further Reading

Holson, Laura M. 2016. "Nina Jacobson Has Her Revenge on Hollywood's Old-Boy Network. *The New York Times*, December 6. https://nyti.ms/2jSOyat

Human Rights Campaign. 2016. "Nina Jacobson Receives the HRC Visibility Award." *YouTube*, video, 24:02, March 20. https://www.youtube.com/watch?v=27L2NnO2LRc

Karpel, Ari. 2013. "How Hunger Games Producer Nina Jacobson Shepherds Great Stories to the Screen." *Fast Company*, November 23. https://www.fastcompany.com/3022192/how-hunger-games-producer-nina-jacobson-shepherds-great-stories-to-the-screen

Lambe, Stacy. 2016. "How American Crime Story Producer Nina Jacobson Is Making Audiences Face a Harsh Reality." *ET*, March 18. http://www.etonline.com/news/184642_how_american_crime_story_producer_nina_jacobson_is_making_audiences_face_a_harsh_reality

McCue, Matt. 2014. "How Getting Fired Led Hunger Games Producer Nina Jacobson to Success." *Fortune*, November 7. http://fortune.com/2014/11/07/hunger-games

The Numbers. "Box Office History for Hunger Games Movies." *The Numbers*. https://www.the-numbers.com/movies/franchise/Hunger-Games#tab=summary

THRnetwork. 2016. "The People v. O.J. Simpson' Producer Nina Jacobson on Creating 'Outside' Her 'Experience.'" *The Hollywood Reporter,* June 21. YouTube, 5:07, https://www.youtube.com/watch?v=UmHPf7Vq7pQ

Thompson, Anne. 2016. "How 'The People v. O.J. Simpson' Producers Made the Switch from Film to Anthology TV." *IndieWire*, August 1. http://www.indiewire.com/2016/08/people-v-oj-simpson-nina-jacobson-brad-simpson-producers-interview-emmys-1201712070

Verhoeven, Beatrice. 2017. "Hunger Games Producer Rips Hollywood 'Conventional Wisdom' about Diversity as 'Bulls—Prejudice.' *The Wrap*, October 3. https://www.thewrap.com/hunger-games-producer-nina-jacobson-slams-hollywoods-bias-as-prejudice-disguised-as-conventional-wisdom

Werk It: The Podcast. 2017. "Nina Jacobson on Being a Hollywood Boss." Accessed January 30, 2018. https://www.wnycstudios.org/story/nina-jacobson-being-hollywood-boss

Langley, Donna (1968–)

Donna Langley was the first British woman to ever run a Hollywood studio and, for a time, until Stacey Snider rose up the ranks of 20th Century Fox Film in 2016, was the only female studio head in town. Her work for Universal has allowed the once-flailing studio to become one of the most successful in Hollywood by prioritizing diversity, both in the kinds of stories the studio was telling and the kind of filmmakers that were telling them.

The current chairman of Universal Pictures—answering only to Jeff Shell, Chairman of Universal Filmed Entertainment Group—oversees all aspects of Universal's production and marketing operations worldwide, which include Focus Features and the DreamWorks Animation department. Before joining Universal in 2001, Donna Langley had her start in New Line Cinema, where she worked on such films as Mike Myers's *Austin Powers: The Spy Who Shagged Me* (1999) and Jennifer Lopez's *The Cell* (2000).

She started work at Universal in 2001, and eight years later, Langley was appointed to the co-chairman position, alongside Adam Fogelson. The following years proved to be "challenging" and plagued by a "revolving door of owners" (Masters 2015). This led to a string of expensive miscalculations that failed to bring the desired success at the box office, such as *Public Enemies* (2009), *Funny People* (2009), *Scott Pilgrim vs. the World* (2010), *R.I.P.D* (2013), and *47 Ronin* (2013). Concerning these years, Langley expresses the difficulty of running a studio and struggling to salvage troubled productions: "you're doing triage every day." This inevitably prevented her from thinking about "strategy" and gaining "momentum" (Masters 2015).

Her strategy was revealed a few years later and consisted, quite simply and perhaps old-fashioned of a diverse slate of films that served everyone, including underserved audiences, while not backing away from originality. Working within contemporary millennial Hollywood and bereft from superhero intellectual properties—except from having distribution rights for the Marvel character Hulk, a tricky position—Langley has helped Universal support a wide-ranging slate of films, pursued their own possible franchises (from nurturing *Fast & Furious*, to *Pitch Perfect*, to *The Purge*), and backed up unconventional films. She helped promote talent diverse both in terms of gender, like affording directing opportunities to Angelina Jolie, Sam Taylor-Johnson, and Elizabeth Banks, as well as in terms of race, by developing films such as *Ride Along* (2014) and *Straight Outta Compton* (2015). She has also bolstered franchises such as the Jason Bourne series, while acquiring the juggernaut book *Fifty Shades of Grey.*

Both 2015 and 2017 were banner years for Universal under Langley's creative leadership. In 2015, the studio reached the then highest-grossing domestic, international, and worldwide box office of any single year in any film studio's history. That year, Universal's *Furious 7, Jurassic World,* and Illumination's *Minions* reached a new milestone: the first time any studio ever tallied three films to cross $1 billion at the worldwide box office. In 2017, Langley and Universal's success continued with an array of big franchise films and low-budget films, once again supporting a strategy of having a diverse slate of films that catered to all audiences, outside of just the usual "young white males" (Masters 2015): *Fifty Shades Darker, The Fate of the Furious*, Illumination's *Despicable Me 3,* and *Girls Trip. Split* and *Get Out*, two of the year's most surprising hits, were the result of a 10-year deal Langley has in place with Jason Blum and Blumhouse. Apart from her strategy, her relationships with creative filmmakers and producers has made her someone reliable who people return to partner with, such as Judd Apatow, Elizabeth Banks, and Ice Cube.

Despite the recent hits, Langley attempted to emulate Marvel's superhero shared universe. By removing the once horror characters (Frankenstein, Dracula, and others) to the action adventure genre, the results proved dismaying results. Tom Cruise's *The Mummy* (2017) was a disappointment at the box office, after the equally disappointing *Dracula Untold* (2014).

Langley was named *The Hollywood Reporter*'s Executive of the Year in 2015, being regularly featured in the publication's Top 100 Women in Entertainment issues. She was also honored with the 2016 Pioneer of the Year Award from the Will Rogers Motion Picture Pioneers Foundation. Langley is an ambassador for Vital Voices Global Ambassadors Program, a program that provides women with the resources and coaching to help their endeavors. She is on the advisory board of Chrysalis and was also a key founder of *The Hollywood Reporter*'s Women in Film Mentorship program.

Langley received the Producers Guild of America's 2018 Milestone Award at the 29th Annual Producers Guild Awards. Producers Guild Awards chairs Donald De Line and Amy Pascal praised her "stewardship of tentpole event films," but also the fashion in which she "built her studio into a home for smart, talented, passionate filmmakers—especially for those who color outside the lines or don't fit into Hollywood's usual boxes" (McNary 2017). Previous recipients include Clint Eastwood, Steven Spielberg, Sherry Lansing, Bob Iger, and Tom Rothman.

Ana Cabral Martins

See also: Lansing, Sherry; Pascal, Amy

Further Reading

Dawtrey, Adam. 2009. "Universal Picks First British Woman to Run a Hollywood Studio." *The Guardian*, October 8. http://www.theguardian.com/film/2009/oct/08/donna-langley-universal-pictures

Holman, Jordyn. 2014. "Donna Langley Provides Resources and Mentorship to Women in Vital Voices Program." *Variety*, October 7. http://variety.com/2014/film/features/donna-langley-mentors-women-in-vital-voices-program-1201323085

Masters, Kim. 2015. "Donna Langley: The Secret Weapon Behind Hollywood's Biggest Box-Office Year Ever." *The Hollywood Reporter*, December 9. https://www.hollywoodreporter.com/features/donna-langley-secret-weapon-behind-845931

McNary, Dave. 2017. "Donna Langley to Get Producers Guild's Milestone Award." *Variety*, October 25. http://variety.com/2017/film/news/donna-langley-producers-guild-milestone-award-1202598603

Morfoot, Addie, and Diane Garrett. 2018. "Donna Langley on Universal Success and the 'Fate of the Movie Gods.'" *Variety*, January 19. http://variety.com/2018/film/awards/donna-langley-on-universal-success-fate-movie-gods-1202667869

Walker, Tim. 2015. "Film Studio Promotes Female Talent over Superhero Films to Top the Box Office." *The Independent*, August 22. http://www.independent.co.uk/arts-entertainment/films/news/universal-pictures-studio-promotes-female-talent-over-superhero-films-to-top-box-office-10467630.html

Lansing, Sherry (1944–)

A groundbreaking pioneer, the first woman to lead production at a major movie studio, a University of California Regent, creator of The Sherry Lansing Foundation—the name Sherry Lansing is huge. Having a star on the Hollywood Walk of Fame and being the recipient of the Jean Hersholt Humanitarian Award from the Academy of Motion Picture Arts and Sciences doesn't even begin to cover the list of awards and honors Lansing has received over the years for achievements in film history and philanthropy in the nonprofit world. Although the 1980 *New York Times* headline "Former Model Named Head of Fox Productions" still irritates her, Lansing now uses the incident as a means of pointing out what strides women in the movie business have made. After all, the announcement of a woman running a studio would not make the front page today as shocking news, and both the diminishment of her achievements and experience would less likely be a focus.

After growing up in Chicago and earning a bachelor's of science degree at Northwestern University, Lansing taught high school math and English in Watts, East Los Angeles, while going to casting calls after school. Indeed, she did work briefly as a model in television commercials for Max Factor and an as actor in such films as *Rio Lobo* (1970) and a 1971 episode of *Ironside*. While on the set of *Loving* (1970), Lansing made smart suggestions on script changes and was offered a part-time job behind the camera as a script reader for producer Ray Wagner. Within six months, she was synopsizing full time, eventually invited into story conferences, and after a year and a half, moved on to work with a major television producer, Leonard Stern Associates. Making her way through the ranks, Lansing became executive story editor at Metro-Goldwyn-Mayer (MGM) and then executive vice president of creative affairs there. Her talents led to a hire as vice president (VP) in charge of production at Columbia, followed by a senior VP position, before moving on to the presidency at 20th Century Fox in 1980.

Sherry Lansing at Variety's 1st Annual Power of Women Luncheon at the Beverly Wilshire Hotel in Los Angeles, California, on September 24, 2009. Lansing became the first female studio head in Hollywood history when she was hired as the president of production at 20th Century Fox. She would go on to have a very successful tenure as Chairman and CEO of Paramount Pictures. As a partner in Jaffe/Lansing Productions, Lansing produced *Fatal Attraction* (1987). The film received an Academy Award nomination for Best Picture. (Carrienelson1/Dreamstime.com)

Lansing credits the women's movement as well as her love of moviemaking itself as a tremendous help, enabling her to persevere in a time when everyday sexism was common. For example, when she became head of MGM's story department, the expected raise in salary was not forthcoming. A senior executive admitted that she was not making the equivalent of a man because she was not married with a family to support, an inequality she just had to accept at the time. Sherry describes putting her head down, overpreparing, and overworking to rise up the ladder. Jane Fonda was one of the first strong women role models she encountered, an inspiration for Lansing to find her own voice and speak her own mind.

The *Times* headline might have also trumpeted that Lansing was only 35 years old at the time of her Fox appointment and became one of the highest-paid female executives in any industry. She had just helmed the 1979 Columbia triumphs *Kramer vs. Kramer*, winning five Academy Awards including Best Picture, and *The China Syndrome*, nominated for four Oscars. Alan Hirschfield, the chief operations officer (COO) at Fox and former president of Columbia, brought on Lansing in part because of her relative youth, telling the press that audiences were trending down in age and he believed that she could attract younger moviemakers to engage a younger audience. Sherry's mother, on the other hand, was worried, "Well, no one's going to marry you now" (Galloway 2017, 97).

Winning the Women in Film Crystal Award in 1981, Lansing presided over Fox for three years with hits like *Chariots of Fire* (1981, winner of four Oscars, including Best Picture), Golden Globe–nominated *Taps* (1981), and *The Verdict* (1982), nominated for five Academy Awards. Yet the sexism, of course, followed her to Fox. When oil magnate Marvin Davis bought the studio and she first introduced herself, he assumed that she was an assistant there to serve coffee, not the president of the studio.

Citing the heavy administrative duties of the Fox presidency and a desire for a more hands-on approach to producing, she teamed up with Stanley Jaffe, who had been executive vice president of worldwide production at Columbia. The independent production company of Jaffe-Lansing turned out successes such as *Fatal Attraction* (1987), which garnered them a Best Picture Oscar nomination; *The Accused* (1988), the drama focused on the issue of blaming the victim in rape cases for which Jodie Foster won the Best Actress Academy Award; and *Black Rain* (1989), nominated for two Oscars.

After the partnership dissolved, Lansing stepped in as chairperson and CEO of Paramount Pictures in 1992, overseeing three Best Picture Oscar winners: *Forrest Gump* (1994), *Braveheart* (1995), and *Titanic* (1997, still the second highest-grossing movie of all time). Her impressive 12-year tenure there includes a 1996 star on the Hollywood Walk of Fame, the first female studio executive to be so honored, and *Ladies' Home Journal* ranked her as number 16 on their 2001 list of the most powerful women in America. By 2002, she was named *The Hollywood Reporter*'s most powerful woman.

The Paramount years include what Hollywood insiders dub "Sherry Lansing movies," films like *The First Wives Club* (1996) or *Kiss the Girls* (1997) about women who fight back or will not be ignored. However, Sherry was losing the passion that had made her such a great executive or producer on more than 200 films, and even with a purported $25 million contract, she was looking for a new driving force in her life. Not considering retiring at age 60, she turned her attention to activism and philanthropy through The Sherry Lansing Foundation (SLF). This new life's work resulted in the Jean Hersholt Humanitarian Award from the Academy of Motion Picture Arts and Sciences in 2007.

Lansing's foundation is a nonprofit organization dedicated to raising awareness and funding for cancer research and encore career opportunities, a program designed to retrain retired and midcareer professionals to serve as math and science teachers in California public schools. She is also the co-founder of the Big Sisters of Greater Los Angeles Future Fund, which provides college scholarships to deserving "Little Sisters," and serves on numerous boards, including the Regents of the University of California, American Cancer Society Cancer Action Network, Carter Center, and Entertainment Industry Foundation. The lengthy list of nonprofit activities and awards is ongoing, including an honorary doctorate in fine arts from the American Film Institute and induction into the National Women's Hall of Fame in 2017, reflecting her life as a pioneer, business leader, and visionary during her film career and afterwards. *The Hollywood Reporter* honored Sherry with the enduring legacy of naming the Sherry Lansing Leadership Award, given annually to recognize groundbreaking achievement and strong ideals in the entertainment industry.

Promoting his April 2017 authorized biography *Leading Lady: Sherry Lansing and the Making of a Hollywood Groundbreaker*, Stephen Galloway calls her "the most powerful woman Hollywood has ever known." Former colleagues describe Sherry as different from the cliché of the female executive who clawed her way to the top—not holding other women down, but raising them up. Lansing continues to serve as an example to young people trying to make it in the film industry, her message focusing on resiliency, never giving up, and not taking "no" for an answer. She points to education as an important foundation for success. Her knowledge of literature and story structure were key to landing her first job in a time when there were few film schools. She also knew math, and her comfort with numbers and the ability to read a budget were critical to her rise in the producing world.

Lansing credits her mother, a teenage Jewish refugee from Nazi Germany, as an early role model who took over her husband's small real estate development business when he died; Sherry was nine years old. By her actions, mother showed daughter that she could lead an empowered life and be self-sufficient. Following Lansing's achievements, many other women have stepped into key Hollywood corporate roles. With such a stellar rise to positions of power over men, she has had to endure mean-spirited comments and rumors of "sleeping her way to the top"—yet her record as a producer and studio executive speaks for itself. Eighty percent of the films released by Sherry Lansing were profitable, including 6 out of 10 of the highest-grossing films in the history of Paramount and one of the most successful track records in the history of the film industry. "She has been a trailblazer in our business and has all of that special and unique experience that comes with being first. In the years that I have known her, she hasn't lost a step," said Viacom Entertainment Group chairman Jonathan Dolgen (quoted in Galloway 2002, 18).

Angela Beauchamp

See also: Steel, Dawn

Further Reading

Galloway, Stephen. 2002. "*The Hollywood Reporter*'s 2002 Women in Entertainment Power 100." *Hollywood Reporter* 376(17), 18–27.

Galloway, Stephen. 2017. *Leading Lady: Sherry Lansing and the Making of a Hollywood Groundbreaker.* New York: Crown Archetype.

Plotkin, Janis. 2009. "Sherry Lansing." *Jewish Women's Archive*, March 1. https://jwa.org/encyclopedia/article/lansing-sherry

Staff. 2009. "Sherry Lansing Named First Female Studio Production Head." *History*, April 1. https://www.history.com/this-day-in-history/sherry-lansing-named-first-female-studio-production-head

Pascal, Amy (1958–)

Amy Pascal is unique in the history of Hollywood producers, for after rising to the top of the studio system as co-chairman of Sony Pictures Entertainment, she was forced to resign from her position after an international incident of geopolitical consequences—an intriguing career arc if ever there were one.

Pascal got her start in the business as a secretary for the independent production company Kestrel Films, then became the vice president of production at 20th Century Fox in 1986, and joined Columbia Pictures shortly before its sale to Japanese electronics giant Sony in 1988. A project of particular note that Pascal developed during her time at Columbia is *A League of Their Own* (1992), directed by Penny Marshall. Telling the largely forgotten tale of the All-American Girls Professional Baseball League, the film has gone on to become something of a modern feminist classic, with memorable performances from Geena Davis, Lori Petty, and Madonna. The film signaled Pascal's early career interest in women's issues.

Pascal was named co-chairperson of Sony Pictures Entertainment in September 2006. Pascal's time at Sony was marked by the production of a number of successful blockbusters, including the film adaptations of Dan Brown's *Da Vinci Code* novels and the continuation of the James Bond series with Daniel Craig in the titular role. In a prescient move, Pascal greenlit *Spider-Man* (2002) starring Tobey Maguire, which rejuvenated the superhero genre, one that came to dominate tentpole filmmaking in Hollywood for the foreseeable future.

Pascal has publicly reflected on her position as the first female head of a major Hollywood studio throughout her career. In an interview with *Forbes* for their "most powerful women in the world" list, Pascal was asked about her role in creating more opportunities for female-centric films. She replied: "I think it is my responsibility. Because I love movies about women. I love women. I've always cared about making movies about women my entire career. We probably hire more female directors here—if there are any—we do it because we want to and we do it because we have to. We made lots of movies with Nora Ephron, with Nancy Meyers, with Catherine Hardwicke, with Kathryn Bigelow. That's an agenda for us" (Silverstein 2013).

Pascal's name was splashed across headlines in late 2014 in an event that sent shockwaves through Hollywood and generated a response from no less than the president of the United States, Barack Obama. In apparent retaliation for the content of the soon-to-be-released film *The Interview*—a comedy starring James Franco and Seth Rogan about a plot to assassinate Kim Jong-un—the so-called "Guardians of Peace," a group with ties to North Korea, broke into the computer systems of Sony Pictures Entertainment, the parent company of the film's distributor, Columbia Pictures. The group leaked internal emails and various other company records with damning results for Pascal and her producer, Scott Rudin.

The leaking of Sony's dirty laundry caused quite a media stir, especially among the entertainment press and the trade magazines. Some noted at the time Pascal's potential hypocrisy stemming from several emails in which she speaks rather dismissively of other women in Hollywood (Merlan 2015). In reference to a possible film of the life of Cleopatra starring Angelina Jolie, Pascal wrote of the superstar: "I'm not destroying my career over a minimally talented spoiled brat who thought nothing of shoving this off her plate for eighteen months so she could go direct a movie. I have no desire to be making a movie with her, or anybody, that she runs and that we don't. She's a camp event and a celebrity and that's all and the last thing anybody needs is to make a giant bomb with her that any fool could see coming." In another email, Pascal refers to Megan Ellison, the producer of Oscar-winning films like *Zero Dark Thirty* (2009), as "this bipolar 28-year-old lunatic" (Merlan 2015). In another controversial and much commented-upon exchange between Pascal and Rudin, the cinematic tastes of President Obama were discussed. In language that was widely seen as racially insensitive, Pascal suggested Obama's favorite films in recent years were likely the African American–themed *Django Unchained* (2012) and *The Butler* (2013).

Pascal did not survive the negative attention focused on Sony in the wake of the cyber-attack. In February 2015, it was announced that Pascal would be stepping down from her position as co-chairman of Sony Entertainment Pictures and chairman of its motion picture group. Subsequently, she accepted a new production deal that would keep her within Sony Studios (Lang 2015). In the months after her effective firing, Pascal had occasion to reflect on the experience and reckon with the potential consequences for women working in Hollywood. In an interview with magazine editor Tina Brown, Pascal reiterated her commitment to providing further opportunities going forward: "I think that the most important thing that we can do in our business is make movies with female protagonists and movies with female villains and movies where . . . the plot of the movie is about them, where their actions have consequences in the story. Because the worst thing you can do is just be on the sidelines" (McNary 2015). One of the first projects as part of her newly formed production company was the 2016 reboot of the beloved 80s action-comedy *Ghostbusters*, this time re-imagined with an all-female cast.

Jason LaRivière

See also: Bigelow, Kathryn; Ellison, Megan; Ephron, Nora; Langley, Donna; Marshall, Penny; Meyers, Nancy

Further Reading

Begley, Sarah. 2014. "Who Is Amy Pascal? Meet the Exec Tangled Up in Sony's Leaked Emails." *Time,* December 14. http://time.com/3631735/amy-pascal-sony-hack

Lang, Brent. 2015. "Sony's Amy Pascal Stepping Down as Co-Chairman." *Variety,* February 5. http://variety.com/2015/film/news/sonys-amy-pascal-stepping-down-as-co-chairman-1201424905

McNary, Dave. 2015. "Amy Pascal Talks Getting 'Fired,' Sony Hack and Angelina Jolie Emails in Candid Interview." *Variety*, February 11. http://variety.com/2015/film/news/amy-pascal-sony-angelina-jolie-obama-hack-the-interview-1201431167

Merlan, Anna. 2015. "Amy Pascal's Girl Power Platitudes about Women in Movies Fall Flat." *Jezebel*, February 12. http://jezebel.com/amy-pascals-girl-power-platitudes-about-women-in-movies-1685478345

Silverstein, Melissa, 2013. "Sony Head Amy Pascal on Women Directors: The Whole System Is Geared for Them To Fail." *Indiewire*, May 23. http://blogs.indiewire.com/womenandhollywood/sony-head-amy-pascal-on-women-directors-the-whole-system-is-geared-for-them-to-fail

Pickford, Mary (1892–1979)

Mary Pickford was an absolute force in early Hollywood. She was one of the first female film stars, but she wasn't content to stay in front of the camera. She also wrote, produced, and distributed films. She was one of the co-founders of United Artists, and she was one of only three female founding members of the Academy of Motion Picture Arts and Sciences. With her movies, business acumen, and the sheer force of her celebrity, she played an integral role in shaping the film industry and in making Hollywood what it is today.

Producer and silent movie star Mary Pickford on the beach with a motion picture camera, circa 1916. Pickford was a leading pioneer in early Hollywood. In addition to being a major movie star, she co-founded Pickford-Fairbanks Studios with Douglas Fairbanks and eventually created the United Artists film studio with Fairbanks, D.W. Griffith, and Charlie Chaplin. She was also one of the original 36 founders of the Academy of Motion Picture Arts and Sciences. (Library of Congress)

There was no way Pickford could have known this was in store for her when she began acting. Born Gladys Louise Smith in Toronto in 1892 (though she later claimed it was 1893), she was the oldest of three children. Her father left when she was three, and he died shortly thereafter. In order to make ends meet, her mother had to take in boarders, and one couple worked for the local theater. They needed children to play extras in a play called *The Silver King.* Gladys and her little sister joined the cast to earn a little extra money, and thus Mary Pickford got her start on the stage at the age of seven.

Acting was an easy way to make money for the struggling family, so all four of them took various parts in shows both in Toronto and on the road. Gladys stood out in these shows and became an audience favorite. To capitalize on her success, the whole family moved to New York City where Gladys was determined to make it on Broadway. She begged a maid to ask actress Blanche Bates for a recommendation, and Bates agreed without even seeing her. With that reference in hand, she auditioned for director David Belasco, who cast her on the spot. He also required that she change her name. Together, they decided on Mary Pickford, using her mother's name, Marie, and that of her maternal grandfather, John Pickford Hennessey.

After her Broadway debut, *The Warrens of Virginia,* ended its run, Pickford kept her new name and, at her mother's prompting, tried out for a job with a motion picture company. Though initially wary of the new medium and eager to return to the stage, Pickford grew to prefer being on film. After she joined Biograph Company at the age of 17, she returned to the stage only once, in 1913, to star in *A Good Little Devil.* From that point on, movies were her focus.

When Pickford joined Biograph Company, the going rate for actors was $5 per day. She negotiated with D. W. Griffith, the company's main director, to earn $10 per day, with a $40 weekly minimum. This willingness to fight for her own interests and ability to negotiate on her own behalf characterized her film career. After gaining fame as "The Biograph Girl," she left the company the next year to work for Carl Laemmle at the rate of $175 per week. A year later, she switched to the Majestic Company for $225 per week. She later worked for Biograph once more, and then for Famous Players, where she eventually earned full control of her pictures and a salary of $10,000 per week. Finally, in 1919, she joined with D. W. Griffith, Douglas Fairbanks, and Charlie Chaplin to form United Artists, a company that was drastically different from the major film studios of the time.

In the early days of Hollywood, movie studios owned every part of the production process, including the theaters that showed their films. United Artists took a different approach. It didn't produce any films and instead acted as a distributor for independently produced movies. This allowed the artists much greater control over their films. Though the studio system reigned supreme for decades after United Artists was founded, its legacy is apparent in the current film industry, where independent films are often picked up by larger companies for distribution.

The idea of independent films was very important to Pickford, and, in 1941, she became one of the founders of the Society of Independent Motion Picture Producers. It was this society that eventually brought an end to the studio system by suing Paramount for violating antitrust laws. This led to the Supreme Court requiring all of the major studios to sell their theaters in 1948 and opened the door for the modern film era.

Pickford was also involved in creating one of the most recognized names in Hollywood: Oscar. She was one of only three women included in the founding members of the Academy of Motion Picture Arts and Sciences

Pickford, while exceedingly talented and driven, was also very lucky to enter the movie industry when it was new. Because it was not yet prestigious, women were granted much greater creative freedom than they were in other, better established, artistic fields. She took advantage of this temporary ability to control and made an incredibly successful career. However, while not controlled by the studios, she was still not completely free to make the movies she wanted.

Known as "America's Sweetheart," Pickford gained fame for playing children. Even in her thirties, she still regularly played characters ranging from 10 to 15 years in age. As she grew and sought more adult roles, audiences still demanded to see her in the types of films that made her famous. In order to please both herself and her fans, she alternated between playing adults and children. Notably, in *Little Lord Fauntleroy* (1936), she played both the titular child and his mother. Finally, in 1928, Mary cut her signature ringlets into a chic bob in an emotional response to the death of her mother. Her haircut was so shocking to American audiences that it made the front page of *The New York Times*.

Her next movie after the cut was *Coquette* (1929), her first film with sound. It earned her an Oscar for Best Actress in a Leading Role and was her last successful movie. The transition to sound was hard on a lot of Hollywood stars, and Pickford was no exception. After a few lackluster performances, she eventually retired from acting in 1933. After that, she focused exclusively on producing before retiring for good in the 1950s.

Like her career, Mary Pickford's personal life was also filled with drama. Pickford met her first husband, Owen Moore, when she was just starting to make it big at Biograph. Despite her mother's protestations, the couple married in 1911. Her fame and his alcoholism took a toll on the relationship, and they separated. While they were apart, she fell in love with Douglas Fairbanks, and Pickford and Moore filed for divorce in 1920. This was exceptionally risky on Pickford's part, as her entire reputation was based on being innocent and childlike.

Luckily, when she married Fairbanks later the same month, the public rejoiced. They were two of the biggest stars at the time, and their fans loved that they were together. They were so popular that when they toured London on their honeymoon, fans actually pulled Mary out of their car through the open window. Their home in Beverly Hills was named "Pickfair" and was a prime destination for celebrities, politicians, and even visiting heads of state. They were two of the first actors to leave their handprints outside Grauman's Chinese Theatre. The couple remained happy for a while, but Fairbanks's affair with another woman ended their relationship in 1933.

Pickford married her third and final husband, Charles "Buddy" Rogers, in 1937. They adopted two children and remained married until Pickford's death in 1979.

Mary Pickford's legacy continues in the very existence of the film industry. She helped motion pictures gain popularity, and she was one of the first big movie stars. She had incredible power in early Hollywood, and she made business decisions that are still influencing movies today. Her ideas about film distribution and artist control were revolutionary at the time but commonplace now. Another child star with famous ringlets, Shirley Temple, is perhaps Pickford's most direct successor, but Pickford's influence goes far beyond her childish roles. Mary Pickford helped establish the cult of celebrity. She wasn't just an actress; she was a national fascination. The entire way America treats movie stars can be traced back to Mary Pickford and the beginning of the Hollywood era.

However, her legacy extends even further. In her life, Mary Pickford was exceptionally charitable. She helped to establish the Motion Picture Relief Fund (MPRF), an organization designed to help struggling members of the film industry. After the rise of talkies ended the careers of many involved in silent films, the MPRF played a large role in helping them back to their feet. It was also a wonderful safety net during the Depression, helping thousands of film employees per year. Pickford spearheaded many fundraisers for the organization, and she pushed for everyone to pledge one half of 1 percent of their earnings to the fund, a donation later formalized by the Screen Actors Guild. The MPRF currently exists as the Motion Picture & Television Fund Foundation, and it is still helping those in need.

Furthermore, Pickford donated generously to the Actors Fund and the Jewish Home for the Aging, now named the Los Angeles Jewish Home. She also traveled all across the country to sell war bonds during World War I, and she acted in a short film designed to boost the troops' morale.

Mary continued to give after her death. Her will stipulated that much of her estate go to a foundation. The Mary Pickford Foundation, which she created in the 1950s, finally became a full-fledged charity with the money from her estate. Today it offers scholarships, endowments, and a silent film library to further the study of Hollywood's roots.

Mary Pickford was a fantastically talented actress, a shrewd businesswoman, and an extremely generous soul. She is remembered for these traits along with the profound impact she had on Hollywood as a whole.

Audrey Curtis

See also: Bara, Theda; Loos, Anita; Marion, Frances; Mathis, June

Further Reading

Eyman, Scott. 1990. *Mary Pickford: America's Sweetheart.* New York: Donald I. Fine, Inc.

Fischer, Lucy, ed. 2009. *American Cinema of the 1920s: Themes and Variations.* New Brunswick, NJ: Rutgers University Press.

Pawlak, Deborah Ann. 2011. *Bringing Up Oscar: The Story of the Men and Women Who Founded the Academy.* New York: Pegasus Books.

Schmidt, Christel, ed. 2012. *Mary Pickford: Queen of the Movies.* Lexington: University Press of Kentucky.

Sova, Dawn B. 1998. *Women in Hollywood: From Vamp to Studio Head.* New York: Fromm International.

Turner, Erin H. 1999. *More than Petticoats: Remarkable American Women.* Helena, MT: Twodot.

Snider, Stacey (1961–)

When Stacey Snider became the executive officer and chairwoman of 20th Century Fox in 2017 (succeeding Jim Gianopulos), it was one more step in a successful career in the film business. Snider graduated with a degree in law from UCLA Law School in 1985 and began her work as an assistant at Simpson-Bruckheimer Productions before quickly moving on to the position of director of development at Guber-Peters Co. at Warner Bros. In 1992, Snider was named president of production at Tri Star (now Columbia Pictures/Sony Pictures Entertainment) and thus became the highest-ranking female executive at a Hollywood studio. During her time with Tri Star, the company made movies such as *Philadelphia* (1993), *Seven Years in Tibet* (1997), and *Godzilla* (1998). In 1999, Snider became the CEO of Universal Pictures. Under her leadership, Universal made films such as *A Beautiful Mind* (2001), *Gladiator* (2000), *Erin Brockovich* (2000), and *The Pianist* (2002). The immense international box office success of these and other films put Snider at number 2 on a 2002 list of the 100 most powerful women in Hollywood published by *The Hollywood Reporter.* In 2006, she left Universal to serve as co-chairwoman and CEO of DreamWorks Pictures. During Snider's leadership, DreamWorks created successful films such as *The Kite Runner* (2007) and *Transformers. Revenge of the Fallen* (2009). However, her time with the label was also marked by continuous sale negotiations (Paramount Pictures, DreamWorks Studios, Amblin Partners) and unsettled investments and ownership issues as well as battles in the management structure. When Snider began her work as a CEO at 20th Century Fox in 2016, the media anticipated conflicts between her and president Emma Watts. A sexist plot of catfights had been spun, but Snider proved to be professional and settled in her new role.

As the CEO of one of the big film studios, Snider makes influential production and marketing decisions. Under her leadership, the focus is on popular family productions that can be marketed beyond the screening of a movie in the cinemas. Her interest is also on new technologies that not only broaden the possibilities of moviemaking but also enhance the viewing experience. Her management style is clear-cut. Marc Shmugher, vice chairman of Universal during Snider's leadership, said about her: "Stacey is an extraordinary leader who never stops asking questions. She has a great creative and legalistic mind, and she has challenged everyone in the organization to be responsible all the time: have they thought of everything, followed through on everything, have they been flawless in the undertaking on all of their projects, all of the time" (Dunkley 2001). Snider is said to frequent the movie theaters and watch new releases regularly on Sundays.

Andrea Zittlau

Further Reading

Dunkley, Cathy. 2001. "Showmen of the Year." *Variety*, August 27, 45.

Lang, Brent. 2017. "Fox's Stacey Snider Gets Candid about Netflix, Diversity, and the Future of Wolverine." *Los Angeles Times*, September 20. http://variety.com/2017/film/features/stacey-snider-21st-century-fox-first-year-1202563799/

Steel, Dawn (1946–1997)

Dawn Steel, once known as "the most powerful woman in Hollywood" (Smith 1987), was the first woman to head a major motion picture studio, Columbia Studios, "the highest executive position ever reached by a woman in the film industry" (Harmetz 1990). Prior to this role, Steel was the president of production at Paramount Motion Picture Group. Able to greenlight or reject film ideas, the studio, under her tenure, oversaw more than 100 films in development annually, a "record in contemporary Hollywood" (Smith 1987, 211). Films she advocated for and helped develop during her career include *Flashdance* (1983), *Footloose* (1984), *Top Gun* (1986), *When Harry Met Sally* (1989), *Ghostbusters II* (1989), *Cool Runnings* (1993), and *City of Angels* (1998), which is dedicated to her memory. Many of these films portray the plight of the outcast or marginalized via gender or economic status, topics dear to Steel due to her poor upbringing and struggles against sexism in the entertainment industry. Steel's legacy is simultaneously her success in understanding public interest in films and her advocacy for female empowerment in the entertainment industry during a period where men were reluctant to hire women.

Steel's first job at Paramount was in marketing. Tasked with merchandising the overschedule and overbudget *Star Trek: The Motion Picture* (1979), Steel convinced McDonald's to create commercials of Klingon aliens from the film eating there; this was, as Steel notes, the first movie tie-in of its kind and earned her a promotion to vice president of production by then-president of Paramount Michael Eisner. Attributing her initial success to creative marketing and her own energy, Steel demonstrated her ability to read the public audience with commercially successful films *Flashdance* and *Footloose* for young adults and rejecting suggestions to turn *Beverly Hills Cop* (1984) into a drama. Unlike many other studios and agents in Hollywood who prepared "packages" of scripts, directors, and stars, Steel and Paramount prioritized the script and control over the products. In 1985, after the abrupt departures of top executives such as Eisner, Barry Diller, and Jeffrey Katzenberg,

Steel was promoted to production chief, only the second woman after Sherry Lansing to lead a major film production department. Surprisingly fired from Paramount in 1987 while giving birth, Steel was hired by Columbia to succeed the dismissed David Puttnam and subsequently became the first female major studio head from 1987 to 1990, when the studio was sold to Sony. In the following years, Steel led Steel Pictures in a deal with The Walt Disney Company from 1990 to 1993 and Atlas Entertainment with husband Charles Roven from 1994 to her passing.

A key aspect of Steel's success was her ability to navigate complex relationships and male power structures in Hollywood during a period where women were rarely trusted with the responsibility of overseeing production budgets. Steel and other women were always aware of the differences in treatment compared to male colleagues, such as limitations into where female employees could go, their power in meetings, and the language used. Frustrated, Steel retained a mantra of refusing to cry (which implied weakness) in front of male executives, and was careful to note how well she was treated by many in her public engagements and autobiography (Steel 1993). Executives were impressed and aware of her tenacity as "the most determined woman in the business" (Masters 1993; Weinraub 1997a). Dismissing claims that her looks equated her career, Steel instead insisted the men she worked for valued that "I made them laugh and entertained them. And the other thing was that I could identify a good idea. Not a lot of people can do that. That was my gift" (Steel 1993; Weinraub 1997b).

Early in her career, Steel was "threatened" by other women in the industry, feeling their presence and the prevailing notion that only one woman could rise would prevent her success. In reflecting upon her transformation into advocate, she stated, "If there was only room for one woman in a room, I wanted to be her. I'm not proud of it. I certainly don't feel that way now" (Weinraub 1993). As her impact at studios and in film production increased, however, so did her awareness of the necessity of aiding women and furthering their careers. Cognizant of other women trailblazers before her, such as Lansing, Steel confronted her own discomfort with power as production chief, saying, "I have a responsibility to other women because I am in this position. I just want to make sure I honor them" (Smith 1987, 255). This responsibility saw numerous female writers, producers, directors, and others find jobs in Steel's films. Nora Ephron's first directorial job came from Steel and, upon Steel's death, said she "was the first woman to understand that part of her responsibility was to make sure that eventually there were lots of other powerful women. She hired women as executives, women as producers and directors, women as marketing people" (Weinraub 1997a). Many of her films similarly allowed for diversity in female roles.

Renee Ann Drouin

See also: Lansing, Sherry

Further Reading

Abramowitz, Rachel. 2000. *Is that a Gun in Your Pocket?: Women's Experience of Power in Hollywood.* New York: Random House.

Harmetz, Aljean. 1990. "Dawn Steel Quits Columbia Picture Post." *The New York Times*, January 9. https://www.nytimes.com/1990/01/09/arts/dawn-steel-quits-columbia-pictures-post.html

Masters, Kim. 1993. "Dawn Steel, Showing Her Mettle; The Fallen Studio Exec Plugs into a New Source of Power." *The Washington Post*, October 11.

Smith, Liz. 1987. "Dawn Steel: The Most Powerful Woman in Hollywood." *Vogue*, January 1.

Steel, Dawn. 1993. *They Can Kill You But They Can't Eat You: Lessons from the Front.* New York: Pocket Books.

Weinraub, Bernard. 1997a. "Dawn Steel, Studio Chief and Producer, Dies at 51." *The New York Times*, December 22. https://www.nytimes.com/1997/12/22/movies/dawn-steel-studio-chief-and-producer-dies-at-51.html

Weinraub, Bernard. 1997b. "Dawn Steel Muses from the Top of Hollywood's Heap." *The New York Times*, August 30. http://www.nytimes.com/1993/08/30/movies/dawn-steel-muses-from-the-top-of-hollywood-s-heap.html

Interview with Sherry Lansing

How was your father's love of story an inspiration for you to go into the movie business?

My father is probably the strongest reason that I got into the movie business. We used to go to the Museum of Science and Industry and watch the silent movies at the Nickelodeon. I saw what pleasure it gave him. I watched him laugh, I watched him be moved, I watched the effect that movies had on him. That seemed to me such an extraordinary thing, to be able to affect people's emotions. So that's really when I got interested.

What makes a good script, and how do you decide whether it should be made into a film?

I've always felt that filmmaking is not a passive experience. That if you read a good script, it should invoke an emotional response. It should make you cry, make you laugh, make you frightened, etc. If you're not engaged emotionally, that usually is not a good sign. You should also root for the characters, and by that I don't mean they have to be the stereotypical "good guys." I just mean that you should care about them. They should be morally complex, like we see in so many great television shows today such as Bryan Cranston's character Walter White in *Breaking Bad.* You care about them and you'll root for them even though they are morally complex. So if it had those two elements, I knew it was a good script.

I always trusted my instincts when it came to deciding which scripts I should develop. A script had to first contain those two elements, but then something about it had to strike me in the gut. Finally, I'd then always apply fiscal responsibility. If I thought it should cost 20 million but it would actually cost 200 million, then that meant we couldn't make the movie right now. But I never gave up on a good script and would put it on the shelf and wait, and wait, and sometimes I'd wait a decade until I could make it. It's heartbreaking sometimes because there are moments when you really want to make a movie, but the numbers aren't making sense and you just can't. But it doesn't mean that you can't find a way to do it later. Either way, you had to be extraordinarily passionate about the story and not give up. If you do give up, then you knew that you didn't have enough passion for it to begin with.

You should always try and get the right elements attached to the script first, not the other way around. Saying: "I like this movie star or director, even though I don't like the script" isn't right. The deal should never drive the decision; that's where you get in trouble. People often think if it's a good deal they should do it even though they don't believe in the material. But you can't make a movie if you don't believe in the material or you don't think it's fiscally responsible.

What is the key to overcoming discouragement? What has enabled you to be successful in the film industry as well as the nonprofit world with The Sherry Lansing Foundation?

You first have to start with a passion for something. It's like falling in love. You have that passion, whether it's turning a script into a movie or entering the nonprofit world to fund cancer research. That passion is so great that it overcomes any disappointment that you might have. The mission is greater than you so you try to almost never take anything personally. They didn't like the script? They're not interested in funding cancer research? It's not about me. It's about something bigger. It's not about me. It's about getting this movie made. It's not about me, it's about health care. Whatever it is, it's *not* about me. So, you know that any rejection you're experiencing isn't personal.

Then, I do believe you have to have great resiliency. You have to be able to pick yourself up after you've been knocked down. There's a wonderful saying from Sumner Redstone that goes, "Success is not built on success. It's built on failure . . . and picking yourself up and trying again." There's another from Winston Churchill that's great as well: "Success is going from failure to failure without losing your enthusiasm." It's a great quote and I think it's really true. The way to cultivate resiliency is to not take anything personally, and you accomplish that by having a passion and believing that the mission is bigger than your own indignity, hurts, or whatever it is. You concentrate on your mission while you're enduring rejection. Maybe they're being sexist or maybe they don't like the script and you believe in it, or the director doesn't want to do it. If you really believe that it's bigger than yourself, it's not about you and you are passionate about it, you will keep going. You will keep going for many, many decades. You know, we formed Stand Up to Cancer 10 years ago. We're every bit as passionate about it, probably even more so now, because we've experienced such loss among friends and people that we cared about.

Every cause *you believe in* is worthy. You believe that you want to get the movie made, and so therefore you will, within reason, endure rejection. You don't have to endure cruelty, but you'll endure rejection. You'll endure whatever it takes to get it done. The greatest trait that I learned from my mother was resiliency. To pick yourself up or, as she used to say: "pull your socks up and move on."

Another key thing is to not dwell in the past. Don't listen to all the noise that's surrounding you and don't get sucked into all that negativity. Just keep moving and keep trying to get it done, whatever you're doing. It's very pragmatic advice. You know, someone said to me the other day, "When you were the head of the studio, there was so much pressure." I said, you just can't think about that. You just have to think about the movie. The movies saved me. Wanting to get these movies done and concentrating just on that alone saved me from all the other noise. It enabled me to focus on the task at hand.

Can you speak to the presence of female executives and the spirit of sisterhood in the film industry now?

You know, that's what's changed. I think that's such an interesting thing. When I was making my way in the business, there weren't a lot of women there that were ahead of me . . . although there were some wonderful male mentors. I worked with great men who were very supportive of women. But at first, it really did feel like there was only room for one woman at the table and so we were wary of each other. That saddens me more than I can possibly tell you. It wasn't until later in my career, as women started to come up into more executive roles that it changed. We started to realize that a victory for one was a victory for all.

I've been gone from the entertainment industry for 13 years, but *The Hollywood Reporter* kindly named an award after me [the "Sherry Lansing Award"], so I attend this "Women in Entertainment Breakfast" that *The Hollywood Reporter* hosts to give the award. When I'm there I see these women, and they are best friends! They call each other up for jobs, and say, "Look, this job isn't right for me. You should do this." They have a sisterhood that is so wonderful to see. That only existed, I would say, in the last third of my career, but didn't exist in the first two-thirds. I have benefited from that in the sense that many of my best girlfriends became women in the industry. The value of female friendship and the value of sharing your problems or insecurities is now so precious. Stand Up to Cancer was created by eight women.

So those days of being the only woman at the table are long, long over and it's fantastic. When I think about the progress of the women's movement, I think about how foolish we were in the beginning. Then again, maybe tokenism needed to happen first, this idea that "we're only going to hire one woman. Okay, we can check that box." I mean, without getting into the whole #MeToo of it all, look at what women have accomplished! Just look at what they've done. The power of women is astounding today. That wasn't the way that it was when I was growing up, but you know, we quickly adapted. I must say several of my closest friends in the world are women in the entertainment business and we're forever giving each other advice. My girlfriends are, other than my husband and my family, the most valuable thing in my life.

Business executives can have a ruthless image, but your reputation for kindness precedes you. How has your empathy been a strength in the business world?

I've been a producer. So it was very hard for me to be cut-throat when passing on material because I had been there. And as you know, I think *Fatal Attraction* was passed on by, I don't know, over 36 directors, something like that. I know what it feels like to want to do something. I also know that I'm wrong as much as I'm right.

So I returned every phone call. I did every pass myself. And I always would end it with, "This is just my feeling, and when it's a huge hit, you can tell the story about how I passed on it" because you're going to be wrong a lot of times and no one has all the answers.

You also need luck. I mean, that's just a fact. Anybody who has had a great career has to look back and say, "Without luck, I couldn't have done it. Yes, I worked hard. Yes, I did this. Yes, I had resiliency. Yes, I overworked. Yes, I was passionate." But you need luck. So I understood how painful it was to be rejected, I felt great empathy and I never felt that I had all the answers. I felt if I passed on material directly and honestly, that I was giving every project and person the dignity that everyone deserves and the dignity that I would have wanted when I was a producer. I hated it when I would just get no response, and that's how I would sometimes know someone passed when I was a producer. I really hated that.

How do you guard against things like burnout and overwhelm?

I try to keep a balanced life, which is hard because the work is seven days a week. But I try to always find time once or twice a week to have lunch with a girlfriend, or a friend, and just get away from it all. Even before I was married, I had an active social life. After I got married, my husband and my two boys were wonderfully supportive. But throughout my career, I've always tried to make time for family and friends. I didn't always do a good job of it, but I tried to make time. Sometimes work was responsible for certain relationships ending because I preferred the work over the relationship, but that was a pretty good sign that the relationship wasn't the right relationship.

Interestingly enough, I always felt that if I stopped living a life outside of work I couldn't make good movies, because how can you write about love or do a move about love if you've never been in love? How can you do a movie about being hurt if you've never been hurt? If you don't know about life and don't participate in life, then how can you make movies that are going to touch people? So I always try to have time, free time for fun and travel. Travel was a wonderful way to keep my life in balance. I felt if I didn't strive for a balanced life, then I actually would not be a good executive or a good producer, because I'd become a machine.

Stuntwomen

Introduction

The work of stuntwomen in film is typically underappreciated. When a stuntwoman doubles for an actress in some death-defying act, she contributes to the story by making it more believable and making the film itself more exciting for audiences to watch. Doubling for the stars has often meant others have received credit for their work.

The story of stuntwomen in Hollywood cinema was not a steady progression or rise from obscurity to prominence. Prior to the 1920s during the silent era, stuntwomen such as Helen Gibson, who is regarded as the first professional stuntwoman in Hollywood history, went from stunt-doubling to becoming stars themselves since they were able to perform daring stunt work and convincingly act as well. At a time when women were still denied the right to vote based on the Victorian belief that their constitution was too delicate to occupy the public sphere, women like Helen Gibson were captured on film doing stunts or "gags" such as leaping onto moving trains, riding horses standing up, and dangling by rope from a bridge.

After the rise of the studio system in the 1920s, however, the number of stuntwomen began to dwindle along with the number of women in many other occupations of the Hollywood film industry as the cost of production rose and fewer producers were willing to put women in key filmmaking positions. Men of smaller size replaced stuntwomen, wearing wigs and dresses, and stuntwomen certainly were not considered the stars—they distinctly doubled for them. It would not be until the decline of the studio system and the start of the countercultural revolution in the late 1960s that the number of stuntwomen would steadily begin to increase. Today, stuntwomen like Zoë Bell harken back to the silent era tradition, making the transition from doubling for an actress to being the star actress who performs her own stunts. When one considers the skintight costumes women are typically asked to wear today, performing stunts without padding can make the job even more perilous than it is for their male peers.

It was not until 2001 with the formation of the Taurus World Stunt Awards that achievements in stunt work were recognized by the industry. A category for best stunt work still does not exist at the Academy Awards.

Laura L .S. Bauer

Bell, Zoë (1978–)

Despite the series of biographies and collected interviews with stuntmen and stuntwomen that have appeared since the explosive yet short-lived popularity of low-budget action films in the 1970s, the dearth of work on the "stuntie" in film and media studies (and in the popular press) is widely unrecognized. Scholars such as Jacob Smith, Miranda Janis Banks, and Lauren Steimer speak to the perplexing yet historically necessitated position of stunt performers as both "hypervisible [actors] . . . and *invisible* film laborers" (Steimer 2009, 363). Moreover, the female stunting star, though a long-standing figure in Asian cinema, is almost nonexistent in the United States.

New Zealander stuntwoman and actress Zoë Bell. Bell is well known for her stunt work doubling for actress Lucy Lawless in the *Xena: Warrior Princess* television series (1995–2001), and for Uma Thurman in Quentin Tarantino's *Kill Bill: Volume 1* (2003) and *Kill Bill: Volume 2* (2004). She made a notable transition to acting when Tarantino cast her to play herself in *Grindhouse* and *Death Proof* in 2007. Bell has won three Taurus World Stunt Awards. (Photo by Zoë Bell)

Zoë Bell (also known as "Zoë the Cat") is a prominent stuntwoman and actress who has performed in various films and television productions. Most notably, she is recognized for her roles as a stunt double for actress Lucy Lawless in the television series *Xena: Warrior Princess* and for actress Uma Thurman in Quentin Tarantino's action films, *Kill Bill: Vol. 1* (2003) and *Kill Bill: Vol. 2* (2004). Bell's extensive training in gymnastics and tae kwon do undoubtedly inform her work in the martial arts and action genres. Her role as primary stunt double for Lawless in *Xena*, for instance, required Bell to perform stunts while regularly suspended on a rigged harness ("wire-fu") in the show's effort to mimic both Hong Kong *wuxia* and kung-fu films. Such wirework and flying, kicking, and twirling sequences necessitated a foundation in gymnastics and martial arts, which are considered Bell's specialties. In turn, the additional training Bell received under the guidance of stunt coordinator Peter Bell in hybrid wire-fu techniques while working on *Xena* helped to cement her role as stunt double in Tarantino's *wuxia*-inspired series. While filming in China under the tutelage of choreographer Yuen Woo Ping, Bell acclimated to Hong Kong–style harness work, and her unique performance style evolved to include *wushu* and *samurai* expertise.

Bell, a native of Waiheke Island, New Zealand, was raised by her parents Andrew and Tish Bell, a doctor and nurse, respectively. In interviews, Bell has revealed that Waiheke Island provided an idyllic backdrop to nurture her athleticism and love of movement. Her father helped introduce Bell to stunt work when he treated a stuntman for a head injury and returned with an industry contact for Bell. Following her father's chance encounter, Bell performed her first professional stunt in *Shortland Street*, a New Zealand soap opera. After *Xena*, also filmed in New Zealand, ended its run in 2001, Bell visited the United States for a *Xena* convention, where she met fellow stuntwoman Jeannie Epper. Epper played a pivotal role in mentoring Bell and in assisting the start of Bell's career in the United States. Both Epper and Bell were the focus of Amanda Micheli's documentary, *Double Dare* (2004), which captured the struggles of these women—Epper as a veteran stuntwoman and Bell as a newcomer—to secure work in Hollywood. Micheli's documentary suggests that Epper was instrumental in facilitating Bell's encounter with Tarantino's stunt scout, Kenny Lesco. After starring as a stunt double in the *Kill Bill* series, Bell was cast as herself in Tarantino's half of the double-feature, *Grindhouse Presents: Death Proof* (2007).

In recruiting Bell for *Death Proof* (2007), Tarantino helped her break the boundaries of the Hollywood caste system and make the rare transition to female action star. She has since not only acted in several movies but also starred *and* co-produced in the action-horror film, *Raze* (2013). Of the difficulties inherent in her transition, Bell stated: "I've definitely made the transition into acting over doubling, just because I needed to make it clear to myself, so that I fully committed. Being perceived as an actor by the outside world, rather than as a stunt girl who does dialogue, has been a part of the challenge in front of me" (Radish 2014). Although Bell acknowledges the gender disparities that still exist in the stunt (and film) industry today, she fully embraces the growing interest in powerful and complex female action heroes in film. As Steimer (2009) concedes, Bell's groundbreaking work on *Xena*, as well as the documentary on her early career and her starring role in *Grindhouse* (2007), "have helped to bring about the recent resurgence of the stunting star" (380).

Bell has received various accolades for her stunt performances in feature films. Among her many nominations, Bell and stuntwoman Monica Staggs)won a Taurus World Stunt Award in 2005 in the categories Best Overall Stunt by a Stunt Woman and Best Fight for their trailer fight in *Kill Bill: Volume 2* (2004). She won an award for Best Overall Stunt by a Stunt Woman with stuntwoman Tracy Keehn-Dashnaw in 2007 for their stunt performances on a 1970 Dodge Challenger in *Grindhouse* (2007). Most recently, Bell won a Maverick Movie Award alongside stuntmen Ryan Happy and Chris Torres for the movie *Reflections* (2008) and the Indie Icon Award at the Las Vegas International Film Festival in 2013 for *Raze* (2013).

Jennifer A. Lopez-Lam

See also: Epper, Jeannie

Further Reading

Banks, Miranda Janis. 2006. *Bodies of Work: Rituals of Doubling and the Erasure of Film/TV Production Labor*. Ann Arbor: University of Michigan.

Collier, Sean. 2009. "Interview: Zoë Bell." *Verbicide Magazine*, 25, February 12. www.verbicidemagazine.com/2009/03/10/interview-zoe-bell/

Conley, Kevin. 2007. "Stunt Woman Zoe Bell Is on Fire," *Marie Claire*. April 8, http://www.marieclaire.com/celebrity/a384/zoe-bell

IMDb. 2015. "Zoë Bell." http://www.imdb.com/name/nm1057928

Radish, Christina. 2014. "Zoe Bell Talks RAZE, Transitioning from Stuntwoman to Actress, Juggling Acting and Producing, and More." *Collider*, February 15. http://collider.com/zoe-bell-raze-interview

Smith, Jacob. 2004. "Seeing Double: Stunt Performance and Masculinity." *Journal of Film and Video* 56(3): 35–53.

Steimer, Lauren. 2009. "From *Wuxia* to *Xena*: Translation and the Body Spectacle of Zoë Bell." *Discourse* 31(3): 359–390.

Epper, Jeannie (1941–)

Though most film buffs would not recognize her by sight, Jeannie Epper is a true Hollywood icon. Born Jean Luann Epper more than 70 years ago, Jeannie maintains her vital role as part of four generations of Hollywood stuntpeople—a family institution known simply as "the Eppers." A female pioneer in the realm of stunt work, Jeannie's 50-year career is proof of the Eppers' staying power, as this matriarch and mentor remains active in the field of movie stunts despite the supposed limitations of her gender, or her age.

While the Epper family "may not be the most famous . . . or the flashiest . . . their roots undoubtedly go the deepest" where the Hollywood stunt profession and its often dangerous "gags" are concerned (Nashawaty 2007, 91). Jeannie and her five siblings, Margo, Gary, Tony, Andy, and Stephanie Epper, owe many of their special abilities to their father, one of Hollywood's original stuntmen, John Epper. In the 1960s, John doubled for the likes of actors Gary Cooper, Errol Flynn, and Ronald Reagan, most often stepping in when a tricky stunt on horseback was required. Jeannie's own career as a stunt double began at the age of nine, when she successfully rode a horse bareback down a steep cliff to cinch a particularly tricky scene with traditional Epper panache. After this first rush of on-set adrenaline, Jeannie was devoted to her craft and later came to realize that "perhaps her first love was indeed the stunt world" (Della Cava 2007).

At a time when men often served as doubles for female actors, however, Jeannie had to blaze her own trail in the stunt world. TV stunt work for women did not become common enough to pursue as a career until the mid-to-late 1970s. Thus, it was Jeannie's early work as a regular stand-in for Lynda Carter on *Wonder Woman* (1975–1979) and for Kate Jackson on *Charlie's Angels* (1976) that solidified her position in the profession. Work in action feature films soon followed, with Jeannie completing Kathleen Turner's celebrated downhill mudslide in one of 1984's major movie productions, *Romancing the Stone*. Jeannie's work on the big screen continued through the late 1990s and well into the more recent 2000s, where she perfected stunts for *Catch Me If You Can* (2002), *Minority Report* (2002), and *Kill Bill: Vol. 2* (2004). To date, Jeannie has completed nearly 150 feature film and television stunts—and this figure is a conservative estimate at best.

Extensive, long-term work in such a risky and physically demanding business has led Jeannine to encounter her share of dangerous narrow escapes. Trapped in and burned by a collapsing, fire-filled building while filming the television show *Lancer* (circa 1968), Jeannine later awoke in the hospital with much of her hair singed by the fire but the doll from the scene still firmly clutched in her hands. Just a few years later, another stunt double accidentally hit Jeannie with a picture frame—despite advance warning from Jeannie to take a step back—cracking her skull on the set of *Foxy Brown* (1974). Reportedly a born-again Christian and "deeply religious," Epper prays before each stunt. She states, "As far as I'm concerned, whenever I do a stunt, it's 150 percent going to work out" (Nashawaty 2007, 95). In 2000 at the age of 59, Epper put her faith to the test in a different way by stepping forward to donate a kidney to her good friend, actor Ken Howard. Both recovered from the consequent surgeries, and despite a doctor's dire warning, Jeannie was able to return to her profession as a stunt double.

Currently listed as treasurer of the United Stuntwomen's Association, Epper also serves as champion for female newcomers in her field. Epper's dedication to the business and its young women is in part the focus of Amanda Micheli's acclaimed 2004 documentary, *Double Dare*. The film follows Epper and a younger counterpart, Zoë Bell, through the various trials and tribulations that greet new and seasoned stuntwomen alike. Micheli notes that while Epper "deserves to be a leading stunt coordinator," she has taken on this coveted role for a few films, as such employment has been slow to come in the still male-dominated field (Della Cava 2007).

In 2007, the Taurus Stunt Awards paid tribute to Epper's commitment to her profession by granting her the Taurus Lifetime Achievement Award, honoring her for 50 years of success in stunt work. "[C]onsidered by many to be the greatest stuntwoman who's ever lived," Jeannie continues to seek work in Hollywood, despite being over 70 years of age (Nashawaty 2007, 94). While all of her brothers and sisters have retired from the stunt business, Jeannie persists. As of this writing, her most recent work was in the 2015 film *Hot Pursuit*. While Jeannie steadfastly refuses to retire, she does confess that she now chooses her roles a little more carefully, as the bruises do not heal quite as quickly and easily as in the past. Despite the ever-present physical dangers and the enduring inequality, Jeannie has stated, quite simply, that she loves doing stunts: "'It's where I'm the most alive'" (Osgood and Lee 2014). "When they call, it's hard to say no"—and thankfully, they do keep calling (Della Cava 2007).

Cindy Marlow McClenagan

See also: Bell, Zoë

Further Reading

Della Cava, Marco R. 2007. "Epper Pulls Out All the Stunts." *USA Today*, March 2. Accessed June 18, 2015. http://eds.a.ebscohost.com/eds/detail/detail?vid=2&sid=b88dedae-0ee8-4cf0-a492-fed4c506de4a%40sessionmgr4004&hid=4202&bdata=JnNpdGU9ZWRzLWxpdmU%3d#db=edsgao&AN=edsgcl.161044897

Micheli, Amanda, dir. 2004. *Double Dare*. DVD. New York: Film Buff.

Nashawaty, Chris. 2007. "Danger Is Their Middle Name." *Entertainment Weekly* 959/960: 90–98.

Osgood, Charles, and Cowan Lee. 2014. "Stunt Performers Taking a Fall in This Spring's Biggest Hit." *CBS News Sunday Morning Newspaper Source*, April 4.

Evans, Debbie (1958–)

Born in Lakewood, California, stuntwoman Debbie Evans is no stranger to Hollywood or to the action film industry of the late 20th and early 21st centuries. However, since the majority of Evans's work has come as a stunt driver, trick rider, and body double, her name and face may not be as recognizable as her finely honed skills. With over 200 stunt credits, dating from 1973's *The Young and the Restless* to 2015's *Monster Trucks*, Evans is considered one of Hollywood's top professional stuntwomen. A pioneer in the field of female stunt work, Evans proved early on that women were capable of achieving stunts—vehicular, mechanical, and practical—on par with their male counterparts.

Evans did not set out to pursue a career in stunt work, but it did follow naturally from an active childhood encouraged by a motorcycle "daredevil" of a father (Adams 2001). David Evans, who raced Steve McQueen in the documentary *On Any Sunday* (1971), first introduced his daughter Debbie to riding motorcycles at the young age of six. Soon after, Debbie participated in her first motorcycle observed trials at the age of nine, competing against males her age, as there was no class for females at any age. She eventually received an "expert" rank in motorcycle trials classification, becoming the first woman ever to claim such a title. A five-year sponsorship by Yamaha in the 1970s led to one of Debbie's famous pre-show and half-time competition "tricks": doing a headstand on a motorcycle seat while balancing herself—and the cycle, sans kickstand—perfectly. Her trick career had begun.

Stuntwoman Debbie Evans receiving her statuette for winning the Best Overall Stunt by a Woman for *Superman Returns* (2006), at the 2007 Taurus World Stunt Awards. Her transition into film stunt work stemmed from her exceptional ability as one of the best female motorcycle riders in observed trials competition in the United States. Evans is now considered one of Hollywood's top stuntwomen. (M. Phillips/WireImage/Getty Images)

In the late 1970s, Evans took her talents to additional "firsts" on an even larger stage—that of Hollywood film. Her break into the film industry was a motorcycle stunt jump over a 30-foot ravine for the movie *Deathsport* (1978), starring David Carradine). She credits her motorcycle trial riding as crucial to her success with this first stunt, and with the many that followed, suggesting that she "treats each stunt like . . . a trials section" (Van Beveren 1999). Shortly after filming *Deathsport,* Evans became the only female to compete in the 1979 CBS Stunt Competition, in which she placed a very respectable second overall. Evans has worked as a stuntwoman in television and film ever since, including early work as Lynda Carter's double in the television series *Wonder Woman* (1975–1979). Her TV super-hero practice fed the growth of Evans's stunt career through the 1980s and 1990s. In the early 2000s, highly acclaimed work in film blockbusters such as *Charlie's Angels* (2001)—where "she fell down a bell-tower shaft and cartwheeled down a set of stairs" (Adams 2001)—and stunt work for *The Fast and the Furious* (2001), *The Matrix Reloaded* (2003), and *Mr. and Mrs. Smith* (2005), solidified her high-profile position in the industry. In addition to her talent for manipulating fast motorcycles and speeding vehicles of all sorts, Evans's innate athletic ability has allowed her to hone various martial arts and sport skills, including the ability to water ski, snowboard, rappel, rock climb, and scuba dive.

Awards have also come naturally to Evans. In 1998, she became the top American motorcycle rider in the unofficial Women's Trials World Championship. Evans is also the winner of several Taurus World Stunt Awards (2002, 2004, and 2007) for stunt work as Michelle Rodriguez's body double in *The Fast and the Furious,* and as Carrie-Ann Moss's stunt double in the now famous Ducati scene for *The Matrix Reloaded.* The early 2000s are peppered with other Taurus World Stunt Award nominations and additional awards for ensemble trick or stunt work. In 2003, Evans returned to her roots in motorcycle competition, winning the final round of the Federation of International Motorcyclists (FIM) European Championship. That same year the American Motorcycle Association (AMA) inducted her into the Motorcycle Hall of Fame.

The daredevil tradition runs strong in Debbie Evans's family with her sister, Donna Evans, also working in the Hollywood stunt industry, as well as husband, Lane Leavitt, and two of their three children (so far). Leavitt and Evans joined forces to create a successful business venture, the stunt-work agency Leavittation, Inc. With a hint of admiration, husband Leavitt notes, "[Debbie's] pain tolerance is so high. On *Batman & Robin* (1997), she broke her ankle. She taped it up and she finished the night's work with a broken ankle" (Weir 2006). And what is Evans's advice for avoiding injury and executing a great stunt? "Just go with the fall. Try not to fight it, relax into it . . . and if you are in a dress, always keep your legs together" (Adams 2001).

Cindy Marlow McClenagan

Further Reading

Adams, Jason. 2001. "She's All Splat." *Sports Illustrated Women* 3(6): 68.

AMA Motorcycle Hall of Fame. 2003. "Debbie Evans." http://www.motorcyclemuseum.org/halloffame/detail.aspx?RacerID=300.

Griffins, John. 2003. "Double Dare: For Sisters, Debbie and Donna Evans, Dangling from Mountaintops Is All in a Day's Work." *Reader's Digest* 162(970): 104–110.

Van Beveren, Anne. 1999. "Pretty Trick." *Free 2 Wheel* December: 16–19, 29.

Weir, Bill. 2006. "Hollywood's Stunt Family." *Good Morning America* (ABC). *Regional Business News*. http://eds.a.ebscohost.com/eds/detail/detail?vid=2&sid=16cf9940-1ddc-43dd-a86ef259aa8aace2%40sessionmgr4005&hid=4202&bdata=JnNpdGU9ZWRzLWxpdmU%3d#db=bwh&AN=35080899.

Gibson, Helen (1891–1977)

Known as the "Girl with Nine Lives" and "Daredevil Helen," Helen Gibson is widely regarded as the first professional stuntwoman in film history. She was also one of the top "serial queens"—actresses who were famous for starring in short action films—and starred in the popular adventure series *The Hazards of Helen*. Gibson worked as a stunt double and extra with a film career that spanned 51 years. As a serial star, she was famous for death-defying stunts such as jumping from a bridge onto a speeding train and driving a motorcycle up a wooden ramp, through a wooden gate, and into a speeding train car. She is an official inductee of the Hollywood Stuntmen's Hall of Fame and inspired an award in her name for the Action Icon Awards, an annual ceremony that celebrates the achievements of professional stuntwomen. Gibson was fearless, and her daring work inspired countless women to follow in her nimble footsteps.

Helen Gibson was born Rose August Werner on August 27, 1891, in Cleveland, Ohio, to Swiss and German immigrant parents. At the age of 18, she moved to the Miller Brothers' 101 Ranch in Oklahoma to learn horseback riding after seeing a rodeo performance at the Luna Park fairground in Cleveland. She very quickly became a leading rider for the Miller Brothers' traveling Western show, which then led to work as an extra for short Westerns. In between her work as an extra in early Western films, she performed in rodeos in Los Angeles, where she met her husband Edmund "Hoot" Gibson, who would later become a popular Western star. In 1915, she was hired by the Kalem Film Company to do stunt work for Helen Holmes in the successful railroad series—a highly specific genre of short films that revolved around adventures on trains—*The Hazards of Helen*.

While *The Hazards of Helen* is often referred to as a "serial," it was really a series, since each episode was self-contained and did not feature the cliffhanger ending that defined the serial. The episodes of a series could be shown out of order, which many exhibitors did with *The Hazards of Helen*. In the series and serials of the 1910s, the starring female characters were usually the heroines, and they subverted the gender norms of their time through their dangerous physical stunts and acts of bravery. Aside from *The Hazards of Helen*, the most famous of these films was *The Perils of Pauline* starring Pearl White.

Although serial queens like Pearl White, Helen Holmes, and Grace Cunard were famous for doing their own action scenes, doubles were sometimes used for the more dangerous stunts. Gibson closely resembled Helen Holmes and was first hired as her stunt double in 1915. Later that year, Holmes left the Kalem Film Company to start a production company with her husband, and Gibson was recast in the lead role. The studio made Gibson change her name from Rose to Helen to match the character. The recasting and name change proved confusing for filmgoers. *Motion Picture Magazine* received many letters from fans asking whether

Helen Gibson and Helen Holmes were the same person. Holmes led *The Hazards of Helen* for 48 episodes and Gibson the remaining 71. After the series ended, Gibson was hired by the Universal Pictures Company to do more railroad films, including the popular series *A Daring Daughter*, which featured her famous motorcycle stunt.

Gibson considered her most dangerous stunt to be one from the episode "A Girl's Grit" from *The Hazards of Helen*. In this scene, she jumped onto the top of a speeding train from the roof of a railroad station. In 1968, Gibson recalled this near-death experience in an article for *Film Review*: "The distance between station roof and train top was accurately measured, and I practiced the jump with the train standing still. The train had to be moving on camera for about a quarter mile and its accelerating velocity was timed to the second. I was not nervous as the train approached, and leapt without hesitation. I landed right, but the train's motion made me roll toward the end of the car. I caught hold of an air vent and hung on, allowing my body to dangle over the edge to increase the effect on the screen. I suffered only a few bruises" (Gibson 1968, 34).

Serials were banned in many American cities in 1921 due to concerns regarding the female characters' unfeminine behaviors and the sexual overtones of the villain's capture and torture of the heroine (often with rope binding). The censorship of the genre coincided with Gibson's declining stardom and financial ruin.

In 1920, Gibson had divorced Hoot Gibson and created her own production company, Helen Gibson Productions. Unfortunately, her foray into production failed, and she was forced to declare bankruptcy before her company's first film *No Man's Woman* was completed. The next year, she starred in William Bertram's *The Wolverine* and was scheduled to appear in the director's next film before suffering from appendicitis and losing the role. After another failed production and a serious injury, she went to work for the Ringling Bros./Barnum & Bailey circus as a rodeo performer for several years.

In 1927, she returned to Hollywood to work as a stunt double for older actresses, including Marie Dressler, May Robson, and Ethel Barrymore. She was still performing dangerous stunts at the age of 44, including a long fall down a flight of stairs in the 1938 film *The Condemned Women*. According to the *Los Angeles Times*, she received $50 for the stunt and $25 for the reshoot the following day. Her last role was a bit part as a horse driver in the 1962 Western *The Man Who Shot Liberty Valance*. Helen Gibson died at the age of 86 on October 10, 1977.

Megan Heatherly

Further Reading

Bean, Jennifer M. 2001. "Technologies of Early Stardom and the Extraordinary Body." *Camera Obscura*. 16(3): 8–57.

Calderazzo, John. 1989. "Actors in the Sky." *The Georgia Review*. 43(4): 769–781.

Gibson, Helen. 1968. "In Very Early Days Screen Acting Was Often a Matter of Guts." *Films in Review* 19: 28–34.

Gregory, Mollie. 2015. *Stuntwomen: The Untold Hollywood Story*. Lexington: University Press of Kentucky.

Rainey, Buck. 1999. *Serials and Series: A World Filmography, 1912–1956.* Jefferson, NC: McFarland & Company.

Stamp, Shelley. 2004. "An Awful Struggle between Love and Ambition: Serial Heroines, Serial Stars, and Their Female Fans." In *The Silent Cinema Reader.* Edited by Lee Grieveson and Peter Krämer. London, New York: Routledge, 210–225.

Interview with Zoë Bell

What's the life of a stuntwoman like? Do you work on multiple projects at the same time or just one?

It's an ever-changing industry, especially for a woman. Everybody's career has a different shape and path, but the work usually depends on the particular skill set and how the stunt person got into it.

I went quite a few years before I was hired regularly on jobs. Typically, if you're doubling a female doing action, you were on it for the length of the show because you were probably a predominant character like I was on *Xena: Warrior Princess.* There isn't usually a lot of background action that involves women. You might be a villager fleeing or something like that. So if it's mostly soldiers or warriors, the doubles were usually men. *Xena* was quite different, obviously, because there were warrior women in it, which was awesome. I feel like, as a woman, you're either getting short stints or you're on for the duration, and there's not that much work in short stints as there is for men. Men would be a day here and a day there, a week on that project and two weeks on this project. They would skip about like that. There's not as much of that kind of work available for a woman, at least not enough to make a living. If you were doubling for the length of a show, though, that was a sweet spot to be in.

It seems like a lot of guys can have a career not having to look like the actor in question because they can be background. They can be the gangster, thug, soldier, etc. But it's different when it comes to roles available for women. There's more demand for stuntwomen to aesthetically match the actress they double (whether they're short or tall, etc.). So there's pressure to have plain features that don't stand out; women with distinct features will find it much more difficult to have a constant stream of work.

What's it like working in such a physically demanding, male-dominated profession?

It's funny, I think one of the interesting things is that it does seem like an obviously male-dominated profession because it's perceived as being aggressive, athletic, and all those things that, for a long time, were far more associated with men than they were with women. I've not worked in any other industry or any other department so I can only speak to my personal experience. But it seems like once the women's movement got started, more female action roles started happening. I'm thinking of shows like *Xena* and *Alias.*

I've also always felt that if I had the skill set and the right attitude, I was willing to improve, listen when I needed to listen, and know when to speak up if I had an opinion, and if I just worked really hard, those boys would respect it. If you're an athlete, and you step up, and you have something good to offer, most of them will—not always willingly—but most will at some point come around and respect you because there comes a point where you've just got to give credit where credit is due.

It's hard to get your foot in the door to show what you can do. While doubling for *Xena*, I was in a harness 75 percent of the time and kicking the asses of the boys who might otherwise judge me on a daily basis. I think there is something sporting in the stuntperson world, there's this unspoken understanding: you knock a guy on his ass in a bar to win respect. So the old boys and I would get in a scrap and then get over it.

I don't know, it's an understanding that's a challenge to convey in words because it exists on a primal level, and it's deeply associated with being masculine, although I think both men and women have it. When I'm working with intelligent, talented, experienced men, they quickly recognize I'm also intelligent, talented, and experienced because I can show them I'm physically capable.

Do you think there's a certain personality type that's drawn to stunt work?

It's not often that you come across a really sort of insular, introverted person who's drawn to performing in front of a bunch of people and throwing themselves off buildings, or even doing martial arts. There's a lot of nerds that are stuntpeople because they've been the nerds that studied martial arts emphatically when they were little. Maybe they didn't fit in or they loved Bruce Lee, so they studied martial arts.

I don't think "thrill-seeking" would accurately describe why I'm drawn to stunt work though; it's more like there's a certain satisfaction when you pull off something really physically demanding. I've always liked going fast, and I like being up high, but it's never consciously about the risk. If I think I'm going to die or get hurt, I just experience anxiety. That doesn't sound fun to me. But the accomplishment and the execution and the problem solving to perform this thing or make something work, that's where I get my satisfaction. Impressing people on set like the director or the stunt coordinator with pulling it off—getting those kinds of reactions out of people, are the things that really get me going. The collaboration, the teamwork, I love.

As a kid I used to love to climb trees and the higher the better. I used to love jumping off stuff. I like falling. I like going fast. but I don't feel as though any of it is an adrenaline thing. There's a freedom to it for me, it feels liberating.

So it's extremely difficult when I get hurt. Injuries are my least favorite topic. Some people are really proud of it and are like, "I got this or that," and they love to compare war stories and notes and I get it. I don't even have a judgment around it. It's more just, for me personally, being hurt is the most miserable time for me. When I'm incapacitated, I start freaking out asking "Who am I if I don't have these abilities?" I start to suffer a full-on identity crisis when I'm physically limited, because knowing what my body is capable of is massively satisfying.

What's your favorite thing about being a stuntwoman?

My favorite experience about being a stuntperson is functioning within the stunt team. Having an unspoken language that happens between you and your team members when it's going right. The physics of it all becomes an instinctive conversation. Knowing that I can trust those people, that I can lean on those people, and knowing that I can push my boundaries because I trust that they have my back. I'm capable of so much more because they are there. That is one of the most beautiful feelings. We are not all badasses. Those moments are really beautiful. They might be people you don't necessarily ever want to drink a beer with, that might drive you batty outside of work. But in that moment, we know we have each other. Ninety-nine percent of what I do, I couldn't do without other people. Who it is in the forefront of the shop is like the lead singer of the band. But without a band, they're just a person and a microphone, you know?

It's also not just figuring out how to make gags work, but figuring out how we can make the flight, the gag, or the action serve the story. That's part of problem solving. Figuring where to put the camera so it looks like the heaviest impact or it looks fast. If I have to move the camera to aid that. It's not just problem solving, it's also enhancing and figuring out how to make something fresh, and new, and shocking. Audiences are savvy, so you have to keep a step ahead. If you're going for a normal fight and there's one massive move, you could go five massive moves in a row. The first one could be the most insane, incredible thing you've ever seen, but if you don't build up to it, it gets boring. You've got to fit the rules of the world that you're in and you've got to stick to it because these days, people are like, "What? If he can jump over that building, how come he can't jump over that car?" People think like that now.

And people now know we exist. People didn't used to really know about stuntpeople. They thought we were all daredevils. There was the assumption that it was the actors doing it the whole time and you didn't really get spoken about. It was behind the magician's curtain. I sort of miss those days, actually.

People used to come to me (more so on *Kill Bill* than on *Xena*) and say, "Doesn't it upset you that Uma gets all the credit for all the stuff that you've actually done?" No! Of course not, that's my job. My job is to make it look like this character is capable—and it's her job too! Both of our jobs is to make this character, The Bride, look like everything that she and I do is that character. You're not meant to watch it thinking it's Uma Thurman. You're meant to watch it and think it's The Bride. If they can tell it was me, then I messed up.

How did you get interested in acting, and what has it been like to act yourself in *Death Proof*?

I remember watching Uma being The Bride and I never thought, "I can do that." It was more, "Man. Imagine that!" Imagine doing both sides: establishing the character and then figuring out what the action feels or looks like. Uma establishes something and that informs who I become as The Bride.

When I was doing *Death Proof* I was terrified of acting. Sometimes, when I was really self-conscious and couldn't figure out how to act like Zoë the character as opposed to just myself, who was incredibly scared and nervous, I approached it like as a stuntwoman which meant turning off my emotions. But that mentality would sometimes mess me up. It wasn't until *Kill Bill*, when Quentin was like, "No, no. I need that. I need some of those emotions in your work, please" that I came to appreciate how emotions could inform my work as a stuntwoman. If you break down the stunt when I'm on the bonnet of the car in *Death Proof*, I had to act in order to make the sequence and the stunt amazing.

Now, the only way I could feel safe enough to act while doing the stunt was because I had ultimate faith in the team supporting me. Tracy Keehn-Dashnaw, who was driving the car. Buddy Joe Hooker, who was driving Kurt's car. The guy working the camera car and the arm, and Quentin's direction and my coordinator watching from the outside. I got to push my boundaries because I knew those guys were keeping me safe and what we had put in place was keeping me safe. I was able to throw myself around and put my feet in scary spots and do all of those things that, had I not felt safe, that chase sequence would have been boring because I would have just been white-knuckled, hugging myself to the bonnet of the car at all times.

I can't reveal exactly what we did, but there were a ton of professionals and safety measures put in place. So when people are like, "Oh, sweet, I'm going to try it!" When people start getting on cars with two belts, never having done anything like this before, and the person driving the car isn't a professional, and they don't have a safety I feel like I have to speak to it a bit. What we did out there wasn't easy and it's not safe.

Visual and Special Effects

Introduction

In the earliest days of cinema, filmmakers were quick to notice the potential the medium had for special effects. The realization that there was an illusion created by separate frames coming together that produced smooth, continuous movement meant that the manipulation of individual frames could produce a visual trick effect on screen. Simple in-camera techniques in which an effect is created solely within the camera are some of the earliest examples of special effects in cinema. The first jump-cut (where there is a break in continuous action), for example, was discovered accidentally by Georges Méliès in his short film *The Vanishing Lady* (1896).

Since then, optical effects (in which images are created photographically with the camera) and mechanical effects, which are achieved during live-action shooting (including techniques that range from animatronics to atmospheric effects such as fabricating wind or snow) have evolved, pushed forward by various advances in technology. Since the development of computer-generated imagery (CGI) in the 1970s, a distinction between special effects (SFX, SPFX, or FX) and visual effects (VFX) has emerged. Special effects encompasses optical and mechanical effects, which typically occur during live-action shooting, whereas visual effects refers to images generated or modified, commonly occurring during post-production (with a great amount of careful planning in pre-production and production). Superimpositions, compositing, claymation, miniatures, matte paintings, stop motion, split-screen technology, motion control, FX makeup, CGI, animatronics, animated CGI, motion capture, and 3D all fall under the umbrella category of visual and special effects, and all require specific skill sets and training to execute.

Although the Oscar category for Best Special Effects would not exist until 1938, the first Academy Award given for special effects was called "Best Engineering Effects," which was awarded to Roy Pomeroy in 1928 for *Wings* (1927) and David O. Selznick petitioned the Academy to recognize the then groundbreaking stop-motion animation created by Willis O'Brien for *King Kong* (1933) but was denied. It is fair to say that special effects has a long history, and yet this is one occupation in Hollywood where women remain extremely underrepresented.

Women did not begin to enter the field of special effects until the late 1970s, and some of the first women on the scene can be attributed to the efforts of Patricia Rose Duignan. Duignan was the production assistant on the first *Star Wars* movie in 1977 (she would later go on to be the production supervisor on *Star Wars: Return of the Jedi* in 1983 and director of marketing at Industrial Light & Magic [ILM] for many years afterward). While there, Duignan was the force behind hiring women such as Peg Hunter, Mary Walter, and Lori J. Nelson at ILM. Many more prominent women would begin their careers in special effects in the 1990s. Sara Bennett would be the first woman VFX supervisor to win an Oscar for her work in *Ex Machina* in 2015—Bennett is only the third woman nominated in the category, which was also won by Suzanne Benson in 1986 for her work on *Aliens*.

Laura L. S. Bauer

Bennett, Sara (Unknown–)

Best known for her work on the first four Harry Potter movies, the television series *Dr. Who* and *Sherlock*, and the film *Ex Machina* (2014), Sara Bennett is a British visual effects supervisor specializing in 2D effects. In addition to her vast portfolio, which frequently spans across both the small and big screens, in 2013, Bennett co-founded the visual effects production company, Milk. Prior to the launch of Milk, she was head of 2D at Mill TV & Film from 2005 onward. As a respected and award-winning artist, Bennett has advocated for more opportunities for women in a male-dominated industry as well as mentored young women interested in visual effects.

Visual effects supervisor Sara Bennett holding her Oscar for Best Achievement in Visual Effects for her work on *Ex Machina* (2014), at the 2016 Vanity Fair Oscar Party at Wallis Annenberg Center for the Performing Arts on February 28, 2016, in Beverly Hills, California. (Alberto E. Rodriguez/WireImage)

Bennett's work has not gone unnoticed. For their work on the movie *Ex Machina*, Bennett and Andrew Whitehurst, Paul Norris, and Mark Williams Ardington of Double Negative, a British motion picture visual effects and computer animation company, beat some impressive competitors for the 2016 Best Visual Effects Academy Award: *Mad*

Max: Fury Road, The Martian, Star Wars: The Force Awakens, and *The Revenant.* Interestingly, Bennett also worked on *The Martian* although she wasn't part of the nominated team at the 2016 Academy Awards. For her work on *Ex Machina,* Bennett was additionally nominated for a 2016 British Academy Award (BAFTA).

In *Ex Machina*, an eccentric CEO selects a programmer to evaluate the artificial intelligence and conduct a Turing test of a robot named Ava. While Double Negative's Whitehurst, Norris, and Williams Ardington created Ava, Bennett and her team at Milk created Ava's world—both her point of view and other special effects in the film. To show the audience the world through Ava's eyes, one critic noted how Bennett "incorporated modern-day software with a dash of traditional science fiction filters" to ultimately create a robot an "audience could fall in love with" (Woerner 2016). Having Bennett's female perspective would prove invaluable.

Bennett is only the third woman to be nominated for a Best Visual Effects Oscar in the Academy Award's 86-year history, and only the second woman to win. She is the first female supervisor to take home the statue. The last woman nominated was Pamela Easley for *Cliffhanger* in 1993, marking a 22-year absence of women in the category. The last and only other female artist awarded the Academy Award for Visual Effects was Suzanne M. Benson for *Aliens* in 1986.

It is not just the Academy of Motion Picture Arts and Sciences, however, that has honored Bennett. In addition to winning an Oscar, Bennett won a primetime Emmy for her work on *Sherlock* and was nominated for a BAFTA in 2010 for her work on *Merlin*. In total, she boasts 10 award nominations and 2 wins.

The acknowledgement of her work has helped raise awareness about the lack of recognition as well as the lack of opportunities for women in the field. "It is tragic that she is only the second female to win and the first VFX supervisor to win. I can certainly see the balance being addressed with more women coming in at [the] entry level, but there is a lot more work to be done," stated Will Cohen, a Milk co-founder (Pennington 2016).

As a co-founder of Milk and head of Milk's 2D effects, Bennett has not only supported greater diversity within the field but also has made a concerted effort to hire more women. In a 2016 interview, she stated, "I'm very aware if two people came in for the same job, a man and a woman, and they're both equally skilled and both great at what they do, I'd naturally pick the female because it's important to change the ratio up a little bit. I think we're currently at 70 percent men, 30 percent women" (Woerner 2016). Bennett believes that greater diversity can lead to a better work environment and better art.

In 2017, Milk was awarded £2m by BGF (Business Growth Fund) to expand their studios; the company believes it is poised to grow based on increasing content demands due to streaming services like Netflix and Amazon. With this growth, Bennett and her colleagues will likely continue their work on improving gender equity in the field. As mentioned after her 2016 Academy Award win, Bennett remarked, "I would *love* to see more women in prominent creative roles in our industry—I was a little shocked to find out I was the third ever female VFX Oscar nominee" (Reid 2016).

Melissa Vosen Callens

Further Reading

Giardina, Carolyn. 2016. "Oscars: 'Ex Machina' Wins for Visual Effects." *The Hollywood Reporter*, February 28. https://www.hollywoodreporter.com/behind-screen/2016-oscars-visual-effects-award-870731

IMDb. 2017. "Sara Bennett." Accessed December 17, 2017. http://www.imdb.com/name/nm1025904

Investment News. 2017. "Visual Effects Company Gets BGF Funding to Expand Studio." *Investment News*, June 21. https://www.bgf.co.uk/visual-effects-company-gets-bgf-funding-expand-studio

Pennington, Adrian. 2016. "'Ex Machina's Sara Bennett First Woman VFX Supervisor to Win Oscar." *Screen Daily*, February 29. https://www.screendaily.com/production/ex-machinas-sara-bennett-first-woman-vfx-supervisor-to-win-oscar/5100954.article

Reid, Natalie. 2016. "We're Celebrating!" *Milk*, March 1. http://www.milk-vfx.com/2016/03/01/were-celebrating-milks-sara-bennett-is-first-female-vfx-oscar-winner-in-twenty-three-years

"Sara Bennett." 2017. Accessed December 22, 2017. https://www.pearsoncollegelondon.ac.uk/escape-studios/advisory-board/sara-bennett.html

Woerner, Meredith. 2016. "Oscars 2016: 'Ex Machina' Is Trying to Bust through the Men-Only Visual Effects Club." *Los Angeles Times*, February 26. http://www.latimes.com/entertainment/herocomplex/la-et-hc-oscars-vfx-woman-20160226-story.html

De Quattro, Lindy (1969–)

Whether analogue, digital, or technological experimental, visual effects have always been a hybrid of science and art. From the outset, visual effects supervisor Lindy De Quattro seemed to intuitively pursue this connection between the magic of art and the ideas of science and technology.

Growing up in Silicon Valley, De Quattro was surrounded by computers and their potential. However, in addition to her affinity for mathematics, science, and video games, she had a strong interest in fine art. De Quattro was finally able to combine these two affections when she started college, double-majoring in fine art and computer science at the University of California, Berkeley. Recognizing that her interests could best be linked to the field of visual effects, she went on to receive a master's of science degree in computer science at the University of Southern California, followed by a master's of fine arts degree in film, video, and computer animation from the University of Southern California School of Cinema-Television.

Having graduated in the 1990s De Quattro began her career at a time when digital effects were only just getting established within the film industry. Her first professional experience was as a digital artist at Sony Hi-Definition Center. She then went on to RGA/LA and Warner Digital Studios before landing at Industrial Light & Magic in 1997, where she ascended through the ranks as technical director and sequence supervisor before finally earning the coveted position of VFX supervisor in 2007 on *Rush Hour 3*.

Lindy De Quattro's unique ability to marry art and technology has served her well, as she is currently one of the few female visual effects supervisors in the United States. At the supervisor level, competing in a male-dominated field hasn't been an easy task. De Quattro has witnessed the preferential treatment given to men as male colleagues with less experience have been hired for projects denied to her. Furthermore, the majority of big-budgeted blockbuster films have male VFX supervisors, but De Quattro has proven to be the exception, having worked on a wide range of films that not only include the superhero/science fiction/fantasy blockbuster but drama and comedy as well. Some of the groundbreaking effects for which De Quattro is acknowledged today for include the smoke in *Wild Wild West* (1999), the raining frogs in *Magnolia* (1999), the ocean swells in *The Perfect Storm* (2000), the clouds in *Peter Pan* (2003), the three brides dying in *Van Helsing* (2004), and the water effects in *Poseidon* (2006). She has also been the visual effects supervisor for *The Great Gatsby* (2013), a digital artist for *Harry Potter and the Half-Blood Prince* (2009), and was responsible for creating the "Hall of Containment" sequence in *Minority Report* (2002). All in all, there have been more than 30 movies to which Lindy De Quattro has contributed her technical expertise, mostly as a digital artist or visual effects supervisor. Besides these features, she has also been the VFX supervisor on the Wanda Wuhan Movie Park experience in China named Ultimate Energy.

Visual effects supervisor Lindy De Quattro in her office at Industrial Light & Magic in San Francisco, California. De Quattro is noted for providing her technical expertise on a number of films that rely heavily on special effects such as *The Perfect Storm* (2000), *Minority Report* (2002), *Pacific Rim* (2013), and *Downsizing* (2017). *Pacific Rim* and *Downsizing* were nominated for several visual effects awards. (Photo by Chris Hawkinson)

Lindy De Quattro's most critical acclaim as a VFX supervisor so far has been for the technical innovation on fluid and particle simulation in her work on *Pacific Rim* (2013) for which she won the 2013 Hollywood Post Alliance (HPA) Award for Outstanding Visual Effects in a Feature Film. Her work on *Pacific Rim* was also nominated for Best Special Visual Effects at the 2014 British Academy of Film and Television Arts (BAFTA) Awards, the 2014 Seattle Film Critics Awards, the 2014 International Online Cinema Awards (INOCA), and the 2014 Gold Derby Awards. Her other notable film, *Downsizing* (2017), was formally recognized for the artistry involved in shrinking people as seamlessly as possible. For her work on *Downsizing* Lindy de Quattro and her team were nominated for the VES (Visual Effects Society) Award for Outstanding Supporting Visual Effects in a Photoreal Feature (2018).

Over the last two decades, Lindy de Quattro has not only worked with some of the best-known directors of our time, such as Steven Spielberg, Wolfgang Petersen, and Baz Luhrmann, but she has also been mentored and promoted by many great visual effects artists like Mike Fink, Wendy Rogers, Joe Letteri, Scott Farrar, Bill George, Dennis Muren, and John Knoll. One can look forward to seeing more of De Quattro's work in the decades to come and, thanks to the precedent she is setting, the visual effects work of the women who are sure to follow, thanks to her example.

Katrin von Kap-herr

Further Reading

Chan, Charmaine. "Women in Visual Effects: 'Lindy De Quattro.'" Accessed January 31, 2018. http://www.womeninvfx.com/profiles/lindy.html

Grau, Oliver. 2007. "Remember the Phantasmagoria! Illusion Politics of the Eighteenth Century and Its Multimedial Afterlife." In *MediaArtHistories*. Edited by Oliver Grau. Cambridge, London: The MIT Press, 137–161.

Industrial Light & Magic. n.d. "Lindy De Quattro." Accessed January 31, 2018. https://www.ilm.com/people/lindy-de-quattro

Seymour, Mike. 2018. "Downsizing Matt Damon." *FX Guide*, January 5. https://www.fxguide.com/featured/downsizing-matt-damon

Douglas, Charlene Eberle (Unknown–)

It can be said with little argument that some of the most iconic scenes of any Superman film are the Man of Steel taking flight. At first confused for a bird or a plane, Superman soars across the sky, his iconic red cape dragging in the wind behind him. Part of the team that works to bring scenes like this to reality are the people working in virtual effects (VFX). In the latest Superman incarnation *Man of Steel* (2013), the iconic flight scenes, laser eye action, explosions, and many other visual effects bringing a sense of awe and spectacle to the film are thanks to the talents of VFX producer Charlene Eberle. It is not Eberle's skills and talent as a VFX professional that makes her a Hollywood heroine, however. It is not even, necessarily, her tenacity to work in an industry notorious for grueling schedules in exchange for little to no attention from the mass public. Eberle is a Hollywood heroine because she is willing to offer her time and knowledge to act as a mentor for future generations of young women in a field where issues concerning gender equality are now more in the open than ever before.

Over the last few years it's become quite common knowledge—even among non-industry insiders—that there is a gap between the number of women working in tech industries, including the fields of digital effects, compared to men, but it was in 2014 that more fervent focus on issues of sexism in the tech industries and, especially Hollywood, came into public discussion. In the field of VFX, there appears to be gender equality in some departments; however, the majority of the departments are still male dominated. In a research study examining over 2,000 of the highest-grossing U.S. box office films between 1994 and 2013, film producer, writer, and teacher Stephen Follows (2014) indicated that only 17.5 percent of a film crew in the VFX department was made up of women. What Follows's study does not make clear is the distinction between crew "on-set" versus anyone who may be working on the film in a studio, possibly even outsourced as many VFX houses tend to be by the bigger studios (Teich and Syed 2015). As such, the issue of gender disparity is a complex one: Is it a question of a culture of sexism in the industry, or an active choice made by women, or are they interrelated? There are several roles in VXF ranging from working onset to in-office. While working as a VFX supervisor, Eberle noted, "I think a lot of women would like to deal more with the money angle and being in the office . . . I think women who are in visual FX start out maybe as a coordinator and eventually end up, just out of natural default, in a producer type role rather than sitting in the trenches getting dirty" (Dunlop 2015, 2). Noted for 16 hours or more workdays stretching for weeks at a time, and traveling to several locations at a moment's notice, a VXF supervisor's position can be hectic and can leave little room for a traditional and more situated lifestyle. Although Eberle notes that it may not only be due to a woman's choice, she does not deny the gender inequalities that do exist in the industry. In terms of examining pay in the VFX industry, for example, Eberle noted women making 25 percent to 30 percent less than their male counterparts for the same job requiring the same skill sets (Dunlop 2015).

With the time-consuming schedule and gender inequality issues in the industry ranging from hiring practices to income disparities, there are, without question, challenges facing women who are currently working in or attempting to get into the field. Trying to help even the odds in a way, Eberle is mentoring women filmmakers as part of a special contest hosted by the Women in Film + Television Vancouver (WIFTV). The WIFTV is a local chapter of the Women in Film + Television International (WIFTI), which developed in 1989 in response to a lack of leadership opportunities for women in film and television. And these women are in more than good hands. Eberle's work experience includes a wide range of positions in visual effects, including producing the visual effects on a variety of films such as *The Wolf of Wall Street* (2014), *I, Robot* (2004), and *The Fantastic Four* (2005). In 2014, Eberle became the VFX executive producer for the visual effects studio Imagine Engine, Inc., providing VFX for films such as *Jurassic World* (2015) and more. At that time she helmed the visual effects production team of the *Point Break* (2015) remake. She is an invaluable source of information and guide on the industry. "I would love to help women in film," says Eberle, "I think there is not enough support for females in this industry of film. Being able to give women some insight to how VFX can help with the movie in ways they may not know is valuable. Knowledge in all aspect of film is huge" (De Bock, 2015, 1).

For a woman—let alone any person—to truly make it in the VFX field, they must love it; they must be passionate about the work. Knowing what kind of challenges to expect, however, and how to overcome them can be vital in helping to make it a little easier to love the work. Women in the industry, like Eberle, who have not only already been there, done that but been there, done that and then some, and are now passing on the knowledge to incoming generations, are the voices who help continue to stand up for a better, more equal, and fair industry; a better, more equal, and fair world.

Elaine Venter

Further Reading

De Bock, Katja. 2015. "Meet VFX Producer, #FromOutDarkSide Mentor Charlene Eberle." Accessed January 5, 2015. https://wiftv.wordpress.com/2015/12/14/meet-vfx-producer-fromourdarkside-mentor-charlene-eberle/#more-2445

Dunlop, Renee. 2015. "Women in the Field." *CG Society*. Accessed October 25, 2015. http://www.cgsociety.org/index.php/CGSFeatures/CGSFeatureSpecial/women_in_the_field

Follows, Stephen. 2014. "Gender within Film Crews." Accessed December 20, 2015. http://stephenfollows.com/hg4h4/Gender_Within_Film_Crews-stephenfollows_com.pdf

Image Engine. 2016. "Crew: Charlene Eberle Visual Effects Executive Producer." Accessed January 3, 2016. http://image-engine.com/crew/charlene-eberle

IMDb. "Charlene Eberle Douglas." Accessed June 15, 2015. http://www.imdb.com/name/nm0248065

Teich, Sonya, and Raqi Syed. 2015. "Visual Effects: The Gender Bias behind the Screen." *TechCrunch*. Accessed October 25, 2015. http://techcrunch.com/2015/02/02/women-in-vfx-high-tech-yet-not-tech

Women in Film + Television Vancouver (WITV). 2015. "Mission + History." Accessed January 5, 2015. http://www.womeninfilm.ca/Mission_Statement.html

Goulekas, Karen (1962–)

In cinema few things are more important than not losing the audience over badly done visual effects. This is why a trained eye for details is required during the production process so that effects do not fall out of the picture later.

Visual effects supervisor Karen Goulekas follows this paradigm and pays special attention to every visual and computer-generated element. Over the years she has not only worked with famous directors like James Cameron, Luc Besson, Roland Emmerich, Sam Raimi, Rian Johnson, and many more, but she has also tried to carry a story so far that people are moved beyond film watching. Her great enthusiasm for stories may be due to the fact that she first wanted to become a writer before she discovered the potential of visual effects. For her, *The Day after Tomorrow* (2004) is still one of the most important cinematic contributions of our time, as it generated an awareness of climate change. The visual effects are thus key elements of the narrative, as they credibly show a catastrophic storm with multiple twisters as the result of global warming, which leads to the collapse of civilization in the film plot. It is only logical that Goulekas's work as visual effects supervisor on *The Day after Tomorrow* was appreciated accordingly by two awards as well as two nominations: the BAFTA Award for Achievement in Special Visual Effects, the VES (Visual Effects Society) Award for Best Single Visual Effect of the Year, and nominations for the Academy Award Best Visual Effects, as well as the Saturn Award for Best Special Effects.

While only a few women work as visual effects supervisors, Goulekas has always been privileged in doing high-profile work from the beginning of her career. After finishing her studies in television production at the University of Connecticut in 1984, Goulekas began working as a digital artist. Since she has always been into video games, she was thrilled when she came across a 3D computer in 1984 and started flying 3D objects around on the screen. This enthusiasm for visual effects has never let go of her.

But it was not until Goulekas won two Emmy Awards in 1992 as an animation supervisor for the Barcelona Summer Olympics on NBC in the categories Best Graphic Design and Best Technical Team Studio while doing animated logos for commercials as a freelance digital artist that she decided to switch to the film business. One year later she already worked on her first movie, *Last Action Hero* (1993), as a digital effects artist, followed by *True Lies* (1994). In 1995 she became the digital effects supervisor at Boss Films, but shortly thereafter switched to Digital Domain, where she worked on well-known movies with famous directors like *Strange Days* (1995), *Apollo 13* (1995), *The Fifth Element* (1997), and *Titanic* (1997). For *The Fifth Element* she received her first award as a digital effects supervisor in film: the BAFTA Achievement Award for Special Visual Effects.

Visual effects supervisor Karen Goulekas on the beach near her home in Marina Del Rey, California. For both *The Fifth Element* (1997) and *The Day After Tomorrow* (2004), Goulekas won awards from the British Academy of Film and Television Arts (BAFTA) for Best Special Visual Effects.

After gaining enough experience at a studio, Goulekas decided to work independently and left Digital Domain in 1998. Her first film as associate visual effects supervisor was *Godzilla* (1998), which got her an Academy Award Long List Nomination, as well as the Saturn Award for Best Visual Effects. To this date, Goulekas has supervised over 30 films, including *Spider-Man* (2002) and *Green Lantern* (2011). Goulekas has also recently gained further professional experience as a producer of *The Green Ghost* (2017).

However, it would be wrong to think that Goulekas's sense for detail is only expressed in cinematic visual effects, because she also cares about precise and to-the-point explanations used in film. Here her fondness for writing resurfaces. In 2001 she wrote a long overdue glossary where she provided a "simple and clear-cut explanation" (Goulekas 2001, vii) for over 7,000 visual effects terms. Goulekas's ambition was to generate a common language between filmmakers and effects artists all over the world. Since the film and visual effects industry has grown considerably over the last decades, it has always been a challenge for her "to keep up with the ever-changing language and terminology used in everyday conversation among visual effects professionals" (Goulekas 2001, vii). With this book, she is the first to have compiled such an extensive glossary of cinematic terms within the effects industry. However, this publication is not the only one by Goulekas. She has also written two subchapters in *The VES Handbook of Visual Effects*, on the topics of post-visualization and on-set data acquisition, in which she contributes her experience on the film *10,000 BC* (2008).

Karen Goulekas's abilities are not limited to the cinema alone but also extend to other fields. Her releases under the abbreviation "KEG" (aka Karen E. Goulekas) bear witness to this. In 2009 she started her own blog and began writing limericks, mostly based on real yet often unbelievable headlines. In 2013 she reprinted these limericks in an anthology. Karen Goulekas also works as a photo artist shooting pictures on her travels around the world. So far she has five available art collections, whose paper prints can be purchased on her KEG Art website. Goulekas also runs her own YouTube channel, "KEG," where she recently released two self-written and self-edited critical rap music videos about President Donald Trump.

Goulekas is a woman of many interests and talents. It will be interesting to discover to which areas her interests will shift in the future and which exciting things beyond effects, logos, art, rap songs, lyrics and scientific texts we can still expect.

Katrin von Kap-herr

Further Reading

Failes, Ian. 2016. "Karen Goulekas." In *Masters of FX. Behind the Scenes with Geniuses of Visual and Special Effects.* London: Ilex, 66–75.

Goulekas, Karen. 2001. *Visual Effects in a Digital World: A Comprehensive Glossary of over 7000 Visual Effects Terms*. San Francisco: Morgan Kaufmann.

Goulekas, Karen. 2013. *The Daily Limerick, Volume 1: Sep. 15, 2012–Sep. 14, 2013: A Year in Review. 365 Daily Topical Limericks Based on Real—Often Unbelievable—News Headlines*. CreateSpace Independent Publishing Platform, Marina Del Rey, CA: KEG Press.

Goulekas, Karen. 2015a. "On-Set Data Acquisition." In *The VES Handbook of Visual Effects: Industry Standard VFX Practices and Procedures*. Edited by Jeffrey A. Okun and Susan Zwerman, Burlington, MA: Focal Press, 139–152.

Goulekas, Karen. 2015b. "Postvis." In *The VES Handbook of Visual Effects: Industry Standard VFX Practices and Procedures.* Edited by Jeffrey A. Okun and Susan Zwerman, Waltham: Focal Press, 57–61.

KEG Art. n.d.a "KEG Art. By KEG" Accessed March 25, 2018. http://www.kegart.com

KEG FX. n.d.b "KEG FX. Karen E. Goulekas" Accessed March 25, 2018. http://kegfx.com/Keg/Index.html

KEG Limerick Blogspot. 2014. "KEG Limerick. Karen E. Goulekas" Accessed March 25, 2018. http://keglimerick.blogspot.de

KEG Rap. n.d. "KEG KEG" Accessed March 25, 2018. https://www.youtube.com/channel/UCAGOtq7-npDBqLB319rBGww

Nelson, Lori J. (Unknown–)

As one of the pioneering women in visual effects, Lori J. Nelson has had a storied career spanning over 30 years in the effects industry. Nelson has worked on over 40 films, first as a visual effects (VFX) optical coordinator and later as a VFX producer for the majority of her career.

Nelson has been described as a "pioneer woman" in the VFX industry (Lee 2014). She began her career in 1985 at the landmark Industrial Light & Magic (ILM), the special effects unit within Lucasfilm. And she wasn't alone. Nelson worked alongside several other pioneering women in the pre-computer visual effects industry at ILM. Rather than computer-generated imagery, Nelson and her female cohort worked in optical effects, creating visual effects by manipulating light. Up until the 1970s, most positions in optical effects were held by men, but the women's liberation movement helped break down barriers and open the door for women interested in the art of optical trickery.

Like many who make history, Nelson stumbled upon effects work almost by accident. While working for a temporary employment agency, Nelson was offered a position as a receptionist at ILM. She started off at a desk, answering phones, corresponding with potential employees, and giving tours of the ILM campus. However, her superiors quickly realized that Nelson could offer more and quizzed her on how to accomplish specific effects shots. She impressed them enough with her answers that they ended up hiring her permanently in the newly created optical coordinator position at the company.

During the optical era of visual effects, most shots were composed of a combination of live-action, models, miniatures, explosions, matte paintings, and blue screens. The job of the optical lineup crew, where Nelson worked as a coordinator early in her career, was to map out the process of combining all of these elements for the optical printer cameraman. This was a high-pressure position that required long hours, and mistakes were not tolerated. But it also allowed Nelson to cut her teeth in the VFX business and ultimately helped her grow into the leading producer she eventually became.

As an optical coordinator, Nelson helped bring fantastic elements to life in films like *Star Trek IV: The Voyage Home* (1986), *Willow* (1988), *Who Framed Roger Rabbit* (1988), *Indiana Jones and the Last Crusade* (1989), *Ghostbusters II* (1989), *Back to the Future II* (1989), and *Batman Returns* (1992). Nelson's tenure at ILM resulted in some of the most celebrated examples of optical effects in cinematic history. *Who Framed Roger Rabbit* won the Academy Award for Best Visual Effects, the BAFTA Film Award for Best Special Effects, and the Saturn Award for Best Special Effects. *Back to the Future II* won the Academy Award for Best Visual Effects, the BAFTA Film Award for Best Special Effects, and the Saturn Award for Best Special Effects.

Along with the rest of the industry, Nelson transitioned to digital VFX in the early 1990s, acting as digital coordinator on *The Last Action Hero* (1993) before graduating to the role of producer. As a VFX producer and supervisor, Nelson has worked on films like *Matilda* (1996), *The Fast and the Furious* (2001), *Men in Black II* (2002), *Fast and Furious* (2009), *The Green Hornet* (2011), *42* (2013), and *The SpongeBob Movie: Sponge Out of Water* (2015).

Nelson has also left her mark at a number of leading visual effects and animation studios. Throughout her long career, she has worked at ILM, Boss Film Studios, Hammerhead Productions, EFILM, Warner Bros. Animation, Luma Pictures, and Rhythm & Hues, among others.

John Vanderhoef

Further Reading

Lee, Jennifer. 2014. "Female Special Effects Pioneers Share Stories from *Star Wars*, *Back to the Future*, and Beyond." *The Mary Sue*, May 9. http://www.themarysue.com/women-in-visual-effects

Nelson, Lori J. 2009. "Success Story: Lori Nelson." In *The Visual Effects Producer: Understanding the Art and Business of VFX*. Edited by Charles Finance and Susan Zwerman. New York: Focal Press.

Interview with Karen Goulekas

How would you explain your profession and its contribution to a film, and what's your schedule like?

I'm a visual special effects (VFX) supervisor, so I am involved from the start of pre-production, then principal photography and through to the end of post production. I supervise the creation of all the VFX in a film.

During prep, the work schedule is pretty much 10-hour days. During the shoot, I am with the crew so we are on a minimum of 12 hours (actually, more often like 13 or 14 hours). During post, we start out at around 10 hours, but it can quickly escalate to many more hours as we approach the deadline!

What makes you good at what you do?

I think that what makes me a bit different from many, not all, supervisors, is being able to multitask the creative, technical, and financial. The primary job of the VFX supervisor is to create high-quality work that best portrays the director's vision and helps support the story. However, I'm also very involved with the budget and quite often do the VFX budget myself. This is something that not all supervisors do. I do it because it's important to me to be creative in how the money is spent in order to get the highest-quality vendors and artists involved.

The 5th Element and *The Day after Tomorrow* are two that I am still very proud of—and not just because they both won BAFTAs. *The 5th Element* was very creative and inventive for its time, and *The Day after Tomorrow* pushed the envelope for its technical achievements at the time it was created. In terms of the biggest bang for the buck, I would say that *Looper* definitely takes the cake. That was my first indy from start to finish, and we really pulled off seamless effects work on a much smaller budget than I had normally been accustomed to.

Did you have a mentor? Were there any women in your field you could look up to? Do you feel you began with any advantages?

I would have to say my mentor is that chief engineer from the first TV station. He was a super-smart guy and when he saw my interest in animation, he taught me how to do the basic programming language needed to really make the Dubner sing. I had never touched a computer during college, no math beyond algebra and God knows I had never taken any programming courses—but there I was, with his help, writing little programs to do super-cool animations exploding all over my screen.

The first woman I ran into doing 3D animation was when I first applied for a job as a Dubner artist at a production company in Boston. She was leaving the post house to go to film school. I never really got to know her that well, as she was leaving as I was coming in.

After that, I didn't come across any other women doing animation I don't think until I went to Digital Domain in 1993, and there were quite a few there, the most I had ever seen for sure! But the ratio was still heavily weighted toward men.

I respected a lot of the women I was working with along the way, but they were mostly producers and very few women digital artists until I got to Digital Domain. There, they had gathered really experienced artists, all with about 10 years of experience, which is right about where I was at when I got there. So there was a whole lot of mutual respect across the board for both men and women alike.

I had no particular advantages in terms of getting into the film industry, but I did have the advantage that my parents paid for college for me; a lot of people don't get that perk.

Do you have children or dependents?

I intentionally chose not to have any children because I knew I would not be happy being 50 percent mom and 50 percent career. And I definitely did not want to be a 100 percent stay-at-home mom. I decided I would be happier being able to focus 100 percent on my career, and I think this is one of the biggest reasons I have been able to stay relevant. It takes a lot of time and energy to do this; it's not something you can do only half-time.

Have you ever felt discriminated against in your field simply because of your gender or identity?

Of course I have run across men who were chauvinists, but I always dealt with them very straight on so they usually backed off. But you are going to find chauvinists in any workplace, and you will also find a lot of men who are fantastic. The same goes for women: some aren't cool while others are great! I would say I generally have more male friends than female, and I really enjoy hanging out with the boys, so I don't recall ever feeling left out because of my gender.

One thing that has always happened though, is that whenever I first arrive on a film set almost everyone assumes I am the VFX producer rather than the VFX supervisor. I attribute this to the fact that a lot more women tend to occupy that role than that of a VFX supervisor, but I also think it's because the VFX supervisor role is a creative and technical role, and there is a tendency to assume that job will be performed by a guy. I could be wrong, but that is just what I always think when I have to keep correcting them from calling me VFX producer instead of VFX supervisor.

Is there ageism in your field?

I think that ageism is probably more of any issue than gender. It is generally assumed that the younger ones coming up will know more about the latest technologies. And, if you are a middle-aged woman, even more likely for people to assume that you don't know about all the latest stuff. It's strange but true. However, once I go in for the interview they quickly figure out that I still act like a kid and have the energy to match, so still getting the gigs.

I can't say that I've really had many conversations about sexism in general. It is more likely to come up if I feel a guy is treating me differently because I'm a woman, but that really doesn't happen much. While it happened from time to time when I was younger, I can't think of a time in later years when it did. I think that age and experience are likely to earn more respect from the get-go than someone that is deemed to be young for their particular role.

If your field is male dominated, any thoughts on how to support more women and minorities coming into your field?

Women VFX supervisors are a rare breed, especially on the production side as opposed to working at a facility. I have been among the very few that I can think of over the years, but I attribute it more to the fact that I chose not to have kids so I could focus on that job. I mean if you have kids and can only give the VFX supervisor role part-time attention, how can you possibly keep up with your male and female counterparts [who] don't have kids?

I am not one to conform to any rules in general—including boys-club rules. I never was good with authority figures and rules.

I never think in terms of solidarity with other women or the men as being the enemy. For me, it's pretty black and white. I either like and respect you, regardless of your gender, race, or sexual preference—or I don't like or respect you.)
It's really that simple from my point of view. And I assume others either like me or they don't for whatever reason they choose.

Interview with Lindy De Quattro

How would you explain your craft?

My title is VFX Supervisor, and I work in visual effects (VFX) on feature films. Generally speaking, VFX is the process of creating computer-generated imagery (CGI) outside the scope of a live-action shoot and then seamlessly integrating those images into the live-action footage for a photo-real result. When I first begin a new project, I start by reading the script and creating a shot and asset breakdown for that script. That process allows me to determine how many VFX shots are required for that script and how many individual CG assets will need to be built in order to execute those shots. Once I've created the breakdown, then I bid it. Bidding is the process by which I determine the overall cost to execute the work. I do this by evaluating the type of work required for each shot or asset build, the specific artists needed to execute that work and how much time each artist will need for each task. For example, if a hypothetical script said "the dinosaur crashed through the cement wall" then I know I need to build a CG dinosaur and a CG wall, and I know that the director will likely want to cover that action from at least three different angles so I'd bid that as three shots, which each require 3D animation of the dinosaur as well as 3D destruction of the wall, including dust and other particle effects. The final costs are dependent on the VFX company/artists actually doing the work and other variables like tax incentives and rebates.

Once a project is awarded, I work with the live-action production team to determine the needs of the VFX department on set. We run through all the shots and discuss what sets will be built and which will be CG, where we will need green screens, which characters will need motion capture, which shots might need motion control, etc. It takes many meetings and a lot of back and forth with all the other departments to work out all the details of a live-action shoot. It is also part of my job to be present on set during filming of the live-action portion of the film. My job on set is to ensure that any plates captured for VFX shots are done so correctly, i.e., placing and lighting green screens appropriately, adding tracking markers where needed, capturing camera and lighting data to be able to re-create the camera setup in post, doing any motion capture or facial capture that may be necessary, etc. It's also important for me to be there because inevitably things change at the last minute and issues come up that need immediate attention. Scripts change, weather changes, lots of things can happen to throw off the initial plan, and decisions need to be made quickly to keep production on schedule. The time I'm required to be on set for any one film generally falls between three and six months but can be longer or shorter depending on the project.

Our work in post-production frequently begins in the art department. The art department works with me and the director to come up with 2D artwork that accurately represents the characters, environments, and effects that the director is envisioning for the film. It is much faster and therefore less expensive to do this look development in 2D than to try to do it during shot production, so we always try to lock down the look before we begin the 3D builds. Once the designs are approved, then we move into modeling/painting/rigging/lighting of each asset. All of this work is done in the computer by a different artist for each stage of the process. Once the assets are built and approved, we move into shot production, and that is where we spend most of our time. Shot production can be anywhere from three to nine months on a typical feature film project. During shot production, we begin each day with dailies. During dailies, each artist shows their work on the shots they are currently assigned and I give feedback on that work. Then the artist spends the rest of the day executing the changes that I requested and I then see those changes in dailies the following day. Obviously that is a bit of a simplification of the process but that's generally how it works. Periodically I will present our work to the director to make sure that he or she is happy with our progress and to ensure we are moving in the right direction. We will continue on like that until I'm happy with all the shots and all shots are approved by the director.

VFX, like all aspects of film, is ART first and foremost, but it also requires a good understanding of science because what we are really doing is replicating and augmenting reality. I happen to be one of those people who uses both sides of their brains equally so it's always been easy for me to understand both sides of this industry. I can tell an artist what I want to see visually and also discuss with them the best way to execute it technically.

How have you had to adapt over the course of your career to stay relevant?

VFX, as with any tech industry, is always changing and advancing. The types of effects we are creating dictate the technology that we develop in order to meet those needs. Every project is different and has new requirements. We are always redesigning our pipeline and both our hardware and software in order to stay on the cutting edge. It is important as a supervisor to have at least a top-level understanding of all the new techniques that are available so that you know what's in your toolbox. In addition, VFX are being used more and more outside of the film industry. Lately VFX has made a huge contribution to the virtual reality/augmented reality (VR/AR) field, and there has been a lot of new development in that direction. I am constantly reading about and learning new technology so that I can stay relevant in the industry.

I tend to get very caught up in each project I work on and the success of the work becomes very personal to me. I have to remind myself that as long as I'm working hard and doing my best, I need to let go of the things I cannot control. Film is a very collaborative medium, and you need to trust your partners to handle their own responsibilities. I found that if you try to take all of that on yourself, you will be overwhelmed. I have three quotes on my computer at work, they say:

> "It's not what gets done to you, it's what you do with it."
> "Define yourself by what you love, not by what you hate."
> "You say I'm a bitch like it's a bad thing."

These messages remind me to persevere, to stay positive, and to not be ashamed to be powerful even in the face of prejudice, criticism, and skepticism, all of which I face a lot as a woman in a male-dominated industry.

I was at work when I went into labor with my second child. I was finishing up the setup for the "taffy roadway" in the film *Son of the Mask*, and I was typing up notes so another artist could take it over for me while I was out on maternity leave. I had to stop every 10 minutes or so for my contractions and then try to hurry through before the next one. I remember being in the hospital just after the birth and getting an angry email on my BlackBerry from one of my producers wondering why I wasn't in the meeting where they were expecting me. My company has a daycare center on campus, and both of my children came to work with me every day from the age of eight weeks until kindergarten began. That was certainly a huge benefit and support for me as a working mother. It also made birthday parties a lot more fun since the parents of their friends were all my co-workers.

Having children certainly taught me a lot of patience, and it helped me understand that my family is by far the most important thing in my life. Being on location when

I had toddlers was very difficult. Luckily my husband had a job that was flexible enough that he could manage a lot of the child-rearing tasks, and when the kids were very young we had a part-time nanny, but I think those long separations had a lasting impact on my children and certainly on me. We cherish spending time together. I may be one of the only people with teenagers who love to hang out with me, travel with me, and just spend time together. We don't take each other for granted. These days, now that the kids are older, I try to bring them out to visit me when I'm on location. My kids have had some amazing experiences traveling all over the world to visit me on set.

Have you ever felt discriminated against in your field simply because of your gender or identity?

My first 10 years in VFX went pretty smoothly. I had some struggles working in such a collaborative industry. VFX is absolutely a team process, and you have to learn how to work very closely with a lot of other artists, which can be tricky. You have to learn how to disengage your ego from the process and understand that everyone on the team has the same goal in the end, which is the best-looking VFX possible on screen. I certainly came across several men who had an issue taking direction from me because I was female, and I worked with a few supervisors who wouldn't assign me hero tasks because I was female, but overall I didn't run into too much discrimination. Once I was promoted to VFX supervisor, I had to interact with the client side of the industry and that is where I ran into rampant gender discrimination. When my company is bidding a film, they will send out a handful of potential VFX supervisors and then the client (studio, director, producers) will select which ones they want to interview. I almost never get chosen. I've heard comments like, "It's a really tough director and we need someone who can handle him" or "She doesn't have enough *experience*." I was actually told on one superhero project that I didn't have enough experience to even interview for the job (even though I had already supervised several films), and the white male VFX supervisor the studio ended up hiring had never supervised a show before. And the person doing the hiring on that project was a woman. It's not like anyone comes right out and says "we don't want a woman." I'm not sure they even realize that they have a gender bias. It's really this unconscious bias that when most people picture . . . a surgeon, or a senator, or a director, or a VFX supervisor, they picture a white man. And anyone that doesn't fit that mental picture makes them insecure. Are they going to be good enough? Do they know what they're doing? Even if I do get the interview, I still have a low chance of getting the job. I'm a feminine, heterosexual woman. I don't look or act like a man. A lot of women in the film industry present themselves more gender neutral and that seems to be an easier pill for the studios to swallow that a woman who looks like your local soccer mom, but I refuse to change who I am. I know I have a lot to offer and I will just continue to make the most of the opportunities I'm given. That said, it's been very difficult to not get the same opportunities as the male supervisors and to have to "prove myself" over and over again when that's not the case for the men. I've watched numerous men pass me by on the corporate ladder as they easily are crewed to show after show while I sometimes go for long periods without a project. I had to let go of the career I felt

I had earned and that I would have had if I had been male and learn to create opportunities for myself and enjoy the work that I was doing. I still struggle with that. My daughter sometimes says that she wants to be a VFX artist, and I'm not sure how to respond to that. On the one hand the work is so fun and interesting, but I don't want her to have to go through what I have.

Any thoughts on how to support more women and minorities coming into your field? Can inclusion be practiced voluntarily or do we need quotas?

In order to solve the gender issue in the VFX industry, we need to approach it from both ends. What I mean by that is we need to both get more girls into science, technology, engineering, and math (STEM) fields and mentor more girls as they enter the workforce, and at the same time we need to set quotas with all of the studios so that everyone currently working in the industry today gets used to seeing women as the head of the VFX department. Women make up roughly 50 percent of the population and they should make up roughly 50 percent of all VFX supervisors. I categorically reject the ridiculous arguments that there aren't enough qualified women, that women prefer to stay home with their kids, or that it's somehow "unfair" to white men to set quotas. Those are simply excuses to avoid the issue and I'm a big believer in the quote by Eldridge Cleaver: "There is no more neutrality in the world. You either have to be part of the solution, or you're going to be part of the problem." He said it in regard to the plight of black Americans, but I think it is also applicable to the plight of women in the workplace.

I used to be opposed to affirmative action. I remember when I was applying for college and I was told that the University of California (UC) system had implemented affirmative action. I ranted about how unfair it was and that if my scores and grades were higher than another candidate, then I objectively deserved to be accepted over that person. What I failed to realize at that time was that my parents paid for the very best private schools for the first 18 years of my life. They paid for a private tutor to work with me to study for the SAT and to help me write my college application essays. I lived in a 4,500-square-foot home with a swimming pool in a very expensive neighborhood with domestic help. We owned four cars. I got an allowance. I never had to work or worry about money. My parents were happily married for my entire life. I took private tennis lessons to give me my "extracurricular activity." My teachers called on me in class. They graded my papers expecting me to do well. All I ever had to worry about was my schoolwork. I was so privileged. I had every possible advantage to help me get my high grades and my high SAT score. If there was a poor, nonwhite child who lived with her single, working mother, had an after-school job to help pay the bills, sometimes was hungry or homeless because there wasn't enough money to pay the bills and that child was able to get anywhere even remotely close to my SAT score or my grades then they absolutely deserved that slot at UC. I understand now how much harder that girl had to work to get to the same place I got to without even trying. I think that's something you don't really understand deep in your soul until you've lived through it. It's really hard to understand the effects of privilege until you DON'T have it. The VFX industry is strongly dominated by white men. We desperately need more minorities and more women in all levels of the industry and most notably as heads of department.

I recently had a unique experience on set. I worked on a commercial as the VFX supervisor and both the director and the director of photography (DP) were also female. The rest of the crew was fairly well divided between men and women, probably about 60 to 40 percent. It was the most amazing on-set experience I'd ever had. The mood was collaborative and open. Nobody was yelling or criticizing the crew. I didn't have to prove myself repeatedly. My opinion was sought and valued. Obviously this one experience may well have been due to the particular personalities of the people involved and not necessarily their genders, but it gave me such great hope for what could be, and also great sadness for what is being lost by not allowing more women into these roles.

Appendix: More Influential Women in Hollywood

ACTRESSES

Julie Andrews
Lauren Bacall
Kathy Bates
Halle Berry
Cate Blanchett
Clara Bow
Louise Brooks
Sandra Bullock
Joan Crawford
Dorothy Dandridge
Geena Davis
Olivia de Havilland
Dolores del Río
Judi Dench
Judy Garland
Lillian Gish
Susan Hayward
Audrey Hepburn
Holly Hunter
Angelina Jolie
Diane Keaton
Grace Kelly
Nicole Kidman
Hedy Lamarr
Jennifer Lawrence
Vivien Leigh
Frances McDormand
Bette Midler
Marilyn Monroe
Julianne Moore
Pola Negri
Mabel Normand
Natalie Portman
Julia Roberts
Ginger Rogers
Susan Sarandon
Barbara Stanwyck
Barbra Streisand
Gloria Swanson
Elizabeth Taylor
Shirley Temple
Emma Thompson
Lana Turner
Lupe Vélez
Mae West
Kate Winslet
Reese Witherspoon
Anna May Wong

CASTING DIRECTORS

Sarah Finn
Cathy Sandrich Gelfond
Randi Hiller
Sheila Jaffe
Amanda Mackey Johnson
Allison Jones
Lynn Kressel
Julie Lowry-Johnson
Francine Maisler
Jeanne McCarthy

CINEMATOGRAPHERS

Natasha Braier
Caroline Champetier
Charlotte Bruus Christensen
Autumn Durald
Anna Foerster
Agnès Godard
Kirsten Johnson
Kira Kelly
Jessie Maple
Tami Reiker
Sandi Sissel
Quyen Tran

COSTUME DESIGNERS

Jenny Beavan
Sharen Davis
Jacqueline Durran
Lindy Hemming
Dorothy Jeakins
Anna Hill Johnstone
Judianna Makovsky
Ellen Mirojnick
Ruth Morley
Sandy Powell
Ann Roth
Deborah L. Scott
Julie Weiss
Mary Zophres

DIRECTORS

Chantal Akerman
Allison Anders
Gillian Armstrong
Niki Caro
Julie Dash
Claire Denis
Catherine Hardwicke
Mary Harron
Amy Heckerling
Nicole Holofcener
Barbara Kopple
Mimi Leder
Mira Nair
Euzhan Palcy
Kimberly Peirce
Sally Potter
Lynne Ramsay
Dee Rees
Penelope Spheeris
Agnès Varda

EDITORS

Françoise Bonnot
Maryann Brandon
Gabriella Cristiani
Dody Dorn
Adrienne Fazan
Lisa Fruchtman
Dana Glauberman
Tina Hirsch
Alisa Lepselter
Carol Littleton
Marcia Lucas
Mary Jo Markey
Barbara McLean
Susan E. Morse
Blanche Sewell
Claire Simpson
Margaret Sixel
Dorothy Spencer
Yelizaveta Svilova
Mary Sweeney
Eda Warren

FEATURE ANIMATION

Brenda Banks
Lauren Faust
Lillian Friedman
Jennifer Lee
Bianca Majolie
Kazuko Nakamura
Reiko Okuyama
Retta Scott
Rebeca Sugar
Eiko Tanaka

MAKEUP AND HAIRSTYLING ARTISTS

Christine Blundell
Lois Burwell
Julie Dartnell
Camille Friend
Frances Hannon
Ilona Herman
Tami Lane
Robin Mathews
Valli O'Reilly
Jenny Shircore
Lesley Vanderwalt

MUSIC

Lesley Barber
Wendy Carlos
Lisa Coleman
Laura Karpman
Gail Kubik
Mica Levi
Jocelyn Pook
Lolita Ritmanis

PRODUCERS

Darla Kay Anderson
Diablo Cody
Denise Di Novi
Lindsay Doran
Wendy Finerman
Lucy Fisher
Lianne Hallon
Norma Heyman
Debra Hill
Gale Anne Hurd
Lynda Obst
Harriet Parsons
Peggy Rajski
Maggie Renzi
Karen Rosenfelt
Jane Rosenthal
Stacey Sher
Cathy Shulman
Paula Wagner
Paula Weinstein
Laura Ziskin

PRODUCTION DESIGN

Anna Asp
Fay Babcock
Hannah Beachler
Ewa Braun
Sarah Greenwood
Mildred Griffiths
Nancy Haigh
Lilly Kilvert
Karen O'Hara
Jeannine Oppewall
Ida Random
Gretchen Rau
Sandy Reynolds-Wasco
Eve Stewart
Carol Strober
Lisa Thompson
Kristi Zea

SCREENWRITERS

Barbara Benedek
Philippa Boyens
Leslie Dixon
Jane Goldman
Laura Jones
Gloria Katz
Melissa Mathison
Elaine May
Ida May Park
Dorothy Parker
Nicole Perlman
Anna Hamilton Phelan
Melissa Rosenberg
Robin Swicord
Delores Taylor
Barbara Turner
Virginia Van Upp
Fran Walsh
Audrey Wells

SOUND

Gloria S. Borders
Dana Bunescu
Ajae Clearway
Teresa Eckton
Mary H. Ellis
Paula Fairfield
Nelson Ferreira
Sherry Klein
Eliza Paley
Kira Roessler
Lauren Stephens
Becky Sullivan

STUDIO HEADS AND EXECUTIVES

Bonnie Arnold
Kristine Belson
Megan Colligan
Lindsay Doran
Ida Koverman
Sue Kroll
Diane Nelson
Sheila Nevins
Mary Parent
Mireille Soria
Sophie Watts

STUNTWOMEN

LaFaye Baker
Polly Burson
Annie Ellis
Bonnie Happy
Leigh Hennessy
Leslie Hoffman
Julie Ann Johnson
Regina Parton
Helen Thurston
Nancy Thurston

VISUAL AND SPECIAL EFFECTS

Suzanne Benson
Rose Duignan
Pamela Easley
Peg Hunter
Mary Walter

About the Editor and Contributors

EDITOR

LAURA L. S. BAUER is a PhD candidate in the English department of Claremont Graduate University (CGU) and the current film studies editor for *Women's Studies: An Interdisciplinary Journal*, a peer-reviewed scholarly journal published by Taylor & Francis. Ms. Bauer co-edited *All Things Dickinson: An Encyclopedia of Emily Dickinson's World* with Wendy Martin, PhD, and Karen Beth Strovas, PhD (2014). Prior to CGU, Ms. Bauer worked for Steve Small, the former Department Head of Talent at Paradigm Talent Agency in Beverly Hills, California, and film producer Lorenzo di Bonventura, whose production company Di Bonaventura Pictures is based at Paramount Studios in Hollywood, California. Ms. Bauer is also a Laura P. Fernandez Endowed Fellowship recipient and the Vice President of the Sigma Tau Delta International English Honor Society chapter at CGU.

CONTRIBUTORS

ALI M. AMRI is an independent researcher of cultural and film studies from Tunisia. He is currently interested in investigating how the British cultural studies tradition bears on the study of Hollywood cinema. Through an exploration of the changing portrayals of American social minorities in the post–Cold War combats, he is particularly looking to synthesize a cultural approach to the study of genre.

ANGELA BEAUCHAMP is the Department of Cinematic Arts administrator and an adjunct lecturer in film history at the University of New Mexico, after working several years for cinematographer Shane Hurlbut, ASC. Angie holds an MA in Film Theory and Gender Studies from Skidmore College.

ANNIE BERKE, PHD, is an assistant professor of film at Hollins University. She was previously a Beinecke Fellow in New Haven, Connecticut, and the director of programming for the Environmental Film Festival at Yale. Annie has published in the *Historical Journal of Film, Radio, and Television, Feminist Media Histories*, and

Screening the Past and has an article forthcoming in *Camera Obscura: Feminism, Culture, and Media Studies.* She is currently at work on a book for the University of California Press entitled *You Just Type: Women Television Writers in 1950s America.*

RACHEL ROHAC BERNSTEIN is a reference librarian at the Academy of Motion Picture Arts and Sciences' Margaret Herrick Library in Beverly Hills, California. She received her Masters of Library and Information Sciences at the University of California, Los Angeles.

BRYCE N. BIFFLE has a master's degree in musicology at Texas Tech University. Apart from his musicological emphases in film music studies and orchestral music, he is also an active freelance composer, orchestrator, and arranger.

ANGELA BOURASSA is the founder and editor in chief of LA-Screenwriter.com, a leading resource for working and aspiring screenwriters.

CAMILLE BOURGEUS is a doctoral candidate in film studies at the Research Centre for Visual Poetics at the University of Antwerp. Her research is about the cinema of Chinese filmmaker Wang Bing within the context of a perceived "new realist" turn in contemporary art cinema.

BEYZA BOYACIOGLU is a filmmaker and artist from Istanbul. Her work has been exhibited in various venues and festivals, including MoMA Documentary Fortnight, IDFA (International Documentary Filmfestival Amsterdam), RIDM (Montréal International Documentary Festival), Anthology Film Archives, Barbican Centre, and Morelia International Film Festival. She has an MSc in Comparative Media Studies from the Massachusetts Institute of Technology (MIT).

ANKE BROUWERS, PHD, is a lecturer and researcher at the University of Antwerp and KASK School of Arts, Ghent. Her focus is on women in silent film, adaptation, and classical Hollywood narrative.

KIMBERLY MULLENDORE BROWN, DMA, is a professor and director of vocal studies at Wayland Baptist University (Texas). She earned a Master of Music from the University of Alabama and a Doctor of Musical Arts from the University of Memphis. Her research interests center largely upon women's vocal health topics.

SUSAN CABRAL-EBERT has been the president of the IATSE Local 706 Make-up Artists and Hair Stylists Guild for 15 years, and has been an award-winning makeup artist since the late 1970s. She was one of the first female makeup artists to enter the union and is a member of both the Motion Picture Academy and the Television Academy. She is the chairperson for the Make-up Artists and Hair Stylists Guild Awards, edits *The Artisan* magazine for the Guild, is an officer of the California IATSE Council doing legislative work, is on the board of directors of the Hollywood Chamber of Commerce, and has been appointed to the California Film Commission.

MELISSA VOSEN CALLENS, PHD, is currently an assistant professor of instructional design and communication at North Dakota State University, Fargo. Her research and teaching interests include online pedagogy, emerging media, and representations of gender in popular culture. Her writing can be found in *English Journal*, *Dialogue: The Interdisciplinary Journal of Popular Culture and Pedagogy*, and *A Sense of Community: Essays on the Television Series and Its Fandom*, among other publications.

DANIELLE COFER is an English PhD candidate at the University of Rhode Island. She earned her master's degree in English literature and language at California Polytechnic University in Pomona, California. Her current research interests include recovery work focused on 19th-century New England women writers and the preservation of historic cemeteries.

REBEKAH A. CROWE, PHD, is an assistant professor of history at Wayland Baptist University. She received a Masters of Arts in history from Baylor University and a PhD in history from Texas Christian University. Her focus is on women in the American West.

AUDREY CURTIS earned her master's in English from Claremont Graduate University, and she is currently working toward her Juris Doctorate at New York University School of Law.

SARAH DAWSON has a BFA in Creative Producing from Chapman University and received an MA in Media, Culture, and Communication Studies from New York University. She is currently launching a film distribution company that focuses on the distribution of independent films to digital platforms worldwide.

JONATHAN DICKSTEIN, PHD, is an independent scholar. He teaches literature and media studies and researches connections among mathematical logic, narrative theory, and psychoanalysis.

JESS DONOHOE completed a Bachelor of Arts (Honours) in English Literature at the University of Wollongong. Her research focus is on the depiction of professional woman in literature. She is currently pursuing postgraduate studies.

SHAWN DRISCOLL received his master's degree in 2017 from Worcester State University and is currently an Adjunct Professor of History and Political Science at Becker College in Worcester, Massachusetts. His focus is on Vietnam era–America and 1960s counterculture studies.

RENEE ANN DROUIN is a doctoral student of rhetoric and writing at Bowling Green State University. Her focus is on feminist rhetoric, popular culture analysis, and writing center pedagogy.

ERENDIRA ESPINOZA-TABOADA has a master's degree in critical studies from the School of Cinematic Arts at the University of Southern California. Her focus is contemporary Hollywood cinema.

ERIN FABIAN earned her master's at The Bard Graduate Center: Decorative Art, Design History and Material Culture. Her focus is on the significant influence Hollywood costume designers had on American women and the fashion market during the first half of the 20th century.

KWANDA M. M. FORD is a PhD student in Cinema and Media Studies and an Eugene V. Cota Robles Fellow at University of California Los Angeles. She obtained her master's degree in cultural studies with a certificate in Africana studies and media studies emphasis from Claremont Graduate University. Her research draws on the black feminist tradition to study histories and popular culture representations of cross-racial feminist alliances. She has written on freedwoman's narratives, film history, black diaspora popular culture, and critical food studies. Before relocating to Los Angeles, she earned a master's in human services counseling and a bachelor's in liberal arts from National-Louis University (Chicago).

RICHARD FOUNTAIN, PHD, is associate professor of collaborative piano at Wayland Baptist University (Texas), where he teaches applied piano, accompanying, piano literature, and piano pedagogy while maintaining an active solo and collaborative performing schedule. Fountain serves as principal keyboard for Lincoln's Symphony Orchestra and the Lubbock Symphony Orchestra.

CHELSEA GIBBS is a scholar of Hollywood's studio era. She holds a master's degree in critical studies from the University of Southern California's School of Cinematic Arts.

MARK ANDREW HAIN, PHD, is an instructor of film studies at Bowling Green State University. His research interests include audience and star studies with focuses on film and popular music, along with explorations of contemporary fandom of historical media.

SUSAN HARIS is a PhD candidate in Literature and Philosophy in the Department of Humanities and Social Sciences, at the Indian Institute of Technology Delhi, India. Her work explores environmental humanities through a South Asian framework with a particular focus on animals. She is also interested in film noir and late classical Hollywood cinema.

KRISTEN HATCH is associate professor of film and media studies in the School of Humanities at the University of California, Irvine. Her research interests include American film history, histories of gender and sexuality, and cultural studies. She is the author of *Shirley Temple and the Performance of Girlhood* (Rutgers University Press, 2015).

MEGAN HEATHERLY is a recent graduate of the Master's Program in Film and Media Studies at Columbia University and a contributor to the *Women Film Pioneers Project*. Her research focuses on film fan publications of the early to mid-20th century and women's contributions to early Hollywood.

ANDREW HOWE, PHD, is Professor of History at La Sierra University, where he teaches courses in American history, popular culture, and film/television studies. Recent scholarship includes book chapters on fan identification and cultural artifacts associated with *Game of Thrones*, the role of cemeteries and burial rites in the Western genre, and the re-examination of Manifest Destiny in the wake of the passenger pigeon's extinction.

ELEANOR M. HUNTINGTON is a master's student in critical studies at the University of Southern California School of Cinematic Arts. Her focus is on educational and children's media.

ZACH JANSEN earned his MLIS from St. Catherine University (Saint Paul, MN) and has a master's degree in film studies from National University (San Diego, CA). His focus is on silent era films and American films.

ENNURI JO has a master's degree in critical studies from the School of Cinematic Arts at the University of Southern California and is currently in their doctorate program.

KATRIN VON KAP-HERR, DR. PHIL., is a lecturer at the University of Applied Sciences, Potsdam, Germany. Her research is on theories, concepts, and strategies of visual media and media culture. She recently published a book about the double logic of contemporary digital visual effects in Hollywood cinema.

ANTHONY J. KING, PHD, is associate professor of music at Wayland Baptist University (Texas), where he teaches The Marching Pioneers (marching band) and The Real Benchwarmers (basketball pep band). King also teaches applied percussion and plays regularly with the WBU faculty jazz, and orchestral groups in Plainview, Lubbock, and Big Springs.

LIDIA KNIAŹ is a doctoral student at Maria Curie-Sklodowska University in Lublin, Poland, and a 2016 winner of the Second Prize in Poland's contest for the Best MA Thesis in American Studies. Her research interests include science fiction music videos, Afrofuturism, and sound design in film. She is currently working on her dissertation on Afrofuturist music videos.

ALEXANDER LALAMA is a PhD candidate at Claremont Graduate University in Claremont, California. His research interests include Latinx literature and culture studies, hemispheric studies, music and subcultures, and gender studies. He teaches courses in Latinx masculinities, gender and women's studies and multicultural literature.

ROGER W. LANDES, PHD, is professor of practice at Texas Tech University School of Music. His research interests include American popular music, guitar studies, and folk revival.

DEBORAH NADOOLMAN LANDIS, PHD, is the director of the UCLA David C. Copley Center for Costume. Her costume design career includes *Coming to America* (Academy Award nominee), *The Three Amigos*, *Trading Places*, *Raiders of the Lost Ark*, *An American Werewolf in London*, *The Blues Brothers*, *Animal House*, and Michael Jackson's *Thriller*. A two-term past-president of the Costume Designers Guild, Landis is the author of six books, including the catalog for her landmark exhibition, *Hollywood Costume* (2012) at the Victoria & Albert Museum in London.

JASON LARIVIÈRE is currently a doctoral candidate in the department of Media, Culture, and Communication at New York University. His dissertation project considers the theme of compression as a technical and philosophical concept. His writings on film have appeared in *The Brooklyn Rail*.

JUAN LLAMAS-RODRIGUEZ, PHD, is assistant professor of transnational media in the School of Arts, Technology, and Emerging Communication at the University of Texas at Dallas. His research and teaching focuses on media theory, creative labor, and Latin American film and television. His work has been published or is forthcoming in *Feminist Media Histories, Film Quarterly, Jump Cut, and Cinema Journal*.

JENNIFER A. LOPEZ-LAM is a master's candidate in English literature at California Polytechnic University, Pomona. She also has a master's degree in psychology. She is interested in gender politics, the intersection between trauma and memory in contemporary literature, and the nature and function of meta-fiction in trauma narratives.

BREENA L. LORAINE is a PhD candidate in the Department of Musicology and the Graduate Certificate in Early Modern and Eighteenth-Century Studies program at the University of California, Los Angeles. Her research projects focus on film and television music, the contemporary music industry, seventeenth- and eighteenth-century opera, and early sacred music.

ERVIN MALAKAJ, PHD, is assistant professor of German studies at the University of British Columbia.

BROOKE A. MARINE received her BS in Media, Culture, and Communication from New York University and MA in Humanities (Cinema & Media Studies) from The University of Chicago. She currently works as an assistant digital editor for *W* magazine. Her interests include film, television, and media studies in American popular culture.

DIANA E. MARTINEZ, PHD, has a doctorate in film and media studies from the University of Oregon. She is the education director of Film Streams, a nonprofit arthouse organization in Omaha, Nebraska. Her fields of research include media industry studies, women in film, and authorship.

ANA CABRAL MARTINS, PHD, has a doctorate in digital media and is an academic researcher. Her recent work includes "Where Comics and Movies Converge: Days of Future Present," published in *Visions of the Future in Comics: International Perspectives* and "Bending the Mind of *Doctor Strange*" for the magazine *Beneficial Shock.*

BRIAN F. MCCABE, PHD, works on theatrical drama from post-conflict zones, particularly Northern Ireland and the Republic of Ireland. In addition, Brian studies the evolution of poetry in both form and topic in America from the Antebellum period to the present. His interest in this project stems from the desire to promote women's voices, scholarship, and experience in the arts. Dr. McCabe currently teaches at the University of La Verne in California.

SARAH MCCARROLL, PHD, is an associate professor of theater and resident costume designer and costume shop manager at Georgia Southern University. Her work appears in *Theatre, Performance and Cognition: Languages, Bodies and Ecologies* and *Theatre Symposium.* Her professional theater credits include the Utah Shakespeare Festival and Milwaukee Repertory Theater.

KESHIA L. MCCLANTOC is a master's student and teaching assistant in English at the University of Nebraska-Lincoln. Her focus is on queer feminist rhetoric and popular culture.

CINDY MARLOW MCCLENAGAN, PHD, is professor of English and dean of the School of Languages and Literature at Wayland Baptist University in Plainview, Texas. Her areas of research include 19th- and 20th-century America literature, specifically as it relates to African American literature and violent female characters.

BRANDEISE MONK-PAYTON is a doctoral candidate in modern culture and media at Brown University and a Ford Foundation Dissertation Fellow. Her research focuses on race and representation in film, television, and digital media. Specifically, she is interested in the aesthetics and politics of racialized media exposure in public culture.

KELSEY E. MOORE received her master's in Cinema and Media Studies from the University of Southern California. She is also a founding member of the Guardian Princess Alliance. Her research interests include Italian cinema, memory, and postwar Hollywood.

LAUREN MORRISON is a doctoral student in English at Claremont Graduate University. Her focus is in 20th-century American literature with special interest in the appearance, influence, and transformation of religion in mid-century and postmodern narratives.

GRAYSON NOWAK holds a master's degree in film and media studies from Emory University. His master's thesis is "Absurd Parody for Nostalgic Night Owls: Understanding Adult Swim's Offensive Content," though his academic interests range beyond late-night television and include masala Bollywood films, Soviet montage, and film noir.

STEPHANIE OLIVER is an adjunct lecturer in the Media Arts Department at the University of North Texas, where she received her Master of Arts in Critical-Cultural Media Studies. Her academic research interests include the representation of gender and sexuality in contemporary American films, genre studies, and auteur theory.

LANDON PALMER, PHD, is a historian of film, media, and popular music teaching in the Department of Communication at the University of Tampa. He is the author of a forthcoming book on the history of casting musicians in screen roles.

ALAINA PANGELINA is a freelance writer and student of culture, especially in the arts, and journalism. She has most recently been a contributing writer for *Collide* and *WORLD* magazines.

CHRISTINA PARKER-FLYNN, PHD, is Assistant Professor of Film & Literature in the Department of English at Florida State University. She teaches courses in Hitchcock and film theory, adaptation studies, and Hollywood Cinema. Her current research interests include exploring the connection between 19th-century French literature and film theory, as well as the interrelationship between fashion, film, and form.

ERIC PELLERIN is the electronic resources librarian at Medgar Evers College, City University of New York. His research interests include genre theory and Hong Kong cinema. He is the author of "The Simpsons and Television Self-Reflexivity as Critique" from *The Simpsons Did It! Postmodernity in Yellow.*

DONNA R. PHILLIPS is an adjunct instructor in the English department at Citrus College in Glendora, California. She has an MA in 19th-century British literature and writes both fiction and non-fiction.

CELESTE REEB is a doctoral candidate in film at the University of Oregon. She has an MA in English literature from Salisbury University. Her focus is on sound, captioning, and audience studies.

NATASHA RUBIN researches costume design in the movies for the UCLA/TFT David C. Copley Center for Costume Design. She earned her master's degree in film production from the University of Southern California. She is a contributor to *Hollywood Sketchbook: A Century of Costume Illustration* (2012, HarperCollins).

ROBERT SEVENICH has a master's degree in critical studies from the University of Southern California's School of Cinematic Arts. He received his Bachelor of Arts from The College of the Holy Cross in Theatre and Pre-med. His work has been published in the *Middle Ground Journal* and *In Media Res.*

STEFFI SHOOK is a doctoral candidate in media arts and studies at Ohio University. Her background is in film studies, and her current research focuses on video games, gender and sexuality, and marginalized media production.

MICKY SMALL is a writer, director and media artist/scholar. She earned her MFA in Interdisciplinary Digital Media and Performance from Arizona State University and is the founder of Femme Powered Productions. Her focus is on female and queer representation in superhero, action, sci fi and fantasy film, tv and emerging media.

KAREN BETH STROVAS, PHD, is an associate professor of English at Wayland Baptist University in Plainview, Texas, and an assistant editor of Women's Studies: An Inter-disciplinary Journal. Strovas publishes on 19th century novels and their adaptations, and sleep and sleeplessness in literature and film.

SCOTT M. STROVAS, PHD, is an associate professor of music history at Wayland Baptist University (Texas), where he teaches courses in music history and theory, film music, and American music. He has published or presented on such diverse subjects as film and television music, music pedagogy, writing pedagogy, contemporary orchestral music, and jazz.

NICHOLAS TAMARKIN, PHD, is an Equity actor, director, and teacher. He earned his MFA in directing from the University of Wisconsin-Madison.

CARRIE TUPPER is a writer, animator, and creative developer with more than a decade of experience, with an interest in history, intersectional feminism, animation, and resonant storytelling. Based in Atlanta, Georgia, she works on the Glyph Award–winning comic series *Kamikaze* and is also a contributing writer for TheMarySue.com.

ILA TYAGI, PHD, is a Writing Lecturer at Yale-NUS College in Singapore. She completed her PhD in American Studies and Film and Media Studies at Yale University in 2018. Her research fields include the environmental humanities, science and technology, and modern and contemporary Anglo-American literature and visual media. Her writing has appeared in Oxford Bibliographies, Senses of Cinema, and the World Film Locations book series.

JOHN VANDERHOEF, PHD, is an Assistant Professor of Media Studies in the Communications Department at California State University, Dominguez Hills. His research interests include indie media, digital labor, media industries, and discourses around gender, race, and sexuality in media and production cultures.

ELAINE VENTER is a media studies doctoral candidate at Claremont Graduate University. Her dissertation is on the blocking of access to media content based on geographic location—known as geoblocking—from an economic, political, and cultural perspective. She is an assistant professor at Colorado Mesa University in the Mass Communication department teaching a variety of subject matter related to media.

ANNA WEINSTEIN, has a Master of Fine Arts degree and has developed screenplays for Furthur Films and Permoveo Productions. She teaches screenwriting and cinema studies at Auburn University, and she frequently contributes interviews with global female filmmakers to *Film International.* She is series editor of the PERFORM book series (Routledge), which includes volumes on screenwriting, directing, and acting.

CHARLOTTE WYNANT is a postgraduate student of English literature at the University of Antwerp, from which she recently graduated with a Master in Theatre and Film Studies.

JENNIFER A. ZALE, PHD, earned her doctorate from the Department of Communication and Culture (Film and Media Studies) at Indiana University Bloomington. Her main areas of interest are the connections between dance and early cinema, silent film history, and Russian cinema.

JESSICA ZIEGENFUSS is a PhD candidate within UC Irvine's Visual Studies doctoral program. Her dissertation project is a material history of artist Eva Hesse's 1960-era works, speaking directly to the biographical and cultural dimensions of her sculptural mediums. More specifically, her analysis attends to the aesthetic and social role of different modern materials, mainly industrial collage, latex, and plastics, in Hesse's works from the period. More broadly, her research spans the topics of feminist and queer theory, critical theory, ecological studies of art, postminimalism, issues of materiality and art, scientific experimentation in art, and the history of synthetics and the petrochemical industry.

ANDREA ZITTLAU, PHD, teaches in the English Department of the University of Rostock, Germany, and focuses on performance art and experimental film in her research and writing.

Index

Page numbers in **bold** indicate the location of main entries.